Daily Office Readings

Year Two, Volume 2

Compiled and edited by
The Reverend Terence L. Wilson

The Church Hymnal Corporation
800 Second Avenue, New York, NY 10017

The Church Hymnal Corporation wishes to express its appreciation to The National Council of Churches for permission to use its texts, and to Nelson Gruppo for the layout and design.

ISBN 0-89869-107-9

Introduction

Daily Office Readings (DOR) is published in four volumes, two for each year of the Daily Office Lectionary. The selection of the readings is in strict accordance with the Daily Office Lectionary of *The Book of Common Prayer*, pages 936-1000, and has been drawn from *The Common Bible* (Revised Standard Version, an Ecumenical Edition), whose accuracy and wide ecumenical acceptance are generally recognized. The texts in this book may, of course, be replaced by corresponding passages from any of the other versions of the Bible authorized for public worship in this Church.

The readings have been edited for liturgical use, as were the readings in *Lectionary Texts,* in accordance with the suggestions in BCP, page 888. All alternatives cited have been included. In only a very few cases where exactly the same passages are to be read, rather than reprinting an entire passage, page references to a preceding page are given.

All optional passages have also been included. Those which may be omitted (cited in parentheses in the Daily Office Lectionary), have been set off in separate indented paragraphs, and marked with a vertical bar line at the margin. In some of the passages, an opening phrase may have been needed to clarify the context and is printed in italics and set off in brackets. The italicized words should be omitted when the preceding section is read and the continuity of the entire reading is clear.

In this book, citations from the Psalter are placed at the point where psalmody is normally used in the reading of the Daily Offices, before the Lessons. Citations for Morning Prayer are given first, for Evening Prayer second, separated by the symbol ❖ . Where the citation is only for either Morning Prayer or Evening Prayer, the Office is named. This is especially the case in the readings for The Season after Pentecost (volume 2) and in the readings for Holy Days. Page numbers refer to BCP Psalter unless otherwise noted, and are enclosed in brackets. Optional psalmody is enclosed in parentheses; this is true when either an entire Psalm or only part of a Psalm is optional.

The Lessons for Daily Office Holy Days applicable for the part of the year covered by each volume are included at the back of the volume.

For ease of reference, footlines on each page identify the day found on that page.

Because of the importance of the Daily Office in the Anglican tradition, it is hoped these volumes will make the Offices easier to recite, aiding the use of the Office for private or public prayers. These volumes eliminate the need to find three readings for each day in the Bible and to track down those readings which skip around within a given passage. DOR should make it more possible for the laity and clergy alike to develop the habit of reciting the Offices by eliminating much of the work involved. They will also be invaluable for those who are traveling.

The publishers hope this book will enrich participation in worship by all the people, and will assist the clergy and other ministers in worthily proclaiming the Word of God at the daily recitation of the Offices.

Daily Office Readings

Year Two, Volume 2
Eve of Pentecost through Proper 29

Eve of Pentecost

(Evening Prayer)   *Psalm 33* [page 626]

A Reading (Lesson) from the Book of Exodus
[19:3-8a, 16-20]

Moses went up to God, and the Lord called to him out of
the mountain, saying, "Thus you shall say to the house of
Jacob, and tell the people of Israel: You have seen what I
did to the Egyptians, and how I bore you on eagles' wings
and brought you to myself. Now therefore, if you will obey
my voice and keep my covenant, you shall be my own
possession among all peoples; for all the earth is mine, and
you shall be to me a kingdom of priests and a holy nation.
These are the words which you shall speak to the children
of Israel." So Moses came and called the elders of the
people, and set before them all these words which the
Lord had commanded him. And all the people answered
together and said, "All that the Lord has spoken we will
do." On the morning of the third day there were thunders
and lightnings, and a thick cloud upon the mountain, and
a very loud trumpet blast, so that all the people who were
in the camp trembled. Then Moses brought the people out
of the camp to meet God; and they took their stand at the
foot of the mountain. And Mount Sinai was wrapped in
smoke, because the Lord descended upon it in fire; and the

smoke of it went up like the smoke of a kiln, and the whole mountain quaked greatly. And as the sound of the trumpet grew louder and louder, Moses spoke, and God answered him in thunder. And the Lord came down upon Mount Sinai, to the top of the mountain; and the Lord called Moses to the top of the mountain, and Moses went up.

A Reading (Lesson) from the First Letter of Peter [2:4-10]

Come to him, to that living stone, rejected by men, but in God's sight chosen and precious; and like living stones be yourselves built into a spiritual house, to be a holy priesthood, to offer spiritual sacrifices acceptable to God through Jesus Christ. For it stands in scripture: "Behold, I am laying in Zion a stone, a cornerstone chosen and precious, and he who believes in him will not be put to shame." To you therefore who believe, he is precious, but for those who do not believe, "The very stone which the builders rejected has become the head of the corner," and "A stone that will make men stumble, a rock that will make them fall"; for they stumble because they disobey the word, as they were destined to do. But you are a chosen race, a royal priesthood, a holy nation, God's own people, that you may declare the wonderful deeds of him who called you out of darkness into his marvelous light. Once you were no people but now you are God's people; once you had not received mercy but now you have received mercy.

The Day of Pentecost

Psalm 118 [page 760]   ❖   *Psalm 145* [page 801]

A Reading (Lesson) from the Book of Deuteronomy [16:9-12]

Moses summoned all Israel, and said to them, "You shall count seven weeks; begin to count the seven weeks from

the time you first put the sickle to the standing grain. Then
you shall keep the feast of weeks to the Lord your God
with the tribute of a freewill offering from your hand,
which you shall give as the Lord your God blesses you; and
you shall rejoice before the Lord your God, you and your
son and your daughter, your manservant and your
maidservant, the Levite who is within your towns, the
sojourner, the fatherless, and the widow who are among
you, at the place which the Lord your God will choose, to
make his name dwell there. You shall remember that you
were a slave in Egypt; and you shall be careful to observe
these statutes."

A Reading (Lesson) from the Acts of the Apostles
[4:18-21, 23-33]

The rulers, the scribes and the elders called Peter and John
and charged them not to speak or teach at all in the name
of Jesus. But Peter and John answered them, "Whether it
is right in the sight of God to listen to you rather than to
God, you must judge; for we cannot but speak of what
we have seen and heard." And when they had further
threatened them, they let them go, finding no way to
punish them, because of the people; for all men praised
God for what had happened. When they were released
they went to their friends and reported what the chief
priests and the elders had said to them. And when they
heard it, they lifted their voices together to God and said,
"Sovereign Lord, who didst make the heaven and the earth
and the sea and everything in them, who by the mouth of
our father David, thy servant, didst say by the Holy Spirit,
'Why did the Gentiles rage, and the peoples imagine vain
things? The kings of the earth set themselves in array, and
the rulers were gathered together, against the Lord and
against his Anointed'—for truly in this city there were
gathered together against thy holy servant Jesus, whom
thou didst anoint, both Herod and Pontius Pilate, with the
Gentiles and the peoples of Israel, to do whatever thy hand

and thy plan had predestined to take place. And now, Lord, look upon their threats, and grant to thy servants to speak thy word with all boldness, while thou stretchest out thy hand to heal, and signs and wonders are performed through the name of thy holy servant Jesus." And when they had prayed, the place in which they were gathered together was shaken; and they were all filled with the Holy Spirit and spoke the word of God with boldness. Now the company of those who believed were of one heart and soul, and no one said that any of the things which he possessed was his own, but they had everything in common. And with great power the apostles gave their testimony to the resurrection of the Lord Jesus, and great grace was upon them all.

A Reading (Lesson) from the Gospel according to John [4:19-26]

The woman at the well said to Jesus, "Sir, I perceive that you are a prophet. Our fathers worshiped on this mountain; and you say that in Jerusalem is the place where men ought to worship." Jesus said to her, "Woman, believe me, the hour is coming when neither on this mountain nor in Jerusalem will you worship the Father. You worship what you do not know; we worship what we know, for salvation is from the Jews. But the hour is coming, and now is, when the true worshipers will worship the Father in spirit and truth, for such the Father seeks to worship him. God is spirit, and those who worship him must worship in spirit and truth." The woman said to him, "I know that Messiah is coming (he who is called Christ); when he comes, he will show us all things." Jesus said to her, "I who speak to you am he."

On the weekdays which follow, the Readings are taken from the numbered Proper (one through six) which corresponds most closely to the date of Pentecost.

Eve of Trinity Sunday

(Evening Prayer)   *Psalm 104* [page 735]

A Reading (Lesson) from the Book of Ecclesiasticus
[42:15-25]

I will now call to mind the works of the Lord, and will declare what I have seen. By the words of the Lord his works are done. The sun looks down on everything with its light, and the work of the Lord is full of his glory. The Lord has not enabled his holy ones to recount all his marvelous works, which the Lord the Almighty has established that the universe may stand firm in his glory. He searches out the abyss, and the hearts of men, and considers their crafty devices. For the Most High knows all that may be known, and he looks into the signs of the age. He declares what has been and what is to be, and he reveals the tracks of hidden things. No thought escapes him, and not one word is hidden from him. He has ordained the splendors of his wisdom, and he is from everlasting and to everlasting. Nothing can be added or taken away, and he needs no one to be his counselor. How greatly to be desired are all his works, and how sparkling they are to see! All these things live and remain for ever for every need, and are all obedient. All things are twofold, one opposite the other, and he has made nothing incomplete. One confirms the good things of the other, and who can have enough of beholding his glory?

A Reading (Lesson) from the Letter of Paul to the Ephesians [3:14-21]

For this reason I bow my knees before the Father, from whom every family in heaven and on earth is named, that according to the riches of his glory he may grant you to be strengthened with might through his Spirit in the inner man, and that Christ may dwell in your hearts through faith; that you, being rooted and grounded in love, may have power to comprehend with all the saints what is the breadth and length and height and depth, and to know the love of Christ which surpasses knowledge, that you may be filled with all the fulness of God. Now to him who by the power at work within us is able to do far more abundantly than all that we ask or think, to him be glory in the church and in Christ Jesus to all generations, for ever and ever. Amen.

Trinity Sunday

Psalm 146 [page 803], *Psalm 147* [page 804] ❖
Psalm 111 [page 754], *Psalm 112* [page 755],
Psalm 113 [page 756]

A Reading (Lesson) from the Book of Job [38:1-11; 42:1-5]

The Lord answered Job out of the whirlwind: "Who is this that darkens counsel by words without knowledge? Gird up your loins like a man, I will question you, and you shall declare to me. Where were you when I laid the foundation of the earth? Tell me, if you have understanding. Who determined its measurements—surely you know! Or who stretched the line upon it? On what were its bases sunk, or who laid its cornerstone, when the morning stars sang together, and all the sons of God shouted for joy? Or who shut in the sea with doors, when it burst forth from the womb; when I made clouds its garment, and thick darkness its swaddling band, and prescribed bounds for it, and set bars and doors, and said, 'Thus far shall you come, and no farther, and here shall your proud waves be stayed'?" Then Job answered the Lord: "I know that thou canst do all things, and that no purpose of thine can be thwarted. 'Who is this that hides counsel without knowledge?' Therefore I have uttered what I did not understand, things too wonderful for me, which I did not know. 'Hear, and I will speak; I will question you, and you declare to me.' I had heard of thee by the hearing of the ear, but now my eye sees thee."

A Reading (Lesson) from the Revelation to John [19:4-16]

The twenty-four elders and the four living creatures fell down and worshiped God who is seated on the throne, saying, "Amen. Hallelujah!" And from the throne came a voice crying, "Praise our God, all you his servants, you who fear him, small and great." Then I heard what seemed to be the voice of a great multitude, like the sound of many waters and like the sound of mighty thunderpeals, crying, "Hallelujah! For the Lord our God the Almighty reigns. Let us rejoice and exult and give him the glory, for the marriage of the Lamb has come, and his Bride has made herself ready; it was granted her to be clothed with fine linen, bright and pure"—for the fine linen is the righteous deeds of the saints. And the angel said to me, "Write this: Blessed are those who are invited to the marriage supper of the Lamb." And he said to me, "These are true words of God." Then I fell down at his feet to worship him, but he said to me, "You must not do that! I am a fellow servant with you and your brethren who hold the testimony of Jesus. Worship God." For the testimony of Jesus is the spirit of prophecy. Then I saw heaven opened, and behold, a white horse! He who sat upon it is called Faithful and True, and in righteousness he judges and makes war. His eyes are like a flame of fire, and on his head are many diadems; and he has a name inscribed which no one knows but himself. He is clad in a robe dipped in blood, and the name by which he is called is The Word of God. And the armies of heaven, arrayed in fine linen, white and pure, followed him on white horses. From his mouth issues a sharp sword with which to smite the nations, and he will rule them with a rod of iron; he will tread the wine press of the fury of the wrath of God the Almighty. On his robe and on his thigh he has a name inscribed, King of kings and Lord of lords.

A Reading (Lesson) from the Gospel according to John
[1:29-34]

The next day John saw Jesus coming toward him, and said, "Behold, the Lamb of God, who takes away the sin of the world! This is he of whom I said, 'After me comes a man who ranks before me, for he was before me.' I myself did not know him; but for this I came baptizing with water, that he might be revealed to Israel." And John bore witness, "I saw the Spirit descend as a dove from heaven, and it remained on him. I myself did not know him; but he who sent me to baptize with water said to me, 'He on whom you see the Spirit descend and remain, this is he who baptizes with the Holy Spirit.' And I have seen and have borne witness that this is the Son of God."

On the weekdays which follow, the Readings are taken from the numbered Proper (two through seven) which corresponds most closely to the date of Trinity Sunday.

The Season after Pentecost

Proper 1 *Week of the Sunday closest to May 11*

Monday

Psalm 106:1-18 [page 741] ❖ *Psalm 106:19-48* [page 743]

A Reading (Lesson) from the Book of Ezekiel [33:1-11]

The word of the Lord came to me: "Son of man, speak to your people and say to them, If I bring the sword upon a land, and the people of the land take a man from among them, and make him their watchman; and if he sees the sword coming upon the land and blows the trumpet and warns the people; then if any one who hears the sound of the trumpet does not take warning, and the sword comes and takes him away, his blood shall be upon his own head. He heard the sound of the trumpet, and did not take warning; his blood shall be upon himself. But if he had taken warning, he would have saved his life. But if the watchman sees the sword coming and does not blow the trumpet, so that the people are not warned, and the sword comes, and takes any one of them; that man is taken away in his iniquity, but his blood I will require at the watchman's hand. So you, son of man, I have made a watchman for the house of Israel; whenever you hear a word from my mouth, you shall give them warning from me. If I say to the wicked, O wicked man, you shall surely die, and you do not speak to warn the wicked to turn from his way, that wicked man shall die in his iniquity, but his blood I will require at your hand. But if you warn the wicked to turn from his way, and he does not turn from his way; he shall die in his iniquity, but you will have saved your life. And you, son of man, say to the house of Israel, Thus have you said: 'Our transgressions and our sins are upon us, and we waste away because of them; how then can we live?' Say to them, As I live, says the Lord God, I have no pleasure in the death of the wicked, but that the wicked turn from his way and live; turn back, turn back from your evil ways; for why will you die, O house of Israel?"

A Reading (Lesson) from the First Letter of John [1:1-10]

That which was from the beginning, which we have heard, which we have seen with our eyes, which we have looked upon and touched with our hands, concerning the word of life—the life was made manifest, and we saw it, and testify to it, and proclaim to you the eternal life which was with the Father and was made manifest to us—that which we have seen and heard we proclaim also to you, so that you may have fellowship with us; and our fellowship is with the Father and with his Son Jesus Christ. And we are writing this that our joy may be complete. This is the message we have heard from him and proclaim to you, that God is light and in him is no darkness at all. If we say we have fellowship with him while we walk in darkness, we lie and do not live according to the truth; but if we walk in the light, as he is in the light, we have fellowship with one another, and the blood of Jesus his Son cleanses us from all sin. If we say we have no sin, we deceive ourselves, and the truth is not in us. If we confess our sins, he is faithful and just, and will forgive our sins and cleanse us from all unrighteousness. If we say we have not sinned, we make him a liar, and his word is not in us.

A Reading (Lesson) from the Gospel according to Matthew
[9:27-34]

As Jesus passed on from there, two blind men followed him, crying aloud, "Have mercy on us, Son of David." When he entered the house, the blind men came to him; and Jesus said to them, "Do you believe that I am able to do this?" They said to him, "Yes, Lord." Then he touched their eyes, saying, "According to your faith be it done to you." And their eyes were opened. And Jesus sternly charged them, "See that no one knows it." But they went away and spread his fame through all that district. As they were going away, behold, a dumb demoniac was brought to him. And when the demon had been cast out, the dumb man spoke; and the crowds marveled, saying, "Never was anything like this seen in Israel." But the Pharisees said, "He casts out demons by the prince of demons."

Tuesday

(Psalm 120 [page 778]), *Psalm 121* [page 779],
Psalm 122 [page 779], *Psalm 123* [page 780]
❖ *Psalm 124* [page 781], *Psalm 125* [page 781],
Psalm 126 [page 782], *(Psalm 127* [page 782])

A Reading (Lesson) from the Book of Ezekiel [33:21-33]

In the twelfth year of our exile, in the tenth month, on the fifth day of the month, a man who had escaped from Jerusalem came to me and said, "The city has fallen." Now the hand of the Lord had been upon me the evening before the fugitive came; and he had opened my mouth by the time the man came to me in the morning; so my mouth was opened, and I was no longer dumb. The word of the Lord came to me: "Son of man, the inhabitants of these waste places in the land of Israel keep saying, 'Abraham was only one man, yet he got possession of the land; but we are many; the land is surely given us to possess.' Therefore say to them, Thus says the Lord God: You eat flesh with the blood, and lift up your eyes to your idols, and shed blood; shall you then possess the land? You resort to the sword, you commit abominations and each of you defiles his neighbor's wife; shall you then possess the land? Say this to them, Thus says the Lord God: As I live, surely those who are in the waste places shall fall by the sword; and him that is in the open field I will give to the beasts to be devoured; and those who are in strongholds and in caves shall die by pestilence. And I will make the land a desolation and a waste; and her proud might shall come to an end; and the mountains of Israel shall be so desolate that none will pass through. Then they will know that I am the Lord, when I have made the land a desolation and a waste because of all their abonimations which they have committed. As for you, son of man, your people who talk together about you by the walls and at the doors of the houses, say to one another, each to his brother, 'Come, and hear what the word is that comes forth from the Lord.' And they come to you as people come, and they sit before you as my people, and they hear what you say but they will not do it; for with their lips they show much love, but their heart is set on their gain. And, lo, you are to them like one who sings love songs with a beautiful voice and plays well on an instrument, for they hear what you say, but they will not do it. When this comes—and come it will!—then they will know that a prophet has been among them."

A Reading (Lesson) from the First Letter of John [2:1-11]

My little children, I am writing this to you so that you may not sin; but if any one does sin, we have an advocate with the Father, Jesus Christ the righteous; and he is the expiation for our sins, and not for ours only but also for the sins of the whole world. And by this we may be sure that we know him, if we keep his commandments. He who says, "I know him" but disobeys his commandments is a liar, and the truth is not in him; but whoever keeps his word, in him truly love for God is perfected. By this we may be sure that we are in him: he who says he abides in him ought to walk in the same way in which he walked. Beloved, I am writing you no new commandment, but an old commandment which you had from the beginning; the old commandment is the word which you have heard. Yet I am writing you a new commandment, which is true in him and in you, because the darkness is passing away and the true light is already shining. He who says he is in the light and hates his brother is in the darkness still. He who loves his brother abides in the light, and in it there is no cause for stumbling. But he who hates his brother is in the darkness and walks in the darkness, and does not know where he is going, because the darkness has blinded his eyes.

A Reading (Lesson) from the Gospel according to Matthew [9:35—10:4]

Jesus went about all the cities and villages, teaching in their synagogues and preaching the gospel of the kingdom, and healing every disease and every infirmity. When he saw the crowds, he had compassion for them, because they were harassed and helpless, like sheep without a shepherd. Then he said to his disciples, "The harvest is plentiful, but the laborers are few; pray therefore the Lord of the harvest to send out laborers into his harvest." And he called to him his twelve disciples and gave them authority over unclean spirits, to cast them out, and to heal every disease and every infirmity. The names of the twelve apostles are these: first, Simon, who is called Peter, and Andrew his brother; James the son of Zeb'edee, and John his brother; Philip and Bartholomew; Thomas and Matthew the tax collector; James the son of Alphaeus, and Thaddaeus; Simon the Cananaean, and Judas Iscariot, who betrayed him.

Wednesday

Psalm 119:145-176 [page 775]   ❖   *Psalm 128* [page 783], *Psalm 129* [page 784],   *Psalm 130* [page 784]

A Reading (Lesson) from the Book of Ezekiel [34:1-16]

The word of the Lord came to me: "Son of man, prophesy against the shepherds of Israel, prophesy, and say to them, even to the shepherds, Thus says the Lord God: Ho, shepherds of Israel who have been feeding yourselves! Should not shepherds feed the sheep? You eat the fat, you clothe yourselves with the wool, you slaughter the fatlings; but you do not feed the sheep. The weak you have not strengthened, the sick you have not healed, the crippled you have not bound up, the strayed you have not brought back, the lost you have not sought, and with force and harshness you have ruled them. So they were scattered, because there was no shepherd; and they became food for all the wild beasts. My sheep were scattered, they wandered over all the mountains and on every high hill; my sheep were scattered over all the face of the earth, with none to search or seek for them. Therefore, you shepherds, hear the word of the Lord: As I live, says the Lord God, because my sheep have become a prey, and my sheep have become food for all the wild beasts, since there was no shepherd; and because my shepherds have not searched for my sheep, but the shepherds have fed themselves, and have not fed my sheep; therefore, you shepherds, hear the word of the Lord: Thus says the Lord God, Behold, I am against the shepherds; and I will require my sheep at their hand, and put a stop to their feeding the sheep; no longer shall the shepherds feed themselves. I will rescue my sheep from their mouths, that they may not be food for them. For thus says the Lord God: Behold, I, I myself will search for my sheep, and will seek them out. As a shepherd seeks out his flock when some of his sheep have been scattered abroad, so will I seek out my sheep; and I will rescue them from all places where they have been scattered on a day of clouds and thick darkness. And I will bring them out from the peoples, and gather them from the countries, and will bring them into their own land; and I will feed them on the mountains of Israel, by the fountains, and in all the inhabited places of the country. I will feed them with good pasture, and upon the mountain heights of Israel shall be their pasture; there they shall lie down in good grazing land, and on fat pasture they shall feed on the mountains of Israel. I myself will be the shepherd of my sheep, and I will make them lie down, says the Lord God. I will seek the lost, and I will bring back the strayed, and I will bind up the crippled, and I will strengthen the weak, and the fat and the strong I will watch over; I will feed them in justice."

A Reading (Lesson) from the First Letter of John [2:12-17]

I am writing to you, little children, because your sins are forgiven for his sake. I am writing to you, fathers, because you know him who is from the beginning. I am writing to you, young men, because you have overcome the evil one. I write to you, children, because you know the Father. I write to you, fathers, because you know him who is from the beginning. I write to you, young men, because you are strong, and the word of God abides in you, and you have overcome the evil one. Do not love the world or the things in the world. If any one loves the world, love for the Father is not in him. For all that is in the world, the lust of the flesh and the lust of the eyes and the pride of life, is not of the Father but is of the world. And the world passes away, and the lust of it; but he who does the will of God abides for ever.

A Reading (Lesson) from the Gospel according to Matthew [10:5-15]

The twelve apostles Jesus sent out, charging them, "Go nowhere among the Gentiles, and enter no town of the Samaritans, but go rather to the lost sheep of the house of Israel. And preach as you go, saying, 'The kingdom of heaven is at hand.' Heal the sick, raise the dead, cleanse lepers, cast out demons. You received without paying, give without pay. Take no gold, nor silver, nor copper in your belts, no bag for your journey, nor two tunics, nor sandals, nor a staff; for the laborer deserves his food. And whatever town or village you enter, find out who is worthy in it, and stay with him until you depart. As you enter the house, salute it. And if the house is worthy, let your peace come upon it; but if it is not worthy, let your peace return to you. And if any one will not receive you or listen to your words, shake off the dust from your feet as you leave that house or town. Truly, I say to you, it shall be more tolerable on the day of judgment for the land of Sodom and Gomor'rah than for that town."

Thursday

Psalm 131 [page 785], *Psalm 132* [page 785], *(Psalm 133* [page 787]) ❖ *Psalm 134* [page 787], *Psalm 135* [page 788]

A Reading (Lesson) from the Book of Ezekiel [37:21b-28]

"Thus says the Lord God: Behold, I will take the people of Israel from the nations among which they have gone, and

will gather them from all sides, and bring them to their
own land; and I will make them one nation in the land,
upon the mountains of Israel; and one king shall be king
over them all; and they shall be no longer two nations, and
no longer divided into two kingdoms. They shall not defile
themselves any more with their idols and their detestable
things, or with any of their transgressions; but I will save
them from all the backslidings in which they have sinned,
and will cleanse them; and they shall be my people, and
I will be their God. My servant David shall be king over
them; and they shall all have one shepherd. They shall
follow my ordinances and be careful to observe my
statutes. They shall dwell in the land where your fathers
dwelt that I gave to my servant Jacob; they and their
children and their children's children shall dwell there for
ever; and David my servant shall be their prince for ever.
I will make a covenant of peace with them; it shall be an
everlasting covenant with them; and I will bless them and
multiply them, and will set my sanctuary in the midst of
them for evermore. My dwelling place shall be with them;
and I will be their God, and they shall be my people. Then
the nations will know that I the Lord sanctify Israel, when
my sanctuary is in the midst of them for evermore."

A Reading (Lesson) from the First Letter of John [2:18-29]

Children, it is the last hour; and as you have heard that
antichrist is coming, so now many antichrists have come;
therefore we know that it is the last hour. They went out
from us, but they were not of us; for if they had been of us,
they would have continued with us; but they went out,
that it might be plain that they all are not of us. But you
have been anointed by the Holy One, and you all know.
I write to you, not because you do not know the truth, but
because you know it, and know that no lie is of the truth.
Who is the liar but he who denies that Jesus is the Christ?
This is the antichrist, he who denies the Father and the
Son. No one who denies the Son has the Father. He who

confesses the Son has the Father also. Let what you heard from the beginning abide in you. If what you heard from the beginning abides in you, then you will abide in the Son and in the Father. And this is what he has promised us, eternal life. I write this to you about those who would deceive you; but the anointing which you received from him abides in you, and you have no need that any one should teach you; as his anointing teaches you about everything, and is true, and is no lie, just as it has taught you, abide in him. And now, little children, abide in him, so that when he appears we may have confidence and not shrink from him in shame at his coming. If you know that he is righteous, you may be sure that every one who does right is born of him.

A Reading (Lesson) from the Gospel according to Matthew [10:16-23]

Jesus charged the twelve apostles, "Behold, I send you out as sheep in the midst of wolves; so be wise as serpents and innocent as doves. Beware of men; for they will deliver you up to councils, and flog you in their synagogues, and you will be dragged before governors and kings for my sake, to bear testimony before them and the Gentiles. When they deliver you up, do not be anxious how you are to speak or what you are to say; for what you are to say will be given to you in that hour; for it is not you who speak, but the Spirit of your Father speaking through you. Brother will deliver up brother to death, and the father his child, and children will rise against parents and have them put to death; and you will be hated by all for my name's sake. But he who endures to the end will be saved. When they persecute you in one town, flee to the next; for truly, I say to you, you will not have gone through all the towns of Israel, before the Son of man comes."

Friday

Psalm 140 [page 796],   *Psalm 142* [page 798],

❖   *Psalm 141* [page 797],   *Psalm 143:1-11(12)* [page 798]

A Reading (Lesson) from the Book of Ezekiel [39:21-29]

The word of the Lord came to me: "I will set my glory among the nations; and all the nations shall see my judgment which I have executed, and my hand which I have laid on them. The house of Israel shall know that I am the Lord their God, from that day forward. And the nations shall know that the house of Israel went into captivity for their iniquity, because they dealt so treacherously with me that I hid my face from them and gave them into the hand of their adversaries, and they all fell by the sword. I dealt with them according to their uncleanness and their transgressions, and hid my face from them. Therefore thus says the Lord God: Now I will restore the fortunes of Jacob, and have mercy upon the whole house of Israel; and I will be jealous for my holy name. They shall forget their shame, and all the treachery they have practiced against me, when they dwell securely in their land with none to make them afraid, when I have brought them back from the peoples and gathered them from their enemies' lands, and through them have vindicated my holiness in the sight of many nations. Then they shall know that I am the Lord their God because I sent them into exile among the nations, and then gathered them into their own land. I will leave none of them remaining among the nations any more; and I will not hide my face any more from them, when I pour out my Spirit upon the house of Israel, says the Lord God."

A Reading (Lesson) from the First Letter of John [3:1-10]

See what love the Father has given us, that we should be called children of God; and so we are. The reason why the world does not know us is that it did not know him. Beloved, we are God's children now; it does not yet appear what we shall be, but we know that when he appears we shall be like him, for we shall see him as he is. And every one who thus hopes in him purifies himself as he is pure. Every one who commits sin is guilty of lawlessness; sin is lawlessness. You know that he appeared to take away sins, and in him there is no sin. No one who abides in him sins; no one who sins has either seen him or known him. Little children, let no one deceive you. He who does right is righteous, as he is righteous. He who commits sin is of the devil; for the devil has sinned from the beginning. The reason the Son of God appeared was to destroy the works of the devil. No one born of God commits sin; for God's nature abides in him, and he cannot sin because he is born of God. By this it may be seen who are the children of God, and who are the children of the devil: whoever does not do right is not of God, nor he who does not love his brother.

A Reading (Lesson) from the Gospel according to Matthew
[10:24-33]

Jesus charged the twelve apostles, "A disciple is not above his teacher, nor a servant above his master; it is enough for the disciple to be like his teacher, and the servant like his master. If they have called the master of the house Be-el'zebul, how much more will they malign those of his household. So have no fear of them; for nothing is covered that will not be revealed, or hidden that will not be known. What I tell you in the dark, utter in the light; and what you hear whispered, proclaim upon the housetops. And do not fear those who kill the body but cannot kill the soul; rather fear him who can destroy both soul and body in hell. Are not two sparrows sold for a penny? And not one of them will fall to the ground without your Father's will. But even the hairs of your head are all numbered. Fear not, therefore; you are of more value than many sparrows. So every one who acknowledges me before men, I also will acknowledge before my Father who is in heaven; but whoever denies me before men, I also will deny before my Father who is in heaven."

Saturday

Psalm 137: 1-6 (7-9) [page 792],   *Psalm 144* [page 801]
❖ *Psalm 104* [page 735]

A Reading (Lesson) from the Book of Ezekiel [47:1-12]

A man, whose appearance was like bronze, brought me back to the door of the temple; and behold, water was issuing from below the threshold of the temple toward the east (for the temple faced east); and the water was flowing down from below the south end of the threshold of the temple, south of the altar. Then he brought me out by way of the north gate, and led me round on the outside to the outer gate, that faces toward the east; and the water was coming out on the south side. Going on eastward with a line in his hand, the man measured a thousand cubits, and then led me through the water; and it was ankle-deep. Again he measured a thousand, and led me through the water; and it was knee-deep. Again he measured a thousand, and led me through the water; and it was up to the loins. Again he measured a thousand, and it was a river that I could not pass through, for the water had risen; it was deep enough to swim in, a river that could not be passed through. And he said to me, "Son of man, have you seen this?" Then he led me back along the bank of the river. As I went back, I saw upon the bank of the river very many trees on the one side and on the other. And he said to me, "This water flows toward the eastern region and goes down into the Arabah; and when it enters the stagnant waters of the sea, the water will become fresh. And wherever the river goes every living creature which swarms will live, and there will be very many fish; for this water goes there, that the waters of the sea may become fresh; so everything will live where the river goes. Fishermen will stand beside the sea; from En-ge'di to En-eg'laim it will be a place for the spreading of nets; its fish will be of very many kinds, like the fish of the Great Sea. But its swamps and marshes will not become fresh; they are to be left for salt. And on the banks, on both sides of the river, there will grow all kinds of trees for food. Their leaves will not wither nor their fruit fail, but they will bear fresh fruit every month, because the water for them flows from the sanctuary. Their fruit will be for food, and their leaves for healing."

A Reading (Lesson) from the First Letter of John [3:11-18]

For this is the message which you have heard from the beginning, that we should love one another, and not be like Cain who was of the evil one, and murdered his brother. And why did he murder him? Because his own deeds were evil and his brother's righteous. Do not wonder, brethren, that the world hates you. We know that we have passed out of death into life, because we love the brethren. He who does not love abides in death. Any one who hates his brother is a murderer, and you know that no murderer has eternal life abiding in him. By this we know love, that he laid down his life for us; and we ought to lay down our lives for the brethren. But if any one has the world's goods and sees his brother in need, yet closes his heart against him, how does God's love abide in him? Little children, let us not love in word or speech but in deed and in truth.

A Reading (Lesson) from the Gospel according to Matthew [10:34-42]

Jesus charged the twelve apostles, "Do not think that I have come to bring peace on earth; I have not come to bring peace, but a sword. For I have come to set a man against his father, and a daughter against her mother, and a daughter-in-law against her mother-in-law; and a man's foes will be those of his own household. He who loves father or mother more than me is not worthy of me; and he who loves son or daughter more than me is not worthy of me; and he who does not take his cross and follow me is not worthy of me.He who finds his life will lose it, and he who loses his life for my sake will find it. He who receives you receives me, and he who receives me receives him who sent me. He who receives a prophet because he is a prophet shall receive a prophet's reward, and he who receives a righteous man because he is a righteous man shall receive a righteous man's reward. And whoever gives to one of these little ones even a cup of cold water because he is a disciple, truly, I say to you, he shall not lose his reward."

Proper 2   *Week of the Sunday closest to May 18*

Monday

Psalm 1 [page 585],   *Psalm 2* [page 586],
Psalm 3 [page 587]   ❖   *Psalm 4* [page 587],
Psalm 7 [page 590]

A Reading (Lesson) from the Book of Proverbs [3:11-20]

My son, do not despise the Lord's discipline or be weary of his reproof, for the Lord reproves him whom he loves, as a father the son in whom he delights. Happy is the man who finds wisdom, and the man who gets understanding, for the gain from it is better than gain from silver and its profit better than gold. She is more precious than jewels, and nothing you desire can compare with her. Long life is in her right hand; in her left hand are riches and honor. Her ways are ways of pleasantness, and all her paths are peace. She is a tree of life to those who lay hold of her; those who hold her fast are called happy. The Lord by wisdom founded the earth; by understanding he established the heavens; by his knowledge the deeps broke forth, and the clouds drop down the dew.

A Reading (Lesson) from the First Letter of John
[3:18—4:6]

Little children, let us not love in word or speech but in deed and in truth. By this we shall know that we are of the truth, and reassure our hearts before him whenever our hearts condemn us; for God is greater than our hearts, and he knows everything. Beloved, if our hearts do not condemn us, we have confidence before God; and we receive from him whatever we ask, because we keep his commandments and do what pleases him. And this is his commandment, that we should believe in the name of his Son Jesus Christ and love one another, just as he has commanded us. All who keep his commandments abide in him, and he in them. And by this we know that he abides in us, by the Spirit which he has given us. Beloved, do not believe every spirit, but test the spirits to see whether they are of God; for many false prophets have gone out into the world. By this you know the Spirit of God: every spirit which confesses that Jesus Christ has come in the flesh is of God, and every spirit which does not confess Jesus is not of God. This is the spirit of antichrist, of which you heard that it was coming, and now it is in the world already. Little children, you are of God, and have overcome them; for he who is in you is greater than he who is in the world. They are of the world, therefore what they say is of the world, and the world listens to them. We are of God. Whoever knows God listens to us, and he who is not of God does not listen to us. By this we know the spirit of truth and the spirit of error.

A Reading (Lesson) from the Gospel according to Matthew
[11:1-6]

When Jesus had finished instructing his twelve disciples, he went on from there to teach and preach in their cities. Now when John heard in prison about the deeds of the Christ, he sent word by his disciples and said to him, "Are you he who is to come, or shall we look for another?" And Jesus answered them, "Go and tell John what you hear and see: the blind receive their sight and the lame walk, lepers are cleansed and the deaf hear, and the dead are raised up, and the poor have good news preached to them. And blessed is he who takes no offense at me."

Tuesday

Psalm 5 [page 588], *Psalm 6* [page 589] ❖
Psalm 10 [page 594], *Psalm 11* [page 596]

A Reading (Lesson) from the Book of Proverbs [4:1-27]

Hear, O sons, a father's instruction, and be attentive, that you may gain insight; for I give you good precepts: do not forsake my teaching. When I was a son with my father, tender, the only one in the sight of my mother, he taught me, and said to me, "Let your heart hold fast my words; keep my commandments, and live; do not forget, and do not turn away from the words of my mouth. Get wisdom; get insight. Do not forsake her, and she will keep you; love her, and she will guard you. The beginning of wisdom is this: Get wisdom, and whatever you get, get insight. Prize her highly, and she will exalt you; she will honor you if you embrace her. She will place on your head a fair garland; she will bestow on you a beautiful crown." Hear, my son, and accept my words, that the years of your life may be many. I have taught you the way of wisdom; I have led you in the paths of uprightness. When you walk, your step will not be hampered; and if you run, you will not stumble. Keep hold of instruction, do not let go; guard her, for she is your life. Do not enter the path of the wicked, and do not walk in the way of evil men. Avoid it; do not go on it; turn away from it and pass on. For they cannot sleep unless they have done wrong; they are robbed of sleep unless they have made some one stumble. For they eat the bread of wickedness and drink the wine of violence. But the path of the righteous is like the light of dawn, which shines brighter and brighter until full day. The way of the wicked is like deep darkness; they do not know over what they stumble. My son, be attentive to my words; incline your ear to my sayings. Let them not escape from your sight; keep them within your heart. For they are life to him who finds them, and healing to all his flesh. Keep your heart with all vigilance; for from it flow the springs of life. Put away from you crooked speech, and put devious talk far from you. Let your eyes look directly forward, and your gaze be straight before you. Take heed to the path of your feet, then all your ways will be sure. Do not swerve to the right or to the left; turn your foot away from evil.

A Reading (Lesson) from the First Letter of John [4:7-21]

Beloved, let us love one another; for love is of God, and he who loves is born of God and knows God. He who does not love does not know God; for God is love. In this the love of God was made manifest among us, that God sent his only Son into the world, so that we might live through him. In this is love, not that we loved God but that he loved us and sent his Son to be the expiation for our sins. Beloved, if God so loved us, we also ought to love one another. No man has ever seen God; if we love one another, God abides in us and his love is perfected in us. By this we know that we abide in him and he in us, because he has given us of his own Spirit. And we have seen and testify that the Father has sent his Son as the Savior of the world. Whoever confesses that Jesus is the Son of God, God abides in him, and he in God. So we know and believe the love God has for us. God is love, and he who abides in love abides in God, and God abides in him. In this is love perfected with us, that we may have confidence for the day of judgment, because as he is so are we in this world. There is no fear in love, but perfect love casts out fear. For fear has to do with punishment, and he who fears is not perfected in love. We love, because he first loved us. If any one says, "I love God," and hates his brother, he is a liar; for he who does not love his brother whom he has seen, cannot love God whom he has not seen. And this commandment we have from him, that he who loves God should love his brother also.

A Reading (Lesson) from the Gospel according to Matthew [11:7-15]

As John's disciples went away, Jesus began to speak to the crowds concerning John: "What did you go out into the wilderness to behold? A reed shaken by the wind? Why then did you go out? To see a man clothed in soft raiment? Behold, those who wear soft raiment are in kings' houses. Why then did you go out? To see a prophet? Yes, I tell you, and more than a prophet. This is he of whom it is written, 'Behold, I send my messenger before thy face, who shall prepare thy way before thee.' Truly, I say to you, among those born of women there has risen no one greater than John the Baptist; yet he who is least in the kingdom of heaven is greater than he. From the days of John the Baptist until now the kingdom of heaven has suffered violence, and men of violence take it by force. For all the prophets and the law prophesied until John; and if you are willing to accept it, he is Eli'jah who is to come. He who has ears to hear, let him hear."

Wednesday

Psalm 119:1-24 [page 763]   ❖   *Psalm 12* [page 597], *Psalm 13* [page 597],   *Psalm 14* [page 598]

A Reading (Lesson) from the Book of Proverbs [6:1-19]

My son, if you have become surety for your neighbor, have given your pledge for a stranger; if you are snared in the utterance of your lips, caught in the words of your mouth; then do this, my son, and save yourself, for you have come into your neighbor's power: go, hasten, and importune your neighbor. Give your eyes no sleep and your eyelids no slumber; save yourself like a gazelle from the hunter, like a bird from the hand of the fowler. Go to the ant, O sluggard; consider her ways, and be wise. Without having any chief, officer or ruler, she prepares her food in summer, and gathers her sustenance in harvest. How long will you lie there, O sluggard? When will you arise from your sleep? A little sleep, a little slumber, a little folding of the hands to rest, and poverty will come upon you like a vagabond, and want like an armed man. A worthless person, a wicked man, goes about with crooked speech, winks with his eyes, scrapes with his feet, points with his finger, with perverted heart devises evil, continually sowing discord; therefore calamity will come upon him suddenly; in a moment he will be broken beyond healing. There are six things which the Lord hates, seven which are an abomination to him: haughty eyes, a lying tongue, and hands that shed innocent blood, a heart that devises wicked plans, feet that make haste to run to evil, a false witness who breathes out lies, and a man who sows discord among brothers.

A Reading (Lesson) from the First Letter of John [5:1-12]

Every one who believes that Jesus is the Christ is a child of God, and every one who loves the parent loves the child. By this we know that we love the children of God, when we love God and obey his commandments. For this is the love of God, that we keep his commandments. And his commandments are not burdensome. For whatever is born of God overcomes the world; and this is the victory that overcomes the world, our faith. Who is it that overcomes the world but he who believes that Jesus is the Son of God? This is he who came by water and blood, Jesus Christ, not with the water only but with the water and the blood. And the Spirit is the witness, because the Spirit is the truth. There are three witnesses, the Spirit, the water, and the blood; and these three agree. If we receive the testimony of men, the testimony of God is greater; for this is the testimony of God that he has borne witness to his Son. He who believes in the Son of God has the testimony in himself. He who does not believe God has made him a liar, because he has not believed in the testimony that God has borne to his Son. And this is the testimony, that God gave us eternal life, and this life is in his Son. He who has the Son has life; he who has not the Son of God has not life.

A Reading (Lesson) from the Gospel according to Matthew [11:16-24]

Jesus said to the crowds, "To what shall I compare this generation? It is like children sitting in the market places and calling to their playmates, 'We piped to you, and you did not dance; we wailed, and you did not mourn.' For John came neither eating nor drinking, and they say, 'He has a demon'; the Son of man came eating and drinking, and they say, 'Behold, a glutton and a drunkard, a friend of tax collectors and sinners!' Yet wisdom is justified by her deeds." Then he began to upbraid the cities where most of his mighty works had been done, because they did not repent. "Woe to you, Chora'zin! woe to you, Beth-sa'ida! for if the mighty works done in you had been done in Tyre and Sidon, they would have repented long ago in sackcloth and ashes. But I tell you, it shall be more tolerable on the day of judgment for Tyre and Sidon than for you. And you, Caper'na-um, will you be exalted to heaven? You shall be brought down to Hades. For if the mighty works done in you had been done in Sodom, it would have remained until this day. But I tell you that it shall be more tolerable on the day of judgment for the land of Sodom than for you."

Thursday

Psalm 18:1-20 [page 602]   ❖   *Psalm 18:21-50* [page 604]

A Reading (Lesson) from the Book of Proverbs [7:1-27]

My son, keep my words and treasure up my commandments with you; keep my commandments and live, keep my teachings as the apple of your eye; bind them on your fingers, write them on the tablet of your heart. Say to wisdom, "You are my sister," and call insight your intimate friend; to preserve you from the loose woman, from the adventuress with her smooth words. For at the window of my house I have looked out through my lattice, and I have seen among the simple, I have perceived among the youths, a young man without sense, passing along the street near her corner, taking the road to her house in the twilight, in the evening, at the time of night and darkness. And lo, a woman meets him, dressed as a harlot, wily of heart. She is loud and wayward, her feet do not stay at home; now in the street, now in the market, and at every corner she lies in wait. She seizes him and kisses him, and with impudent face she says to him: "I had to offer sacrifices, and today I have paid my vows; so now I have come out to meet you, to seek you eagerly, and I have found you. I have decked my couch with coverings, colored spreads of Egyptian linen; I have perfumed my bed with myrrh, aloes, and cinnamon. Come, let us take our fill of love till morning; let us delight ourselves with love. For my husband is not at home; he has gone on a long journey; he took a bag of money with him; at full moon he will come home." With much seductive speech she persuades him; with her smooth talk she compels him. All at once he follows her, as an ox goes to the slaughter, or as a stag is caught fast till an arrow pierces its entrails; as a bird rushes into a snare; he does not know that it will cost him his life. And now, O sons, listen to me, and be attentive to the words of my mouth. Let not your heart turn aside to her ways, do not stray into her paths; for many a victim has she laid low; yea, all her slain are a mighty host. Her house is the way to Sheol, going down to the chambers of death.

A Reading (Lesson) from the First Letter of John [5:13-21]

I write this to you who believe in the name of the Son of God, that you may know that you have eternal life. And this is the confidence which we have in him, that if we ask anything according to his will he hears us. And if we know that he hears us in whatever we ask, we know that we have obtained the requests made of him. If any one sees his brother committing what is not a mortal sin, he will ask, and God will give him life for those whose sin is not mortal. There is sin which is mortal; I do not say that one is to pray for that. All wrongdoing is sin, but there is sin which is not mortal. We know that any one born of God does not sin, but He who was born of God keeps him, and the evil one does not touch him. We know that we are of God, and the whole world is in the power of the evil one. And we know that the Son of God has come and has given us understanding, to know him who is true; and we are in him who is true, in his Son Jesus Christ. This is the true God and eternal life. Little children, keep yourselves from idols.

A Reading (Lesson) from the Gospel according to Matthew [11:25-30]

Jesus declared, "I thank thee, Father, Lord of heaven and earth, that thou hast hidden these things from the wise and understanding and revealed them to babes; yea, Father, for such was thy gracious will. All things have been delivered to me by my Father; and no one knows the Son except the Father, and no one knows the Father except the Son and any one to whom the Son chooses to reveal him. Come to me, all who labor and are heavy laden, and I will give you rest. Take my yoke upon you, and learn from me; for I am gentle and lowly in heart, and you will find rest for your souls. For my yoke is easy, and my burden is light."

Friday

Psalm 16 [page 599],   *Psalm 17* [page 600]
❖   *Psalm 22* [page 610]

A Reading (Lesson) from the Book of Proverbs [8:1-21]

Does not wisdom call, does not understanding raise her
voice? On the heights beside the way, in the paths she takes
her stand; beside the gates in front of the town, at the
entrance of the portals she cries aloud: "To you, O men, I
call, and my cry is to the sons of men. O simple ones, learn
prudence; O foolish men, pay attention. Hear, for I will
speak noble things, and from my lips will come what is
right; for my mouth will utter truth; wickedness is an
abomination to my lips. All the words of my mouth are
righteous; there is nothing twisted or crooked in them.
They are all straight to him who understands and right to
those who find knowledge. Take my instruction instead of
silver, and knowledge rather than choice gold; for wisdom
is better than jewels, and all that you may desire cannot
compare with her. I, wisdom, dwell in prudence, and I find
knowledge and discretion. The fear of the Lord is hatred of
evil. Pride and arrogance and the way of evil and perverted
speech I hate. I have counsel and sound wisdom, I have
insight, I have strength. By me kings reign, and rulers
decree what is just; by me princes rule, and nobles govern
the earth. I love those who love me, and those who seek me
diligently find me. Riches and honor are with me, enduring
wealth and prosperity. My fruit is better than gold, even
fine gold, and my yield than choice silver. I walk in the way
of righteousness, in the paths of justice, endowing with
wealth those who love me, and filling their treasuries."

A Reading (Lesson) from the Second Letter of John [1-13]

The elder to the elect lady and her children, whom I love in
the truth, and not only I but also all who know the truth,
because of the truth which abides in us and will be with us

for ever: Grace, mercy, and peace will be with us, from God the Father and from Jesus Christ the Father's Son, in truth and love. I rejoiced greatly to find some of your children following the truth, just as we have been commanded by the Father. And now I beg you, lady, not as though I were writing you a new commandment, but the one we have had from the beginning, that we love one another. And this is love, that we follow his commandments; this is the commandment, as you have heard from the beginning, that you follow love. For many deceivers have gone out into the world, men who will not acknowledge the coming of Jesus Christ in the flesh; such a one is the deceiver and the antichrist. Look to yourselves, that you may not lose what you have worked for, but may win a full reward. Any one who goes ahead and does not abide in the doctrine of Christ does not have God; he who abides in the doctrine has both the Father and the Son. If any one comes to you and does not bring this doctrine, do not receive him into the house or give him any greeting; for he who greets him shares his wicked work. Though I have much to write to you, I would rather not use paper and ink, but I hope to come to see you and talk with you face to face, so that our joy may be complete. The children of your eldest sister greet you.

A Reading (Lesson) from the Gospel according to Matthew
[12:1-14]

At that time Jesus went through the grainfields on the sabbath; his disciples were hungry, and they began to pluck heads of grain and to eat. But when the Pharisees saw it, they said to him, "Look, your disciples are doing what is not lawful to do on the sabbath." He said to them, "Have you not read what David did, when he was hungry, and those who were with him: how he entered the house of God and ate the bread of the Presence, which it was not lawful for him to eat nor for those who were with him, but only for the priests? Or have you not read in the law how on the sabbath the priests in the temple profane the sabbath, and are guiltless? I tell you, something greater than the temple is here. And if you had known what this means, 'I desire mercy, and not sacrifice,' you would not have condemned the guiltless. For the Son of man is lord of the sabbath." And he went on from there, and entered their synagogue. And behold, there was a man with a withered hand. And they asked him, "Is it lawful to heal on the sabbath?" so that they might accuse him. He said to them, "What man of you, if he has one sheep and it falls into a pit on the sabbath, will not lay hold of it and lift it out? Of how much more value is a man than a sheep! So it is lawful to do good on the sabbath." Then he said to the man, "Stretch out your hand." And the man stretched it out, and it was restored, whole like the other. But the Pharisees went out and took counsel against him, how to destroy him.

Saturday

Psalm 20 [page 608], *Psalm 21:1-7(8-14)* [page 608]
❖ *Psalm 110:1-5(6-7)* [page 753], *Psalm 116* [page 759], *Psalm 117* [page 760]

A Reading (Lesson) from the Book of Proverbs [8:22-36]

Wisdom cries aloud: "The Lord created me at the beginning of his work, the first of his acts of old. Ages ago I was set up, at the first, before the beginning of the earth. When there were no depths I was brought forth, when there were no springs abounding with water. Before the mountains had been shaped, before the hills, I was brought forth; before he had made the earth with its fields, or the first of the dust of the world. When he established the heavens, I was there, when he drew a circle on the face of the deep, when he made firm the skies above, when he established the fountains of the deep, when he assigned to the sea its limit, so that the waters might not transgress his command, when he marked out the foundations of the earth, then I was beside him, like a master workman; and I was daily his delight, rejoicing before him always, rejoicing in his inhabited world and delighting in the sons of men. And now, my sons, listen to me: happy are those who keep my ways. Hear instruction and be wise, and do not neglect it. Happy is the man who listens to me, watching daily at my gates, waiting beside my doors. For he who finds me finds life and obtains favor from the Lord; but he who misses me injures himself; all who hate me love death."

A Reading (Lesson) from the Third Letter of John [1-15]

The elder to the beloved Ga'ius, whom I love in the truth. Beloved, I pray that all may go well with you and that you may be in health, I know that it is well with your soul. For I greatly rejoiced when some of the brethren arrived and testified to the truth of your life, as indeed you do follow the truth. No greater joy can I have than this, to hear that my children follow the truth. Beloved, it is a loyal thing you do when you render any service to the brethren, especially to strangers, who have testified to your love before the church. You will do well to send them on their journey as befits God's service. For they have set out for his sake and have accepted nothing from the heathen. So we ought to support such men, that we may be fellow workers in the truth. I have written something to the church; but Diot'rephes, who likes to put himself first, does not acknowledge my authority. So if I come, I will bring up what he is doing, prating against me with evil words. And not content with that, he refuses to welcome the brethren, and also stops those who want to welcome them and puts them out of the church. Beloved, do not imitate evil but imitate good. He who does good is of God; he who does evil has not seen God. Deme'trius has testimony from every one, and from the truth itself; I testify to him too, and you know my testimony is true. I had much to write to you, but

I would rather not write with pen and ink; I hope to see you soon, and we will talk together face to face. Peace be with you. The friends greet you. Greet the friends, every one of them.

A Reading (Lesson) from the Gospel according to Matthew [12:15-21]

Jesus, aware that the Pharisees took counsel against him, how to destroy him, withdrew from there. And many followed him, and he healed them all, and ordered them not to make him known. This was to fulfil what was spoken by the prophet Isaiah: "Behold, my servant whom I have chosen, my beloved with whom my soul is well pleased. I will put my Spirit upon him, and he shall proclaim justice to the Gentiles. He will not wrangle or cry aloud, nor will any one hear his voice in the streets; he will not break a bruised reed or quench a smoldering wick, till he brings justice to victory; and in his name will the Gentiles hope."

Proper 3 *Week of the Sunday closest to May 25*

Sunday

Psalm 148 [page 805], *Psalm 149* [page 807], *Psalm 150* [page 807] ❖ *Psalm 114* [page 756], *Psalm 115* [page 757]

A Reading (Lesson) from the Book of Proverbs [9:1-12]

Wisdom has built her house, she has set up her seven pillars. She has slaughtered her beasts, she has mixed her wine, she has also set her table. She has sent out her maids to call from the highest places in the town, "Whoever is simple, let him turn in here!" To him who is without sense she says, "Come, eat of my bread and drink of the wine I have mixed. Leave simpleness, and live, and walk in the way of insight." He who corrects a scoffer gets himself abuse, and he who reproves a wicked man incurs injury. Do not reprove a scoffer, or he will hate you; reprove a wise man, and he will love you. Give instruction to a wise man, and he will be still wiser; teach a righteous man and he will increase in learning. The fear of the Lord is the beginning of wisdom, and the knowledge of the Holy One is insight. For by me your days will be multiplied, and years will be added to your life. If you are wise, you are wise for yourself; if you scoff, you alone will bear it.

A Reading (Lesson) from the Acts of the Apostles [8:14-25]

When the apostles at Jerusalem heard that Samar'ia had received the word of God, they sent to them Peter and John, who came down and prayed for them that they might receive the Holy Spirit; for it had not yet fallen on any of them, but they had only been baptized in the name of the Lord Jesus. Then they laid their hands on them and they received the Holy Spirit. Now when Simon saw that the Spirit was given through the laying on of the apostles' hands, he offered them money, saying, "Give me also this power, that any one on whom I lay my hands may receive the Holy Spirit." But Peter said to him, "Your silver perish with you, because you thought you could obtain the gift of God with money! You have neither part nor lot in this matter, for your heart is not right before God. Repent therefore of this wickedness of yours, and pray to the Lord that, if possible, the intent of your heart may be forgiven you. For I see that you are in the gall of bitterness and in the bond of iniquity." And Simon answered, "Pray for me to the Lord, that nothing of what you have said may come upon me." Now when they had testified and spoken the word of the Lord, they returned to Jerusalem, preaching the gospel to many villages of the Samaritans.

A Reading (Lesson) from the Gospel according to Luke
[10:25-28, 38-42]

Behold, a lawyer stood up to put Jesus to the test, saying,
"Teacher, what shall I do to inherit eternal life?" He said to
him, "What is written in the law? How do you read?" And
he answered, "You shall love the Lord your God with all
your heart, and with all your soul, and with all your
strength, and with all your mind; and your neighbor as
yourself." And he said to him, "You have answered right;
do this, and you will live." Now as they went on their way,
he entered a village; and a woman named Martha received
him into her house. And she had a sister called Mary, who
sat at the Lord's feet and listened to his teaching. But
Martha was distracted with much serving; and she went to
him and said, "Lord, do you not care that my sister has left
me to serve alone? Tell her then to help me." But the Lord
answered her, "Martha, Martha, you are anxious and
troubled about many things; one thing is needful. Mary
has chosen the good portion, which shall not be taken
away from her."

Monday

Psalm 25 [page 614] ❖ *Psalm 9* [page 593],
Psalm 15 [page 599]

A Reading (Lesson) from the Book of Proverbs [10:1-12]

A wise son makes a glad father, but a foolish son is a
sorrow to his mother. Treasures gained by wickedness do
not profit, but righteousness delivers from death. The Lord
does not let the righteous go hungry, but he thwarts the
craving of the wicked. A slack hand causes poverty, but the
hand of the diligent makes rich. A son who gathers in
summer is prudent, but a son who sleeps in harvest brings
shame. Blessings are on the head of the righteous, but the
mouth of the wicked conceals violence. The memory of the

righteous is a blessing, but the name of the wicked will rot. The wise of heart will heed commandments, but a prating fool will come to ruin. He who walks in integrity walks securely, but he who perverts his ways will be found out. He who winks the eye causes trouble, but he who boldly reproves makes peace. The mouth of the righteous is a fountain of life, but the mouth of the wicked conceals violence. Hatred stirs up strife, but love covers all offenses.

A Reading (Lesson) from the First Letter of Paul to Timothy [1:1-17]

Paul, an apostle of Christ Jesus by command of God our Savior and of Christ Jesus our hope, To Timothy, my true child in the faith: Grace, mercy, and peace from God the Father and Christ Jesus our Lord. As I urged you when I was going to Macedo'nia, remain at Ephesus that you may charge certain persons not to teach any different doctrine, nor to occupy themselves with myths and endless genealogies which promote speculations rather than the divine training that is in faith; whereas the aim of our charge is love that issues from a pure heart and a good conscience and sincere faith. Certain persons by swerving from these have wandered away into vain discussion, desiring to be teachers of the law, without understanding either what they are saying or the things about which they make assertions. Now we know that the law is good, if any one uses it lawfully, understanding this, that the law is not laid down for the just but for the lawless and disobedient, for the ungodly and sinners, for the unholy and profane, for murderers of fathers and murderers of mothers, for manslayers, immoral persons, sodomites, kidnapers, liars, perjurers, and whatever else is contrary to sound doctrine, in accordance with the glorious gospel of the blessed God with which I have been entrusted. I thank him who has given me strength for this, Christ Jesus our Lord, because he judged me faithful by appointing me to his service, though I formerly blasphemed and persecuted and insulted him; but I received mercy because I had acted ignorantly in unbelief, and the grace of our Lord overflowed for me with the faith and love that are in Christ Jesus. The saying is sure and worthy of full acceptance, that Christ Jesus came into the world to save sinners. And I am the foremost of sinners; but I received mercy for this reason, that in me, as the foremost, Jesus Christ might display his perfect patience for an example to those who were to believe in him for eternal life. To the King of ages, immortal, invisible, the only God, be honor and glory for ever and ever. Amen.

A Reading (Lesson) from the Gospel according to Matthew [12:22-32]

A blind and dumb demoniac was brought to Jesus, and he healed him, so that the dumb man spoke and saw. And all the people were amazed, and said, "Can this be the Son of David?" But when the Pharisees heard it they said, "It is only by Be-el'zebul, the prince of demons, that this man casts out demons." Knowing their thoughts, he said to them, "Every kingdom divided against itself is laid waste, and no city or house divided against itself will stand; and if Satan casts out Satan, he is divided against himself; how then will his kingdom stand? And if I cast out demons by Be-el'zebul, by whom do your sons cast them out? Therefore they shall be your judges. But if it is by the Spirit of God that I cast out demons, then the kingdom of God has come upon you. Or how can one enter a strong man's house and plunder his goods, unless he first binds the strong man? Then indeed he may plunder his house. He who is not with me is against me, and he who does not gather with me scatters. Therefore I tell you, every sin and blasphemy will be forgiven men, but the blasphemy against the Spirit will not be forgiven. And whoever speaks against the Holy Spirit will not be forgiven, either in this age or in the age to come."

Tuesday

Psalm 26 [page 616]   *Psalm 28* [page 619]   ❖
Psalm 36 [page 632],   *Psalm 39* [page 638]

A Reading (Lesson) from the Book of Proverbs [15:16-33]

Better is a little with the fear of the Lord than great
treasure and trouble with it. Better is a dinner of herbs
where love is than a fatted ox and hatred with it. A
hot-tempered man stirs up strife, but he who is slow to
anger quiets contention. The way of a sluggard is
overgrown with thorns, but the path of the upright is a
level highway. A wise son makes a glad father, but a
foolish man despises his mother. Folly is a joy to him who
has no sense, but a man of understanding walks aright.
Without counsel plans go wrong, but with many advisers
they succeed. To make an apt answer is a joy to a man, and
a word in season, how good it is! The wise man's path
leads upward to life, that he may avoid Sheol beneath.
The Lord tears down the house of the proud, but maintains
the widow's boundaries. The thoughts of the wicked are
an abomination to the Lord, the words of the pure are
pleasing to him. He who is greedy for unjust gain makes
trouble for his household, but he who hates bribes will
live. The mind of the righteous ponders how to answer,
but the mouth of the wicked pours out evil things. The
Lord is far from the wicked, but he hears the prayer of the
righteous. The light of the eyes rejoices the heart, and good
news refreshes the bones. He whose ear heeds wholesome
admonition will abide among the wise. He who ignores
instruction despises himself, but he who heeds admonition
gains understanding. The fear of the Lord is instruction in
wisdom, and humility goes before honor.

*A Reading (Lesson) from the First Letter of Paul
to Timothy* [1:18—2:8]

This charge I commit to you, Timothy, my son, in accordance with the prophetic utterances which pointed to you, that inspired by them you may wage the good warfare, holding faith and a good conscience. By rejecting conscience, certain persons have made shipwreck of their faith, among them Hymenae'us and Alexander, whom I have delivered to Satan that they may learn not to blaspheme. First of all, then, I urge that supplications, prayers, intercessions, and thanksgivings be made for all men, for kings and all who are in high positions, that we may lead a quiet and peaceable life, godly and respectful in every way. This is good, and it is acceptable in the sight of God our Savior, who desires all men to be saved and to come to the knowledge of the truth. For there is one God, and there is one mediator between God and men, the man Christ Jesus, who gave himself as a ransom for all, the testimony to which was borne at the proper time. For this I was appointed a preacher and apostle (I am telling the truth, I am not lying), a teacher of the Gentiles in faith and truth. I desire then that in every place the men should pray, lifting holy hands without anger or quarreling.

A Reading (Lesson) from the Gospel according to Matthew [12:33-42]

Jesus said to the Pharisees, "Either make the tree good, and its fruit good; or make the tree bad, and its fruit bad; for the tree is known by its fruit. You brood of vipers! How can you speak good, when you are evil? For out of the abundance of the heart the mouth speaks. The good man out of his good treasure brings forth good, and the evil man out of his evil treasure brings forth evil. I tell you, on the day of judgment men will render account for every careless word they utter; for by your words you will be justified, and by your words you will be condemned." Then some of the scribes and Pharisees said to him, "Teacher, we wish to see a sign from you." But he answered them, "An evil and adulterous generation seeks for a sign;

but no sign shall be given to it except the sign of the prophet Jonah. For as Jonah was three days and three nights in the belly of the whale, so will the Son of man be three days and three nights in the heart of the earth. The men of Nin'eveh will arise at the judgment with this generation and condemn it; for they repented at the preaching of Jonah, and behold, something greater than Jonah is here. The queen of the South will arise at the judgment with this generation and condemn it; for she came from the ends of the earth to hear the wisdom of Solomon, and behold, something greater than Solomon is here."

Wednesday

Psalm 38 [page 636]   ❖   *Psalm 119:25-48* [page 765]

A Reading (Lesson) from the Book of Proverbs [17:1-20]

Better is a dry morsel with quiet than a house full of feasting with strife. A slave who deals wisely will rule over a son who acts shamefully, and will share the inheritance as one of the brothers. The crucible is for silver, and the furnace is for gold, and the Lord tries hearts. An evildoer listens to wicked lips; and a liar gives heed to a mischievous tongue. He who mocks the poor insults his Maker; he who is glad at calamity will not go unpunished. Grandchildren are the crown of the aged, and the glory of sons is their fathers. Fine speech is not becoming to a fool; still less is false speech to a prince. A bribe is like a magic stone in the eyes of him who gives it; wherever he turns he prospers. He who forgives an offense seeks love, but he who repeats a matter alienates a friend. A rebuke goes deeper into a man of understanding than a hundred blows into a fool. An evil man seeks only rebellion, and a cruel messenger will be sent against him. Let a man meet a she-bear robbed of her cubs, rather than a fool in his folly. If a man returns evil for good, evil will not depart from his house. The beginning of strife is like letting out water; so quit before the quarrel breaks out. He who justifies the wicked and he who condemns the righteous are both alike an abomination to the Lord. Why should a fool have a price in his hand to buy wisdom, when he has no mind? A friend loves at all times, and a brother is born for adversity. A man without sense gives a pledge, and becomes surety in the presence of his neighbor. He who loves transgression loves strife; he who makes his door high seeks destruction. A man of crooked mind does not prosper, and one with a perverse tongue falls into calamity.

A Reading (Lesson) from the First Letter of Paul to Timothy [3:1-16]

The saying is sure: If any one aspires to the office of bishop, he desires a noble task. Now a bishop must be above reproach, the husband of one wife, temperate, sensible, dignified, hospitable, an apt teacher, no drunkard, not violent but gentle, not quarrelsome, and no lover of money. He must manage his own household well, keeping his children submissive and respectful in every way; for if a man does not know how to manage his own household, how can he care for God's church? He must not be a recent convert, or he may be puffed up with conceit and fall into the condemnation of the devil; moreover he must be well thought of by outsiders, or he may fall into reproach and the snare of the devil. Deacons likewise must be serious, not double-tongued, not addicted to much wine, not greedy for gain; they must hold the mystery of the faith with a clear conscience. And let them also be tested first; then if they prove themselves blameless let them serve as deacons. The women likewise must be serious, no slanderers, but temperate, faithful in all things. Let deacons be the husband of one wife, and let them manage their children and their households well; for those who serve well as deacons gain a good standing for themselves and also great confidence in the faith which is in Christ Jesus. I hope to come to you soon, but I am writing these instructions to you so that, if I am delayed, you may know how one ought to behave in the household of God, which is the church of the living God, the pillar and bulwark of the truth. Great indeed, we confess, is the mystery of our religion: He was manifested in the flesh, vindicated in the Spirit, seen by angels, preached among the nations, believed on in the world, taken up in glory.

A Reading (Lesson) from the Gospel according to Matthew [12:43-50]

Jesus answered the scribes and the Pharisees, "When an unclean spirit has gone out of a man, he passes through waterless places seeking rest, but he finds none. Then he says, 'I will return to my house from which I came.' And when he comes he finds it empty, swept, and put in order. Then he goes and brings with him seven other spirits more evil than himself, and they enter and dwell there; and the last state of that man becomes worse than the first. So shall it be also with this evil generation." While he was still speaking to the people, behold, his mother and his brothers stood outside, asking to speak to him. But he replied to the man who told him, "Who is my mother, and who are my brothers?" And stretching out his hand toward his disciples, he said, "Here are my mother and my brothers! For whoever does the will of my Father in heaven is my brother, and sister, and mother."

Thursday

Psalm 37:1-18 [page 633] ❖ *Psalm 37:19-42* [page 634]

A Reading (Lesson) from the Book of Proverbs [21:30—22:6]

No wisdom, no understanding, no counsel, can avail against the Lord. The horse is made ready for the day of battle, but the victory belongs to the Lord. A good name is to be chosen rather than great riches, and favor is better than silver or gold. The rich and the poor meet together; the Lord is the maker of them all. A prudent man sees danger and hides himself; but the simple go on, and suffer for it. The reward for humility and fear of the Lord is riches and honor and life. Thorns and snares are in the way of the perverse; he who guards himself will keep far from them. Train up a child in the way he should go, and when he is old he will not depart from it.

A Reading (Lesson) from the First Letter of Paul to Timothy [4:1-16]

Now the Spirit expressly says that in later times some will depart from the faith by giving heed to deceitful spirits and doctrines of demons, through the pretensions of liars whose consciences are seared, who forbid marriage and enjoin abstinence from foods which God created to be received with thanksgiving by those who believe and know the truth. For everything created by God is good, and nothing is to be rejected if it is received with thanksgiving; for then it is consecrated by the word of God and prayer. If you put these instructions before the brethren, you will be a good minister of Christ Jesus, nourished on the words of the faith and of the good doctrine which you have followed. Have nothing to do with godless and silly myths. Train yourself in godliness; for while bodily training is of some value, godliness is of value in every way, as it holds promise for the present life and also for the life to come. The saying is sure and worthy of full acceptance. For to this end we toil and strive, because we have our hope set on the living God, who is the Savior of all men, especially of those who believe. Command and teach these things. Let no one despise your youth, but set the believers an example in speech and conduct, in love, in faith, in purity. Till I come, attend to the public reading of scripture, to preaching, to teaching. Do not neglect the gift you have, which was given you by prophetic utterance when the council of elders laid their hands upon you. Practice these duties, devote yourselves to them, so that all may see your progress. Take heed to yourself and to your teaching; hold to that, for by so doing you will save both yourself and your hearers.

A Reading (Lesson) from the Gospel according to Matthew [13:24-30]

Another parable Jesus put before the crowd, saying, "The kingdom of heaven may be compared to a man who sowed good seed in his field; but while men were sleeping, his enemy came and sowed weeds among the wheat, and went away. So when the plants came up and bore grain, then the weeds appeared also. And the servants of the householder came and said to him, 'Sir, did you not sow good seed in your field? How then has it weeds?' He said to them, 'An enemy has done this.' The servants said to him, 'Then do you want us to go and gather them?' But he said, 'No; lest in gathering the weeds you root up the wheat along with them. Let both grow together until the harvest; and at harvest time I will tell the reapers, Gather the weeds first and bind them in bundles to be burned, but gather the wheat into my barn.' "

Friday

Psalm 31 [page 622]   ❖   *Psalm 35* [page 629]

A Reading (Lesson) from the Book of Proverbs [23:19-21,29—24:2]

Hear, my son, and be wise, and direct your mind in the way. Be not among winebibbers, or among gluttonous eaters of meat; for the drunkard and the glutton will come to poverty, and drowsiness will clothe a man with rags. Who has woe? Who has sorrow? Who has strife? Who has complaining? Who has wounds without cause? Who has redness of eyes? Those who tarry long over wine, those who go to try mixed wine. Do not look at wine when it is red, when it sparkles in the cup and goes down smoothly. At the last it bites like a serpent, and stings like an adder. Your eyes will see strange things, and your mind utter perverse things. You will be like one who lies down in the midst of the sea, like one who lies on the top of a mast. "They struck me," you will say, "but I was not hurt; they beat me, but I did not feel it. When shall I awake? I will seek another drink." Be not envious of evil men, nor desire to be with them; for their minds devise violence, and their lips talk of mischief.

A Reading (Lesson) from the First Letter of Paul to Timothy [5:17-22(23-25)]

Let the elders who rule well be considered worthy of double honor, especially those who labor in preaching and teaching; for the scripture says, "You shall not muzzle an ox when it is treading out the grain," and, "The laborer deserves his wages." Never admit any charge against an elder except on the evidence of two or three witnesses. As for those who persist in sin, rebuke them in the presence of all, so that the rest may stand in fear. In the presence of God and of Christ Jesus and the elect angels I charge you to keep these rules without favor, doing nothing from partiality. Do not be hasty in the laying on of hands, nor participate in another man's sins; keep yourself pure.

No longer drink only water, but use a little wine for the sake of your stomach and your frequent ailments. The sins of some men are conspicuous, pointing to judgment, but the sins of others appear later. So also good deeds are conspicuous; and even when they are not, they cannot remain hidden.

A Reading (Lesson) from the Gospel according to Matthew
[13:31-35]

Another parable Jesus put before the crowd, saying, "The
kingdom of heaven is like a grain of mustard seed which a
man took and sowed in his field; it is the smallest of all
seeds, but when it has grown it is the greatest of shrubs,
and becomes a tree, so that the birds of the air come and
make nests in its branches." He told them another parable.
"The kingdom of heaven is like leaven which a woman took
and hid in three measures of flour, till it was all leavened."
All this Jesus said to the crowds in parables; indeed he said
nothing to them without a parable. This was to fulfil what
was spoken by the prophet: "I will open my mouth in
parables, I will utter what has been hidden since the
foundation of the world."

Saturday

Psalm 30 [page 621],   *Psalm 32* [page 624]   ❖
Psalm 42 [page 643],   *Psalm 43* [page 644]

A Reading (Lesson) from the Book of Proverbs [25:15-28]

With patience a ruler may be persuaded, and a soft tongue
will break a bone. If you have found honey, eat only
enough for you, lest you be sated with it and vomit it. Let
your foot be seldom in your neighbor's house, lest he
become weary of you and hate you. A man who bears false
witness against his neighbor is like a war club, or a sword,
or a sharp arrow. Trust in a faithless man in time of
trouble is like a bad tooth or a foot that slips. He who sings
songs to a heavy heart is like one who takes off a garment
on a cold day, and like vinegar on a wound. If your enemy
is hungry, give him bread to eat; and if he is thirsty, give
him water to drink; for you will heap coals of fire on his
head, and the Lord will reward you. The north wind brings
forth rain; and a backbiting tongue, angry looks. It is

better to live in a corner of the housetop than in a house shared with a contentious woman. Like cold water to a thirsty soul, so is good news from a far country. Like a muddied spring or a polluted fountain is a righteous man who gives way before the wicked. It is not good to eat much honey, so be sparing of complimentary words. A man without self-control is like a city broken into and left without walls.

A Reading (Lesson) from the First Letter of Paul to Timothy [6:6-21]

There is great gain in godliness with contentment; for we brought nothing into the world, and we cannot take anything out of the world; but if we have food and clothing, with these we shall be content. But those who desire to be rich fall into temptation, into a snare, into many senseless and hurtful desires that plunge men into ruin and destruction. For the love of money is the root of all evils; it is through this craving that some have wandered away from the faith and pierced their hearts with many pangs. But as for you, man of God, shun all this; aim at righteousness, godliness, faith, love, steadfastness, gentleness. Fight the good fight of the faith; take hold of the eternal life to which you were called when you made the good confession in the presence of many witnesses. In the presence of God who gives life to all things, and of Christ Jesus who in his testimony before Pontius Pilate made the good confession, I charge you to keep the commandment unstained and free from reproach until the appearing of our Lord Jesus Christ; and this will be made manifest at the proper time by the blessed and only Sovereign, the King of kings and Lord of lords, who alone has immortality and dwells in unapproachable light, whom no man has ever seen or can see. To him be honor and eternal dominion. Amen. As for the rich in this world, charge them not to be haughty, nor to set their hopes on uncertain riches but on God who richly furnishes us with everything to enjoy. They are to do good, to be rich in good deeds, liberal and generous, thus laying up for themselves a good foundation for the future, so that they may take hold of the life which is life indeed. O Timothy, guard what has been entrusted to you. Avoid the godless chatter and contradictions of what is falsely called knowledge, for by professing it some have missed the mark as regards the faith. Grace be with you.

A Reading (Lesson) from the Gospel according to Matthew [13:36-43]

Jesus left the crowds and went into the house. And his disciples came to him, saying, "Explain to us the parable of the weeds of the field." He answered, "He who sows the good seed is the Son of man; the field is the world, and the good seed means the sons of the kingdom; the weeds are the sons of the evil one, and the enemy who sowed them is the devil; the harvest is the close of the age, and the reapers are angels. Just as the weeds are gathered and burned with fire, so will it be at the close of the age. The Son of man will send his angels, and they will gather out of his kingdom all causes of sin and all evildoers, and throw them into the furnace of fire; there men will weep and gnash their teeth. Then the righteous will shine like the sun in the kingdom of their Father. He who has ears, let him hear."

Proper 4 *Week of the Sunday closest to June 1*

Sunday

Psalm 63:1-8(9-11) [page 670], *Psalm 98* [page 727]
❖ *Psalm 103* [page 733]

A Reading (Lesson) from the Book of Ecclesiastes [1:1-11]

The words of the Preacher, the son of David, king in

Jerusalem. Vanity of vanities, says the Preacher, vanity of vanities! All is vanity. What does man gain by all the toil at which he toils under the sun? A generation goes, and a generation comes, but the earth remains for ever. The sun rises and the sun goes down, and hastens to the place where it rises. The wind blows to the south, and goes round to the north; round and round goes the wind, and on its circuits the wind returns. All streams run to the sea, but the sea is not full; to the place where the streams flow, there they flow again. All things are full of weariness; a man cannot utter it; the eye is not satisfied with seeing, nor the ear filled with hearing. What has been is what will be, and what has been done is what will be done; and there is nothing new under the sun. Is there a thing of which it is said, "See, this is new"? It has been already, in the ages before us. There is no remembrance of former things, nor will there be any remembrance of later things yet to happen among those who come after.

A Reading (Lesson) from the Acts of the Apostles [8:26-40]

An angel of the Lord said to Philip, "Rise and go toward the south to the road that goes down from Jerusalem to Gaza." This is a desert road. And he rose and went. And behold, an Ethiopian, a eunuch, a minister of Candace, the queen of the Ethiopians, in charge of all her treasure, had come to Jerusalem to worship and was returning; seated in his chariot, he was reading the prophet Isaiah. And the Spirit said to Philip, "Go up and join this chariot." So Philip ran to him, and heard him reading Isaiah the prophet, and asked, "Do you understand what you are reading?" And he said, "How can I, unless some one guides me?" And he invited Philip to come up and sit with him. Now the passage of the scripture which he was reading was this: "As a sheep led to the slaughter or a lamb before its shearer is dumb, so he opens not his mouth. In his humiliation justice was denied him. Who can describe his generation? For his life is taken up from the earth."

And the eunuch said to Philip, "About whom, pray, does the prophet say this, about himself or about some one else?" Then Philip opened his mouth, and beginning with this scripture he told him the good news of Jesus. And as they went along the road they came to some water, and the eunuch said, "See, here is water! What is to prevent my being baptized?" And he commanded the chariot to stop, and they both went down into the water, Philip and the eunuch, and he baptized him. And when they came up out of the water, the Spirit of the Lord caught up Philip; and the eunuch saw him no more, and went on his way rejoicing. But Philip was found at Azo'tus, and passing on he preached the gospel to all the towns till he came to Caesare'a.

A Reading (Lesson) from the Gospel according to Luke [11:1-13]

Jesus was praying in a certain place, and when he ceased, one of his disciples said to him, "Lord, teach us to pray, as John taught his disciples." And he said to them, "When you pray, say: Father, hallowed be thy name. Thy kingdom come. Give us each day our daily bread; and forgive us our sins, for we ourselves forgive every one who is indebted to us; and lead us not into temptation." And he said to them, "Which of you who has a friend will go to him at midnight and say to him, 'Friend, lend me three loaves; for a friend of mine has arrived on a journey, and I have nothing to set before him'; and he will answer from within, 'Do not bother me; the door is now shut, and my children are with me in bed; I cannot get up and give you anything'? I tell you, though he will not get up and give him anything because he is his friend, yet because of his importunity he will rise and give him whatever he needs. And I tell you, Ask, and it will be given you; seek, and you will find; knock, and it will be opened to you. For every one who asks receives, and he who seeks finds, and to him who knocks it will be opened. What father among you, if his son asks for a fish, will instead of a fish give him a serpent; or if he asks for an egg, will give him a scorpion? If you then, who are evil, know how to give good gifts to your children, how much more will the heavenly Father give the Holy Spirit to those who ask him!"

Monday

Psalm 41 [page 641], *Psalm 52* [page 657] ❖
Psalm 44 [page 645]

A Reading (Lesson) from the Book of Ecclesiastes
[2:1-15]

I said to myself, "Come now, I will make a test of pleasure; enjoy yourself." But behold, this also was vanity. I said of laughter, "It is mad," and of pleasure, "What use is it?" I searched with my mind how to cheer my body with wine—my mind still guiding me with wisdom—and how to lay hold on folly, till I might see what was good for the sons of men to do under heaven during the few days of their life. I made great works; I built houses and planted vineyards for myself; I made myself gardens and parks, and planted in them all kinds of fruit trees. I made myself pools from which to water the forest of growing trees. I bought male and female slaves, and had slaves who were born in my house; I had also great possessions of herds and flocks, more than any who had been before me in Jerusalem. I also gathered for myself silver and gold and the treasure of kings and provinces; I got singers, both men and women, and many concubines, man's delight. So I became great and surpassed all who were before me in Jerusalem; also my wisdom remained with me. And whatever my eyes desired I did not keep from them; I kept my heart from no pleasure, for my heart found pleasure in all my toil, and this was my reward for all my toil. Then I considered all that my hands had done and the toil I had spent in doing it, and behold, all was vanity and a striving after wind, and there was nothing to be gained under the sun. So I turned to consider wisdom and madness and folly; for what can the man do who comes after the king? Only what he has already done. Then I saw that wisdom excels folly as light excels darkness. The wise man has his eyes in his head, but the fool walks in darkness; and yet I perceived that one fate comes to all of them. Then I said to myself, "What befalls the fool will befall me also; why then have I been so very wise?" And I said to myself that this also is vanity.

A Reading (Lesson) from the Letter of Paul to the Galatians [1:1-17]

Paul an apostle—not from men nor through man, but through Jesus Christ and God the Father, who raised him from the dead—and all the brethren who are with me, To the churches of Galatia: Grace to you and peace from God the Father and our Lord Jesus Christ, who gave himself for our sins to deliver us from the present evil age, according to the will of our God and Father; to whom be the glory for ever and ever. Amen. I am astonished that you are so quickly deserting him who called you in the grace of Christ and turning to a different gospel—not that there is another gospel, but there are some who trouble you and want to pervert the gospel of Christ. But even if we, or an angel from heaven, should preach to you a gospel contrary to that which we preached to you, let him be accursed. As we have said before, so now I say again, If any one is preaching to you a gospel contrary to that which you received, let him be accursed. Am I now seeking the favor of men, or of God? Or am I trying to please men? If I were still pleasing men, I should not be a servant of Christ. For I would have you know, brethren, that the gospel which was preached by me is not man's gospel. For I did not receive it from man, nor was I taught it, but it came through a revelation of Jesus Christ. For you have heard of my former life in Judaism, how I persecuted the church of God violently and tried to destroy it; and I advanced in Judaism beyond many of my own age among my people, so extremely zealous was I for the traditions of my fathers. But when he who had set me apart before I was born, and had called me through his grace, was pleased to reveal his Son to me, in order that I might preach him among the Gentiles, I did not confer with flesh and blood, nor did I go up to Jerusalem to those who were apostles before me, but I went away into Arabia; and again I returned to Damascus.

A Reading (Lesson) from the Gospel according to Matthew [13:44-52]

Jesus said to the disciples, "The kingdom of heaven is like treasure hidden in a field, which a man found and covered up; then in his joy he goes and sells all that he has and buys that field. Again, the kingdom of heaven is like a merchant in search of fine pearls, who, on finding one pearl of great value, went and sold all that he had and bought it. Again, the kingdom of heaven is like a net which was thrown into the sea and gathered fish of every kind; when it was full, men drew it ashore and sat down and sorted the good into vessels but threw away the bad. So it will be at the close of the age. The angels will come out and separate the evil from the righteous, and throw them into the furnace of fire; there men will weep and gnash their teeth. Have you understood all this?" They said to him, "Yes." And he said to them, "Therefore every scribe who has been trained for the kingdom of heaven is like a householder who brings out of his treasure what is new and what is old."

Tuesday

Psalm 45 [page 647]   ❖   *Psalm 47* [page 650], *Psalm 48* [page 651]

A Reading (Lesson) from the Book of Ecclesiastes
[2:16-26]

For of the wise man as of the fool there is no enduring remembrance, seeing that in the days to come all will have been long forgotten. How the wise man dies just like the fool! So I hated life, because what is done under the sun was grievous to me; for all is vanity and a striving after wind. I hated all my toil in which I had toiled under the sun, seeing that I must leave it to the man who will come after me; and who knows whether he will be a wise man or a fool? Yet he will be master of all for which I toiled and used my wisdom under the sun. This also is vanity. So I turned about and gave my heart up to despair over all the toil of my labors under the sun, because sometimes a man who has toiled with wisdom and knowledge and skill must leave all to be enjoyed by a man who did not toil for it. This also is vanity and a great evil. What has a man from all the toil and strain with which he toils beneath the sun? For all his days are full of pain, and his work is a vexation; even in the night his mind does not rest. This also is vanity. There is nothing better for a man than that he should eat and drink, and find enjoyment in his toil. This also, I saw, is from the hand of God; for apart from him who can eat or who can have enjoyment? For to the man who pleases him God gives wisdom and knowledge and joy; but to the sinner he gives the work of gathering and heaping, only to give to one who pleases God. This also is vanity and a striving after wind.

A Reading (Lesson) from the Letter of Paul to the Galatians [1:18—2:10]

After three years I went up to Jerusalem to visit Cephas, and remained with him fifteen days. But I saw none of the other apostles except James the Lord's brother. (In what I am writing to you, before God, I do not lie!) Then I went into the regions of Syria and Cili′cia. And I was still not known by sight to the churches of Christ in Judea; they only heard it said, "He who once persecuted us is now preaching the faith he once tried to destroy." And they glorified God because of me. Then after fourteen years I went up again to Jerusalem with Barnabas, taking Titus along with me. I went up by revelation; and I laid before them (but privately before those who were of repute) the gospel which I preach among the Gentiles, lest somehow I should be running or had run in vain. But even Titus, who was with me, was not compelled to be circumcised, though he was a Greek. But because of false brethren secretly brought in, who slipped in to spy out our freedom which we have in Christ Jesus, that they might bring us into bondage—to them we did not yield submission even for a moment, that the truth of the gospel might be preserved for you. And from those who were reputed to be something (what they were makes no difference to me; God shows no partiality)—those, I say, who were of repute added nothing to me; but on the contrary, when they saw that I had been entrusted with the gospel to the uncircumcised, just as Peter had been entrusted with the gospel to the circumcised (for he who worked through Peter for the mission to the circumcised worked through me also for the Gentiles), and when they perceived the grace that was given to me, James and Cephas and John, who were reputed to be pillars, gave to me and Barnabas the right hand of fellowship, that we should go to the Gentiles and they to the circumcised; only they would have us remember the poor, which very thing I was eager to do.

A Reading (Lesson) from the Gospel according to Matthew [13:53-58]

When Jesus had finished these parables, he went away from there, and coming to his own country he taught them in their synagogue, so that they were astonished, and said, "Where did this man get this wisdom and these mighty works? Is not this the carpenter's son? Is not his mother called Mary? And are not his brothers James and Joseph and Simon and Judas? And are not all his sisters with us? Where then did this man get all this?" And they took offense at him. But Jesus said to them, "A prophet is not without honor except in his own country and in his own house." And he did not do many mighty works there, because of their unbelief.

Wednesday

Psalm 119:49-72 [page 767] ❖ *Psalm 49* [page 652], (*Psalm 53* [page 658])

A Reading (Lesson) from the Book of Ecclesiastes [3:1-15]

For everything there is a season, and a time for every matter under heaven: a time to be born, and a time to die; a time to plant, and a time to pluck up what is planted; a time to kill, and a time to heal; a time to break down, and a time to build up; a time to weep, and a time to laugh; a time to mourn, and a time to dance; a time to cast away stones, and a time to gather stones together; a time to embrace, and a time to refrain from embracing; a time to seek, and a time to lose; a time to keep, and a time to cast away; a time to rend, and a time to sew; a time to keep silence, and a time to speak; a time to love, and a time to hate; a time for war, and a time for peace. What gain has the worker from his toil? I have seen the business that God has given to the sons of men to be busy with. He has made everything beautiful in its time; also he has put eternity into man's mind, yet so that he cannot find out what God has done from the beginning to the end. I know that there is nothing better for them than to be happy and enjoy themselves as long as they live; also that it is God's gift to man that every one should eat and drink and take pleasure in all his toil. I know that whatever God does endures for ever; nothing can be added to it, nor anything taken from it; God has made it so, in order that men should fear before him. That which is, already has been; that which is to be, already has been; and God seeks what has been driven away.

A Reading (Lesson) from the Letter of Paul to the Galatians [2:11-21]

When Cephas came to Antioch I opposed him to his face, because he stood condemned. For before certain men came from James, he ate with the Gentiles; but when they came he drew back and separated himself, fearing the circumcision party. And with him the rest of the Jews acted insincerely, so that even Barnabas was carried away by their insincerity. But when I saw that they were not straightfoward about the truth of the gospel, I said to Cephas before them all, "If you, though a Jew, live like a Gentile and not like a Jew, how can you compel the Gentiles to live like Jews?" We ourselves, who are Jews by birth and not Gentile sinners, yet who know that a man is not justified by works of the law but through faith in Jesus Christ, even we have believed in Christ Jesus, in order to be justified by faith in Christ, and not by works of the law, because by works of the law shall no one be justified. But if, in our endeavor to be justified in Christ, we ourselves were found to be sinners, is Christ then an agent of sin? Certainly not! But if I build up again those things which I tore down, then I prove myself a transgressor. For I through the law died to the law, that I might live to God. I have been crucified with Christ; it is no longer I who live, but Christ who lives in me; and the life I now live in the flesh I live by faith in the Son of God, who loved me and gave himself for me. I do not nullify the grace of God; for if justification were through the law, then Christ died to no purpose.

A Reading (Lesson) from the Gospel according to Matthew
[14:1-12]

Herod the tetrarch heard about the fame of Jesus; and he said to his servants, "This is John the Baptist, he has been raised from the dead; that is why these powers are at work in him." For Herod had seized John and bound him and put him in prison, for the sake of Hero'di-as, his brother Philip's wife; because John said to him, "It is not lawful for you to have her." And though he wanted to put him to death, he feared the people, because they held him to be a prophet. But when Herod's birthday came, the daughter of Hero'di-as danced before the company, and pleased Herod, so that he promised with an oath to give her whatever she might ask. Prompted by her mother, she said, "Give me the head of John the Baptist here on a platter." And the king was sorry; but because of his oaths and his guests he commanded it to be given; he sent and had John beheaded in the prison, and his head was brought on a platter and given to the girl, and she brought it to her mother. And his disciples came and took the body and buried it; and they went and told Jesus.

Thursday

Psalm 50 [page 654]   ❖   *(Psalm 59* [page 665],
Psalm 60 [page 667])   or   *Psalm 8* [page 592],
Psalm 84 [page 707]

A Reading (Lesson) from the Book of Ecclesiastes
[3:16—4:3]

Moreover I saw under the sun that in the place of justice, even there was wickedness, and in the place of righteousness, even there was wickedness. I said in my heart, God will judge the righteous and the wicked, for he has appointed a time for every matter, and for every work.

I said in my heart with regard to the sons of men that God is testing them to show them that they are but beasts. For the fate of the sons of men and the fate of beasts is the same; as one dies, so dies the other. They all have the same breath, and man has no advantage over the beasts; for all is vanity. All go to one place; all are from the dust, and all turn to dust again. Who knows whether the spirit of man goes upward and the spirit of the beast goes down to the earth? So I saw that there is nothing better than that a man should enjoy his work, for that is his lot; who can bring him to see what will be after him? Again I saw all the oppressions that are practiced under the sun. And behold, the tears of the oppressed, and they had no one to comfort them! On the side of the oppressors there was power, and there was no one to comfort them. And I thought the dead who are already dead more fortunate than the living who are still alive; but better than both is he who has not yet been, and has not seen the evil deeds that are done under the sun.

A Reading (Lesson) from the Letter of Paul to the Galatians [3:1-14]

O foolish Galatians! Who has bewitched you, before whose eyes Jesus Christ was publicly portrayed as crucified? Let me ask you only this: Did you receive the Spirit by works of the law, or by hearing with faith? Are you so foolish? Having begun with the Spirit, are you now ending with the flesh? Did you experience so many things in vain—if it really is in vain. Does he who supplies the Spirit to you and works miracles among you do so by works of the law, or by hearing with faith? Thus Abraham "believed God, and it was reckoned to him as righteousness." So you see that it is men of faith who are the sons of Abraham. And the scripture, foreseeing that God would justify the Gentiles by faith, preached the gospel beforehand to Abraham, saying, "In you shall all

the nations be blessed." So then, those who are men of
faith are blessed with Abraham who had faith. For all who
rely on works of the law are under a curse; for it is written,
"Cursed be every one who does not abide by all things
written in the book of the law, and do them." Now it is
evident that no man is justified before God by the law; for
"He who through faith is righteous shall live"; but the law
does not rest on faith, for "He who does them shall live
by them." Christ redeemed us from the curse of the law,
having become a curse for us—for it is written, "Cursed be
every one who hangs on a tree"—that in Christ Jesus the
blessing of Abraham might come upon the Gentiles, that
we might receive the promise of the Spirit through faith.

A Reading (Lesson) from the Gospel according to Matthew
[14:13-21]

When Jesus heard that John had been beheaded by Herod,
he withdrew from there in a boat to a lonely place apart.
But when the crowds heard it, they followed him on foot
from the towns. As he went ashore he saw a great throng;
and he had compassion on them, and healed their sick.
When it was evening, the disciples came to him and said,
"This is a lonely place, and the day is now over; send the
crowds away to go into the villages and buy food for
themselves." Jesus said, "They need not go away; you give
them something to eat." They said to him, "We have only
five loaves here and two fish." And he said, "Bring them
here to me." Then he ordered the crowds to sit down on
the grass; and taking the five loaves and the two fish he
looked up to heaven, and blessed, and broke and gave the
loaves to the disciples, and the disciples gave them to the
crowds. And they all ate and were satisfied. And they took
up twelve baskets full of the broken pieces left over. And
those who ate were about five thousand men, besides
women and children.

Friday

Psalm 40 [page 640],   *Psalm 54* [page 659]   ❖
Psalm 51 [page 656]

A Reading (Lesson) from the Book of Ecclesiastes [5:1-7]

Guard your steps when you go to the house of God; to
draw near to listen is better than to offer the sacrifice of
fools; for they do not know that they are doing evil. Be not
rash with your mouth, nor let your heart be hasty to utter
a word before God, for God is in heaven, and you upon
earth; therefore let your words be few. For a dream comes
with much business, and a fool's voice with many words.
When you vow a vow to God, do not delay paying it; for
he has no pleasure in fools. Pay what you vow. It is better
that you should not vow than that you should vow and not
pay. Let not your mouth lead you into sin, and do not say
before the messenger that it was a mistake; why should
God be angry at your voice, and destroy the work of your
hands? For when dreams increase, empty words grow
many: but do you fear God.

*A Reading (Lesson) from the Letter of Paul
to the Galatians* [3:15-22]

To give a human example, brethren: no one annuls even a
man's will, or adds to it, once it has been ratified. Now the
promises were made to Abraham and to his offspring. It
does not say, "And to offsprings," referring to many; but,
referring to one, "And to your offspring," which is Christ.
This is what I mean: the law, which came four hundred
and thirty years afterward, does not annul a covenant
previously ratified by God, so as to make the promise void.
For if the inheritance is by the law, it is no longer by
promise; but God gave it to Abraham by a promise. Why
then the law? It was added because of transgressions, till
the offspring should come to whom the promise had

been made; and it was ordained by angels through an intermediary. Now an intermediary implies more than one; but God is one. Is the law then against the promises of God? Certainly not; for if a law had been given which could make alive, then righteousness would indeed be by the law. But the scripture consigned all things to sin, that what was promised to faith in Jesus Christ might be given to those who believe.

A Reading (Lesson) from the Gospel according to Matthew
[14:22-36]

Jesus made the disciples get into the boat and go before him to the other side, while he dismissed the crowds. And after he had dismissed the crowds, he went up on the mountain by himself to pray. When evening came, he was there alone, but the boat by this time was many furlongs distant from the land, beaten by the waves; for the wind was against them. And in the fourth watch of the night he came to them, walking on the sea. But when the disciples saw him walking on the sea, they were terrified, saying, "It is a ghost!" And they cried out for fear. But immediately he spoke to them, saying, "Take heart, it is I; have no fear." And Peter answered him, "Lord, if it is you, bid me come to you on the water." He said, "Come." So Peter got out of the boat and walked on the water and came to Jesus; but when he saw the wind, he was afraid, and beginning to sink he cried out, "Lord, save me." Jesus immediately reached out his hand and caught him, saying to him, "O man of little faith, why did you doubt?" And when they got into the boat, the wind ceased. And those in the boat worshiped him, saying, "Truly you are the Son of God." And when they had crossed over, they came to land at Gennes'aret. And when the men of that place recognized him, they sent round to all that region and brought to him all that were sick, and besought him that they might only touch the fringe of his garment; and as many as touched it were made well.

Saturday

Psalm 55 [page 660]   ❖   *Psalm 138* [page 793],
Psalm 139:1-17(18-23) [page 794]

A Reading (Lesson) from the Book of Ecclesiastes
[5:8-20]

If you see in a province the poor oppressed and justice and
right violently taken away, do not be amazed at the matter;
for the high official is watched by a higher, and there
are yet higher ones over them. But in all, a king is an
advantage to a land with cultivated fields. He who loves
money will not be satisfied with money; nor he who loves
wealth, with gain: this also is vanity. When goods increase,
they increase who eat them; and what gain has their owner
but to see them with his eyes? Sweet is the sleep of a
laborer, whether he eats little or much; but the surfeit of
the rich will not let him sleep. There is a grievous evil
which I have seen under the sun: riches were kept by their
owner to his hurt, and those riches were lost in a bad
venture; and he is father of a son, but he has nothing in his
hand. As he came from his mother's womb he shall go
again, naked as he came, and shall take nothing for his
toil, which he may carry away in his hand. This also is a
grievous evil: just as he came, so shall he go; and what gain
has he that he toiled for the wind, and spent all his days in
darkness and grief, in much vexation and sickness and
resentment? Behold, what I have seen to be good and to be
fitting is to eat and drink and find enjoyment in all the toil
with which one toils under the sun the few days of his life
which God has given him, for this is his lot. Every man
also to whom God has given wealth and possessions and
power to enjoy them, and to accept his lot and find
enjoyment in his toil—this is the gift of God. For he will
not much remember the days of his life because God keeps
him occupied with joy in his heart.

*A Reading (Lesson) from the Letter of Paul
to the Galatians* [3:23—4:11]

Before faith came, we were confined under the law, kept
under restraint until faith should be revealed. So that the
law was our custodian until Christ came, that we might be
justified by faith. But now that faith has come, we are no
longer under a custodian; for in Christ Jesus you are all
sons of God, through faith. For as many of you as were
baptized into Christ have put on Christ. There is neither
Jew nor Greek, there is neither slave nor free, there is
neither male nor female; for you are all one in Christ Jesus.
And if you are Christ's, then you are Abraham's offspring,
heirs according to the promise. I mean that the heir, as
long as he is a child, is not better than a slave, though he is
the owner of all the estate; but he is under guardians and
trustees until the date set by the father. So with us; when
we were children, we were slaves to the elemental spirits of
the universe. But when the time had fully come, God sent
forth his Son, born of woman, born under the law, to
redeem those who were under the law, so that we might
receive adoption as sons. And because you are sons, God
has sent the Spirit of his Son into our hearts, crying,
"Abba! Father!" So through God you are no longer a slave
but a son, and if a son then an heir. Formerly, when you
did not know God, you were in bondage to beings that by
nature are no gods; but now that you have come to know
God, or rather to be known by God, how can you turn
back again to the weak and beggarly elemental spirits,
whose slaves you want to be once more? You observe days,
and months, and seasons, and years! I am afraid I have
labored over you in vain.

A Reading (Lesson) from the Gospel according to Matthew
[15:1-20]

Pharisees and scribes came to Jesus from Jerusalem and
said, "Why do your disciples transgress the tradition of the

elders? For they do not wash their hands when they eat."
He answered them, "And why do you transgress the
commandment of God for the sake of your tradition? For
God commanded, 'Honor your father and your mother,'
and, 'He who speaks evil of father or mother, let him
surely die.' But you say, 'If any one tells his father or his
mother, What you would have gained from me is given
to God, he need not honor his father.' So, for the sake of
your tradition, you have made void the word of God. You
hypocrites! Well did Isaiah prophesy of you, when he said:
'This people honors me with their lips, but their heart is far
from me; in vain do they worship me, teaching as doctrines
the precepts of men.'" And he called the people to him and
said to them, "Hear and understand: not what goes into
the mouth defiles a man, but what comes out of the mouth,
this defiles a man." Then the disciples came and said to
him, "Do you know that the Pharisees were offended when
they heard this saying?" He answered, "Every plant which
my heavenly Father has not planted will be rooted up. Let
them alone; they are blind guides. And if a blind man leads
a blind man, both will fall into a pit." But Peter said to
him, "Explain the parable to us." And he said, "Are you
also still without understanding? Do you not see that
whatever goes into the mouth passes into the stomach, and
so passes on? But what comes out of the mouth proceeds
from the heart, and this defiles a man. For out of the heart
come evil thoughts, murder, adultery, fornication, theft,
false witness, slander. These are what defile a man; but to
eat with unwashed hands does not defile a man."

Proper 5   *Week of the Sunday closest to June 8*

Sunday

Psalm 24 [page 613],   *Psalm 29* [page 620]   ❖
Psalm 8 [page 592],   *Psalm 84* [page 707]

A Reading (Lesson) from the Book of Ecclesiastes
[6:1-12]

There is an evil which I have seen under the sun, and it
lies heavy upon men: a man to whom God gives wealth,
possessions, and honor, so that he lacks nothing of all that
he desires, yet God does not give him power to enjoy them,
but a stranger enjoys them; this is vanity; it is a sore
affliction. If a man begets a hundred children, and lives
many years, so that the days of his years are many, but he
does not enjoy life's good things, and also has no burial,
I say that an untimely birth is better off than he. For it
comes into vanity and goes into darkness, and in darkness
its name is covered; moreover it has not seen the sun or
known anything; yet it finds rest rather than he. Even
though he should live a thousand years twice told, yet
enjoy no good—do not all go to the one place? All the toil
of man is for his mouth, yet his appetite is not satisfied. For
what advantage has the wise man over the fool? And what
does the poor man have who knows how to conduct
himself before the living? Better is the sight of the eyes than
the wandering of desire; this also is vanity and a striving
after wind. Whatever has come to be has already been
named, and it is known what man is, and that he is not
able to dispute with one stronger than he. The more
words, the more vanity, and what is man the better? For
who knows what is good for man while he lives the few
days of his vain life, which he passes like a shadow? For
who can tell man what will be after him under the sun?

A Reading (Lesson) from the Acts of the Apostles [10:9-23]

The next day, when the servants of Cornelius were on their
journey and coming near Joppa, Peter went up on the
housetop to pray, about the sixth hour. And he became
hungry and desired something to eat; but while they were
preparing it, he fell into a trance and saw the heaven
opened, and something descending, like a great sheet, let

down by four corners upon the earth. In it were all kinds of animals and reptiles and birds of the air. And there came a voice to him, "Rise, Peter; kill and eat." But Peter said, "No, Lord; for I have never eaten anything that is common or unclean." And the voice came to him again a second time, "What God has cleansed, you must not call common." This happened three times, and the thing was taken up at once to heaven. Now while Peter was inwardly perplexed as to what the vision which he had seen might mean, behold, the men that were sent by Cornelius, having made inquiry for Simon's house, stood before the gate and called out to ask whether Simon who was called Peter was lodging there. And while Peter was pondering the vision, the Spirit said to him, "Behold, three men are looking for you. Rise and go down, and accompany them without hesitation; for I have sent them." And Peter went down to the men and said, "I am the one you are looking for; what is the reason for your coming?" And they said, "Cornelius, a centurion, an upright and God-fearing man, who is well spoken of by the whole Jewish nation, was directed by a holy angel to send for you to come to his house, and to hear what you have to say." So he called them in to be his guests. The next day he rose and went off with them, and some of the brethren from Joppa accompanied him.

A Reading (Lesson) from the Gospel according to Luke
[12:32-40]

Jesus said to his disciples, "Fear not, little flock, for it is your Father's good pleasure to give you the kingdom. Sell your possessions, and give alms; provide yourselves with purses that do not grow old, with a treasure in the heavens that does not fail, where no thief approaches and no moth destroys. For where your treasure is, there will your heart be also. Let your loins be girded and your lamps burning, and be like men who are waiting for their master to come home from the marriage feast, so that they may open to him at once when he comes and knocks. Blessed are those servants whom the master finds awake when he comes; truly, I say to you, he will gird himself and have them sit at table, and he will come and serve them. If he comes in the second watch, or in the third, and finds them so, blessed are those servants! But know this, that if the householder had known at what hour the thief was coming, he would not have left his house to be broken into. You also must be ready; for the Son of man is coming at an unexpected hour."

Monday

Psalm 56 [page 662], *Psalm 57* [page 663], *(Psalm 58* [page 664]) ❖ *Psalm 64* [page 671], *Psalm 65* [page 672]

A Reading (Lesson) from the Book of Ecclesiastes [7:1-14]

A good name is better than precious ointment; and the day of death, than the day of birth. It is better to go to the house of mourning than to go to the house of feasting; for this is the end of all men, and the living will lay it to heart. Sorrow is better than laughter, for by sadness of countenance the heart is made glad. The heart of the wise is in the house of mourning; but the heart of fools is in the house of mirth. It is better for a man to hear the rebuke of the wise than to hear the song of fools. For as the crackling of thorns under a pot, so is the laughter of the fools; this also is vanity. Surely oppression makes the wise man foolish, and a bribe corrupts the mind. Better is the end of a thing than its beginning; and the patient in spirit is better than the proud in spirit. Be not quick to anger, for anger lodges in the bosom of fools. Say not, "Why were the former days better than these?" For it is not from wisdom that you ask this. Wisdom is good with an inheritance, an advantage to those who see the sun. For the protection of wisdom is like the protection of money; and the advantage of knowledge is that wisdom preserves the life of him who has it. Consider the work of God; who can make straight what he has made crooked? In the day of prosperity be joyful, and in the day of adversity consider; God has made the one as well as the other, so that man may not find out anything that will be after him.

A Reading (Lesson) from the Letter of Paul to the Galatians [4:12-20]

Brethren, I beseech you, become as I am, for I also have become as you are. You did me no wrong; you know it was because of a bodily ailment that I preached the gospel to you at first; and though my condition was a trial to you, you did not scorn or despise me, but received me as an angel of God, as Christ Jesus. What has become of the satisfaction you felt? For I bear you witness that, if possible, you would have plucked out your eyes and given them to me. Have I then become your enemy by telling you the truth? They make much of you, but for no good purpose; they want to shut you out, that you may make much of them. For a good purpose it is always good to be made much of, and not only when I am present with you. My little children, with whom I am again in travail until Christ be formed in you! I could wish to be present with you now and to change my tone, for I am perplexed about you.

A Reading (Lesson) from the Gospel according to Matthew [15:21-28]

Jesus went away from there and withdrew to the district of Tyre and Sidon. And behold, a Canaanite woman from that region came out and cried, "Have mercy on me, O Lord, Son of David; my daughter is severely possessed by a demon." But he did not answer her a word. And his disciples came and begged him, saying, "Send her away, for she is crying after us." He answered, "I was sent only to the lost sheep of the house of Israel." But she came and knelt before him, saying, "Lord, help me." And he answered, "It is not fair to take the children's bread and throw it to the dogs." She said, "Yes, Lord, yet even the dogs eat the crumbs that fall from their masters' table." Then Jesus answered her, "O woman, great is your faith! Be it done for you as you desire." And her daughter was healed instantly.

Tuesday

Psalm 61 [page 668],   *Psalm 62* [page 669]   ❖
Psalm 68:1-20(21-23)24-36 [page 676]

A Reading (Lesson) from the Book of Ecclesiastes
[8:14—9:10]

There is a vanity which takes place on earth, that there are righteous men to whom it happens according to the deeds of the wicked, and there are wicked men to whom it happens according to the deeds of the righteous. I said that this also is vanity. And I commend enjoyment, for man has no good thing under the sun but to eat, and drink, and enjoy himself, for this will go with him in his toil through the days of life which God gives him under the sun. When I applied my mind to know wisdom, and to see the business that is done on earth, how neither day nor night one's eyes see sleep; then I saw all the work of God, that man cannot find out the work that is done under the sun. However much man may toil in seeking, he will not find it out; even though a wise man claims to know, he cannot find it out. but all this I laid to heart, examining it all, how the righteous and the wise and their deeds are in the hand of God; whether it is love or hate man does not know. Everything before them is vanity, since one fate comes to all, to the righteous and the wicked, to the good and the evil, to the clean and the unclean, to him who sacrifices and him who does not sacrifice. As is the good man, so is the sinner; and he who swears is as he who shuns an oath. This is an evil in all that is done under the sun, that one fate comes to all; also the hearts of men are full of evil, and madness is in their hearts while they live, and after that they go to the dead. But he who is joined with all the living has hope, for a living dog is better than a dead lion. For the living know that they will die, but the dead know nothing, and they have no more reward; but the memory of them is lost. Their love and their hate and their envy have already perished, and they have no more for ever any share in all that is done under the sun. Go, eat your bread with enjoyment, and drink your wine with a merry heart; for God has already approved what you do. Let your garments be always white; let not oil be lacking on your head. Enjoy life with the wife whom you love, all the days of your vain life which he has given you under the sun, because that is your portion in life and in your toil at which you toil under the sun. Whatever your hand finds to do, do it with your might; for there is no work or thought or knowledge or wisdom in Sheol, to which you are going.

A Reading (Lesson) from the Letter of Paul to the Galations [4:21-31]

Tell me, you who desire to be under law, do you not hear the law? For it is written that Abraham had two sons, one by a slave and one by a free woman. But the son of the slave was born according to the flesh, the son of the free woman through promise. Now this is an allegory: these women are two covenants. One is from Mount Sinai, bearing children for slavery; she is Hagar. Now Hagar is Mount Sinai in Arabia; she corresponds to the present Jerusalem, for she is in slavery with her children. But the Jerusalem above is free, and she is our mother. For it is written, "Rejoice, O barren one who does not bear; break forth and shout, you who are not in travail; for the children of the desolate one are many more than the children of her that is married." Now we, brethren, like Isaac, are children of promise. But as at that time he who was born according to the flesh persecuted him who was born according to the Spirit, so it is now. But what does the scripture say? "Cast out the slave and her son; for the son of the slave shall not inherit with the son of the free woman." So, brethren, we are not children of the slave but of the free woman.

A Reading (Lesson) from the Gospel according to Matthew [15:29-39]

Jesus went on from Tyre and Sidon and passed along the Sea of Galilee. And he went up on the mountain, and sat down there. And great crowds came to him, bringing with them the lame, the maimed, the blind, the dumb, and many others, and they put them at his feet, and he healed them, so that the throng wondered, when they saw the dumb speaking, the maimed whole, the lame walking, and the blind seeing; and they glorified the God of Israel. Then Jesus called his disciples to him and said, "I have compassion on the crowd, because they have been with me now three days, and have nothing to eat; and I am unwilling to send them away hungry, lest they faint on the way." And the disciples said to him, "Where are we to get bread enough in the desert to feed so great a crowd?" And Jesus said to them, "How many loaves have you?" They said, "Seven, and a few small fish." And commanding the crowd to sit down on the ground, he took the seven loaves and the fish, and having given thanks he broke them and gave them to the disciples, and the disciples gave them to the crowds. And they all ate and were satisfied; and they took up seven baskets full of the broken pieces left over. Those who ate were four thousand men, besides women and children. And sending away the crowds, he got into the boat and went to the region of Mag'adan.

Wednesday

Psalm 72 [page 685] ❖ *Psalm 119:73-96* [page 769]

A Reading (Lesson) from the Book of Ecclesiastes
[9:11-18]

Again I saw that under the sun the race is not to the swift,
nor the battle to the strong, nor bread to the wise, nor
riches to the intelligent, nor favor to the men of skill; but
time and chance happen to them all. For man does not
know his time. Like fish which are taken in an evil net, and
like birds which are caught in a snare, so the sons of men
are snared at an evil time, when it suddenly falls upon
them. I have also seen this example of wisdom under the
sun, and it seemed great to me. There was a little city with
few men in it; and a great king came against it and
besieged it, building great siegeworks against it. But there
was found in it a poor wise man, and he by his wisdom
delivered the city. Yet no one remembered that poor man.
But I say that wisdom is better than might, though the
poor man's wisdom is despised, and his words are not
heeded. The words of the wise heard in quiet are better
than the shouting of a ruler among fools. Wisdom is better
than weapons of war, but one sinner destroys much good.

*A Reading (Lesson) from the Letter of Paul
to the Galatians* [5:1-15]

For freedom Christ has set us free; stand fast therefore,
and do not submit again to a yoke of slavery. Now I, Paul,
say to you that if you receive circumcision, Christ will be
of no advantage to you. I testify again to every man who
receives circumcision that he is bound to keep the whole
law. You are severed from Christ, you who would be
justified by the law; you have fallen away from grace. For
through the Spirit, by faith, we wait for the hope of
righteousness. For in Christ Jesus neither circumcision nor
uncircumcision is of any avail, but faith working through

love. You were running well; who hindered you from obeying the truth? This persuasion is not from him who calls you. A little leaven leavens the whole lump. I have confidence in the Lord that you will take no other view than mine; and he who is troubling you will bear his judgment, whoever he is. But if I, brethren, still preach circumcision, why am I still persecuted? In that case the stumbling block of the cross has been removed. I wish those who unsettle you would mutilate themselves! For you were called to freedom, brethren; only do not use your freedom as an opportunity for the flesh, but through love be servants of one another. For the whole law is fulfilled in one word, "You shall love your neighbor as yourself." But if you bite and devour one another take heed that you are not consumed by one another.

A Reading (Lesson) from the Gospel according to Matthew [16:1-12]

The Pharisees and Sad'ducees came, and to test him they asked him to show them a sign from heaven. He answered them, "When it is evening, you say, 'It will be fair weather; for the sky is red.' And in the morning, 'It will be stormy today, for the sky is red and threatening.' You know how to interpret the appearance of the sky, but you cannot interpret the signs of the times. An evil and adulterous generation seeks for a sign, but no sign shall be given to it except the sign of Jonah." So he left them and departed. When the disciples reached the other side, they had forgotten to bring any bread. Jesus said to them, "Take heed and beware of the leaven of the Pharisees and Sad'ducees." And they discussed it among themselves, saying, "We brought no bread." But Jesus, aware of this, said, "O men of little faith, why do you discuss among yourselves the fact that you have no bread? Do you not yet perceive? Do you not remember the five loaves of the five thousand, and how many baskets you gathered? Or the seven loaves of the four thousand, and how many baskets you gathered? How is it that you fail to perceive that I did not speak about bread? Beware of the leaven of the Pharisees and Sad'ducees." Then they understood that he did not tell them to beware of the leaven of bread, but of the teaching of the Pharisees and Sad'ducees.

Thursday

(Psalm 70 [page 682]*), Psalm 71* [page 683]
❖ *Psalm 74* [page 689]

A Reading (Lesson) from the Book of Ecclesiastes [11:1-8]

Cast your bread upon the waters, for you will find it after many days. Give a portion to seven, or even to eight, for you know not what evil may happen on earth. If the clouds are full of rain, they empty themselves on the earth; and if a tree falls to the south or to the north, in the place where the tree falls, there it will lie. He who observes the wind will not sow; and he who regards the clouds will not reap. As you do not know how the spirit comes to the bones in the womb of a woman with child, so you do not know the work of God who makes everything. In the morning sow your seed, and at evening withhold not your hand; for you do not know which will prosper, this or that, or whether both alike will be good. Light is sweet, and it is pleasant for the eyes to behold the sun. For if a man lives many years, let him rejoice in them all; but let him remember that the days of darkness will be many. All that comes is vanity.

A Reading (Lesson) from the Letter of Paul to the Galatians [5:16-24]

But I say, walk by the Spirit, and do not gratify the desires of the flesh. For the desires of the flesh are against the Spirit, and the desires of the Spirit are against the flesh; for these are opposed to each other, to prevent you from doing what you would. But if you are led by the Spirit you are not under the law. Now the works of the flesh are plain: fornication, impurity, licentiousness, idolatry, sorcery, enmity, strife, jealousy, anger, selfishness, dissension, party spirit, envy, drunkenness, carousing, and the like. I warn you, as I warned you before, that those who do such things shall not inherit the kingdom of God. But the fruit of the Spirit is love, joy, peace, patience, kindness, goodness, faithfulness, gentleness, self-control; against such there is no law. And those who belong to Christ Jesus have crucified the flesh with its passions and desires.

A Reading (Lesson) from the Gospel according to Matthew [16:13-20]

When Jesus came into the district of Caesare'a Philippi, he asked his disciples, "Who do men say that the Son of man is?" And they said, "Some say John the Baptist, others say Eli'jah, and others Jeremiah or one of the prophets." He said to them, "But who do you say that I am?" Simon Peter replied, "You are the Christ, the Son of the living God." And Jesus answered him, "Blessed are you, Simon Bar-Jona! For flesh and blood has not revealed this to you, but my Father who is in heaven. And I tell you, you are Peter, and on this rock I will build my church, and the powers of death shall not prevail against it. I will give you the keys of the kingdom of heaven, and whatever you bind on earth shall be bound in heaven, and whatever you loose on earth shall be loosed in heaven." Then he strictly charged the disciples to tell no one that he was the Christ.

Friday
Psalm 69:1-23(24-30)31-38 [page 679] ❖
Psalm 73 [page 687]

A Reading (Lesson) from the Book of Ecclesiastes [11:9—12:14]

Rejoice, O young man, in your youth, and let your heart cheer you in the days of your youth; walk in the ways of your heart and the sight of your eyes. But know that for all these things God will bring you into judgment. Remove vexation from your mind, and put away pain from your body; for youth and the dawn of life are vanity. Remember also your Creator in the days of your youth, before the evil days come, and the years draw nigh, when you will say, "I have no pleasure in them"; before the sun and the light and the moon and the stars are darkened and the clouds return after the rain; in the day when the keepers of the house tremble, and the strong men are bent, and the grinders cease because they are few, and those that look through the windows are dimmed, and the doors on the street are shut; when the sound of the grinding is low, and one rises up at the voice of a bird, and all the daughters of song are brought low; they are afraid also of what is high, and terrors are in the way; the almond tree blossoms, the grasshopper drags itself along and desire fails; because man goes to his eternal home, and the mourners go about the streets; before the silver cord is snapped, or the golden bowl is broken, or the pitcher is broken at the fountain, or the wheel broken at the cistern, and the dust returns to the earth as it was, and the spirit returns to God who gave it. Vanity of vanities, says the Preacher; all is vanity. Besides being wise, the Preacher also taught the people knowledge, weighing and studying and arranging proverbs with great care. The Preacher sought to find pleasing words, and uprightly he wrote words of truth. The sayings of the wise are like goads, and like nails firmly fixed are the collected sayings which are given by one Shepherd. My son, beware of anything beyond these. Of making many books there is no end, and much study is a weariness of the flesh. The end of the matter; all has been heard. Fear God, and keep his commandments; for this is the whole duty of man. For God will bring every deed into judgment, with every secret thing, whether good or evil.

*A Reading (Lesson) from the Letter of Paul
to the Galatians* [5:25—6:10]

If we live by the Spirit, let us also walk by the Spirit. Let us
have no self-conceit, no provoking of one another, no envy
of one another. Brethren, if a man is overtaken in any
trespass, you who are spiritual should restore him in a
spirit of gentleness. Look to yourself, lest you too be
tempted. Bear one another's burdens, and so fulfil the law
of Christ. For if any one thinks he is something, when he is
nothing, he deceives himself. But let each one test his own
work, and then his reason to boast will be in himself alone
and not in his neighbor. For each man will have to bear his
own load. Let him who is taught the word share all good
things with him who teaches. Do not be deceived; God is
not mocked, for whatever a man sows, that he will also
reap. For he who sows to his own flesh will from the flesh
reap corruption; but he who sows to the Spirit will from
the Spirit reap eternal life. And let us not grow weary in
welldoing, for in due season we shall reap, if we do not
lose heart. So then, as we have opportunity, let us do
good to all men, and especially to those who are of the
household of faith.

A Reading (Lesson) from the Gospel according to Matthew
[16:21-28]

After Peter's confession Jesus began to show his disciples
that he must go to Jerusalem and suffer many things from
the elders and chief priests and scribes, and be killed, and
on the third day be raised. And Peter took him and began
to rebuke him, saying, "God forbid, Lord! This shall never
happen to you." But he turned and said to Peter, "Get
behind me, Satan! You are a hindrance to me; for you are
not on the side of God, but of men." Then Jesus told his
disciples, "If any man would come after me, let him deny
himself and take up his cross and follow me. For whoever
would save his life will lose it, and whoever loses his life

for my sake will find it. For what will it profit a man, if he gains the whole world and forfeits his life? Or what shall a man give in return for his life? For the Son of man is to come with his angels in the glory of his Father, and then he will repay every man for what he has done. Truly, I say to you, there are some standing here who will not taste death before they see the Son of man coming in his kingdom."

Saturday

Psalm 75 [page 691],   *Psalm 76* [page 692]   ❖
Psalm 23 [page 612],   *Psalm 27* [page 617]

A Reading (Lesson) from the Book of Numbers [3:1-13]

These are the generations of Aaron and Moses at the time when the Lord spoke with Moses on Mount Sinai. These are the names of the sons of Aaron: Nadab the first-born, and Abi'hu, and Elea'zar, and Ith'amar; these are the names of the sons of Aaron, the anointed priests, whom he ordained to minister in the priest's office. But Nadab and Abi'hu died before the Lord when they offered unholy fire before the Lord in the wilderness of Sinai; and they had no children. So Elea'zar and Ith'amar served as priests in the lifetime of Aaron their father. And the Lord said to Moses, "Bring the tribe of Levi near, and set them before Aaron the priest, that they may minister to him. They shall perform duties for him and for the whole congregation before the tent of meeting, as they minister at the tabernacle; they shall have charge of all the furnishings of the tent of meeting, and attend to the duties for the people of Israel as they minister at the tabernacle. And you shall give the Levites to Aaron and his sons; they are wholly given to him from among the people of Israel. And you shall appoint Aaron and his sons, and they shall attend to their priesthood; but if any one else comes near, he shall be put to death." And the Lord said to Moses, "Behold, I have taken the Levites from among the people of Israel instead of every first-born that opens the womb among the people of Israel. The Levites shall be mine, for all the first-born are mine; on the day that I slew all the first-born in the land of Egypt, I consecrated for my own all the first-born in Israel, both of man and of beast; they shall be mine: I am the Lord."

A Reading (Lesson) from the Letter of Paul to the Galatians [6:11-18]

See with what large letters I am writing to you with my own hand. It is those who want to make a good showing in the flesh that would compel you to be circumcised, and only in order that they may not be persecuted for the cross of Christ. For even those who receive circumcision do not themselves keep the law, but they desire to have you circumcised that they may glory in your flesh. But far be it from me to glory except in the cross of our Lord Jesus Christ, by which the world has been crucified to me, and I to the world. For neither circumcision counts for anything, nor uncircumcision, but a new creation. Peace and mercy be upon all who walk by this rule, upon the Israel of God. Henceforth let no man trouble me; for I bear on my body the marks of Jesus. The grace of our Lord Jesus Christ be with your spirit, brethren. Amen.

A Reading (Lesson) from the Gospel according to Matthew [17:1-13]

After six days Jesus took with him Peter and James and John his brother, and led them up a high mountain apart. And he was transfigured before them, and his face shone like the sun, and his garments became white as light. And behold, there appeared to them Moses and Eli'jah, talking with him. And Peter said to Jesus, "Lord, it is well that we are here; if you wish, I will make three booths here, one for you and one for Moses and one for Eli'jah." He was still speaking, when lo, a bright cloud overshadowed them, and a voice from the cloud said, "This is my beloved Son, with whom I am well pleased; listen to him." When the disciples heard this, they fell on their faces, and were filled with awe. But Jesus came and touched them, saying, "Rise, and have no fear." And when they lifted up their eyes, they saw no one but Jesus only. And as they were coming down the mountain, Jesus commanded them, "Tell no one this vision, until the Son of man is raised from the dead." And the disciples asked him, "Then why do the scribes say that first Eli'jah must come?" He replied, "Eli'jah does come, and he is to restore all things; but I tell you that Eli'jah has already come, and they did not know him, but did to him whatever they pleased. So also the Son of man will suffer at their hands." Then the disciples understood that he was speaking to them of John the Baptist.

Proper 6   *Week of the Sunday closest to June 15*

Sunday

Psalm 93 [page 722],   *Psalm 96* [page 725]   ❖
Psalm 34 [page 627]

A Reading (Lesson) from the Book of Numbers   [6:22-27]

The Lord said to Moses, "Say to Aaron and his sons, Thus you shall bless the people of Israel: you shall say to them, The Lord bless you and keep you: The Lord make his face to shine upon you, and be gracious to you: The Lord lift up his countenance upon you, and give you peace. So shall they put my name upon the people of Israel, and I will bless them."

A Reading (Lesson) from the Acts of the Apostles   [13:1-12]

In the church at Antioch there were prophets and teachers, Barnabas, Simeon who was called Niger, Lucius of Cyre'ne, Man'a-en a member of the court of Herod the tetrarch, and Saul. While they were worshiping the Lord and fasting, the Holy Spirit said, "Set apart for me Barnabas and Saul for the work to which I have called them." Then after fasting and praying they laid their hands on them and sent them off. So, being sent out by the Holy Spirit, they went down to Seleu'cia; and from there they sailed to Cyprus. When they arrived at Sal'amis, they proclaimed the word of God in the synagogues of the Jews. And they had John to assist them. When they had gone through the whole island as far as Paphos, they came upon a certain magician, a Jewish false prophet, named Bar-Jesus. He was with the proconsul, Sergius Paulus, a man of intelligence, who summoned Barnabas and Saul and sought to hear the word of God. But El'ymas the magician (for that is the meaning of his name) withstood them, seeking to turn away the proconsul from the faith. But Saul, who is also called Paul, filled with the Holy Spirit, looked intently at him and said, "You son of the devil, you enemy of all righteousness, full of all deceit and villainy, will you not stop making crooked the straight paths of the Lord? And now, behold, the hand of the Lord is upon you, and you shall be blind and unable to see the sun for a time." Immediately mist and darkness fell upon him and he went about seeking people to lead him by the hand. Then the proconsul believed, when he saw what had occurred, for he was astonished at the teaching of the Lord.

A Reading (Lesson) from the Gospel according to Luke
[12:41-48]

Peter said, "Lord, are you telling this parable for us or for all?" And the Lord said, "Who then is the faithful and wise steward, whom his master will set over his household, to give them their portion of food at the proper time? Blessed is that servant whom his master when he comes will find so doing. Truly, I say to you, he will set him over all his possessions. But if that servant says to himself, 'My master is delayed in coming,' and begins to beat the menservants and the maidservants, and to eat and drink and get drunk, the master of that servant will come on a day when he does not expect him and at an hour he does not know, and will punish him, and put him with the unfaithful. And that servant who knew his master's will, but did not make ready or act according to his will, shall receive a severe beating. But he who did not know, and did what deserved a beating, shall receive a light beating. Every one to whom much is given, of him will much be required; and of him to whom men commit much they will demand all the more."

Monday

Psalm 80 [page 702] ❖ *Psalm 77* [page 693]
(Psalm 79 [page 701])

A Reading (Lesson) from the Book of Numbers
[9:15-23;10:29-36]

On the day that the tabernacle was set up, the cloud covered the tabernacle, the tent of the testimony; and at evening it was over the tabernacle like the appearance of fire until morning. So it was continually; the cloud covered it by day, and the appearance of fire by night. And whenever the cloud was taken up from over the tent, after that the people of Israel set out; and in the place where the cloud settled down, there the people of Israel encamped. At the command of the Lord the people of Israel set out, and at the command of the Lord they encamped; as long as the cloud rested over the tabernacle, they remained in camp. Even when the cloud continued over the tabernacle many days, the people of Israel kept the charge of the Lord, and did not set out. Sometimes the cloud was a few days over the tabernacle, and according to the command of the Lord they remained in camp; then according to the command of the Lord they set out. And sometimes the cloud remained from evening until morning; and when the cloud was taken up in the morning, they set out, or if it continued for a day and a night, when the cloud was taken up they set out. Whether it was two days, or a month, or a longer time, that the cloud continued over the tabernacle, abiding there, the people of Israel remained in camp and did not set out; but when it was taken up they set out. At the command of the Lord they encamped, and at the command of the Lord they set out; they kept the charge of the Lord, at the command of the Lord by Moses. And Moses said to Hobab, the son of Reu'el the Mid'ianite, Moses' father-in-law, "We are setting out for the place of which the Lord said, 'I will give it to you'; come with us, and we will do you good; for the Lord has promised good to Israel." But he said to him, "I will not go; I will depart to my own land and to my kindred." And he said, "Do not leave us, I pray you, for you know how we are to encamp in the wilderness, and you will serve as eyes for us. And if you go with us, whatever good the Lord will do to us, the same will we do to you." So they set out from the mount of the Lord three days' journey; and the ark of the covenant of the Lord went before them three days' journey, to seek out a resting place for them. And the cloud of the Lord was over them by day, whenever they set out from the camp. And whenever the ark set out, Moses said, "Arise, O Lord, and let thy enemies be scattered; and let them that hate thee flee before thee." And when it rested, he said, "Return, O Lord, to the ten thousand thousands of Israel."

A Reading (Lesson) from the Letter of Paul to the Romans [1:1-15]

Paul, a servant of Jesus Christ, called to be an apostle, set apart for the gospel of God which he promised beforehand through his prophets in the holy scriptures, the gospel concerning his Son, who was descended from David according to the flesh and designated Son of God in power according to the Spirit of holiness by his resurrection from the dead, Jesus Christ our Lord, through whom we have received grace and apostleship to bring about the obedience of faith for the sake of his name among all the nations, including yourselves who are called to belong to Jesus Christ; To all God's beloved in Rome, who are called to be saints: Grace to you and peace from God our Father and the Lord Jesus Christ. First, I thank my God through Jesus Christ for all of you, because your faith is proclaimed in all the world. For God is my witness, whom I serve with my spirit in the gospel of his Son, that without ceasing I mention you always in my prayers, asking that somehow by God's will I may now at last succeed in coming to you. For I long to see you, that I may impart to you some spiritual gift to strengthen you, that is, that we may be mutually encouraged by each other's faith, both yours and mine. I want you to know, brethren, that I have often intended to come to you (but thus far have been prevented), in order that I may reap some harvest among you as well as among the rest of the Gentiles. I am under obligation both to Greeks and to barbarians, both to the wise and to the foolish: so I am eager to preach the gospel to you also who are in Rome.

A Reading (Lesson) from the Gospel according to Matthew [17:14-21]

When Jesus and his disciples came to the crowd, a man came up to him and kneeling before him said, "Lord, have mercy on my son, for he is an epileptic and he suffers terribly; for often he falls into the fire, and often into the water. And I brought him to your disciples, and they could not heal him." And Jesus answered, "O faithless and perverse generation, how long am I to be with you? How long am I to bear with you? Bring him here to me." And Jesus rebuked him, and the demon came out of him, and the boy was cured instantly. Then the disciples came to Jesus privately and said, "Why could we not cast it out?" He said to them, "Because of your little faith. For truly,

I say to you, if you have faith as a grain of mustard seed, you will say to this mountain, 'Move from here to there,' and it will move; and nothing will be impossible to you."

Tuesday

Psalm 78:1-39 [page 694]   ❖   *Psalm 78:40-72* [page 698]

A Reading (Lesson) from the Book of Numbers [11:1-23]

The people complained in the hearing of the Lord about their misfortunes; and when the Lord heard it, his anger was kindled, and the fire of the Lord burned among them, and consumed some outlying parts of the camp. Then the people cried to Moses; and Moses prayed to the Lord, and the fire abated. So the name of that place was called Tab'erah, because the fire of the Lord burned among them. Now the rabble that was among them had a strong craving; and the people of Israel also wept again, and said, "O that we had meat to eat! We remember the fish we ate in Egypt for nothing, the cucumbers, the melons, the leeks, the onions, and the garlic; but now our strength is dried up, and there is nothing at all but this manna to look at." Now the manna was like coriander seed, and its appearance like that of bdellium. The people went about and gathered it, and ground it in mills or beat it in mortars, and boiled it in pots, and made cakes of it; and the taste of it was like the taste of cakes baked with oil. When the dew fell upon the camp in the night, the manna fell with it. Moses heard the people weeping throughout their families, every man at the door of his tent; and the anger of the Lord blazed hotly, and Moses was displeased. Moses said to the Lord, "Why hast thou dealt ill with thy servant? And why have I not found favor in thy sight, that thou dost lay this burden of all this people upon me? Did I conceive all this people? Did I bring them forth, that thou shouldst say to me, 'Carry them in your bosom, as a nurse carries the sucking child, to the land which thou didst swear to give their fathers?' Where am I to get meat to give to all this people? For they weep before me and say, 'Give us meat, that we may eat.' I am not able to carry all this people alone, the burden is too heavy for me. If thou wilt deal thus with me, kill me at once, if I find favor in thy sight, that I may not see my wretchedness." And the Lord said to Moses, "Gather for me seventy men of the elders of Israel, whom you know to be the elders of the people and officers over them; and bring them to the tent of meeting, and let them take their stand there with you. And I will come down and talk with you there; and I will take some of the spirit which is upon you and put it upon them; and they shall bear the burden of the people with you, that you may not bear it yourself alone. And say to the people, 'Consecrate yourselves for tomorrow, and you shall eat meat; for you have wept in the hearing of the Lord, saying, "Who will give us meat to eat? For it was well with us in Egypt." Therefore the Lord will give you meat, and you shall eat. You shall not eat one day, or two days, or five days, or ten days, or twenty days, but a whole month, until it comes out at your nostrils and becomes loathsome to you, because you have rejected the Lord who is among you, and have wept before him, saying, "Why did we come forth out of Egypt?"'" But Moses said, "The people among whom I am number six hundred thousand on foot; and thou hast said, 'I will give them meat, that they may eat a whole month!" Shall flocks and herds be slaughtered for them, to suffice them? Or shall all the fish of the sea be gathered together for them, to suffice them?" And the Lord said to Moses, "Is the Lord's hand shortened? Now you shall see whether my word will come true for you or not."

*A Reading (Lesson) from the Letter of Paul
to the Romans* [1:16-25]

I am not ashamed of the gospel: it is the power of God for salvation to every one who has faith, to the Jew first and also to the Greek. For in it the righteousness of God is revealed through faith for faith; as it is written, "He who through faith is righteous shall live." For the wrath of God is revealed from heaven against all ungodliness and wickedness of men who by their wickedness suppress the truth. For what can be known about God is plain to them, because God has shown it to them. Ever since the creation of the world his invisible nature, namely, his eternal power and deity, has been clearly perceived in the things that have been made. So they are without excuse; for although they knew God they did not honor him as God or give thanks to him, but they became futile in their thinking and their senseless minds were darkened. Claiming to be wise, they became fools, and exchanged the glory of the immortal God for images resembling mortal man or birds or animals or reptiles. Therefore God gave them up in the lusts of their hearts to impurity, to the dishonoring of their bodies among themselves, because they exchanged the truth about God for a lie and worshiped and served the creature rather than the Creator, who is blessed for ever! Amen.

A Reading (Lesson) from the Gospel according to Matthew [17:22-27]

As they were gathering in Galilee, Jesus said to the disciples, "The Son of man is to be delivered into the hands of men, and they will kill him, and he will be raised on the third day." And they were greatly distressed. When they came to Caper′na-um, the collectors of the half-shekel tax went up to Peter and said, "Does not your teacher pay the tax?" He said, "Yes." And when he came home, Jesus spoke to him first, saying, "What do you think, Simon? From whom do kings of the earth take toll or tribute? From their sons or from others?" And when he said, "From others," Jesus said to him, "Then the sons are free. However, not to give offense to them, go to the sea and cast a hook, and take the first fish that comes up, and when you open its mouth you will find a shekel; take that and give it to them for me and for yourself."

Wednesday

Psalm 119:97-120 [page 771] ❖ *Psalm 81* [page 704], *Psalm 82* [page 705]

A Reading (Lesson) from the Book of Numbers
[11:24-33 (34-35)]

Moses went out and told the people the words of the Lord; and he gathered seventy men of the elders of the people, and placed them round about the tent. Then the Lord came down in the cloud and spoke to him, and took some of the spirit that was upon him and put it upon the seventy elders; and when the spirit rested upon them, they prophesied. But they did so no more. Now two men remained in the camp, one named Eldad, and the other named Medad, and the spirit rested upon them; they were among those registered, but they had not gone out to the tent, and so they prophesied in the camp. And a young man ran and told Moses, "Eldad and Medad are prophesying in the camp." And Joshua the son of Nun, the minister of Moses, one of his chosen men, said, "My lord Moses, forbid them." But Moses said to him, "Are you jealous for my sake? Would that all the Lord's people were prophets, that the Lord would put his spirit upon them!" And Moses and the elders of Israel returned to the camp. And there went forth a wind from the Lord, and it brought quails from the sea, and let them fall beside the camp, about a day's journey on this side and a day's journey on the other side, round about the camp, and about two cubits above the face of the earth. And the people rose all that day, and all night, and all the next day, and gathered the quails; he who gathered least gathered ten homers; and they spread them out for themselves all around the camp. While the meat was yet between their teeth, before it was consumed, the anger of the Lord was kindled against the people, and the Lord smote the people with a very great plague.

Therefore the name of that place was called Kib'roth-hatta'avah, because there they buried the people who had the craving. From Kib'roth-hatta'avah the people journeyed to Haze'roth; and they remained at Haze'roth.

A Reading (Lesson) from the Letter of Paul to the Romans [1:28—2:11]

Since they did not see fit to acknowledge God, God gave them up to a base mind and to improper conduct. They were filled with all manner of wickedness, evil, covetousness, malice. Full of envy, murder, strife, deceit, malignity, they are gossips, slanderers, haters of God, insolent, haughty, boastful, inventors of evil, disobedient to parents, foolish, faithless, heartless, ruthless. Though they know God's decree that those who do such things deserve to die, they not only do them but approve those who practice them. Therefore you have no excuse, O man, whoever you are, when you judge another; for in passing judgment upon him you condemn yourself, because you, the judge, are doing the very same things. We know that the judgment of God rightly falls upon those who do such things. Do you suppose, O man, that when you judge those who do such things and yet do them yourself, you will escape the judgment of God? Or do you presume upon the riches of his kindness and forbearance and patience? Do you not know that God's kindness is meant to lead you to repentance? But by your hard and impenitent heart you are storing up wrath for yourself on the day of wrath when God's righteous judgment will be revealed. For he will render to every man according to his works: to those who by patience in well-doing seek for glory and honor and immortality, he will give eternal life; but for those who are factious and do not obey the truth, but obey wickedness, there will be wrath and fury. There will be tribulation and distress for every human being who does evil, the Jew first and also the Greek, but glory and honor and peace for every one who does good, the Jew first and also the Greek. For God shows no partiality.

A Reading (Lesson) from the Gospel according to Matthew [18:1-9]

When they were in Caper'na-um, the disciples came to Jesus, saying, "Who is the greatest in the kingdom of heaven?" And calling to him a child, he put him in the midst of them, and said, "Truly, I say to you, unless you turn and become like children, you will never enter the kingdom of heaven. Whoever humbles himself like this child, he is the greatest in the kingdom of heaven. Whoever receives one such child in my name receives me; but whoever causes one of these little ones who believe in me to sin, it would be better for him to have a great millstone fastened round his neck and to be drowned in the depth of the sea. Woe to the world for temptations to sin! For it is necessary that temptations come, but woe to the man by whom the temptation comes! And if your hand or your foot causes you to sin, cut it off and throw it away; it is better for you to enter life maimed or lame than with two hands or two feet to be thrown into the eternal fire. And if your eye causes you to sin, pluck it out and throw it away; it is better for you to enter life with one eye than with two eyes to be thrown into the hell of fire."

Thursday

(Psalm 83 [page 706]*)* or *Psalm 34* [page 627] ❖
Psalm 85 [page 708], *Psalm 86* [page 709]

A Reading (Lesson) from the Book of Numbers [12:1-16]

Miriam and Aaron spoke against Moses because of the Cushite woman whom he had married, for he had married a Cushite woman; and they said, "Has the Lord indeed spoken only through Moses? Has he not spoken through us also?" And the Lord heard it. Now the man Moses was very meek, more than all men that were on the face of the earth. And suddenly the Lord said to Moses and to Aaron and Miriam, "Come out, you three, to the tent of meeting." And the three of them came out. And the Lord came down in a pillar of cloud, and stood at the door of the tent, and called Aaron and Miriam; and they both came forward. And he said, "Hear my words: If there is a prophet among you, I the Lord make myself known to him in a vision, I speak with him in a dream. Not so with my servant Moses; he is entrusted with all my house. With him I speak mouth to mouth, clearly, and not in dark speech; and he beholds the form of the Lord. Why then were you not afraid to speak against my servant Moses?" And the anger of the Lord was kindled against them, and he departed; and when the cloud removed from over the tent, behold, Miriam was leprous, as white as snow. And Aaron turned towards Miriam, and behold, she was leprous. And Aaron said to Moses, "Oh, my lord, do not punish us because we have done foolishly and have sinned. Let her not be as one dead, of whom the flesh is half consumed when he comes out of his mother's womb." And Moses cried to the Lord, "Heal her, O God, I beseech thee." But the Lord said to Moses, "If her father had but spit in her face, should she not be shamed seven days? Let her be shut up outside the camp seven days, and after that she may be brought in again." So Miriam was shut up outside the camp seven days; and the people did not set out on the march till Miriam was brought in again. After that the people set out from Haze'roth, and encamped in the wilderness of Paran.

A Reading (Lesson) from the Letter of Paul to the Romans [2:12-24]

All who have sinned without the law will also perish without the law, and all who have sinned under the law will be judged by the law. For it is not the hearers of the law who are righteous before God, but the doers of the law who will be justified. When Gentiles who have not the law do by nature what the law requires, they are a law to themselves, even though they do not have the law. They show that what the law requires is written on their hearts, while their conscience also bears witness and their conflicting thoughts accuse or perhaps excuse them on that day when, according to my gospel, God judges the secrets of men by Christ Jesus. But if you call yourself a Jew and rely upon the law and boast of your relation to God and know his will and approve what is excellent, because you are instructed in the law, and if you are sure that you are a guide to the blind, a light to those who are in darkness, a corrector of the foolish, a teacher of children, having in the law the embodiment of knowledge and truth—you then who teach others, will you not teach yourself? While you preach against stealing, do you steal? You who say that one must not commit adultery, do you commit adultery? You who abhor idols, do you rob temples? You who boast in the law, do you dishonor God by breaking the law? For, as it is written, "The name of God is blasphemed among the Gentiles because of you."

A Reading (Lesson) from the Gospel according to Matthew
[18:10-20]

Jesus said to the disciples, "See that you do not despise one of these little ones; for I tell you that in heaven their angels always behold the face of my Father who is in heaven. What do you think? If a man has a hundred sheep, and one of them has gone astray, does he not leave the ninety-nine on the mountains and go in search of the one that went astray? And if he finds it, truly, I say to you, he rejoices over it more than over the ninety-nine that never went astray. So it is not the will of my Father who is in heaven that one of these little ones should perish. If your brother sins against you, go and tell him his fault, between you and him alone. If he listens to you, you have gained your brother. But if he does not listen, take one or two others along with you, that every word may be confirmed by the evidence of two or three witnesses. If he refuses to listen to them, tell it to the church; and if he refuses to listen even to the church, let him be to you as a Gentile and a tax collector. Truly, I say to you, whatever you bind on earth shall be bound in heaven, and whatever you loose on earth shall be loosed in heaven. Again I say to you, if two of you agree on earth about anything they ask, it will be done for them by my Father in heaven. For where two or three are gathered in my name, there am I in the midst of them."

Friday

Psalm 88 [page 712]   ❖   *Psalm 91* [page 719],
Psalm 92 [page 720]

A Reading (Lesson) from the Book of Numbers
[13:1-3,21-30]

The Lord said to Moses, "Send men to spy out the land of Canaan, which I give to the people of Israel; from each tribe of their fathers shall you send a man, every one a leader among them." So Moses sent them from the wilderness of Paran, according to the command of the Lord, all of them men who were heads of the people of Israel. So they went up and spied out the land from the wilderness of Zin to Rehob, near the entrance of Hamath. They went up into the Negeb, and came to Hebron; and Ahi'man, Sheshai, and Talmai, the descendants of Anak, were there. (Hebron was built seven years before Zo'an in Egypt.) And they came to the Valley of Eshcol, and cut down from there a branch with a single cluster of grapes, and they carried it on a pole between two of them; they brought also some pomegranates and figs. That place was called the Valley of Eshcol, because of the cluster which the men of Israel cut down from there. At the end of forty days they returned from spying out the land. And they came to Moses and Aaron and to all the congregation of the people of Israel in the wilderness of Paran, at Kadesh; they brought back word to them and to all the congregation, and showed them the fruit of the land. And they told him, "We came to the land to which you sent us; it flows with milk and honey, and this is its fruit. Yet the people who dwell in the land are strong, and the cities are fortified and very large; and besides, we saw the descendants of Anak there. The Amal'ekites dwell in the land of the Negeb; the Hittites, the Jeb'usites, and the Amorites dwell in the hill country; and the Canaanites dwell by the sea, and along the Jordan." But Caleb quieted the people before Moses, and said, "Let us go up at once, and occupy it; for we are well able to overcome it."

A Reading (Lesson) from the Letter of Paul to the Romans [2:25—3:8]

Circumcision indeed is of value if you obey the law; but if you break the law, your circumcision becomes uncircumcision. So, if a man who is uncircumcised keeps the precepts of the law, will not his uncircumcision be regarded as circumcision? Then those who are physically uncircumcised but keep the law will condemn you who have the written code and circumcision but break the law. For he is not a real Jew who is one outwardly, nor is true circumcision something external and physical. He is a Jew who is one inwardly, and real circumcision is a matter of the heart, spiritual and not literal. His praise is not from men but from God. Then what advantage has the Jew? Or what is the value of circumcision? Much in every way. To begin with, the Jews are entrusted with the oracles of God. What if some were unfaithful? Does their faithlessness nullify the faithfulness of God? By no means! Let God be true though every man be false, as it is written, "That thou mayest be justified in thy words, and prevail when thou art judged." But if our wickedness serves to show the justice of God, what shall we say? That God is unjust to inflict wrath on us? (I speak in a human way.) By no means! For then how could God judge the world? But if through my falsehood God's truthfulness abounds to his glory, why am I still being condemned as a sinner? And why not do evil that good may come?—as some people slanderously charge us with saying. Their condemnation is just.

A Reading (Lesson) from the Gospel according to Matthew
[18:21-35]

Peter came up and said to Jesus, "Lord, how often shall my brother sin against me, and I forgive him? As many as seven times?" Jesus said to him, "I do not say to you seven times, but seventy times seven. Therefore the kingdom of heaven may be compared to a king who wished to settle accounts with his servants. When he began the reckoning, one was brought to him who owed him ten thousand talents; and as he could not pay, his lord ordered him to be sold, with his wife and children and all that he had, and payment to be made. So the servant fell on his knees, imploring him, 'Lord, have patience with me, and I will pay you everything.' And out of pity for him the lord of that servant released him and forgave him the debt. But that same servant, as he went out, came upon one of his fellow servants who owed him a hundred denarii; and seizing him by the throat he said, 'Pay what you owe.' So his fellow servant fell down and besought him, 'Have patience with me, and I will pay you.' He refused and went and put him in prison till he should pay the debt. When his fellow servants saw what had taken place, they were greatly distressed, and they went and reported to their lord all that had taken place. Then his lord summoned him and said to him, 'You wicked servant! I forgave you all that debt because you besought me; and should not you have had mercy on your fellow servant, as I had mercy on you?' And in anger his lord delivered him to the jailers, till he should pay all his debt. So also my heavenly Father will do to every one of you, if you do not forgive your brother from your heart."

Saturday

Psalm 87 [page 711],   *Psalm 90* [page 717]   ❖
Psalm 136 [page 789]

A Reading (Lesson) from the Book of Numbers
[13:31—14:25]

The men who had gone up with Caleb into the land of Canaan said, "We are not able to go up against the people; for they are stronger than we." So they brought to the people of Israel an evil report of the land which they had spied out, saying, "The land, through which we have gone, to spy it out, is a land that devours its inhabitants; and all the people that we saw in it are men of great stature. And there we saw the Nephilim (the sons of Anak, who come from the Nephilim); and we seemed to ourselves like grasshoppers, and so we seemed to them." Then all the congregation raised a loud cry; and the people wept that night. And all the people of Israel murmured against Moses and Aaron; the whole congregation said to them, "Would that we had died in the land of Egypt! Or would that we had died in this wilderness! Why does the Lord bring us into this land, to fall by the sword? Our wives and our little ones will become a prey; would it not be better for us to go back to Egypt?" And they said to one another, "Let us choose a captain, and go back to Egypt." Then Moses and Aaron fell on their faces before all the assembly of the congregation of the people of Israel. And Joshua the son of Nun and Caleb the son of Jephun'neh, who were among those who had spied out the land, rent their clothes, and said to all the congregation of the people of Israel, "The land, which we passed through to spy it out, is an exceedingly good land. If the Lord delights in us, he will bring us into this land and give it to us, a land which flows with milk and honey. Only, do not rebel against the Lord; and do not fear the people of the land, for they are bread for us; their protection is removed from them, and the Lord is with us; do not fear them." But all the congregation said to stone them with stones. Then the glory of the Lord appeared at the tent of meeting to all the people of Israel. And the Lord said to Moses, "How long will this people despise me? And how long will they not believe in me, in spite of all the signs which I have wrought among them? I will strike them with the pestilence and disinherit them, and I will make of you a nation greater and mightier than they." But Moses said to the Lord, "Then the Egyptians will hear of it, for thou didst bring up this people in thy might from among them, and they will tell the inhabitants of this land. They have heard that thou, O Lord, art in the midst of this people; for thou, O Lord, art seen face to face, and thy cloud stands over them and thou goest before them, in a pillar of cloud by day and in a pillar of fire by night. Now if thou dost kill this people as one man, then the nations who have heard thy fame will say, 'Because the Lord was not able to bring this people into the land which he swore to give to them, therefore he has slain them in the wilderness.' And now, I pray thee, let the power of the Lord be great as thou hast promised, saying 'The Lord is slow to anger, and abounding in steadfast love, forgiving iniquity and transgression, but he will by no means clear the guilty, visiting the iniquity of fathers upon children, upon the third and upon the fourth generation.' Pardon the iniquity of this people, I pray thee, according to the greatness of thy steadfast love, and according as thou hast forgiven this people, from Egypt even until now." Then the Lord said, "I have pardoned, according to your work; but truly, as I live, and as all the earth shall be filled with the glory of the Lord, none of the men who have seen my glory and my signs which I wrought in Egypt and in the wilderness, and yet have put me to the proof these ten times and have not hearkened to my voice, shall see the land which I swore to give to their fathers; and none of those who despised me shall see it. But my servant Caleb, because he has a different spirit and has followed me fully, I will bring into the land into which he went, and his descendants shall possess it. Now, since the Amal'ekites and the Canaanites dwell in the valleys, turn tomorrow and set out for the wilderness by the way to the Red Sea."

A Reading (Lesson) from the Letter of Paul to the Romans [3:9-20]

What then? Are we Jews any better off? No, not at all; for I have already charged that all men, both Jews and Greeks, are under the power of sin, as it is written: "None is righteous, no, not one; no one understands, no one seeks for God. All have turned aside, together they have gone wrong; no one does good, not even one." "Their throat is an open grave, they use their tongues to deceive." "The venom of asps is under their lips." "Their mouth is full of curses and bitterness." "Their feet are swift to shed blood, in their paths are ruin and misery, and the way of peace they do not know." "There is no fear of God before their eyes." Now we know that whatever the law says it speaks to those who are under the law, so that every mouth may be stopped, and the whole world may be held accountable to God. For no human being will be justified in his sight by works of the law, since through the law comes knowledge of sin.

A Reading (Lesson) from the Gospel according to Matthew [19:1-12]

When Jesus had finished these sayings, he went away from Galilee and entered the region of Judea beyond the Jordan; and large crowds followed him, and he healed them there.

And Pharisees came up to him and tested him by asking, "Is it lawful to divorce one's wife for any cause?" He answered, "Have you not read that he who made them from the beginning made them male and female, and said, 'For this reason a man shall leave his father and mother and be joined to his wife, and the two shall become one flesh'? So they are no longer two but one flesh. What therefore God has joined together, let not man put asunder." They said to him, "Why then did Moses command one to give a certificate of divorce, and to put her away?" He said to them, "For your hardness of heart Moses allowed you to divorce your wives, but from the beginning it was not so. And I say to you: whoever divorces his wife, except for unchastity, and marries another, commits adultery." The disciples said to him, "If such is the case of a man with his wife, it is not expedient to marry." But he said to them, "Not all men can receive this saying, but only those to whom it is given. For there are eunuchs who have been so from birth, and there are eunuchs who have been made eunuchs by men, and there are eunuchs who have made themselves eunuchs for the sake of the kingdom of heaven. He who is able to receive this, let him receive it."

Proper 7 *Week of the Sunday closest to June 22*

Sunday

Psalm 66 [page 673], *Psalm 67* [page 675] ❖
Psalm 19 [page 606], *Psalm 46* [page 649]

A Reading (Lesson) from the Book of Numbers [14:26-45]

The Lord said to Moses and to Aaron, "How long shall this wicked congregation murmur against me? I have heard the murmurings of the people of Israel, which they murmur against me. Say to them, 'As I live,' says the Lord, 'what you have said in my hearing I will do to you: your dead bodies shall fall in this wilderness; and of all your number, numbered from twenty years old and upward, who have murmured against me, not one shall come into the land where I swore that I would make you dwell, escept Caleb the son of Jephun'neh and Joshua the son of Nun. But your little ones, who you said would become a prey, I will bring in, and they shall know the land which you have despised. But as for you, your dead bodies shall fall in this wilderness. And your children shall be shepherds in the wilderness forty years, and shall suffer for your faithlessness, until the last of your dead bodies lies in the wilderness. According to the number of the days in which you spied out the land, forty days, for every day a year, you shall bear your iniquity, forty years, and you shall know my displeasure.' I, the Lord, have spoken; surely this will I do to all this wicked congregation that are gathered together against me: in this wilderness they shall come to a full end, and there they shall die." And the men whom Moses sent to spy out the land, and who returned and made all the congregation to murmur against him by bringing up an evil report against the land, the men who brought up an evil report of the land, died by plague before the Lord. But Joshua the son of Nun and Caleb the son of Jephun'neh remained alive, of those men who went to spy out the land. And Moses told these words to all the people of Israel, and the people mourned greatly. And they rose early in the morning, and went up to the heights of the hill country, saying, "See, we are here, we will go up to the place which the Lord has promised; for we have sinned." But Moses said, "Why now are you transgressing the command of the Lord, for that will not succeed? Do not go up lest you be struck down before your enemies, for the Lord is not among you. For there the Amal'ekites and the Canaanites are before you, and you shall fall by the sword; because you have turned back from following the Lord, the Lord will not be with you." But they presumed to go up to the heights of the hill country, although neither the ark of the covenant of the Lord, nor Moses, departed out of the camp. Then the Amal'ekites and the Canaanites who dwelt in that hill country came down, and defeated them and pursued them, even to Hormah.

A Reading (Lesson) from the Acts of the Apostles [15:1-12]

Some men came down from Judea and were teaching the brethren, "Unless you are circumcised according to the custom of Moses, you cannot be saved." And when Paul and Barnabas had no small dissension and debate with them, Paul and Barnabas and some of the others were appointed to go up to Jerusalem to the apostles and the elders about this question. So, being sent on their way by the church, they passed through both Phoeni'cia and Samar'ia, reporting the conversion of the Gentiles, and they gave great joy to all the brethren. When they came to Jerusalem, they were welcomed by the church and the apostles and the elders, and they declared all that God had done with them. But some believers who belonged to the party of the Pharisees rose up, and said, "It is necessary to circumcise them, and to charge them to keep the law of Moses." The apostles and the elders were gathered together to consider this matter. And after there had been much debate, Peter rose and said to them, "Brethren, you know that in the early days God made choice among you, that by my mouth the Gentiles should hear the word of the gospel and believe. And God who knows the heart bore witness to them, giving them the Holy Spirit just as he did to us; and he made no distinction between us and them, but cleansed their hearts by faith. Now therefore why do you make trial of God by putting a yoke upon the neck of the disciples which neither our fathers nor we have been able to bear? But we believe that we shall be saved through the grace of the Lord Jesus, just as they will." And all the assembly kept silence; and they listened to Barnabas and Paul as they related what signs and wonders God had done through them among the Gentiles.

A Reading (Lesson) from the Gospel according to Luke
[12:49-56]

Jesus said to his disciples, "I came to cast fire upon the earth; and would that it were already kindled! I have a baptism to be baptized with; and how I am constrained until it is accomplished! Do you think that I have come to give peace on earth? No, I tell you, but rather division; for henceforth in one house there will be five divided, three against two and two against three; they will be divided, father against son and son against father, mother against daughter and daughter against her mother, mother-in-law against her daughter-in-law and daughter-in-law against her mother-in-law." He also said to the multitudes, "When you see a cloud rising in the west, you say at once, 'A shower is coming'; and so it happens. And when you see the south wind blowing, you say, 'There will be scorching heat'; and it happens. You hypocrites! You know how to interpret the appearance of earth and sky; but why do you not know how to interpret the present time?"

Monday

Psalm 89:1-18 [page 713]   ❖   *Psalm 89:19-52* [page 715]

A Reading (Lesson) from the Book of Numbers [16:1-19]

Korah the son of Izhar, son of Kohath, son of Levi, and Dathan and Abi'ram the sons of Eli'ab, and On the son of Peleth, sons of Reuben, took men; and they rose up before Moses, with a number of the people of Israel, two hundred and fifty leaders of the congregation, chosen from the assembly, well-known men; and they assembled themselves together against Moses and against Aaron, and said to them, "You have gone too far! For all the congregation are holy, every one of them, and the Lord is among them; why then do you exalt yourselves above the assembly of the Lord?" When Moses heard it, he fell on his face; and he said to Korah and all his company, "In the morning the Lord will show who is his, and who is holy, and will cause him to come near to him; him whom he will choose he will cause to come near to him. Do this: take censers, Korah and all his company; put fire in them and put incense upon them before the Lord tomorrow, and the man whom the Lord chooses shall be the holy one. You have gone too far, sons of Levi!" And Moses said to Korah, "Hear now, you sons of Levi: is it too small a thing for you that the God of Israel has separated you from the congregation of Israel, to bring you near to himself, to do service in the tabernacle of the Lord, and to stand before the congregation to minister to them; and that he has brought you near him, and all your brethren the sons of Levi with you? And would you seek the priesthood also? Therefore it is against the Lord that you and all your company have gathered together; what is Aaron that you murmur against him?" And Moses sent to call Dathan and Abi'ram the sons of Eli'ab; and they said, "We will not come up. Is it a small thing that you have brought us up out of a land flowing with milk and honey, to kill us in the wilderness, that you must also make yourself a prince over us? Moreover you have not brought us into a land flowing with milk and honey, nor given us inheritance of fields and vineyards. Will you put out the eyes of these men? We will not come up." And Moses was very angry, and said to the Lord, "Do not respect their offering. I have not taken one ass from them, and I have not harmed one of them." And Moses said to Korah, "Be present, you and all your company, before the Lord, you and they, and Aaron, tomorrow; and let every one of you take his censer, and put incense upon it, and every one of you bring before the Lord his censer, two hundred and fifty censers; you also, and Aaron, each his censer." So every man took his censer, and they put fire in them and laid incense upon them, and they stood at the entrance of the tent of meeting with Moses and Aaron. Then Korah assembled all the congregation against them at the entrance of the tent of meeting. And the glory of the Lord appeared to all the congregation.

A Reading (Lesson) from the Letter of Paul to the Romans [3:21-31]

Now the righteousness of God has been manifested apart from law, although the law and the prophets bear witness to it, the righteousness of God through faith in Jesus Christ for all who believe. For there is no distinction; since all have sinned and fall short of the glory of God, they are justified by his grace as a gift, through the redemption which is in Christ Jesus, whom God put forward as an expiation by his blood, to be received by faith. This was to show God's righteousness, because in his divine forbearance he had passed over former sins; it was to prove at the present time that he himself is righteous and that he justifies him who has faith in Jesus. Then what becomes of our boasting? It is excluded. On what principle? On the principle of works? No, but on the principle of faith. For we hold that a man is justified by faith apart from works of law. Or is God the God of Jews only? Is he not the God of Gentiles also? Yes, of Gentiles also, since God is one; and he will justify the circumcised on the ground of their faith and the uncircumcised through their faith. Do we then overthrow the law by this faith? By no means! On the contrary, we uphold the law.

A Reading (Lesson) from the Gospel according to Matthew [19:13-22]

Children were brought to Jesus that he might lay his hands on them and pray. The disciples rebuked the people; but Jesus said, "Let the children come to me, and do not hinder them; for to such belongs the kingdom of heaven." And he laid his hands on them and went away. And behold, one came up to him, saying, "Teacher, what good deeds must I do, to have eternal life?" And he said to him, "Why do you ask me about what is good? One there is who is good. If you would enter life, keep the commandments." He said to him, "Which?" And Jesus said, "You shall not kill, You shall not commit adultery, You shall not steal, You shall not bear false witness, Honor your father and mother, and, You shall love your neighbor as yourself." The young man said to him, "All these I have observed; what do I still lack?" Jesus said to him, "If you would be perfect, go, sell what you possess and give to the poor, and you will have treasure in heaven; and come, follow me." When the young man heard this he went away sorrowful; for he had great possessions.

Tuesday

Psalm 97 [page 726], *Psalm 99* [page 728], *(Psalm 100* [page 729]) ❖ *Psalm 94* [page 722], *(Psalm 95* [page 724])

A Reading (Lesson) from the Book of Numbers [16:20-35]

The Lord said to Moses and to Aaron, "Separate yourselves from among this congregation, that I may consume them in a moment." And they fell on their faces, and said, "O God, the God of the spirits of all flesh, shall one man sin, and wilt thou be angry with all the congregation?" And the Lord said to Moses, "Say to the congregation, Get away from about the dwelling of Korah, Dathan, and Abi'ram." Then Moses rose and went to Dathan and Abi'ram; and the elders of Israel followed him. And he said to the congregation, "Depart, I pray you, from the tents of these wicked men, and touch nothing of theirs, lest you be swept away with all their sins." So they got away from the dwelling of Korah, Dathan, and Abi'ram; and Dathan and Abi'ram came out and stood at the door of their tents, together with their wives, their sons, and their little ones. And Moses said, "Hereby you shall know that the Lord has sent me to do all these works, and that it has not been of my own accord. If these men die the common death of all men, or if they are visited by the fate of all men, then the Lord has not sent me. But if the Lord creates something new, and the ground opens its mouth, and swallows them up, with all that belongs to them, and they go down alive into Sheol, then you shall know that these men have despised the Lord." And as he finished speaking all these words, the ground under them split asunder; and the earth opened its mouth and swallowed them up, with their households and all the men that belonged to Korah and all their goods. So they and all that belonged to them went down alive into Sheol; and the earth closed over them, and they perished from the midst of the assembly. And all Israel that were round about them fled at their cry; for they said, "Lest the earth swallow us up!" And fire came forth from the Lord, and consumed the two hundred and fifty men offering the incense.

A Reading (Lesson) from the Letter of Paul to the Romans [4:1-12]

What then shall we say about Abraham, our forefather according to the flesh? For if Abraham was justified by works, he has something to boast about, but not before God. For what does the scripture say? "Abraham believed God, and it was reckoned to him as righteousness." Now to one who works, his wages are not reckoned as a gift but as his due. And to one who does not work but trusts him who justifies the ungodly, his faith is reckoned as righteousness. So also David pronounces a blessing upon the man to whom God reckons righteousness apart from works: "Blessed are those who iniquities are forgiven, and whose sins are covered; blessed is the man against whom the Lord will not reckon his sin." Is this blessing pronounced only upon the circumcised, or also upon the uncircumcised? We say that faith was reckoned to

Abraham as righteousness. How then was it reckoned to him? Was it before or after he had been circumcised? It was not after, but before he was circumcised. He received circumcision as a sign or seal of the righteousness which he had by faith while he was still uncircumcised. The purpose was to make him the father of all who believe without being circumcised and who thus have righteousness reckoned to them, and likewise the father of the circumcised who are not merely circumcised but also follow the example of the faith which our father Abraham had before he was circumcised.

A Reading (Lesson) from the Gospel according to Matthew [19:23-30]

Jesus said to his disciples, "Truly, I say to you, it will be hard for a rich man to enter the kingdom of heaven. Again I tell you, it is easier for a camel to go through the eye of a needle than for a rich man to enter the kingdom of God." When the disciples heard this they were greatly astonished, saying, "Who then can be saved?" But Jesus looked at them and said to them, "With men this is impossible, but with God all things are possible." Then Peter said in reply, "Lo, we have left everything and followed you. What then shall we have?" Jesus said to them, "Truly, I say to you, in the new world, when the Son of man shall sit on his glorious throne, you who have followed me will also sit on twelve thrones, judging the twelve tribes of Israel. And every one who has left houses or brothers or sisters or father or mother or children or lands, for my name's sake, will receive a hundredfold, and inherit eternal life. But many that are first will be last, and the last first."

Wednesday

Psalm 101 [page 730], *Psalm 109:1-4 (5-19) 20-30* [page 750] ❖ *Psalm 119:121-144* [page 773]

A Reading (Lesson) from the Book of Numbers [16:36-50]

The Lord said to Moses, "Tell Elea'zar the son of Aaron the priest to take up the censers out of the blaze; then scatter the fire far and wide. For they are holy, the censers of these men who have sinned at the cost of their lives; so let them be made into hammered plates as a covering for the altar, for they offered them before the Lord; therefore they are holy. Thus they shall be a sign to the people of Israel." So Elea'zar the priest took the bronze censers, which those who were burned had offered; and they were hammered out as a covering for the altar, to be a reminder to the people of Israel, so that no one who is not a priest, who is not of the descendants of Aaron, should draw near to burn incense before the Lord, lest he become as Korah and as his company—as the Lord said to Elea'zar through Moses. But on the morrow all the congregation of the people of Israel murmured against Moses and against Aaron, saying, "You have killed the people of the Lord." And when the congregation had assembled against Moses and against Aaron, they turned toward the tent of meeting; and behold, the cloud covered it, and the glory of the Lord appeared. And Moses and Aaron came to the front of the tent of meeting, and the Lord said to Moses, "Get away from the midst of this congregation, that I may consume them in a moment." And they fell on their faces. And Moses said to Aaron, "Take your censer, and put fire therein from off the altar, and lay incense on it, and carry it quickly to the congregation, and make atonement for them; for wrath has gone forth from the Lord, the plague has begun." So Aaron took it as Moses said, and ran into the midst of the assembly; and behold, the plague had already begun among the people; and he put on the incense, and made atonement for the people. And he stood between the dead and the living; and the plague was stopped. Now those who died by the plague were fourteen thousand seven hundred, besides those who died in the affair of Korah. And Aaron returned to Moses at the entrance of the tent of meeting, when the plague was stopped.

A Reading (Lesson) from the Letter of Paul to the Romans [4:13-25]

The promise to Abraham and his descendants, that they should inherit the world, did not come through the law but through the righteousness of faith. If it is the adherents of the law who are to be the heirs, faith is null and the promise is void. For the law brings wrath, but where there is no law there is no transgression. That is why it depends on faith, in order that the promise may rest on grace and be guaranteed to all his descendants—not only to the adherents of the law but also to those who share the faith of Abraham, for he is the father of us all, as it is written, "I have made you the father of many nations"—in the presence of the God in whom he believed, who gives life to the dead and calls into existence the things that do not exist. In hope he believed against hope, that he should become the father of many nations; as he had been told, "So shall your descendants be." He did not weaken in faith when he considered his own body, which was as good as dead because he was about a hundred years old, or when he considered the barrenness of Sarah's womb. No distrust made him waver concerning the promise of God, but he grew strong in his faith as he gave glory to God, fully convinced that God was able to do what he had promised. That is why his faith was "reckoned to him as righteousness." But the words, "it was reckoned to him," were written not for his sake alone, but for ours also. It will be reckoned to us who believe in him that raised from the dead Jesus our Lord, who was put to death for our trespasses and raised for our justification.

A Reading (Lesson) from the Gospel according to Matthew
[20:1-16]

Jesus said to his disciples, "The kingdom of heaven is like a householder who went out early in the morning to hire laborers for his vineyard. After agreeing with the laborers for a denarius a day, he sent them into his vineyard. And going out about the third hour he saw others standing idle in the market place; and to them he said, 'You go into the vineyard too, and whatever is right I will give you.' So they went. Going out again about the sixth hour and the ninth hour, he did the same. And about the eleventh hour he went out and found others standing; and he said to them, 'Why do you stand here idle all day?' They said to him, 'Because no one has hired us.' He said to them, 'You go into the vineyard too.' And when evening came, the owner of the vineyard said to his steward, 'Call the laborers and pay them their wages, beginning with the last, up to the first.' And when those hired about the eleventh hour came, each of them received a denarius. Now when the first came, they thought they would receive more; but each of them also received a denarius. And on receiving it they grumbled at the householder, saying, 'These last worked only one hour, and you have made them equal to us who have borne the burden of the day and the scorching heat.' But he replied to one of them, 'Friend, I am doing you no wrong; did you not agree with me for a denarius? Take what belongs to you, and go; I choose to give this last as I give to you. Am I not allowed to do what I choose with what belongs to me? Or do you begrudge my generosity?' So the last will be first, and the first last."

Thursday

Psalm 105:1-22 [page 738] ❖
Psalm 105:23-45 [page 739]

A Reading (Lesson) from the Book of Numbers [17:1-11]

The Lord said to Moses, "Speak to the people of Israel,
and get from them rods, one for each fathers' house, from
all their leaders according to their fathers' houses, twelve
rods. Write each man's name upon his rod, and write
Aaron's name upon the rod of Levi. For there shall be one
rod for the head of each fathers' house. Then you shall
deposit them in the tent of meeting before the testimony,
where I meet with you. And the rod of the man whom I
choose shall sprout; thus I will make to cease from me the
murmurings of the people of Israel, which they murmur
against you." Moses spoke to the people of Israel; and all
their leaders gave him rods, one for each leader, according
to their fathers' houses, twelve rods; and the rod of Aaron
was among their rods. And Moses deposited the rods
before the Lord in the tent of the testimony. And on the
morrow Moses went into the tent of the testimony; and
behold, the rod of Aaron for the house of Levi had
sprouted and put forth buds, and produced blossoms, and
it bore ripe almonds. Then Moses brought out all the rods
from before the Lord to all the people of Israel; and they
looked, and each man took his rod. And the Lord said to
Moses, "Put back the rod of Aaron before the testimony,
to be kept as a sign for the rebels, that you may make an
end of their murmurings against me, lest they die." Thus
did Moses; as the Lord commanded him, so he did.

*A Reading (Lesson) from the First Letter of Paul
to the Romans* [5:1-11]

Since we are justified by faith, we have peace with God
through our Lord Jesus Christ. Through him we have
obtained access to this grace in which we stand, and we
rejoice in our hope of sharing the glory of God. More than
that, we rejoice in our sufferings, knowing that suffering
produces endurance, and endurance produces character,
and character produces hope, and hope does not

disappoint us, because God's love has been poured into our hearts through the Holy Spirit which has been given to us. While we were still weak, at the right time, Christ died for the ungodly. Why, one will hardly die for a righteous man—though perhaps for a good man one will dare even to die. But God shows his love for us in that while we were yet sinners Christ died for us. Since, therefore, we are now justified by his blood, much more shall we be saved by him from the wrath of God. For if while we were enemies we were reconciled to God by the death of his Son, much more, now that we are reconciled, shall we be saved by his life. Not only so, but we also rejoice in God through our Lord Jesus Christ, through whom we have now received our reconciliation.

A Reading (Lesson) from the Gospel according to Matthew
[20:17-28]

As Jesus was going up to Jerusalem, he took the twelve disciples aside, and on the way he said to them, "Behold, we are going up to Jerusalem; and the Son of man will be delivered to the chief priests and scribes, and they will condemn him to death, and deliver him to the Gentiles to be mocked and scourged and crucified, and he will be raised on the third day." Then the mother of the sons of Zeb'edee came up to him, with her sons, and kneeling before him she asked him for something. And he said to her, "What do you want?" She said to him, "Command that these two sons of mine may sit, one at your right hand and one at your left, in your kingdom." But Jesus answered, "You do not know what you are asking. Are you able to drink the cup that I am to drink?" They said to him, "We are able." He said to them, "You will drink my cup, but to sit at my right hand and at my left is not mine to grant, but it is for those for whom it has been prepared by my Father." And when the ten heard it, they were indignant at the two brothers. But Jesus called them to him and said, "You know that the rulers of the Gentiles lord it over them, and their great men exercise authority over them. It shall not be so among you; but whoever would be great among you must be your servant, and whoever would be first among you must be your slave; even as the Son of man came not to be served but to serve, and to give his life as a ransom for many."

Friday

Psalm 102 [page 731] ❖ *Psalm 107:1-32* [page 746]

A Reading (Lesson) from the Book of Numbers [20:1-13]

The people of Israel, the whole congregation, came into the wilderness of Zin in the first month, and the people stayed in Kadesh; and Miriam died there, and was buried there. Now there was no water for the congregation; and they assembled themselves together against Moses and against Aaron. And the people contended with Moses, and said, "Would that we had died when our brethren died before the Lord! Why have you brought the assembly of the Lord into this wilderness, that we should die here, both we and our cattle? And why have you made us come up out of Egypt, to bring us to this evil place? It is no place for grain, or figs, or vines, or pomegranates; and there is no water to drink." Then Moses and Aaron went from the presence of the assembly to the door of the tent of meeting, and fell on their faces. And the glory of the Lord appeared to them, and the Lord said to Moses, "Take the rod, and assemble the congregation, you and Aaron your brother, and tell the rock before their eyes to yield water; so you shall bring water out of the rock for them; so you shall give drink to the congregation and their cattle." And Moses took the rod from before the Lord, as he commanded him. And Moses and Aaron gathered the assembly together before the rock, and he said to them, "Hear now, you rebels; shall we bring forth water for you out of this rock?" And Moses lifted up his hand and struck the rock with his rod twice; and water came forth abundantly, and the congregation drank, and their cattle. And the Lord said to Moses and Aaron, "Because you did not believe in me, to sanctify me in the eyes of the people of Israel, therefore you shall not bring this assembly into the land which I have given them." These are the waters of Mer'ibah, where the people of the Lord contended with the Lord, and he showed himself holy among them.

A Reading (Lesson) from the Letter of Paul to the Romans [5:12-21]

As sin came into the world through one man and death through sin, and so death spread to all men because all men sinned—sin indeed was in the world before the law was given, but sin is not counted where there is no law. Yet death reigned from Adam to Moses, even over those whose sins were not like the transgression of Adam, who was a type of the one who was to come. But the free gift is not like the trespass. For if many died through one man's trespass, much more have the grace of God and the free gift in the grace of that one man Jesus Christ abounded for many. And the free gift is not like the effect of that one man's sin. For the judgment following one trespass brought condemnation, but the free gift following many trespasses brings justification. If, because of one man's trespass, death reigned through that one man, much more will those who receive the abundance of grace and the free gift of righteousness reign in life through the one man Jesus Christ. Then as one man's trespass led to condemnation for all men, so one man's act of righteousness leads to acquittal and life for all men. For as by one man's disobedience many were made sinners, so by one man's obedience many will be made righteous. Law came in, to increase the trespass; but where sin increased, grace abounded all the more, so that, as sin reigned in death, grace also might reign through righteousness to eternal life through Jesus Christ our Lord.

A Reading (Lesson) from the Gospel according to Matthew
[20:29-34]

As they went out to Jericho, a great crowd followed Jesus. And behold, two blind men sitting by the roadside, when they heard that Jesus was passing by, cried out, "Have mercy on us, Son of David!" The crowd rebuked them, telling them to be silent; but they cried out the more, "Lord, have mercy on us, Son of David!" And Jesus stopped and called them, saying, "What do you want me to do for you?" They said to him, "Lord, let our eyes be opened." And Jesus in pity touched their eyes, and immediately they received their sight and followed him.

Saturday

Psalm 107:33-43 [page 748]   *Psalm 108:1-6 (7-13)* [page 749]
❖   *Psalm 33* [page 626]

A Reading (Lesson) from the Book of Numbers [20:14-29]

Moses sent messengers from Kadesh to the king of Edom, "Thus says your brother Israel: You know all the adversity that has befallen us; how our fathers went down to Egypt, and we dwelt in Egypt a long time; and the Egyptians dealt harshly with us and our fathers; and when we cried to the Lord, he heard our voice, and sent an angel and brought us forth out of Egypt; and here we are in Kadesh, a city on the edge of your territory. Now let us pass through your land. We will not pass through field or vineyard, neither will we drink water from a well; we will go along the King's Highway, we will not turn aside to the right hand or to the left, until we have passed through your territory." But Edom said to him, "You shall not pass through, lest I come out with the sword against you." And the people of Israel said to him, "We will go up by the highway; and if we drink of your water, I and my cattle, then I will pay for it; let me only pass through on foot, nothing more." But he said, "You shall not pass through." And Edom came out against them with many men, and with a strong force. Thus Edom refused to give Israel passage through his territory; so Israel turned away from him. And they journeyed from Kadesh, and the people of Israel, the whole congregation, came to Mount Hor. And the Lord said to Moses and Aaron at Mount Hor, on the border of the land of Edom, "Aaron shall be gathered to his people; for he shall not enter the land which I have given to the people of Israel, because you rebelled against my command at the waters of Mer'ibah. Take Aaron and Elea'zor his son, and bring them up to Mount Hor; and strip Aaron of his garments, and put them upon Elea'zar his son; and Aaron shall be gathered to his people, and shall die there." Moses did as the Lord commanded; and they went up Mount Hor in the sight of all the congregation. And Moses stripped Aaron of his garments, and put them upon Elea'zar his son; and Aaron died there at the top of the mountain. Then Moses and Elea'zar came down from the mountain. And when all the congregation saw that Aaron was dead, all the house of Israel wept for Aaron thirty days.

A Reading (Lesson) from the Letter of Paul to the Romans [6:1-11]

What shall we say then? Are we to continue in sin that grace may abound? By no means! How can we who died to sin still live in it? Do you now know that all of us who have been baptized into Christ Jesus were baptized into his death? We were buried therefore with him by baptism into death, so that as Christ was raised from the dead by the glory of the Father, we too might walk in newness of life. For if we have been united with him in a death like his, we shall certainly be united with him in a resurrection like his. We know that our old self was crucified with him so that the sinful body might be destroyed, and we might no longer be enslaved to sin. For he who has died is freed from sin. But if we have died with Christ, we believe that we shall also live with him. For we know that Christ being raised from the dead will never die again; death no longer has dominion over him. The death he died he died to sin, once for all, but the life he lives he lives to God. So you also must consider yourselves dead to sin and alive to God in Christ Jesus.

A Reading (Lesson) from the Gospel according to Matthew [21:1-11]

When Jesus and the disciples drew near to Jerusalem and came to Beth'phage, to the Mount of Olives, then Jesus sent two disciples, saying to them, "Go into the village opposite you, and immediately, you will find an ass tied, and a colt with her; untie them and bring them to me. If any one says anything to you, you shall say, 'The Lord has need of them,' and he will send them immediately." This took place to fulfil what was spoken by the prophet, saying, "Tell the daughter of Zion, Behold, your king is coming to you, humble, and mounted on an ass, and on a colt, the foal of an ass." The disciples went and did as Jesus had directed them; they brought the ass and the colt, and put their garments on them, and he sat thereon. Most of the crowd spread their garments on the road, and others cut branches from the trees and spread them on the road. And the crowds that went before him and that followed him shouted, "Hosanna to the Son of David! Blessed is he who comes in the name of the Lord! Hosanna in the highest!" And when he entered Jerusalem, all the city was stirred, saying, "Who is this?" And the crowds said, "This is the prophet Jesus from Nazareth of Galilee."

Proper 8   *Week of the Sunday closest to June 29*

Sunday

Psalm 118 [page 760]   ❖   *Psalm 145* [page 801]

A Reading (Lesson) from the Book of Numbers
[21:4-9,21-35]

From Mount Hor they set out by the way to the Red Sea,
to go around the land of Edom; and the people became
impatient on the way. And the people spoke against God
and against Moses, "Why have you brought us up out of
Egypt to die in the wilderness? For there is no food and no
water, and we loathe this worthless food." Then the Lord
sent fiery serpents among the people, and they bit the
people, so that many people of Israel died. And the people
came to Moses, and said, "We have sinned, for we have
spoken against the Lord and against you; pray to the Lord,
that he take away the serpents from us." So Moses prayed
for the people. And the Lord said to Moses, "Make a fiery
serpent, and set it on a pole; and every one who is bitten,
when he sees it, shall live." So Moses made a bronze
serpent, and set it on a pole; and if a serpent bit any man,
he would look at the bronze serpent and live. Then Israel
sent messengers to Sihon king of the Amorites, saying,
"Let me pass through your land; we will not turn aside into
field or vineyard; we will not drink the water of a well; we
will go by the King's Highway, until we have passed
through your territory." But Sihon would not allow Israel
to pass through his territory. He gathered all his men
together, and went out against Israel to the wilderness, and
came to Jahaz, and fought against Israel. And Israel slew
him with the edge of the sword, and took possession of his
land from the Arnon to the Jabbok, as far as to the
Ammonites; for Jazer was the boundary of the
Ammonites. And Israel took all these cities, and Israel
settled in all the cities of the Amorites, in Heshbon, and in
all its villages. For Heshbon was the city of Sihon the king
of the Amorites, who had fought against the former king
of Moab and taken all his land out of his hand, as far as
the Arnon. Therefore the ballad singers say, "Come to
Heshbon, let it be built, let the city of Sihon be established.
For fire went forth from Heshbon, flame from the city of

Sihon. It devoured Ar of Moab, the lords of the heights of the Arnon. Woe to you, O Moab! You are undone, O people of Chemosh! He has made his sons fugitives, and his daughters captives, to an Amorite king, Sihon. So their posterity perished from Heshbon, as far as Dibon, and we laid waste until fire spread to Med'eba." Thus Israel dwelt in the land of the Amorites. And Moses sent to spy out Jazer; and they took its villages, and dispossessed the Amorites that were there. Then they turned and went up by the way to Bashan; and Og the king of Bashan came out against them, he and all his people, to battle at Ed're-i. But the Lord said to Moses, "Do not fear him; for I have given him into your hand, and all his people, and his land; and you shall do to him as you did to Sihon king of the Amorites, who dwelt at Heshbon." So they slew him, and his sons, and all his people, until there was not one survivor left to him; and they possessed his land.

A Reading (Lesson) from the Acts of the Apostles
[17:(12-21)22-34]

Many of the Jews at Beroe'a believed, with not a few Greek women of high standing as well as men. But when the Jews of Thessaloni'ca learned that the word of God was proclaimed by Paul at Beroe'a also, they came there too, stirring up and inciting the crowds. Then the brethren immediately sent Paul off on his way to the sea, but Silas and Timothy remained there. Those who conducted Paul brought him as far as Athens; and receiving a command for Silas and Timothy to come to him as soon as possible, they departed. Now while Paul was waiting for them at Athens, his spirit was provoked within him as he saw that the city was full of idols. So he argued in the synagogue with the Jews and the devout persons, and in the market place every day with those who chanced to be there. Some also of the Epicurean and Stoic philosophers met him. And some said, "What would this babbler say?" Others said, "He seems to be a preacher of foreign divinities"—because he preached Jesus and the resurrection. And they took hold of him and brought him to the Are-op'agus, saying, "May we know what this new teaching is which you present? For you bring some strange things to our ears; we wish to know therefore what these things mean." Now all the Athenians and the foreigners who lived there spent their time in nothing except telling or hearing something new.

[*Paul was brought to the Are-op'agus by the Epicurean and Stoic philosophers, who said to him, "May we know what this new teaching is which you present?"*] So Paul, standing in the middle of the Are-op'agus, said: "Men of Athens, I perceive that in every way you are very religious. For as I passed along, and observed the objects of your worship, I found also an altar with this inscription, 'To an unknown god.' What therefore you worship as unknown, this I proclaim to you. The God who made the world and everything in it, being Lord of heaven and earth, does not live in shrines made by man, nor is he served by human hands, as though he needed anything, since he himself gives to all men life and breath and everything. And he made from one every nation of men to live on all the face of the earth, having determined allotted periods and the boundaries of their habitation, that they should seek God, in the hope that they might feel after him and find him. Yet he is not far from each one of us, for 'In him we live and move and have our being'; as even some of your poets have said, 'For we are indeed his offspring.' Being then God's offspring, we ought not to think that the Deity is like gold, or silver, or stone, a representation by the art and imagination of man. The times of ignorance God overlooked, but now he commands all men everywhere to repent, because he has fixed a day on which he will judge the world in righteousness by a man whom he has appointed, and of this he has given assurance to all men by raising him from the dead." Now when they heard of the resurrection of the dead, some mocked; but others said, "We will hear you again about this." So Paul went out from among them. But some men joined him and believed, among them Dionys'ius the Are-op'agite and a woman named Dam'aris and others with them.

A Reading (Lesson) from the Gospel according to Luke [13:10-17]

Jesus was teaching in one of the synagogues on the sabbath. And there was a woman who had had a spirit of infirmity for eighteen years; she was bent over and could not fully straighten herself. And when Jesus saw her, he called her and said to her, "Woman, you are freed from your infirmity." And he laid his hands upon her, and immediately she was made straight, and she praised God. But the ruler of the synagogue, indignant because Jesus had healed on the sabbath, said to the people, "There are six days on which work ought to be done; come on those days and be healed, and not on the sabbath day." Then the Lord answered him, "You hypocrites! Does not each of you on the sabbath untie his ox or his ass from the manger, and lead it away to water it? And ought not this woman, a daughter of Abraham whom Satan bound for eighteen years, be loosed from this bond on the sabbath day? As he said this, all his adversaries were put to shame; and all the people rejoiced at all the glorious things that were done by him.

Monday

Psalm 106:1-18 [page 741] ❖ *Psalm 106:19-48* [page 743]

A Reading (Lesson) from the Book of Numbers [22:1-21]

The people of Israel set out, and encamped in the plains of Moab beyond the Jordan at Jericho. And Balak the son of Zippor saw all that Israel had done to the Amorites. And

Moab was in great dread of the people, because they were many; Moab was overcome with fear of the people of Israel. And Moab said to the elders of Mid'ian, "This horde will now lick up all that is round about us, as the ox licks up the grass of the field." So Balak the son of Zippor, who was king of Moab at that time, sent messengers to Balaam the son of Be'or at Pethor, which is near the River, in the land of Amaw to call him, saying, "Behold, a people has come out of Egypt; they cover the face of the earth, and they are dwelling opposite me. Come now, curse this people for me, since they are too mighty for me; perhaps I shall be able to defeat them and drive them from the land; for I know that he whom you bless is blessed, and he whom you curse is cursed." So the elders of Moab and the elders of Mid'ian departed with the fees for divination in their hand; and they came to Balaam, and gave him Balak's message. And he said to them, "Lodge here this night, and I will bring back word to you, as the Lord speaks to me"; so the princes of Moab stayed with Balaam. And God came to Balaam and said, "Who are these men with you?" And Balaam said to God, "Balak the son of Zippor, king of Moab, has sent to me, saying, 'Behold, a people has come out of Egypt, and it covers the face of the earth; now come, curse them for me; perhaps I shall be able to fight against them and drive them out.'" God said to Balaam, "You shall not go with them; you shall not curse the people, for they are blessed." So Balaam rose in the morning, and said to the princes of Balak, "Go to your own land; for the Lord has refused to let me go with you." So the princes of Moab rose and went to Balak, and said, "Balaam refuses to come with us." Once again Balak sent princes, more in number and more honorable than they. And they came to Balaam and said to him, "Thus says Balak the son of Zippor: 'Let nothing hinder you from coming to me; for I will surely do you great honor, and whatever you say to me I will do; come, curse this people for me.'" But Balaam answered and said to the servants of Balak, "Though Balak were to give me his house full of silver and gold, I could not go beyond the command of the Lord my God, to do less or more. Pray, now, tarry here this night also, that I may know what more the Lord will say to me." And God came to Balaam at night and said to him, "If the men have come to call you, rise, go with them; but only what I bid you, that shall you do." So Balaam rose in the morning, and saddled his ass, and went with the princess of Moab.

A Reading (Lesson) from the Letter of Paul to the Romans [6:12-23]

Let not sin therefore reign in your mortal bodies, to make you obey their passions. Do not yield your members to sin as instruments of wickedness, but yield yourselves to God as men who have been brought from death to life, and your members to God as instruments of righteousness. For sin will have no dominion over you, since you are not under law but under grace. What then? Are we to sin because we are not under law but under grace? By no means! Do you not know that if you yield yourselves to any one as obedient slaves, you are slaves of the one whom you obey, either of sin, which leads to death, or of obedience, which leads to righteousness? But thanks be to God, that you who were once slaves of sin have become obedient from the heart to the standard of teaching to which you were committed, and, having been set free from sin, have become slaves of righteousness. I am speaking in human terms, because of your natural limitations. For just as you once yielded your members to impurity and to greater and greater iniquity, so now yield your members to righteousness for sanctification. When you were slaves of sin, you were free in regard to righteousness. But then what return did you get from the things of which you are now ashamed? The end of those things is death. But now that you have been set free from sin and have become slaves of God, the return you get is sanctification and its end, eternal life. For the wages of sin is death, but the free gift of God is eternal life in Christ Jesus our Lord.

A Reading (Lesson) from the Gospel according to Matthew
[21:12-22]

Jesus entered the temple of God and drove out all who sold and bought in the temple, and he overturned the tables of the moneychangers and the seats of those who sold pigeons. He said to them, "It is written, 'My house shall be called a house of prayer'; but you make it a den of robbers." And the blind and the lame came to him in the temple, and he healed them. But when the chief priests and the scribes saw the wonderful things that he did, and the children crying out in the temple, "Hosanna to the Son of David!" they were indignant; and they said to him, "Do you hear what these are saying?" And Jesus said to them, "Yes; have you never read, 'Out of the mouth of babes and sucklings thou hast brought perfect praise'?" And leaving them, he went out of the city to Bethany and lodged there. In the morning, as he was returning to the city, he was hungry. And seeing a fig tree by the wayside he went to it, and found nothing on it but leaves only. And he said to it, "May no fruit ever come from you again!" And the fig tree withered at once. When the disciples saw it they marveled, saying, "How did the fig tree wither at once?" And Jesus answered them, "Truly, I say to you, if you have faith and never doubt, you will not only do what has been done to the fig tree, but even if you say to this mountain, 'Be taken up and cast into the sea,' it will be done. And whatever you ask in prayer, you will receive, if you have faith."

Tuesday

(*Psalm 120* [page 778]), *Psalm 121* [page 779],
Psalm 122 [page 779], *Psalm 123* [page 780] ❖
Psalm 124 [page 781], *Psalm 125* [page 781],
Psalm 126 [page 782], (*Psalm 127* [page 782])

A Reading (Lesson) from the Book of Numbers [22:21-38]

Balaam rose in the morning, and saddled his ass, and went with the princes of Moab. But God's anger was kindled because he went; and the angel of the Lord took his stand in the way as his adversary. Now he was riding on the ass, and his two servants were with him. And the ass saw the angel of the Lord standing in the road, with a drawn sword in his hand; and the ass turned aside out of the road, and went into the field; and Balaam struck the ass, to turn her into the road. Then the angel of the Lord stood in a narrow path between the vineyards, with a wall on either side. And when the ass saw the angel of the Lord, she pushed against the wall, and pressed Balaam's foot against the wall; so he struck her again. Then the angel of the Lord went ahead, and stood in a narrow place, where there was no way to turn either to the right or to the left. When the ass saw the angel of the Lord, she lay down under Balaam; and Balaam's anger was kindled, and he struck the ass with his staff. Then the Lord opened the mouth of the ass, and she said to Balaam, "What have I done to you, that you have struck me these three times?" And Balaam said to the ass, "Because you have made sport of me. I wish I had a sword in my hand, for then I would kill you." And the ass said to Balaam, "Am I not your ass, upon which you have ridden all your life long to this day? Was I ever accustomed to do so to you?" And he said, "No." Then the Lord opened the eyes of Balaam, and he saw the angel of the Lord standing in the way, with his drawn sword in his hand; and he bowed his head, and fell on his face. And the angel of the Lord said to him, "Why have you struck your ass these three times? Behold, I have come forth to withstand you, because your way is perverse before me; and the ass saw me, and turned aside before me these three times. If she had not turned aside from me, surely just now I would have slain you and let her live." Then Balaam said to the angel of the Lord, "I have sinned, for I did not know that thou didst stand in the road against me. Now therefore, if it is evil in thy sight, I will go back again." And the angel of the Lord said to Balaam, "Go with the men; but only the word which I bid you, that shall you speak." So Balaam went on with the princes of Balak. When Balak heard that Balaam had come, he went out to meet him at the city of Moab, on the boundary formed by the Arnon, at the extremity of the boundary. And Balak said to Balaam, "Did I not send to you to call you? Why did you not come to me? Am I not able to honor you?" Balaam said to Balak, "Lo, I have come to you! Have I now any power at all to speak to anything? The word that God puts in my mouth, that must I speak."

A Reading (Lesson) from the Letter of Paul to the Romans [7:1-12]

Do you not know, brethren—for I am speaking to those who know the law—that the law is binding on a person only during his life? Thus a married woman is bound by law to her husband as long as he lives; but if her husband dies she is discharged from the law concerning the husband. Accordingly, she will be called an adulteress if she lives with another man while her husband is alive. But if her husband dies she is free from that law, and if she marries another man she is not an adulteress. Likewise, my brethren, you have died to the law through the body of Christ, so that you may belong to another, to him who has been raised from the dead in order that we may bear fruit for God. While we were living in the flesh, our sinful passions, aroused by the law, were at work in our members to bear fruit for death. But now we are discharged from the law, dead to that which held us captive, so that we serve not under the old written code but in the new life of the Spirit. What then shall we say? That the law is sin? By no means! Yet, if it had not been for the law, I should not have known sin. I should not have known what it is to covet if the law had not said, "You shall not covet." But sin, finding opportunity in the commandment, wrought in me all kinds of covetousness. Apart from the law sin lies dead. I was once alive apart from the law, but when the commandment came, sin revived and I died; the very commandment which promised life proved to be death to me. For sin, finding opportunity in the commandment, deceived me and by it killed me. So the law is holy, and the commandment is holy and just and good.

A Reading (Lesson) from the Gospel according to Matthew [21:23-32]

When Jesus entered the temple, the chief priests and the elders of the people came up to him as he was teaching, and said, "By what authority are you doing these things, and who gave you this authority?" Jesus answered them, "I also will ask you a question; and if you tell me the answer, then I also will tell you by what authority I do these things. The baptism of John, whence was it? From heaven or from men?" And they argued with one another, "If we say, 'From heaven,' he will say to us, 'Why then did you not believe him?' But if we say, 'From men,' we are afraid of the multitude; for all hold that John was a prophet." So they answered Jesus, "We do not know." And he said to them, "Neither will I tell you by what authority I do these things. What do you think? A man had two sons; and he went to the first and said, 'Son, go and work in the vineyard today.' And he answered, 'I will not'; but afterward he repented and went. And he went to the second and said the same; and he answered, 'I go, sir,' but did not go. Which of the two did the will of the father?" They said, "The first." Jesus said to them, "Truly, I say to you, the tax collectors and the harlots go into the kingdom of God before you. For John came to you in the way of righteousness, and you did not believe him, but the tax collectors and the harlots believed him; and even when you saw it, you did not afterward repent and believe him."

Wednesday

Psalm 119:145-176 [page 775] ❖
Psalm 128 [page 783],   *Psalm 129* [page 784],
Psalm 130 [page 784]

A Reading (Lesson) from the Book of Numbers
[22:41—23:12]

On the morrow Balak took Balaam and brought him up to
Bamoth-ba'al; and from there he saw the nearest of the
people. And Balaam said to Balak, "Build for me here
seven altars, and provide for me here seven bulls and seven
rams." Balak did as Balaam had said; and Balak and
Balaam offered on each altar a bull and a ram. And
Balaam said to Balak, "Stand beside your burnt offering,
and I will go; perhaps the Lord will come to meet me; and
whatever he shows me I will tell you." And he went to a
bare height. And God met Balaam; and Balaam said to
him, "I have prepared the seven altars, and I have offered
upon each altar a bull and a ram." And the Lord put a
word in Balaam's mouth, and said, "Return to Balak, and
thus you shall speak." And he returned to him, and lo, he
and all the princes of Moab were standing beside his burnt
offering. And Balaam took up his discourse, and said,
"From Aram Balak has brought me, the king of Moab from
the eastern mountains: 'Come, curse Jacob for me, and
come, denounce Israel!' How can I curse whom God has
not cursed? How can I denounce whom the Lord has not
denounced? For from the top of the mountains I see him,
from the hills I behold him; lo, a people dwelling alone,
and not reckoning itself among the nations! Who can
count the dust of Jacob, or number the fourth part of
Israel? Le me die the death of the righteous, and let my end
be like his!" And Balak said to Balaam, "What have you
done to me? I took you to curse my enemies, and behold,
you have done nothing but bless them." And he answered,
"Must I not take heed to speak what the Lord puts in my
mouth?"

*A Reading (Lesson) from the Letter of Paul
to the Romans* [7:13-25]

Did that which is good, then, bring death to me? By no
means! It was sin, working death in me through what is
good, in order that sin might be shown to be sin, and
through the commandment might become sinful beyond
measure. We know that the law is spiritual; but I am
carnal, sold under sin. I do not understand my own
actions. For I do not do what I want, but I do the very
thing I hate. Now if I do what I do not want, I agree that
the law is good. So then it is no longer I that do it, but sin
which dwells within me. For I know that nothing good
dwells within me, that is, in my flesh. I can will what is
right, but I cannot do it. For I do not do the good I want,
but the evil I do not want is what I do. Now if I do what I
do not want, it is no longer I that do it, but sin which
dwells within me. So I find it to be a law that when I want
to do right, evil lies close at hand. For I delight in the law
of God, in my inmost self, but I see in my members another
law at war with the law of my mind and making me
captive to the law of sin which dwells in my members.
Wretched man that I am! Who will deliver me from this
body of death? Thanks be to God through Jesus Christ our
Lord! So then, I of myself serve the law of God with my
mind, but with my flesh I serve the law of sin.

A Reading (Lesson) from the Gospel according to Matthew
[21:33-46]

Jesus said to the chief priests and the elders of the people,
"Hear another parable. There was a householder who
planted a vineyard, and set a hedge around it, and dug a
wine press in it, and built a tower, and let it out to tenants,
and went into another country. When the season of fruit
drew near, he sent his servants to the tenants, to get his
fruit; and the tenants took his servants and beat one, killed
another, and stoned another. Again he sent other servants,

more than the first; and they did the same to them. Afterward he sent his son to them, saying, 'They will respect my son.' But when the tenants saw the son, they said to themselves, 'This is the heir; come, let us kill him and have his inheritance.' And they took him and cast him out of the vineyard, and killed him. When therefore the owner of the vineyard comes, what will he do to those tenants?" They said to him, "He will put those wretches to a miserable death, and let out the vineyard to other tenants who will give him the fruits in their seasons." Jesus said to them, "Have you never read in the scriptures: 'The very stone which the builders rejected has become the head of the corner; this was the Lord's doing, and it is marvelous in our eyes'? Therefore I tell you, the kingdom of God will be taken away from you and given to a nation producing the fruits of it." When the chief priests and the Pharisees heard his parables, they perceived that he was speaking about them. But when they tried to arrest him, they feared the multitudes, because they held him to be a prophet.

Thursday

Psalm 131 [page 785],   *Psalm 132* [page 785],
(Psalm 133 [page 787])   ❖   *Psalm 134* [page 787],
Psalm 135 [page 788]

A Reading (Lesson) from the Book of Numbers [23:11-26]

Balak said to Balaam, "What have you done to me? I took you to curse my enemies, and behold, you have done nothing but bless them." And he answered, "Must I not take heed to speak what the Lord puts in my mouth?" And Balak said to him, "Come with me to another place, from which you may see them; you shall see only the nearest of them, and shall not see them all; then curse them for me from there." And he took him to the field of Zophim, to the top of Pisgah, and built seven altars, and offered a bull and a ram on each altar. Balaam said to Balak, "Stand here beside your burnt offering, while I meet the Lord yonder." And the Lord met Balaam, and put a word in his mouth, and said, "Return to Balak, and thus shall you speak." And he came to him, and, lo, he was standing beside his burnt offering, and the princes of Moab with him. And Balak said to him, "What has the Lord spoken?" And Balaam took up his discourse, and said, "Rise, Balak, and hear; hearken to me, O son of Zippor: God is not man, that he should lie, or a son of man, that he should repent. Has he said, and will he not do it? Or has he spoken, and will he not fulfil it? Behold, I received a command to bless: he has blessed, and I cannot revoke it. He has not beheld misfortune in Jacob; nor has he seen trouble in Israel. The Lord their God is with them, and the shout of a king is among them. God brings them out of Egypt; they have as it were the horns of the wild ox. For there is no enchantment against Jacob, no divination against Israel; now it shall be said of Jacob and Israel, 'What has God wrought!' Behold, a people! As a lioness it rises up and as a lion it lifts itself; it does not lie down till it devours the prey, and drinks the blood of the slain." And Balak said to Balaam, "Neither curse them at all, nor bless them at all." But Balaam answered Balak, "Did I not tell you, 'All that the Lord says, that I must do'?"

A Reading (Lesson) from the Letter of Paul to the Romans [8:1-11]

There is therefore now no condemnation for those who are in Christ Jesus. For the law of the Spirit of life in Christ Jesus has set me free from the law of sin and death. For God has done what the law, weakened by the flesh, could not do: sending his own Son in the likeness of sinful flesh and for sin, he condemned sin in the flesh, in order that the just requirement of the law might be fulfilled in us, who walk not according to the flesh but according to the Spirit. For those who live according to the flesh set their minds on the things of the flesh, but those who live according to the Spirit set their minds on the things of the Spirit. To set the mind on the flesh is death, but to set the mind on the Spirit is life and peace. For the mind that is set on the flesh is hostile to God; it does not submit to God's law, indeed it cannot; and those who are in the flesh cannot please God. But you are not in the flesh, you are in the Spirit, if in fact the Spirit of God dwells in you. And one who does not have the Spirit of Christ does not belong to him. But if Christ is in you, although your bodies are dead because of sin, your spirits are alive because of righteousness. If the Spirit of him who raised Jesus from the dead dwells in you, he who raised Christ Jesus from the dead will give life to your mortal bodies also through his Spirit which dwells in you.

A Reading (Lesson) from the Gospel according to Matthew
[22:1-14]

Again Jesus spoke to the chief priests and the Pharisees in parables, saying, "The kingdom of heaven may be compared to a king who gave a marriage feast for his son, and sent his servants to call those who were invited to the marriage feast; but they would not come. Again he sent other servants, saying, 'Tell those who are invited, Behold, I have made ready my dinner, my oxen and my fat calves are killed, and everything is ready; come to the marriage feast.' But they made light of it and went off, one to his farm, another to his business, while the rest seized his servants, treated them shamefully, and killed them. The king was angry, and he sent his troops and destroyed those murderers and burned their city. Then he said to his servants, 'The wedding is ready, but those invited were not worthy. Go therefore to the thoroughfares, and invite to the marriage feast as many as you find.' And those servants went out into the streets and gathered all whom they found, both bad and good; so the wedding hall was filled with guests. But when the king came in to look at the guests, he saw there a man who had no wedding garment; and he said to him, 'Friend, how did you get in here without a wedding garment?' And he was speechless. Then the king said to the attendants, 'Bind him hand and foot, and cast him into the outer darkness; there men will weep and gnash their teeth.' For many are called, but few are chosen."

Friday

Psalm 140 [page 796], *Psalm 142* [page 798] ❖
Psalm 141 [page 797], *Psalm 143:1-11(12)* [page 798]

A Reading (Lesson) from the Book of Numbers [24:1-13]

When Balaam saw that it pleased the Lord to bless Israel, he did not go, as at other times, to look for omens, but set his face toward the wilderness. And Balaam lifted up his eyes, and saw Israel encamping tribe by tribe. And the Spirit of God came upon him, and he took up his discourse, and said, "The oracle of Balaam the son of Be'or, the oracle of the man whose eye is opened, the oracle of him who hears the words of God, who sees the vision of the Almighty, falling down, but having his eyes uncovered: how fair are your tents, O Jacob, your encampments, O Israel! Like valleys that stretch afar, like gardens beside a river, like aloes that the Lord has planted, like cedar trees beside the waters. Water shall flow from his buckets, and his seed shall be in many waters, his king shall be higher than Agag, and his kingdom shall be exalted. God brings him out of Egypt; he has as it were the horns of the wild ox, he shall eat up the nations his adversaries, and shall break their bones in pieces, and pierce them through with his arrows. He couched, he lay down, like a lion, and like a lioness; who will rouse him up? Blessed be every one who blesses you, and cursed be every one who curses you." And Balak's anger was kindled against Balaam, and he struck his hands together; and Balak said to Balaam, "I called you to curse my enemies, and behold, you have blessed them these three times. Therefore now flee to your place; I said, 'I will certainly honor you,' but the Lord has held you back from honor." And Balaam said to Balak, "Did I not tell your messengers whom you sent to me, 'If Balak should give me his house full of silver and gold, I would not be able to go beyond the word of the Lord, to do either good or bad of my own will; what the Lord speaks, that will I speak'?"

A Reading (Lesson) from the Letter of Paul to the Romans [8:12-17]

So then, brethren, we are debtors, not to the flesh, to live according to the flesh—for if you live according to the flesh you will die, but if by the Spirit you put to death the deeds of the body you will live. For all who are led by the Spirit of God are sons of God. For you did not receive the spirit of slavery to fall back into fear, but you have received the spirit of sonship. When we cry, "Abba! Father!" it is the Spirit himself bearing witness with our spirit that we are children of God, and if children, then heirs, heirs of God and fellow heirs with Christ, provided we suffer with him in order that we may also be glorified with him.

A Reading (Lesson) from the Gospel according to Matthew [22:15-22]

The Pharisees went and took counsel how to entangle Jesus in his talk. And they sent their disciples to him, along with the Hero'di-ans, saying, "Teacher, we know that you are true, and teach the way of God truthfully, and care for no man; for you do not regard the position of men. Tell us, then, what you think. Is it lawful to pay taxes to Caesar, or not?" But Jesus, aware of their malice, said, "Why put me to the test, you hypocrites? Show me the money for the tax." And they brought him a coin. And Jesus said to them,

"Whose likeness and inscription is this?" They said,
"Caesar's." Then he said to them, "Render therefore to
Caesar the things that are Caesar's, and to God the things
that are God's." When they heard it, they marveled; and
they left him and went away.

Saturday

Psalm 137:1-6(7-9) [page 792], *Psalm 144* [page 801]
❖ *Psalm 104* [page 735]

A Reading (Lesson) from the Book of Numbers [24:12-25]

Balaam said to Balak, "Did I not tell your messengers
whom you sent to me, 'If Balak should give me his house
full of silver and gold, I would not be able to go beyond the
word of the Lord, to do either good or bad of my own will;
what the Lord speaks, that will I speak'? And now, behold,
I am going to my people; come, I will let you know what
this people will do to your people in the latter days." And
he took up his discourse, and said, "The oracle of Balaam
the son of Be'or, the oracle of the man whose eye is opened,
the oracle of him who hears the words of God, and knows
the knowledge of the Most High, who sees the vision of the
Almighty, falling down, but having his eyes uncovered: I
see him, but not now; I behold him, but not nigh; a star
shall come forth out of Jacob, and a scepter shall rise out
of Israel; it shall crush the forehead of Moab, and break
down all the sons of Sheth. Edom shall be dispossessed,
Se'ir also, his enemies, shall be dispossessed, while Israel
does valiantly. By Jacob shall dominion be exercised, and
the survivors of cities be destroyed!" Then he looked on
Am'alek, and took up his discourse, and said, "Am'alek
was the first of the nations, but in the end he shall come to
destruction." And he looked on the Ken'ite, and took up
his discourse, and said, "Enduring is your dwelling place,
and your nest is set in the rock; nevertheless Kain shall be

wasted. How long shall Asshur take you away captive?"
And he took up his discourse, and said, "Alas, who shall
live when God does this? But ships shall come from Kittim
and shall afflict Asshur and Eber; and he also shall come to
destruction." Then Balaam rose, and went back to his
place; and Balak also went his way.

*A Reading (Lesson) from the Letter of Paul
to the Romans* [8:18-25]

I consider that the sufferings of this present time are not
worth comparing with the glory that is to be revealed to
us. For the creation waits with eager longing for the
revealing of the sons of God; for the creation was
subjected to futility, not of its own will but by the will of
him who subjected it in hope; because the creation itself
will be set free from its bondage to decay and obtain the
glorious liberty of the children of God. We know that the
whole creation has been groaning in travail together until
now; and not only the creation, but we ourselves, who
have the first fruits of the Spirit, groan inwardly as we wait
for adoption as sons, the redemption of our bodies. For in
this hope we were saved. Now hope that is seen is not
hope. For who hopes for what he sees? But if we hope for
what we do not see, we wait for it with patience.

A Reading (Lesson) from the Gospel according to Matthew
[22:23-40]

The same day Sad'ducees came to Jesus, who say that there
is no resurrection; and they asked him a question, saying,
"Teacher, Moses said, 'If a man dies, having no children, his
brother must marry the widow, and raise up children for
his brother.' Now there were seven brothers among us; the
first married, and died, and having no children left his wife
to his brother. So too the second and third, down to the
seventh. After them all, the woman died. In the
resurrection, therefore, to which of the seven will she be

wife? For they all had her." But Jesus answered them, "You are wrong, because you know neither the scriptures nor the power of God. For in the resurrection they neither marry nor are given in marriage, but are like angels in heaven. And as for the resurrection of the dead, have you not read what was said to you by God, 'I am the God of Abraham, and the God of Isaac, and the God of Jacob'? He is not God of the dead, but of the living." And when the crowd heard it, they were astonished at his teaching. But when the Pharisees heard that he had silenced the Sad'ducees, they came together. And one of them, a lawyer, asked him a question, to test him. "Teacher, which is the great commandment in the law?" And he said to him, "You shall love the Lord your God with all your heart, and with all your soul, and with all your mind. This is the great and first commandment. And a second is like it, You shall love your neighbor as yourself. On these two commandments depend all the law and the prophets."

Proper 9 *Week of the Sunday closest to July 6*

Sunday

Psalm 146 [page 803], *Psalm 147* [page 804] ❖
Psalm 111 [page 754], *Psalm 112* [page 755],
Psalm 113 [page 756]

A Reading (Lesson) from the Book of Numbers [27:12-23]

The Lord said to Moses, "Go up into this mountain of Ab'arim, and see the land which I have given to the people of Israel. And when you have seen it, you also shall be gathered to your people, as your brother Aaron was gathered, because you rebelled against my word in the wilderness of Zin during the strife of the congregation, to sanctify me at the waters before their eyes." (These are the waters of Mer'ibah of Kadesh in the wilderness of Zin.)

Moses said to the Lord, "Let the Lord, the God of the spirits of all flesh, appoint a man over the congregation, who shall go out before them and come in before them, who shall lead them out and bring them in; that the congregation of the Lord may not be as sheep which have no shepherd." And the Lord said to Moses, "Take Joshua the son of Nun, a man in whom is the spirit, and lay your hand upon him; cause him to stand before Elea'zar the priest and all the congregation, and you shall commission him in their sight. You shall invest him with some of your authority, that all the congregation of the people of Israel may obey. And he shall stand before Elea'zar the priest, who shall inquire for him by the judgment of the Urim before the Lord; at his word they shall go out, and at his word they shall come in, both he and all the people of Israel with him, the whole congregation." And Moses did as the Lord commanded him; he took Joshua and caused him to stand before Elea'zar the priest and the whole congregation, and he laid his hands upon him, and commissioned him as the Lord directed through Moses.

A Reading (Lesson) from the Acts of the Apostles
[19:11-20]

God did extraordinary miracles by the hands of Paul, so that handkerchiefs or aprons were carried away from his body to the sick, and diseases left them and the evil spirits came out of them. Then some of the itinerant Jewish exorcists undertook to pronounce the name of the Lord Jesus over those who had evil spirits, saying, "I adjure you by the Jesus whom Paul preaches." Seven sons of a Jewish high priest named Sceva were doing this. But the evil spirit answered them, "Jesus I know, and Paul I know; but who are you?" And the man in whom the evil spirit was leaped on them, mastered all of them, and overpowered them, so that they fled out of that house naked and wounded. And this became known to all residents of Ephesus, both Jews and Greeks; and fear fell upon them all; and the name of the Lord Jesus was extolled. Many also of those who were now believers came, confessing and divulging their practices. And a number of those who practiced magic arts brought their books together and burned them in the sight of all; and they counted the value of them and found it came to fifty thousand pieces of silver. So the word of the Lord grew and prevailed mightily.

A Reading (Lesson) from the Gospel according to Mark [1:14-20]

After John was arrested, Jesus came into Galilee, preaching the gospel of God, and saying, "The time is fulfilled, and the kingdom of God is at hand; repent, and believe in the gospel." And passing along by the Sea of Galilee, he saw Simon and Andrew the brother of Simon casting a net in the sea; for they were fishermen. And Jesus said to them, "Follow me and I will make you become fishers of men." And immediately they left their nets and followed him. And going on a little farther, he saw James the son of Zeb'edee and John his brother, who were in their boat mending the nets. And immediately he called them; and they left their father Zeb'edee in the boat with the hired servants, and followed him.

Monday

Psalm 1 [page 585], *Psalm 2* [page 586], *Psalm 3* [page 587] ❖ *Psalm 4* [page 587], *Psalm 7* [page 590]

A Reading (Lesson) from the Book of Numbers [32:1-6,16-27]

The sons of Reuben and the sons of Gad had a very great multitude of cattle; and they saw the land of Jazer and the land of Gilead, and behold, the place was a place for cattle. So the sons of Gad and the sons of Reuben came and said to Moses and to Elea'zar the priest and to the leaders of the congregation, "At'aroth, Dibon, Jazer, Nimrah, Heshbon, Elea'leh, Sebam, Nebo, and Be'on, the land which the Lord smote before the congregation of Israel, is a land for cattle; and your servants have cattle." And they said, "If we have found favor in your sight, let this land be given to your servants for a possession; do not take us across the Jordan." But Moses said to the sons of Gad and to the sons of Reuben, "Shall your brethren go to the war while you sit here?" Then they came near to him, and said, "We will build sheepfolds here for our flocks, and cities for our little ones, but we will take up arms, ready to go before the people of Israel, until we have brought them to their place; and our little ones shall live in the fortified cities because of the inhabitants of the land. We will not return to our homes until the people of Israel have inherited each his inheritance. For we will not inherit with them on the other side of the Jordan and beyond; because our inheritance has come to us on this side of the Jordan to the east." So Moses said to them, "If you will do this, if you will take up arms to go before the Lord for the war, and every armed man of you will pass over the Jordan before the Lord, until he has driven out his enemies from before him and the land is subdued before the Lord; then after that you shall return and be free of obligation to the Lord and to Israel; and this land shall be your possession before the Lord. But if you will not do so, behold, you have sinned against the Lord; and be sure your sin will find you out. Build cities for your little ones, and folds for your sheep; and do what you have promised." And the sons of Gad and the sons of Reuben said to Moses, "Your servants will do as my lord commands. Our little ones, our wives, our flocks, and all our cattle, shall remain there in the cities of Gilead; but your servants will pass over, every man who is armed for war, before the Lord to battle, as my lord orders."

*A Reading (Lesson) from the Letter of Paul
to the Romans* [8:26-30]

Likewise the Spirit helps us in our weakness; for we do not
know how to pray as we ought, but the Spirit himself
intercedes for us with sighs too deep for words. And he
who searches the hearts of men knows what is the mind of
the Spirit, because the Spirit intercedes for the saints
according to the will of God. We know that in everything
God works for good with those who love him, who are
called according to his purpose. For those whom he
foreknew he also predestined to be conformed to the image
of his Son, in order that he might be the first-born among
many brethren. And those whom he predestined he also
called; and those whom he called he also justified; and
those whom he justified he also glorified.

A Reading (Lesson) from the Gospel according to Matthew
[23:1-12]

Jesus said to the crowds and to his disciples, "The scribes
and the Pharisees sit on Moses' seat; so practice and
observe whatever they tell you, but not what they do; for
they preach, but do not practice. They bind heavy burdens,
hard to bear, or lay them on men's shoulders; but they
themselves will not move them with their finger. They do
all their deeds to be seen by men; for they make their
phylacteries broad and their fringes long, and they love the
place of honor at feasts and the best seats in the
synagogues, and salutations in the market places, and
being called rabbi by men. But you are not to be called
rabbi, for you have one teacher, and you are all brethren.
And call no man your father on earth, for you have one
Father, who is in heaven. Neither be called masters, for
you have one master, the Christ. He who is greatest among
you shall be your servant; whoever exalts himself will be
humbled, and whoever humbles himself will be exalted."

Tuesday

Psalm 5 [page 588],   *Psalm 6* [page 589]   ❖
Psalm 10 [page 594],   *Psalm 11* [page 596]

A Reading (Lesson) from the Book of Numbers
[35:1-3,9-15, 30-34]

The Lord said to Moses in the plains of Moab by the
Jordan at Jericho, "Command the people of Israel, that
they give to the Levites, from the inheritance of their
possession, cities to dwell in; and you shall give to the
Levites pasture lands round about the cities. The cities
shall be theirs to dwell in, and their pasture lands shall be
for their cattle and for their livestock and for all their
beasts." And the Lord said to Moses, "Say to the people of
Israel, When you cross the Jordan into the land of Canaan,
then you shall select cities to be cities of refuge for you,
that the manslayer who kills any person without intent
may flee there. The cities shall be for you a refuge from the
avenger, that the manslayer may not die until he stands
before the congregation for judgment. And the cities which
you give shall be your six cities of refuge. You shall give
three cities beyond the Jordan, and three cities in the land
of Canaan, to be cities of refuge. These six cities shall be
for refuge for the people of Israel, and for the stranger and
for the sojourner among them, that any one who kills any
person without intent may flee there. If any one kills a
person, the murderer shall be put to death on the evidence
of witnesses; but no person shall be put to death on the
testimony of one witness. Moreover you shall accept no
ransom for the life of a murderer, who is guilty of death;
but he shall be put to death. And you shall accept no
ransom for him who has fled to his city of refuge, that he
may return to dwell in the land before the death of the high
priest. You shall not thus pollute the land in which you
live; for blood pollutes the land, and no expiation can be
made for the land, for the blood that is shed in it, except by

the blood of him who shed it. You shall not defile the land in which you live, in the midst of which I dwell; for I the Lord dwell in the midst of the people of Israel."

A Reading (Lesson) from the Letter of Paul to the Romans [8:31-39]

What then shall we say to this? If God is for us, who is against us? He who did not spare his own Son but gave him up for us all, will he not also give us all things with him? Who shall bring any charge against God's elect? It is God who justifies; who is to condemn? Is it Christ Jesus, who died, yes, who was raised from the dead, who is at the right hand of God, who indeed intercedes for us? Who shall separate us from the love of Christ? Shall tribulation, or distress, or persecution, or famine, or nakedness, or peril, or sword? As it is written, "For thy sake we are being killed all the day long; we are regarded as sheep to be slaughtered." No, in all these things we are more than conquerors through him who loved us. For I am sure that neither death, nor life, nor angels, nor principalities, nor things present, nor things to come, nor powers, nor height, nor depth, nor anything else in all creation, will be able to separate us from the love of God in Christ Jesus our Lord.

A Reading (Lesson) from the Gospel according to Matthew [23:13-26]

Jesus said to the crowds and to his disciples, "But woe to you, scribes and Pharisees, hypocrites! because you shut the kingdom of heaven against men; for you neither enter yourselves, nor allow those who would enter to go in. Woe to you, scribes and Pharisees, hypocrites! for you traverse sea and land to make a single proselyte, and when he becomes a proselyte, you make him twice as much a child of hell as yourselves. Woe to you, blind guides, who say, 'If any one swears by the temple, it is nothing; but if any one swears by the gold of the temple, he is bound by his oath.'

You blind fools! For which is greater, the gold or the temple that has made the gold sacred? And you say, 'If any one swears by the altar, it is nothing; but if any one swears by the gift that is on the altar, he is bound by his oath.' You blind men! For which is greater, the gift or the altar that makes the gift sacred? So he who swears by the altar, swears by it and by everything on it; and he who swears by the temple, swears by it and by him who dwells in it; and he who swears by heaven, swears by the throne of God and by him who sits upon it. Woe to you, scribes and Pharisees, hypocrites! for you tithe mint and dill and cummin, and have neglected the weightier matters of the law, justice and mercy and faith; these you ought to have done, without neglecting the others. You blind guides, straining out a gnat and swallowing a camel! Woe to you, scribes and Pharisees, hypocrites! for you cleanse the outside of the cup and of the plate, but inside they are full of extortion and rapacity. You blind Pharisee! first cleanse the inside of the cup and of the plate, that the outside also may be clean."

Wednesday

Psalm 119:1-24 [page 763] ❖ *Psalm 12* [page 597], *Psalm 13* [page 597], *Psalm 14* [page 598]

A Reading (Lesson) from the Book of Deuteronomy [1:1-18]

These are the words that Moses spoke to all Israel beyond the Jordan in the wilderness, in the Arabah over against Suph, between Paran and Tophel, Laban, Haze'roth, and Diz'ahab. It is eleven days' journey from Horeb by the way of Mount Se'ir to Ka'desh-bar'nea. And in the fortieth year, on the first day of the eleventh month, Moses spoke to the people of Israel according to all that the Lord had given him in commandment to them, after he had defeated Sihon the king of the Amorites, who lived in Heshbon, and Og the king of Bashan, who lived in Ash'taroth and in Ed're-i. Beyond the Jordan, in the land of Moab, Moses undertook to explain this law, saying, "The Lord our God said to us in Horeb, 'You have stayed long enough at this mountain; turn and take your journey and go to the hill country of the Amorites, and to all their neighbors in the Arabah, in the hill country and in the lowland, and in the Negeb, and by the seacoast, the land of the Canaanites, and Lebanon, as far as the great river, the river Eu-phra'tes. Behold, I have set the land before you; go in and take possession of the land which the Lord swore to your fathers, to Abraham, to Isaac, and to Jacob, to give to them and to their descendants after them.' At that time I said to you, 'I am not able alone to bear you; the Lord your God has multiplied you, and behold, you are this day as the stars of heaven for multitude. May the Lord, the God of your fathers, make you a thousand times as many as you are, and bless you, as he has promised you! How can I bear alone the weight and burden of you and your strife? Choose wise, understanding, and experienced men, according to your tribes, and I will appoint them as your heads.' And you answered me, 'The thing that you have spoken is good for us to do.' So I took the heads of your tribes, wise and experienced men, and set them as heads over you, commanders of thousands, commanders of hundreds, commanders of fifties, commanders of tens, and officers, throughout your tribes. And I charged your judges at that time, 'Hear the cases between your brethren, and judge righteously between a man and his brother or the alien that is with him. You shall not be partial in judgment; you shall hear the small and the great alike; you shall not be afraid of the face of man, for the judgment is God's; and the case that is too hard for you, you shall bring to me, and I will hear it.' And I commanded you at that time all the things that you should do."

*A Reading (Lesson) from the Letter of Paul
to the Romans* [9:1-18]

I am speaking the truth in Christ, I am not lying; my conscience bears me witness in the Holy Spirit, that I have great sorrow and unceasing anguish in my heart. For I could wish that I myself were accursed and cut off from Christ for the sake of my brethren, my kinsmen by race. They are Israelites, and to them belong the sonship, the glory, the covenants, the giving of the law, the worship, and the promises; to them belong the patriarchs, and of their race, according to the flesh, is the Christ. God who is over all be blessed for ever. Amen. But it is not as though the word of God had failed. For not all who are descended from Israel belong to Israel, and not all are children of Abraham because they are his descendants; but "Through Isaac shall your descendants be named." This means that it is not the children of the flesh who are the children of God, but the children of the promise are reckoned as descendants. For this is what the promise said, "About this time I will return and Sarah shall have a son." And not only so, but also when Rebecca had conceived children by one man, our forefather Isaac, though they were not yet born and had done nothing either good or bad, in order that God's purposes of election might continue, not because of works but because of his call, she was told, "The elder will serve the younger." As it is written, "Jacob I loved, but Esau I hated." What shall we say then? Is there injustice on God's part? By no means! For he says to Moses, "I will have mercy on whom I have mercy, and I will have compassion on whom I have compassion." So it depends not upon man's will or exertion, but upon God's mercy. For the scripture says to Pharaoh, "I have raised you up for the very purpose of showing my power in you, so that my name may be proclaimed in all the earth." So then he has mercy upon whomever he wills, and he hardens the heart of whomever he wills.

A Reading (Lesson) from the Gospel according to Matthew
[23:27-39]

Jesus said to the crowds and to his disciples, "Woe to you, scribes and Pharisees, hypocrites! for you are like whitewashed tombs, which outwardly appear beautiful, but within they are full of dead men's bones and all uncleanness. So you also outwardly appear righteous to men, but within you are full of hypocrisy and iniquity. Woe to you, scribes and Pharisees, hypocrites! for you build the tombs of the prophets and adorn the monuments of the righteous, saying, 'If we had lived in the days of our fathers, we would not have taken part with them in shedding the blood of the prophets.' Thus you witness against yourselves, that you are sons of those who murdered the prophets. Fill up, then, the measure of your fathers. You serpents, you brood of vipers, how are you to escape being sentenced to hell? Therefore I send you prophets and wise men and scribes, some of whom you will kill and crucify, and some you will scourge in your synagogues and persecute from town to town, that upon you may come all the righteous blood shed on earth, from the blood of innocent Abel to the blood of Zechari'ah the son of Barachi'ah, whom you murdered between the sanctuary and the altar. Truly, I say to you, all this will come upon this generation. O Jerusalem, Jerusalem, killing the prophets and stoning those who are sent to you! How often would I have gathered your children together as a hen gathers her brood under her wings, and you would not! Behold, your house is forsaken and desolate. For I tell you, you will not see me again, until you say, 'Blessed is he who comes in the name of the Lord.' "

Thursday

Psalm 18:1-20 [page 602]   ❖   *Psalm 18:21-50* [page 604]

A Reading (Lesson) from the Book of Deuteronomy
[3:18-28]

These are the words that Moses spoke to all Israel beyond the Jordan in the wilderness, "I commanded you at that time, saying, 'The Lord your God has given you this land to possess; all your men of valor shall pass over armed before your brethren the people of Israel. But your wives, your little ones, and your cattle (I know that you have many cattle) shall remain in the cities which I have given you, until the Lord gives rest to your brethren, as to you, and they also occupy the land which the Lord your God gives them beyond the Jordan; then you shall return every man to his possession which I have given you.' And I commanded Joshua at that time, 'Your eyes have seen all that the Lord your God has done to these two kings; so will the Lord do to all the kingdoms into which you are going over. You shall not fear them; for it is the Lord your God who fights for you.' And I besought the Lord at that time, saying, 'O Lord God, thou hast only begun to show thy servant thy greatness and thy mighty hand; for what god is there in heaven or on earth who can do such works and mighty acts as thine? Let me go over, I pray, and see the good land beyond the Jordan, that goodly hill country, and Lebanon.' But the Lord was angry with me on your account, and would not hearken to me; and the Lord said to me, 'Let it suffice you; speak no more to me of this matter. Go up to the top of Pisgah, and lift up your eyes westward and northward and southward and eastward, and behold it with your eyes; for you shall not go over this Jordan. But charge Joshua, and encourage and strengthen him; for he shall go over at the head of this people, and he shall put them in possession of the land which you shall see.'"

A Reading (Lesson) from the Letter of Paul to the Romans [9:19-33]

You shall say to me then, "Why does he still find fault? For who can resist his will?" But who are you, a man, to answer back to God? Will what is molded say to its molder, "Why have you made me thus?" Has the potter no right over the clay, to make out of the same lump one vessel for beauty and another for menial use? What if God, desiring to show his wrath and to make known his power, has endured with much patience the vessels of wrath made for destruction, in order to make known the riches of his glory for the vessels of mercy, which he has prepared beforehand for glory, even us whom he has called, not from the Jews only but also from the Gentiles? As indeed he says in Hose'a, "Those who were not my people I will call 'my people,' and her who was not beloved I will call 'my beloved.'" "And in the very place where it was said to them, 'You are not my people,' they will be called 'sons of the living God.'" And Isaiah cries out concerning Israel: "Though the number of the sons of Israel be as the sand of the sea, only a remnant of them will be saved; for the Lord will execute his sentence upon the earth with rigor and dispatch." And as Isaiah predicted, "If the Lord of hosts had not left us children, we would have fared like Sodom and been made like Gomor'rah." What shall we say, then? That Gentiles who did not pursue righteousness have attained it, that is, righteousness through faith; but that Israel who pursued the righteousness which is based on law did not succeed in fulfilling that law. Why? Because they did not pursue it through faith, but as if it were based on works. They have stumbled over the stumbling stone, as it is written, "Behold, I am laying in Zion a stone that will make men stumble, a rock that will make them fall; and he who believes in him will not be put to shame."

A Reading (Lesson) from the Gospel according to Matthew [24:1-14]

Jesus left the temple and was going away, when his disciples came to point out to him the buildings of the temple. But he answered them, "You see all these, do you not? Truly, I say to you, there will not be left here one stone upon another, that will not be thrown down." As he sat on the Mount of Olives, the disciples came to him privately, saying, "Tell us, when will this be, and what will be the sign of your coming and of the close of the age?" And Jesus answered them, "Take heed that no one leads you astray. For many will come in my name, saying, 'I am the Christ,' and they will lead many astray. And you will hear of wars and rumors of wars; see that you are not alarmed; for this must take place, but the end is not yet. For nation will rise against nation, and kingdom against kingdom, and there will be famines and earthquakes in various places: all this is but the beginning of the birth-pangs. Then they will deliver you up to tribulation, and put you to death; and you will be hated by all nations for my name's sake. And then many will fall away, and betray one another, and hate one another. And many false prophets will arise and lead many astray. And because wickedness is multiplied, most men's love will grow cold. But he who endures to the end will be saved. And this gospel of the kingdom will be preached throughout the whole world, as a testimony to all nations; and then the end will come."

Friday

Psalm 16 [page 599],   *Psalm 17* [page 600]   ❖
Psalm 22 [page 610]

A Reading (Lesson) from the Book of Deuteronomy
[31:7-13,24—32:4]

Moses summoned Joshua, and said to him in the sight of all Israel, "Be strong and of good courage; for you shall go with this people into the land which the Lord has sworn to their fathers to give them; and you shall put them in possession of it. It is the Lord who goes before you; he will be with you, he will not fail you or forsake you; do not fear or be dismayed." And Moses wrote this law, and gave it to the priests the sons of Levi, who carried the ark of the covenant of the Lord, and to all the elders of Israel. And

Moses commanded them, "At the end of every seven years, at the set time of the year of release, at the feast of booths, when all Israel comes to appear before the Lord your God at the place which he will choose, you shall read this law before all Israel in their hearing. Assemble the people, men, women, and little ones, and the sojourner within your towns, that they may hear and learn to fear the Lord your God, and be careful to do all the words of this law, and that their children, who have not known it, may hear and learn to fear the Lord your God, as long as you live in the land which you are going over the Jordan to possess." When Moses had finished writing the words of this law in a book, to the very end, Moses commanded the Levites who carried the ark of the covenant of the Lord, "Take this book of the law, and put it by the side of the ark of the covenant of the Lord your God, that it may be there for a witness against you. For I know how rebellious and stubborn you are; behold, while I am yet alive with you, today you have been rebellious against the Lord; how much more after my death! Assemble to me all the elders of your tribes, and your officers, that I may speak these words in their ears and call heaven and earth to witness against them. For I know that after my death you will surely act corruptly, and turn aside from the way which I have commanded you; and in the days to come evil will befall you, because you will do what is evil in the sight of the Lord, provoking him to anger through the work of your hands." Then Moses spoke the words of this song until they were finished, in the ears of all the assembly of Israel: "Give ear, O heavens, and I will speak; and let the earth hear the words of my mouth. May my teaching drop as the rain, my speech distil as the dew, as the gentle rain upon the tender grass, and as the showers upon the herb. For I will proclaim the name of the Lord. Ascribe greatness to our God! The Rock, his work is perfect; for all his ways are justice. A God of faithfulness and without iniquity, just and right is he."

*A Reading (Lesson) from the Letter of Paul
to the Romans* [10:1-13]

Brethren, my heart's desire and prayer to God for them is
that they may be saved. I bear them witness that they have
a zeal for God, but it is not enlightened. For, being
ignorant of the righteousness that comes from God, and
seeking to establish their own, they did not submit to
God's righteousness. For Christ is the end of the law, that
every one who has faith may be justified. Moses writes
that the man who practices the righteousness which is
based on the law shall live by it. But the righteousness
based on faith says, Do not say in your heart, "Who will
ascend into heaven?" (that is, to bring Christ down) or
"Who will descend into the abyss?" (that is, to bring Christ
up from the dead). But what does it say? The word is near
you, on your lips and in your heart (that is, the word of
faith which we preach); because, if you confess with your
lips that Jesus is Lord and believe in your heart that God
raised him from the dead, you will be saved. For man
believes with his heart and so is justified, and he confesses
with his lips and so is saved. The scripture says, "No one
who believes in him will be put to shame." For there is no
distinction between Jew and Greek; the same Lord is Lord
of all and bestows his riches upon all who call upon him.
For, "every one who calls upon the name of the Lord will
be saved."

A Reading (Lesson) from the Gospel according to Matthew
[24:15-31]

Jesus said to the disciples, "When you see the desolating
sacrilege spoken of by the prophet Daniel, standing in the
holy place (let the reader understand), then let those who
are in Judea flee to the mountains; let him who is on the
housetop not go down to take what is in his house; and let
him who is in the field not turn back to take his mantle.
And alas for those who are with child and for those who

give suck in those days! Pray that your flight may not be in winter or on a sabbath. For then there will be great tribulation, such as has not been from the beginning of the world until now, no, and never will be. And if those days had not been shortened, no human being would be saved; but for the sake of the elect those days will be shortened. Then if any one says to you, 'Lo, here is the Christ!' or 'There he is!' do not believe it. For false Christs and false prophets will arise and show great signs and wonders, so as to lead astray, if possible, even the elect. Lo, I have told you beforehand. So, if they say to you, 'Lo, he is in the wilderness,' do not go out; if they say, 'Lo, he is in the inner rooms,' do not believe it. For as the lightning comes from the east and shines as far as the west, so will be the coming of the Son of man. Wherever the body is, there the eagles will be gathered together. Immediately after the tribulation of those days the sun will be darkened, and the moon will not give its light, and the stars will fall from heaven, and the powers of the heavens will be shaken; then will appear the sign of the Son of man in heaven, and then all the tribes of the earth will mourn, and they will see the Son of man coming on the clouds of heaven with power and great glory; and he will send out his angels with a loud trumpet call, and they will gather his elect from the four winds, from one end of heaven to the other."

Saturday

Psalm 20 [page 608],   *Psalm 21:1-7 (8-14)* [page 608]
❖   *Psalm 110:1-5 (6-7)* [page 753],   *Psalm 116* [page 759],
Psalm 117 [page 760]

A Reading (Lesson) from the Book of Deuteronomy
[34:1-12]

Moses went up from the plains of Moab to Mount Nebo, to the top of Pisgah, which is opposite Jericho. And the

Lord showed him all the land, Gilead as far as Dan, all Naph'tali, the land of E'phraim and Manas'seh, all the land of Judah as far as the Western Sea, the Negeb, and the Plain, that is, the valley of Jericho the city of palm trees, as far as Zo'ar. And the Lord said to him, "This is the land of which I swore to Abraham, to Isaac, and to Jacob, 'I will give it to your descendants.' I have let you see it with your eyes, but you shall not go over there." So Moses the servant of the Lord died there in the land of Moab, according to the word of the Lord, and he buried him in the valley in the land of Moab opposite Beth-pe'or; but no man knows the place of his burial to this day. Moses was a hundred and twenty years old when he died; his eye was not dim, nor his natural force abated. And the people of Israel wept for Moses in the plains of Moab thirty days; then the days of weeping and mourning for Moses were ended. And Joshua the son of Nun was full of the spirit of wisdom, for Moses had laid his hands upon him; so the people of Israel obeyed him, and did as the Lord had commanded Moses. And there has not arisen a prophet since in Israel like Moses, whom the Lord knew face to face, none like him for all the signs and the wonders which the Lord sent him to do in the land of Egypt, to Pharaoh and to all his servants and to all his land, and for all the mighty power and all the great and terrible deeds which Moses wrought in the sight of all Israel.

A Reading (Lesson) from the Letter of Paul to the Romans [10:14-21]

But how are men to call upon him in whom they have not believed? And how are they to believe in him of whom they have never heard? And how are they to hear without a preacher? And how can men preach unless they are sent? As it is written, "How beautiful are the feet of those who preach good news!" But they have not all obeyed the gospel; for Isaiah says, "Lord, who has believed what he has heard from us?" So faith comes from what is heard, and what is heard comes by the preaching of Christ. But I ask, have they not heard? Indeed they have; for "Their voice has gone out to all the earth, and their words to the ends of the world." Again I ask, did Israel not understand? First Moses says, "I will make you jealous of those who are not a nation; with a foolish nation I will make you angry." Then Isaiah is so bold as to say, "I have been found by those who did not seek me; I have shown myself to those who did not ask for me." But of Israel he says, "All day long I have held out my hands to a disobedient and contrary people."

A Reading (Lesson) from the Gospel according to Matthew [24:32-51]

Jesus said to the disciples, "From the fig tree learn its lesson: as soon as its branch becomes tender and puts forth its leaves, you know that summer is near. So also, when you see all these things, you know that he is near, at the very gates. Truly, I say to you, this generation will not pass away till all these things take place. Heaven and earth will pass away, but my words will not pass away. But of that day and hour no one knows, not even the angels of heaven, nor the Son, but the Father only. As were the days of Noah, so will be the coming of the Son of man. For as in those days before the flood they were eating and drinking, marrying and giving in marriage, until the day when Noah entered the ark, and they did not know until the flood came and swept them all away, so will be the coming of the Son of man. Then two men will be in the field; one is taken and one is left. Two women will be grinding at the mill; one is taken and one is left. Watch therefore, for you do not know on what day your Lord is coming. But know this, that if the householder had known in what part of the night the thief was coming, he would have watched and would not have let his house be broken into. Therefore you also must be ready; for the Son of man is coming at an hour you do not expect. Who then is the faithful and wise servant, whom his master has set over his household, to give them their food at the proper time? Blessed is that servant whom his master when he comes will find so doing. Truly, I say to you, he will set him over all his possessions. But if that wicked servant says to himself, 'My master is delayed,' and begins to beat his fellow servants, and eats and drinks with the drunken, the master of that servant will come on a day when he does not expect him and at an hour he does not know, and will punish him, and put him with the hypocrites; there men will weep and gnash their teeth."

Proper 10 *Week of the Sunday closest to July 13*

Sunday

Psalm 148 [page 805],   *Psalm 149* [page 807],
Psalm 150 [page 807] ❖ *Psalm 114* [page 756],
Psalm 115 [page 757]

A Reading (Lesson) from the Book of Joshua [1:1-18]

After the death of Moses the servant of the Lord, the Lord said to Joshua the son of Nun, Moses' minister, "Moses my servant is dead; now therefore arise, go over this Jordan, you and all this people, into the land which I am giving to them, to the people of Israel. Every place that the sole of your foot will tread upon I have given to you, as I promised to Moses. From the wilderness and this Lebanon as far as the great river, the river Eu-phra'tes, all the land of the Hittites to the Great Sea toward the going down of the sun shall be your territory. No man shall be able to stand before you all the days of your life; as I was with Moses, so I will be with you; I will not fail you or forsake you. Be strong and of good courage; for you shall cause this people to inherit the land which I swore to their fathers to give them. Only be strong and very courageous, being careful to do according to all the law which Moses my servant commanded you; turn not from it to the right hand or to the left, that you may have good success wherever you go. This book of the law shall not depart out of your mouth, but you shall meditate on it day and night, that you may be careful to do according to all that is written in it; for then you shall make your way prosperous, and then you shall have good success. Have I not commanded you? Be strong and of good courage; be not frightened, neither be dismayed; for the Lord your God is with you wherever you go." Then Joshua commanded the officers of the people, "Pass through the camp, and command the people, 'Prepare your provisions; for within three days you are to pass over this Jordan, to go in to take possession of the land which the Lord your God gives you to possess.'" And to the Reubenites, the Gadites, and the half-tribe of Manas'seh, Joshua said, "Remember the word which Moses the servant of the Lord commanded you, saying, 'The Lord your God is providing you a place of rest, and will give you this land.' Your wives, your little ones, and your cattle shall remain in the land which Moses gave you beyond the Jordan; but all the men of valor among you shall pass over armed before your brethren and shall help them, until the Lord gives rest to your brethren as well as to you, and they also take possession of the land which the Lord your God is giving them; then you shall return to the land of your possession, and shall possess it, the land which Moses the servant of the Lord gave you beyond the Jordan toward the sunrise." And they answered Joshua, "All that you have commanded us we will do, and wherever you send us we will go. Just as we obeyed Moses in all things, so we will obey you; only may the Lord your God be with you, as he was with Moses! Whoever rebels against your commandment and disobeys your words, whatever you command him, shall be put to death. Only be strong and of good courage."

A Reading (Lesson) from the Acts of the Apostles [21:3-15]

When we had come in sight of Cyprus, leaving it on the left we sailed to Syria, and landed at Tyre; for there the ship was to unload its cargo. And having sought out the disciples, we stayed there for seven days. Through the Spirit they told Paul not to go on to Jerusalem. And when our days there were ended, we departed and went on our journey; and they all, with wives and children, brought us on our way till we were outside the city; and kneeling down on the beach we prayed and bade one another farewell. Then we went on board the ship, and they returned home. When we had finished the voyage from Tyre, we arrived at Ptolema'is; and we greeted the brethren and stayed with them for one day. On the morrow we departed and came to Caesare'a; and we entered the house of Philip the evangelist, who was one of the seven, and stayed with him. And he had four unmarried daughters, who prophesied. While we were staying for some days, a prophet named Ag'abus came down from Judea. And coming to us he took Paul's girdle and bound his own feet and hands, and said, "Thus says the Holy Spirit, 'So shall the Jews at Jerusalem bind the man who owns this girdle and deliver him into the hands of the Gentiles.'" When we heard this, we and the people there begged him not to go up to Jerusalem. Then Paul answered, "What are you doing, weeping and breaking my heart? For I am ready not only to be imprisoned but even to die at Jerusalem for the name of the Lord Jesus." And when he would not be persuaded, we ceased and said, "The will of the Lord be done."

A Reading (Lesson) from the Gospel according to Mark [1:21-27]

Jesus, Simon and Andrew, James and John, went into Caper'na-um; and immediately on the sabbath he entered the synagogue and taught. And they were astonished at his teaching, for he taught them as one who had authority, and not as the scribes. And immediately there was in their synagogue a man with an unclean spirit; and he cried out, "What have you to do with us, Jesus of Nazareth? Have you come to destroy us? I know who you are, the Holy One of God." But Jesus rebuked him, saying, "Be silent, and come out of him!" And the unclean spirit, convulsing him and crying with a loud voice, came out of him. And they were all amazed, so that they questioned among themselves, saying, "What is this? A new teaching! With authority he commands even the unclean spirits, and they obey him."

Monday

Psalm 25 [page 614]   ❖   *Psalm 9* [page 593],
Psalm 15 [page 599]

A Reading (Lesson) from the Book of Joshua [2:1-14]

Joshua the son of Nun sent two men secretly from Shittim as spies, saying, "Go, view the land, especially Jericho." And they went, and came into the house of a harlot whose name was Rahab, and lodged there. And it was told the king of Jericho "Behold, certain men of Israel have come here tonight to search out the land." Then the king of Jericho sent to Rahab, saying, "Bring forth the men that have come to you, who entered your house; for they have come to search out all the land." But the woman had taken the two men and hidden them; and she said, "True, men came to me, but I did not know where they came from; and when the gate was to be closed, at dark, the men went out; where the men went I do not know; pursue them quickly, for you will overtake them." But she had brought them up to the roof, and hid them with the stalks of flax which she had laid in order on the roof. So the men pursued after them on the way to Jordan as far as the fords; and as soon as the pursuers had gone out, the gate was shut. Before they lay down, she came up to them on the roof, and said to the men, "I know that the Lord has given you the land, and that the fear of you has fallen upon us, and that all the inhabitants of the land melt away before you. For we have heard how the Lord dried up the water of the Red Sea before you when you came out of Egypt, and what you did to the two kings of the Amorites that were beyond the Jordan, to Sihon and Og, whom you utterly destroyed. And as soon as we heard it, our hearts melted, and there was no courage left in any man, because of you; for the Lord your God is he who is God in heaven above and on earth beneath. Now then, swear to me by the Lord that as I have dealt kindly with you, you also will deal kindly with my father's house, and give me a sure sign, and save alive my father and mother, my brothers and sisters, and all who belong to them, and deliver our lives from death." And the men said to her, "Our life for yours! If you do not tell this business of ours, then we will deal kindly and faithfully with you when the Lord gives us the land."

A Reading (Lesson) from the Letter of Paul to the Romans [11:1-12]

I ask, then, has God rejected his people? By no means! I myself am an Israelite, a descendant of Abraham, a member of the tribe of Benjamin. God has not rejected his people whom he foreknew. Do you not know what the scripture says of Eli'jah, how he pleads with God against Israel? "Lord, they have killed thy prophets, they have demolished thy altars, and I alone am left, and they seek my life." But what is God's reply to him? "I have kept for myself seven thousand men who have not bowed the knee to Ba'al." So too at the present time there is a remnant, chosen by grace. But if it is by grace, it is no longer on the basis of works; otherwise grace would no longer be grace. What then? Israel failed to obtain what it sought. The elect obtained it, but the rest were hardened, as it is written, "God gave them a spirit of stupor, eyes that should not see and ears that should not hear, down to this very day." And David says, "Let their table become a snare and a trap, a pitfall and a retribution for them; let their eyes be darkened so that they cannot see, and bend their backs for ever." So I ask, have they stumbled so as to fall? By no means! But through their trespass salvation has come to the Gentiles, so as to make Israel jealous. Now if their trespass means riches for the world, and if their failure means riches for the Gentiles, how much more will their full inclusion mean!

A Reading (Lesson) from the Gospel according to Matthew [25:1-13]

Jesus said to the disciples, "Then the kingdom of heaven shall be compared to ten maidens who took their lamps and went to meet the bridegroom. Five of them were foolish, and five were wise. For when the foolish took their lamps, they took no oil with them; but the wise took flasks of oil with their lamps. As the bridegroom was delayed, they all slumbered and slept. But at midnight there was a cry, 'Behold, the bridegroom! Come out to meet him.' Then all those maidens rose and trimmed their lamps. And the foolish said to the wise, 'Give us some of your oil, for our lamps are going out.' But the wise replied, 'Perhaps there will not be enough for us and for you; go rather to the dealers and buy for yourselves.' And while they went to buy, the bridegroom came, and those who were ready went in with him to the marriage feast; and the door was shut. Afterward the other maidens came also, saying, 'Lord, lord, open to us.' But he replied, 'Truly, I say to you, I do not know you.' Watch therefore, for you know neither the day nor the hour."

Tuesday

Psalm 26 [page 616],   *Psalm 28* [page 619]   ❖
Psalm 36 [page 632],   *Psalm 39* [page 638]

A Reading (Lesson) from the Book of Joshua [2:15-24]

Rahab let the two men whom Joshua the son of Nun had sent secretly from Shittim as spies down by a rope through the window, for her house was built into the city wall, so that she dwelt in the wall. And she said to them, "Go into the hills, lest the pursuers meet you; and hide yourselves there three days, until the pursuers have returned; then afterward you may go your way." The men said to her, "We will be guiltless with respect to this oath of yours which you have made us swear. Behold, when we come into the land, you shall bind this scarlet cord in the window through which you let us down; and you shall gather into your house your father and mother, your brothers, and all your father's household. If any one goes out of the doors of your house into the street, his blood shall be upon his head, and we shall be guiltless; but if a hand is laid upon any one who is with you in the house, his blood shall be on our head. But if you tell this business of ours, then we shall be guiltless with respect to your oath which you have made us swear." And she said, "According to your words, so be it." Then she sent them away, and they departed; and she bound the scarlet cord in the window. They departed, and went into the hills, and remained there three days, until the pursuers returned; for the pursuers had made search all along the way and found nothing. Then the two men came down again from the hills, and passed over and came to Joshua the son of Nun; and they told him all that had befallen them. And they said to Joshua, "Truly the Lord has given all the land into our hands; and moreover all the inhabitants of the land are fainthearted because of us."

A Reading (Lesson) from the Letter of Paul to the Romans [11:13-24]

Now I am speaking to you Gentiles. Inasmuch then as I am an apostle to the Gentiles, I magnify my ministry in order to make my fellow Jews jealous, and thus save some of them. For if their rejection means the reconciliation of the world, what will their acceptance mean but life from the dead? If the dough offered as first fruits is holy, so is the whole lump; and if the root is holy, so are the branches. But if some of the branches were broken off, and you, a wild olive shoot, were grafted in their place to share the richness of the olive tree, do not boast over the branches. If you do boast, remember it is not you that support the root, but the root that supports you. You will say, "Branches were broken off so that I might be grafted in." That is true. They were broken off because of their unbelief, but you stand fast only through faith. So do not become proud, but stand in awe. For if God did not spare the natural branches, neither will he spare you. Note then the kindness and the severity of God: severity toward those who have fallen, but God's kindness to you, provided you continue in his kindness; otherwise you too will be cut off. And even the others, if they do not persist in their unbelief, will be grafted in, for God has the power to graft them in again. For if you have been cut from what is by nature a wild olive tree, and grafted, contrary to nature, into a cultivated olive tree, how much more will these natural branches be grafted back into their own olive tree.

A Reading (Lesson) from the Gospel according to Matthew
[25:14-30]

Jesus said to the disciples, "For it will be as when a man going on a journey called his servants and entrusted to them his property; to one he gave five talents, to another two, to another one, to each according to his ability. Then he went away. He who had received the five talents went at once and traded with them; and he made five talents more. So also, he who had the two talents made two talents more. But he who had received the one talent went and dug in the ground and hid his master's money. Now after a long time the master of those servants came and settled accounts with them. And he who had received the five talents came forward, bringing five talents more, saying, 'Master, you delivered to me five talents; here I have made five talents more.' His master said to him, 'Well done, good and faithful servant; you have been faithful over a little, I will set you over much; enter into the joy of your master.' And he also who had the two talents came forward, saying, 'Master, you delivered to me two talents; here I have made two talents more.' His master said to him, 'Well done, good and faithful servant; you have been faithful over a little, I will set you over much; enter into the joy of your master.' He also who had received the one talent came forward, saying, 'Master, I knew you to be a hard man, reaping where you did not sow, and gathering where you did not winnow; so I was afraid, and I went and hid your talent in the ground. Here you have what is yours.' But his master answered him, 'You wicked and slothful servant! You knew that I reap where I have not sowed, and gather where I have not winnowed? Then you ought to have invested my money with the bankers, and at my coming I should have received what was my own with interest. So take the talent from him, and give it to him who has the ten talents. For to every one who has will more be given, and he will have abundance; but from him who has not, even what he has will be taken away. And cast the worthless servant into the outer darkness; there men will weep and gnash their teeth.' "

Wednesday

Psalm 38 [page 636] ❖ *Psalm 119:25-48* [page 765]

A Reading (Lesson) from the Book of Joshua [3:1-13]

Early in the morning Joshua rose and set out from Shittim, with all the people of Israel; and they came to the Jordan, and lodged there before they passed over. At the end of three days the officers went through the camp and commanded the people, "When you see the ark of the covenant of the Lord your God being carried by the Levitical priests, then you shall set out from your place and follow it, that you may know the way you shall go, for you have not passed this way before. Yet there shall be a space between you and it, a distance of about two thousand cubits; do not come near it." And Joshua said to the people, "Sanctify yourselves; for tomorrow the Lord will do wonders among you." And Joshua said to the priests, "Take up the ark of the covenant, and pass on before the people." And they took up the ark of the covenant, and went before the people. And the Lord said to Joshua, "This day I will begin to exalt you in the sight of all Israel, that they may know that, as I was with Moses, so I will be with you. And you shall command the priests who bear the ark of the covenant, 'When you come to the brink of the waters of the Jordan, you shall stand still in the Jordan.' " And Joshua said to the people of Israel, "Come hither, and hear the words of the Lord your God." And Joshua said, "Hereby you shall know that the living God is among you, and that he will without fail drive out from before you the Canaanites, the Hittites, the Hivites, the Per'izzites, the Gir'gashites, the Amorites, and the Jeb'usites. Behold, the ark of the covenant of the Lord of all the earth is to pass over before you into the Jordan. Now therefore take twelve men from the tribes of Israel, from each tribe a man. And when the soles of the feet of the priests who bear the ark of the Lord, the Lord of all the earth, shall rest in the waters of the Jordan, the waters of the Jordan shall be stopped from flowing, and the waters coming down from above shall stand in one heap."

A Reading (Lesson) from the Letter of Paul to the Romans [11:25-36]

Lest you be wise in your own conceits, I want you to understand this mystery, brethren: a hardening has come upon part of Israel, until the full number of the Gentiles come in, and so all Israel will be saved; as it is written, "The Deliverer will come from Zion, he will banish ungodliness from Jacob"; "and this will be my covenant with them when I take away their sins." As regards the gospel they are enemies of God, for your sake; but as regards election they are beloved for the sake of their forefathers. For the gifts and the call of God are irrevocable. Just as you were once disobedient to God but now have received mercy because of their disobedience, so they have now been disobedient in order that by the mercy shown to you they also may receive mercy. For God has consigned all men to disobedience, that he may have mercy upon all. O the depth of the riches and wisdom and knowledge of God! How unsearchable are his judgments and how inscrutable his ways! "For who has known the mind of the Lord, or who has been his counselor?" "Or who has given a gift to him that he might be repaid?" For from him and through him and to him are all things. To him be glory for ever. Amen.

A Reading (Lesson) from the Gospel according to Matthew [25:31-46]

Jesus said to the disciples, "When the Son of man comes in his glory, and all the angels with him, then he will sit on his glorious throne. Before him will be gathered all the nations, and he will separate them one from another as a shepherd separates the sheep from the goats, and he will place the sheep at his right hand, but the goats at the left. Then the King will say to those at his right hand, 'Come, O blessed of my Father, inherit the kingdom prepared for you from the foundation of the world; for I was hungry and you gave me food, I was thirsty and you gave me drink, I was a stranger and you welcomed me, I was naked and you clothed me, I was sick and you visited me, I was in prison and you came to me.' Then the righteous will answer him, 'Lord, when did we see thee hungry and feed thee, or thirsty and give thee drink? And when did we see thee a stranger and welcome thee, or naked and clothe thee? And when did we see thee sick or in prison and visit thee?' And the King will answer them, "Truly, I say to you, as you did it to one of the least of these my brethren, you did it to me.' Then he will say to those at his left hand, 'Depart from me, you cursed, into the eternal fire prepared for the devil and his angels; for I was hungry and you gave me no food, I was thirsty and you gave me no drink, I was a stranger and you did not welcome me, naked and you did not clothe me, sick and in prison and you did not visit me.' Then they also will answer, 'Lord, when did we see thee hungry or thirsty or a stranger or naked or sick or in prison, and did not minister to thee?' Then he will answer them, 'Truly, I say to you, as you did it not to one of the least of these, you did it not to me.' And they will go away into eternal punishment, but the righteous into eternal life."

Thursday

Psalm 37:1-18 [page 633] ❖ *Psalm 37:19-42* [page 634]

A Reading (Lesson) from the Book of Joshua [3:14—4:7]

When the people set out from their tents, to pass over the Jordan with the priests bearing the ark of the covenant before the people, and when those who bore the ark had come to the Jordan, and the feet of the priests bearing the ark were dipped in the brink of the water (the Jordan overflows all its banks throughout the time of harvest), the waters coming down from above stood and rose up in a heap far off, at Adam, the city that is beside Zarethan, and those flowing down toward the sea of the Arabah, the Salt Sea, were wholly cut off; and the people passed over opposite Jericho. And while all Israel were passing over on dry ground, the priests who bore the ark of the covenant of the Lord stood on dry ground in the midst of the Jordan, until all the nation finished passing over the Jordan. When all the nation had finished passing over the Jordan, the Lord said to Joshua, "Take twelve men from the people, from each tribe a man, and command them, 'Take twelve stones from here out of the midst of the Jordan, from the very place where the priests' feet stood, and carry them over with you, and lay them down in the place where you lodge tonight.'" Then Joshua called the twelve men from the people of Israel, whom he had appointed, a man from each tribe; and Joshua said to them, "Pass on before the ark of the Lord your God into the midst of the Jordan, and take up each of you a stone upon his shoulder, according to the number of the tribes of the people of Israel, that this may be a sign among you, when your children ask in time to come, 'What do those stones mean to you?' Then you shall tell them that the waters of the Jordan were cut off before the ark of the covenant of the Lord; when it passed over the Jordan, the waters of the Jordan were cut off. So these stones shall be to the people of Israel a memorial for ever."

A Reading (Lesson) from the Letter of Paul to the Romans [12:1-8]

I appeal to you therefore, brethren, by the mercies of God, to present your bodies as a living sacrifice, holy and acceptable to God, which is your spiritual worship. Do not be conformed to this world but be transformed by the renewal of your mind, that you may prove what is the will of God, what is good and acceptable and perfect. For by the grace given to me I bid every one among you not to think of himself more highly than he ought to think, but to think with sober judgment, each according to the measure of faith which God has assigned him. For as in one body we have many members, and all the members do not have the same function, so we, though many, are one body in Christ, and individually members one of another. Having gifts that differ according to the grace given to us, let us use them; if prophecy, in proportion to our faith; if service, in our serving; he who teaches, in his teaching; he who exhorts, in his exhortation; he who contributes, in liberality; he who gives aid, with zeal; he who does acts of mercy, with cheerfulness.

A Reading (Lesson) from the Gospel according to Matthew [26:1-16]

When Jesus had finished all these sayings, he said to his disciples, "You know that after two days the Passover is coming, and the Son of man will be delivered up to be crucified." Then the chief priests and the elders of the people gathered in the palace of the high priest, who was called Ca'iaphas, and took counsel together in order to arrest Jesus by stealth and kill him. But they said, "Not during the feast, lest there be a tumult among the people." Now when Jesus was at Bethany in the house of Simon the leper, a woman came up to him with an alabaster flask of very expensive ointment, and she poured it on his head, as he sat at table. But when the disciples saw it, they were indignant, saying, "Why this waste? For the ointment might have been sold for a large sum, and given to the poor." But Jesus, aware of this, said to them, "Why do you trouble the woman? For she has done a beautiful thing to me. For you always have the poor with you, but you will not always have me. In pouring this ointment on my body she has done it to prepare me for burial. Truly, I say to you, wherever this gospel is preached in the whole world, what she has done will be told in memory of her." Then one of the twelve, who was called Judas Iscariot, went to the chief priests and said, "What will you give me if I deliver him to you?" And they paid him thirty pieces of silver. And from that moment he sought an opportunity to betray him.

Friday

Psalm 31 [page 622]   ❖   *Psalm 35* [page 629]

A Reading (Lesson) from the Book of Joshua
[4:19—5:1,10-15]

The people came up out of the Jordan on the tenth day of
the first month, and they encamped in Gilgal on the east
border of Jericho. And those twelve stones, which they
took out of the Jordan, Joshua set up in Gilgal. And he said
to the people of Israel, "When your children ask their
fathers in time to come, 'What do these stones mean?' then
you shall let your children know, 'Israel passed over this
Jordan on dry ground.' For the Lord your God dried up
the waters of the Jordan for you until you passed over, as
the Lord your God did to the Red Sea, which he dried up
for us until we passed over, so that all the people of the
earth may know that the hand of the Lord is mighty; that
you may fear the Lord your God for ever." When all the
kings of the Amorites that were beyond the Jordan to the
west, and all the kings of the Canaanites that were by the
sea, heard that the Lord had dried up the waters of the
Jordan for the people of Israel until they had crossed over,
their heart melted, and there was no longer any spirit in
them, because of the people of Israel. While the people of
Israel were encamped in Gilgal they kept the passover on
the fourteenth day of the month at evening in the plains of
Jericho. And on the morrow after the passover, on that
very day, they ate of the produce of the land, unleavened
cakes and parched grain. And the manna ceased on the
morrow, when they ate of the produce of the land; and the
people of Israel had manna no more, but ate of the fruit of
the land of Canaan that year. When Joshua was by Jericho,
he lifted up his eyes and looked, and behold, a man stood
before him with his drawn sword in his hand; and Joshua
went to him and said to him, "Are you for us, or for our
adversaries?" And he said, "No; but as commander of the
army of the Lord I have now come." And Joshua fell on his
face to the earth, and worshiped him, and said to him,
"What does my lord bid his servant?" And the commander

of the Lord's army said to Joshua, "Put off your shoes from your feet; for the place where you stand is holy." And Joshua did so.

A Reading (Lesson) from the Letter of Paul to the Romans [12:9-21]

Let love be genuine; hate what is evil, hold fast to what is good; love one another with brotherly affection; outdo one another in showing honor. Never flag in zeal, be aglow with the Spirit, serve the Lord. Rejoice in your hope, be patient in tribulation, be constant in prayer. Contribute to the needs of the saints, practice hospitality. Bless those who persecute you; bless and do not curse them. Rejoice with those who rejoice, weep with those who weep. Live in harmony with one another; do not be haughty, but associate with the lowly; never be conceited. Repay no one evil for evil, but take thought for what is noble in the sight of all. If possible, so far as it depends upon you, live peaceably with all. Beloved, never avenge yourselves, but leave it to the wrath of God; for it is written, "Vengeance is mine, I will repay, says the Lord." No, "if your enemy is hungry, feed him; if he is thirsty, give him drink; for by so doing you will heap burning coals upon his head." Do not be overcome by evil, but overcome evil with good.

A Reading (Lesson) from the Gospel according to Matthew [26:17-25]

On the first day of Unleavened Bread, the disciples came to Jesus, saying, "Where will you have us prepare for you to eat the passover?" He said, "Go into the city to a certain one, and say to him, 'The Teacher says, My time is at hand; I will keep the passover at your house with my disciples.'" And the disciples did as Jesus had directed them, and they prepared the passover. When it was evening, he sat at table with the twelve disciples; and as they were eating, he said, "Truly, I say to you, one of you will betray me." And they were very sorrowful, and began to say to him one after another, "Is it I, Lord?" He answered, "He who has dipped his hand in the dish with me, will betray me. The Son of man goes as it is written of him, but woe to that man by whom the Son of man is betrayed! It would have been better for that man if he had not been born." Judas, who betrayed him, said, "Is it I, Master?" He said to him, "You have said so."

Saturday

Psalm 30 [page 621], *Psalm 32* [page 624] ❖
Psalm 42 [page 643], *Psalm 43* [page 644]

A Reading (Lesson) from the Book of Joshua [6:1-14]

Jericho was shut up from within and from without because of the people of Israel; none went out, and none came in. And the Lord said to Joshua, "See, I have given into your hand Jericho, with its king and mighty men of valor. You shall march around the city, all the men of war going around the city once. Thus shall you do for six days. And seven priests shall bear seven trumpets of rams' horns before the ark; and on the seventh day you shall march around the city seven times, the priests blowing the trumpets. And when they make a long blast with the ram's horn, as soon as you hear the sound of the trumpet, then all the people shall shout with a great shout; and the wall of the city will fall down flat, and the people shall go up every man straight before him." So Joshua the son of Nun called the priests and said to them, "Take up the ark of the covenant, and let seven priests bear seven trumpets of rams' horns before the ark of the Lord." And he said to the people, "Go forward; march around the city, and let the armed men pass on before the ark of the Lord." And as Joshua had commanded the people, the seven priests bearing the seven trumpets of rams' horns before the Lord went forward, blowing the trumpets, with the ark of the covenant of the Lord following them. And the armed men went before the priests who blew the trumpets, and the rear guard came after the ark, while the trumpets blew continually. But Joshua commanded the people, "You shall not shout or let your voice be heard, neither shall any word go out of your mouth, until the day I bid you shout; then you shall shout." So he caused the ark of the Lord to compass the city, going about it once; and they came into the camp, and spent the night in the camp. Then Joshua rose early in the morning, and the priests took up the ark of the Lord. And the seven priests bearing the seven trumpets of rams' horns before the ark of the Lord passed on, blowing the trumpets continually; and the armed men went before them, and the rear guard came after the ark of the Lord, while the trumpets blew continually. And the second day they marched around the city once, and returned into the camp. So they did for six days.

A Reading (Lesson) from the Letter of Paul to the Romans [13:1-7]

Let every person be subject to the governing authorities. For there is no authority except from God, and those that exist have been instituted by God. Therefore he who resists the authorities resists what God has appointed, and those who resist will incur judgment. For rulers are not a terror to good conduct, but to bad. Would you have no fear of him who is in authority? Then do what is good, and you will receive his approval, for he is God's servant for your good. But if you do wrong, be afraid, for he does not bear the sword in vain; he is the servant of God to execute his wrath on the wrongdoer. Therefore one must be subject, not only to avoid God's wrath but also for the sake of conscience. For the same reason you also pay taxes, for the authorities are ministers of God, attending to this very thing. Pay all of them their dues, taxes to whom taxes are due, revenue to whom revenue is due, respect to whom respect is due, honor to whom honor is due.

A Reading (Lesson) from the Gospel according to Matthew
[26:26-35]

Now as they were eating the passover, Jesus took bread, and blessed, and broke it, and gave it to the disciples and said, "Take, eat; this is my body." And he took a cup, and when he had given thanks he gave it to them, saying, "Drink of it, all of you; for this is my blood of the covenant, which is poured out for many for the forgiveness of sins. I tell you I shall not drink again of this fruit of the vine until that day when I drink it new with you in my Father's kingdom." And when they had sung a hymn, they went out to the Mount of Olives. Then Jesus said to them, "You will all fall away because of me this night; for it is written, 'I will strike the shepherd, and the sheep of the flock will be scattered.' But after I am raised up, I will go before you to Galilee." Peter declared to him, "Though they all fall away because of you, I will never fall away." Jesus said to him, "Truly, I say to you, this very night, before the cock crows, you will deny me three times." Peter said to him, "Even if I must die with you, I will not deny you." And so said all the disciples.

Proper 11 *Week of the Sunday closest to July 20*

Sunday

Psalm 63:1-8(9-11) [page 670],   *Psalm 98* [page 727] ❖
Psalm 103 [page 733]

A Reading (Lesson) from the Book of Joshua [6:15-27]

On the seventh day the people of Israel rose early at the dawn of day, and marched around Jericho in the same manner seven times; it was only on that day that they marched around the city seven times. And at the seventh time, when the priests had blown the trumpets, Joshua said to the people, "Shout; for the Lord has given you the city. And the city and all that is within it shall be devoted to the Lord for destruction; only Rahab the harlot and all who are with her in her house shall live, because she hid the messengers that we sent. But you, keep yourselves from the things devoted to destruction, lest when you have devoted them you take any of the devoted things and make the camp of Israel a thing for destruction, and bring trouble upon it. But all silver and gold, and vessels of bronze and iron, are sacred to the Lord; they shall go into the treasury of the Lord." So the people shouted, and the trumpets were blown. As soon as the people heard the sound of the trumpet, the people raised a great shout, and the wall fell down flat, so that the people went up into the city, every man straight before him, and they took the city. Then they utterly destroyed all in the city, both men and women, young and old, oxen, sheep, and asses, with the edge of the sword. And Joshua said to the two men who had spied out the land, "Go into the harlot's house, and bring out from it the woman, and all who belong to her, as you swore to her." So the young men who had been spies went in, and brought our Rahab, and her father and mother and brothers and all who belonged to her; and they brought all her kindred, and set them outside the camp of Israel. And they burned the city with fire, and all within it; only the silver and gold, and the vessels of bronze and of iron, they put into the treasury of the house of the Lord. But Rahab the harlot, and her father's household, and all who belonged to her, Joshua saved alive; and she dwelt in Israel to this day, because she hid the messengers whom Joshua sent to spy out Jericho. Joshua laid an oath upon them at that time, saying, "Cursed before the Lord be the man that rises up and rebuilds this city, Jericho. At the cost of his first-born shall he lay its foundation, and at the cost of his youngest son shall he set up its gates." So the Lord was with Joshua; and his fame in all the land.

A Reading (Lesson) from the Acts of the Apostles
[22:30—23:11]

On the morrow, desiring to know the real reason why the Jews accused Paul, the tribune unbound him, and commanded the chief priests and all the council to meet, and he brought Paul down and set him before them. And Paul, looking intently at the council, said, "Brethren, I have lived before God in all good conscience up to this day." And the high priest Anani'as commanded those who stood by him to strike him on the mouth. Then Paul said to him, "God shall strike you, you whitewashed wall! Are you sitting to judge me according to the law, and yet contrary to the law you order me to be struck?" Those who stood by said, " Would you revile God's high priest?" And Paul said, "I did not know, brethren, that he was the high priest; for it is written, 'You shall not speak evil of a ruler of your people.' " But when Paul perceived that one part were Sad'ducees and the other Pharisees, he cried out in the council, "Brethren, I am a Pharisee, a son of Pharisees; with respect to the hope and the resurrection of the dead I am on trial." And when he had said this, a dissension arose between the Pharisees and the Sad'ducees; and the assembly was divided. For the Sad'ducees say that there is no resurrection, nor angel, nor spirit; but the Pharisees acknowledge them all. Then a great clamor arose; and some of the scribes of the Pharisees' party stood up and contended, "We find nothing wrong in this man. What if a spirit or an angel spoke to him?" And when the dissension became violent, the tribune, afraid that Paul would be torn in pieces by them, commanded the soldiers to go down and take him by force from among them and bring him into the barracks. The following night the Lord stood by him and said, "Take courage, for as you have testified about me at Jerusalem, so you must bear witness also at Rome."

A Reading (Lesson) from the Gospel according to Mark
[2:1-12]

When Jesus returned to Caper'na-um after some days, it
was reported that he was at home. And many were
gathered together, so that there was no longer room for
them, not even about the door; and he was preaching the
word to them. And they came, bringing to him a paralytic
carried by four men. And when they could not get near
him because of the crowd, they removed the roof above
him; and when they had made an opening, they let down
the pallet on which the paralytic lay. And when Jesus saw
their faith, he said to the paralytic, "My son, your sins are
forgiven." Now some of the scribes were sitting there,
questioning in their hearts, "Why does this man speak
thus? Is it blasphemy! Who can forgive sins but God
alone?" And immediately Jesus, perceiving in his spirit that
they thus questioned within themselves, said to them,
"Why do you question thus in your hearts? Which is easier,
to say to the paralytic, 'Your sins are forgiven,' or to say,
'Rise, take up your pallet and walk'? But that you many
know that the Son of man has authority on earth to forgive
sins"—he said to the paralytic—"I say to you, rise, take up
your pallet and go home." And he rose, and immediately
took up the pallet and went out before them all; so that
they were all amazed and glorified God, saying, "We never
saw anything like this!"

Monday

Psalm 41 [page 641],   *Psalm 52* [page 657]   ❖
Psalm 44 [page 645]

A Reading (Lesson) from the Book of Joshua [7:1-13]

The people of Israel broke faith in regard to the devoted
things; for Achan the son of Carmi, son of Zabdi, son of
Zerah, of the tribe of Judah, took some of the devoted

things; and the anger of the Lord burned against the people of Israel. Joshua sent men from Jericho to Ai, which is near Beth-a'ven, east of Bethel, and said to them, "Go up and spy out the land." And the men went up and spied out Ai. And they returned to Joshua, and said to him, "Let not all the people go up, but let about two or three thousand men go up and attack Ai; do not make the whole people toil up there, for they are but few." So about three thousand went up there from the people; and they fled before the men of Ai, and the men of Ai killed about thirty-six men of them, and chased them before the gate as far as Sheb'arim, and slew them at the descent. And the hearts of the people melted, and became as water. Then Joshua rent his clothes, and fell to the earth upon his face before the ark of the Lord until the evening, he and the elders of Israel; and they put dust upon their heads. And Joshua said, "Alas, O Lord God, why hast thou brought this people over the Jordan at all, to give us into the hands of the Amorites, to destroy us? Would that we had been content to dwell beyond the Jordan! O Lord, what can I say, when Israel has turned their backs before their enemies! For the Canaanites and all the inhabitants of the land will hear of it, and will surround us, and cut off our name from the earth; and what wilt thou do for thy great name?" The Lord said to Joshua, "Arise, why have you thus fallen upon your face? Israel has sinned; they have transgressed my covenant which I commanded them; they have taken some of the devoted things; they have stolen, and lied, and put them among their own stuff. Therefore the people of Israel cannot stand before their enemies; they turn their backs before their enemies, because they have become a thing for destruction. I will be with you no more, unless you destroy the devoted things from among you. Up, sanctify the people, and say, 'Sanctify yourselves for tomorrow; for thus says the Lord, God of Israel, "There are devoted things in the midst of you, O Israel; you cannot stand before your enemies, until you take away the devoted things from among you." ' "

*A Reading (Lesson) from the Letter of Paul
to the Romans* [13:8-14]

Owe no one anything, except to love one another; for he
who loves his neighbor has fulfilled the law. The
commandments, "You shall not commit adultery, You
shall not kill, You shall not steal, You shall not covet," and
any other commandment, are summed up in this sentence,
"You shall love your neighbor as yourself." Love does no
wrong to a neighbor; therefore love is the fulfilling of the
law. Besides this you know what hour it is, how it is full
time now for you to wake from sleep. For salvation is
nearer to us now than when we first believed; the night is
far gone, the day is at hand. Let us then cast off the works
of darkness and put on the armor of light; let us conduct
ourselves becomingly as in the day, not in reveling and
drunkenness, not in debauchery and licentiousness, not in
quarreling and jealousy. But put on the Lord Jesus Christ,
and make no provision for the flesh, to gratify its desires.

A Reading (Lesson) from the Gospel according to Matthew
[26:36-46]

Jesus went with his disciples to a place called Gethsem'ane,
and he said to them, "Sit here, while I go yonder and pray."
And taking with him Peter and the two sons of Zeb'edee,
he began to be sorrowful and troubled. Then he said to
them, "My soul is very sorrowful, even to death; remain
here, and watch with me." And going on a little farther he
fell on his face and prayed, "My Father, if it be possible, let
this cup pass from me; nevertheless, not as I will, but as
thou wilt." And he came to the disciples and found them
sleeping; and he said to Peter, "So, could you not watch
with me one hour? Watch and pray that you may not enter
into temptation; the spirit indeed is willing, but the flesh is
weak." Again, for the second time, he went away and
prayed, "My Father, if this cannot pass unless I drink it,
thy will be done." And again he came and found them

sleeping, for their eyes were heavy. So, leaving them again, he went away and prayed for the third time, saying the same words. Then he came to the disciples and said to them, "Are you still sleeping and taking your rest? Behold, the hour is at hand, and the Son of man is betrayed into the hands of sinners. Rise, let us be going; see, my betrayer is at hand."

Tuesday

Psalm 45 [page 647] ❖ *Psalm 47* [page 650],
Psalm 48 [page 651]

A Reading (Lesson) from the Book of Joshua [8:1-22]

The Lord said to Joshua, "Do not fear or be dismayed; take all the fighting men with you, and arise, go up to Ai; see, I have given into your hand the king of Ai, and his people, his city, and his land; and you shall do to Ai and its king as you did to Jericho and its king; only its spoil and its cattle you shall take as booty for yourselves; lay an ambush against the city, behind it." So Joshua arose, and all the fighting men, to go up to Ai; and Joshua chose thirty thousand mighty men of valor, and sent them forth by night. And he commanded them, "Behold, you shall lie in ambush against the city, behind it; do not go very far from the city, but hold yourselves all in readiness; and I, and all the people who are with me, will approach the city. And when they come out against us, as before, we shall flee before them; and they will come out after us, till we have drawn them away from the city; for they will say, 'They are fleeing from us, as before.' So we will flee from them; then you shall rise up from the ambush, and seize the city; for the Lord your God will give it into your hand. And when you have taken the city, you shall set the city on fire, doing as the Lord has bidden; see, I have commanded you." So Joshua sent them forth; and they went to the place of ambush, and lay between Bethel and Ai, to the west of Ai; but Joshua spent that night among the people. And Joshua arose early in the morning and mustered the people, and went up, with the elders of Israel, before the people to Ai. And all the fighting men who were with him went up, and drew near before the city, and encamped on the north side of Ai, with a ravine between them and Ai. And he took about five thousand men, and set them in ambush between Bethel and Ai, to the west of the city. So they stationed the forces, the main encampment which was north of the city and its rear guard west of the city. But Joshua spent that night in the valley. And when the king of Ai saw this he and all his people, the men of the city, made haste and went out early to the descent toward the Arabah to meet Israel in battle; but he did not know that there was an ambush against him behind the city. And Joshua and all Israel made a pretense of being beaten before them, and fled in the direction of the wilderness. So all the people who were in the city were called together to pursue them, and as they pursued Joshua they were drawn away from the city. There was not a man left in Ai or Bethel, who did not go out after Israel; they left the city open, and pursued Israel. Then the Lord said to Joshua, "Stretch out the javelin that is in your hand toward Ai; for I will give it into your hand." And Joshua stretched out the javelin that was in his hand toward the city. And the ambush rose quickly out of their place, and as soon as he had stretched out his hand, they ran and entered the city and took it; and they made haste to set the city on fire, So when the men of Ai looked back, behold, the smoke of the city went up to heaven; and they had no power to flee this way or that, for the people that fled to the wilderness turned back upon the pursuers. And when Joshua and all Israel saw that the ambush had taken the city, and that the smoke of the city went up, then they turned back and smote the men of Ai. And the others came forth from the city against them; so they were in the midst of Israel, some on this side, and some on that side; and Israel smote them, until there was left none that survived or escaped.

*A Reading (Lesson) from the Letter of Paul
to the Romans* [14:1-12]

As for the man who is weak in faith, welcome him, but not
for disputes over opinions. One believes he may eat
anything, while the weak man eats only vegetables.Let not
him who eats despise him who abstains, and let not him
who abstains pass judgment on him who eats; for God has
welcomed him. Who are you to pass judgment on the
servant of another? It is before his own master that he
stands or falls. And he will be upheld, for the Master is
able to make him stand. One man esteems one day as
better than another, while another man esteems all days
alike. Let every one be fully convinced in his own mind. He
who observes the day, observes it in honor of the Lord. He
also who eats, eats in honor of the Lord, since he gives
thanks to God; while he who abstains, abstains in honor of
the Lord and gives thanks to God. None of us lives to
himself, and none of us dies to himself. If we live, we live to
the Lord, and if we die, we die to the Lord; so then,
whether we live or whether we die, we are the Lord's. For
to this end Christ died and lived again, that he might be
Lord both of the dead and of the living. Why do you pass
judgment on your brother? Or you, why do you despise
your brother? For we shall all stand before the judgment
seat of God; for it is written, "As I live, says the Lord,
every knee shall bow to me, and every tongue shall give
praise to God." So each of us shall give account of himself
to God.

A Reading (Lesson) from the Gospel according to Matthew
[26:47-56]

While Jesus was still speaking, Judas came, one of the
twelve, and with him a great crowd with swords and clubs,
from the chief priests and the elders of the people. Now the
betrayer had given them a sign, saying, "The one I shall
kiss is the man; seize him." And he came up to Jesus at
once and said, "Hail, Master!" And he kissed him. Jesus

said to him, "Friend, why are you here?" Then they came up and laid hands on Jesus and seized him. And behold, one of those who were with Jesus stretched out his hand and drew his sword, and struck the slave of the high priest, and cut off his ear. Then Jesus said to him, "Put your sword back into its place; for all who take the sword will perish by the sword. Do you think that I cannot appeal to my Father, and he will at once send me more than twelve legions of angels? But how then should the scriptures be fulfilled, that it must be so?" At that hour Jesus said to the crowds, "Have you come out as against a robber, with swords and clubs to capture me? Day after day I sat in the temple teaching, and you did not seize me. But all this has taken place, that the scriptures of the prophets might be fulfilled." Then all the disciples forsook him and fled.

Wednesday

Psalm 119:49-72 [page 767]   ❖   *Psalm 49* [page 652],
(Psalm 53 [page 658])

A Reading (Lesson) from the Book of Joshua [8:30-35]

Joshua built an altar in Mount Ebal to the Lord, the God of Israel, as Moses the servant of the Lord had commanded the people of Israel, as it is written in the book of the law of Moses, "an altar of unhewn stones, upon which no man has lifted an iron tool"; and they offered on it burnt offerings to the Lord, and sacrificed peace offerings. And there, in the presence of the people of Israel, he wrote upon the stones a copy of the law of Moses, which he had written. And all Israel, sojourner as well as home-born, with their elders and officers and their judges, stood on opposite sides of the ark before the Levitical priests who carried the ark of the covenant of the Lord, half of them in front of Mount Ger'izim and half of them in front of Mount Ebal, as Moses the servant of the Lord had commanded at the first, that they should bless the people of Israel. And afterward he read all the words of the law, the blessing and the curse, according to all that is written in the book of the law. There was not a word of all that Moses commanded which Joshua did not read before all the assembly of Israel, and the women, and the little ones, and the sojourners who lived among them.

A Reading (Lesson) from the Letter of Paul to the Romans [14:13-23]

Let us no more pass judgment on one another, but rather decide never to put a stumbling block or hindrance in the way of a brother. I know and am persuaded in the Lord Jesus that nothing is unclean in itself; but it is unclean for any one who thinks it unclean. If your brother is being injured by what you eat, you are no longer walking in love. Do not let what you eat cause the ruin of one for whom Christ died. So do not let your good be spoken of as evil. For the kingdom of God is not food and drink but righteousness and peace and joy in the Holy Spirit; he who thus serves Christ is acceptable to God and approved by men. Let us then pursue what makes for peace and for mutual upbuilding. Do not, for the sake of food, destroy the work of God. Everything is indeed clean, but it is wrong for any one to make others fall by what he eats; it is right not to eat meat or drink wine or do anything that makes your brother stumble. The faith that you have, keep between yourself and God; happy is he who has no reason to judge himself for what he approves. But he who has doubts is condemned, if he eats, because he does not act from faith; for whatever does not proceed from faith is sin.

A Reading (Lesson) from the Gospel according to Matthew [26:57-68]

Those who had seized Jesus led him to Caïaphas the high priest, where the scribes and the elders had gathered. But Peter followed him at a distance, as far as the courtyard of the high priest, and going inside he sat with the guards to see the end. Now the chief priests and the whole council sought false testimony against Jesus that they might put him to death, but they found none, though many false witnesses came forward. At last two came forward and said, "This fellow said, 'I am able to destroy the temple of God, and to build it in three days.'" And the high priest stood up and said, "Have you no answer to make?" What is it that these men testify against you?" But Jesus was silent. And the high priest said to him, "I adjure you by the living God, tell us if you are the Christ, the Son of God." Jesus said to him, "You have said so. But I tell you, hereafter you will see the Son of man seated at the right hand of Power, and coming on the clouds of heaven." Then the high priest tore his robes, and said, "He has uttered blasphemy. Why do we still need witnesses? You have now heard his blasphemy. What is your judgment?" They answered, "He deserves death." Then they spat in his face, and struck him; and some slapped him, saying, "Prophesy to us, you Christ! Who is it that struck you?"

Thursday

Psalm 50 [page 654]   ❖   (*Psalm 59* [page 665],
Psalm 60 [page 667])   or   *Psalm 66* [page 673],
Psalm 67 [page 675]

A Reading (Lesson) from the Book of Joshua [9:3-21]

When the inhabitants of Gibeon heard what Joshua had done to Jericho and to Ai, they on their part acted with cunning, and went and took worn-out sacks upon their asses, and wineskins, worn-out and torn and mended, with worn-out, patched sandals on their feet, and worn-out clothes; and all their provisions were dry and moldy. And they went to Joshua in the camp at Gilgal, and said to him and to the men of Israel, "We have come from a far country; so now make a covenant with us." But the men of Israel said to the Hivites, "Perhaps you live among us; then how can we make a covenant with you?" They said to Joshua, "We are your servants." And Joshua said to them, "Who are you? And where do you come from?" They said to him, "From a very far country your servants have come, because of the name of the Lord your God; for we have heard a report of him, and all that he did in Egypt, and all that he did to the two kings of the Amorites who were beyond the Jordan, Sihon the king of Heshbon, and Og king of Bashan, who dwelt in Ash'taroth. And our elders and all the inhabitants of our country said to us, 'Take provisions in your hand for the journey, and go to meet them, and say to them, "We are your servants; come now, make a covenant with us."' Here is our bread; it was still warm when we took it from our houses as our food for the journey, on the day we set forth to come to you, but now, behold, it is dry and moldy; these wineskins were new when we filled them, and behold, they are burst; and these garments and shoes of ours are worn out from the very long journey." So the men partook of their provisions, and did not ask direction from the Lord. And Joshua made peace with them, and made a covenant with them, to let them live; and the leaders of the congregation swore to them. At the end of three days after they made a covenant with them, they heard that they were their neighbors, and that they dwelt among them. And the people of Israel set out and reached their cities on the third day. Now their cities were Gibeon, Chephi'rah, Be-er'oth, and Kir'iath-je'arim. But the people of Israel did not kill them, because the leaders of the congregation had sworn to them by the Lord, the God of Israel. Then all the congregation murmured against the leaders. But all the leaders said to all the congregation, "We have sworn to them by the Lord, the God of Israel, and now we may not touch them. This we will do to them, and let them live, lest wrath be upon us, because of the oath which we swore to them." And the

leaders said to them, "Let them live." So they became
hewers of wood and drawers of water for all the
congregation, as the leaders had said of them.

*A Reading (Lesson) from the Letter of Paul
to the Romans* [15:1-13]

We who are strong ought to bear with the failings of the
weak, and not to please ourselves; let each of us please his
neighbor for his good, to edify him. For Christ did not
please himself; but, as it is written, "The reproaches of
those who reproached thee fell on me." For whatever was
written in former days was written for our instruction, that
by steadfastness and by the encouragement of the
scriptures we might have hope. May the God of
steadfastness and encouragement grant you to live in such
harmony with one another, in accord with Christ Jesus,
that together you may with one voice glorify the God and
Father of our Lord Jesus Christ. Welcome one another,
therefore, as Christ has welcomed you, for the glory of
God. For I tell you that Christ became a servant to the
circumcised to show God's truthfulness, in order to
confirm the promises given to the patriarchs, and in order
that the Gentiles might glorify God for his mercy. As it is
written, "Therefore I will praise thee among the Gentiles,
and sing to thy name"; and again it is said, "Rejoice, O
Gentiles, with his people"; and again, "Praise the Lord, all
Gentiles, and let all the peoples praise him"; and further
Isaiah says, "The root of Jesse shall come, he who rises to
rule the Gentiles; in him shall the Gentiles hope." May the
God of hope fill you with all joy and peace in believing, so
that by the power of the Holy Spirit you may abound in
hope.

A Reading (Lesson) from the Gospel according to Matthew
[26:69-75]

Peter was sitting outside in the courtyard. And a maid
came up to him, and said, "You also were with Jesus the

Galilean." But he denied it before them all, saying, "I do not know what you mean." And when he went out to the porch, another maid saw him, and she said to the bystanders, "This man was with Jesus of Nazareth." And again he denied it with an oath, "I do not know the man." After a little while the bystanders came up and said to Peter, "Certainly you are also one of them, for your accent betrays you." Then he began to invoke a curse on himself and to swear, "I do not know the man." And immediately the cock crowed. And Peter remembered the saying of Jesus, "Before the cock crows, you will deny me three times." And he went out and wept bitterly.

Friday

Psalm 40 [page 640], *Psalm 54* [page 659] ❖
Psalm 51 [page 656]

A Reading (Lesson) from the Book of Joshua [9:22—10:15]

Joshua summoned the Gibeonites, and he said to them, "Why did you deceive us, saying, 'We are very far from you,' when you dwell among us? Now therefore you are cursed, and some of you shall always be slaves, hewers of wood and drawers of water for the house of my God." They answered Joshua, "Because it was told to your servants for certainty that the Lord your God had commanded his servant Moses to give you all the land, and to destroy all the inhabitants of the land from before you; so we feared greatly for our lives because of you, and did this thing. And now, behold, we are in your hand: do as it seems good and right in your sight to do to us." So he did to them, and delivered them out of the hand of the people of Israel; and they did not kill them. But Joshua made them that day hewers of wood and drawers of water for the congregation and for the altar of the Lord, to continue to this day, in the place which he should choose. When Ado'ni-ze'dek king of Jerusalem heard how Joshua had taken Ai, and had utterly destroyed it, doing to Ai and its king as he had done to Jericho and its king, and how the inhabitants of Gibeon had made peace with Israel and were among them, he feared greatly, because Gibeon was a great city, like one of the royal cities, and because it was greater than Ai, and all its men were mighty. So Ado′ni-ze′dek king of Jerusalem sent to Hoham king of Hebron, to Piram king of Jarmuth, to Japhi′a king of Lachish, and to Debir king of Eglon, saying, "Come up to me and help me, and let us smite Gibeon; for it has made peace with Joshua and with the people of Israel." Then the five kings of the Amorites, the king of Jerusalem, the king of Hebron, the king of Jarmuth, the king of Lachish, and the king of Eglon, gathered their forces, and went up with all their armies and encamped against Gibeon, and made war against it. And the men of Gibeon sent to Joshua at the camp in Gilgal, saying, "Do not relax your hand from your servants; come up to us quickly, and save us, and help us; for all the kings of the Amorites that dwell in the hill country are gathered against us." So Joshua went up from Gilgal, he and all the people of war with him, and all the mighty men of valor. And the Lord said to Joshua, "Do not fear them, for I have given them into your hands; there shall not a man of them stand before you." So Joshua came upon them suddenly, having marched up all night from Gilgal. And the Lord threw them into a panic before Israel, who slew them with a great slaughter at Gibeon, and chased them by the way of the ascent of Beth-horon, and smote them as far as Aze′kah and Makke′dah. And as they fled before Israel, while they were going down the ascent of Beth-horon, the Lord threw down great stones from heaven upon them as far as Aze′kah, and they died; there were more who died because of the hailstones than the men of Israel killed with the sword. Then spoke Joshua to the Lord in the day when the Lord gave the Amorites over to the men of Israel; and he said in the sight of Israel, "Sun, stand thou still at Gibeon, and thou Moon in the valley of

Aïjalon." And the sun stood still, and the moon stayed, until the nation took vengeance on their enemies. Is this not written in the Book of Jashar? The sun stayed in the midst of heaven, and did not hasten to go down for about a whole day. There has been no day like it before or since, when the Lord hearkened to the voice of a man; for the Lord fought for Israel. Then Joshua returned, and all Israel with him, to the camp at Gilgal.

A Reading (Lesson) from the Letter of Paul to the Romans [15:14-24]

I myself am satisfied about you, my brethren, that you yourselves are full of goodness, filled with all knowledge, and able to instruct one another. But on some points I have written to you very boldly by way of reminder, because of the grace given me by God to be a minister of Christ Jesus to the Gentiles in the priestly service of the gospel of God, so that the offering of the Gentiles may be acceptable, sanctified by the Holy Spirit. In Christ Jesus, then, I have reason to be proud of my work for God. For I will not venture to speak of anything except what Christ has wrought through me to win obedience from the Gentiles, by word and deed, by the power of signs and wonders, by the power of the Holy Spirit, so that from Jerusalem and as far round as Illyr'icum I have fully preached the gospel of Christ, thus making it my ambition to preach the gospel, not where Christ has already been named, lest I build on another man's foundation, but as it is written, "They shall see who have never been told of him, and they shall understand who have never heard of him." This is the reason why I have so often been hindered from coming to you. But now, since I no longer have any room for work in these regions, and since I have longed for many years to come to you, I hope to see you in passing as I go to Spain, and to be sped on my journey there by you, once I have enjoyed your company for a little.

A Reading (Lesson) from the Gospel according to Matthew
[27:1-10]

When morning came, all the chief priests and the elders of the people took counsel against Jesus to put him to death; and thy bound him and led him away and delivered him to Pilate the governor. When Judas, his betrayer, saw that he was condemned, he repented and brought back the thirty pieces of silver to the chief priest and the elders, saying, "I have sinned in betraying innocent blood." They said, "What is that to us? See to it yourself." And throwing down the pieces of silver in the temple, he departed; and he went and hanged himself. But the chief priests, taking the pieces of silver, said, "It is not lawful to put them into the treasury, since they are blood money." So they took counsel, and bought with them the potter's field, to bury strangers in. Therefore that field has been called the Field of Blood to this day. Then was fulfilled what had been spoken by the prophet Jeremiah, saying, "And they took the thirty pieces of silver, the price of him on whom a price had been set by some of the sons of Israel, and they gave them for the potter's field, as the Lord directed me."

Saturday

Psalm 55 [page 660]   ❖   *Psalm 138* [page 793],
Psalm 139:1-17(18-23) [page 794]

A Reading (Lesson) from the Book of Joshua [23:1-16]

A long time afterward, when the Lord had given rest to Israel from all their enemies round about, and Joshua was old and well advanced in years, Joshua summoned all Israel, their elders and heads, their judges and officers, and said to them, "I am now old and well advanced in years; and you have seen all that the Lord your God has done to all these nations for your sake, for it is the Lord your God who has fought for you. Behold, I have allotted to you as an inheritance for your tribes those nations that remain, along with all the nations that I have already cut off, from the Jordan to the Great Sea in the west. The Lord your God will push them back before you, and drive them out of your sight; and you shall possess their land, as the Lord your God promised you. Therefore be very steadfast to keep and do all that is written in the book of the law of Moses, turning aside from it neither to the right hand nor to the left, that you may not be mixed with these nations left here among you, or make mention of the names of their gods, or swear by them, or serve them, or bow down yourselves to them, but cleave to the Lord your God as you have done to this day. For the Lord has driven out before you great and strong nations; and as for you, no man has been able to withstand you to this day. One man of you puts to flight a thousand, since it is the Lord your God who fights for you, as he promised you. Take good heed to yourselves, therefore, to love the Lord your God. For if you turn back, and join the remnant of these nations left here among you, and make marriages with them, so that you marry their women and they yours, know assuredly that the Lord your God will not continue to drive out these nations before you; but they shall be a snare and a trap for you, a scourge on your sides, and thorns in your eyes, till you perish from off this good land which the Lord your God has given you. And now I am about to go the way of all the earth, and you know in your hearts and souls, all of you, that not one thing has failed of all the good things which the Lord your God promised concerning you; all have come to pass for you, not one of them has failed. But just as all the good things which the Lord your God promised concerning you have been fulfilled for you, so the Lord will bring upon you all the evil things, until he has destroyed you from off this good land which the Lord your God has given you, if you transgress the covenant of the Lord your God, which he commanded you, and go and serve other gods and bow down to them. Then the anger of the Lord will be kindled against you, and you shall perish quickly from off the good land which he has given to you."

*A Reading (Lesson) from the Letter of Paul
to the Romans* [15:25-33]

At present, however, I am going to Jerusalem with aid for
the saints. For Macedo'nia and Acha'ia have been pleased
to make some contribution for the poor among the saints
at Jerusalem; they were pleased to do it, and indeed they
are in debt to them, for if the Gentiles have come to share
in their spiritual blessings, they ought also to be of service
to them in material blessings. When therefore I have
completed this, and have delivered to them what has been
raised, I shall go on by way of you to Spain; and I know
that when I come to you I shall come in the fulness of the
blessing of Christ. I appeal to you, brethren, by our Lord
Jesus Christ and by the love of the Spirit, to strive together
with me in your prayers to God on my behalf, that I may
be delivered from the unbelievers in Judea, and that my
service for Jerusalem may be acceptable to the saints, so
that by God's will I may come to you with joy and be
refreshed in your company. The God of peace be with you
all. Amen.

A Reading (Lesson) from the Gospel according to Matthew
[27:11-23]

Jesus stood before the governor; and the governor asked
him, "Are you the King of the Jews?" Jesus said, "You
have said so." But when he was accused by the chief priests
and elders, he made no answer. Then Pilate said to him,
"Do you not hear how many things they testify against
you?" But he gave him no answer, not even to a single
charge; so that the governor wondered greatly. Now at the
feast the governor was accustomed to release for the crowd
any one prisoner whom they wanted. And they had then a
notorious prisoner, called Barab'bas. So when they had
gathered, Pilate said to them, "Whom do you want me to
release for you, Barab'bas or Jesus who is called Christ?"

For he knew that it was out of envy that they had delivered him up. Besides, while he was sitting on the judgment seat, his wife sent word to him, "Have nothing to do with that righteous man, for I have suffered much over him today in a dream." Now the chief priests and the elders persuaded the people to ask for Barab'bas and destroy Jesus. The governor again said to them, "Which of the two do you want me to release for you?" And they said, "Barab'bas." Pilate said to them, "Then what shall I do with Jesus who is called Christ?" They all said, "Let him be crucified." And he said, "Why, what evil has he done?" But they shouted all the more, "Let him be crucified."

Proper 12   *Week of the Sunday closest to July 27*

Sunday

Psalm 24 [page 613],   *Psalm 29* [page 620]   ❖
Psalm 8 [page 592],   *Psalm 84* [page 707]

A Reading (Lesson) from the Book of Joshua [24:1-15]

Joshua gathered all the tribes of Israel to Shechem, and summoned the elders, the heads, the judges, and the officers of Israel; and they presented themselves before God. And Joshua said to all the people, "Thus says the Lord, the God of Israel, 'Your father lived of old beyond the Eu-phra'tes, Terah, the father of Abraham and of Nahor; and they served other gods. Then I took your father Abraham from beyond the River and led him through all the land of Canaan, and made his offspring many. I gave him Isaac; and to Isaac I gave Jacob and Esau. And I gave Esau the hill country of Se'ir to possess, but Jacob and his children went down to Egypt. And I sent Moses and Aaron, and I plagued Egypt with what I did in the midst of it; and afterwards I brought you out. Then I brought your fathers out of Egypt, and you came to the sea; and the Egyptians pursued your fathers with chariots and horsemen to the Red Sea. And when they cried to the Lord, he put darkness between you and the Egyptians, and made the sea come upon them and cover them; and your eyes saw what I did to Egypt; and you lived in the wilderness a long time. Then I brought you to the land of the Amorites, who lived on the other side of the Jordan; they fought with you, and I gave them into your hand, and you took possession of their land, and I destroyed them before you. Then Balak the son of Zippor, king of Moab, arose and fought against Israel; and he sent and invited Balaam the son of Be'or to curse you, but I would not listen to Balaam; therefore he blessed you; so I delivered you out of his hand. And you went over the Jordan and came to Jericho, and the men of Jericho fought against you, and also the Amorites, the Per'izzites, the Canaanites, the Hittites, the Gir'gashites, the Hivites, and the Jeb'usites; and I gave them into your hand. And I sent the hornet before you, which drove them out before you, the two kings of the Amorites; it was not by your sword or by your bow. I gave you a land on which you had not labored, and cities which you had not built, and you dwell therein; you eat the fruit of vineyards and oliveyards which you did not plant.' Now therefore fear the Lord, and serve him in sincerity and in faithfulness; put away the gods which your fathers served beyond the River, and in Egypt, and serve the Lord. And if you be unwilling to serve the Lord, choose this day whom you will serve, whether the gods your fathers served in the region beyond the River, or the gods of the Amorites in whose land you dwell; but as for me and my house, we will serve the Lord."

A Reading (Lesson) from the Acts of the Apostles
[28:23-31]

When the local leaders of the Jews had appointed a day for Paul to speak to them, they came to him at his lodging in great numbers. And he expounded the matter to them from morning till evening, testifying to the kingdom of God and trying to convince them about Jesus both from the law of Moses and from the prophets. And some were convinced by what he said, while others disbelieved. So, as they disagreed among themselves, they departed, after Paul had made one statement: "The Holy Spirit was right in saying to your fathers through Isaiah the prophet: 'Go to this people, and say, You shall indeed hear but never understand, and you shall indeed see but never perceive. For this people's heart has grown dull, and their ears are heavy of hearing, and their eyes they have closed; lest they should perceive with their eyes, and hear with their ears, and understand with their heart, and turn for me to heal them.' Let it be known to you then that this salvation of God has been sent to the Gentiles; they will listen." And he lived there two whole years at his own expense, and welcomed all who came to him, preaching the kingdom of God and teaching about the Lord Jesus Christ quite openly and unhindered.

A Reading (Lesson) from the Gospel according to Mark
[2:23-28]

One sabbath Jesus was going through the grainfields; and as they made their way his disciples began to pluck heads of grain. And the Pharisees said to him, "Look, why are they doing what is not lawful on the sabbath?" And he said to them, "Have you never read what David did, when he was in need and was hungry, he and those who were with him: how he entered the house of God, when Abi'athar was high priest, and ate the bread of the Presence, which is not lawful for any but the priests to eat, and also gave it to those who were with him?" And he said to them, "The sabbath was made for man, not man for the Sabbath; so the Son of man is lord even of the sabbath."

Monday

Psalm 56 [page 662],   *Psalm 57* [page 663],
(Psalm 58 [page 664])   ❖   *Psalm 64* [page 671],
Psalm 65 [page 672]

A Reading (Lesson) from the Book of Joshua [24:16-33]

The people answered Joshua, "Far be it from us that we should forsake the Lord, to serve other gods; for it is the Lord our God who brought us and our fathers up from the land of Egypt, out of the house of bondage, and who did those great signs in our sight, and preserved us in all the way that we went, and among all the peoples through whom we passed; and the Lord drove out before us all the peoples, the Amorites who lived in the land; therefore we also will serve the Lord, for he is our God." But Joshua said to the people, "You cannot serve the Lord; for he is a holy God; he is a jealous God; he will not forgive your transgressions or your sins. If you forsake the Lord and serve foreign gods, he will turn and do you harm, and consume you, after having done you good." And the poeple said to Joshua, "Nay; but we will serve the Lord." Then Joshua said to the people, "You are witnesses against yourselves that you have chosen the Lord, to serve him." And they said, "We are witnesses." He said, "Then put away the foreign gods which are among you, and incline your heart to the Lord, the God of Israel." And the people said to Joshua, "The Lord our God we will serve, and his voice we will obey." So Joshua made a covenant with the people that day, and made statutes and ordinances for them at Shechem. And Joshua wrote these words in the book of the law of God; and he took a great stone, and set it up there under the oak in the sanctuary of the Lord. And Joshua said to all the people, "Behold, this stone shall be a witness against us; for it has heard all the words of the Lord which he spoke to us; therefore it shall be a witness against you, lest you deal falsely with your God." So

Joshua sent the people away, every man to his inheritance. After these things Joshua the son of Nun, the servant of the Lord, died, being a hundred and ten years old. And they buried him in his own inheritance at Tim'nath-se'rah, which is in the hill country of E'phraim, north of the mountain of Ga'ash. And Israel served the Lord all the days of Joshua, and all the days of the elders who outlived Joshua and had known all the work which the Lord did for Israel. The bones of Joseph which the people of Israel brought up from Egypt were buried at Shechem, in the portion of ground which Jacob bought from the sons of Hamor the father of Shechem for a hundred pieces of money; it became an inheritance of the descendants of Joseph. And Elea'zar the son of Aaron died; and they buried him at Gib'e-ah, the town of Phin'ehas his son, which had been given him in the hill country of E'phraim.

A Reading (Lesson) from the Letter of Paul to the Romans [16:1-16]

I commend to you our sister Phoebe, a deaconess of the church at Cen'chre-ae, that you may receive her in the Lord as befits the saints, and help her in whatever she may require from you, for she has been a helper of many and of myself as well. Greet Prisca and Aquila, my fellow workers in Christ Jesus, who risked their necks for my life, to whom not only I but also all the churches of the Gentiles give thanks; greet also the church in their house. Greet my beloved Epae'netus, who was the first convert in Asia for Christ. Greet Mary, who has worked hard among you. Greet Androni'cus and Ju'nias, my kinsmen and my fellow prisoners; they are men of note among the apostles, and they were in Christ before me. Greet Amplia'tus, my beloved in the Lord. Greet Urba'nus, our fellow worker in Christ, and my beloved Stachys. Greet Apel'les, who is approved in Christ. Greet those who belong to the family of Aristobu'lus. Greet my kinsman Hero'dion. Greet those in the Lord who belong to the family of Narcis'sus. Greet

those workers in the Lord, Tryphae'na and Trypho'sa.
Greet the beloved Persis, who has worked hard in the
Lord. Greet Rufus, eminent in the Lord, also his mother
and mine. Greet Asyn'critus, Phlegon, Hermes, Pat'robas,
Hermas, and the brethren who are with them. Greet
Philol'ogus, Julia, Nereus and his sister, and Olym'pas, and
all the saints who are with them. Greet one another with a
holy kiss. All the churches of Christ greet you.

A Reading (Lesson) from the Gospel according to Matthew
[27:24-31]

When Pilate saw that he was gaining nothing, but rather
that a riot was beginning, he took water and washed his
hands before the crowd, saying, "I am innocent of this
man's blood; see to it yourselves." And all the people
answered, "His blood be on us and on our children!" Then
he released for them Barab'bas, and having scourged Jesus,
delivered him to be crucified. Then the soldiers of the
governor took Jesus into the praetorium, and they
gathered the whole battalion before him. And they
stripped him and put a scarlet robe upon him, and plaiting
a crown of thorns they put it on his head, and put a reed in
his right hand. And kneeling before him they mocked him,
saying, "Hail, King of the Jews!" And they spat upon him,
and took the reed and struck him on the head. And when
they had mocked him, they stripped him of the robe, and
put his own clothes on him, and led him away to crucify him

Tuesday

Psalm 61 [page 668], *Psalm 62* [page 669] ❖
Psalm 68:1-20(21-23)24-36 [page 676]

A Reading (Lesson) from the Book of Judges [2:1-5,11-23]

The angel of the Lord went up from Gilgal to Bochim. And
he said, "I brought you up from Egypt, and brought you

into the land which I swore to give to your fathers. I said, 'I will never break my covenant with you, and you shall make no covenant with the inhabitants of this land; you shall break down their altars.' But you have not obeyed my command. What is this you have done? So now I say, I will not drive them out before you; but they shall become adversaries to you, and their gods shall be a snare to you." When the angel of the Lord spoke these words to all the people of Israel, the people lifted up their voices and wept. And they called the name of that place Bochim; and they sacrificed there to the Lord. And the people of Israel did what was evil in the sight of the Lord and served the Ba'als; and they forsook the Lord, the God of their fathers, who had brought them out of the land of Egypt; they went after other gods, from among the gods of the peoples who were round about them, and bowed down to them; and they provoked the Lord to anger. They forsook the Lord, and served the Ba'als and the Ash'taroth. So the anger of the Lord was kindled against Israel, and he gave them over to plunderers, who plundered them; and he sold them into the power of their enemies round about, so that they could no longer withstand their enemies. Whenever they marched out, the hand of the Lord was against them for evil, as the Lord had warned, and as the Lord had sworn to them; and they were in sore straits. Then the Lord raised up judges, who saved them out of the power of those who plundered them. And yet they did not listen to their judges; for they played the harlot after other gods and bowed down to them; they soon turned aside from the way in which their fathers had walked, who had obeyed the commandments of the Lord, and they did not do so. Whenever the Lord raised up judges for them, the Lord was with the judge, and he saved them from the hand of their enemies all the days of the judge; for the Lord was moved to pity by their groaning because of those who afflicted and oppressed them. But whenever the judge died, they turned back and behaved worse than their fathers, going after other gods, serving them and bowing down to them; they did not drop any of their practices or their stubborn ways. So the anger of the Lord was kindled against Israel; and he said, "Because this people have transgressed my covenant, which I commanded their fathers, and have not obeyed my voice, I will not henceforth drive out before them any of the nations that Joshua left when he died, that by them I may test Israel, whether they will take care to walk in the way of the Lord as their fathers did, or not." So the Lord left those nations, not driving them out at once, and he did not give them into the power of Joshua.

A Reading (Lesson) from the Letter of Paul to the Romans [16:17-27]

I appeal to you, brethren, to take note of those who create dissensions and difficulties, in opposition to the doctrine which you have been taught; avoid them. For such persons do not serve our Lord Christ, but their own appetites, and by fair and flattering words they deceive the hearts of the simple-minded. For while your obedience is known to all, so that I rejoice over you, I would have you wise as to what is good and guileless as to what is evil; then the God of peace will soon crush Satan under your feet. The grace of our Lord Jesus Christ be with you. Timothy, my fellow worker, greets you; so do Lucius and Jason and Sosip'ater, my kinsmen. I Tertius, the writer of this letter, greet you in the Lord. Ga'ius, who is host to me and to the whole church, greets you. Eras'tus, the city treasurer, and our brother Quartus, greet you. Now to him who is able to strengthen you, according to my gospel and the preaching of Jesus Christ, according to the revelation of the mystery which was kept secret for long ages but is now disclosed and through the prophetic writings is made known to all nations, according to the command of the eternal God, to bring about the obedience of faith—to the only wise God be glory for evermore through Jesus Christ! Amen.

A Reading (Lesson) from the Gospel according to Matthew
[27:32-44]

As the soldiers and Jesus went out of the praetorium, they
came upon a man of Cyre'ne, Simon by name; this man
they compelled to carry Jesus' cross. And when they came
to a place called Gol'gotha (which means the place of a
skull), they offered him wine to drink, mingled with gall;
but when he tasted it, he would not drink it. And when
they had crucified him, they divided his garments among
them by casting lots; then they sat down and kept watch
over him there. And over his head they put the charge
against him, which read, "This is Jesus the King of the
Jews." Then two robbers were crucified with him, one on
the right and one on the left. And those who passed by
derided him, wagging their heads and saying, "You who
would destroy the temple and build it in three days, save
yourself! If you are the Son of God, come down from the
cross." So also the chief priests, with the scribes and elders,
mocked him, saying, "He saved others; he cannot save
himself. He is the King of Israel; let him come down from
the cross, and we will believe in him. He trusts in God; let
God deliver him now, if he desires him; for he said, 'I am
the Son of God.'" And the robbers who were crucified with
him also reviled him in the same way.

Wednesday

Psalm 72 [page 685]   ❖   *Psalm 119:73-96* [page 769]

A Reading (Lesson) from the Book of Judges [3:12-30]

The people of Israel again did what was evil in the sight of
the Lord; and the Lord strengthened Eglon the king of
Moab against Israel, because they had done what was evil
in the sight of the Lord. He gathered to himself the
Ammonites and the Amal'ekites, and went and defeated
Israel; and they took possession of the city of palms. And

the people of Israel served Eglon the king of Moab eighteen years. But when the people of Israel cried to the Lord, the Lord raised up for them a deliverer, Ehud, the son of Gera, the Benjaminite, a left-handed man. The people of Israel sent tribute by him to Eglon the king of Moab. And Ehud made for himself a sword with two edges, a cubit in length; and he girded it on his right thigh under his clothes. And he presented the tribute to Eglon king of Moab. Now Eglon was a very fat man. And when Ehud had finished presenting the tribute, he sent away the people that carried the tribute. But he himself turned back at the sculptured stones near Gilgal, and said, "I have a secret message for you, O king." And he commanded, "Silence." And all his attendants went out from his presence. And Ehud came to him, as he was sitting alone in his cool roof chamber. And Ehud said, "I have a message from God for you." And he arose from his seat. And Ehud reached with his left hand, took the sword from his right thigh, and thrust it into his belly; and the hilt also went in after the blade, and the fat closed over the blade, for he did not draw the sword out of his belly; and the dirt came out. Then Ehud went out into the vestibule, and closed the doors of the roof chamber upon him, and locked them. When he had gone, the servants came; and when they saw that the doors of the roof chamber were locked, they thought, "He is only relieving himself in the closet of the cool chamber." And they waited till they were utterly at a loss; but when he still did not open the doors of the roof chamber, they took the key and opened them; and there lay their lord dead on the floor. Ehud escaped while they delayed, and passed beyond the sculptured stones, and escaped to Se-i'rah. When he arrived, he sounded the trumpet in the hill country of E'phraim; and the people of Israel went down with him from the hill country, having him at their head. And he said to them, "Follow after me; for the Lord has given your enemies the Moabites into your hand." So they went down after him, and seized the fords of the Jordan against the Moabites, and allowed not a man to pass over. And they killed at that time about ten thousand of the Moabites, all strong, able-bodied men; not a man escaped. So Moab was subdued that day under the hand of Israel. And the land had rest for eighty years.

A Reading (Lesson) from the Acts of the Apostles [1:1-14]

In the first book, O The-oph'ilus, I have dealt with all that Jesus began to do and teach, until the day when he was taken up, after he had given commandment through the Holy Spirit to the apostles whom he had chosen. To them he presented himself alive after his passion by many proofs, appearing to them during forty days, and speaking of the kingdom of God. And while staying with them he charged them not to depart from Jerusalem, but to wait for the promise of the Father, which, he said, "you heard from me, for John baptized with water, but before many days you shall be baptized with the Holy Spirit." So when they had come together, they asked him, "Lord, will you at this time restore the kingdom to Israel?" He said to them, "It is not for you to know times or seasons which the Father has fixed by his own authority. But you shall receive power when the Holy Spirit has come upon you; and you shall be my witnesses in Jerusalem and in all Judea and Samar'ia and to the end of the earth." And when he had said this, as they were looking on, he was lifted up, and a cloud took him out of their sight. And while they were gazing into heaven as he went, behold, two men stood by them in white robes, and said, "Men of Galilee, why do you stand looking into heaven? This Jesus, who was taken up from you into heaven, will come in the same way as you saw him go into heaven." Then they returned to Jerusalem from the mount called Olivet, which is near Jerusalem, a sabbath day's journey away; and when they had entered, they went up to the upper room, where they were staying, Peter and John and James and Andrew, Philip and Thomas, Bartholomew and Matthew, James the son of

Alphaeus and Simon the Zealot and Judas the son of James. All these with one accord devoted themselves to prayer, together with the women and Mary the mother of Jesus, and with his brothers.

A Reading (Lesson) from the Gospel according to Matthew [27:45-54]

From the sixth hour there was darkness over all the land until the ninth hour. And about the ninth hour Jesus cried with a loud voice, "Eli, Eli, la'ma sabach-tha'ni?" that is, "My God, my God, why hast thou forsaken me?" And some of the bystanders hearing it said, "This man is calling Eli'jah." And one of them at once ran and took a sponge, filled it with vinegar, and put it on a reed, and gave it to him to drink. But the others said, "Wait, let us see whether Eli'jah will come to save him." And Jesus cried again with a loud voice and yielded up his spirit. And behold, the curtain of the temple was torn in two, from top to bottom; and the earth shook, and the rocks were split; the tombs also were opened, and many bodies of the saints who had fallen asleep were raised, and coming out of the tombs after his resurrection they went into the holy city and appeared to many. When the centurion and those who were with him, keeping watch over Jesus, saw the earthquake and what took place, they were filled with awe, and said, "Truly this was the Son of God!"

Thursday

(Psalm 70 [page 682]), *Psalm 71* [page 683] ❖ *Psalm 74* [page 689]

A Reading (Lesson) from the Book of Judges [4:4-23]

Deb'orah, a prophetess, the wife of Lap'pidoth, was judging Israel at that time. She used to sit under the palm of Deb'orah between Ramah and Bethel in the hill country of E'phraim; and the people of Israel came up to her for judgment. She sent and summoned Barak the son of Abin'o-am from Kedesh in Naph'tali, and said to him, "The Lord, the God of Israel, commands you, 'Go, gather your men at Mount Tabor, taking ten thousand from the tribe of Naph'tali and the tribe of Zeb'ulun. And I will draw out Sis'era, the general of Jabin's army, to meet you by the river Kishon with his chariots and his troops; and I will give him into your hand.'" Barak said to her, "If you will go with me, I will go; but if you will not go with me, I will not go." And she said, "I will surely go with you; nevertheless, the road on which you are going will not lead to your glory, for the Lord will sell Sis'era into the hand of a woman." Then Deb'orah arose, and went with Barak to Kedesh. And Barak summoned Zeb'ulun and Naph'tali to Kedesh; and ten thousand men went up at his heels; and Deb'orah went up wth him. Now Heber the Ken'ite had separated from the Ken'ites, the descendants of Hobab the father-in-law of Moses, and had pitched his tent as far away as the oak in Za-anan'nim, which is near Kedesh. When Sis'era was told that Barak the son of Abin'o-am had gone up to Mount Tabor, Sis'era called out all his chariots, nine hundred chariots of iron, and all the men who were with him, from Haro'sheth-ha-goiim to the river Kishon. And Deb'orah said to Barak, "Up! For this is the day in which the Lord has given Sis'era into your hand. Does not the Lord go out before you?" So Barak went down from Mount Tabor with ten thousand men following him. And the Lord routed Sis'era and all his chariots and all his army before Barak at the edge of the sword; and Sis'era alighted from his chariot and fled away on foot. And Barak pursued the chariots and the army to Haro'sheth-ha-goiim, and all the army of Sis'era fell by the edge of the sword; not a man was left. But Sis'era fled away on foot to the tent of Ja'el, the wife of Heber the Ken'ite; for there was peace between Jabin the king of Hazor and the house of Heber the Ken'ite.

And Ja'el came out to meet Sis'era, and said to him, "Turn aside, my lord, turn aside to me; have no fear." So he turned aside to her into the tent, and she covered him with a rug. And he said to her, "Pray, give me a little water to drink; for I am thirsty." So she opened a skin of milk and gave him a drink and covered him. And he said to her, "Stand at the door of the tent, and if any man comes and asks you, 'Is any one here?' say, No." But Ja'el the wife of Heber took a tent peg, and took a hammer in her hand, and went softly to him and drove the peg into his temple, till it went down into the ground, as he was lying fast asleep from weariness. So he died. And behold, as Barak pursued Sis'era, Ja'el went out to meet him, and said to him, "Come, and I will show you the man whom you are seeking." So he went in to her tent; and there lay Sis'era dead, with the tent peg in his temple. So on that day God subdued Jabin the king of Canaan before the people of Israel.

A Reading (Lesson) from the Acts of the Apostles [1:15-26]

In those days Peter stood up among the brethren (the company of persons was about a hundred and twenty), and said, "Brethren, the scripture had to be fulfilled, which the Holy Spirit spoke beforehand by the mouth of David, concerning Judas who was guide to those who arrested Jesus. For he was numbered among us, and was allotted his share in this ministry. (Now this man bought a field with the reward of his wickedness; and falling headlong he burst open in the middle and all his bowels gushed out. And it became known to all the inhabitants of Jerusalem, so that the field was called in their language Akel'dama, that is, Field of Blood.) For it is written in the book of Psalms, 'Let the habitation become desolate, and let there be no one to live in it'; and 'His office let another take.' So one of the men who have accompanied us during all the time that the Lord Jesus went in and out among us; beginning from the baptism of John until the day when he was taken up from us—one of these men must become with us a witness to his resurrection." And they put forward two, Joseph called Barsabbas, who was surnamed Justus, and Matthi'as. And they prayed and said, "Lord, who knowest the hearts of all men, show which one of these two thou hast chosen to take the place in this ministry and apostleship from which Judas turned aside, to go to his own place." And they cast lots for them, and the lot fell on Matthi'as; and he was enrolled with the eleven apostles.

A Reading (Lesson) from the Gospel according to Matthew [27:55-66]

There were also many women at Gol'gotha, looking on from afar, who had followed Jesus from Galilee, ministering to him; among whom were Mary Mag'dalene, and Mary the mother of James and Joseph, and the mother of the sons of Zeb'edee. When it was evening, there came a rich man from Arimathe'a, named Joseph, who also was a disciple of Jesus. He went to Pilate and asked for the body of Jesus. Then Pilate ordered it to be given to him. And Joseph took the body, and wrapped it in a clean linen shroud, and laid it in his own new tomb, which he had hewn in the rock; and he rolled a great stone to the door of the tomb, and departed. Mary Mag'dalene and the other Mary were there, sitting opposite the sepulchre. Next day, that is, after the day of Preparation, the chief priests and the Pharisees gathered before the Pilate and said, "Sir, we remember how that imposter said, while he was still alive, 'After three days I will rise again.' Therefore order the sepulchre to be made secure until the third day, lest his disciples go and steal him away, and tell the people, 'He has risen from the dead,' and the last fraud will be worse than the first." Pilate said to them, "You have a guard of soldiers; go, make it as secure as you can." So they went and made the sepulchre secure by sealing the stone and setting a guard.

Friday

Psalm 69:1-23(24-30)31-38 [page 679] ❖
Psalm 73 [page 687]

A Reading (Lesson) from the Book of Judges [5:1-18]

Then sang Deb'orah and Barak the son of Abin'o-am on the day Jabin the king of Hazor was killed: "That the leaders took the lead in Israel, that the people offered themselves willingly, bless the Lord! Hear, O kings; give ear, O princes; to the Lord I will sing, I will make melody to the Lord, the God of Israel. Lord, when thou didst go forth from Se'ir, when thou didst march from the region of Edom, the earth trembled, and the heavens dropped, yea, the clouds dropped water. The mountains quaked before the Lord, yon Sinai before the Lord, the God of Israel. In the days of Shamgar, son of Anath, in the days of Ja'el, caravans ceased and the travelers kept to the byways. The peasantry ceased in Israel, they ceased until you arose, Deb'orah, arose as a mother in Israel. When new gods were chosen, then war was in the gates. Was shield or spear to be seen among forty thousand in Israel? My heart goes out to the commanders of Israel who offered themselves willingly among the people. Bless the Lord. Tell of it, you who ride on tawny asses, you who sit on rich carpets and you who walk by the way. To the sound of musicians at the watering places, there they repeat the triumphs of the Lord, the triumphs of his peasantry in Israel. Then down to the gates marched the people of the Lord. Awake, awake, Deb'orah! Awake, awake, utter a song! Arise, Barak, lead away your captives, O son of Abin'o-am. Then down marched the remnant of the noble; the people of the Lord marched down for him against the mighty. From E'phraim they set out thither into the valley, following you, Benjamin, with your kinsmen; from Machir marched down the commanders, and from Zeb'ulun those who bear the marshal's staff; the princes of Is'sachar came with

Deb'orah, and Is'sachar faithful to Barak; into the valley
they rushed forth at his heels. Among the clans of Reuben
there were great searchings of heart. Why did you tarry
among the sheepfolds, to hear the piping for the flocks?
Among the clans of Reuben there were great searchings of
heart. Gilead stayed beyond the Jordan; and Dan, why did
he abide with the ships? Asher sat still at the coast of the
sea, settling down by his landings. Zeb'ulun is a people that
jeoparded their lives to the death; Naph'tali too, on the
heights of the field."

A Reading (Lesson) from the Acts of the Apostles [2:1-21]

When the day of Pentecost had come, they were all
together in one place. And suddenly a sound came from
heaven like the rush of a mighty wind, and it filled all the
house where they were sitting. And there appeared to them
tongues as of fire, distributed and resting on each one of
them. And they were all filled with the Holy Spirit and
began to speak in other tongues, as the Spirit gave them
utterance. Now there were dwelling in Jerusalem Jews,
devout men from every nation under heaven. And at this
sound the multitude came together, and they were
bewildered, because each one heard them speaking in his
own language. And they were amazed and wondered,
saying, "Are not all these who are speaking Galileans? And
how is it that we hear, each of us in his own native
language? Par'thians and Medes and Elamites and residents
of Mesopota'mia, Judea and Cappado'cia, Pontus and Asia,
Phryg'ia and Pamphyl'ia, Egypt and the parts of Libya
belonging to Cyre'ne, and visitors from Rome, both Jews
and proselytes, Cretans and Arabians, we hear them telling
in our own tongues the mighty works of God." And all
were amazed and perplexed, saying to one another, "What
does this mean?" But others mocking said, "They are filled
with new wine." But Peter, standing with the eleven, lifted
up his voice and addressed them, "Men of Judea and all
who dwell in Jerusalem, let this be known to you, and give

ear to my words. For these men are not drunk, as you suppose, since it is only the third hour of the day; but this is what was spoken by the prophet Jo'el: 'And in the last days it shall be, God declares, that I will pour out my Spirit upon all flesh, and your sons and your daughters shall prophesy, and your young men shall see visions, and your old men shall dream dreams; yea, and on my menservants and my maidservants in those days I will pour out my Spirit; and they shall prophesy. And I will show wonders in the heaven above and signs on the earth beneath, blood, and fire, and vapor of smoke; the sun shall be turned into darkness and the moon into blood, before the day of the Lord comes, the great and manifest day. And it shall be that whoever calls on the name of the Lord shall be saved.' "

A Reading (Lesson) from the Gospel according to Matthew [28:1-10]

After the sabbath, toward the dawn of the first day of the week, Mary Mag'dalene and the other Mary went to see the sepulchre. And behold, there was a great earthquake; for an angel of the Lord descended from heaven and came and rolled back the stone, and sat upon it. His appearance was like lightning, and his raiment white as snow. And for fear of him the guards trembled and became like dead men. But the angel said to the women, "Do not be afraid; for I know that you seek Jesus who was crucified. He is not here; for he has risen, as he said. Come, see the place where he lay. Then go quickly and tell his disciples that he has risen from the dead, and behold, he is going before you to Galilee; there you will see him. Lo, I have told you." So they departed quickly from the tomb with fear and great joy, and ran to tell his disciples. And behold, Jesus met them and said, "Hail!" And they came up and took hold of his feet and worshiped him. Then Jesus said to them, "Do not be afraid; go and tell my brethren to go to Galilee, and there they will see me."

Saturday

Psalm 75 [page 691],   *Psalm 76* [page 692]   ❖
Psalm 23 [page 612],   *Psalm 27* [page 617]

A Reading (Lesson) from the Book of Judges [5:19-31]

Then sang Deb'orah and Barak the son of Abin'o-am on the day Jabin the king of Hazor was killed: "The kings came, they fought; then fought the kings of Canaan, at Ta'anach, by the waters of Megid'do; they got no spoils of silver. From heaven fought the stars, from their courses they fought against Sis'era. The torrent Kishon swept them away, the onrushing torrent, the torrent Kishon. March on, my soul, with might! Then loud beat the horses' hoofs with the galloping, galloping of his steeds. Curse Meroz, says the angel of the Lord, curse bitterly its inhabitants, because they came not to the help of the Lord, to the help of the Lord against the mighty. Most blessed of women be Ja'el, the wife of Heber the Ken'ite, of tent-dwelling women most blessed. He asked water and she gave him milk, she brought him curds in a lordly bowl. She put her hand to the tent peg and her right hand to the workmen's mallet; she struck Sis'era a blow, she crushed his head, she shattered and pierced his temple. He sank, he fell, he lay still at her feet; at her feet he sank, he fell; where he sank, there he fell dead. Out of the window she peered, the mother of Sis'era gazed through the lattice: 'Why is his chariot so long in coming? Why tarry the hoofbeats of his chariots?' Her wisest ladies make answer, nay, she gives answer to herself, 'Are they not finding and dividing the spoil?—A maiden or two for every man; spoil of dyed stuffs for Sis'era, spoil of dyed stuffs embroidered, two pieces of dyed work embroidered for my neck as spoil?' So perish all thine enemies, O Lord! But thy friends be like the sun as he rises in his might." And the land had rest for forty years.

A Reading (Lesson) from the Acts of the Apostles [2:22-36]

Peter, standing with the eleven, lifted up his voice and addressed the devout men, "Men of Israel, hear these words: Jesus of Nazareth, a man attested to you by God with mighty works and wonders and signs which God did through him in your midst, as you yourselves know—this Jesus, delivered up according to the definite plan and foreknowledge of God, you crucified and killed by the hands of lawless men. But God raised him up, having loosed the pangs of death, because it was not possible for him to be held by it. For David says concerning him, 'I saw the Lord always before me, for he is at my right hand that I may not be shaken; therefore my heart was glad, and my tongue rejoiced; moreover my flesh will dwell in hope. For thou wilt not abandon my soul to Hades, nor let the Holy One see corruption. Thou hast made known to me the ways of life; thou wilt make me full of gladness with thy presence.' Brethren, I may say to you confidently of the patriarch David that he both died and was buried, and his tomb is with us to this day. Being therefore a prophet, and knowing that God had sworn with an oath to him that he would set one of his descendants upon his throne, he foresaw and spoke of the resurrection of the Christ, that he was not abandoned to Hades, nor did his flesh see corruption. This Jesus God raised up, and of that we all are witnesses. Being therefore exalted at the right hand of God, and having received from the Father the promise of the Holy Spirit, he has poured out this which you see and hear. For David did not ascend into the heavens; but he himself says, 'The Lord said to my Lord, Sit at my right hand, till I make thy enemies a stool for thy feet.' Let all the house of Israel therefore know assuredly that God has made him both Lord and Christ, this Jesus whom you crucified."

A Reading (Lesson) from the Gospel according to Matthew
[28:11-20]

While the women were going to tell the disciples, behold, some of the guard went into the city and told the chief priests all that had taken place. And when they had assembled with the elders and taken counsel, they gave a sum of money to the soldiers and said, "Tell people, 'His disciples came by night and stole him away while we were asleep.' And if this comes to the governor's ears, we will satisfy him and keep you out of trouble." So they took the money and did as they were directed; and this story has been spread among the Jews to this day. Now the eleven disciples went to Galilee, to the mountain to which Jesus had directed them. And when they saw him they worshiped him; but some doubted. And Jesus came and said to them, "All authority in heaven and on earth has been given to me. Go therefore and make disciples of all nations, baptizing them in the name of the Father and of the Son and of the Holy Spirit, teaching them to observe all that I have commanded you; and lo, I am with you always, to the close of the age."

Proper 13 *Week of the Sunday closest to August 3*

Sunday

Psalm 93 [page 722], *Psalm 96* [page 725] ❖
Psalm 34 [page 627]

A Reading (Lesson) from the Book of Judges [6:1-24]

The people of Israel did what was evil in the sight of the Lord; and the Lord gave them into the hand of Midʹian seven years. And the hand of Midʹian prevailed over Israel; and because of Midʹian the people of Israel made for themselves the dens which are in the mountains, and the caves and the strongholds. For whenever Israelites put in seed the Mid'ianites and the Amal'ekites and the people of the East would come up and attack them; they would encamp against them and destroy the produce of the land, as far as the neighborhood of Gaza, and leave no sustenance in Israel, and no sheep or ox or ass. For they would come up with their cattle and their tents, coming like locusts for number; both they and their camels could not be counted; so that they wasted the land as they came in. And Israel was brought very low because of Mid'ian; and the people of Israel cried for help to the Lord. When the people of Israel cried to the Lord on account of the Mid'ianites, the Lord sent a prophet to the people of Israel; and he said to them, "Thus says the Lord, the God of Israel: I led you up from Egypt, and brought you out of the house of bondage; and I delivered you from the hand of the Egyptians, and from the hand of all who oppressed you, and drove them out before you, and gave you their land; and I said to you, 'I am the Lord your God; you shall not pay reverence to the gods of the Amorites, in whose land you dwell.' But you have not given heed to my voice." Now the angel of the Lord came and sat under the oak at Ophrah, which belonged to Jo'ash the Abiez'rite, as his son Gideon was beating out wheat in the wine press, to hide it from the Mid'ianites. And the angel of the Lord appeared to him and said to him, "The Lord is with you, you mighty man of valor." And Gideon said to him, "Pray, sir, if the Lord is with us, why then has all this befallen us? And where are all his wonderful deeds which our fathers recounted to us, saying, 'Did not the Lord bring us up from Egypt?' But now the Lord has cast us off, and given us into the hand of Mid'ian." And the Lord turned to him and said, "Go in this might of yours and deliver Israel from the hand of Mid'ian; do not I send you?" And he said to him, "Pray, Lord, how can I deliver Israel? Behold, my clan is the weakest in Manas'seh, and I am the least in my family."

And the Lord said to him, "But I will be with you, and you shall smite the Midʹianites as one man." And he said to him, "If now I have found favor with thee, then show me a sign that it is thou who speakest with me. Do not depart from here, I pray thee, until I come to thee, and bring out my present, and set it before thee." And he said, "I will stay till you return." So Gideon went into his house and prepared a kid, and unleavened cakes from an ephah of flour; the meat he put in a basket, and the broth he put in a pot, and brought them to him under the oak and presented them. And the angel of God said to him, "Take the meat and the unleavened cakes, and put them on this rock, and pour the broth over them." And he did so. Then the angel of the Lord reached out the tip of the staff that was in his hand, and touched the meat and the unleavened cakes; and there sprang up fire from the rock and consumed the flesh and the unleavened cakes; and the angel of the Lord vanished from his sight. Then Gideon perceived that he was the angel of the Lord; and Gideon said, "Alas, O Lord God! For now I have seen the angel of the Lord face to face." But the Lord said to him, "Peace be to you; do not fear, you shall not die." Then Gideon built an altar there to the Lord, and called it, The Lord is peace. To this day it still stands at Ophrah, which belongs to the Abiezʹrites.

A Reading (Lesson) from the Second Letter of Paul to the Corinthians [9:6-15]

The point is this: he who sows sparingly will also reap sparingly, and he who sows bountifully will also reap bountifully. Each one must do as he has made up his mind, not reluctantly or under compulsion, for God loves a cheerful giver. And God is able to provide you with every blessing in abundance, so that you may always have enough of everything and may provide in abundance for every good work. As it is written, "He scatters abroad, he gives to the poor; his righteousness endures for ever." He who supplies seed to the sower and bread for food will supply and multiply your resources and increase the harvest of your righteousness. You will be enriched in every way for great generosity, which through us will produce thanksgiving to God; for the rendering of this service not only supplies the wants of the saints but also overflows in many thanksgivings to God. Under the test of this service, you will glorify God by your obedience in ackowledging the gospel of Christ, and by the generosity of your contribution for them and for all others; while they long for you and pray for you, because of the surpassing grace of God in you. Thanks be to God for his inexpressible gift!

A Reading (Lesson) from the Gospel according to Mark
[3:20-30]

The crowd came together again, so that Jesus and his disciples could not even eat. And when his family heard it, they went out to seize him, for people were saying, "He is beside himself." And the scribes who came down from Jerusalem said, "He is possessed by Be-el'zebul, and by the prince of demons he casts out the demons." And he called them to him, and said to them in parables, "How can Satan cast out Satan? If a kingdom is divided against itself, that kingdom cannot stand. And if a house is divided against itself, that house will not be able to stand. And if Satan has risen up against himself and is divided, he cannot stand, but is coming to an end. But no one can enter a strong man's house and plunder his goods, unless he first binds the strong man; then indeed he may plunder his house. Truly, I say to you, all sins will be forgiven the sons of men, and whatever blasphemies they utter; but whoever blasphemes against the Holy Spirit never has forgiveness, but is guilty of an eternal sin"—for they had said, "He has an unclean spirit."

Monday

Psalm 80 [page 702]   ❖   *Psalm 77* [page 693],
(Psalm 79 [page 701])

A Reading (Lesson) from the Book of Judges [6:25-40]

That night the Lord said to Gideon, "Take your father's
bull, the second bull seven years old, and pull down the
altar of Ba'al which your father has, and cut down the
Ashe'rah that is beside it; and build an altar to the Lord
your God on top of the stronghold here, with stones laid in
due order; then take the second bull, and offer it as a burnt
offering with the wood of the Ashe'rah which you shall cut
down." So Gideon took ten men of his servants, and did as
the Lord had told him; but because he was too afraid of his
family and the men of the town to do it by day, he did it by
night. When the men of the town rose early in the
morning, behold, the altar of Ba'al was broken down, and
the Ashe'rah beside it was cut down, and the second bull
was offered upon the altar which had been built. And they
said to one another, "Who has done this thing?" And after
they had made search and inquired, they said, "Gideon the
son of Jo'ash had done this thing." Then the men of the
town said to Jo'ash, "Bring out your son, that he may die,
for he has pulled down the altar of Ba'al and cut down the
Ashe'rah beside it." But Jo'ash said to all who were arrayed
against him, "Will you contend for Ba'al? Or will you
defend his cause? Whoever contends for him shall be put
to death by morning. If he is a god, let him contend for
himself, because his altar has been pulled down."
Therefore on that day he was called Jerubba'al, that is to
say, "Let Ba'al contend against him," because he pulled
down his altar. Then all the Mid'ianites and the Amal'ekites
and the people of the East came together, and crossing the
Jordan they encamped in the Valley of Jezreel. But the
Spirit of the Lord took possession of Gideon; and he
sounded the trumpet, and the Abiez'rites were called out to

follow him. And he sent messengers throughout all
Manas'seh; and they too were called out to follow him.
And he sent messengers to Asher, Zeb'ulun, and Naph'tali;
and they went up to meet them. Then Gideon said to God,
"If thou wilt deliver Israel by my hand, as thou hast said,
behold, I am laying a fleece of wool on the threshing floor;
if there is dew on the fleece alone, and it is dry on all the
ground, then I shall know that thou wilt deliver Israel by
my hand, as thou hast said." And it was so. When he rose
early next morning and squeezed the fleece, he wrung
enough dew from the fleece to fill a bowl with water. Then
Gideon said to God, "Let not thy anger burn against me,
let me speak but this once; pray, let me make trial only this
once with the fleece; pray, let it be dry only on the fleece,
and on all the ground let there be dew." And God did so
that night; for it was dry on the fleece only, and on all the
ground there was dew.

A Reading (Lesson) from the Acts of the Apostles [2:37-47]

When the devout men heard what Peter had said they were
cut to the heart, and said to Peter and the rest of the
apostles, "Brethren, what shall we do?" And Peter said to
them, "Repent, and be baptized every one of you in the
name of Jesus Christ for the forgiveness of your sins; and
you shall receive the gift of the Holy Spirit. For the
promise is to you and to your children and to all that are
far off, every one whom the Lord our God calls to him."
And he testified with many other words and exhorted
them, saying, "Save yourselves from this crooked
generation." So those who received his word were
baptized, and there were added that day about three
thousand souls. And they devoted themselves to the
apostles' teaching and fellowship, to the breaking of bread
and the prayers. And fear came upon every soul; and many
wonders and signs were done through the apostles. And all
who believed were together and had all things in common;

and they sold their possessions and goods and distributed them to all, as any had need. And day by day, attending the temple together and breaking bread in their homes, they partook of food with glad and generous hearts, praising God and having favor with all the people. And the Lord added to their number day by day those who were being saved.

A Reading (Lesson) from the Gospel according to John
[1:1-18]

In the beginning was the Word, and the Word was with God, and the Word was God. He was in the beginning with God; all things were made through him, and without him was not anything made that was made. In him was life, and the life was the light of men. The light shines in the darkness, and the darkness has not overcome it. There was a man sent from God, whose name was John. He came for testimony, to bear witness to the light, that all might believe through him. He was not the light, but came to bear witness to the light. The true light that enlightens every man was coming into the world. He was in the world, and the world was made through him, yet the world knew him not. He came to his own home, and his own people received him not. But to all who received him who believed in his name, he gave power to become children of God; who were born, not of blood nor of the will of the flesh nor of the will of man, but of God. And the Word became flesh and dwelt among us, full of grace and truth; we have beheld his glory, glory as of the only Son from the Father. (John bore witness to him, and cried, "This was he of whom I said, 'He who comes after me ranks before me, for he was before me.'") And from his fulness have we all received, grace upon grace. For the law was given through Moses; grace and truth came through Jesus Christ. No one has ever seen God; the only Son, who is in the bosom of the Father, he has made him known.

Tuesday

Psalm 78:1-39 [page 694]   ❖   *Psalm 78:40-72* [page 698]

A Reading (Lesson) from the Book of Judges [7:1-18]

Jerubba'al (that is, Gideon) and all the people who were with him rose early and encamped beside the spring of Harod; and the camp of Mid'ian was north of them, by the hill of Moreh, in the valley. The Lord said to Gideon, "The people with you are too many for me to give the Mid'ianites into their hand, lest Israel vaunt themselves against me, saying, 'My own hand has delivered me.' Now therefore proclaim in the ears of the people, saying, 'Whoever is fearful and trembling, let him return home.'" And Gideon tested them; twenty-two thousand returned, and ten thousand remained. And the Lord said to Gideon, "The people are still too many; take them down to the water and I will test them for you there; and he of whom I say to you, 'This man shall go with you,' shall go with you; and any of whom I say to you, 'This man shall not go with you,' shall not go." So he brought the people down to the water; and the Lord said to Gideon, "Every one that laps the water with his tongue, as a dog laps, you shall set by himself; likewise every one that kneels down to drink." And the number of those that lapped, putting their hands to their mouths, was three hundred men; but all the rest of the people knelt down to drink water. And the Lord said to Gideon, "With the three hundred men that lapped I will deliver you, and give the Mid'ianites into your hand; and let all the others go every man to his home." So he took the jars of the people from their hands, and their trumpets; and he sent all the rest of Israel every man to his tent, but retained the three hundred men; and the camp of Mid'ian was below him in the valley. That same night the Lord said to him, "Arise, go down against the camp; for I have given it into your hand. But if you fear to go down, go down to the camp with Purah your servant; and you shall hear what they say, and afterward your hands shall be strengthened to go down against the camp." Then he went down with Purah his servant to the outposts of the armed men that were in the camp. And the Mid'ianites and the Amal'ekites and all the people of the East lay along the valley like locusts for multitude; and their camels were without number, as the sand which is upon the seashore for multitude. When Gideon came, behold, a man was telling a dream to his comrade; and he said, "Behold, I dreamed a dream; and lo, a cake of barley bread tumbled into the camp of Mid'ian, and came to the tent, and struck it so that it fell, and turned it upside down, so that the tent lay flat." And his comrade answered, "This is no other than the sword of Gideon the son of Jo'ash, a man of Israel; into his hand God has given Mid'ian and all the host." When Gideon heard the telling of the dream and its interpretation, he worshiped; and he returned to the camp of Israel, and said, "Arise; for the Lord has given the host of Mid'ian into your hand." And he divided the three hundred men into three companies, and put trumpets into the hands of all of them and empty jars, with torches inside the jars. And he said to them, "Look at me, and do likewise; when I come to the outskirts of the camp, do as I do. When I blow the trumpet, I and all who are with me, then blow the trumpets also on every side of all the camp, and shout, 'For the Lord and for Gideon.'"

A Reading (Lesson) from the Acts of the Apostles [3:1-11]

Peter and John were going up to the temple at the hour of prayer, the ninth hour. And a man lame from birth was being carried, whom they laid daily at the gate of the temple which is called Beautiful to ask alms of those who entered the temple. Seeing Peter and John about to go into the temple, he asked for alms. And Peter directed his gaze at him, with John, and said, "Look at us." And he fixed his attention upon them, expecting to receive something from them. But Peter said, "I have no silver and gold, but I give you what I have; in the name of Jesus Christ of Nazareth, walk." And he took him by the right hand and raised him up; and immediately his feet and ankles were made strong. And leaping up he stood and walked and entered the temple with them, walking and leaping and praising God. And all the people saw him walking and praising God, and recognized him as the one who sat for alms at the Beautiful Gate of the temple; and they were filled with wonder and amazement at what had happened to him. While he clung to Peter and John, all the people ran together to them in the portico called Solomon's, astounded.

A Reading (Lesson) from the Gospel according to John
[1:19-28]

This is the testimony of John, when the Jews sent priests and Levites from Jerusalem to ask him, "Who are you?" He confessed, he did not deny, but confessed, "I am not the Christ." And they asked him, "What then? Are you Eli'jah?" He said, "I am not." "Are you the prophet?" And he answered, "No." They said to him then, "Who are you? Let us have an answer for those who sent us. What do you say about yourself?" He said, "I am the voice of one crying in the wilderness, 'Make straight the way of the Lord,' as the prophet Isaiah said." Now they had been sent from the Pharisees. They asked him, "Then why are you baptizing, if you are neither the Christ, nor Eli'jah, nor the prophet?" John answered them, "I baptize with water; but among you stands one whom you do not know, even he who comes after me, the thong of whose sandal I am not worthy to untie." This took place in Bethany beyond the Jordan, where John was baptizing.

Wednesday

Psalm 119:97-120 [page 771] ❖ *Psalm 81* [page 704]
Psalm 82 [page 705]

A Reading (Lesson) from the Book of Judges [7:19—8:12]

Gideon and the hundred men who were with him came to
the outskirts of the camp at the beginning of the middle
watch, when they had just set the watch; and they blew the
trumpets and smashed the jars that were in their hands.
And the three companies blew the trumpets and broke the
jars, holding in their left hands the torches, and in their
right hands the trumpets to blow; and they cried, "A
sword for the Lord and for Gideon!" They stood every
man in his place round about the camp, and all the army
ran; they cried out and fled. When they blew the three
hundred trumpets, the Lord set every man's sword against
his fellow and against all the army; and the army fled as far
as Beth-shit'tah toward Zer'erah, as far as the border of
A'bel-meho'lah, by Tabbath. And the men of Israel were
called out from Naph'tali and from Asher and from all
Manas'seh, and they pursued after Mid'ian. And Gideon
sent messengers throughout all the hill country of
E'phraim, saying, "Come down against the Mid'ianites and
seize the waters against them, as far as Beth-bar'ah, and
also the Jordan." So all the men of E'phraim were called
out, and they seized the waters as far as Beth-bar'ah, and
also the Jordan. And they took the two princes of Mid'ian,
Oreb and Zeeb; they killed Oreb at the rock of Oreb, and
Zeeb they killed at the wine press of Zeeb, as they pursued
Mid'ian; and they brought the heads of Oreb and Zeeb to
Gideon beyond the Jordan. And the men of E'phraim said
to him, "What is this that you have done to us, not to call
us when you went to fight with Mid'ian?" And they
upbraided him violently. And he said to them, "What have
I done now in comparison with you? Is not the gleaning of
the grapes of E'phraim better than the vintage of Abi-e'zer?

God has given into your hands the princes of Mid'ian, Oreb and Zeeb; what have I been able to do in comparison with you?" Then their anger against him was abated, when he had said this. And Gideon came to the Jordan and passed over, he and the three hundred men who were with him, faint yet pursuing. So he said to the men of Succoth, "Pray, give loaves of bread to the people who follow me; for they are faint, and I am pursuing after Zebah and Zalmun'na, the kings of Mid'ian." And the officials of Succoth said, "Are Zebah and Zalmun'na already in your hand, that we should give bread to your army?" And Gideon said, "Well then, when the Lord has given Zebah and Zalmun'na into my hand, I will flail your flesh with the thorns of the wilderness and with briers." And from there he went up to Penu'el, and spoke to them in the same way; and the men of Penu'el answered him as the men of Succoth had answered. And he said to the men of Penu'el, "When I come again in peace, I will break down this tower." Now Zebah and Zalmun'na were in Karkor with their army, about fifteen thousand men, all who were left of all the army of the people of the East; for there had fallen a hundred and twenty thousand men who drew the sword. And Gideon went up by the caravan route east of Nobah and Jog'behah, and attacked the army; for the army was off its guard. And Zebah and Zalmun'na fled; and he pursued them and took the two kings of Mid'ian, Zebah and Zalmun'na, and he threw all the army into a panic.

A Reading (Lesson) from the Acts of the Apostles [3:12-26]

When Peter saw the people run together to them in the portico called Solomon's he addressed the people, "Men of Israel, why do you wonder at this, or why do you stare at us, as though by our own power or piety we had made him walk? The God of Abraham and of Isaac and of Jacob, the God of our fathers, glorified his servant Jesus, whom you delivered up and denied in the presence of Pilate, when he had decided to release him. But you denied the Holy and Righteous One, and asked for a murderer to be granted to you, and killed the Author of life, whom God raised from the dead. To this we are witnesses. And his name, by faith in his name, has made this man strong whom you see and know; and the faith which is through Jesus has given the man this perfect health in the presence of you all. And now, brethren, I know that you acted in ignorance, as did also your rulers. But what God foretold by the mouth of all the prophets, that his Christ should suffer, he thus fulfilled. Repent therefore, and turn again, that your sins may be blotted out, that times of refreshing may come from the presence of the Lord, and that he may send the Christ appointed for you, Jesus, whom heaven must receive until the time for establishing all that God spoke by the mouth of his holy prophets of old. Moses said, 'The Lord God will raise up for you a prophet from your brethren as he raised me up. You shall listen to him in whatever he tells you. And it shall be that every soul that does not listen to that prophet shall be destroyed from the people.' And all the prophets who have spoken, from Samuel and those who came afterwards, also proclaimed these days. You are the sons of the prophets and of the covenant which God gave to your fathers, saying to Abraham, 'And in your posterity shall all the families of the earth be blessed.' God, having raised up his servant, sent him to you first, to bless you in turning every one of you from your wickedness."

A Reading (Lesson) from the Gospel according to John [1:29-42]

The next day John saw Jesus coming toward him, and said, "Behold, the Lamb of God, who takes away the sin of the world! This is he of whom I said, 'After me comes a man who ranks before me, for he was before me.' I myself did not know him; but for this I came baptizing with water, that he might be revealed to Israel." And John bore witness, "I saw the Spirit descend as a dove from heaven, and it remained on him. I myself did not know him; but he who sent me to baptize with water said to me, 'He on whom you see the Spirit descend and remain, this is he who baptizes with the Holy Spirit.' And I have seen and have borne witness that this is the Son of God." The next day again John was standing with two of his disciples; and he looked at Jesus as he walked, and said, "Behold, the Lamb of God!" The two disciples heard him say this, and they followed Jesus. Jesus turned, and saw them following, and said to them, "What do you seek?" And they said to him, "Rabbi" (which means Teacher), "where are you staying?" He said to them, "Come and see." They came and saw where he was staying; and they stayed with him that day, for it was about the tenth hour. One of the two who heard John speak, and followed him, was Andrew, Simon Peter's brother. He first found his brother Simon, and said to him, "We have found the Messiah" (which means Christ). He brought him to Jesus. Jesus looked at him, and said, "So you are Simon the son of John? You shall be called Cephas" (which means Peter).

Thursday

(*Psalm 83* [page 706]) or *Psalm 145* [page 801] ❖
Psalm 85 [page 708], *Psalm 86* [page 709]

A Reading (Lesson) from the Book of Judges [8:22-35]

The men of Israel said to Gideon, "Rule over us, you and your son and your grandson also; for you have delivered us out of the hand of Mid'ian." Gideon said to them, "I will not rule over you, and my son will not rule over you; the Lord will rule over you." And Gideon said to them, "Let me make a request of you; give me every man of you the earrings of his spoil." (For they had golden earrings, because they were Ish'maelites.) And they answered, "We will willingly give them." And they spread a garment, and every man cast in it the earrings of his spoil. And the weight of the golden earrings that he requested was one thousand seven hundred shekels of gold; besides the crescents and the pendants and the purple garments worn by the kings of Mid'ian, and besides the collars that were about the necks of the camels. And Gideon made an ephod of it and put it in his city, in Ophrah; and all Israel played the harlot after it there, and it became a snare to Gideon and to his family. So Mid'ian was subdued before the people of Israel, and they lifted up their heads no more. And the land had rest forty years in the days of Gideon. Jerubba'al the son of Jo'ash went and dwelt in his own house. Now Gideon had seventy sons, his own offspring, for he had many wives. And his concubine who was in Shechem also bore him a son, and he called his name Abim'elech. And Gideon the son of Jo'ash died in a good old age, and was buried in the tomb of Jo'ash his father, at Ophrah of the Abiez'rites. As soon as Gideon died, the people of Israel turned again and played the harlot after the Ba'als, and made Ba'al-be'rith their god. And the people of Israel did not remember the Lord their God, who had rescued them from the hand of all their enemies on every side; and they did not show kindness to the family of Jerubba'al (that is, Gideon) in return for all the good that he had done to Israel.

A Reading (Lesson) from the Acts of the Apostles [4:1-12]

As Peter and John were speaking to the people, the priests and the captain of the temple and the Sad'ducees came upon them, annoyed because they were teaching the people and proclaiming in Jesus the resurrection from the dead. And they arrested them and put them in custody until the morrow, for it was already evening. But many of those who heard the word believed; and the number of the men came to about five thousand. On the morrow their rulers and elders and scribes were gathered together in Jerusalem, with Annas the high priest and Ca'iaphas and

John and Alexander, and all who were of the high-priestly family. And when they had set them in the midst, they inquired, "By what power or by what name did you do this?" Then Peter, filled with the Holy Spirit, said to them, "Rulers of the people and elders, if we are being examined today concerning a good deed done to a cripple, by what means this man has been healed, be it known to you all, and to all the people of Israel, that by the name of Jesus Christ of Nazareth, whom you crucified, whom God raised from the dead, by him this man is standing before you well. This is the stone which was rejected by you builders, but which has become the head of the corner. And there is salvation in no one else, for there is no other name under heaven given among men by which we must be saved."

A Reading (Lesson) from the Gospel according to John [1:43-51]

The next day Jesus decided to go to Galilee. And he found Philip and said to him, "Follow me." Now Philip was from Beth-sa'ida, the city of Andrew and Peter. Philip found Nathan'a-el, and said to him, "We have found him of whom Moses in the law and also the prophets wrote, Jesus of Nazareth, the son of Joseph." Nathan'a-el said to him, "Can anything good come out of Nazareth?" Philip said to him, "Come and see." Jesus saw Nathan'a-el coming to him, and said of him, "Behold, an Israelite indeed, in whom is no guile!" Nathan'a-el said to him, "How do you know me?" Jesus answered him, "Before Philip called you, when you were under the fig tree, I saw you." Nathan'a-el answered him, "Rabbi, you are the Son of God! You are the King of Israel!" Jesus answered him, "Because I said to you, I saw you under the fig tree, do you believe? You shall see greater things than these." And he said to him, "Truly, truly, I say to you, you will see heaven opened, and the angels of God ascending and descending upon the Son of man."

Friday

Psalm 88 [page 712] ❖ *Psalm 91* [page 719],
Psalm 92 [page 720]

A Reading (Lesson) from the Book of Judges [9:1-16,19-21]

Abim'elech the son of Jerubba'al went to Shechem to his
mother's kinsmen and said to them and to the whole clan
of his mother's family, "Say in the ears of all the citizens of
Shechem, 'Which is better for you, that all seventy of the
sons of Jerubba'al rule over you, or that one rule over you?'
Remember also that I am your bone and your flesh." And
his mother's kinsmen spoke all these words on his behalf
on the ears of all the men of Shechem; and their hearts
inclined to follow Abim'elech, for they said, "He is our
brother." And they gave him seventy pieces of silver out of
the house of Ba'al-be'rith with which Abim'elech hired
worthless and reckless fellows, who followed him. And he
went to his father's house at Ophrah, and slew his brothers
the sons of Jerubba'al, seventy men, upon one stone; but
Jotham the youngest son of Jerubba'al was left, for he hid
himself. And all the citizens of Shechem came together,
and all Beth-millo, and they went and made Abim'elech
king, by the oak of the pillar at Shechem. When it was told
to Jotham, he went and stood on the top of Mount
Ger'izim, and cried aloud and said to them, "Listen to me,
you men of Shechem, that God may listen to you. The trees
once went forth to annoint a king over them; and they said
to the olive tree, 'Reign over us.' But the olive tree said to
them, 'Shall I leave my fatness, by which gods and men are
honored, and go to sway over the trees?' And the trees said
to the fig tree, 'Come you, and reign over us.' But the fig
tree said to them, 'Shall I leave my sweetness and my good
fruit, and go sway over the trees?' And the trees said to the
vine, 'Come you, and reign over us.' But the vine said to
them, 'Shall I leave my wine which cheers gods and men,
and go to sway over the trees?' Then all the trees said to

the bramble, 'Come you, and reign over us.' And the bramble said to the trees, 'If in good faith you are anointing me king over you; then come and take refuge in my shade; but if not, let fire come out of the bramble and devour the cedars of Lebanon.' Now therefore, if you acted in good faith and honor when you made Abim'elech king, and if you have dealt well with Jerubba'al and his house, and have done to him as his deeds deserved, if you then have acted in good faith and honor with Jerubba'al and with his house this day, then rejoice in Abim'elech, and let him also rejoice in you; but if not, let fire come out from Abim'elech, and devour the citizens of Shechem, and Beth-millo; and let fire come out from the citizens of Shechem and from Beth-millo, and devour Abim'elech." And Jotham ran away and fled, and went to Beer and dwelt there, for fear of Abim'elech his brother.

A Reading (Lesson) from the Acts of the Apostles [4:13-31]

When the rulers and elders and scribes saw the boldness of Peter and John, and perceived that they were uneducated, common men, they wondered; and they recognized that they had been with Jesus. But seeing the man that had been healed standing beside them, they had nothing to say in opposition. But when they had commanded them to go aside out of the council, they conferred with one another, saying, "What shall we do with these men? For that a notable sign has been performed through them is manifest to all the inhabitants of Jerusalem, and we cannot deny it. But in order that it may spread no further among the people, let us warn them to speak no more to any one in this name." So they called them and charged them not to speak or teach at all in the name of Jesus. But Peter and John answered them, "Whether it is right in the sight of God to listen to you rather than to God, you must judge; for we cannot but speak of what we have seen and heard." And when they had further threatened them, they let them go, finding no way to punish them, because of the people; for all men praised God for what had happened. For the man on whom this sign of healing was performed was more than forty years old. When they were released they went to their friends and reported what the chief priests and the elders had said to them. And when they heard it, they lifted their voices together to God and said, "Sovereign Lord, who didst make the heaven and the earth and the sea and everything in them, who by the mouth of our father David, they servant, didst say by the Holy Spirit, 'Why did the Gentiles rage, and the peoples imagine vain things? The kings of the earth set themselves in array, and the rulers were gathered together, against the Lord and against his Anointed'—for truly in this city there were gathered together against thy holy servant Jesus, whom thou didst anoint, both Herod and Pontius Pilate, with the Gentiles and the peoples of Israel, to do whatever thy hand and thy plan had predestined to take place. And now, Lord, look upon their threats, and grant to thy servants to speak thy word with all boldness, while thou stretchest out thy hand to heal, and signs and wonders are performed through the name of thy holy servant Jesus." And when they had prayed, the place in which they were gathered together was shaken; and they were all filled with the Holy Spirit and spoke the word of God with boldness.

A Reading (Lesson) from the Gospel according to John
[2:1-12]

On the third day there was a marriage at Cana in Galilee, and the mother of Jesus was there; Jesus also was invited to the marriage, with his disciples. When the wine gave out, the mother of Jesus said to him, "They have no wine." And Jesus said to her, "O woman, what have you to do with me? My hour has not yet come." His mother said to the servants, "Do whatever he tells you." Now six stone jars were standing there, for the Jewish rites of purification, each holding twenty or thirty gallons. Jesus said to them, "Fill the jars with water." And they filled them up to the brim. He said to them, "Now draw some out, and take it to the steward of the feast." So they took it. When the steward of the feast tasted the water now become wine, and did not know where it came from (though the servants who had drawn the water knew), the steward of the feast called the bridegroom and said to him, "Every man serves the good wine first; and when men have drunk freely, then the poor wine; but you have kept the good wine until now." This, the first of his signs, Jesus did at Cana in Galilee, and manifested his glory; and his disciples believed in him. After this he went down to Caper′na-um, with his mother and his brothers and his disciples; and there they stayed for a few days.

Saturday

Psalm 87 [page 711], *Psalm 90* [page 717] ❖
Psalm 136 [page 789]

A Reading (Lesson) from the Book of Judges
[9:22-25,50-57]

Abim′elech ruled over Israel three years. And God sent an evil spirit between Abim′elech and the men of Shechem; and the men of Shechem dealt treacherously with Abim′elech; that the violence done to the seventy sons of Jerubba′al might come and their blood be laid upon Abim′elech their brother, who slew them, and upon the men of Shechem, who strengthened his hands to slay his brothers. And the men of Shechem put men in ambush against him on the mountain tops, and they robbed all who passed by them along that way; and it was told Abim′elech. Then Abim′elech went to Thebez, and encamped against Thebez, and took it. But there was a strong tower within the city, and all the people of the city fled to it, all the men and women, and shut themselves in; and they went to the roof of the tower. And Abim'elech came to the tower, and fought against it, and drew near to the door of the tower to burn it with fire. And a certain woman threw an upper millstone upon Abim'elech's head, and crushed his skull. Then he called hastily to the young man his armor-bearer, and said to him, "Draw your sword and kill me, lest men say of me, 'A woman killed him.'" And his young man thrust him through, and he died. And when the men of Israel saw that Abim'elech was dead, they departed every man to his home. Thus God requited the crime of Abim'elech, which he committed against his father in killing his seventy brothers; and God also made all the wickedness of the men of Shechem fall back upon their heads, and upon them came the curse of Jotham the son of Jerubba'al.

A Reading (Lesson) from the Acts of the Apostles
[4:32—5:11]

The company of those who believed were of one heart and soul, and no one said that any of the things which he possessed was his own, but they had everything in common. And with great power the apostles gave their testimony to the resurrection of the Lord Jesus, and great grace was upon them all. There was not a needy person among them, for as many as were possessors of lands or houses sold them, and brought the proceeds of what was sold and laid it at the apostles' feet; and distribution was made to each as any had need. Thus Joseph who was surnamed by the apostles Barnabas (which means, Son of encouragement), a Levite, a native of Cyprus, sold a field which belonged to him, and brought the money and laid it at the apostles' feet. But a man named Anani'as with his wife Sapphi'ra sold a piece of property, and with his wife's knowledge he kept back some of the proceeds, and brought only a part and laid it at the apostles' feet. But

Peter said, "Anani'as, why has Satan filled your heart to lie to the Holy Spirit and to keep back part of the proceeds of the land? While it remained unsold, did it not remain your own? And after it was sold, was it not at your disposal? How is it that you have contrived this deed in your heart? You have not lied to men but to God." When Anani'as heard these words, he fell down and died. And great fear came upon all who heard of it. The young men rose and wrapped him up and carried him out and buried him. After an interval of about three hours his wife came in, not knowing what had happened. And Peter said to her, "Tell me whether you sold the land for so much." And she said, "Yes, for so much." But Peter said to her, "How is it that you have agreed together to tempt the Spirit of the Lord? Hark, the feet of those that have buried your husband are at the door, and they will carry you out." Immediately she fell down at his feet and died. When the young men came in they found her dead, and they carried her out and buried her beside her husband. And great fear came upon the whole church, and upon all who heard of these things.

A Reading (Lesson) from the Gospel according to John
[2:13-25]

The Passover of the Jews was at hand, and Jesus went up to Jerusalem. In the temple he found those who were selling oxen and sheep and pigeons, and the money-changers at their business. And making a whip of cords, he drove them all, with the sheep and oxen, out of the temple; and he poured out the coins of the money-changers and overturned their tables. And he told those who sold the pigeons, "Take these things away; you shall not make of my Father's house a house of trade." His disciples remembered that it was written, "Zeal for thy house will consume me." The Jews then said to him, "What sign have you to show us for doing this?" Jesus answered them, "Destroy this temple, and in three days I will raise it up."

The Jews then said, "It has taken forty-six years to build this temple, and will you raise it up in three days?" But he spoke of the temple of his body. When therefore he was raised from the dead, his disciples remembered that he had said this; and they believed the scripture and the word which Jesus had spoken. Now when he was in Jerusalem at the Passover feast, many believed in his name when they saw the signs which he did; but Jesus did not trust himself to them, because he knew all men and needed no one to bear witness of man; for he himself knew what was in man.

Proper 14   *Week of the Sunday closest to August 10*

Sunday

Psalm 66 [page 673],   *Psalm 67* [page 675]   ❖
Psalm 19 [page 606],   *Psalm 46* [page 649]

A Reading (Lesson) from the Book of Judges
[11:1-11,29-40]

Jephthah the Gileadite was a mighty warrior, but he was the son of a harlot. Gilead was the father of Jephthah. And Gilead's wife also bore him sons; and when his wife's sons grew up, they thrust Jephthah out, and said to him, "You shall not inherit in our father's house; for you are the son of another woman." Then Jephthah fled from his brothers, and dwelt in the land of Tob; and worthless fellows collected round Jephthah, and went raiding with him. After a time the Ammonites made war against Israel. And when the Ammonites made war against Israel, the elders of Gilead went to bring Jephthah from the land of Tob; and they said to Jephthah, "Come and be our leader, that we may fight with the Ammonites." But Jephthah said to the elders of Gilead, "Did you not hate me, and drive me out of my father's house? Why have you come to me now when you are in trouble?" And the elders of Gilead said to

Jephthah, "That is why we have turned to you now, that you may go with us and fight with the Ammonites, and be our head over all the inhabitants of Gilead." Jephthah said to the elders of Gilead, "If you bring me home again to fight with the Ammonites, and the Lord gives them over to me, I will be your head." And the elders of Gilead said to Jephthah, "The Lord will be witness between us; we will surely do as you say." So Jephthah went with the elders of Gilead, and the people made him head and leader over them; and Jephthah spoke all his words before the Lord at Mizpah. Then the Spirit of the Lord came upon Jephthah, and he passed through Gilead and Manas'seh, and passed on to Mizpah of Gilead, and from Mizpah of Gilead he passed on to the Ammonites. And Jephthah made a vow to the Lord, and said, "If thou wilt give the Ammonites into my hand, then whoever comes forth from the doors of my house to meet me, when I return victorious from the Ammonites, shall be the Lord's, and I will offer him up for a burnt offering." So Jephthah crossed over to the Ammonites to fight against them; and the Lord gave them into his hand. And he smote them from Aro'er to the neighborhood of Minnith, twenty cities, and as far as Abel-keramim, with a very great slaughter. So the Ammonites were subdued before the people of Israel. Then Jephthah came to his home at Mizpah; and behold, his daughter came out to meet him with timbrels and with dances; she was his only child; beside her he had neither son nor daughter. And when he saw her, he rent his clothes, and said, "Alas, my daughter! you have brought me very low, and you have become the cause of great trouble to me; for I have opened my mouth to the Lord, and I cannot take back my vow." And she said to him, "My father, if you have opened your mouth to the Lord, do to me according to what has gone forth from your mouth, now that the Lord has avenged you on your enemies, on the Ammonites." And she said to her father, "Let this thing be done for me; let me alone two months, that I may go and wander on the mountains, and bewail my virginity, I and my companions." And he said, "Go." And he sent her away for two months; and she departed, she and her companions, and bewailed her virginity upon the mountains. And at the end of two months, she returned to her father, who did with her according to his vow which he had made. She had never known a man. And it became a custom in Israel that the daughters of Israel went year by year to lament the daughter of Jephthah the Gileadite four days in the year.

A Reading (Lesson) from the Second Letter of Paul to the Corinthians [11:21b-31]

Whatever any one dares to boast of—I am speaking as a fool—I also dare to boast of that. Are they Hebrews? So am I. Are they Israelites? So am I. Are they descendants of Abraham? So am I. Are they servants of Christ? I am a better one—I am talking like a madman—with far greater labors, far more imprisonments, with countless beatings, and often near death. Five times I have received at the hands of the Jews the forty lashes less one. Three times I have been beaten with rods; once I was stoned. Three times I have been shipwrecked; a night and a day I have been adrift at sea; on frequent journeys, in danger from rivers, danger from robbers, danger from my own people, danger from Gentiles, danger in the city, danger in the wilderness, danger at sea, danger from false brethren; in toil and hardship, through many a sleepless night, in hunger and thirst, often without food, in cold and exposure. And, apart from other things, there is the daily pressure upon me of my anxiety for all the churches. Who is weak, and I am not weak? Who is made to fall, and I am not indignant? If I must boast, I will boast of the things that show my weakness. The God and Father of the Lord Jesus, he who is blessed for ever, knows that I do not lie.

A Reading (Lesson) from the Gospel according to Mark [4:35-41]

On that day, when evening had come, Jesus said to the disciples, "Let us go across to the other side." And leaving the crowd, they took him with them in the boat, just as he was. And other boats were with him. And a great storm of wind arose, and the waves beat into the boat, so that the boat was already filling. But he was in the stern, asleep on the cushion; and they woke him and said to him, "Teacher, do you not care if we perish?" And he awoke and rebuked the wind, and said to the sea, "Peace! Be still!" And the wind ceased, and there was a great calm. He said to them, "Why are you afraid? Have you no faith?" And they were filled with awe, and said to one another, "Who then is this, that even wind and sea obey him?"

Monday

Psalm 89:1-18 [page 713]   ❖   *Psalm 89:19-52* [page 715]

A Reading (Lesson) from the Book of Judges [12:1-7]

The men of E'phraim were called to arms, and they crossed to Zaphon and said to Jephthah, "Why did you cross over to fight against the Ammonites, and did not call us to go with you? We will burn your house over you with fire." And Jephthah said to them, "I and my people had a great feud with the Ammonites; and when I called you, you did not deliver me from their hand. And when I saw that you would not deliver me, I took my life in my hand, and crossed over against the Ammonites, and the Lord gave them into my hand; why then have you come up to me this day, to fight against me?" Then Jephthah gathered all the men of Gilead and fought with E'phraim; and the men of Gilead smote E'phraim, because they said, "You are fugitives of E'phraim, you Gileadites, in the midst of E'phraim and Manas'seh." And the Gileadites took the fords of the Jordan against the E'phraimites. And when any of the fugitives of E'phraim said, "Let me go over," the men of Gilead said to him, "Are you an E'phraimite?" When he said, "No," they said to him, "Then say Shibboleth," and he said, "Sibboleth," for he could not pronounce it right; then they seized him and slew him at the fords of the Jordan. And there fell at that time forty-two thousand of the E'phraimites. Jephthah judged Israel six years. Then Jephthah the Gileadite died, and was buried in his city of Gilead.

A Reading (Lesson) from the Acts of the Apostles [5:12-26]

Now many signs and wonders were done among the people by the hands of the apostles. And they were all together in Solomon's Portico. None of the rest dared join them, but the people held them in high honor. And more than ever believers were added to the Lord, multitudes both of men and women, so that they even carried out the sick into the streets, and laid them on beds and pallets, that as Peter came by at least his shadow might fall on some of them. The people also gathered from the towns around Jerusalem, bringing the sick and those afflicted with unclean spirits, and they were all healed. But the high priest rose up and all who were with him, that is, the party of the Sad'ducees, and filled with jealousy they arrested the apostles and put them in the common prison. But at night the angel of the Lord opened the prison doors and brought them out and said, "Go and stand in the temple and speak to the people all the words of this Life." And when they heard this, they entered the temple at daybreak and taught. Now the high priest came and those who were with him and called together the council and all the senate of Israel, and sent to the prison to have them brought. But when the officers came, they did not find them in the prison, and they returned and reported, "We found the prison securely locked and the sentries standing at the doors, but when we opened it we found no one inside." Now when the captain of the temple and the chief priests heard these words, they were much perplexed about them, wondering what this would come to. And some one came and told them, "The men whom you put in prison are standing in the temple and teaching the people." Then the captain with the officers went and brought them, but without violence, for they were afraid of being stoned by the people.

A Reading (Lesson) from the Gospel according to John
[3:1-21]

There was a man of the Pharisees, named Nicodémus, a ruler of the Jews. This man came to Jesus by night and said to him, "Rabbi, we know that you are a teacher come from God; for no one can do these signs that you do, unless God is with him." Jesus answered him, "Truly, truly, I say to you, unless one is born anew, he cannot see the kingdom of God." Nicodémus said to him, "How can a man be born when he is old? Can he enter a second time into his mother's womb and be born?" Jesus answered, "Truly, truly, I say to you, unless one is born of water and the Spirit, he cannot enter the kingdom of God. That which is born of the flesh is flesh, and that which is born of the Spirit is spirit. Do not marvel that I said to you, 'You must be born anew.' The wind blows where it wills, and you hear the sound of it, but you do not know whence it comes or whither it goes; so it is with every one who is born of the Spirit." Nicodémus said to him, "How can this be?" Jesus answered him, "Are you a teacher of Israel, and yet you do not understand this? Truly, truly, I say to you, we speak of what we know, and bear witness to what we have seen; but you do not receive our testimony. If I have told you earthly things and you do not believe, how can you believe if I tell you heavenly things? No one has ascended into heaven but he who descended from heaven, the Son of man. And as Moses lifted up the serpent in the wilderness, so must the Son of man be lifted up, that whoever believes in him may have eternal life." For God so loved the world that he gave his only Son, that whoever believes in him should not perish but have eternal life. For God sent the Son into the world, not to condemn the world, but that the world might be saved through him. He who believes in him is not condemned; he who does not believe is condemned already, because he has not believed in the name of the only Son of God. And this is the judgment, that the light has come into the world, and men loved darkness rather than light, because their deeds were evil. For every one who does evil hates the light, and does not come to the light, lest his deeds should be exposed. But he who does what is true comes to the light, that it may be clearly seen that his deeds have been wrought in God.

Tuesday

Psalm 97 [page 726], *Psalm 99* [page 728],
(Psalm 100 [page 729]) ❖ *Psalm 94* [page 722],
(Psalm 95 [page 724])

A Reading (Lesson) from the Book of Judges [13:1-15]

The people of Israel again did what was evil in the sight of the Lord; and the Lord gave them into the hand of the Philistines for forty years. And there was a certain man of Zorah, of the tribe of the Danites, whose name was Mano'ah; and his wife was barren and had no children. And the angel of the Lord appeared to the woman and said to her, "Behold, you are barren and have no children; but you shall conceive and bear a son. Therefore beware, and drink no wine or strong drink, and eat nothing unclean, for lo, you shall conceive and bear a son. No razor shall come upon his head, for the boy shall be a Nazirite to God from birth; and he shall begin to deliver Israel from the hand of the Philistines." Then the woman came and told her husband, "A man of God came to me, and his countenance was like the countenance of the angel of God, very terrible; I did not ask him whence he was, and he did not tell me his name; but he said to me, 'Behold, you shall conceive and bear a son; so then drink no wine or strong drink, and eat nothing unclean, for the boy shall be a Nazirite to God from birth to the day of his death.'" Then Mano'ah entreated the Lord, and said, "O, Lord, I pray thee, let the man of God whom thou didst send come again to us, and teach us what we are to do with the boy that will be born." And God listened to the voice of Mano'ah, and the angel of God came again to the woman as she sat in the field; but Mano'ah her husband was not with her. And the woman ran in haste and told her husband, "Behold, the man who came to me the other day has appeared to me." And Mano'ah arose and went after his wife, and came to the man and said to him, "Are you the man who spoke to this woman?" And he said, "I am." And Mano'ah said, "Now when your words come true, what is to be the boy's manner of life, and what is he to do?" And the angel of the Lord said to Mano'ah, "Of all that I said to the woman let her beware. She may not eat of anything that comes from the vine, neither let her drink wine or strong drink, or eat any unclean thing; all that I commanded her let her observe." Mano'ah said to the angel of the Lord, "Pray, let us detain you, and prepare a kid for you."

A Reading (Lesson) from the Acts of the Apostles [5:27-42]

When the captain with the officers had brought the apostles, they set them before the council. And the high priest questioned them, saying, "We strictly charged you not to teach in this name, yet here you have filled Jerusalem with your teaching and you intend to bring this man's blood upon us." But Peter and the apostles answered, "We must obey God rather than men. The God of our fathers raised Jesus whom you killed by hanging him on a tree. God exalted him at his right hand as Leader and Savior, to give repentance to Israel and forgiveness of sins. And we are witnesses to these things, and so is the Holy Spirit whom God has given to those who obey him." When they heard this they were enraged and wanted to kill them. But a Pharisee in the council named Gama'liel, a teacher of the law, held in honor by all the people, stood up and ordered the men to be put outside for a while. And he said to them, "Men of Israel, take care what you do with these men. For before these days Theu'das arose, giving himself out to be somebody, and a number of men, about four hundred, joined him; but he was slain and all who followed him were dispersed and came to nothing. After him Judas the Galilean arose in the days of the census and drew away some of the people after him; he also perished, and all who followed him were scattered. So in the present case I tell you, keep away from these men and let them alone; for if this plan or this undertaking is of men, it will fail; but if it is of God, you will not be able to overthrow them. You might even be found opposing God!" So they took his advice, and when they had called in the apostles, they beat them and charged them not to speak in the name of Jesus, and let them go. Then they left the presence of the council, rejoicing that they were counted worthy to suffer dishonor for the name. And every day in the temple and at home they did not cease teaching and preaching Jesus as the Christ.

A Reading (Lesson) from the Gospel according to John
[3:22-36]

Jesus and his disciples went into the land of Judea; there he remained with them and baptized. John also was baptizing at Ae'non near Salim, because there was much water there; and people came and were baptized. For John had not yet been put in prison. Now a discussion arose between John's disciples and a Jew over purifying. And they came to John, and said to him, "Rabbi, he who was with you beyond the Jordan, to whom you bore witness, here he is, baptizing, and all are going to him." John answered, "No one can receive anything except what is given him from heaven. You yourselves bear me witness, that I said, I am not the Christ, but I have been sent before him. He who has the bride is the bridegroom; the friend of the bridegroom, who stands and hears him, rejoices greatly at the bridegroom's voice; therefore this joy of mine is now full. He must increase, but I must decrease." He who comes from above is above all; he who is of the earth belongs to the earth, and of the earth he speaks; he who comes from heaven is above all. He bears witness to what he has seen and heard, yet no one receives his testimony; he who receives his testimony sets his seal to this, that God is true. For he whom God has sent utters the words of God, for it is not by measure that he gives the Spirit; the Father loves the Son, and has given all things into his hand. He who believes in the Son has eternal life; he who does not obey the Son shall not see life, but the wrath of God rests upon him.

Wednesday

Psalm 101 [page 730],   *Psalm 109:1-4(5-19)20-30*
[page 750] ❖ *Psalm 119:121-144* [page 773]

A Reading (Lesson) from the Book of Judges [13:15-24]

Mano'ah said to the angel of the Lord, "Pray, let us detain you, and prepare a kid for you." And the angel of the Lord said to Mano'ah, "If you detain me, I will not eat of your food; but if you make ready a burnt offering, then offer it to the Lord." (For Mano'ah did not know that he was the angel of the Lord.) And Mano'ah said to the angel of the Lord, "What is your name, so that, when your words come true, we may honor you?" And the angel of the Lord said to him, "Why do you ask my name, seeing it is wonderful?" So Mano'ah took the kid with the cereal offering, and offered it upon the rock to the Lord, to him who works wonders. And when the flame went up toward heaven from the altar, the angel of the Lord ascended in the flame of the altar while Mano'ah and his wife looked on; and they fell on their faces to the ground. The angel of the Lord appeared no more to Mano'ah and to his wife. Then Mano'ah knew that he was the angel of the Lord. And Mano'ah said to his wife, "We shall surely die, for we have seen God." But his wife said to him, "If the Lord had meant to kill us, he would not have accepted a burnt offering and a cereal offering at our hands, or shown us all these things, or now announced to us such things as these." And the woman bore a son, and called his name Samson; and the boy grew, and the Lord blessed him.

A Reading (Lesson) from the Acts of the Apostles [6:1-15]

Now in these days when the disciples were increasing in number, the Hellenists murmured against the Hebrews because their widows were neglected in the daily distribution. And the twelve summoned the body of the disciples and said, "It is not right that we should give up preaching the word of God to serve tables. Therefore, brethren, pick out from among you seven men of good repute, full of the Spirit and of wisdom, whom we may appoint to this duty. But we will devote ourselves to prayer and to the ministry of the word." And what they said pleased the whole multitude, and they chose Stephen, a man full of faith and of the Holy Spirit, and Philip, and Proch'orus, and Nica'nor, and Timon, and Par'menas, and Nicola'us, a proselyte of Antioch. These they set before the apostles, and they prayed and laid their hands upon them. And the word of God increased; and the number of the disciples multiplied greatly in Jerusalem, and a great many of the priests were obedient to the faith. And Stephen, full of grace and power, did great wonders and signs among the people. Then some of those who belonged to the synagogue of the Freedmen (as it was called), and of the Cyre'nians, and of the Alexandrians, and of those from Cili'cia and Asia, arose and disputed with Stephen. But they could not withstand the wisdom and the Spirit with which he spoke. Then they secretly instigated men, who said, "We have heard him speak blasphemous words against Moses and God." And they stirred up the people and the elders and the scribes, and they came upon him and seized him and brought him before the council, and set up false witnesses who said, "This man never ceases to speak words against this holy place and the law; for we have heard him say that this Jesus of Nazareth will destroy this place, and will change the customs which Moses delivered to us." And gazing at him, all who sat in the council saw that his face was like the face of an angel.

A Reading (Lesson) from the Gospel according to John
[4:1-26]

When the Lord knew that the Pharisees had heard that Jesus was making and baptizing more disciples than John (although Jesus himself did not baptize, but only his disciples), he left Judea and departed again to Galilee. He had to pass through Samar'ia. So he came to a city of Samar'ia, called Sy'char, near the field that Jacob gave to his son Joseph. Jacob's well was there, and so Jesus, wearied as he was with his journey, sat down beside the well. It was about the sixth hour. There came a woman of Samar'ia to draw water. Jesus said to her, "Give me a drink." For his disciples had gone away into the city to buy food. The Samaritan women said to him, "How is it that you, a Jew, ask a drink of me, a woman of Samar'ia?" For Jews have no dealings with Samaritans. Jesus answered her, "If you knew the gift of God, and who it is that is saying to you, 'Give me a drink,' you would have asked him, and he would have given you living water." The woman said to him, "Sir, you have nothing to draw with, and the well is deep; where do you get that living water? Are you greater than our father Jacob, who gave us the well, and drank from it himself, and his sons, and his cattle?" Jesus said to her, "Every one who drinks of this water will thirst again, but whoever drinks of the water that I shall give him will never thirst; the water that I shall give him will become in him a spring of water welling up to eternal life." The woman said to him, "Sir, give me this water, that I may not thirst, nor come here to draw." Jesus said to her, "Go, call your husband, and come here." The woman answered him, "I have no husband." Jesus said to her, "You are right in saying, 'I have no husband'; for you have had five husbands, and he whom you now have is not your husband; this you said truly." The woman said to him, "Sir, I perceive that you are a prophet. Our fathers worshiped on this mountain; and you say that in Jerusalem is the place where men ought to worship." Jesus said to her, 'Woman, believe me, the hour is coming when neither on this mountain nor in Jerusalem will you worship the Father. You worship what you do not know; we worship what we know, for salvation is from the Jews. But the hour is coming, and now is, when the true worshipers will worship the Father in spirit and truth, for such the Father seeks to worship him. God is spirit, and those who worship him must worship him in spirit and truth." The woman said to him, "I know that Messiah is coming (he who is called Christ); when he comes, he will show us all things." Jesus said to her, "I who speak to you am he."

Thursday

Psalm 105:1-22 [page 738] ❖ *Psalm 105:23-45* [page 739]

A Reading (Lesson) from the Book of Judges [14:1-19]

Samson went down to Timnah, and at Timnah he saw one of the daughters of the Philistines. Then he came up, and told his father and mother, "I saw one of the daughters of

the Philistines at Timnah; now get her for me as my wife."
But his father and mother said to him, "Is there not a
woman among the daughters of your kinsmen, or among
all our people, that you must go to take a wife from the
uncircumcised Philistines?" But Samson said to his father,
"Get her for me; for she pleases me well." His father and
mother did not know that it was from the Lord; for he was
seeking an occasion against the Philistines. At that time the
Philistines had dominion over Israel. Then Samson went
down with his father and mother to Timnah, and he came
to the vineyards of Timnah. And behold, a young lion
roared against him; and the Spirit of the Lord came
mightily upon him, and he tore the lion asunder as one
tears a kid; and he had nothing in his hand. But he did not
tell his father or his mother what he had done. Then he
went down and talked with the woman; and she pleased
Samson well. And after a while he returned to take her;
and he turned aside to see the carcass of the lion, and
behold, there was a swarm of bees in the body of the lion,
and honey. He scraped it out into his hands, and went on,
eating as he went; and he came to his father and mother,
and gave some to them, and they ate. But he did not tell
them that he had taken the honey from the carcass of the
lion. And his father went down to the woman, and Samson
made a feast there; for so the young men used to do. And
when the people saw him, they brought thirty companions
to be with him. And Samson said to them, "Let me now
put a riddle to you; if you can tell me what it is, within the
seven days of the feast, and find it out, then I will give you
thirty linen garments and thirty festal garments; but if you
cannot tell me what it is, then you shall give me thirty linen
garments and thirty festal garments." And they said to
him, "Put your riddle, that we may hear it." And he said to
them, "Out of the eater came something to eat. Out of the
strong came something sweet." And they could not in three
days tell what the riddle was. On the fourth day they said
to Samson's wife, "Entice your husband to tell us what the

riddle is, lest we burn you and your father's house with fire. Have you invited us here to impoverish us?" And Samson's wife wept before him, and said, "You only hate me, you do not love me; you have put a riddle to my countrymen, and you have not told me what it is." And he said to her, "Behold, I have not told my father nor my mother, and shall I tell you?" She wept before him the seven days that their feast lasted; and on the seventh day he told her, because she pressed him hard. Then she told the riddle to her countrymen. And the men of the city said to him on the seventh day before the sun went down, "What is sweeter than honey? What is stronger than a lion?" And he said to them, "If you had not plowed with my heifer, you would not have found out my riddle." And the Spirit of the Lord came mightily upon him, and went down to Ash'kelon and killed thirty men of the town, and took their spoil and gave the festal garments to those who had told the riddle. In hot anger he went back to his father's house.

A Reading (Lesson) from the Acts of the Apostles
[6:15—7:16]

Gazing at Stephen, all who sat in the council saw that his face was like the face of an angel. And the high priest said, "Is this so?" And Stephen said: "Brethren and fathers, hear me. The God of glory appeared to our father Abraham, when he was in Mesopota'mia, before he lived in Haran, and said to him, 'Depart from your land and from your kindred and go into the land which I will show you.' Then he departed from the land of the Chalde'ans, and lived in Haran. And after his father died, God removed him from there into this land in which you are now living; yet he gave him no inheritance in it, not even a foot's length, but promised to give it to him in possession and to his posterity after him, though he had no child. And God spoke to this effect, that his posterity would be aliens in a land belonging to others, who would enslave them and ill-treat them four hundred years. 'But I will judge the nation which they serve,' said God, 'and after that they shall come out and worship me in this place.' And he gave him the covenant of circumcision. And so Abraham became the father of Isaac, and circumcised him on the eighth day; and Isaac became the father of Jacob, and Jacob of the twelve patriarchs. And the patriarchs, jealous of Joseph, sold him into Egypt; but God was with him, and rescued him out of all his afflictions, and gave him favor and wisdom before Pharaoh, king of Egypt, who made him governor over Egypt and over all his household. Now there came a famine throughout all Egypt and Canaan, and great affliction, and our fathers could find no food. But when Jacob heard that there was grain in Egypt, he sent forth our fathers the first time. And at the second visit Joseph made himself known to his brothers, and Joseph's family became known to Pharaoh. And Joseph sent and called to him Jacob his father and all his kindred, seventy-five souls; and Jacob went down into Egypt. And he died, himself and our fathers, and they were carried back to Shechem and laid in the tomb that Abraham had bought for a sum of silver from the sons of Hamor in Shechem."

A Reading (Lesson) from the Gospel according to John
[4:27-42]

As Jesus was talking to the woman at the well his disciples came. They marveled that he was talking with a woman, but none said, "What do you wish?" or, "Why are you talking with her?" So the woman left her water jar, and went away into the city, and said to the people, "Come, see a man who told me all that I ever did. Can this be the Christ?" They went out of the city and were coming to him. Meanwhile the disciples besought him, saying, "Rabbi, eat." But he said to them, "I have food to eat of which you do not know." So the disciples said to one another, "Has any one brought him food?" Jesus said to them, "My food is to do the will of him who sent me, and to accomplish his work. Do you not say, 'There are yet four months, then comes the harvest'? I tell you, lift up your eyes, and see how the fields are already white for harvest. He who reaps receives wages, and gathers fruit for eternal life, so that sower and reaper may rejoice together. For here the saying holds true, 'One sows and another reaps.' I sent you to reap that for which you did not labor; others have labored, and you have entered into their labor." Many Samaritans from that city believed in him because of the woman's testimony, "He told me all that I ever did." So when the Samaritans came to him, they asked him to stay with them; and he stayed there two days. And many more believed because of his word. They said to the woman, "It is no longer because of your words that we believe, for we have heard for ourselves, and we know that this is indeed the Savior of the world."

Friday

Psalm 102 [page 731] ❖ *Psalm 107:1-32* [page 746]

A Reading (Lesson) from the Book of Judges [14:20—15:20]

Samson's wife was given to his companion, who had been his best man. After a while, at the time of wheat harvest, Samson went to visit his wife with a kid; and he said, "I will go in to my wife in the chamber." But her father would not allow him to go in. And her father said, "I really thought that you utterly hated her; so I gave her to your companion. Is not her younger sister fairer than she? Pray take her instead." And Samson said to them, "This time I shall be blameless in regard to the Philistines, when I do them mischief." So Samson went and caught three hundred foxes, and took torches; and the turned them tail to tail, and put a torch between each pair of tails. And when he had set fire to the torches, he let the foxes go into the standing grain of the Philistines, and burned up the shocks and the standing grain, as well as the olive orchards. Then the Philistines said, "Who has done this?" And they said, "Samson, the son-in-law of the Timnite, because he has taken his wife and given her to his companion." And the Philistines came up, and burned her and her father with fire. And Samson said to them, "If this is what you do, I swear I will be avenged upon you, and after that I will quit." And he smote them hip and thigh with great slaughter; and he went down and stayed in the cleft of the rock of Etam. Then the Philistines came up and encamped in Judah, and made a raid on Lehi. And the men of Judah said, "Why have you come up against us?" They said, "We have come up to bind Samson, to do to him as he did to us." Then three thousand men of Judah went down to the cleft of the rock of Etam, and said to Samson, "Do you not know that the Philistines are rulers over us? What then is this that you have done to us?" And he said to them, "As they did to me, so have I done to them." And they said to him, "We have come down to bind you, that we may give you into the hands of the Philistines." And Samson said to them, "Swear to me that you will not fall upon me yourselves." They said to him, "No; we will only bind you and give you into their hands; we will not kill you." So they bound him with two new ropes, and brought him up from the rock. When they came to Lehi, the Philistines came shouting to meet him; and the Spirit of the Lord came mightily upon him, and the ropes which were on his arms became as flax that has caught fire, and his bonds melted off his hands. And he found a fresh jawbone of an ass, and put out his hand and seized it, and with it he slew a thousand men. And Samson said, "With the jawbone of an ass, heaps upon heaps, with the jawbone of an ass have I slain a thousand men." When he had finished speaking, he threw away the jawbone out of his hand; and that place was called Ra'math-le'hi. And he was very thirsty, and he called on the Lord and said, "Thou hast granted this great deliverance by the hand of thy servant; and shall I now die of thirst, and fall into the hands of the uncircumcised?"

And God split open the hollow place that is at Lehi, and there came water from it; and when he drank, his spirit returned, and he revived. Therefore the name of it was called En-hak'kore; it is at Lehi to this day. And he judged Israel in the days of the Philistines twenty years.

A Reading (Lesson) from the Acts of the Apostles [7:17-29]

Stephen said to the high priest and to the council: "As the time of the promise drew near, which God had granted to Abraham, the people grew and multiplied in Egypt till there arose over Egypt another king who had not known Joseph. He dealt craftily with our race and forced our fathers to expose their infants, that they might not be kept alive. At this time Moses was born, and was beautiful before God. And he was brought up for three months in his father's house; and when he was exposed, Pharaoh's daughter adopted him and brought him up as her own son. And Moses was instructed in all the wisdom of the Egyptians, and he was mighty in his words and deeds. When he was forty years old, it came into his heart to visit his brethren, the sons of Israel. And seeing one of them being wronged, he defended the oppressed man and avenged him by striking the Egyptian. He supposed that his brethren understood that God was giving them deliverance by his hand, but they did not understand. And on the following day he appeared to them as they were quarreling and would have reconciled them, saying, 'Men, you are brethren, why do you wrong each other?' But the man who was wronging his neighbor thrust him aside, saying, 'Who made you a ruler and a judge over us? Do you want to kill me as you killed the Egyptian yesterday?' At this retort Moses fled, and bcame an exile in the land of Mid'ian, where he became the father of two sons."

A Reading (Lesson) from the Gospel according to John
[4:43-54]

After two days in Samaria Jesus departed to Galilee. For
Jesus himself testified that a prophet has no honor in his
own country. So when he came to Galilee, the Galileans
welcomed him, having seen all that he had done in
Jerusalem at the feast, for they too had gone to the feast.
So he came again to Cana in Galilee, where he had made
the water wine. And at Caper'na-um there was an official
whose son was ill. When he heard that Jesus had come
from Judea to Galilee, he went and begged him to come
down and heal his son, for he was at the point of death.
Jesus therefore said to him, "Unless you see signs and
wonders you will not believe." The official said to him,
"Sir, come down before my child dies." Jesus said to him,
"Go; your son will live." The man believed the word that
Jesus spoke to him and went his way. As he was going
down, his servants met him and told him that his son was
living. So he asked them the hour when he began to mend,
and they said to him, "Yesterday at the seventh hour the
fever left him." The father knew that was the hour when
Jesus had said to him, "Your son will live"; and he himself
believed, and all his household. This was now the second
sign that Jesus did when he had come from Judea to
Galilee.

Saturday

Psalm 107:33-43 [page 748],   *Psalm 108:1-6(7-13)* [page 749]
❖   *Psalm 33* [page 626]

A Reading (Lesson) from the Book of Judges [16:1-14]

Samson went to Gaza, and there he saw a harlot, and he
went in to her. The Gazites were told, "Samson has come
here," and they surrounded the place and lay in wait for
him all night at the gate of the city. They kept quiet all

night, saying, "Let us wait till the light of the morning; then we will kill him." But Samson lay till midnight, and at midnight he arose and took hold of the doors of the gate of the city and the two posts, and pulled them up, bar and all, and put them on his shoulders and carried them to the top of the hill that is before Hebron. After this he loved a woman in the valley of Sorek, whose name was Deli′lah. And the lords of the Philistines came to her and said to her, "Entice him, and see wherein his great strength lies, and by what means we may overpower him, that we may bind him to subdue him; and we will give you eleven hundred pieces of silver." And Deli′lah said to Samson, "Please tell me wherein your great strength lies, and how you might be bound, that one could subdue you." And Samson said to her, "If they bind me with seven fresh bowstrings which have not been dried, then I shall become weak, and be like any other man." Then the lords of the Philistines brought her seven fresh bowstrings which had not been dried, and she bound him with them. Now she had men lying in wait in an inner chamber. And she said to him, "The Philistines are upon you, Samson!" But he snapped the bowstrings, as a string of tow snaps when it touches the fire. So the secret of his strength was not known. And Deli′lah said to Samson, "Behold, you have mocked me, and told me lies; please tell me how you might be bound." And he said to her, "If they bind me with new ropes that have not been used, then I shall become weak, and be like any other man." So Deli′lah took new ropes and bound him with them, and said to him, "The Philistines are upon you, Samson!" And the men lying in wait were in an inner chamber. But he snapped the ropes off his arms like a thread. And Deli′lah said to Samson, "Until now you have mocked me, and told me lies; tell me how you might be bound." And he said to her, "If you weave the seven locks of my head with the web and make it tight with the pin, then I shall become weak, and be like any other man." So while he slept, Deli′lah took the seven locks of his head and wove them into the web. And she made them tight with the pin, and said to him, "The Philistines are upon you, Samson!" But he awoke from his sleep, and pulled away the pin, the loom, and the web.

A Reading (Lesson) from the Acts of the Apostles [7:30-43]

Stephen said to the high priest and to the council: "When forty years had passed, an angel appeared to Moses in the wilderness of Mount Sinai, in a flame of fire in a bush. When Moses saw it he wondered at the sight; and as he drew near to look, the voice of the Lord came, 'I am the God of your fathers, the God of Abraham and of Isaac and of Jacob.' And Moses trembled and did not dare to look. And the Lord said to him, 'Take off the shoes from your feet, for the place where you are standing is holy ground. I have surely seen the ill-treatment of my people that are in Egypt and heard their groaning, and I have come down to deliver them. And now come, I will send you to Egypt.' This Moses whom they refused, saying, 'Who made you a ruler and a judge?' God sent as both ruler and deliverer by the hand of the angel that appeared to him in the bush. He led them out, having performed wonders and signs in Egypt and at the Red Sea, and in the wilderness for forty years. This is the Moses who said to the Israelites, 'God will raise up for you a prophet from your brethren as he raised me up.' This is he who was in the congregation in the wilderness with the angel who spoke to him at Mount Sinai, and with our fathers; and he received living oracles to give to us. Our fathers refused to obey him, but thrust him aside, and in their hearts they turned to Egypt, saying to Aaron, 'Make for us gods to go before us; as for this Moses who led us out from the land of Egypt, we do not know what has become of him.' And they made a calf in those days, and offered a sacrifice to the idol and rejoiced in the works of their hands. But God turned and gave them over to worship the host of heaven, as it is written in the book of the prophets: 'Did you offer to me slain beasts and sacrifices, forty years in the wilderness, O house of Israel?

And you took up the tent of Moloch, and the star of the god Rephan, the figures which you made to worship; and I will remove you beyond Babylon.'"

A Reading (Lesson) from the Gospel according to John
[5:1-18]

After his second sign there was a feast of the Jews, and Jesus went up to Jerusalem. Now there is in Jerusalem by the Sheep Gate a pool, in Hebrew called Beth-za'tha, which has five porticoes. In these lay a multitude of invalids, blind, lame, paralyzed. One man was there, who had been ill for thirty-eight years. When Jesus saw him and knew that he had been lying there a long time, he said to him, "Do you want to be healed?" The sick man answered him, "Sir, I have no man to put me into the pool when the water is troubled, and while I am going another steps down before me." Jesus said to him, "Rise, take up your pallet, and walk." And at once the man was healed, and he took up his pallet and walked. Now that day was the sabbath. So the Jews said to the man who was cured, "It is the sabbath, it is not lawful for you to carry your pallet." But he answered them, "The man who healed me said to me, 'Take up your pallet, and walk.'" They asked him, "Who is the man who said to you, 'Take up your pallet, and walk'?" Now the man who had been healed did not know who it was, for Jesus had withdrawn, as there was a crowd in the place. Afterward, Jesus found him in the temple, and said to him, "See, you are well! Sin no more, that nothing worse befall you." The man went away and told the Jews that it was Jesus who had healed him. And this was why the Jews persecuted Jesus, because he did this on the sabbath. But Jesus answered them, "My Father is working still, and I am working." This was why the Jews sought all the more to kill him, because he not only broke the sabbath but also called God his own Father, making himself equal with God.

Proper 15 *Week of the Sunday closest to August 17*

Sunday

Psalm 118 [page 760] ❖ *Psalm 145* [page 801]

A Reading (Lesson) from the Book of Judges [16:15-31]

Delilah said to Samson, "How can you say, 'I love you,' when your heart is not with me? You have mocked me these three times, and you have not told me wherein your great strength lies." And when she pressed him hard with her words day after day, and urged him, his soul was vexed to death. And he told her all his mind, and said to her, "A razor has never come upon my head; for I have been a Nazirite to God from my mother's womb. If I be shaved, then my strength will leave me, and I shall become weak, and be like any other man." When Delilah saw that he had told her all his mind, she sent and called the lords of the Philistines, saying, "Come up this once, for he has told me all his mind." Then the lords of the Philistines came up to her, and brought the money in their hands. She made him sleep upon her knees; and she called a man, and had him shave off the seven locks of his head. Then she began to torment him, and his strength left him. And she said, "The Philistines are upon you, Samson!" And he awoke from his sleep, and said, "I will go out as at other times, and shake myself free." And he did not know that the Lord had left him. And the Philistines seized him and gouged out his eyes, and brought him down to Gaza, and bound him with bronze fetters; and he ground at the mill in the prison. But the hair of his head began to grow again after it had been shaved. Now the lords of the Philistines gathered to offer a great sacrifice to Dagon their god, and to rejoice; for they said, "Our god has given Samson our enemy into our hand." And when the people saw him, they praised their god; for they said, "Our god has given our enemy into our hand, the ravager of our country, who has slain many of us." And when their hearts were merry, they said, "Call Samson, that he may make sport for us." So they called Samson out of the prison, and he made sport before them. They made him stand between the pillars; and Samson said to the lad who held him by the hand, "Let me feel the pillars on which the house rests, that I may lean against them." Now the house was full of men and women; all the lords of the Philistines were there, and on the roof there were about three thousand men and women, who looked on while Samson made sport. Then Samson called to the Lord and said, "O Lord God, remember me, I pray thee, and strengthen me, I pray thee, only this once, O God, that I may be avenged upon the Philistines for one of my two eyes." And Samson grasped the two middle pillars upon which the house rested, and he leaned his weight upon them, his right hand on the one and his left hand on the other. And Samson said, "Let me die with the Philistines." Then he bowed with all his might; and the house fell upon the lords and upon all the people that were in it. So the dead whom he slew at his death were more than those whom he had slain during his life. Then his brothers and all his family came down and took him and brought him up and buried him between Zorah and Esh'ta-ol in the tomb of Mano'ah his father. He had judged Israel twenty years.

A Reading (Lesson) from the Second Letter of Paul to the Corinthians [13:1-11]

This is the third time I am coming to you. Any charge must be sustained by the evidence of two or three witnesses. I warned those who sinned before and all the others, and I warn them now while absent, as I did when present on my second visit, that if I come again I will not spare them—since you desire proof that Christ is speaking in me. He is not weak in dealing with you, but is powerful in you. For he was crucified in weakness, but lives by the power of God. For we are weak in him, but in dealing with you we shall live with him by the power of God. Examine yourselves, to see whether you are holding to your faith. Test yourselves. Do you not realize that Jesus Christ is in you?—unless indeed you fail to meet the test! I hope you will find out that we have not failed. But we pray God that you may not do wrong—not that we may appear to have met the test, but that you may do what is right, though we may seem to have failed. For we cannot do anything against the truth, but only for the truth. For we are glad when we are weak and you are strong. What we pray for is your improvement. I write this while I am away from you, in order that when I come I may not have to be severe in my use of the authority which the Lord has given me for building up and not for tearing down. Finally, brethren, farewell. Mend your ways, heed my appeal, agree with one another, live in peace, and the God of love and peace will be with you.

A Reading (Lesson) from the Gospel according to Mark
[5:25-34]

There was a woman who had had a flow of blood for twelve years, and who had suffered much under many physicians, and had spent all that she had, and was no better but rather grew worse. She had heard the reports about Jesus, and came up behind him in the crowd and touched his garment. For she said, "If I touch even his garments, I shall be made well." And immediately the hemorrhage ceased; and she felt in her body that she was healed of her disease. And Jesus, perceiving in himself that power had gone forth from him, immediately turned about in the crowd, and said, "Who touched my garments?" And his disciples said to him, "You see the crowd pressing around you, and yet you say, 'Who touched me?'" And he looked around to see who had done it. But the woman, knowing what had been done to her, came in fear and trembling and fell down before him, and told him the whole truth. And he said to her, "Daughter, your faith has made you well; go in peace, and be healed of your disease."

Monday

Psalm 106:1-18 [page 741] ❖ *Psalm 106:19-48* [page 743]

A Reading (Lesson) from the Book of Judges [17:1-13]

There was a man of the hill country of E'phraim, whose name was Micah. And he said to his mother, "The eleven hundred pieces of silver which were taken from you, about which you uttered a curse, and also spoke it in my ears, behold, the silver is with me; I took it." And his mother said, "Blessed be my son by the Lord." And he restored the eleven hundred pieces of silver to his mother; and his mother said, "I consecrate the silver to the Lord from my hand for my son, to make a graven image and a molten image; now therefore I will restore it to you." So when he restored the money to his mother, his mother took two hundred pieces of silver, and gave it to the silversmith, who made it into a graven image and a molten image; and it was in the house of Micah. And the man Micah had a shrine, and he made an ephod and teraphim, and installed one of his sons, who became his priest. In those days there was no king in Israel; every man did what was right in his own eyes. Now there was a young man of Bethlehem in Judah, of the family of Judah, who was a Levite; and he sojourned there. And the man departed from the town of Bethlehem in Judah, to live where he could find a place; and as he journeyed, he came to the hill country of E'phraim to the house of Micah. And Micah said to him, "From where do you come?" And he said to him, "I am a Levite of Bethlehem in Judah, and I am going to sojourn where I may find a place." And Micah said to him, "Stay with me, and be to me a father and a priest, and I will give you ten pieces of silver a year, and a suit of apparel, and your living." And the Levite was content to dwell with the man; and the young man became to him like one of his sons. And Micah installed the Levite, and the young man became his priest, and was in the house of Micah. Then Micah said, "Now I know that the Lord will prosper me, because I have a Levite as a priest."

A Reading (Lesson) from the Acts of the Apostles
[7:44—8:1a]

Stephen said to the high priest and to the council: "Our fathers had the tent of witness in the wilderness, even as he who spoke to Moses directed him to make it, according to the pattern that he had seen. Our fathers in turn brought it in with Joshua when they dispossessed the nations which God thrust out before our fathers. So it was until the days of David, who found favor in the sight of God and asked leave to find a habitation for the God of Jacob. But it was Solomon who built a house for him. Yet the Most High does not dwell in houses made with hands; as the prophet says, 'Heaven is my throne, and earth my footstool. What house will you build for me, says the Lord, or what is the place of my rest? Did not my hand make all these things?' You stiff-necked people, uncircumcised in heart and ears, you always resist the Holy Spirit. As your fathers did, so do you. Which of the prophets did not your fathers persecute? And they killed those who announced beforehand the coming of the Righteous One, whom you have now betrayed and murdered, you who received the law as delivered by angels and did not keep it." Now when they heard these things they were enraged, and they ground their teeth against him. But he, full of the Holy Spirit, gazed into heaven and saw the glory of God, and Jesus standing at the right hand of God; and he said, "Behold, I see the heavens opened, and the Son of man standing at the right hand of God." But they cried out with a loud voice and stopped their ears and rushed together upon him. Then they cast him out of the city and stoned him; and the witnesses laid down their garments at the feet of a young man named Saul. And as they were stoning Stephen, he prayed, "Lord Jesus, receive my spirit." And he knelt down and cried with a loud voice, "Lord, do not hold this sin against them." And when he had said this, he fell asleep. And Saul was consenting to his death.

A Reading (lesson) fromt he Gospel according to John [5:19-29]

Jesus said to the Jews, "Truly, truly, I say to you, the Son can do nothing of his own accord, but only what he sees the Father doing; for whatever he does, that the Son does likewise. For the Father loves the Son, and shows him all that he himself is doing; and greater works than these will he show him, that you may marvel. For as the Father raises the dead and gives them life, so also the Son gives life to whom he will. The Father judges no one, but has given all judgment to the Son, that all may honor the Son, even as they honor the Father. He who does not honor the Son does not honor the Father who sent him. Truly, truly, I say to you, he who hears my word and believes him who sent me, has eternal life; he does not come into judgment, but has passed from death to life. Truly, truly, I say to you, the hour is coming, and now is, when the dead will hear the voice of the Son of God, and those who hear will live. For as the Father has life in himself, so he has granted the Son also to have life in himself, and has given him authority to execute judgment, because he is the Son of man. Do not marvel at his; for the hour is coming when all who are in the tombs will hear his voice and come forth, those who have done good, to the resurrection of life, and those who have done evil, to the resurrection of judgment."

Tuesday

(*Psalm 120* [page 778]),   *Psalm 121* [page 779],
Psalm 122 [page 779],   *Psalm 123* [page 780]   ❖
Psalm 124 [page 781],   *Psalm 125* [page 781],
Psalm 126 [page 782],   (*Psalm 127* [page 782])

A Reading (Lesson) from the Book of Judges [18:1-15]

In those days there was no king in Israel. And in those days
the tribe of the Danites was seeking for itself an inheritance
to dwell in; for until then no inheritance among the tribes
of Israel had fallen to them. So the Danites sent five able
men from the whole number of their tribe, from Zorah and
from Esh'ta-ol, to spy out the land and to explore it; and
they said to them, "Go and explore the land." And they
came to the hill country of E'phraim, to the house of
Micah, and lodged there. When they were by the house of
Micah, they recognized the voice of the young Levite; and
they turned aside and said to him, "Who brought you
here? What are you doing in this place? What is your
business here?" And he said to them, "Thus and thus has
Micah dealt with me; he has hired me, and I have become
his priest." And they said to him, "Inquire of God, we pray
thee, that we may know whether the journey on which we
are setting out will succeed." And the priest said to them,
"Go in peace. The journey on which you go is under the eye
of the Lord." Then the five men departed, and came to
La'ish, and saw the people who were there, how they dwelt
in security, after the manner of the Sido'nians, quiet and
unsuspecting, lacking nothing that is in the earth, and
possessing wealth, and how they were far from the
Sido'nians and had no dealings with any one. And when
they came to their brethren at Zorah and Esh'ta-ol, their
brethren said to them, "What do you report?" They said,
"Arise, and let us go up against them; for we have seen the
land, and behold, it is very fertile. And will you do
nothing? Do not be slow to go, and enter in and possess
the land. When you go, you will come to an unsuspecting
people. The land is broad; yea, God has given it into your
hands, a place where there is no lack of anything that is in
the earth." And six hundred men of the tribe of Dan,
armed with weapons of war, set forth from Zorah and
Esh'ta-ol, and went up and encamped at Kir'iath-je'arim in
Judah. On this account that place is called Ma'haneh-dan

to this day; behold, it is west of Kir'iath-je'arim. And they passed on from there to the hill country of E'phraim, and came to the house of Micah. Then the five men who had gone to spy out the country of La'ish said to their brethren, "Do you know that in these houses there are an ephod, teraphim, a graven image, and a molten image? Now therefore consider what you will do." And they turned aside thither, and came to the house of the young Levite, at the home of Micah, and asked him of his welfare.

A Reading (Lesson) from the Acts of the Apostles [8:1-13]

Saul was consenting to Stephen's death. And on the day he was stoned a great persecution arose against the church in Jerusalem; and they were all scattered throughout the region of Judea and Samar'ia, except the apostles. Devout men buried Stephen, and made great lamentation over him. But Saul was ravaging the church, and entering house after house, he dragged off men and women and committed them to prison. Now those who were scattered went about preaching the word. Philip went down to a city of Samar'ia, and proclaimed to them the Christ. And the multitudes with one accord gave heed to what was said by Philip, when they heard him and saw the signs which he did. For unclean spirits came out of many who were possessed, crying with a loud voice; and many who were paralyzed or lame were healed. So there was much joy in that city. But there was a man named Simon who had previously practiced magic in the city and amazed the nation of Samar'ia, saying that he himself was somebody great. They all gave heed to him, from the least to the greatest, saying, "This man is that power of God, which is called Great." And they gave heed to him, because for a long time he had amazed them with his magic. But when they believed Philip as he preached good news about the kingdom of God and the name of Jesus Christ, they were baptized, both men and women. Even Simon himself believed, and after being baptized he continued with Philip. And seeing signs and great miracles performed, he was amazed.

A Reading (Lesson) from the Gospel according to John [5:30-47]

Jesus said to the Jews, "I can do nothing on my own authority; as I hear, I judge; and my judgment is just, because I seek not my own will but the will of him who sent me. If I bear witness to myself, my testimony is not true; there is another who bears witness to me, and I know that the testimony which he bears to me is true. You sent to John, and he has borne witness to the truth. Not that the testimony which I receive is from man; but I say this that you may be saved. He was a burning and shining lamp, and you were willing to rejoice for a while in his light. But the testimony which I have is greater than that of John; for the works which the Father has granted me to accomplish, these very works which I am doing, bear me witness that the Father has sent me. And the father who sent me has himself borne witness to me. His voice you have never heard, his form you have never seen; and you do not have his word abiding in you, for you do not believe him whom he has sent. You search the scriptures, because you think that in them you have eternal life; and it is they that bear witness to me; yet you refuse to come to me that you may have life. I do not receive glory from men. But I know that you have not the love of God within you. I have come in my Father's name, and you do not receive me; if another comes in his own name, him you will receive. How can you believe, who receive glory from one another and do not seek the glory that comes from the only God? Do not think that I shall accuse you to the Father; it is Moses who accuses you, on whom you set your hope. If you believed Moses, you would believe me, for he wrote of me. But if you do not believe his writings, how will you believe my words?"

Wednesday

Psalm 119:145-176 [page 775]   ❖   *Psalm 128* [page 783],
Psalm 129 [page 784],   *Psalm 130* [page 784]

A Reading (Lesson) from the Book of Judges [18:16-31]

The six hundred men of the Danites, armed with their
weapons of war, stood by the entrance of the gate; and the
five men who had gone to spy out the land went up, and
entered and took the graven image, the ephod, the
teraphim, and the molten image, while the priest stood by
the entrance of the gate with the six hundred men armed
with weapons of war. And when these went into Micah's
house and took the graven image, the ephod, the teraphim,
and the molten image, the priest said to them, "What are
you doing?" And they said to him, "Keep quiet, put your
hand upon your mouth, and come with us, and be to us a
father and a priest. Is it better for you to be priest to the
house of one man, or to be priest to a tribe and family in
Israel?" And the priest's heart was glad, he took the ephod,
and the teraphim, and the graven image, and went in the
midst of the people. So they turned and departed, putting
the little ones and the cattle and the goods in front of them.
When they were a good way from the home of Micah, the
men who were in the houses near Micah's house were
called out, and they overtook the Danites. And they
shouted to the Danites, who turned round and said to
Micah, "What ails you that you come with such a
company?" And he said, "You take my gods which I made,
and the priest, and go away, and what have I left? How
then do you ask me, 'What ails you?' " And the Danites
said to him, "Do not let your voice be heard among us, lest
angry fellows fall upon you, and you lose your life with the
lives of your household." Then the Danites went their way;
and when Micah saw that they were too strong for him, he
turned and went back to his home. And taking what
Micah had made, and the priest who belonged to him, the

Danites came to La'ish, to a people quiet and unsuspecting, and smote them with the edge of the sword, and burned the city with fire. And there was no deliverer because it was far from Sidon, and they had no dealings with any one. It was in the valley which belongs to Beth-re'hob. And they rebuilt the city, and dwelt in it. And they named the city Dan, after the name of Dan their ancestor, who was born to Israel; but the name of the city was La'ish at the first. And the Danites set up the graven image for themselves; and Jonathan the son of Gershom, son of Moses, and his sons were priests to the tribe of the Danites until the day of the captivity of the land. So they set up Micah's graven image which he made, as long as the house of God was at Shiloh.

Acts 8:14-25 [page 40 above]

A Reading (Lesson) from the Gospel according to John [6:1-15]

Jesus went to the other side of the Sea of Galilee, which is the Sea of Tibe'ri-as. And a multitude followed him, because they saw the signs which he did on those who were diseased. Jesus went up on the mountain, and there sat down with his disciples. Now the Passover, the feast of the Jews, was at hand. Lifting up his eyes, then, and seeing that a multitude was coming to him, Jesus said to Philip, "How are we to buy bread, so that these people may eat?" This he said to test him, for he himself knew what he would do. Philip answered him, "Two hundred denarii would not buy enough bread for each of them to get a little." One of his disciples, Andrew, Simon Peter's brother, said to him, "There is a lad here who has five barley loaves and two fish; but what are they among so many?" Jesus said, "Make the people sit down." Now there was much grass in the place; so the men sat down, in number about five thousand. Jesus then took the loaves, and when he had given thanks, he distributed them to those who were seated; so also the fish, as much as they wanted. And when they had eaten their fill, he told his disciples, "Gather up the fragments left over, that nothing may be lost." So they gathered them up and filled twelve baskets with fragments from the five barley loaves, left by those who had eaten. When the people saw the sign which he had done, they said, "This is indeed the prophet who is to come into the world!" Perceiving then that they were about to come and take him by force to make him king, Jesus withdrew again to the mountain by himself.

Thursday

Psalm 131 [page 785], *Psalm 132* [page 785], *(Psalm 133* [page 787]) ❖ *Psalm 134* [page 787], *Psalm 135* [page 788]

A Reading (Lesson) from the Book of Job [1:1-22]

There was a man in the land of Uz, whose name was Job; and that man was blameless and upright, one who feared God, and turned away from evil. There were born to him seven sons and three daughters. He had seven thousand sheep, three thousand camels, five hundred yoke of oxen, and five hundred she-asses, and very many servants; so that this man was the greatest of all the people of the east. His sons used to go and hold a feast in the house of each on his day; and they would send and invite their three sisters to eat and drink with them. And when the days of the feast had run their course, Job would send and sanctify them, and he would rise early in the morning and offer burnt offerings according to the number of them all; for Job said, "It may be that my sons have sinned, and cursed God in their hearts." Thus Job did continually. Now there was a day when the sons of God came to present themselves before the Lord, and Satan also came among them. The Lord said to Satan, "Whence have you come?" Satan answered the Lord, "From going to and fro on the earth, and from walking up and down on it." And the Lord said to Satan, "Have you considered my servant Job, that there is none like him on the earth, a blameless and upright man, who fears God and turns away from evil?" Then Satan answered the Lord, "Does Job fear God for nought? Hast thou not put a hedge about him and his house and all that he has, on every side? Thou hast blessed the work of his hands, and his possessions have increased in the land. But put forth thy hand now, and touch all that he has, and he will curse thee to thy face." And the Lord said to Satan, "Behold, all that he has is in your power; only upon himself do not put forth your hand." So Satan went forth from the presence of the Lord. Now there was a day when his sons and daughters were eating and drinking wine in their eldest brother's house; and there came a messenger to Job, and said, "The oxen were plowing and the asses feeding beside them; and the Sabe'ans fell upon them and took them, and slew the servants with the edge of the sword; and I alone have escaped to tell you." While he was yet speaking, there came another, and said, "The fire of God fell from heaven and burned up the sheep and the servants, and consumed them; and I alone have escaped to tell you." While he was yet speaking, there came another, and said, "The Chalde'ans formed three companies, and made a raid upon the camels and took them, and slew the servants with the edge of the sword; and I alone have escaped to tell you." While he was yet speaking, there came another, and said, "Your sons and daughters were eating and drinking wine in their eldest brother's house; and behold, a great wind came across the wilderness, and struck the four corners of the house, and it fell upon the young people, and they are dead; and I alone have escaped to tell you." Then Job arose, and rent his robe, and shaved his head, and fell upon the ground, and worshiped. And he said, "Naked I came from my mother's womb, and naked shall I return; the Lord gave, and the Lord has taken away; blessed be the name of the Lord." In all this Job did not sin or charge God with wrong.

Acts 8:26-40   [page 55 above]

A Reading (Lesson) from the Gospel according to John
[6:16-27]

When evening came, Jesus' disciples went down to the sea, got into a boat, and started across the sea to Caper'na-um. It was now dark, and Jesus had not yet come to them. The sea rose because a strong wind was blowing. When they had rowed about three or four miles, they saw Jesus walking on the sea and drawing near to the boat. They were frightened, but he said to them, "It is I; do not be afraid." Then they were glad to take him into the boat, and immediately the boat was at the land to which they were going. On the next day the people who remained on the other side of the sea saw that there had been only one boat there, and that Jesus had not entered the boat with his disciples, but that his disciples had gone away alone. However, boats from Tibe'ri-as came near the place where they ate the bread after the Lord had given thanks. So when the people saw that Jesus was not there, nor his disciples, they themselves got into the boats and went to Caper'na-um, seeking Jesus. When they found him on the other side of the sea, they said to him, "Rabbi, when did you come here?" Jesus answered them, "Truly, truly, I say to you, you seek me, not because you saw signs, but because you ate your fill of the loaves. Do not labor for the food which perishes, but for the food which endures to eternal life, which the Son of man will give to you; for on him has God the Father set his seal."

Friday

Psalm 140 [page 796],   *Psalm 142* [page 798]   ❖
Psalm 141 [page 797],   *Psalm 143:1-11(12)* [page 798]

A Reading (Lesson) from the Book of Job [2:1-13]

Again there was a day when the sons of God came to present themselves before the Lord, and Satan also came among them to present himself before the Lord. And the Lord said to Satan, "Whence have you come?" Satan answered the Lord, "From going to and fro on the earth, and from walking up and down on it." And the Lord said to Satan, "Have you considered my servant Job, that there is none like him on the earth, a blameless and upright man, who fears God and turns away from evil? He still holds fast his integrity, although you moved me against him, to destroy him without cause." Then Satan answered the Lord, "Skin for skin! All that a man has he will give for his life. But put forth thy hand now, and touch his bone and his flesh, and he will curse thee to thy face." And the Lord said to Satan, "Behold, he is in your power; only spare his life." So Satan went forth from the presence of the Lord, and afflicted Job with loathsome sores from the sole of his foot to the crown of his head. And he took a potsherd with which to scrape himself, and sat among the ashes. Then his wife said to him, "Do you still hold fast your integrity? Curse God, and die." But he said to her, "You speak as one of the foolish women would speak. Shall we receive good at the hand of God, and shall we not receive evil?" In all this Job did not sin with his lips. Now when Job's three friends heard of all this evil that had come upon him, they came each from his own place, El'iphaz the Te'manite, Bildad the Shuhite, and Zophar the Na'amathite. They made an appointment together to come to condole with him and comfort him. And when they saw him from afar, they did not recognize him; and they raised their voices and wept; and they rent their robes and sprinkled dust upon their heads toward heaven. And they sat with him on the ground seven days and seven nights, and no one spoke a word to him, for they saw that his suffering was very great.

A Reading (Lesson) from the Acts of the Apostles [9:1-9]

Saul, still breathing threats and murder against the disciples of the Lord, went to the high priest and asked him for letters to the synagogues at Damascus, so that if he found any belonging to the Way, men or women, he might bring them bound to Jerusalem. Now as he journeyed he approached Damascus, and suddenly a light from heaven flashed about him. And he fell to the ground and heard a voice saying to him, "Saul, Saul, why do you persecute me?" And he said, "Who are you, Lord?" And he said, "I am Jesus, whom you are persecuting; but rise and enter the city, and you will be told what you are to do." The men who were traveling with him stood speechless, hearing the voice but seeing no one. Saul arose from the ground; and when his eyes were opened, he could see nothing; so they led him by the hand and brought him into Damascus. And for three days he was without sight, and neither ate nor drank.

A Reading (Lesson) from the Gospel according to John [6:27-40]

Jesus answered the people, "Do not labor for the food which perishes, but for the food which endures to eternal life, which the Son of man will give to you; for on him has God the Father set his seal." Then they said to him, "What must we do, to be doing the works of God?" Jesus answered them, "This is the work of God, that you believe in him whom he has sent." So they said to him, "Then what sign do you do, that we may see, and believe you? What work do you perform? Our fathers ate the manna in the wilderness; as it is written, 'He gave them bread from heaven to eat.'" Jesus then said to them, "Truly, truly, I say to you, it was not Moses who gave you the bread from heaven; my Father gives you the true bread from heaven. For the bread of God is that which comes down from heaven, and gives life to the world." They said to him,

"Lord, give us this bread always." Jesus said to them, "I am the bread of life; he who comes to me shall not hunger, and he who believes in me shall never thirst. But I said to you that you have seen me and yet do not believe. All that the Father gives me will come to me; and him who comes to me I will not cast out. For I have come down from heaven, not to do my own will, but the will of him who sent me; and this is the will of him who sent me, that I should lose nothing of all that he has given me, but raise it up at the last day. For this is the will of my Father, that every one who sees the Son and believes in him should have eternal life; and I will raise him up at the last day."

Saturday

Psalm 137:1-6(7-9) [page 792],   *Psalm 144* [page 801]   ❖
Psalm 104 [page 735]

A Reading (Lesson) from the Book of Job [3:1-26]

After seven days of sitting with his friends Job opened his mouth and cursed the day of his birth. And Job said: "Let the day perish wherein I was born, and the night which said, 'A man-child is conceived.' Let that day be darkness! May God above not seek it, nor light shine upon it. Let gloom and deep darkness claim it. Let clouds dwell upon it; let the blackness of the day terrify it. That night—let thick darkness seize it! let it not rejoice among the days of the year, let it not come into the number of the months. Yea, let that night be barren; let no joyful cry be heard in it. Let those curse it who curse the day, who are skilled to rouse up Leviathan. Let the stars of its dawn be dark; let it hope for light, but have none, nor see the eyelids of the morning; because it did not shut the doors of my mother's womb, nor hide trouble from my eyes. Why did I not die at birth, come forth from the womb and expire? Why did the knees receive me? Or why the breasts, that I should suck?

For then I should have lain down and been quiet; I should have slept; then I should have been at rest, with kings and counselors of the earth who rebuilt ruins for themselves, or with princes who had gold, who filled their houses with silver. Or why was I not as a hidden untimely birth, as infants that never see the light? There the wicked cease from troubling, and there the weary are at rest. There the prisoners are at ease together; they hear not the voice of the taskmaster. The small and the great are there, and the slave is free from his master. Why is light given to him that is in misery, and life to the bitter in soul, who long for death, but it comes not, and dig for it more than for hid treasures; who rejoice exceedingly, and are glad, when they find the grave? Why is light given to a man whose way is hid, whom God has hedged in? For my sighing comes as my bread, and my groanings are poured out like water. For the thing that I fear comes upon me, and what I dread befalls me. I am not at ease, nor am I quiet; I have no rest; but trouble comes."

A Reading (Lesson) from the Acts of the Apostles
[9:10-19a]

There was a disciple at Damascus named Anani'as. The Lord said to him in a vision, "Anani'as." And he said, "Here I am, Lord." And the Lord said to him, "Rise and go to the street called Straight, and inquire in the house of Judas for a man of Tarsus named Saul; for behold, he is praying, and he has seen a man named Anani'as come in and lay his hands on him so that he might regain his sight." But Anani'as answered, "Lord, I have heard from many about this man, how much evil he has done to thy saints at Jerusalem; and here he has authority from the chief priests to bind all who call upon thy name." But the Lord said to him, "Go, for he is a chosen instrument of mine to carry my name before the Gentiles and kings and the sons of Israel; for I will show him how much he must suffer for the sake of my name." So Anani'as departed and entered the house. And laying his hands on him he said, "Brother Saul, the Lord Jesus who appeared to you on the road by which you came, has sent me that you may regain your sight and be filled with the Holy Spirit." And immediately something like scales fell from his eyes and he regained his sight. Then he rose and was baptized, and took food and was strengthened.

A Reading (Lesson) from the Gospel according to John [6:41-51]

The Jews murmured at Jesus, because he said, "I am the bread which came down from heaven." They said, "Is not this Jesus, the son of Joseph, whose father and mother we know? How does he now say, 'I have come down from heaven'?" Jesus answered them, "Do not murmur among yourselves. No one can come to me unless the Father who sent me draws him; and I will raise him up at the last day. It is written in the prophets, 'And they shall all be taught by God.' Every one who has heard and learned from the Father comes to me. Not that any one has seen the Father except him who is from God; he has seen the Father. Truly, truly, I say to you, he who believes has eternal life. I am the bread of life. Your fathers ate manna in the wilderness, and they died. This is the bread which comes down from heaven, that a man may eat of it and not die. I am the living bread which came down from heaven; if any one eats of this bread, he will live for ever; and the bread which I shall give for the life of the world is my flesh."

Proper 16   *Week of the Sunday closest to August 24*

Sunday

Psalm 146 [page 803],   *Psalm 147* [page 804]   ❖
Psalm 111 [page 754],   *Psalm 112* [page 755],
Psalm 113 [page 756]

A Reading (Lesson) from the Book of Job [4:1-6,12-21]

El'iphaz the Te'manite answered: "If one ventures a word with you, will you be offended? Yet who can keep from speaking? Behold, you have instructed many, and you have strengthened the weak hands. Your words have upheld him who was stumbling, and you have made firm the feeble knees. But now it has come to you, and you are impatient; it touches you, and you are dismayed. Is not your fear of God your confidence, and the integrity of your ways your hope? Now a word was brought to me stealthily, my ear received the whisper of it. Amid thoughts from visions of the night, when deep sleep falls on men, dread came upon me, and trembling, which made all my bones shake. A spirit glided past my face; the hair of my flesh stood up. It stood still, but I could not discern its appearance. A form was before my eyes; there was silence, than I heard a voice: 'Can mortal man be righteous before God? Can a man be pure before his Maker? Even in his servants he puts no trust, and his angels he charges with error; how much more those who dwell in houses of clay, whose foundation is in the dust, who are crushed before the moth. Between morning and evening they are destroyed; they perish for ever without any regarding it. If their tent-cord is plucked up within them, do they not die, and that without wisdom?'"

A Reading (Lesson) from the Revelation to John [4:1-11]

After this I looked, and lo, in heaven an open door! And the first voice, which I had heard speaking to me like a trumpet, said, "Come up hither, and I will show you what must take place after this." At once I was in the Spirit, and lo, a throne stood in heaven, with one seated on the throne! And he who sat there appeared like jasper and carnelian, and round the throne was a rainbow that looked like an emerald. Round the throne were twenty-four thrones, and seated on the thrones were twenty-four elders, clad in white garments, with golden crowns upon their heads. From the throne issue flashes of lightning, and voices and peals of thunder, and before the throne burn seven torches of fire, which are the seven spirits of God; and before the throne there is as it were a sea of glass, like crystal. And round the throne, on each side of the throne, are four living creatures, full of eyes in front and behind: the first living creature like a lion, the second living creature like an ox, the third living creature with the face of a man, and the fourth living creature like a flying eagle. And the four living creatures, each of them with six wings, are full of eyes all round and within, and day and night they never cease to sing, "Holy, holy, holy, is the Lord God Almighty, who was and is and is to come!" And whenever the living creatures give glory and honor and thanks to him who is seated on the throne, who lives for ever and ever, the twenty-four elders fall down before him who is seated on the throne and worship him who lives for ever and ever; they cast their crowns before the throne, singing, "Worthy art thou, our Lord and God, to receive glory and honor and power, for thou didst create all things, and by thy will they existed and were created."

A Reading (Lesson) from the Gospel according to Mark
[6:1-6a]

Jesus went away from there and came to his own country; and his disciples followed him. And on the sabbath he began to teach in the synagogue; and many who heard him were astonished, saying, "Where did this man get all this? What is the wisdom given to him? What mighty works are wrought by his hands! Is not this the carpenter, the son of Mary and brother of James and Joses and Judas and Simon, and are not his sisters here with us?" And they took offense at him. And Jesus said to them, "A prophet is not without honor, except in his own country, and among his own kin, and in his own house." And he could do no mighty work there, except that he laid his hands upon a few sick people and healed them. And he marveled because of their unbelief.

Monday

Psalm 1 [page 585], *Psalm 2* [page 586],
Psalm 3 [page 587], ❖ *Psalm 4* [page 587],
Psalm 7 [page 590]

A Reading (Lesson) from the Book of Job
[4:1;5:1-11,17-21,26-27]

El'iphaz the Te'manite answered: "Call now; is there any one who will answer you? To which of the holy ones will you turn? Surely vexation kills the fool, and jealousy slays the simple. I have seen the fool taking root, but suddenly I cursed his dwelling. His sons are far from safety, they are crushed in the gate, and there is no one to deliver them. His harvest the hungry eat, and he takes it even out of thorns; and the thirsty pant after his wealth. For affliction does not come from the dust, nor does trouble sprout from the ground; but man is born to trouble as the sparks fly upward. As for me, I would seek God, and to God would I commit my cause; who does great things and unsearchable, marvelous things without number: he gives rain upon the earth and sends waters upon the fields; he sets on high those who are lowly, and those who mourn are lifted to safety. Behold, happy is the man whom God reproves; therefore despise not the chastening of the Almighty. For he wounds, but he binds up; he smites, but his hands heal. He will deliver you from six troubles; in seven there shall no evil touch you. In famine he will redeem you from death, and in war from the power of the sword. You shall be hid from the scourge of the tongue, and shall not fear destruction when it comes. You shall come to your grave in ripe old age, as a shock of grain comes up to the threshing floor in its season. Lo, this we have searched out; it is true. Hear, and know it for your good."

A Reading (Lesson) from the Acts of the Apostles
[9:19b-31]

For several days Saul was with the disciples at Damascus.
And in the synagogues immediately he proclaimed Jesus,
saying, "He is the Son of God." And all who heard him
were amazed, and said, "Is not this the man who made
havoc in Jerusalem of those who called on this name? And
he has come here for this purpose, to bring them bound
before the chief priests." But Saul increased all the more in
strength, and confounded the Jews who lived in Damascus
by proving that Jesus was the Christ. When many days had
passed, the Jews plotted to kill him, but their plot became
known to Saul. They were watching the gates day and
night, to kill him; but his disciples took him by night and
let him down over the wall, lowering him in a basket. And
when he had come to Jerusalem he attempted to join the
disciples; and they were all afraid of him, for they did not
believe that he was a disciple. But Barnabas took him, and
brought him to the apostles, and declared to them how on
the road he had seen the Lord, who spoke to him, and how
at Damascus he had preached boldly in the name of Jesus.
So he went in and out among them at Jerusalem, preaching
boldly in the name of the Lord. And he spoke and disputed
against the Hellenists; but they were seeking to kill him.
And when the brethren knew it, they brought him down to
Caesare′a, and sent him off to Tarsus. So the church
throughout all Judea and Galilee and Samar′ia had peace
and was built up; and walking in the fear of the Lord and
in the comfort of the Holy Spirit it was multiplied.

A Reading (Lesson) from the Gospel according to John
[6:52-59]

The Jews disputed among themselves, saying, "How can
this man give us his flesh to eat?" So Jesus said to them,
"Truly, truly, I say to you, unless you eat the flesh of the Son
of man and drink his blood, you have no life in you; he

who eats my flesh and drinks my blood has eternal life, and I will raise him up at the last day. For my flesh is food indeed, and my blood is drink indeed. He who eats my flesh and drinks my blood abides in me, and I in him. As the living Father sent me, and I live because of the Father, so he who eats me will live because of me. This is the bread which came down from heaven, not such as the fathers ate and died; he who eats this bread will live for ever." This he said in the synagogue, as he taught at Caper'na-um.

Tuesday

Psalm 5 [page 588], *Psalm 6* [page 589]   ❖
Psalm 10 [page 594], *Psalm 11* [page 596]

A Reading (Lesson) from the Book of Job [6:1-4,8-15,21]

Job answered: "O that my vexation were weighed, and all my calamity laid in the balances! For then it would be heavier than the sand of the sea; therefore my words have been rash. For the arrows of the Almighty are in me; my spirit drinks of their poison; the terrors of God are arrayed against me. O that I might have my request, and that God would grant my desire; that it would please God to crush me, that he would let loose his hand and cut me off! This would be my consolation; I would even exult in pain unsparing; for I have not denied the words of the Holy One. What is my strength, that I should wait? And what is my end, that I should be patient? Is my strength the strength of stones, or is my flesh bronze? In truth I have no help in me, and any resource is driven from me. He who withholds kindness from a friend forsakes the fear of the Almighty. My brethren are treacherous as a torrent-bed, as freshets that pass away. Such you have now become to me; you see my calamity, and are afraid."

A Reading (Lesson) from the Acts of the Apostles
[9:32-43]

As Peter went here and there among them all, he came
down also to the saints that lived at Lydda. There he found
a man named Aene'as, who had been bedridden for eight
years and was paralyzed. And Peter said to him, "Aene'as,
Jesus Christ heals you; rise and make your bed." And
immediately he rose. And all the residents of Lydda and
Sharon saw him, and they turned to the Lord. Now there
was at Joppa a disciple named Tabitha, which means
Dorcas. She was full of good works and acts of charity. In
those days she fell sick and died; and when they had
washed her, they laid her in an upper room. Since Lydda
was near Joppa, the disciples, hearing that Peter was there,
sent two men to him entreating him, "Please come to us
without delay." So Peter rose and went with them. And
when he had come, they took him to the upper room. All
the widows stood beside him weeping, and showing tunics
and other garments which Dorcas made while she was
with them. But Peter put them all outside and knelt down
and prayed; then turning to the body he said, "Tabitha,
rise." And she opened her eyes, and when she saw Peter she
sat up. And he gave her his hand and lifted her up. Then
calling the saints and widows he presented her alive. And it
became known throughout all Joppa, and many believed
in the Lord. And he stayed in Joppa for many days with
one Simon, a tanner.

A Reading (Lesson) from the Gospel according to John
[6:60-71]

Many of Jesus' disciples, when they heard it, said, "This is
a hard saying; who can listen to it?" But Jesus, knowing in
himself that his disciples murmured at it, said to them,
"Do you take offense at this? Then what if you were to see
the Son of man ascending where he was before? It is the

spirit that gives life, the flesh is of no avail; the words that I
have spoken to you are spirit and life. But there are some
of you that do not believe." For Jesus knew from the first
who those were that did not believe, and who it was that
would betray him. And he said, "This is why I told you
that no one can come to me unless it is granted him by the
Father." After this many of his disciples drew back and no
longer went about with him. Jesus said to the twelve, "Do
you also wish to go away?" Simon Peter answered him,
"Lord, to whom shall we go? You have the words of eternal
life; and we have believed, and have come to know, that
you are the Holy One of God." Jesus answered them, "Did
I not choose you, the twelve, and one of you is a devil?" He
spoke of Judas the son of Simon Iscariot, for he, one of the
twelve, was to betray him.

Wednesday

Psalm 119:1-24 [page 763] ❖ *Psalm 12* [page 597],
Psalm 13 [page 597], *Psalm 14* [page 598]

A Reading (Lesson) from the Book of Job [6:1;7:1-21]

Job answered: "Has not man a hard service upon earth,
and are not his days like the days of a hireling? Like a
slave who longs for the shadow, and like a hireling who
looks for his wages, so I am allotted months of emptiness,
and nights of misery are apportioned to me. When I lie
down I say, 'When shall I arise?' But the night is long, and I
am full of tossing till the dawn. My flesh is clothed with
worms and dirt; my skin hardens, then breaks out afresh.
My days are swifter than a weaver's shuttle, and come to
their end without hope. Remember that my life is a breath;
my eye will never again see good. The eye of him who sees
me will behold me no more; while thy eyes are upon me, I
shall be gone. As the cloud fades and vanishes, so he who

goes down to Sheol does not come up; he returns no more to his house, nor does his place know him any more. Therefore I will not restrain my mouth; I will speak in the anguish of my spirit; I will complain in the bitterness of my soul. Am I the sea, or a sea monster, that thou settest a guard over me? When I say, 'My bed will comfort me, my couch will ease my complaint,' then thou dost scare me with reams and terrify me with visions, so that I would choose strangling and death rather than my bones. I loathe my life; I would not live for ever. Let me alone, for my days are a breath. What is man, that thou dost make so much of him, and that thou dost set thy mind upon him, dost visit him every morning, and test him every moment? How long wilt thou not look away from me, nor let me alone till I swallow my spittle? If I sin, what do I do to thee, thou watcher of men? Why hast thou made me thy mark? Why have I become a burden to thee? Why dost thou not pardon my transgression and take away my iniquity? For now I shall lie in the earth; thou wilt seek me, but I shall not be."

A Reading (Lesson) from the Acts of the Apostles
[10:1-16]

At Caesare'a there was a man named Cornelius, a centurion of what was known as the Italian Cohort, a devout man who feared God with all his household, gave alms liberally to the people, and prayed constantly to God. About the ninth hour of the day he saw clearly in a vision an angel of God coming in and saying to him, "Cornelius." And he stared at him in terror, and said, "What is it, Lord?" And he said to him, "Your prayers and your alms have ascended as a memorial before God. And now send men to Joppa, and bring one Simon who is called Peter; he is lodging with Simon, a tanner, whose house is by the seaside." When the angel who spoke to him had departed, he called two of his servants and a devout soldier from among those that waited on him, and having related everything to them, he sent them to Joppa. The next day, as they were on their journey and coming near the city, Peter went up on the housetop to pray, about the sixth hour. And he became hungry and desired something to eat; but while they were preparing it, he fell into a trance and saw the heaven opened, and something descending, like a great sheet, let down by four corners upon the earth. In it were all kinds of animals and reptiles and birds of the air. And there came a voice to him, "Rise, Peter; kill and eat." But Peter said, "No, Lord; for I have never eaten anything that is common or unclean." And the voice came to him again a second time, "What God has cleansed, you must not call common." This happened three times, and the thing was taken up at once to heaven.

A Reading (Lesson) from the Gospel according to John [7:1-13]

Jesus went about in Galilee; he would not go about in Judea, because the Jews sought to kill him. Now the Jews' feast of Tabernacles was at hand. So his brothers said to him, "Leave here and go to Judea, that your disciples may see the works you are doing. For no man works in secret if he seeks to be known openly. If you do these things, show yourself to the world." For even his brothers did not believe in him. Jesus said to them, "My time has not yet come, but your time is always here. The world cannot hate you, but it hates me because I testify of it that its works are evil. Go to the feast yourselves; I am not going up to this feast, for my time has not yet fully come." So saying, he remained in Galilee. But after his brothers had gone up to the feast, then he also went up, not publicly but in private. The Jews were looking for him at the feast, and saying, "Where is he?" And there was much muttering about him among the people. While some said, "He is a good man," others said, "No, he is leading the people astray." Yet for fear of the Jews no one spoke openly of him.

Thursday

Psalm 18:1-20 [page 602], ❖ *Psalm 18:21-50* [page 604]

A Reading (Lesson) from the Book of Job [8:1-10,20-22]

Bildad the Shuhite answered: "How long will you say these things, and the words of your mouth be a great wind? Does God pervert justice? Or does the Almighty pervert the right? If your children have sinned against him, he has delivered them into the power of their transgression. If you will seek God and make supplication to the Almighty, if you are pure and upright, surely then he will rouse himself for you and reward you with a rightful habitation. And though your beginning was small, your latter days will be very great. For inquire, I pray you, of bygone ages, and consider what the fathers have found; for we are but of yesterday, and know nothing, for our days on earth are a shadow. Will they not teach you, and tell you, and utter words out of their understanding? Behold, God will not reject a blameless man, nor take the hand of evildoers. He will yet fill your mouth with laughter, and your lips with shouting. Those who hate you will be clothed with shame, and the tent of the wicked will be no more."

A Reading (Lesson) from the Acts of the Apostles [10:17-33]

While Peter was inwardly perplexed as to what the vision which he had seen might mean, behold, the men that were sent by Cornelius, having made inquiry for Simon's house, stood before the gate and called out to ask whether Simon who was called Peter was lodging there. And while Peter was pondering the vision, the Spirit said to him, "Behold, three men are looking for you. Rise and go down, and accompany them without hesitation; for I have sent them." And Peter went down to the men and said, "I am the one you are looking for; what is the reason for your coming?"

And they said, "Cornelius, a centurion, an upright and God-fearing man, who is well spoken of by the whole Jewish nation, was directed by a holy angel to send for you to come to his house, and to hear what you have to say." So he called them in to be his guests. The next day he rose and went off with them, and some of the brethren from Joppa accompanied him. And on the following day they entered Caesare′a. Cornelius was expecting them and had called together his kinsmen and close friends. When Peter entered, Cornelius met him and fell down at his feet and worshiped him. But Peter lifted him up, saying, "Stand up; I too am a man." And as he talked with him, he went in and found many persons gathered; and he said to them, "You yourselves know how unlawful it is for a Jew to associate with or to visit any one of another nation; but God has shown me that I should not call any man common or unclean. So when I was sent for, I came without objection. I ask then why you sent for me." And Cornelius said, "Four days ago, about this hour, I was keeping the ninth hour of prayer in my house; and behold, a man stood before me in bright apparel, saying, 'Cornelius, your prayer has been heard and your alms have been remembered before God. Send therefore to Joppa and ask for Simon who is called Peter; he is lodging in the house of Simon, a tanner, by the seaside.' So I sent to you at once, and you have been kind enough to come. Now therefore we are all here present in the sight of God, to hear all that you have been commanded by the Lord."

A Reading (Lesson) from the Gospel according to John
[7:14-36]

About the middle of the feast of Tabernacles Jesus went up into the temple and taught. The Jews marveled at it, saying, "How is it that this man has learning, when he has never studied?" So Jesus answered them, "My teaching is not mine, but his who sent me; if any man's will is to do his will, he shall know whether the teaching is from God or whether I am speaking on my own authority. He who speaks on his own authority seeks his own glory; but he who seeks the glory of him who sent him is true, and in him there is no falsehood. Did not Moses give you the law? Yet none of you keeps the law. Why do you seek to kill me?" The people answered, "You have a demon! Who is seeking to kill you?" Jesus answered, "I did one deed, and you all marvel at it. Moses gave you circumcision (not that it is from Moses, but from the fathers), and you circumcise a man upon the sabbath. If on the sabbath a man receives circumcision, so that the law of Moses may not be broken, are you angry with me because on the sabbath I made a man's whole body well? Do not judge by appearances, but judge with right judgment." Some of the people of Jerusalem therefore said, "Is not this the man whom they seek to kill? And here he is, speaking openly, and they say nothing to him! Can it be that the authorities really know that this is the Christ? Yet we know where this man comes from." So Jesus proclaimed, as he taught in the temple, "You know me, and you know where I come from? But I have not come of my own accord; he who sent me is true, and him you do not know. I know him, for I come from him, and he sent me." So they sought to arrest him; but no one laid hands on him, because his hour had not yet come. Yet many of the people believed in him; they said, "When the Christ appears, will he do more signs than this man has done?" The Pharisees heard the crowd thus muttering about him, and the chief priests and Pharisees sent officers to arrest him. Jesus then said, "I shall be with you a little longer, and then I go to him who sent me; you will seek me and you will not find me; where I am you cannot come." The Jews asked one another, "Where does this man intend to go that we shall not find him? Does he intend to go to the Dispersion among the Greeks and teach the Greeks? What does he mean by saying, 'You will seek me and you will not find me,' and, 'Where I am you cannot come'?"

Friday

Psalm 16 [page 599],   *Psalm 17* [page 600]   ❖
Psalm 22 [page 610]

A Reading (Lesson) from the Book of Job [9:1-15, 32-35]

Job answered: "Truly I know that it is so: But how can a man be just before God? If one wished to contend with him, one could not answer him once in a thousand times. He is wise in heart, and mighty in strength—who has hardened himself against him, and succeeded?—he who removes mountains, and they know it not, when he overturns them in his anger; who shakes the earth out of its place, and its pillars tremble; who commands the sun, and it does not rise; who seals up the stars; who alone stretched out the heavens, and trampled the waves of the sea; who made the Bear and Orion, the Plei'ades and the chambers of the south; who does great things beyond understanding, and marvelous things without number. Lo, he passes by me, and I see him not; he moves on, but I do not perceive him. Behold, he snatches away; who can hinder him? Who will say to him, 'What doest thou'? God will not turn back his anger; beneath him bowed the helpers of Rahab. How then can I answer him, choosing my words with him? Though I am innocent I cannot answer him; I must appeal for mercy to my accuser. For he is not a man, as I am, that I might answer him, that we should come to trial together. There is no umpire between us, who might lay his hand upon us both. Let him take his rod away from me, and let not dread of him terrify me. Then I would speak without fear of him, for I am not so in myself."

A Reading (Lesson) from the Acts of the Apostles
[10:34-48]

Peter opened his mouth and said: "Truly I perceive that God shows no partiality, but in every nation any one who fears him and does what is right is acceptable to him. You know the word which he sent to Israel, preaching good news of peace by Jesus Christ (he is Lord of all), the word which was proclaimed throughout all Judea, beginning from Galilee after the baptism which John preached: how God anointed Jesus of Nazareth with the Holy Spirit and with power; how he went about doing good and healing all that were oppressed by the devil, for God was with him. And we are witnesses to all that he did both in the country of the Jews and in Jerusalem. They put him to death by hanging him on a tree; but God raised him on the third day and made him manifest; not to all the people but to us who were chosen by God as witnesses, who ate and drank with him after he rose from the dead. And he commanded us to preach to the people, and to testify that he is the one ordained by God to be judge of the living and the dead. To him all the prophets bear witness that every one who believes in him receives forgiveness of sins through his name." While Peter was still saying this, the Holy Spirit fell on all who heard the word. And the believers from among the circumcised who came with Peter were amazed, because the gift of the Holy Spirit had been poured out even on the Gentiles. For they heard them speaking in tongues and extolling God. Then Peter declared, "Can any one forbid water for baptizing these people who have received the Holy Spirit just as we have?" And he commanded them to be baptized in the name of Jesus Christ. Then they asked him to remain for some days.

A Reading (Lesson) from the Gospel according to John
[7:37-52]

On the last day of the feast of Tabernacles, the great day, Jesus stood up and proclaimed, "If any one thirst, let him come to me and drink. He who believes in me, as the scripture has said, 'Out of his heart shall flow rivers of living water.'" Now this he said about the Spirit, which those who believed in him were to receive, for as yet the

Spirit had not been given, because Jesus was not yet glorified. When they heard these words, some of the people said, "this is really the prophet." Others said, "This is the Christ." But some said, "Is the Christ to come from Galilee? Has not the scripture said that the Christ is descended from David, and comes from Bethlehem, the village where David was?" So there was a division among the people over him. Some of them wanted to arrest him, but no one laid hands on him. The officers then went back to the chief priests and Pharisees, who said to them, "Why did you not bring him?" The officers answered, "No man ever spoke like this man!" The Pharisees answered them, "Are you led astray, you also? Have any of the authorities or of the Pharisees believed in him? But this crowd, who do not know the law, are accursed." Nicodemus, who had gone to him before, and who was one of them, said to them, "Does our law judge a man without first giving him a hearing and learning what he does?" They replied, "Are you from Galilee too? Search and you will see that no prophet is to rise from Galilee."

Saturday

Psalm 20 [page 608], *Psalm 21:1-7(8-14)* [page 608] ❖
Psalm 110:1-5(6-7) [page 753], *Psalm 116* [page 759],
Pslam 117 [page 760]

A Reading (Lesson) from the Book of Job [9:1;10:1-9, 16-22]

Job answered: "I loathe my life; I will give free utterance to my complaint; I will speak in the bitterness of my soul. I will say to God, Do not condemn me; let me know why thou dost contend against me. Does it seem good to thee to oppress, to despise the work of thy hands and favor the designs of the wicked? Hast thou eyes of flesh? Dost thou see as man sees? Are thy days as the days of man, or thy years as man's years, that thou dost seek out my iniquity

and search for my sin, although thou knowest that I am
not guilty, and there is none to deliver out of thy hand?
Thy hands fashioned and made me; and now thou dost
turn about and destroy me. Remember that thou hast
made me of clay; and wilt thou turn me to dust again? And
if I lift myself up, thou dost hunt me like a lion, and again
work wonders against me; thou dost renew thy witness
against me, and increase thy vexation toward me; thou
dost bring fresh hosts against me. Why didst thou bring me
forth from the womb? Would that I had died before any
eye had seen me, and were as though I had not been,
carried from the womb to the grave. Are not the days of
my life few? Let me alone, that I may find a little comfort
before I go whence I shall not return, to the land of gloom
and deep darkness, the land of gloom and chaos, where
light is as darkness."

A Reading (Lesson) from the Acts of the Apostles [11:1-18]

The apostles and the brethren who were in Judea heard
that the Gentiles also had received the word of God. So
when Peter went up to Jerusalem, the circumcision party
criticized him, saying, "Why did you go to uncircumcised
men and eat with them?" But Peter began and explained to
them in order: "I was in the city of Joppa praying; and in a
trance I saw a vision, something descending, like a great
sheet, let down from heaven by four corners; and it came
down to me. Looking at it closely I observed animals and
beasts of prey and reptiles and birds of the air. And I heard
a voice saying to me, 'Rise, Peter; kill and eat.' But I said,
'No, Lord; for nothing common or unclean has ever
entered my mouth.' But the voice answered a second time
from heaven, 'What God has cleansed you must not call
common.' This happened three times, and all was drawn
up again into heaven. At that very moment three men
arrived at the house in which we were, sent to me from
Caesare'a. And the Spirit told me to go with them, making
no distinction. These six brethren also accompanied me,

and we entered the man's house. And he told us how he had seen the angel standing in his house and saying, 'Send to Joppa and bring Simon called Peter; he will declare to you a message by which you will be saved, you and all your household.' As I began to speak, the Holy Spirit fell on them just as on us at the beginning. And I remembered the word of the Lord, how he said, 'John baptized with water, but you shall be baptized with the Holy Spirit.' If then God gave the same gift to them as he gave to us when we believed in the Lord Jesus Christ, who was I that I could withstand God?" When they heard this they were silenced. And they glorified God, saying, "Then to the Gentiles also God has granted repentance unto life."

A Reading (Lesson) from the Gospel according to John
[8:12-20]

Again Jesus spoke to the Pharisees, saying, "I am the light of the world; he who follows me will not walk in darkness, but will have the light of life." The Pharisees then said to him, "You are bearing witness to yourself; your testimony is not true." Jesus answered, "Even if I do bear witness to myself, my testimony is true, for I know whence I have come and whither I am going, but you do not know whence I come or whither I am going. You judge according to the flesh, I judge no one. Yet even if I do judge, my judgment is true, for it is not I alone that judge, but I and he who sent me. In your law it is written that the testimony of two men is true; I bear witness to myself, and the Father who sent me bears witness to me." They said to him therefore, "Where is your Father?" Jesus answered, "You know neither me nor my Father; if you knew me, you would know my Father also." These words he spoke in the treasury, as he taught in the temple; but no one arrested him, because his hour had not yet come.

Proper 17 *Week of the Sunday closest to August 31*

Sunday

Psalm 148 [page 805],   *Psalm 149* [page 807],
Psalm 150 [page 807]   ❖   *Psalm 114* [page 756],
Psalm 115 [page 757]

A Reading (Lesson) from the Book of Job [11:1-9, 13-20]

Zophar the Na'amathite answered: "Should a multitude of
words go unanswered, and a man full of talk be
vindicated? Should your babble silence men, and when you
mock, shall no one shame you? For you say, 'My doctrine
is pure, and I am clean in God's eyes.' But oh, that God
would speak, and open his lips to you, and that he would
tell you the secrets of wisdom! For he is manifold in
understanding. Know then that God exacts of you less
than your guilt deserves. Can you find out the deep things
of God? Can you find out the limit of the Almighty? It is
higher than heaven—what can you do? Deeper than
Sheol—what can you know? Its measure is longer than the
earth, and broader than the sea. If you set your heart
aright, you will stretch out your hands toward him. If
iniquity is in your hand, put it far away, and let not
wickedness dwell in your tents. Surely then you will lift up
your face withou blemish; you will be secure, and will not
fear. You will forget your misery; you will remember it as
waters that have passed away. And your life will be
brighter than the noonday; its darkness will be like the
morning. And you will have confidence, because there is
hope; you will be protected and take your rest in safety.
You will lie down, and none will make you afraid; many
will entreat your favor. But the eyes of the wicked will fail;
all way of escape will be lost to them, and their hope is to
breathe their last."

A Reading (Lesson) from the Revelation to John [5:1-14]

I saw in the right hand of him who was seated on the throne a scroll written within and on the back, sealed with seven seals; and I saw a strong angel proclaiming with a loud voice, "Who is worthy to open the scroll and break its seals?" And no one in heaven or on earth or under the earth was able to open the scroll or to look into it, and I wept much that no one was found worthy to open the scroll or to look into it. Then one of the elders said to me, "Weep not; lo, the Lion of the tribe of Judah, the Root of David, has conquered, so that he can open the scroll and its seven seals." And between the throne and the four living creatures and among the elders, I saw a Lamb standing, as though it had been slain, with seven horns and with seven eyes, which are the seven spirits of God sent out into all the earth; and he went and took the scroll from the right hand of him who was seated on the throne. And when he had taken the scroll, the four living creatures and the twenty-four elders fell down before the Lamb, each holding a harp, and with golden bowls full of incense, which are the prayers of the saints; and they sang a new song, saying, "Worthy art thou to take the scroll and to open its seals, for thou wast slain and by thy blood didst ransom men for God from every tribe and tongue and people and nation, and hast made them a kingdom and priests to our God, and they shall reign on earth." Then I looked, and I heard around the throne and the living creatures and the elders the voice of many angels, numbering myriads of myriads and thousands of thousands, saying with a loud voice, "Worthy is the Lamb who was slain, to receive power and wealth and wisdom and might and honor and glory and blessing!" And I heard every creature in heaven and on earth and under the earth and in the sea, and all therein, saying, "To him who sits upon the throne and to the Lamb be blessing and honor and glory and might for ever and ever!" And the four living creatures said, "Amen!" and the elders fell down and worshiped.

A Reading (Lesson) from the Gospel according to Matthew
[5:1-12]

Seeing the crowds, Jesus went up on the mountain, and when he sat down his disciples came to him. And he opened his mouth and taught them, saying: "Blessed are the poor in spirit, for theirs is the kingdom of heaven. Blessed are those who mourn, for they shall be comforted. Blessed are the meek, for they shall inherit the earth. Blessed are those who hunger and thirst for righteousness, for they shall be satisfied. Blessed are the merciful, for they shall obtain mercy. Blessed are the pure in heart, for they shall see God. Blessed are the peacemakers, for they shall be called sons of God. Blessed are those who are persecuted for righteousness' sake, for theirs is the kingdom of heaven. Blessed are you when men revile you and persecute you and utter all kinds of evil against you falsely on my account. Rejoice and be glad, for your reward is great in heaven, for so men persecuted the prophets who were before you."

Monday

Psalm 25 [page 614]   ❖   *Psalm 9* [page 593],
Psalm 15 [page 599]

A Reading (Lesson) from the Book of Job [12:1-6,13-25]

Job answered: "No doubt you are the people, and wisdom will die with you. But I have understanding as well as you; I am not inferior to you. Who does not know such things as these? I am a laughingstock to my friends; I, who called upon God and he answered me, a just and blameless man, am a laughingstock. In the thought of one who is at ease there is contempt for misfortune; it is ready for those whose feet slip. The tents of robbers are at peace, and those who provoke God are secure, who bring their god in their hand. With God are wisdom and might; he has counsel and understanding. If he tears down, none can rebuild; if he shuts a man in, none can open. If he withholds the waters, they dry up; if he sends them out, they overwhelm the land. With him are strength and wisdom; the deceived and the deceiver are his. He leads counselors away stripped, and judges he makes fools. He looses the bonds of kings, and binds a waistcloth on their loins. He leads priests away stripped, and overthrows the mighty. He deprives of speech those who are trusted, and takes away the discernment of the elders. He pours contempt on princes, and looses the belt of the strong. He uncovers the deeps out of darkness, and brings deep darkness to light. He makes nations great, and he destroys them; he enlarges nations, and leads them away. He takes away understanding from the chiefs of the people of the earth, and makes them wander in a pathless waste. They grope in the dark without a light; and he makes them stagger like a drunken man."

A Reading (Lesson) from the Acts of the Apostles
[11:19-30]

Those who were scattered because of the persecution that arose over Stephen traveled as far as Phoeni'cia and Cyprus and Antioch, speaking the word to none except Jews. But there were some of them, men of Cyprus and Cyre'ne, who on coming to Antioch spoke to the Greeks also, preaching the Lord Jesus. And the hand of the Lord was with them, and a great number that believed turned to the Lord. News of this came to the ears of the church in Jerusalem, and they sent Barnabas to Antioch. When he came and saw the grace of God, he was glad; and he exhorted them all to remain faithful to the Lord with steadfast purpose; for he was a good man, full of the Holy Spirit and of faith. And a large company was added to the Lord. So Barnabas went to Tarsus to look for Saul; and when he had found him, he brought him to Antioch. For a whole year they met with the church, and taught a large company of people; and in Antioch the disciples were for the first time called Christians. Now in these days prophets came down from Jerusalem to Antioch. And one of them named Ag'abus stood up and foretold by the Spirit that there would be a great famine over all the world; and this took place in the days of Claudius. And the disciples determined, every one according to his ability, to send relief to the brethren who lived in Judea; and they did so, sending it to the elders by the hand of Barnabas and Saul.

A Reading (Lesson) from the Gospel according to John [8:21-32]

Again Jesus said to the Pharisees, "I go away, and you will seek me and die in your sin; where I am going, you cannot come." Then said the Jews, "Will he kill himself, since he says, 'Where I am going, you cannot come'?" He said to them, "You are from below, I am from above; you are of this world, I am not of this world. I told you that you would die in your sins, for you will die in your sins unless you believe that I am he." They said to him, "Who are you?" Jesus said to them, "Even what I have told you from the beginning. I have much to say about you and much to judge; but he who sent me is true, and I declare to the world what I have heard from him." They did not understand that he spoke to them of the Father. So Jesus said, "When you have lifted up the Son of man, then you will know that I am he, and that I do nothing on my own authority but speak thus as the Father taught me. And he who sent me is with me; he has not left me alone, for I always do what is pleasing to him." As he spoke thus, many believed in him. Jesus then said to the Jews who had believed in him, "If you continue in my word, you are truly my disciples, and you will know the truth, and the truth will make you free."

Tuesday

Psalm 26 [page 616], *Psalm 28* [page 619] ❖
Psalm 36 [page 632], *Psalm 39* [page 638]

A Reading (Lesson) from the Book of Job
[12:1;13:3-17,21-27]

Job answered: "I would speak to the Almighty, and I desire to argue my case with God. As for you, you whitewash with lies; worthless physicians are you all. Oh that you would keep silent, and it would be your wisdom! Hear now my reasoning, and listen to the pleadings of my lips. Will you speak falsely for God, and speak deceitfully for him? Will you show partiality toward him, will you plead the case for God? Will it be well with you when he searches you out? Or can you deceive him, as one deceives a man? He will surely rebuke you if in secret you show partiality. Will not his majesty terrify you, and the dread of him fall upon you? Your maxims are proverbs of ashes, your defenses are defenses of clay. Let me have silence, and I will speak, and let come on me what may. I will take my flesh in my teeth, and put my life in my hand. Behold, he will slay me; I have no hope; yet I will defend my ways to his face. This will be my salvation, that a godless man shall not come before him. Listen carefully to my words, and let my declaration be in your ears. Withdraw thy hand far from me, and let not dread of thee terrify me. Then call, and I will answer; or let me speak, and do thou reply to me. How many are my iniquities and my sins? Make me know my transgression and my sin. Why dost thou hide thy face, and count me as thy enemy? Wilt thou frighten a driven leaf and pursue dry chaff? For thou writest bitter things against me, and makest me inherit the iniquities of my youth. Thou puttest my feet in the stocks, and watchest all my paths; thou settest a bound to the soles of my feet."

A Reading (Lesson) from the Acts of the Apostles [12:1-17]

About that time Herod the king laid violent hands upon
some who belonged to the church. He killed James the
brother of John with the sword; and when he saw that it
pleased the Jews, he proceeded to arrest Peter also. This
was during the days of Unleavened Bread. And when he
had seized him, he put him in prison, and delivered him to
four squads of soldiers to guard him, intending after the
Passover to bring him out to the people. So Peter was kept
in prison; but earnest prayer for him was made to God by
the church. The very night when Herod was about to bring
him out, Peter was sleeping between two soldiers, bound
with two chains, and sentries before the door were
guarding the prison; and behold, an angel of the Lord
appeared, and a light shone in the cell; and he struck Peter
on the side and woke him, saying, "Get up quickly." And
the chains fell off his hands. And the angel said to him,
"Dress yourself and put on your sandals." And he did so.
And he said to him, "Wrap your mantle around you and
follow me." And he went out and followed him; he did not
know that what was done by the angel was real, but
thought he was seeing a vision. When they had passed the
first and the second guard, they came to the iron gate
leading into the city. It opened to them of its own accord,
and they went out and passed on through the street; and
immediately the angel left him. And Peter came to himself,
and said, "Now I am sure that the Lord has sent his angel
and rescued me from the hand of Herod and from all that
the Jewish people were expecting." When he realized this,
he went to the house of Mary, the mother of John, whose
other name was Mark, where many were gathered
together and were praying. And when he knocked at the
door of the gateway, a maid named Rhoda came to
answer. Recognizing Peter's voice, in her joy she did not
open the gate but ran in and told that Peter was standing at
the gate. They said to her, "You are mad." But she insisted

that it was so. They said, "It is his angel!" But Peter continued knocking; and when they opened, they saw him and were amazed. But motioning to them with his hand to be silent, he described to them how the Lord had brought him out of the prison. And he said, "Tell this to James and to the brethren." Then he departed and went to another place.

A Reading (Lesson) from the Gospel according to John
[8:33-47]

The Jews who believed in Jesus answered him, "We are descendants of Abraham, and have never been in bondage to any one. How is it that you say, 'You will be made free'?" Jesus answered them, "Truly, truly, I say to you, every one who commits sin is a slave to sin. The slave does not continue in the house for ever; the son continues for ever. So if the Son makes you free, you will be free indeed. I know that you are descendants of Abraham; yet you seek to kill me, because my word finds no place in you. I speak of what I have seen with my Father, and you do what you have heard from your father." They answered him, "Abraham is our father." Jesus said to them, "If you were Abraham's children, you would do what Abraham did, but now you seek to kill me, a man who has told you the truth which I heard from God; this is not what Abraham did. You do what your father did." They said to him, "We were not born of fornication; we have one Father, even God." Jesus said to them, "If God were your Father, you would love me, for I proceeded and came forth from God; I came not of my own accord, but he sent me. Why do you not understand what I say? It is because you cannot bear to hear my word. You are of your father the devil, and your will is to do your father's desires. He was a murderer from the beginning, and has nothing to do with the truth, because there is no truth in him. When he lies, he speaks according to his own nature, for he is a liar and the father of lies. But, because I tell the truth, you do not believe me.

Which of you convicts me of sin? If I tell the truth, why do you not believe me? He who is of God hears the words of God; the reason why you do not hear them is that you are not of God."

Wednesday

Psalm 38 [page 636]   ❖   *Psalm 119:25-48* [page 765]

A Reading (Lesson) from the Book of Job [12:1;14:1-22]

Job answered: "Man that is born of a woman is of few days, and full of trouble. He comes forth like a flower, and withers; he flees like a shadow, and continues not. And dost thou open thy eyes upon such a one and bring him into judgment with thee? Who can bring a clean thing out of an unclean? There is not one. Since his days are determined, and the number of his months is with thee, and thou hast appointed his bounds that he cannot pass, look away from him, and desist, that he may enjoy, like a hireling, his day. For there is hope for a tree, if it be cut down, that it will sprout again, and that it shoots will not cease. Though its root grow old in the earth, and its stump die in the ground, yet at the scent of water it will bud and put forth branches like a young plant. But man dies, and is laid low; man breathes his last, and where is he? As waters fail from a lake, and a river wastes away and dries up, so man lies down and rises not again; till the heavens are no more he will not awake, or be roused out of his sleep. Oh that thou wouldest hide me in Sheol, that thou wouldest conceal me until thy wrath be past, that thou wouldest appoint me a set time, and remember me! If a man die, shall he live again? All the days of my service I would wait, till my release should come. Thou wouldest call, and I would answer thee; thou wouldest long for the work of thy hands. For then thou wouldest number my steps, thou wouldest not keep watch over my sin; my transgression would be sealed up in a bag, and thou wouldest cover over my iniquity. But the mountain falls and crumbles away, and the rock is removed from its place; the waters wear away the stones; the torrents wash away the soil of the earth; so thou destroyest the hope of man. Thou prevailest for ever against him, and he passes; thou changest his countenance, and sendest him away. His sons come to honor, and he does not know it; they are brought low, and he perceives it not. He feels only the pain of his own body, and he mourns only for himself."

A Reading (Lesson) from the Acts of the Apostles
[12:18-25]

When day came, there was no small stir among the soldiers over what had become of Peter. And when Herod had sought for him and could not find him, he examined the sentries and ordered that they should be put to death. Then he went down from Judea to Caesare'a, and remained there. Now Herod was angry with the people of Tyre and Sidon; and they came to him in a body, and having persuaded Blastus, the king's chamberlain, they asked for peace, because their country depended on the king's country for food. On an appointed day Herod put on his royal robes, took his seat upon the throne, and made an oration to them. And the people shouted, "The voice of a god, and not of man!" Immediately an angel of the Lord smote him, because he did not give God the glory; and he was eaten by worms and died. But the word of God grew and multiplied. And Barnabas and Saul returned from Jerusalem when they had fulfilled their mission, bringing with them John whose other name was Mark.

A Reading (Lesson) from the Gospel according to John
[8:47-59]

Jesus said to the Jews, "He who is of God hears the words of God; the reason why you do not hear them is that you are not of God." The Jews answered him, "Are we not right in saying that you are a Samaritan and have a demon?" Jesus answered, "I have not a demon; but I honor my Father, and you dishonor me. Yet I do not seek my own glory; there is One who seeks it and he will be the judge. Truly, truly, I say to you, if any one keeps my word, he will never see death." The Jews said to him, "Now we know that you have a demon. Abraham died, as did the prophets; and you say, 'If any one keeps my word, he will never taste death.' Are you greater than our father Abraham, who died? And the prophets died! Who do you claim to be?" Jesus answered, "If I glorify myself, my glory is nothing; it is my Father who glorifies me, of whom you say that he is your God. But you have not known him; I know him. If I said, I do not know him, I should be a liar like you; but I do know him and I keep his word. Your father Abraham rejoiced that he was to see my day; he saw it and was glad." The Jews then said to him, "You are not yet fifty years old, and have you seen Abraham?" Jesus said to them, "Truly, truly, I say to you, before Abraham was, I am." So they took up stones to throw at him; but Jesus hid himself, and went out of the temple.

Thursday

Psalm 37:1-18 [page 633]   ❖   *Psalm 37:19-42* [page 634]

A Reading (Lesson) from the Book of Job
[16:16-22;17:1,13-16]

Job answered: "My face is red with weeping, and on my eyelids is deep darkness; although there is no violence in my hands, and my prayer is pure. O earth, cover not my blood, and let my cry find no resting place. Even now, behold, my witness is in heaven, and he that vouches for me is on high. My friends scorn me; my eye pours out tears to God, that he would maintain the right of a man with God, like that of a man with his neighbor. For when a few years have come I shall go the way whence I shall not return. My spirit is broken, my days are extinct, the grave is ready for me. If I look for Sheol as my house, if I spread my couch in darkness, if I say to the pit, 'You are my father,' and to the worm, 'My mother,' or 'My sister,' where then is my hope? Who will see my hope? Will it go down to the bars of Sheol? Shall we descend together into the dust?"

Acts 13:1-12 [page 87 above]

A Reading (Lesson) from the Gospel according to John
[9:1-17]

As Jesus passed by, he saw a man blind from his birth. And his disciples asked him, "Rabbi, who sinned, this man or his parents, that he was born blind?" Jesus answered, "It was not that this man sinned, or his parents, but that the works of God might be made manifest in him. We must work the works of him who sent me, while it is day; night comes, when no one can work. As long as I am in the world, I am the light of the world." As he said this, he spat on the ground and made clay of the spittle and anointed the man's eyes with the clay, saying to him, "Go, wash in the pool of Silo'am" (which means Sent). So he went and washed and came back seeing. The neighbors and those who had seen him before as a beggar, said, "Is not this the man who used to sit and beg?" Some said, "It is he"; others said, "No, but he is like him." He said, "I am the man." They said to him, "Then how were your eyes opened?" He answered, "The man called Jesus made clay and anointed my eyes and said to me, 'Go to Silo'am and wash'; so I went and washed and received my sight." They said to him, "Where is he?" He said, "I do not know." They brought to the Pharisees the man who had formerly been blind. Now it was a sabbath day when Jesus made the clay and opened his eyes. The Pharisees again asked him how he had received his sight. And he said to them, "He put clay on my eyes, and I washed, and I see." Some of the Pharisees said, "This man is not from God, for he does not keep the sabbath." But others said, "How can a man who is a sinner do such signs?" There was a division among them. So they again said to the blind man, "What do you say about him, since he has opened your eyes?" He said, "He is a prophet."

Friday

Psalm 31 [page 622] ❖ *Psalm 35* [page 629]

A Reading (Lesson) from the Book of Job [19:1-7,14-27]

Job answered: "How long will you torment me, and break me in pieces with words? These ten times you have cast reproach upon me; are you not ashamed to wrong me? And even if it be true that I have erred, my error remains with myself. If indeed you magnify yourselves against me, and make my humiliation an argument against me, know then that God has put me in the wrong, and closed his net about me. Behold, I cry out, 'Violence!' but I am not answered; I call aloud, but there is no justice. My kinsfolk and my close friends have failed me; the guests in my house have forgotten me; my maidservants count me as a stranger; I have become an alien in their eyes. I call to my servant, but he gives me no answer; I must beseech him with my mouth. I am repulsive to my wife, loathsome to the sons of my own mother. Even young children despise me; when I rise they talk against me. All my intimate friends abhor me, and those whom I loved have turned against me. My bones cleave to my skin and to my flesh, and I have escaped by the skin of my teeth. Have pity on me, have pity on me, O you my friends, for the hand of God has touched me! Why do you, like God, pursue me? Why are you not satisfied with my flesh? Oh that my words were written! Oh that they were inscribed in a book! Oh that with an iron pen and lead they were graven in the rock for ever! For I know that my Redeemer lives, and at last he will stand upon the earth; and after my skin has been thus destroyed, then from my flesh I shall see God, whom I shall see on my side, and my eyes shall behold, and not another. My heart faints within me!"

A Reading (Lesson) from the Acts of the Apostles
[13:13-25]

Paul and his company set sail from Paphos, and came to Perga in Pamphylia. And John left them and returned to Jerusalem; but they passed on from Perga and came to Antioch of Pisidia. And on the sabbath day they went into the synagogue and sat down. After the reading of the law and the prophets, the rulers of the synagogue sent to them, saying, "Brethren, if you have any word of exhortation for the people, say it." So Paul stood up, and motioning with his hands, said: "Men of Israel, and you that fear God, listen. The God of this people Israel chose our fathers and made the people great during their stay in the land of Egypt, and with uplifted arm he led them out of it. And for about forty years he bore with them in the wilderness. And when he had destroyed seven nations in the land of Canaan, he gave them their land as an inheritance, for about four hundred and fifty years. And after that he gave them judges until Samuel the prophet. Then they asked for a king; and God gave them Saul the son of Kish, a man of the tribe of Benjamin, for forty years. And when he had removed him, he raised up David to be their king; of whom he testified and said, 'I have found in David the son of Jesse a man after my heart, who will do all my will.' Of this man's posterity God has brought to Israel a Savior, Jesus, as he promised. Before his coming John had preached a baptism of repentance to all the people of Israel. And as John was finishing his course, he said, 'What do you suppose that I am? I am not he. No, but after me one is coming, the sandals of whose feet I am not worthy to untie.'"

A Reading (Lesson) from the Gospel according to John
[9:18-41]

The Jews did not believe that he had been blind and had
received his sight, until they called the parents of the man
who had received his sight, and asked them, "Is this your
son, who you say was born blind? How then does he now
see?" His parents answered, "We know that this is our son,
and that he was born blind; but how he now sees we do
not know, nor do we know who opened his eyes. Ask him;
he is of age, he will speak for himself." His parents said
this because they feared the Jews, for the Jews had already
agreed that if any one should confess him to be Christ, he
was to be put out of the synagogue. Therefore his parents
said, "He is of age, ask him." So for the second time they
called the man who had been blind, and said to him, "Give
God the praise; we know that this man is a sinner." He
answered, "Whether he is a sinner, I do not know; one
thing I know, that though I was blind, now I see." They
said to him, "What did he do to you? How did he open
your eyes?" He answered them, "I have told you already,
and you would not listen. Why do you want to hear it
again? Do you too want to become his disciples?" And
they reviled him, saying, "You are his disciple, but we are
disciples of Moses. We know that God has spoken to
Moses, but as for this man, we do not know where he
comes from." The man answered, "Why, this is a marvel!
You do not know where he comes from, and yet he opened
my eyes. We know that God does not listen to sinners, but
if any one is a worshiper of God and does his will, God
listens to him. Never since the world began has it been
heard that any one opened the eyes of a man born blind. If
this man were not from God, he could do nothing." They
answered him, "You were born in utter sin, and would you
teach us?" And they cast him out. Jesus heard that they
had cast him out, and having found him he said, "Do you
believe in the Son of man?" He answered, "And who is he,
sir, that I may believe in him?" Jesus said to him, "You

have seen him, and it is he who speaks to you." He said, "Lord, I believe"; and he worshiped him. Jesus said, "For judgment I came into this world, that those who do not see may see, and that those who see may become blind." Some of the Pharisees near him heard this, and they said to him, "Are we also blind?" Jesus said to them, "If you were blind, you would have no guilt; but now that you say, 'We see,' your guilt remains."

Saturday

Psalm 30 [page 621], *Psalm 32* [page 624] ❖
Psalm 42 [page 643], *Psalm 43* [page 644]

A Reading (Lesson) from the Book of Job
[22:1-4,21—23:7]

El′iphaz the Te′manite answered: "Can a man be profitable to God? Surely he who is wise is profitable to himself. Is it any pleasure to the Almighty if you are righteous, or is it gain to him if you make your ways blameless? Is it for your fear of him that he reproves you, and enters into judgment with you? Agree with God, and be at peace; thereby good will come to you. Receive instruction from his mouth, and lay up his words in your heart. If you return to the Almighty and humble yourself, if you remove unrighteousness far from your tents, if you lay gold in the dust, and gold of Ophir among the stones of the torrent bed, and if the Almighty is your gold, and your precious silver; then you will delight yourself in the Almighty, and lift up your face to God. You will make your prayer to him, and he will hear you; and you will pay your vows. You will decide on a matter, and it will be established for you, and light will shine on your ways. For God abases the proud, but he saves the lowly. He delivers the innocent man; you will be delivered through the cleanness of your hands." Then Job answered: "Today also my complaint is bitter, his hand is heavy in spite of my groaning. Oh, that I knew where I might find him, that I might come even to his seat! I would lay my case before him and fill my mouth with arguments. I would learn what he would answer me, and understand what he would say to me. Would he contend with me in the greatness of his power? No; he would give heed to me. There an upright man could reason with him, and I should be acquitted for ever by my judge."

A Reading (Lesson) from the Acts of the Apostles
[13:26-43]

Paul stood up in the synagogue in Antioch, and motioning with his hands said: "Brethren, sons of the family of Abraham, and those among you that fear God, to us has been sent the message of this salvation. For those who live in Jerusalem and their rulers, because they did not recognize him nor understand the utterances of the prophets which are read every sabbath, fulfilled these by condemning him. Though they could charge him with nothing deserving death, yet they asked Pilate to have him killed. And when they had fulfilled all that was written of him, they took him down from the tree, and laid him in a tomb. But God raised him from the dead; and for many days he appeared to those who came up with him from Galilee to Jerusalem, who are now his witnesses to the people. And we bring you the good news that what God promised to the fathers, this he has fulfilled to us their children by raising Jesus; as also it is written in the second psalm, 'Thou art my Son, today I have begotten thee.' And as for the fact that he raised him from the dead, no more to return to corruption, he spoke in this way, 'I will give you the holy and sure blessings of David.' Therefore he says also in another psalm, 'Thou will not let thy Holy One see corruption.' For David, after he had served the counsel of God in his own generation, fell asleep, and was laid with his fathers, and saw corruption; but he whom God raised up saw no corruption. Let it be known to you therefore, brethren, that through this man forgiveness of sins is proclaimed to you, and by him every one that believes is freed from everything from which you could not be freed by the law of Moses. Beware, therefore, lest there come upon you what is said in the prophets: 'Behold, you scoffers, and wonder, and perish; for I do a deed in your days, a deed you will never believe, if one declares it to you.'" As they went out, the people begged that these things might be told them the next sabbath. And when the meeting of the synagogue broke up, many Jews and devout converts to Judaism followed Paul and Barnabas, who spoke to them and urged them to continue in the grace of God.

A Reading (Lesson) from the Gospel according to John
[10:1-18]

Jesus said to the Pharisees, "Truly, truly, I say to you, he who does not enter the sheepfold by the door but climbs in by another way, that man is a thief and a robber; but he who enters by the door is the shepherd of the sheep. To him the gatekeeper opens; the sheep hear his voice, and he calls his own sheep by name and leads them out. When he has brought out all his own, he goes before them, and the sheep follow him, for they know his voice. A stranger they will not follow, but they will flee from him, for they do not know the voice of strangers." This figure Jesus used with them, but they did not understand what he was saying to them. So Jesus again said to them, "Truly, truly, I say to you, I am the door of the sheep. All who came before me are thieves and robbers; but the sheep did not heed them. I am the door; if any one enters by me, he will be saved, and will go in and out and find pasture. The thief comes only to steal and kill and destroy; I came that they may have life, and have it abundantly. I am the good shepherd. The good shepherd lays down his life for the sheep. He who is a hireling and not a shepherd, whose own the sheep are not, sees the wolf coming and leaves the sheep and flees; and the wolf snatches them and scatters them. He flees because he is a hireling and cares nothing for the sheep. I am the good shepherd; I know my own and my own know me, as the Father knows me and I know the Father; and I lay down my life for the sheep. And I have other sheep, that are not of this fold; I must bring them also, and they will heed my voice. So there shall be one flock, one shepherd. For this reason the Father loves me, because I lay down my life, that I may take it again. No one takes it from me, but I lay it down of my own accord. I have power to lay it down, and I have power to take it again; this charge I have received from my Father."

Proper 18   *Week of the Sunday closest to September 7*

Sunday

Psalm 63:1-8(9-11) [page 670],   *Psalm 98* [page 727]   ❖
Psalm 103 [page 733]

A Reading (Lesson) from the Book of Job   [25:1-6;27:1-6]

Bildad the Shuhite answered: "Dominion and fear are with God; he makes peace in his high heaven. Is there any number to his armies? Upon whom does his light not arise? How then can man be righteous before God? How can he who is born of woman be clean? Behold, even the moon is not bright and the stars are not clean in his sight; how much less man, who is a maggot, and the son of man, who is a worm!" And Job again took up his discourse, and said: "As God lives, who has taken away my right, and the Almighty, who has made my soul bitter; as long as my breath is in me, and the spirit of God is in my nostrils; my lips will not speak falsehood, and my tongue will not utter deceit. Far be it from me to say that you are right; till I die I will not put away my integrity from me. I hold fast my righteousness, and will not let it go; my heart does not reproach me for any of my days."

A Reading (Lesson) from the Revelation to John [14:1-7,13]

I looked, and lo, on Mount Zion stood the Lamb, and with him a hundred and forty-four thousand who had his name and his Father's name written on their foreheads. And I heard a voice from heaven like the sound of many waters and like the sound of loud thunder; the voice I heard was like the sound of harpers playing on their harps, and they sing a new song before the four living creatures and before the elders. No one could learn that song except the hundred and forty-four thousand who had been redeemed from the earth. It is these who have not defiled themselves with women, for they are chaste; it is these who follow the Lamb wherever he goes; these have been redeemed from mankind as first fruits for God and the Lamb, and in their mouth no lie was found, for they are spotless. Then I saw another angel flying in midheaven, with an eternal gospel to proclaim to those who dwell on earth, to every nation and tribe and tongue and people; and he said with a loud voice, "Fear God and give him glory, for the hour of his judgment has come; and worship him who made heaven and earth, the sea and the fountains of water." And I heard a voice from heaven saying, "Write this: Blessed are the dead who die in the Lord henceforth." "Blessed indeed," says the Spirit, "That they may rest from their labors, for their deeds follow them!"

A Reading (Lesson) from the Gospel according to Matthew [5:13-20]

Jesus opened his mouth and taught them, saying: "You are the salt of the earth; but if salt has lost its taste, how shall its saltness be restored? It is not longer good for anything except to be thrown out and trodden under foot by men. You are the light of the world. A city set on a hill cannot be hid. Nor do men light a lamp and put it under a bushel, but on a stand, and it gives light to all in the house. Let your light so shine before men, that they may see your good works and give glory to your Father who is in heaven. Think not that I have come to abolish the law and the prophets; I have come not to abolish them but to fulfil them. For truly, I say to you, till heaven and earth pass away, not an iota, not a dot, will pass from the law until all is accomplished. Whoever then relaxes one of the least of these commandments and teaches men so, shall be called least in the kingdom of heaven; but he who does them and teaches them shall be called great in the kingdom of heaven. For I tell you, unless your righteousness exceeds that of the scribes and Pharisees, you will never enter the kingdom of heaven."

Monday

Psalm 41 [page 641],   *Psalm 52* [page 657] ❖
Psalm 44 [page 645]

A Reading (Lesson) from the Book of Job
[32:1-10,19—33:1,19-28]

These three men ceased to answer Job, because he was righteous in his own eyes. Then Eli'hu the son of Bar'achel the Buzite, of the family of Ram, became angry. He was angry at Job because he justified himself rather than God; he was angry also at Job's three friends because they had found no answer, although they had declared Job to be in the wrong. Now Eli'hu had waited to speak to Job because they were older than he. And when Eli'hu saw that there was no answer in the mouth of these three men, he became angry. And Eli'hu the son of Bar'achel the Buzite answered: "I am young in years, and you are aged; therefore I was timid and afraid to declare my opinion to you. I said, 'Let days speak, and many years teach wisdom.' But it is the spirit in a man, the breath of the Almighty, that makes him understand. It is not the old that are wise, nor the aged that understand what is right. Therefore I say, 'Listen to me; let me also declare my opinion.' Behold, my heart is like wine that has no vent; like new wineskins, it is ready to burst. I must speak, that I may find relief; I must open my lips and answer. I will not show partiality to any person or use flattery toward any man. For I do not know how to flatter, else would my Maker soon put an end to me. But now, hear my speech, O Job, and listen to all my words. Man is also chastened with pain upon his bed, and with continual strife in his bones; so that his life loathes bread, and his appetite dainty food. His flesh is so wasted away that it cannot be seen; and his bones which were not seen stick out. His soul draws near the Pit, and his life to those who bring death. If there be for him an angel, a mediator, one of the thousand, to declare to man what is right for him; and he is gracious to him, and says, 'Deliver him from going down into the Pit, I have found a ransom; let his flesh become fresh with youth; let him return to the days of his youthful vigor'; then man prays to God, and he accepts him, he comes into his presence with joy. He recounts to men his salvation, and he sings before men, and says: 'I sinned, and perverted what was right, and it was not requited to me. He has redeemed my soul from going down into the Pit, and my life shall see the light.'"

A Reading (Lesson) from the Acts of the Apostles
[13:44-52]

The next sabbath almost the whole city gathered together to hear the word of God. But when the Jews saw the multitudes, they were filled with jealousy, and contradicted what was spoken by Paul, and reviled him. And Paul and Barnabas spoke out boldly, saying, "It was necessary that the word of God should be spoken first to you. Since you thrust it from you, and judge yourselves unworthy of eternal life, behold, we turn to the Gentiles. For so the Lord has commanded us, saying, 'I have set you to be a light for the Gentiles, that you may bring salvation to the uttermost parts of the earth.'" And when the Gentiles heard this, they were glad and glorified the word of God; and as many as were ordained to eternal life believed. And the word of the Lord spread throughout the region. But the Jews incited the devout women of high standing and the leading men of the city, and stirred up persecution against Paul and Barnabas, and drove them out of their district. But they shook off the dust from their feet against them, and went to Ico'nium. And the disciples were filled with joy and with the Holy Spirit.

A Reading (Lesson) from the Gospel according to John [10:19-30]

There was again a division among the Jews because of these words. Many of them said, "He has a demon, and he is mad; why listen to him?" Others said, "These are not the sayings of one who has a demon. Can a demon open the eyes of the blind?" It was the feast of the Dedication at Jerusalem; it was winter, and Jesus was walking in the temple, in the portico of Solomon. So the Jews gathered round him and said to him, "How long will you keep us in suspense? If you are the Christ, tell us plainly." Jesus answered them, "I told you, and you do not believe. The works that I do in my Father's name, they bear witness to me; but you do not believe, because you do not belong to my sheep. My sheep hear my voice, and I know them, and they follow me; and I give them eternal life, and they shall never perish, and no one shall snatch them out of my hand. My Father, who has given them to me, is greater than all, and no one is able to snatch them out of the Father's hand. I and the Father are one."

Tuesday

Psalm 45 [page 647]   ❖   *Psalm 47* [page 650],
Psalm 48 [page 651]

A Reading (Lesson) from the Book of Job [29:1-20]

Job again took up his discourse, and said: "Oh, that I were as in the months of old, as in the days when God watched over me; when his lamp shone upon my head, and by his light I walked through darkness; as I was in my autumn days, when the friendship of God was upon my tent; when the Almighty was yet with me, when my children were about me; when my steps were washed with milk, and the rock poured out for me streams of oil! When I went out to the gate of the city, when I prepared my seat in the square, the young men saw me and withdrew, and the aged rose and stood; the princes refrained from talking, and laid their hand on their mouth; the voice of the nobles was hushed, and their tongue cleaved to the roof of their mouth. When the ear heard it, it called me blessed, and when the eye saw, it approved; because I delivered the poor who cried, and the fatherless who had none to help him. The blessing of him who was about to perish came upon me, and I caused the widow's heart to sing for joy. I put on righteousness, and it clothed me; my justice was like a robe and a turban. I was eyes to the blind, and feet to the lame. I was a father to the poor, and I searched out the cause of him whom I did not know. I broke the fangs of the unrighteous, and made him drop his prey from his teeth. Then I thought, 'I shall die in my nest, and I shall multiply my days as the sand, my roots spread out to the waters, with the dew all night on my branches, my glory fresh with me, and my bow ever new in my hand.'"

A Reading (Lesson) from the Acts of the Apostles [14:1-18]

At Iconium Paul and Barnabas entered together into the Jewish synagogue, and so spoke that a great company believed, both of Jews and of Greeks. But the unbelieving Jews stirred up the Gentiles and poisoned their minds against the brethren. So they remained for a long time, speaking boldly for the Lord, who bore witness to the word of his grace, granting signs and wonders to be done by their hands. But the people of the city were divided; some sided with the Jews, and some with the apostles. When an attempt was made by both Gentiles and Jews, with their rulers, to molest them and to stone them, they learned of it and fled to Lystra and Derbe, cities of Lycao'nia, and to the surrounding country; and there they preached the gospel. Now at Lystra there was a man sitting, who could not use his feet; he was a cripple from birth, who had never walked. He listened to Paul speaking; and Paul, looking intently at him and seeing that he had faith to be made well, said in a loud voice, "Stand upright on your feet." And he sprang up and walked. And when the crowds saw what Paul had done, they lifted up their voices, saying in Lycao'nian, "The gods have come down to us in the likeness of men!" Barnabas they called Zeus, and Paul, because he was the chief speaker, they called Hermes. And the priest of Zeus, whose temple was in front of the city, brought oxen and garlands to the gates and wanted to offer sacrifice with the people. But when the apostles Barnabas and Paul heard of it, they tore their garments and rushed out among the multitude, crying, "Men, why are you doing this? We also are men, of like nature with you, and bring you good news, that you should turn from these vain things to a living God who made the heaven and the earth and the sea and all that is in them. In past generations he allowed all the nations to walk in their own ways; yet he did not leave himself without witness, for he did good and gave you from heaven rains and fruitful seasons, satisfying your hearts with food and gladness." With these words they scarcely restrained the people from offering sacrifice to them.

A Reading (Lesson) from the Gospel according to John
[10:31-42]

The Jews took up stones again to stone Jesus. He answered them, "I have shown you many good works from the

Father; for which of these do you stone me?" The Jews answered him, "It is not for a good work that we stone you but for blasphemy; because you, being a man, make yourself God." Jesus answered them, "Is it not written in your law, 'I said, you are gods'? If he called them gods to whom the word of God came (and scripture cannot be broken), do you say of him whom the Father consecrated and sent into the world, 'You are blaspheming,' because I said, 'I am the Son of God'? If I am not doing the works of my Father, then do not believe me; but if I do them, even though you do not believe me, believe the works, that you may know and understand that the Father is in me and I am in the Father." Again they tried to arrest him, but he escaped from their hands. He went away again across the Jordan to the place where John at first baptized, and there he remained. And many came to him; and they said, "John did no sign, but everything that John said about this man was true." And many believed in him there.

Wednesday

Psalm 119:49-72 [page 767]   ❖   *Psalm 49* [page 652], *(Psalm 53* [page 658])

A Reading (Lesson) from the Book of Job
[29:1;30:1-2,16-31]

Job again took up his discourse, and said: "But now they make sport of me, men who are younger than I, whose fathers I would have disdained to set with the dogs of my flock. What could I gain from the strength of their hands, men whose vigor is gone? And now my soul is poured out within me; days of affliction have taken hold of me. The night racks my bones, and the pain that gnaws me takes no rest. With violence it seizes my garment; it binds me about like the collar of my tunic. God has cast me into the mire, and I have become like dust and ashes. I cry to thee and

thou dost not answer me; I stand, and thou dost not heed
me. Thou hast turned cruel to me; with the might of thy
hand thou dost persecute me. Thou liftest me up on the
wind, thou makest me ride on it, and thou tossest me
about in the roar of the storm. Yea, I know that thou wilt
bring me to death, and to the house appointed for all
living. Yet does not one in a heap of ruins stretch out of
hand, and in his disaster cry for help? Did not I weep for
him whose day was hard? Was not my soul grieved for the
poor? But when I looked for good, evil came; and when I
waited for light, darkness came. My heart is in turmoil,
and is never still; days of affliction come to meet me. I go
about blackened, but not by the sun; I stand up in the
assembly, and cry for help. I am a brother of jackels, and a
companion of ostriches. My skin turns black and falls
from me, and my bones burn with heat. My lyre is turned
to mourning, and my pipe to the voice of those who
weep."

A Reading (Lesson) from the Acts of the Apostles
[14:19-28]

Jews came to Lystra from Antioch and Ico'nium; and
having persuaded the people, they stoned Paul and dragged
him out of the city, supposing that he was dead. But when
the disciples gathered about him, he rose up and entered
the city; and on the next day he went on with Barnabas to
Derbe. When they had preached the gospel to that city and
had made many disciples, they returned to Lystra and to
Ico'nium and to Antioch, strengthening the souls of the
disciples, exhorting them to continue in the faith, and
saying that through many tribulations we must enter the
kingdom of God. And when they had appointed elders for
them in every church, with prayer and fasting, they
committed them to the Lord in whom they believed. Then
they passed through Pisid'ia, and came to Pamphyl'ia. And
when they had spoken the word in Perga, they went down
to Attali'a; and from there they sailed to Antioch, where

they had been commended to the grace of God for the work which they had fulfilled. And when they arrived, they gathered the church together and declared all that God had done with them, and how he had opened a door of faith to the Gentiles. And they remained no little time with the disciples.

A Reading (Lesson) from the Gospel according to John
[11:1-16]

A certain man was ill, Laz'arus of Bethany, the village of Mary and her sister Martha. It was Mary who anointed the Lord with ointment and wiped his feet with her hair, whose brother Laz'arus was ill. So the sisters sent to Jesus, saying, "Lord, he whom you love is ill." But when Jesus heard it he said, "This illness is not unto death; it is for the glory of God, so that the Son of God may be glorified by means of it." Now Jesus loved Martha and her sister and Laz'arus. So when he heard that he was ill, he stayed two days longer in the place where he was. Then after this he said to the disciples, "Let us go into Judea again." The disciples said to him, "Rabbi, the Jews were but now seeking to stone you, and are you going there again?" Jesus answered, "Are there not twelve hours in the day? If any one walks in the day, he does not stumble, because he sees the light of this world. But if any one walks in the night, he stumbles, because the light is not in him." Thus he spoke, and then he said to them, "Our friend Laz'arus has fallen asleep, but I go to awake him out of sleep." The disciples said to him, "Lord, if he has fallen asleep, he will recover." Now Jesus had spoken of his death, but they thought that he meant taking rest in sleep. Then Jesus told them plainly, "Laz'arus is dead; and for your sake I am glad that I was not there, so that you may believe. But let us go to him." Thomas, called the Twin, said to his fellow disciples, "Let us also go, that we may die with him."

Thursday

Psalm 50 [page 654] ❖ *(Psalm 59* [page 665],
Psalm 60 [page 667])   *or*   *Psalm 93* [page 722],
Psalm 96 [page 725]

A Reading (Lesson) from the Book of Job [29:1;31:1-23]

Job again took up his discourse, and said: "I have made a
covenant with my eyes; how could I look upon a virgin?
What would be my portion from God above, and my
heritage from the Almighty on high? Does not calamity
befall the unrighteous, and disaster the workers of
iniquity? Does not he see my ways, and number all my
steps? If I have walked with falsehood, and my foot has
hastened to deceit; (Let me be weighed in a just balance,
and let God know my integrity!) if my step has turned
aside from the way, and my heart has gone after my eyes,
and if any spot has cleaved to my hands; then let me sow,
and another eat; and let what grows for me be rooted out.
If my heart has been enticed to a woman, and I have lain in
wait at my neighbor's door; then let my wife grind for
another, and let others bow down upon her. For that
would be a heinous crime; that would be an iniquity to be
punished by the judges; for that would be a fire which
consumes unto Abaddon, and it would burn to the root all
my increase. If I have rejected the cause of my manservant
or my maidservant, when they brought a complaint
against me; what then shall I do when God rises up? When
he makes inquiry, what shall I answer him? Did not he
who made me in the womb make him? And did not one
fashion us in the womb? If I have withheld anything that
the poor desired, or have caused the eyes of the widow to
fail, or have eaten my morsel alone, and the fatherless has
not eaten of it (for from his youth I reared him as a father,
and from his mother's womb I guided him) if I have seen
any one perish for lack of clothing, or a poor man without
covering; if his loins have not blessed me, and if he was not

warmed with the fleece of my sheep; if I have raised my hand against the fatherless, because I saw help in the gate; then let my shoulder blade fall from my shoulder, and let my arm be broken from its socket. For I was in terror of calamity from God, and I could not have faced his majesty."

A Reading (Lesson) from the Acts of the Apostles [15:1-11]

Some men came down from Judea and were teaching the brethren, "Unless you are circumcised according to the custom of Moses, you cannot be saved." And when Paul and Barnabas had no small dissension and debate with them, Paul and Barnabas and some of the others were appointed to go up to Jerusalem to the apostles and the elders about this question. So, being sent on their way by the church, they passed through both Phoeni'cia and Samar'ia, reporting the conversion of the Gentiles, and they gave great joy to all the brethren. When they came to Jerusalem, they were welcomed by the church and the apostles and the elders, and they declared all that God had done with them. But some believers who belonged to the party of the Pharisees rose up, and said, "It is necessary to circumcise them, and to charge them to keep the law of Moses." The apostles and the elders were gathered together to consider this matter. And after there had been much debate, Peter rose and said to them, "Brethren, you know that in the early days God made choice among you, that by my mouth the Gentiles should hear the word of the gospel and believe. And God who knows the heart bore witness to them, giving them the Holy Spirit just as he did to us; and he made no distinction between us and them, but cleansed their hearts by faith. Now therefore why do you make trial of God by putting a yoke upon the neck of the disciples which neither our fathers nor we have been able to bear? But we believe that we shall be saved through the grace of the Lord Jesus, just as they will."

A Reading (Lesson) from the Gospel according to John
[11:17-29]

When Jesus came to Bethany, he found that Lazarus had
already been in the tomb four days. Bethany was near
Jerusalem, about two miles off, and many of the Jews had
come to Martha and Mary to console them concerning
their brother. When Martha heard that Jesus was coming,
she went and met him, while Mary sat in the house.
Martha said to Jesus, "Lord, if you had been here, my
brother would not have died. And even now I know that
whatever you ask from God, God will give you." Jesus said
to her, "Your brother will rise again." Martha said, "I
know that he will rise again in the resurrection at the last
day." Jesus said to her, "I am the resurrection and the life;
he who believes in me, though he die, yet shall he live, and
whoever lives and believes in me shall never die. Do you
believe this?" She said to him, "Yes, Lord; I believe that
you are the Christ, the Son of God, he who is coming into
the world." When she had said this, she went and called
her sister Mary, saying quietly. "The Teacher is here and is
calling for you." And when she heard it, she rose quickly
and went to him.

Friday

Psalm 40 [page 640],   *Psalm 54* [page 659]   ❖
Psalm 51 [page 656]

A Reading (Lesson) from the Book of Job   [29:1;31:24-40]

Job again took up his discourse, and said: "If I have made
gold my trust, or called fine gold my confidence; if I have
rejoiced because my wealth was great, or because my hand
had gotten much; if I have looked at the sun when it shone,
or the moon moving in splendor, and my heart has been
secretly enticed, and my mouth has kissed my hand; this
also would be an iniquity to be punished by the judges, for

I should have been false to God above. If I have rejoiced at the ruin of him that hated me, or exulted when evil overtook him (I have not let my mouth sin by asking for his life with a curse); if the men of my tent have not said, 'Who is there that has not been filled with his meat?' (the sojourner has not lodged in the street; I have opened my doors to the wayfarer); if I have concealed my transgressions from men, by hiding my iniquity in my bosom, because I stood in great fear of the multitude, and the contempt of families terrified me, so that I kept silence, and did not go out of doors—Oh, that I had one to hear me! (Here is my signature! let the Almighty answer me!) Oh, that I had the indictment written by my adversary! Surely I would carry it on my shoulder; I would bind it on me as a crown; I would give him an account of all my steps; like a prince I would approach him. If my land has cried out against me, and its furrows have wept together; if I have eaten its yield without payment, and caused the death of its owners; let thorns grow instead of wheat, and foul weeds instead of barley." The words of Job are ended.

A Reading (Lesson) from the Acts of the Apostles
[15:12-21]

All the assembly kept silence; and they listened to Barnabas and Paul as they related what signs and wonders God had done through them among the Gentiles. After they finished speaking, James replied, "Brethren, listen to me. Simeon has related how God first visited the Gentiles, to take out of them a people for his name. And with this the words of the prophets agree, as it is written, 'After this I will return, and I will rebuild the dwelling of David, which has fallen; I will rebuild its ruins, and I will set it up, that the rest of men may seek the Lord, and all the Gentiles who are called by my name, says the Lord, who has made these things known from of old.' Therefore my judgment is that we should not trouble those of the Gentiles who turn to God, but should write to them to abstain from the pollutions of idols and from unchastity and from what is strangled and from blood. For from early generations Moses has had in every city those who preach him, for he is read every sabbath in the synagogues."

A Reading (Lesson) from the Gospel according to John
[11:30-44]

Jesus had not yet come to the village of Bethany, but was still in the place where Martha had met him. When the Jews who were with her in the house, consoling her, saw Mary rise quickly and go out, they followed her, supposing that she was going to the tomb to weep there. Then Mary, when she came where Jesus was and saw him, fell at his feet, saying to him, "Lord, if you had been here, my brother would not have died." When Jesus saw her weeping, and the Jews who came with her also weeping, he was deeply moved in spirit and troubled; and he said, "Where have you laid him?" They said to him, "Lord, come and see." Jesus wept. So the Jews said, "See how he loved him!" But some of them said, "Could not he who opened the eyes of the blind man have kept this man from dying?" Then Jesus, deeply moved again, came to the tomb; it was a cave, and a stone lay upon it. Jesus said, "Take away the stone." Martha, the sister of the dead man, said to him, "Lord, by this time there will be an odor, for he has been dead four days." Jesus said to her, "Did I not tell you that if you would believe you would see the glory of God?" So they took away the stone. And Jesus lifted up his eyes and said, "Father, I thank thee that thou hast heard me. I knew that thou hearest me always, but I have said this on account of the people standing by, that they may believe that thou didst send me." When he had said this, he cried with a loud voice, "Laz'arus, come out." The dead man came out, his hands and feet bound with bandages, and his face wrapped with a cloth. Jesus said to them, "Unbind him, and let him go."

Saturday

Psalm 55 [page 660] ❖ *Psalm 138* [page 793],
Psalm 139:1-17 (18-23) [page 794]

A Reading (Lesson) from the Book of Job [38:1-17]

The Lord answered Job out of the whirlwind: "Who is this
that darkens counsel by words without knowledge? Gird
up your loins like a man, I will question you, and you shall
declare to me. Where were you when I laid the foundation
of the earth? Tell me, if you have understanding. Who
determined its measurements—surely you know! Or who
stretched the line upon it? On what were its bases sunk, or
who laid its cornerstone, when the morning stars sang
together, and all the sons of God shouted for joy? Or who
shut in the sea with doors, when it burst forth from the
womb; when I made clouds its garment, and thick
darkness its swaddling band, and prescribed bounds for it,
and set bars and doors, and said, 'Thus far shall you come,
and no farther, and here shall your proud waves be
stayed'? Have you commanded the morning since your
days began, and caused the dawn to know its place, that it
might take hold of the skirts of the earth, and the wicked
be shaken out of it? It is changed like clay under the seal,
and it is dyed like a garment. From the wicked their light is
withheld, and their uplifted arm is broken. Have you
entered into the springs of the sea, or walked in the
recesses of the deep? Have the gates of death been revealed
to you, or have you seen the gates of deep darkness?"

A Reading (Lesson) from the Acts of the Apostles
[15:22-35]

It seemed good to the apostles and the elders, with the
whole church, to choose men from among them and send
them to Antioch with Paul and Barnabas. They sent Judas
called Barsabbas, and Silas, leading men among the
brethren, with the following letter: "The brethren, both

the apostles and the elders, to the brethren who are of the Gentiles in Antioch and Syria and Cilicia, greeting. Since we have heard that some persons from us have troubled you with words, unsettling your minds, although we gave them no instructions, it has seemed good to us, having come to one accord, to choose men and send them to you with our beloved Barnabas and Paul, men who have risked their lives for the sake of our Lord Jesus Christ. We have therefore sent Judas and Silas, who themselves will tell you the same things by word of mouth. For it has seemed good to the Holy Spirit and to us to lay upon you no greater burden than these necessary things: that you abstain from what has been sacrificed to idols and from blood and from what is strangled and from unchastity. If you keep yourselves from these, you will do well. Farewell." So when they were sent off, they went down to Antioch; and having gathered the congregation together, they delivered the letter. And when they read it, they rejoiced at the exhortation. And Judas and Silas, who were themselves prophets, exhorted the brethren with many words and strengthened them. And after they had spent some time, they were sent off in peace by the brethren to those who had sent them. But Paul and Barnabas remained in Antioch, teaching and preaching the word of the Lord, with many others also.

A Reading (Lesson) from the Gospel according to John [11:45-54]

Many of the Jews therefore, who had come with Mary and had seen what Jesus did in raising Lazarus, believed in him; but some of them went to the Pharisees and told them what Jesus had done. So the chief priests and the Pharisees gathered the council, and said, "What are we to do? For this man performs many signs. If we let him go on thus, every one will believe in him, and the Romans will come and destroy both our holy place and our nation." But one of them, Ca'iaphas, who was high priest that year, said to them, "You know nothing at all; you do not understand that it is expedient for you that one man should die for the people, and that the whole nation should not perish." He did not say this of his own accord, but being the high priest that year he prophesied that Jesus should die for the nation, and not for the nation only, but to gather into one the children of God who are scattered abroad. So from that day on they took counsel how to put him to death. Jesus therefore no longer went about openly among the Jews, but went from there to the country near the wilderness, to a town called E'phraim; and there he stayed with the disciples.

Proper 19   *Week of the Sunday closest to September 14*

Sunday

Psalm 24 [page 613],   *Psalm 29* [page 620]   ❖
Psalm 8 [page 592],   *Psalm 84* [page 707]

A Reading (Lesson) from the Book of Job   [38:1,18-41]

The Lord answered Job out of the whirlwind: "Have you comprehended the expanse of the earth? Declare, if you know all this. Where is the way to the dwelling of light, and where is the place of darkness, that you may take it to its territory and that you may discern the paths to its home? You know, for you were born then, and the number of your days is great! Have you entered the storehouses of the snow, or have you seen the storehouses of the hail, which I have reserved for the time of trouble, for the day of battle and war? What is the way to the place where the light is distributed, or where the east wind is scattered upon the earth? Who has cleft a channel for the torrents of rain, and a way for the thunderbolt, to bring rain on a land where no man is, on the desert in which there is no man; to satisfy the waste and desolate land, and to make the ground put forth grass? Has the rain a father, or who has begotten the drops of dew? From whose womb did the ice come forth, and who has given birth to the hoarfrost of heaven? The waters become hard like stone, and the face of the deep is frozen. Can you bind the chains of the Plei′ades, or loose the cords of Orion? Can you lead forth the Maz′zaroth in their season, or can you guide the Bear with its children? Do you know the ordinances of the heavens? Can you establish their rule on the earth? Can you lift up your voice to the clouds, that a flood of waters may cover you? Can you send forth lightnings, that they may go and say to you, 'Here we are'? Who has put wisdom in the clouds, or given understanding to the mists? Who can number the clouds by wisdom? Or who can tilt the waterskins of the heavens, when the dust runs into a mass and the clods cleave fast together? Can you hunt the prey for the lion, or satisfy the appetite of the young lions, when they crouch in their dens, or lie in wait in their covert? Who provides for the raven its prey, when its young ones cry to God, and wander about for lack of food?"

A Reading (Lesson) from the Revelation to John [18:1-8]

I saw another angel coming down from heaven, having great authority; and the earth was made bright with his splendor. And he called out with a mighty voice, "Fallen, fallen is Babylon the great! It has become a dwelling place of demons, a haunt of every foul spirit, a haunt of every foul and hateful bird; for all nations have drunk the wine of her impure passion, and the kings of the earth have committed fornication with her, and the merchants of the earth have grown rich with the wealth of her wantonness." Then I heard another voice from heaven saying, "Come out of her, my people, lest you take part in her sins, lest you share in her plagues; for her sins are heaped high as heaven, and God has remembered her iniquities. Render to her as she herself has rendered, and repay her double for her deeds; mix a double draught for her in the cup she mixed. As she glorified herself and played the wanton, so give her a like measure of torment and mourning. Since in her heart she says, 'A queen I sit, I am no widow, mourning I shall never see,' so shall her plagues come in a single day, pestilence and mourning and famine, and she shall be burned with fire; for mighty is the Lord God who judges her."

A Reading (Lesson) from the Gospel according to Matthew [5:21-26]

Jesus opened his mouth and taught them, saying: "You have heard that it was said to the men of old, 'You shall not kill; and whoever kills shall be liable to judgment.' But I say to you that every one who is angry with his brother shall be liable to judgment; whoever insults his brother shall be liable to the council, and whoever says, 'You fool!' shall be liable to the hell of fire. So if you are offering your gift at the altar, and there remember that your brother has something against you, leave your gift there before the altar and go; first be reconciled to your brother, and then come and offer your gift. Make friends quickly with your accuser, while you are going with him to court, lest your accuser hand you over to the judge, and the judge to the guard, and you be put in prison; truly, I say to you, you will never get out till you have paid the last penny."

Monday

Psalm 56 [page 662], *Psalm 57* [page 663], ❖ *(Psalm 58* [page 664]) ❖ *Psalm 64* [page 671], *Psalm 65* [page 672]

A Reading (Lesson) from the Book of Job [40:1-24]

The Lord said to Job: "Shall a faultfinder contend with the

Almighty? He who argues with God, let him answer it." Then Job answered the Lord: "Behold, I am of small account; what shall I answer thee? I lay my hand on my mouth. I have spoken once, and I will not answer; twice, but I will proceed no further." Then the Lord answered Job out of the whirlwind: "Gird up your loins like a man; I will question you, and you declare to me. Will you even put me in the wrong? Will you condemn me that you may be justified? Have you an arm like God, and can you thunder with a voice like his? Deck yourself with majesty and dignity; clothe yourself with glory and splendor. Pour forth the overflowings of your anger, and look on every one that is proud, and abase him. Look on every one that is proud, and bring him low; and tread down the wicked where they stand. Hide them all in the dust together; bind their faces in the world below. Then will I also acknowledge to you, that your own right hand can give you victory. Behold, Be'hemoth, which I made as I made you; he eats grass like an ox. Behold, his strength in his loins, and his power in the muscles of his belly. He makes his tail stiff like a cedar; the sinews of his thighs are knit together. His bones are tubes of bronze, his limbs like bars of iron. He is the first of the works of God; let him who made him bring near his sword! For the mountains yield food for him where all the wild beasts play. Under the lotus plants he lies, in the covert of the reeds and in the marsh. For his shade the lotus trees cover him; the willows of the brook surround him. Behold, if the river is turbulent he is not frightened; he is confident though Jordan rushes against his mouth. Can one take him with hooks, or pierce his nose with a snare?"

A Reading (Lesson) from the Acts of the Apostles
[15:36—16:5]

After some days in Antioch Paul said to Barnabas, "Come, let us return and visit the brethren in every city where we

proclaimed the word of the Lord, and see how they are."
And Barnabas wanted to take with them John called
Mark. But Paul thought best not to take with them one
who had withdrawn from them in Pamphyl'ia, and had not
gone with them to the work. And there arose a sharp
contention, so that they separated from each other;
Barnabas took Mark with him and sailed away to Cyprus,
but Paul chose Silas and departed, being commended by
the brethren to the grace of the Lord. And he went through
Syria and Cili'cia, strengthening the churches. And he came
also to Derbe and to Lystra. A disciple was there, named
Timothy, the son of a Jewish woman who was a believer;
but his father was a Greek. He was well spoken of by the
brethren at Lystra and Ico'nium. Paul wanted Timothy to
accompany him; and he took him and circumcised him
because of the Jews that were in those places, for they all
knew that his father was a Greek. As they went on their
way through the cities, they delivered to them for
observance the decisions which had been reached by the
apostles and elders who were at Jerusalem. So the churches
were strengthened in the faith, and they increased in
numbers daily.

A Reading (Lesson) from the Gospel according to John
[11:55—12:8]

The Passover of the Jews was at hand, and many went up
from the country to Jerusalem before the Passover, to
purify themselves. They were looking for Jesus and saying
to one another, "What do you think? That he will not
come to the feast?" Now the chief priests and the Pharisees
had given orders that if any one knew where he was, he
should let them know, so that they might arrest him. Six
days before the Passover, Jesus came to Bethany, where
Laz'arus was, whom Jesus had raised from the dead. There
they made him a supper; Martha served, and Laz'arus was

one of those at table with him. Mary took a pound of costly ointment of pure nard and anointed the feet of Jesus and wiped his feet with her hair; and the house was filled with the fragrance of the ointment. But Judas Iscariot, one of his disciples (he who was to betray him), said, "Why was this ointment not sold for three hundred denarii and given to the poor?" This he said, not that he cared for the poor but because he was a thief, and as he had the money box he used to take what was put into it. Jesus said, "Let her alone, let her keep it for the day of my burial. The poor you always have with you, but you do not always have me."

Tuesday

Psalm 61 [page 668], *Psalm 62* [page 669] ❖
Psalm 68:1-20(21-23)24-36 [page 676]

A Reading (Lesson) from the Book of Job [40:1;41:1-11]

The Lord said to Job: "Can you draw out Leviathan with a fishhook, or press down his tongue with a cord? Can you put a rope in his nose, or pierce his jaw with a hook? Will he make many supplications to you? Will he speak to you soft words? Will he make a covenant with you to take him for your servant for ever? Will you play with him as with a bird, or will you put him on a leash for your maidens? Will traders bargain over him? Will they divide him up among the merchants? Can you fill his skin with harpoons, or his head with fishing spears? Lay hands on him; think of the battle; you will not do it again! Behold, the hope of a man is disappointed; he is laid low even at the sight of him. No one is so fierce that he dares to stir him up. Who then is he that can stand before me? Who has given to me, that I should repay him? Whatever is under the whole heaven is mine."

A Reading (Lesson) from the Acts of the Apostles [16:6-15]

Paul and Silas went through the region of Phryg'ia and
Galatia, having been forbidden by the Holy Spirit to speak
the word in Asia. And when they had come opposite
My'sia, they attempted to go into Bithyn'ia, but the Spirit
of Jesus did not allow them; so, passing by My'sia, they
went down to Tro'as. And a vision appeared to Paul in the
night: a man of Macedo'nia was standing beseeching him
and saying, "Come over to Macedo'nia and help us." And
when he had seen the vision, immediately we sought to go
on into Macedo'nia, concluding that God had called us to
preach the gospel to them. Setting sail therefore from
Tro'as, we made a direct voyage to Sam'othrace, and the
following day to Ne-ap'olis, and from there to Philippi,
which is the leading city of the district of Macedo'nia, and
a Roman colony. We remained in this city some days; and
on the sabbath day we went outside the gate to the
riverside, where we supposed there was a place of prayer;
and we sat down and spoke to the women who had come
together. One who heard us was a woman named Lydia,
from the city of Thyati'ra, a seller of purple goods, who
was a worshiper of God. The Lord opened her heart to
give heed to what was said by Paul. And when she was
baptized, with her household, she besought us, saying,
"If you have judged me to be faithful to the Lord, come
to my house and stay." And she prevailed upon us.

A Reading (Lesson) from the Gospel according to John
[12:9-19]

When the great crowd of the Jews learned that Jesus was in
Bethany, they came, not only on account of Jesus but also
to see Laz'arus, whom he had raised from the dead. So the
chief priests planned to put Laz'arus also to death, because
on account of him many of the Jews were going away and
believing in Jesus. The next day a great crowd who had
come to the feast heard that Jesus was coming to

Jerusalem. So they took branches of palm trees and went out to meet him, crying, "Hosanna! Blessed is he who comes in the name of the Lord, even the King of Israel!" And Jesus found a young ass and sat upon it; as it is written, "Fear not, daughter of Zion; behold, your king is coming, sitting on an ass's colt!" His disciples did not understand this at first; but when Jesus was glorified, then they remembered that this had been written of him and had been done to him. The crowd that had been with him when he called Laz'arus out of the tomb and raised him from the dead bore witness. The reason why the crowd went to meet him was that they heard he had done this sign. The Pharisees then said to one another, "You see that you can do nothing; look, the world has gone after him."

Wednesday

Psalm 72 [page 685]   ❖   *Psalm 119:73-96* [page 769]

A Reading (Lesson) from the Book of Job [42:1-17]

Job answered the Lord: "I know that thou canst do all things, and that no purpose of thine can be thwarted. 'Who is this that hides counsel without knowledge?' Therefore I have uttered what I did not understand, things too wonderful for me, which I did not know. 'Hear, and I will speak; I will question you, and you declare to me.' I had heard of thee by the hearing of the ear, but now my eye sees thee; therefore I despise myself, and repent in dust and ashes." After the Lord had spoken these words to Job, the Lord said to El'iphaz the Te'manite: "My wrath is kindled against you and against your two friends; for you have not spoken of me what is right, as my servant Job has. Now therefore take seven bulls and seven rams, and go to my servant Job, and offer up for yourselves a burnt offering; and my servant Job shall pray for you, for I will accept his prayer not to deal with you according to your folly; for you have not spoken of me what is right, as my servant Job has." So El'iphaz the Te'manite and Bildad the Shuhite and Zophar the Na'amathite went and did what the Lord had told them; and the Lord accepted Job's prayer. And the Lord restored the fortunes of Job, when he had prayed for his friends; and the Lord gave Job twice as much as he had before. Then came to him all his brothers and sisters and all who had known him before, and ate bread with him in his house; and they showed him sympathy and comforted him for all the evil that the Lord had brought upon him; and each of them gave him a piece of money and a ring of gold. And the Lord blessed the latter days of Job more than his beginning; and he had fourteen thousand sheep, six thousand camels, a thousand yoke of oxen, and a thousand she-asses. He had also seven sons and three daughters. And he called the name of the first Jemi'mah; and the name of the second Kezi'ah; and the name of the third Ker'en-hap'puch. And in all the land there were no women so fair as Job's daughters; and their father gave them inheritance among their brothers. And after this Job lived a hundred and forty years, and saw his sons, and his sons' sons, four generations. And Job died, an old man, full of days.

A Reading (Lesson) from the Acts of the Apostles
[16:16-24]

As we were going to the place of prayer, we were met by a slave girl who had a spirit of divination and brought her owners much gain by soothsaying. She followed Paul and us, crying, "These men are servants of the Most High God, who proclaim to you the way of salvation." And this she did for many days. But Paul was annoyed, and turned and said to the spirit, "I charge you in the name of Jesus Christ to come out of her." And it came out that very hour. But when her owners saw that their hope of gain was gone, they seized Paul and Silas and dragged them into the market place before the rulers; and when they had brought them to the magistrates they said, "These men are Jews and they are disturbing our city. They advocate customs which it is not lawful for us Romans to accept or practice." The crowd joined in attacking them; and the magistrates tore the garments off them and gave orders to beat them with rods. And when they had inflicted many blows upon them, they threw them into prison, charging the jailer to keep them safely. Having received this charge, he put them into the inner prison and fastened their feet in the stocks.

A Reading (Lesson) from the Gospel according to John [12:20-26]

Among those who went up to worship at the feast in Jerusalem were some Greeks. So these came to Philip, who was from Beth-sa'ida in Galilee, and said to him, "Sir, we wish to see Jesus." Philip went and told Andrew; Andrew went with Philip and they told Jesus. And Jesus answered them, "The hour has come for the Son of man to be glorified. Truly, truly, I say to you, unless a grain of wheat falls into the earth and dies, it remains alone; but if it dies, it bears much fruit. He who loves his life loses it, and he who hates his life in this world will keep it for eternal life. If any one serves me, he must follow me; and where I am, there shall my servant be also; if any one serves me, the Father will honor him."

Thursday

(Psalm 70 [page 682]), *Psalm 71* [page 683] ❖ *Psalm 74* [page 689]

A Reading (Lesson) from the Book of Job [28:1-28]

Job again took up his discourse, and said: "Surely there is a mine for silver, and a place for gold which they refine. Iron is taken out of the earth, and copper is smelted from the ore. Men put an end to darkness, and search out to the farthest bound the ore in gloom and deep darkness. They open shafts in a valley away from where men live; they are forgotten by travelers, they hang afar from men, they swing to and fro. As for the earth, out of it comes bread; but underneath it is turned up as by fire. Its stones are the place of sapphires, and it has dust of gold. That path no bird of prey knows, and the falcon's eye has not seen it. The proud beasts have not trodden it; the lion has not passed over it. Man puts his hand to the flinty rock, and overturns mountains by the roots. He cuts out channels in the rocks, and his eye sees every precious thing. He binds up the streams so that they do not trickle, and the thing that is hid he brings forth to light. But where shall wisdom be found? And where is the place of understanding? Man does not know the way to it, and it is not found in the land of the living. The deep says, 'It is not in me,' and the sea says, 'It is not with me.' It cannot be gotten for gold, and silver cannot be weighed as its price. It cannot be valued in the gold of Ophir, in precious onyx or sapphire. Gold and glass cannot equal it, nor can it be exchanged for jewels of fine gold. No mention shall be made of coral or of crystal; the price of wisdom is above pearls. The topaz of Ethiopia cannot compare with it, nor can it be valued in pure gold. Whence then comes wisdom? And where is the place of understanding? It is hid from the eyes of all living, and concealed from the birds of the air. Abaddon and Death say, 'We have heard a rumor of it with our ears.' God understands the way to it, and he knows its place. For he looks to the ends of the earth, and sees everything under the heavens. When he gave to the wind its weight, and meted out the waters by measure; when he made a decree for the rain, and a way for the lightning of the thunder; then he saw it and declared it; he established it, and searched it out. And he said to man, 'Behold, the fear of the Lord, that is wisdom; and to depart from evil is understanding.'"

A Reading (Lesson) from the Acts of the Apostles
[16:25-40]

About midnight Paul and Silas were praying and singing hymns to God, and the prisoners were listening to them, and suddenly there was a great earthquake, so that the foundations of the prison were shaken; and immediately all the doors were opened and every one's fetters were unfastened. When the jailor woke and saw that the prison doors were open, he drew his sword and was about to kill himself, supposing that the prisoners had escaped. But Paul cried with a loud voice, "Do not harm yourself, for we are all here." And he called for lights and rushed in, and trembling with fear he fell down before Paul and Silas, and brought them out and said, "Men, what must I do to be saved?" And they said, "Believe in the Lord Jesus, and you will be saved, you and your household." And they spoke the word of the Lord to him and to all that were in his house. And he took them the same hour of the night, and washed their wounds, and he was baptized at once, with all his family. Then he brought them up into his house, and set food before them; and he rejoiced with all his household that he had believed in God. But when it was day, the magistrates sent the police, saying, "Let those men go." And the jailer reported the words to Paul, saying, "The magistrates have sent to let you go; now therefore come out and go in peace." But Paul said to them, "They have beaten us publicly, uncondemned, men who are Roman citizens, and have thrown us into prison; and do they now cast us out secretly? No! let them come themselves and take us out." The police reported these words to the magistrates, and they were afraid when they heard that they were Roman citizens; so they came and apologized to them. And they took them out and asked them to leave the city. So they went out of the prison, and visited Lydia; and when they had seen the brethren, they exhorted them and departed.

A Reading (Lesson) from the Gospel according to John
[12:27-36a]

Jesus said to Philip and Andrew, "Now is my soul troubled. And what shall I say, 'Father, save me from this hour'? No, for this purpose I have come to this hour. Father, glorify thy name." Then a voice came from heaven, "I have glorified it, and I will glorify it again." The crowd standing by heard it and said that it had thundered. Others said, "An angel has spoken to him." Jesus answered, "This voice has come for your sake, not for mine. Now is the judgment of this world, now shall the ruler of this world be cast out; and I, when I am lifted up from the earth, will draw all men to myself." He said this to show by what death he was to die. The crowd answered him, "We have heard from the law that the Christ remains for ever. How can you say that the Son of man must be lifted up? Who is this Son of man?" Jesus said to them, "The light is with you for a little longer. Walk while you have the light, lest the darkness overtake you; he who walks in the darkness does not know where he goes. While you have the light, believe in the light, that you may become sons of light."

Friday

Psalm 69:1-23(24-30)31-38 [page 679]   ❖
Psalm 73 [page 687]

A Reading (Lesson) from the Book of Esther [1:1-4,10-19]

In the days of Ahasu-e′rus, the Ahasu-e′rus who reigned from India to Ethiopia over one hundred and twenty-seven provinces, in those days when King Ahasu-e′rus sat on his royal throne in Susa the capital, in the third year of his reign he gave a banquet for all his princes and servants, the army chiefs of Persia and Media and the nobles and governors of the provinces being before him, while he showed the riches of his royal glory and the splendor and pomp of his majesty for many days, a hundred and eighty days. On the seventh day, when the heart of the king was merry with wine, he commanded Mehu'man, Biztha, Harbo'na, Bigtha and Abag'tha, Zethar and Carkas, the seven eunuchs who served King Ahasu-e'rus as chamberlains, to bring Queen Vashti before the king with her royal crown, in order to show the people and the princes her beauty; for she was fair to behold. But Queen Vashti refused to come at the king's command conveyed by the eunuchs. At this the king was enraged, and his anger burned within him. Then the king said to the wise men who knew the times—for this was the king's procedure toward all who were versed in law and judgment, the men next to him being Carshe'na, Shethar, Adma'tha, Tarshish, Meres, Marse'na, and Memu'can, the seven princes of Persia and Media, who saw the king's face, and sat first in the kingdom—: "According to the law, what is to be done to Queen Vashti, because she has not performed the command of King Ahasu-e'rus conveyed by the eunuchs?" Then Memu'can said in presence of the king and the princes, "Not only to the king has Queen Vashti done wrong, but also to all the princes and all the peoples who are in the provinces of King Ahasu-e'rus. For this deed of the queen will be made known to all women, causing them to look with contempt upon their husbands, since they will say, 'King Ahasu-e'rus commanded Queen Vashti to be brought before him, and she did not come.' This very day the ladies of Persia and Media who have heard of the queen's behavior will be telling it to all the king's princes, and there will be contempt and wrath in plenty. If it please the king, let a royal order go forth from him, and let it be written among the laws of the Persians and the Medes so that it may not be altered, that Vashti is to come no more before King Ahasu-e'rus; and let the king give her royal position to another who is better than she.

or this

A Reading (Lesson) from the Book of Judith [4:1-15]

The people of Israel living in Judea heard of everything that Holofer'nes, the general of Nebuchadnez'zar the king of the Assyrians, had done to the nations, and how he had plundered and destroyed all their temples; they were therefore very greatly terrified at his approach, and were alarmed both for Jerusalem and for the temple of the Lord their God. For they had only recently returned from the captivity, and all the people of Judea were newly gathered together, and the sacred vessels and the altar and the temple had been consecrated after their profanation. So they sent to every district of Samar'ia, and to Kona and Beth-horon and Belma'in and Jericho and to Choba and Aesor'a and the valley of Salem, and immediately seized all the high hilltops and fortified the villages on them and stored up food in preparation for war—since their fields had recently been harvested. And Jo'akim, the high priest, who was in Jerusalem at that time, wrote to the people of Bethu'lia and Betomestha'im, which faces Esdrae'lon opposite the plain near Dothan, ordering them to seize the passes up into the hills, since by them Judea could be invaded, and it was easy to stop any who tried to enter, for the approach was narrow, only wide enough for two men at the most. So the Israelites did as Jo'akim the high priest and the senate of the whole people of Israel, in session at Jerusalem, had given order. And every man of Israel cried out to God with great fervor, and they humbled themselves with much fasting. They and their wives and their children and their cattle and every resident alien and hired laborer and purchased slave—they all girded themselves with sackcloth. And all the men and women of Israel, and their children, living at Jerusalem, prostrated themselves before the temple and put ashes on their heads and spread out their sackcloth before the Lord. They even surrounded the altar with sackcloth and cried out in unison, praying earnestly to the God of Israel not to give up their infants as prey and their wives as booty, and the cities they had inherited to be destroyed, and the sanctuary to be profaned and desecrated to the malicious joy of the Gentiles. So the Lord heard their prayers and looked upon their affliction; for the people fasted many days throughout Judea and in Jerusalem before the sanctuary of the Lord Almighty. And Jo'akim the high priest and all the priests who stood before the Lord and ministered to the Lord, with their loins girded with sackcloth, offered the continual burnt offerings and the vows and freewill offerings of the people. With ashes upon their turbans, they cried out to the Lord with all their might to look with favor upon the whole house of Israel.

A Reading (Lesson) from the Acts of the Apostles [17:1-15]

When Paul, Silas, and Timothy had passed through Amphip'olis and Apollo'nia, they came to Thessaloni'ca, where there was a synagogue of the Jews. And Paul went in, as was his custom, and for three weeks he argued with them from the scriptures, explaining and proving that it was necessary for the Christ to suffer and to rise from the dead, and saying, "This Jesus, whom I proclaim to you, is the Christ." And some of them were persuaded, and joined Paul and Silas; as did a great many of the devout Greeks and not a few of the leading women. But the Jews were jealous, and taking some wicked fellows of the rabble, they gathered a crowd, set the city in a uproar, and attacked the house of Jason, seeking to bring them out to the people. And when they could not find them, they dragged Jason and some of the brethren before the city authorities, crying, "These men who have turned the world upside down have come here also, and Jason has received them; and they are all acting against the decrees of Caesar, saying that there is another king, Jesus." And the people and the city authorities were disturbed when they heard this. And when they had taken security from Jason and the rest, they let them go. The brethren immediately sent Paul and Silas away by night to Beroe'a; and when they arrived they went into the Jewish synagogue. Now these Jews were more noble than those in Thessaloni'ca, for they received the word with all eagerness, examining the scriptures daily to see if these things were so. Many of them therefore believed, with not a few Greek women of high standing as well as men. But when the Jews of Thessaloni'ca learned that the word of God was proclaimed by Paul at Beroe'a also, they came there too, stirring up and inciting the crowds. Then the brethren immediately sent Paul off on his way to the sea, but Silas and Timothy remained there. Those who conducted Paul brought him as far as Athens; and receiving a command for Silas and Timothy to come to him as soon as possible, they departed.

A Reading (Lesson) from the Gospel according to John
[12:36b-43]

When Jesus had said this, he departed and hid himself from the Jews. Though he had done so many signs before them, yet they did not believe in him; it was that the word spoken by the prophet Isaiah might be fulfilled: "Lord, who has believed our report, and to whom has the arm of the Lord been revealed?" Therefore they could not believe. For Isaiah again said, "He has blinded their eyes and hardened their heart, lest they should see with their eyes and perceive with their heart, and turn for me to heal them." Isaiah said this because he saw his glory and spoke of him. Nevertheless many even of the authorities believed in him, but for fear of the Pharisees they did not confess it, lest they should be put out of the synagogue: for they loved the praise of men more than the praise of God.

Saturday

Psalm 75 [page 691],   *Psalm 76* [page 692]   ❖
Psalm 23 [page 612],   *Psalm 27* [page 617]

A Reading (Lesson) from the Book of Esther [2:5-8,15-23]

There was a Jew in Susa the capital whose name was
Mor′decai, the son of Ja′ir, son of Shim′e-i, son of Kish, a
Benjaminite, who had been carried away from Jerusalem
among the captives carried away with Jeconi′ah king of
Judah, whom Nebuchadnez′zar king of Babylon had
carried away. He had brought up Hadas′sah, that is Esther,
the daughter of his uncle, for she had neither father nor
mother; the maiden was beautiful and lovely, and when
her father and mother died, Mor′decai adopted her as his
own daughter. So when the king's order and his edict were
proclaimed, and when many maidens were gathered in
Susa the capital in custody of Hegai, Esther also was taken
into the king's palace and put in custody of Hegai who had
charge of the women. When the turn came for Esther the
daughter of Ab′ihail the uncle of Mor′decai, who had
adopted her as his own daughter, to go in to the king, she
asked for nothing except what Hegai the king's eunuch,
who had charge of the women, advised. Now Esther found
favor in the eyes of all who saw her. And when Esther was
taken to King Ahasu-e′rus into his royal palace in the tenth
month, which is the month of Tebeth, in the seventh year
of his reign, the king loved Esther more than all the
women, and she found grace and favor in his sight more
than all the virgins, so that he set the royal crown on her
head and made her queen instead of Vashti. Then the king
gave a great banquet to all his princes and servants; it was
Esther's banquet. He also granted a remission of taxes to
the provinces, and gave gifts with royal liberality. When
the virgins gathered together the second time, Mor′decai
was sitting at the king's gate. Now Esther had not made

known her kindred or her people, as Mor'decai had charged her; for Esther obeyed Mor'decai just as when she was brought up by him. And in those days, as Mor'decai was sitting at the king's gate, Bigthan and Teresh, two of the king's eunuchs, who guarded the threshold, became angry and sought to lay hands on King Ahasu-e'rus. And this came to the knowledge of Mor'decai, and he told it to Queen Esther, and Esther told the king in the name of Mor'decai. When the affair was investigated and found to be so, the men were both hanged on the gallows. And it was recorded in the Book of the Chronicles in the presence of the king.

or this

A Reading (Lesson) from the Book of Judith [5:1-21]

When Holofer'nes, the general of the Assyrian army, heard that the people of Israel had prepared for war and had closed all the high hilltops and set up barricades in the plains, he was very angry. So he called together all the princes of Moab and the commanders of Ammon and all the governors of the coastland, and said to them, "Tell me, you Canaanites, what people is this that lives in the hill country? What cities do they inhabit? How large is their army, and in what does their power or strength consist? Who rules over them as king, leading their army? And why have they alone, of all who live in the west, refused to come out and meet me?" Then Ach'ior, the leader of all the Ammonites, said to him, "Let my Lord now hear a word from the mouth of your servant, and I will tell you the truth about this people that dwells in the nearby mountain district. No falsehood shall come from your servant's mouth. This people is descended from the Chalde'ans. At one time they lived in Mesopota'mia, because they would not follow the gods of their fathers who were in Chalde'a. For they had left the ways of their ancestors, and they worshiped the God of heaven, the God they had come to know; hence they drove them out from the presence of their gods; and they fled to Mesopota′mia, and lived there for a long time. Then their God commanded them to leave the place where they were living and go to the land of Canaan. There they settled, and prospered, with much gold and silver and very many cattle. When a famine spread over Canaan they went down to Egypt and lived there as long as they had food; and there they became a great multitude—so great that they could not be counted. So the king of Egypt became hostile to them; he took advantage of them and set them to making bricks, and humbled them and made slaves of them. Then they cried out to their God, and he afflicted the whole land of Egypt with incurable plagues; and so the Egyptians drove them out of their sight. Then God dried up the Red Sea before them, and he led them by way of Sinai and Ka′desh-bar′nea, and drove out all the people of the wilderness. So they lived in the land of the Amorites, and by their might destroyed all the inhabitants of Heshbon; and crossing over the Jordan they took possession of all the hill country. And they drove out before them the Canaanites and the Per′izzites and the Jeb′usites and the She′chemites and the Ger′gesites, and lived there a long time. As long as they did not sin against their God they prospered, for the God who hates iniquity is with them. But when they departed from the way which he had appointed for them, they were utterly defeated in many battles and were led away captive to a foreign country; the temple of their God was razed to the ground, and their cities were captured by their enemies. But now they have returned to their God, and have come back from the places to which they were scattered, and have occupied Jerusalem, where their sanctuary is, and have settled in the hill country, because it was uninhabited. Now therefore, my master and lord, if there is any unwitting error in this people and they sin against their God and we find out their offense, then we will go up and defeat them. But if there is no transgression in their nation, then let my lord pass them by; for their Lord will defend them, and their God will protect them, and we shall be put to shame before the whole world."

A Reading (Lesson) from the Acts of the Apostles
[17:16-34]

While Paul was waiting for Silas and Timothy at Athens, his spirit was provoked within him as he saw that the city was full of idols, so he argued in the synagogue with the Jews and the devout persons, and in the market place every day with those who chanced to be there. Some also of the Epicurean and Stoic philosophers met him. And some said, "What would this babbler say?" Others said, "He seems to be a preacher of foreign divinities" — because he preached Jesus and the resurrection. And they took hold of him and brought him to the Are-op'agus, saying, "May we know what this new teaching is which you present? For you bring some strange things to our ears; we wish to know therefore what these things mean." Now all the Athenians and the foreigners who lived there spent their time in nothing except telling or hearing something new. So Paul, standing in the middle of the Are-op'agus, said: "Men of Athens, I perceive that in every way you are very religious. For as I passed along, and observed the objects of your worship, I found also an altar with this inscription, 'To an unknown god.' What therefore you worship as unknown, this I proclaim to you. The God who made the world and everything in it, being Lord of heaven and earth, does not live in shrines made by man, nor is he served by human hands, as though he needed anything, since he himself gives to all men life and breath and everything. And he made from one every nation of men to live on all the face of the earth, having determined allotted periods and the boundaries of their habitation, that they should seek God, in the hope that they might feel after him and find him. Yet he is not far from each one of us, for 'In him we live and move and have our being'; as even some of your poets have said, 'For we are indeed his offspring.' Being then God's offspring, we ought not to think that the Deity is like gold, or silver, or stone, a representation by the art and imagination of man. The times of ignorance God overlooked, but now he commands all men everywhere to repent, because he has fixed a day on which he will judge the world in righteousness by a man whom he has appointed, and of this he has given assurance to all men by raising him from the dead." Now when they heard of the resurrection of the dead, some mocked; but others said, "We will hear you again about this." So Paul went out from among them. But some men joined him and believed, among them Dionsy'ius the Are-op'agite and a woman named Dam'aris and others with them.

A Reading (Lesson) from the Gospel according to John [12:44-50]

Jesus cried out and said, "He who believes in me, believes not in me but in him who sent me. And he who sees me sees him who sent me. I have come as light into the world, that whoever believes in me may not remain in darkness. If any one hears my sayings and does not keep them, I do not judge him; for I did not come to judge the world but to save the world. He who rejects me and does not receive my sayings has a judge; the word that I have spoken will be his judge on the last day. For I have not spoken on my own authority; the Father who sent me has himself given me commandment what to say and what to speak. And I know that his commandment is eternal life. What I say, therefore, I say as the Father has bidden me."

Proper 20   *Week of the Sunday closest to September 21*

Sunday

Psalm 93 [page 722],   *Psalm 96* [page 725]   ❖
Psalm 34 [page 627]

A Reading (Lesson) from the Book of Esther   [3:1—4:3]

After Bigthan and Teresh, two of the king's eunuchs, were
both hanged from the gallows, King Ahasu-e'rus promoted
Haman the Ag'agite, the son of Hammeda'tha, and
advanced him and set his seat above all the princes who
were with him. And all the king's servants who were at the
king's gate bowed down and did obeisance to Haman; for
the king had so commanded concerning him. But
Mor'decai did not bow down or do obeisance. Then the
king's servants who were at the king's gate said to
Mor'decai, "Why do you transgress the king's command?"
And when they spoke to him day after day and he would
not listen to them, they told Haman, in order to see
whether Mor'decai's words would avail; for he had told
them that he was a Jew. And when Haman saw that
Mor'decai did not bow down or do obeisance to him,
Haman was filled with fury. But he disdained to lay hands
on Mor'decai alone. So, as they had made known to him
the people of Mor'decai, Haman sought to destroy all the
Jews, the people of Mor'decai, throughout the whole
kingdom of Ahasu-e'rus. In the first month, which is the
month of Nisan, in the twelfth year of King Ahasu-e'rus,
they cast Pur, that is the lot, before Haman day after day;
and they cast it month after month till the twelfth month,
which is the month of Adar. Then Haman said to King
Ahasu-e'rus, "There is a certain people scattered abroad
and dispersed among the peoples in all the provinces of
your kingdom; their laws are different from those of every

other people, and they do not keep the king's laws, so that it is not for the king's profit to tolerate them. If it please the king, let it be decreed that they be destroyed, and I will pay ten thousand talents of silver into the hands of those who have charge of the king's business, that they may put it into the king's treasuries." So the king took his signet ring from his hand and gave it to Haman the Ag'agite, the son of Hammeda'tha, the enemy of the Jews. And the king said to Haman, "The money is given to you, the people also, to do with them as it seems good to you." Then the king's secretaries were summoned on the thirteenth day of the first month, and an edict, according to all that Haman commanded, was written to the king's satraps and to the governors over all the provinces and to the princes of all the peoples, to every province in its own script and every people in its own language; it was written in the name of King Ahasu-e'rus and sealed with the king's ring. Letters were sent by couriers to all the king's provinces, to destroy, to slay and to annihilate all Jews, young and old, women and children, in one day, the thirteenth day of the twelfth month, which is the month of Adar, and to plunder their goods. A copy of the document was to be issued as a decree in every province by proclamation to all the peoples to be ready for that day. The couriers went in haste by order of the king, and the decree was issued in Susa the capital. And the king and Haman sat down to drink; but the city of Susa was perplexed. When Mor'decai learned all that had been done, Mor'decai rent his clothes and put on sackcloth and ashes, and went out into the midst of the city, wailing with a loud and bitter cry; he went up to the entrance of the king's gate, for no one might enter the king's gate clothed with sackcloth. And in every province, wherever the king's command and his decree came, there was great mourning among the Jews, with fasting and weeping and lamenting, and most of them lay in sackcloth and ashes.

or this

A Reading (Lesson) from the Book of Judith
[5:22—6:4,10-21]

When Ach'ior had finished saying this, all the men standing around the tent began to complain; Holofer'nes' officers and all the men from the seacoast and from Moab insisted that he must be put to death. "For," they said, "we will not be afraid of the Israelites; they are a people of no strength or power for making war. Therefore let us go up, Lord Holofer'nes, and they will be devoured by your vast army." When the disturbance made by the men outside the council died down, Holofer'nes, the commander of the Assyrian army, said to Ach'ior and all the Moabites in the presence of all the foreign contingents: "And who are you, Ach'ior, and you hirelings of E'phraim, to prophesy among us as you have done today and tell us not to make war against the people of Israel because their God will defend them? Who is God except Nebuchadnez'zar? He will send his forces and will destroy them from the face of the earth, and their God will not deliver them—we the king's servants will destroy them as one man. They cannot resist the might of our cavalry. We will burn them up, and their mountains will be drunk with their blood and their fields will be full of their dead. They cannot withstand us, but will utterly perish. So says King Nebuchadnez'zar, the lord of the whole earth. For he has spoken; none of his words shall be in vain." Then Holofer'nes ordered his slaves, who waited on him in his tent, to seize Ach'ior and take him to Bethu'lia and hand him over to the men of Israel. So the slaves took him and led him out of the camp into the plain, and from the plain they went up into the hill country and came to the springs below Bethu'lia. When the men of the city saw them, they caught up their weapons and ran out of the city to the top of the hill, and all the slingers kept them from coming up by casting stones at them. However, they got under the shelter of the hill and they bound Ach'ior and left him lying at the foot of the hill, and returned to their master. Then the men of Israel came down from their city and found him; and they untied him and brought him into Bethu'lia and placed him before the magistrates of their city, who in those days were Uzzi'ah the son of Micah, of the tribe of Simeon, and Chabris the son of Gothon'iel, and Charmis the son of Mel'chiel. They called together all the elders of the city, and all their young men and their women ran to the assembly; and they set Ach'ior in the midst of all their people, and Uzzi'ah asked him what had happened. He answered and told them what had taken place at the council of Holofer'nes, and all that he had said in the presence of the Assyrian leaders, and all that Holofer'nes had said so boastfully against the house of Israel. Then the people fell down and worshiped God, and cried out to him, and said, "O Lord God of heaven, behold their arrogance, and have pity on the humiliation of our people, and look this day upon the faces of those who are consecrated to thee." Then they consoled Ach'ior, and praised him greatly. And Uzzi'ah took him from the assembly to his own house and gave a banquet for the elders; and all that night they called on the God of Israel for help.

A Reading (Lesson) from the Letter of James [1:19-27]

Know this, my beloved brethren. Let every man be quick to hear, slow to speak, slow to anger, for the anger of man does not work the righteousness of God. Therefore put away all filthiness and rank growth of wickedness and receive with meekness the implanted word, which is able to save your souls. But be doers of the word, and not hearers only, deceiving yourselves. For if any one is a hearer of the word and not a doer, he is like a man who observes his natural face in a mirror; for he observes himself and goes away, and at once forgets what he was like. But he who looks into the perfect law, the law of liberty, and perseveres, being no hearer that forgets but a doer that acts, he shall be blessed in his doing. If any one thinks he is religious, and does not bridle his tongue but deceives his heart, this man's religion is vain. Religion that is pure and undefiled before God and the Father is this: to visit orphans and widows in their affliction, and to keep oneself unstained from the world.

A Reading (Lesson) from the Gospel according to Matthew [6:1-6,16-18]

Jesus opened his mouth and taught them, saying, "Beware of practicing your piety before men in order to be seen by them; for then you will have no reward from your Father who is in heaven. Thus, when you give alms, sound no trumpet before you, as the hypocrites do in the synagogues and in the streets, that they may be praised by men. Truly, I say to you, they have received their reward. But when you give alms, do not let your left hand know what your right hand is doing, so that your alms may be in secret; and your Father who sees in secret will reward you. And when you pray, you must not be like the hypocrites; for they love to stand and pray in the synagogues and at the street corners, that they may be seen by men. Truly, I say to you, they have received their reward. But when you pray, go into your room and shut the door and pray to your Father who is in secret; and your Father who sees in secret will reward you. And when you fast, do not look dismal, like the hypocrites, for they disfigure their faces that their fasting may be seen by men. Truly, I say to you, they have received their reward. But when you fast, anoint your head and wash your face, that your fasting may not be seen by men but by your Father who is in secret; and your Father who sees in secret will reward you."

Monday

Psalm 80 [page 702] ❖ *Psalm 77* [page 693],
(Psalm 79 [page 701])

A Reading (Lesson) from the Book of Esther [4:4-17]

When Esther's maids and her eunuchs came and told her
that Mor'decai lay in the entrance of the king's gate in
sackcloth, the queen was deeply distressed; she sent
garments to clothe Mor'decai, so that he might take off his
sackcloth, but he would not accept them. Then Esther
called for Hathach, one of the king's eunuchs, who had
been appointed to attend her, and ordered him to go to
Mor'decai to learn what this was and why it was. Hathach
went out to Mor'decai in the open square of the city in
front of the king's gate, and Mor'decai told him all that had
happened to him, and the exact sum of money that Haman
had promised to pay into the king's treasuries for the
destruction of the Jews. Mor'decai also gave him a copy of
the written decree issued in Susa for their destruction, that
he might show it to Esther and explain it to her and charge
her to go to the king to make supplication to him and
entreat him for her people. And Hathach went and told
Esther what Mor'decai had said. Then Esther spoke to
Hathach and gave him a message for Mor'decai, saying,
"All the king's servants and the people of the king's
provinces know that if any man or woman goes to the king
inside the inner court without being called, there is but one
law; all alike are to be put to death, except the one to
whom the king holds out the golden scepter that he may
live. And I have not been called to come into the king these
thirty days." And they told Mor'decai what Esther had
said. Then Mor'decai told them to return answer to Esther,
"Think not that in the king's palace you will escape any
more than all the other Jews. For if you keep silence at
such a time as this, relief and deliverance will rise for the
Jews from another quarter, but you and your father's
house will perish. And who knows whether you have not

come to the kingdom for such a time as this?" Then Esther told them to reply to Mor'decai, "Go, gather all the Jews to be found in Susa, and hold a fast on my behalf, and neither eat nor drink for three days, night or day. I and my maids will also fast as you do. Then I will go to the king, though it is against the law; and if I perish, I perish." Mor'decai then went away and did everything as Esther had ordered him.

or this

A Reading (Lesson) from the Book of Judith [7:1-7,19-32]

The next day Holofer'nes ordered his whole army, and all the allies who had joined him, to break camp and move against Bethu'lia, and to seize the passes up into the hill country and make war on the Israelites. So all their warriors moved their camp that day; their force of men of war was one hundred and seventy thousand infantry and twelve thousand cavalry, together with the baggage and the foot soldiers handling it, a very great multitude. They encamped in the valley near Bethu'lia, beside the spring, and they spread out in breadth over Dothan as far as Balba'im and in length from Bethu'lia to Cy'amon, which faces Esdrae'lon. When the Israelites saw their vast numbers they were greatly terrified, and every one said to his neighbor, "These men will now lick up the face of the whole land; neither the high mountains nor the valleys nor the hills will bear their weight." Then each man took up his weapons, and when they had kindled fires on their towers they remained on guard all that night. On the second day Holofer'nes led out all his cavalry in full view of the Israelites in Bethu'lia, and examined the approaches to the city, and visited the springs that supplied their water, and seized them and set guards of soldiers over them, and then returned to his army. The people of Israel cried out to the Lord their God, for their courage failed, because all their enemies had surrounded them and there was no way of escape from them. The whole Assyrian army, their infantry, chariots, and cavalry, surrounded them for thirty-four days, until all the vessels of water belonging to every inhabitant of Bethulia were empty; their cisterns were going dry, and they did not have enough water to drink their fill for a single day, because it was measured out to them to drink. Their children lost heart, and the women and young men fainted from thirst and fell down in the streets of the city and in the passages through the gates; there was no strength left in them any longer. Then all the people, the young men, the women, and the children, gathered about Uzzi'ah and the rulers of the city and cried out with a loud voice, and said before all the elders, "God be judge between you and us! For you have done us a great injury in not making peace with the Assyrians. For now we have no one to help us; God has sold us into their hands, to strew us on the ground before them with thirst and utter destruction. Now call them in and surrender the whole city to the army of Holofer'nes and to all his forces, to be plundered. For it would be better for us to be captured by them; for we will be slaves, but our lives will be spared, and we shall not witness the death of our babes before our eyes, or see our wives and children draw their last breath. We call to witness against you heaven and earth and our God, the Lord of our fathers, who punishes us according to our sins and the sins of our fathers. Let him not do this day the things which we have described!" Then great and general lamentation arose throughout the assembly, and they cried out to the Lord God with a loud voice. And Uzzi'ah said to them, "Have courage, my brothers! Let us hold out for five more days; by that time the Lord our God will restore to us his mercy, for he will not forsake us utterly. But if these days pass by, and no help comes for us, I will do what you say." Then he dismissed the people to their various posts, and they went up on the walls and towers of their city. The women and children he sent home. And they were greatly depressed in the city.

A Reading (Lesson) from the Acts of the Apostles [18:1-11]

After speaking in the Are-op'agus Paul left Athens and
went to Corinth. And he found a Jew named Aquila, a
native of Pontus, lately come from Italy with his wife
Priscilla, because Claudius had commanded all the Jews to
leave Rome. And he went to see them; and because he was
of the same trade he stayed with them, and they worked,
for by trade they were tentmakers. And he argued in the
synagogue every sabbath, and persuaded Jews and Greeks.
When Silas and Timothy arrived from Macedo'nia, Paul
was occupied with preaching, testifying to the Jews that
the Christ was Jesus. And when they opposed and reviled
him, he shook out his garments and said to them, "Your
blood be upon your heads! I am innocent. From now on I
will go to the Gentiles." And he left there and went to the
house of a man named Titius Justus, a worshiper of God;
his house was next door to the synagogue. Crispus, the
ruler of the synagogue, believed in the Lord, together with
all his household; and many of the Corinthians hearing
Paul believed and were baptized. And the Lord said to Paul
one night in a vision, "Do not be afraid, but speak and do
not be silent; for I am with you, and no man shall attack
you to harm you; for I have many people in this city." And
he stayed a year and six months, teaching the word of God
among them.

A Reading (Lesson) from the Gospel according to Luke
[(1:1-4);3:1-14]

Inasmuch as many have undertaken to compile a
narrative of the things which have been accomplished
among us, just as they were delivered to us by those
who from the beginning were eyewitnesses and
ministers of the word, it seemed good to me also, having
followed all things closely for some time past, to write
an orderly account for you, most excellent Theoph'ilus,
that you may know the truth concerning the things of
which you have been informed.

In the fifteenth year of the reign of Tibe'ri-us Caesar, Pontius Pilate being governor of Judea, and Herod being tetrarch of Galilee, and his brother Philip tetrarch of the region of Iturae'a and Trachoni'tis, and Lysa'ni-as tetrarch of Abile'ne, in the high-priesthood of Annas and Ca'iaphas, the word of God came to John the son of Zechari'ah in the wilderness; and he went into all the region about the Jordan, preaching a baptism of repentance for the forgiveness of sins. As it is written in the book of the words of Isaiah the prophet, "The voice of one crying in the wilderness: Prepare the way of the Lord, make his paths straight. Every valley shall be filled, and every mountain and hill shall be brought low, and the crooked shall be made straight, and the rough ways shall be made smooth; and all flesh shall see the salvation of God." He said therefore to the multitudes that came out to be baptized by him, "You brood of vipers! Who warned you to flee from the wrath to come? Bear fruits that befit repentance, and do not begin to say to yourselves, 'We have Abraham as our father'; for I tell you, God is able from these stones to raise up children to Abraham. Even now the axe is laid to the root of the trees; every tree therefore that does not bear good fruit is cut down and thrown into the fire." And the multitudes asked him, "What then shall we do?" And he answered them, "He who has two coats, let him share with him who has none; and he who has food, let him do likewise." Tax collectors also came to be baptized, and said to him, "Teacher, what shall we do?" And he said to them, "Collect no more than is appointed you." Soldiers also asked him, "And we, what shall we do?" And he said to them, "Rob no one by violence or by false accusation, and be content with your wages."

Tuesday

Psalm 78:1-39 [page 694]   ❖   *Psalm 78:40-72* [page 698]

A Reading (Lesson) from the Book of Esther [5:1-14]

On the third day Esther put on her royal robes and stood in the inner court of the king's palace, opposite the king's hall. The king was sitting on his royal throne inside the palace opposite the entrance to the palace; and when the king saw Queen Esther standing in the court, she found favor in his sight and he held out to Esther the golden scepter that was in his hand. Then Esther approached and touched the top of the scepter. And the king said to her, "What is it, Queen Esther? What is your request? It shall be given you, even to the half of my kingdom." And Esther said, "If it please the king, let the king and Haman come this day to a dinner that I have prepared for the king." Then said the king, "Bring Haman quickly, that we may do as Esther desires." So the king and Haman came to the dinner that Esther had prepared. And as they were drinking wine, the king said to Esther, "What is your petition? It shall be granted you. And what is your request? Even to the half of my kingdom, it shall be fulfilled." But Esther said, "My petition and my request is: If I have found favor in the sight of the king, and if it please the king to grant my petition and fulfil my request, let the king and Haman come tomorrow to the dinner which I will prepare for them, and tomorrow I will do as the king has said." And Haman went out that day joyful and glad of heart. But when Haman saw Mor'decai in the king's gate, that he neither rose nor trembled before him, he was filled with wrath against Mor'decai. Nevertheless Haman restrained himself, and went home; and he sent and fetched his friends and his wife Zeresh. And Haman recounted to them the splendor of his riches, the number of his sons, all the promotions with which the king had honored him, and how he had advanced him above the princes and the servants of the king. And Haman added, "Even Queen Esther let no one come with the king to the banquet she prepared but myself. And tomorrow also I am invited by her together with the king. Yet all this does me no good, so long as I see Mor'decai the Jew sitting at the king's gate." Then his wife Zeresh and all his friends said to him, "Let a gallows fifty cubits high be made, and in the morning tell the king to have Mor'decai hanged upon it; then go merrily with the king to the dinner." This counsel pleased Haman, and he had the gallows made.

or this

A Reading (Lesson) from the Book of Judith
[8:9-17;9:1,7-10]

When Judith heard the wicked words spoken by the people against the ruler, because they were faint for lack of water, and when she heard all that Uzzi'ah said to them, and how he promised them under oath to surrender the city to the Assyrians after five days, she sent her maid, who was in charge of all she possessed, to summon Chabris and Charmis, the elders of her city. They came to her, and she said to them, "Listen to me, rulers of the people of Bethu'lia! What you have said to the people today is not right; you have even sworn and pronounced this oath between God and you, promising to surrender the city to our enemies unless the Lord turns and helps us within so many days. Who are you, that have put God to the test this day, and are setting yourselves up in the place of God among the sons of men? You are putting the Lord Almighty to the test—but you will never know anything! You cannot plumb the depths of the human heart, nor find out what a man is thinking; how do you expect to search out God, who made all these things, and find out his mind or comprehend his thought? No, my brethren, do not provoke the Lord our God to anger. For if he does not choose to help us within these five days, he has power to protect us within any time he pleases, or even to destroy us in the presence of our enemies. Do not try to bind the purposes of the Lord our God; for God is not like man, to be threatened, nor like a human being, to be won over by pleading. Therefore, while we wait for his deliverance, let us call upon him to help us, and he will hear our voice, if it pleases him." Then Judith fell upon her face, and put ashes on her head, and uncovered the sackcloth she was wearing; and at the very time when that evening's incense was being offered in the house of God in Jerusalem, Judith cried out to the Lord with a loud voice, and said, "Behold now, the Assyrians are increased in their might; they are exalted, with their horses and riders; they glory in the strength of their foot soldiers; they trust in shield and spear, in bow and sling, and know not that thou art the Lord who crushest wars; the Lord is thy name. Break their strength by thy might, and bring down their power in thy anger; for they intend to defile thy sanctuary, and to pollute the tabernacle where thy glorious name rests, and to cast down the horn of thy altar with the sword. Behold their pride, and send thy wrath upon their heads; give to me, a widow, the strength to do what I plan. By the deceit of my lips strike down the slave with the prince and the prince with his servant; crush their arrogance by the hand of a woman."

A Reading (Lesson) from the Acts of the Apostles
[18:12-28]

When Gallio was proconsul of Acha'ia, the Jews made a united attack upon Paul and brought him before the tribunal, saying, "This man is persuading men to worship God contrary to the law." But when Paul was about to open his mouth, Gallio said to the Jews, "If it were a matter of wrongdoing or vicious crime, I should have reason to bear with you, O Jews; but since it is a matter of questions about words and names and your own law, see to it yourselves; I refuse to be a judge of these things." And he drove them from the tribunal. And they all seized Sos'thenes, the ruler of the synagogue, and beat him in front of the tribunal. But Gallio paid no attention to this.

After this Paul stayed many days longer, and then took leave of the brethren and sailed for Syria, and with him Priscilla and Aquila. At Cen'chreae he cut his hair, for he had a vow. And they came to Ephesus, and he left them there; but he himself went into the synagogue and argued with the Jews. When they asked him to stay for a longer period, he declined; but on taking leave of them he said, "I will return to you if God wills," and he set sail from Ephesus. When he had landed at Caesare'a, he went up and greeted the church, and then went down to Antioch. After spending some time there he departed and went from place to place through the region of Galatia and Phryg'ia, strengthening all the disciples. Now a Jew named Apol'los, a native of Alexandria, came to Ephesus. He was an eloquent man, well versed in the scriptures. He had been instructed in the way of the Lord; and being fervent in spirit, he spoke and taught accurately the things concerning Jesus, though he knew only the baptism of John. He began to speak boldly in the synagogue; but when Priscilla and Aquila heard him, they took him and expounded to him the way of God more accurately. And when he wished to cross to Acha'ia, the brethren encouraged him, and wrote to the disciples to receive him. When he arrived, he greatly helped those who through grace had believed, for he powerfully confuted the Jews in public, showing by the scriptures that the Christ was Jesus.

A Reading (Lesson) from the Gospel according to Luke
[3:15-22]

As the people were in expectation, and all men questioned in their hearts concerning John, whether perhaps he were the Christ, John answered them all, "I baptize you with water; but he who is mightier than I is coming, the thong of whose sandals I am not worthy to untie; he will baptize you with the Holy Spirit and with fire. His winnowing fork is in his hand, to clear his threshing floor, and to gather the wheat into his granary, but the chaff he will burn with unquenchable fire." So, with many other exhortations, he preached good news to the people. But Herod the tetrarch, who had been reproved by him for Hero'di-as, his brother's wife, and for all the evil things that Herod had done, added this to them all, that he shut up John in prison. Now when all the people were baptized, and when Jesus also had been baptized and was praying, the heaven was opened, and the Holy Spirit descended upon him in bodily form, as a dove, and a voice came from heaven, "Thou art my beloved Son; with thee I am well pleased."

Wednesday

Psalm 119:97-120 [page 771] ❖ *Psalm 81* [page 704],
Psalm 82 [page 705]

A Reading (Lesson) from the Book of Esther [6:1-14]

On that night the king could not sleep; and he gave orders to bring the book of memorable deeds, the chronicles, and they were read before the king. And it was found written how Mor'decai had told about Bigthana and Teresh, two of the king's eunuchs, who guarded the threshold, and who had sought to lay hands upon King Ahasu-e'rus. And the king said, "What honor or dignity has been bestowed on Mor'decai for this?" The king's servants who attended him said, "Nothing has been done for him." And the king said, "Who is in the court?" Now Haman had just entered the outer court of the king's palace to speak to the king about having Mor'decai hanged on the gallows that he had prepared for him. So the king's servants told him, "Haman is there, standing in the court." And the king said, "Let him come in." So Haman came in, and the king said to him, "What shall be done to the man whom the king delights to honor?" And Haman said to himself, "Whom would the king delight to honor more than me?" And Haman said to the king, "For the man whom the king delights to honor, let royal robes be brought, which the king has worn, and the horse which the king has ridden, and on whose head a royal crown is set; and let the robes and the horse be handed over to one of the king's most noble princes; let him array the man whom the king delights to honor, and let him conduct the man on horseback through the open square of the city, proclaiming before him: 'Thus shall it be done to the man whom the king delights to honor.'" Then the king said to Haman, "Make haste, take the robes and the horse, as you have said, and do so to Mor'decai the Jew who sits at the king's gate. Leave out nothing you have mentioned." So Haman took the robes and the horse, and he arrayed Mor'decai and made him ride through the open square of the city, proclaiming, "Thus shall it be done to the man whom the king delights to honor." Then Mor'decai returned to the king's gate. But Haman hurried to his house, mourning and with his head covered. And Haman told his wife Zeresh and all his friends everything that had befallen him. Then his wise men and his wife Zeresh said to him, "If Mor'decai, before whom you have begun to fall, is of the Jewish people, you will not prevail against him but will surely fall before him." While they were yet talking with him, the king's eunuchs arrived and brought Haman in haste to the banquet that Esther had prepared.

or this

A *Reading (Lesson) from the Book of Judith* [10:1-23]

When Judith had ceased crying out to the God of Israel, and had ended all these words, she rose from where she lay prostrate and called her maid and went down into the house where she lived on sabbaths and on her feast days; and she removed the sackcloth which she had been wearing, and took off her widow's garments, and bathed her body with water, and anointed herself with precious ointment, and combed her hair and put on a tiara, and arrayed herself in her gayest apparel, which she used to wear while her husband Manas'seh was living. And she put sandals on her feet, and put on her anklets and bracelets and rings, and her earrings and all her ornaments, and made herself very beautiful, to entice the eyes of all men who might see her. And she gave her maid a bottle of wine and a flask of oil, and filled the bag with parched grain and a cake of dried fruit and fine bread; and she wrapped up all her vessels and gave them to her to carry. Then they went out to the city gate of Bethu'lia, and found Uzzi'ah standing there with the elders of the city, Chabris and Charmis. When they saw her, and noted how her face was altered and her clothing changed, they greatly admired her beauty, and said to her, "May the God of our fathers grant you favor and fulfil your plans, that the people of Israel may glory and Jerusalem may be exalted." And she worshiped God. Then she said to them, "Order the gate of the city to be opened for me, and I will go out and accomplish the things about which you spoke with me." So they ordered the young men to open the gate for her, as she had said. When they had done this, Judith went out, she and her maid with her; and the men of the city watched her until she had gone down the mountain and passed through the valley and they could no longer see her. The women went straight on through the valley; and an Assyrian patrol met her and took her into custody, and asked her, "To what people do you belong, and where are you coming from, and where are you going?" She replied, "I am a daughter of the Hebrews, but I am fleeing from them, for they are about to be handed over to you to be devoured. I am on my way to the presence of Holofer'nes the commander of your army, to give him a true report; and I will show him a way by which he can go and capture all the hill country without losing one of his men, captured or slain." When the men heard her words, and observed her face—she was in their eyes marvelously beautiful—they said to her, "You have saved your life by hurrying down to the presence of our lord. Go at once to his tent; some of us will escort you and hand you over to him. And when you stand before him, do not be afraid in your heart, but tell him just what you have said, and he will treat you well." They chose from their number a hundred men to accompany her and her maid, and they brought them to the tent of Holofer'nes. There was great excitement in the whole camp, for her arrival was reported from tent to tent, and they came and stood around her as she waited outside the tent of Holofer'nes while they told him about her. And they marveled at her beauty, and admired the Israelites, judging them by her, and every one said to his neighbor, "Who can despise these people, who have women like this among them? Surely not a man of them had better be left alive, for if we let them go they will be able to ensnare the whole world!" Then Holofer'nes' companions and all his servants came out and led her into the tent. Holofer'nes was resting on his bed, under a canopy which was woven with purple and gold and emeralds and precious stones. When they told him of her he came forward to the front of the tent, with silver lamps carried before him. And when Judith came into the presence of Holofer'nes and his servants, they all marveled at the beauty of her face; and she prostrated herself and made obeisance to him, and his slaves raised her up.

A Reading (Lesson) from the Acts of the Apostles [19:1-10]

While Apol'los was at Corinth, Paul passed through the upper country and came to Ephesus. There he found some disciples. And he said to them, "Did you receive the Holy Spirit when you believed?" And they said, "No, we have never even heard that there is a Holy Spirit." And he said, "Into what then were you baptized?" They said, "Into John's baptism." And Paul said, "John baptized with the baptism of repentance, telling the people to believe in the one who was to come after him, that is, Jesus." On hearing this, they were baptized in the name of the Lord Jesus. And when Paul had laid his hands upon them, the Holy Spirit came on them; and they spoke with tongues and prophesied. There were about twelve of them in all. And he entered the synagogue and for three months spoke boldly, arguing and pleading about the kingdom of God; but when some were stubborn and disbelieved, speaking evil of the Way before the congregation, he withdrew from them, taking the disciples with him, and argued daily in the hall of Tyran'nus. This continued for two years, so that all the residents of Asia heard the word of the Lord, both Jews and Greeks.

A Reading (Lesson) from the Gospel according to Luke [4:1-13]

Jesus, full of the Holy Spirit, returned from the Jordan, and was led by the Spirit for forty days in the wilderness, tempted by the devil. And he ate nothing in those days; and when they were ended, he was hungry. The devil said to him, "If you are the Son of God, command this stone to become bread." And Jesus answered him, "It is written, 'Man shall not live by bread alone.'" And the devil took him up, and showed him all the kingdoms of the world in a moment of time, and said to him, "To you I will give all this authority and their glory; for it has been delivered to me, and I give it to whom I will. If you, then, will worship me, it shall all be yours." And Jesus answered him, "It is written, 'You shall worship the Lord your God, and him only shall you serve.'" And he took him to Jerusalem, and set him on the pinnacle of the temple, and said to him, "If you are the Son of God, throw yourself down from here; for it is written, 'He will give his angels charge of you, to guard you,' and 'On their hands they will bear you up, lest you strike your foot against a stone.'" And Jesus answered him, "It is said, 'You shall not tempt the Lord your God.'" And when the devil had ended every temptation, he departed from him until an opportune time.

Thursday

(Psalm 83 [page 706]), or *Psalm 116* [page 759],
Psalm 117 [page 760] ❖ *Psalm 85* [page 708],
Psalm 86 [page 709]

A Reading (Lesson) from the Book of Esther [7:1-10]

The king and Haman went in to feast with Queen Esther.
And on the second day, as they were drinking wine, the
king again said to Esther, "What is your petition, Queen
Esther? It shall be granted to you. And what is your
request? Even to the half of my kingdom, it shall be
fulfilled." Then Queen Esther answered, "If I have found
favor in your sight, O king, and if it please the king, let my
life be given me at my petition, and my people at my
request. For we are sold, I and my people, to be destroyed,
to be slain, and to be annihilated. If we had been sold
merely as slaves, men and women, I would have held my
peace; for our afflication is not to be compared with the
loss to the king." Then King Ahasu-e'rus said to Queen
Esther, "Who is he, and where is he, that would presume
to do this?" And Esther said, "A foe and enemy! This
wicked Haman!" Then Haman was in terror before the
king and the queen. And the king rose from the feast in
wrath and went into the palace garden; but Haman stayed
to beg his life from Queen Esther, for he saw that evil was
determined against him by the king. And the king returned
from the palace garden to the place where they were
drinking wine, as Haman was falling on the couch where
Esther was; and the king said, "Will he even assault the
queen in my presence, in my own house?" As the words
left the mouth of the king, they covered Haman's face.
Then said Harbo'na, one of the eunuchs in attendance on
the king, "Moreover, the gallows which Haman has
prepared for Mor'decai, whose word saved the king, is
standing in Haman's house, fifty cubits high." And the king

said, "Hang him on that." So they hanged Haman on the gallows which he had prepared for Mor'decai. Then the anger of the king abated.

or this

A Reading (Lesson) from the Book of Judith [12:1-20]

Holofer'nes commanded his servants to bring Judith in where his silver dishes were kept, and ordered them to set a table for her with some of his own food and to serve her with his own wine. But Judith said, "I cannot eat it, lest it be an offense; but I will be provided from the things I have brought with me." Holofer'nes said to her, "If your supply runs out, where can we get more like it for you? For none of your people is here with us." Judith replied, "As your soul lives, my lord, your servant will not use up the things I have with me before the Lord carries out by my hand what he has determined to do." Then the servants of Holofer'nes brought her into the tent, and she slept until midnight. Along toward the morning watch she arose, and sent to Holofer'nes and said, "Let my lord now command that your servant be permitted to go out and pray." So Holofer'nes commanded his guards not to hinder her. And she remained in the camp for three days, and went out each night to the valley of Bethu'lia, and bathed at the spring in the camp. When she came up from the spring she prayed the Lord God of Israel to direct her way for the raising up of her people. So she returned clean and stayed in the tent until she ate her food toward the evening. On the fourth day Holofer'nes held a banquet for his slaves only, and did not invite any of his officers. And he said to Bago'as, the eunuch who had charge of his personal affairs, "Go now and persuade the Hebrew woman who is in your care to join us and eat and drink with us. For it will be a disgrace if we let such a woman go without enjoying her company, for if we do not embrace her she will laugh at us." So Bago'as went out from the presence of Holofer'nes, and approached her and said, "This beautiful maidservant will please come to my lord and be honored in his presence, and drink wine and be merry with us, and become today like one of the daughters of the Assyrians who serve in the house of Nebuchadnez'zar." Judith said, "Who am I, to refuse my lord? Surely whatever pleases him I will do at once, and it will be a joy to me until the day of my death!" So she got up and arrayed herself in all her woman's finery, and her maid went and spread on the ground for her before Holofer'nes the soft fleeces which she had received from Bago'as for her daily use, so that she might recline on them when she ate. Then Judith came in and lay down, and Holofer'nes' heart was ravished with her and he was moved with great desire to possess her; for he had been waiting for an opportunity to deceive her, ever since the day he first saw her. So Holofer'nes said to her, "Drink now, and be merry with us!" Judith said, "I will drink now, my lord, because my life means more to me today than in all the days since I was born. Then she took and ate and drank before him what her maid had prepared. And Holofer'nes was greatly pleased with her, and drank a great quantity of wine, much more than he had ever drunk in any one day since he was born.

Acts 19:11-20   [page 145 above]

A Reading (Lesson) from the Gospel according to Luke
[4:14-30]

Jesus returned in the power of the Spirit into Galilee, and a report concerning him went out through all the surrounding country. And he taught in their synagogues, being glorified by all. And he came to Nazareth, where he had been brought up; and he went to the synagogue, as his custom was, on the sabbath day. And he stood up to read; and there was given to him the book of the prophet Isaiah. He opened the book and found the place where it was written, "The spirit of the Lord is upon me, because he has anointed me to preach good news to the poor. He has sent me to proclaim release to the captives and recovering of sight to the blind, to set at liberty those who are oppressed, to proclaim the acceptable year of the Lord." And he closed the book, and gave it back to the attendant, and sat down; and the eyes of all in the synagogue were fixed on him. And he began to say to them, "Today this scripture has been fulfilled in your hearing." And all spoke well of him, and wondered at the gracious words which proceeded out of his mouth; and they said, "Is not this Joseph's son?" And he said to them, "Doubtless you will quote to me this proverb, 'Physician, heal yourself; what we have heard you did at Caper'na-um, do here also in your own country.'" And he said, "Truly, I say to you, no prophet is acceptable in his own country. But in truth, I tell you, there were many widows in Israel in the days of Eli'jah, when the heaven was shut up three years and six months, when there came a great famine over all the land; and Eli'jah was sent to none of them but only to Zar'ephath, in the land of Sidon, to a woman who was a widow. And there were many lepers in Israel in the time of the prophet Eli'sha; and none of them was cleansed, but only Na'aman the Syrian." When they heard this, all in the synagogue were filled with wrath. And they rose up and put him out of the city, and led him to the brow of the hill on which their city was built, that they might throw him down headlong. But passing through the midst of them he went away.

Friday

Psalm 88 [page 712]   ❖   *Psalm 91* [page 719],
Psalm 92 [page 720]

A Reading (Lesson) from the Book of Esther [8:1-8,15-17]

On the day that Haman was hanged on the gallows King Ahasu-e'rus gave to Queen Esther the house of Haman, the enemy of the Jews. And Mor'decai came before the king, for Esther had told what he was to her; and the king took off his signet ring, which he had taken from Haman, and gave it to Mor'decai. And Esther set Mor'decai over the house of Haman. Then Esther spoke again to the king; she fell at his feet and besought him with tears to avert the evil design of Haman the Ag'agite and the plot which he had devised against the Jews. And the king held out the golden scepter to Esther, and Esther rose and stood before the king. And she said, "If it please the king, and if I have found favor in his sight, and if the thing seem right before the king, and I be pleasing in his eyes, let an order be written to revoke the letter devised by Haman the Ag'agite, the son of Hammeda'tha, which he wrote to destroy the Jews who are in all the provinces of the king. For how can endure to see the calamity that is coming to my people? Or how can I endure to see the destruction of my kindred?" Then King Ahasu-e'rus said to Queen Esther and to Mor'decai the Jew, "Behold, I have given Esther the house of Haman, and they have hanged him on the gallows, because he would lay hands on the Jews. And you may write as you please with regard to the Jews, in the name of the king, and seal it with the king's ring; for an edict written in the name of the king and sealed with the king's ring cannot be revoked." Then Mor'decai went out from the presence of the king in royal robes of blue and white, with a great golden crown and a mantle of fine linen and purple, while the city of Susa shouted and rejoiced. The Jews had light and gladness and joy and honor. And in every province and in every city, wherever the king's command and his edict came, there was gladness and joy among the Jews, a feast and a holiday. And many from the peoples of the country declared themselves Jews, for the fear of the Jews had fallen upon them.

or this

A Reading (Lesson) from the Book of Judith [13:1-20]

When evening came, Holofer'nes' slaves quickly withdrew,
and Bago'as closed the tent from outside and shut out the
attendants from his master's presence; and they went to
bed, for they all were weary because the banquet had
lasted long. So Judith was left alone in the tent, with
Holofer'nes stretched out on his bed, for he was overcome
with wine. Now Judith had told her maid to stand outside
the bedchamber and to wait for her to come out, as she did
every day; for she said she would be going out for her
prayers. And she had said the same thing to Bago'as. So
every one went out, and no one, either small or great, was
left in the bedchamber. Then Judith, standing beside his
bed, said in her heart, "O Lord God of all might, look in
this hour upon the work of my hands for the exaltation of
Jerusalem. For now is the time to help thy inheritance, and
to carry out my undertaking for the destruction of the
enemies who have risen up against us." She went up to the
post at the end of the bed, above Holofer'nes' head, and
took down his sword that hung there. She came close to his
bed and took hold of the hair of his head, and said, "Give
me strength this day, O Lord God of Israel!" And she
struck his neck twice with all her might, and severed his
head from his body. Then she tumbled his body off the bed
and pulled down the canopy from the posts; after a
moment she went out, and gave Holofer'nes' head to her
maid, who placed it in her food bag. Then the two of them
went out together, as they were accustomed to go for
prayer; and they passed through the camp and circled
around the valley and went up the mountain to Bethu'lia
and went up to its gates. Judith called out from afar to the
watchmen at the gates, "Open, open the gate! God, our
God, is still with us, to show his power in Israel, and his
strength against our enemies, even as he has done this
day!" When the men of her city heard her voice, they
hurried down to the city gate and called together the elders
of the city. They all ran together, both small and great, for

it was unbelievable that she had returned; they opened the gate and admitted them, and they kindled a fire for light, and gathered around them. Then she said to them with a loud voice, "Praise God, O praise him! Praise God, who has not withdrawn his mercy from the house of Israel, but has destroyed our enemies by my hand this very night!" Then she took the head out of the bag and showed it to them, and said, "See, here is the head of Holofer'nes, the commander of the Assyrian army, and here is the canopy beneath which he lay in his drunken stupor. The Lord has struck him down by the hand of a woman. As the Lord lives, who has protected me in the way I went, it was my face that tricked him to his destruction, and yet he committed no act of sin with me, to defile and shame me." All the people were greatly astonished, and bowed down and worshiped God, and said with one accord, "Blessed art thou, our God, who hast brought into contempt this day the enemies of thy people." And Uzzi'ah said to her, "O daughter, you are blessed by the Most High God above all women on earth; and blessed be the Lord God, who created the heavens and the earth, who has guided you to strike the head of the leader of our enemies. Your hope will never depart from the hearts of men, as they remember the power of God. May God grant this to be a perpetual honor to you, and may he visit you with blessings, because you did not spare your own life when our nation was brought low, but have avenged our ruin, walking in the straight path before our God." And all the people said, "So be it, so be it!"

A Reading (Lesson) from the Acts of the Apostles
[19:21-41]

Now after these events Paul resolved in the Spirit to pass through Macedo'nia and Acha'ia and go to Jerusalem, saying, "After I have been there, I must also see Rome." And having sent into Macedo'nia two of his helpers,

Timothy and Eras'tus, he himself stayed in Asia for a while. About that time there arose no little stir concerning the Way. For a man named Deme'trius, a silversmith, who made silver shrines of Ar'temis, brought no little business to the craftsmen. These he gathered together, with the workmen of like occupation, and said, "Men, you know that from this business we have made our wealth. And you see and hear that not only at Ephesus but almost throughout Asia this Paul has persuaded and turned away a considerable company of people, saying that gods made with hands are not gods. And there is danger not only that this trade of ours may come into disrepute but also that the temple of the great goddess Ar'temis may count for nothing, and that she may even be deposed from her magnificence, she whom all Asia and the world worship." When they heard this they were enraged, and cried out, "Great is Ar'temis of the Ephesians!" So the city was filled with the confusion; and they rushed together into the theater, dragging with them Ga'ius and Aristar'chus, Macedo'nians who were Paul's companions in travel. Paul wished to go in among the crowd, but the disciples would not let him; some of the A'si-archs also, who were friends of his, sent to him and begged him not to venture into the theater. Now some cried one thing, some another; for the assembly was in confusion, and most of them did not know why they had come together. Some of the crowd prompted Alexander, whom the Jews had put forward. And Alexander motioned with his hand, wishing to make a defense to the people. But when they recognized that he was a Jew, for about two hours they all with one voice cried out, "Great is Ar'temis of the Ephesians!" And when the town clerk had quieted the crowd, he said, "Men of Ephesus, what man is there who does not know that the city of the Ephesians is temple keeper of the great Ar'temis, and of the sacred stone that fell from the sky? Seeing then that these things cannot be contradicted, you ought to be quiet and do nothing rash. For you have brought these men here who are neither sacrilegious nor blasphemers of our goddess. If therefore Deme'trius and the craftsmen with him have a complaint against any one, the courts are open, and there are proconsuls; let them bring charges against one another. But if you seek anything further, it shall be settled in the regular assembly. For we are in danger of being charged with rioting today, there being no cause that we can give to justify this commotion." And when he had said this, he dismissed the assembly.

A Reading (Lesson) from the Gospel according to Luke [4:31-37]

Jesus went down to Caper'na-um, a city of Galilee. And he was teaching them on the sabbath; and they were astonished at his teaching, for his word was with authority. And in the synagogue there was a man who had the spirit of an unclean demon; and he cried out with a loud voice, "Ah! What have you to do with us, Jesus of Nazareth? Have you come to destroy us? I know who you are, the Holy One of God!" But Jesus rebuked him, saying, "Be silent, and come out of him!" And when the demon had thrown him down in the midst, he came out of him, having done him no harm. And they were all amazed and said to one another, "What is this word? For with authority and power he commands the unclean spirits, and they come out." And reports of him went out into every place in the surrounding region.

Saturday

Psalm 87 [page 711],   *Psalm 90* [page 717]   ❖
Psalm 136 [page 789]

A Reading (Lesson) from the Book of Hosea [1:1—2:1]

The word of the Lord that came to Hose'a the son of Be-e'ri, in the days of Uzzi'ah, Jotham, Ahaz, and

Hezeki'ah, kings of Judah, and in the days of Jerobo'am the son of Jo'ash, king of Israel. When the Lord first spoke through Hose'a, the Lord said to Hose'a, "Go, take to yourself a wife of harlotry and have children of harlotry, for the land commits great harlotry by forsaking the Lord." So he went and took Gomer the daughter of Dibla'im, and she conceived and bore him a son. And the Lord said to him, "Call his name Jezreel; for yet a little while, and I will punish the house of Jehu for the blood of Jezreel, and I will put an end to the kingdom of the house of Israel. And on that day, I will break the bow of Israel in the valley of Jezreel." She conceived again and bore a duaghter. And the Lord said to him, "Call her name Not pitied, for I will no more have pity on the house of Israel, to forgive them at all. But I will have pity on the house of Judah, and I will deliver them by the Lord their God; I will not deliver them by bow, nor by sword, nor by war, nor by horses, nor by horsemen." When she had weaned Not pitied, she conceived and bore a son. And the Lord said, "Call his name Not my people, for you are not my people and I am not your God." Yet the number of the people of Israel shall be like the sand of the sea, which can be neither measured nor numbered; and in the place where it was said to them, "You are not my people," it shall be said to them, "Sons of the living God." And the people of Judah and the people of Israel shall be gathered together, and they shall appoint for themselves one head; and they shall go up from the land, for great shall be the day of Jezreel. Say to your brother, "My people," and to your sister, "She has obtained pity."

A Reading (Lesson) from the Acts of Apostles [20:1-16]

After the uproar in the theater ceased, Paul sent for the disciples and having exhorted them took leave of them and departed for Macedo'nia. When he had gone through these parts and had given them much encouragement, he came to Greece. There he spent three months, and when a plot was made against him by the Jews as he was about to set sail for Syria, he determined to return through Macedo'nia. Sop'ater of Beroe'a, the son of Pyrrhus, accompanied him; and of the Thessalo'nians, Aristar'chus and Secun'dus; and Ga'ius of Derbe, and Timothy; and the Asians, Tych'icus and Troph'imus. These went on and were waiting for us at Tro'as, but we sailed away from Philippi after the days of Unleavened Bread, and in five days we came to them at Tro'as, where we stayed for seven days. On the first day of the week, when we were gathered together to break bread, Paul talked with them, intending to depart on the morrow; and he prolonged his speech until midnight. There were many lights in the upper chamber where we were gathered. And a young man named Eu'tychus was sitting in the window. He sank into a deep sleep as Paul talked still longer; and being overcome by sleep, he fell down from the third story and was taken up dead. But Paul went down and bent over him, and embracing him said, "Do not be alarmed, for his life is in him." And when Paul had gone up and had broken bread and eaten, he conversed with them a long while, until daybreak, and so departed. And they took the lad away alive, and were not a little comforted. But going ahead to the ship, we set sail for Assos, intending to take Paul aboard there; for so he had arranged, intending himself to go by land. And when he met us at Assos, we took him on board and came to Mityle'ne. And sailing from there we came the following day opposite Chi'os; the next day we touched at Samos; and the day after that we came to Mile'tus. For Paul had decided to sail past Ephesus, so that he might not have to spend time in Asia; for he was hastening to be at Jerusalem, if possible, on the day of Pentecost.

A Reading (Lesson) from the Gospel according to Luke [4:38-44]

Jesus arose and left the synagogue, and entered Simon's house. Now Simon's mother-in-law was ill with a high fever, and they besought him for her. And he stood over her and rebuked the fever, and it left her; and immediately she rose and served them. Now when the sun was setting, all those who had any that were sick with various diseases brought them to him; and he laid his hands on every one of them and healed them. And demons also came out of many, crying, "You are the Son of God!" But he rebuked them, and would not allow them to speak, because they knew that he was the Christ. And when it was day he departed and went into a lonely place. And the people sought him and came to him, and would have kept him from leaving them; but he said to them, "I must preach the good news of the kingdom of God to the other cities also; for I was sent for this purpose." And he was preaching in the synagogues of Judea.

Proper 21 *Week of the Sunday closest to September 28*

Sunday

Psalm 66 [page 673], *Psalm 67* [page 675] ❖
Psalm 19 [page 606], *Psalm 46* [page 649]

A Reading (Lesson) from the Book of Hosea [2:2-14]

"Plead with your mother, plead—for she is not my wife, and I am not her husband—that she put away her harlotry from her face, and her adultery from between her breasts; lest I strip her naked and make her as in the day she was born, and make her like a wilderness, and set her like a parched land, and slay her with thirst. Upon her children also I will have no pity, because they are children of harlotry. For their mother has played the harlot; she that conceived them has acted shamefully. For she said, 'I will go after my lovers, who give me my bread and my water, my wool and my flax, my oil and my drink.' Therefore I will hedge up her way with thorns; and I will build a wall against her, so that she cannot find her paths. She shall pursue her lovers, but not overtake them; and she shall seek them, but shall not find them. Then she shall say, 'I will go and return to my first husband, for it was better with me then than now.' And she did not know that it was I who gave her the grain, the wine, and the oil, and who lavished upon her silver and gold which they used for Ba'al. Therefore I will take back my grain in its time, and my wine in its season; and I will take away my wool and my flax, which were to cover her nakedness. Now I will uncover her lewdness in the sight of her lovers, and no one shall rescue her out of my hand. And I will put an end to all her mirth, her feasts, her new moons, her sabbaths, and all her appointed feasts. And I will lay waste her vines and her fig trees, of which she said, 'These are my hire, which my lovers have given me.' I will make them a forest, and the beasts of the field shall devour them. And I will punish her for the feast days of the Ba'als when she burned incense to them and decked herself with her ring and jewelry, and went after her lovers, and forgot me, says the Lord. Therefore, behold, I will allure her, and bring her into the wilderness, and speak tenderly to her."

A Reading (Lesson) from the Letter of James [3:1-13]

Let not many of you become teachers, my brethren, for you know that we who teach shall be judged with greater strictness. For we all make many mistakes, and if any one makes no mistakes in what he says he is a perfect man, able to bridle his whole body also. If we put bits into the mouths of horses that they may obey us, we guide their whole bodies. Look at the ships also; though they are so great and are driven by strong winds, they are guided by a very small rudder wherever the will of the pilot directs. So the tongue is a little member and boasts of great things. How great a forest is set ablaze by a small fire! And the tongue is a fire. The tongue is an unrighteous world among our members, straining the whole body, setting on fire the cycle of nature, and set on fire by hell. For every kind of beast and bird, of reptile and sea creature, can be tamed and has been tamed by humankind, but no human being can tame the tongue—a restless evil, full of deadly poison. With it we bless the Lord and Father, and with it we curse men, who are made in the likeness of God. From the same mouth come blessing and cursing. My brethren, this ought not to be so. Does a spring pour forth from the same opening fresh water and brackish? Can a fig tree, my brethren, yield olives, or a grapevine figs? No more can salt water yield fresh. Who is wise and understanding among you? By his good life let him show his works in the meekness of wisdom.

Matthew 13:44-52   [page 59 above]

Monday

Psalm 89:1-18 [page 713]   ❖   *Psalm 89:19-52* [page 715]

A Reading (Lesson) from the Book of Hosea [2:14-23]

"Therefore, behold, I will allure her, and bring her into the wilderness, and speak tenderly to her. And there I will give her vineyards, and make the Valley of Achor a door of hope. And there she shall answer as in the days of her youth, as at the time when she came out of the land of Egypt. And in that day, says the Lord, you will call me, 'My husband,' and no longer will you call me, 'My Ba'al.' For I will remove the names of the Ba'als from her mouth, and they shall be mentioned by name no more. And I will make for you a covenant on that day with the beasts of the field, the birds of the air, and the creeping things of the ground; and I will abolish the bow, the sword, and war from the land; and I will make you lie down in safety. And I will betroth you to me for ever; I will betroth you to me in righteousness and in justice, in steadfast love, and in mercy. I will betroth you to me in faithfulness; and you shall know the Lord. And in that day, says the Lord, I will answer the heavens and they shall answer the earth; and the earth shall answer the grain, the wine, and the oil, and they shall answer Jezreel; and I will sow him for myself in the land. And I will have pity on Not pitied, and I will say to Not my people, 'You are my people'; and he shall say, 'Thou art my God.'"

A Reading (Lesson) from the Acts of the Apostles
[20:17-38]

From Miletus Paul sent to Ephesus and called to him the elders of the church. And when they came to him, he said to them: "You yourselves know how I lived among you all the time from the first day that I set foot in Asia, serving the Lord with all humility and with tears and with trials which befell me through the plots of the Jews; how I did not shrink from declaring to you anything that was profitable, and teaching you in public and from house to house, testifying both to Jews and to Greeks of repentance to God and of faith in our Lord Jesus Christ. And now, behold, I am going to Jerusalem, bound in the Spirit, not knowing what shall befall me there; except that the Holy Spirit testifies to me in every city that imprisonment and afflictions await me. But I do not account my life of any value nor as precious to myself, if only I may accomplish my course and the ministry which I received from the Lord Jesus, to testify to the gospel of the grace of God. And now, behold, I know that all you among whom I have gone preaching the kingdom will see my face no more. Therefore I testify to you this day that I am innocent of the blood of all of you, for I did not shrink from declaring to you the whole counsel of God. Take heed to yourselves and to all the flock, in which the Holy Spirit has made you overseers, to care for the church of God which he obtained with the blood of his own Son. I know that after my departure fierce wolves will come in among you, not sparing the flock; and from among your own selves will arise men speaking perverse things, to draw away the disciples after them. Therefore be alert, remembering that for three years I did not cease night or day to admonish every one with tears. And now I commend you to God and to the word of his grace, which is able to build you up and to give you the inheritance among all those who are sanctified. I coveted no one's silver or gold or apparel. You yourselves know that these hands ministered to my necessities, and to those who were with me. In all things I have shown you that by so toiling one must help the weak, remembering the words of the Lord Jesus, how he said, 'It is more blessed to give than to receive.'" And when he had spoken thus, he knelt down and prayed with them all. And they all wept and embraced Paul and kissed him, sorrowing most of all because of the word he had spoken, that they should see his face no more. And they brought him to the ship.

A Reading (Lesson) from the Gospel according to Luke
[5:1-11]

When the people pressed upon Jesus to hear the word of God, he was standing by the lake of Gennes'aret. And he saw two boats by the lake; but the fisherman had gone out of them and were washing their nets. Getting into one of the boats, which was Simon's, he asked him to put out a little from the land. And he sat down and taught the people from the boat. And when he had ceased speaking, he said to Simon, "Put out into the deep and let down your nets for a catch." And Simon answered, "Master, we toiled all night and took nothing! But at your word I will let down the nets." And when they had done this, they enclosed a great shoal of fish; and as their nets were breaking, they beckoned to their partners in the other boat to come and help them. And they came and filled both the boats, so that they began to sink. But when Simon Peter saw it, he fell down at Jesus' knees, saying, "Depart from me, for I am a sinful man, O Lord." For he was astonished, and all that were with him, at the catch of fish which they had taken; and so also were James and John, sons of Zeb'edee, who were partners with Simon. And Jesus said to Simon, "Do not be afraid; henceforth you will be catching men." And when they had brought their boats to land, they left everything and followed him.

Tuesday

Psalm 97 [page 726], *Psalm 99* [page 728], *(Psalm 100* [page 729]) ❖ *Psalm 94* [page 722], *(Psalm 95* [page 724])

A Reading (Lesson) from the Book of Hosea [4:1-10]

Hear the word of the Lord, O people of Israel; for the Lord has a controversy with the inhabitants of the land. There is no faithfulness or kindness, and no knowledge of God in the land; there is swearing, lying, killing, stealing, and committing adultery; they break all bounds and murder follows murder. Therefore the land mourns, and all who dwell in it languish, and also the beasts of the field, and the birds of the air; and even the fish of the sea are taken away. Yet let no one contend, and let none accuse, for with you is my contention, O priest. You shall stumble by day, the prophet also shall stumble with you by night; and I will destroy your mother. My people are destroyed for lack of knowledge; because you have rejected knowledge, I reject you from being a priest to me. And since you have forgotten the law of your God, I will also forget your children. The more they increased, the more they sinned against me; I will change their glory into shame. They feed on the sin of my people; they are greedy for their iniquity. And it shall be like people, like priest; I will punish them for their ways, and requite them for their deeds. They shall eat, but not be satisfied; they shall play the harlot, but not multiply; because they have forsaken the Lord to cherish harlotry.

A Reading (Lesson) from the Acts of the Apostles [21:1-14]

When we had parted from the elders of the church at Ephesus and set sail, we came by a straight course to Cos, and the next day to Rhodes, and from there to Pat′ara. And having found a ship crossing to Phoeni′cia, we went aboard, and set sail. When we had come in sight of Cyprus, leaving it on the left we sailed to Syria, and landed at Tyre; for there the ship was to unload its cargo. And having sought out the disciples, we stayed there for seven days. Through the Spirit they told Paul not to go on to Jerusalem. And when our days there were ended, we departed and went on our journey; and they all, with wives and children, brought us on our way till we were outside the city; and kneeling down on the beach we prayed and bade one another farewell. Then we went on board the ship, and they returned home. When we had finished the voyage from Tyre, we arrived at Ptolema′is; and we greeted the brethren and stayed with them for one day. On the morrow we departed and came to Caesare′a; and we entered the house of Philip the evangelist, who was one of the seven, and stayed with him. And he had four unmarried daughters, who prophesied. While we were staying for some days, a prophet named Ag′abus came down from Judea. And coming to us he took Paul's girdle and bound his own feet and hands, and said, "Thus says the Holy Spirit, 'So shall the Jews at Jerusalem bind the man who owns this girdle and deliver him into the hands of the Gentiles.'" When we heard this, we and the people there begged him not to go up to Jerusalem. Then Paul answered, "What are you doing, weeping and breaking my heart? For I am ready not only to be imprisoned but even to die at Jerusalem for the name of the Lord Jesus." And when he would not be persuaded, we ceased and said, "The will of the Lord be done."

A Reading (Lesson) from the Gospel according to Luke
[5:12-26]

When Jesus was in one of the cities, there came man full of
leprosy; and when he saw Jesus, he fell on his face and
besought him, "Lord, if you will, you can make me clean."
and he stretched out his hand, and touched him, saying, "I
will; be clean." And immediately the leprosy left him. And
he charged him to tell no one; but "go and show yourself
to the priest, and make an offering for your cleansing, as
Moses commanded, for a proof to the people." But so
much the more the report went abroad concerning him;
and great multitudes gathered to hear and to be healed of
their infirmities. But he withdrew to the wilderness and
prayed. On one of those days, as he was teaching, there
were Pharisees and teachers of the law sitting by, who had
come from every village of Galilee and Judea and from
Jerusalem; and the power of the Lord was with him to
heal. And behold, men were bringing on a bed a man who
was paralyzed, and they sought to bring him in and lay
him before Jesus; but finding no way to bring him in,
because of the crowd, they went up on the roof and let him
down with his bed through the tiles into the midst before
Jesus. And when he saw their faith he said, "Man, your
sins are forgiven you." And the scribes and the Pharisees
began to question, saying, "Who is this that speaks
blasphemies? Who can forgive sins but God only?" When
Jesus perceived their questionings, he answered them,
"Why do you question in your hearts? Which is easier, to
say, 'Your sins are forgiven you,' or to say, 'Rise and walk'?
But that you may know that the Son of man has authority
on earth to forgive sins" — he said to the man who was
paralyzed — "I say to you, rise, take up your bed and go
home." And immediately he rose before them, and went
home, glorifying God. And amazement seized them all,
and they glorified God and were filled with awe, saying,
"We have seen strange things today."

Wednesday

Psalm 101 [page 730],
Psalm 109:1-4(5-19) 20-30 [page 750] ❖
Psalm 119:121-144 [page 773]

A Reading (Lesson) from the Book of Hosea [4:11-19]

Wine and new wine take away the understanding. My people inquire of a thing of wood, and their staff gives them oracles. For a spirit of harlotry has led them astray, and they have left their God to play the harlot. They sacrifice on the tops of the mountains, and make offerings upon the hills, under oak, poplar, and terebinth, because their shade is good. Therefore your daughters play the harlot, and your brides commit adultery. I will not punish your daughters when they play the harlot, nor your brides when they commit adultery; for the men themselves go aside with harlots, and sacrifice with cult prostitutes, and a people without understanding shall come to ruin. Though you play the harlot, O Israel, let not Judah become guilty. Enter not into Gilgal, nor go up to Beth-a'ven, and swear not, "As the Lord lives." Like a stubborn heifer, Israel is stubborn; can the Lord now feed them like a lamb in a broad pasture? E'phraim is joined to idols, let him alone. A band of drunkards, they give themselves to harlotry; they love shame more than their glory. A wind has wrapped them in its wings, and they shall be ashamed because of their altars.

A Reading (Lesson) from the Acts of the Apostles
[21:15-26]

After these days of traveling we made ready and went up to Jerusalem. And some of the disciples from Caesare'a went with us, bringing us to the house of Mnason of Cyprus, an early disciple, with whom we should lodge. When we had come to Jerusalem, the brethren received us gladly. On the following day Paul went in with us to James; and all the elders were present. After greeting them, he related one by one the things that God had done among the Gentiles through his ministry. And when they heard it, they glorified God. And they said to him, "You see, brother, how many thousands there are among the Jews of those who have believed; they are all zealous for the law, and they have been told about you that you teach all the Jews who are among the Gentiles to forsake Moses, telling them not to circumcise their children or observe the customs. What then is to be done? They will certainly hear that you have come. Do therefore what we tell you. We have four men who are under a vow; take these men and purify yourself along with them and pay their expenses, so that they may shave their heads. Thus all will know that there is nothing in what they have been told about you but that you yourself live in observance of the law. But as for the Gentiles who have believed, we have sent a letter with our judgment that they should abstain from what has been sacrificed to idols and from blood and from what is strangled and from unchastity." Then Paul took the men, and the next day he purified himself with them and went into the temple, to give notice when the days of purification would be fulfilled and the offering presented for every one of them.

A Reading (Lesson) from the Gospel according to Luke
[5:27-39]

After healing the paralytic Jesus went out, and saw a tax collector, named Levi, sitting at the tax office; and he said to him, "Follow me." And he left everything, and rose and followed him. And Levi made him a great feast in his house; and there was a large company of tax collectors and others sitting at table with them. And the Pharisees and their scribes murmured against his disciples, saying, "Why do you eat and drink with tax collectors and sinners?" And

Jesus answered them, "Those who are well have no need of a physician, but those who are sick; I have not come to call the righteous, but sinners to repentance." And they said to him, "The disciples of John fast often and offer prayers, and so do the disciples of the Pharisees, but yours eat and drink." And Jesus said to them, "Can you make wedding guests fast while the bridegroom is with them? The days will come, when the bridegroom is taken away from them, and then they will fast in those days." He told them a parable also: "No one tears a piece from a new garment and puts it upon an old garment; if he does, he will tear the new, and the piece from the new will not match the old. And no one puts new wine into old wineskins; if he does, the new wine will burst the skins and it will be spilled, and the skins will be destroyed. But new wine must be put into fresh wineskins. And no one after drinking old wine desires new; for he says, 'The old is good.'"

Thursday

Psalm 105:1-22 [page 738]   ❖   *Psalm 105:23-45* [page 739]

A Reading (Lesson) from the Book of Hosea [5:8—6:6]

Blow the horn in Gib'e-ah, the trumpet in Ramah. Sound the alarm at Beth-a'ven; tremble, O Benjamin! E'phraim shall become a desolation in the day of punishment; among the tribes of Israel I declare what is sure. The princes of Judah have become like those who remove the landmark; upon them I will pour out my wrath like water. E'phraim is oppressed, crushed in judgment, because he was determined to go after vanity. Therefore I am like a moth to E'phraim, and like dry rot to the house of Judah. When E'phraim saw his sickness, and Judah his wound, then E'phraim went to Assyria, and sent to the great king. But he is not able to cure you or heal your wound. For I will be like a lion to E'phraim, and like a young lion to the house of Judah. I, even I, will rend and go away, I will carry off, and none shall rescue. I will return again to my place, until they acknowledge their guilt and seek my face, and in their distress they seek me, saying, "Come, let us return to the Lord; for he has torn, that he may heal us; he has stricken, and he will bind us up. After two days he will revive us; on the third day he will raise us up, that we may live before him. Let us know, let us press on to know the Lord; his going forth is sure as the dawn; he will come to us as the showers, as the spring rains that water the earth." What shall I do with you, O E'phraim? What shall I do with you, O Judah? Your love is like a morning cloud, like the dew that goes early away. Therefore I have hewn them by the prophets, I have slain them by the words of my mouth, and my judgment goes forth as the light. For I desire steadfast love and not sacrifice, the knowledge of God, rather than burnt offerings.

A Reading (Lesson) from the Acts of the Apostles
[21:27-36]

When the seven days of the purification were almost completed, the Jews from Asia, who had seen Paul in the temple, stirred up all the crowd, and laid hands on him, crying out, "Men of Israel, help! This is the man who is teaching men everywhere against the people and the law and this place; moreover he also brought Greeks into the temple, and he has defiled this holy place." For they had previously seen Troph'imus the Ephesian with him in the city, and they supposed that Paul had brought him into the temple. Then all the city was aroused, and the people ran together; they seized Paul and dragged him out of the temple, and at once the gates were shut. And as they were trying to kill him, word came to the tribune of the cohort that all Jerusalem was in confusion. He at once took soldiers and centurions, and ran down to them; and when they saw the tribune and the soldiers, they stopped beating

Paul. Then the tribune came up and arrested him, and ordered him to be bound with two chains. He inquired who he was and what he had done. Some in the crowd shouted one thing, some another; and as he could not learn the facts because of the uproar, he ordered him to be brought into the barracks. And when he came to the steps, he was actually carried by the soldiers because of the violence of the crowd; for the mob of the people followed, crying, "Away with him!"

A Reading (Lesson) from the Gospel according to Luke
[6:1-11]

On a sabbath, while Jesus was going through the grainfields, his disciples plucked and ate some heads of grain, rubbing them in their hands. But some of the Pharisees said, "Why are you doing what is not lawful to do on the sabbath?" And Jesus answered, "Have you not read what David did when he was hungry, he and those who were with him: how he entered the house of God, and took and ate the bread of the Presence, which it is not lawful for any but the priests to eat, and also gave it to those with him?" And he said to them, "The Son of man is lord of the sabbath." On another sabbath, when he entered the synagogue and taught, a man was there whose right hand was withered. And the scribes and the Pharisees watched him, to see whether he would heal on the sabbath, so that they might find an accusation against him. But he knew their thoughts, and he said to the man who had the withered hand, "Come and stand here." And he rose and stood there. And Jesus said to them, "I ask you, is it lawful on the sabbath to do good or to do harm, to save life or to destroy it?" And he looked around on them all, and said to him, "Stretch out your hand." And he did so, and his hand was restored. But they were filled with fury and discussed with one another what they might do to Jesus.

Friday

Psalm 102 [page 731]   ❖   *Psalm 107:1-32* [page 746]

A Reading (Lesson) from the Book of Hosea [10:1-15]

Israel is a luxuriant vine that yields its fruit. The more his fruit increased the more altars he built; as his country improved he improved his pillars. Their heart is false; now they must bear their guilt. The Lord will break down their altars, and destroy their pillars. For now they will say: "We have no king, for we fear not the Lord, and a king, what could he do for us?" They utter mere words; with empty oaths they make covenants; so judgment springs up like poisonous weeds in the furrows of the field. The inhabitants of Samar'ia tremble for the calf of Beth-a'ven. Its people shall mourn for it, and its idolatrous priests shall wail over it, over its glory which has departed from it. Yea, the thing itself shall be carried to Assyria, as tribute to the great king. E'phraim shall be put to shame, and Israel shall be ashamed of his idol. Samar'ia's king shall perish, like a chip on the face of the waters. The high places of Aven, the sin of Israel, shall be destroyed. Thorn and thistle shall grow up on their altars; and they shall say to the mountains, Cover us, and to the hills, Fall upon us. From the days of Gib'e-ah, you have sinned, O Israel; there they have continued. Shall not war overtake them in Gib'e-ah? I will come against the wayward people to chastise them; and nations shall be gathered against them when they are chastised for their double iniquity. E'phraim was a trained heifer that loved to thresh, and I spared her fair neck; but I will put E'phraim to the yoke, Judah must plow, Jacob must harrow for himself. Sow for yourselves righteousness, reap the fruit of steadfast love; break up your fallow ground, for it is the time to seek the Lord, that he may come and rain salvation upon you. You have plowed iniquity, you have reaped injustice, you have eaten the fruit of lies. Because you have trusted in your chariots and in the multitude of your warriors, therefore the tumult of war shall arise among your people, and all your fortresses shall be destroyed, as Shalman destroyed Beth-ar'bel on the day of battle; mothers were dashed in pieces with their children. Thus it shall be done to you, O house of Israel, because of your great wickedness. In the storm the king of Israel shall be utterly cut off.

A Reading (Lesson) from the Acts of the Apostles
[21:37—22:16]

As Paul was about to be brought into the barracks, he said to the tribune, "May I say something to you?" And he said, "Do you know Greek? Are you not the Egyptian, then, who recently stirred up a revolt and led the four thousand men of the Assassins out into the wilderness?" Paul replied, "I am a Jew, from Tarsus in Cili'cia, a citizen of no mean city; I beg you, let me speak to the people." And when he had given him leave, Paul, standing on the steps, motioned with his hands to the people; and when there was a great hush, he spoke to them in the Hebrew language, saying: "Brethren and fathers, hear the defense which I now make before you." And when they heard that he addressed them in the Hebrew language, they were the more quiet. And he said: "I am a Jew, born at Tarsus in Cili'cia, but brought up in this city at the feet of Gama'liel, educated according to the strict manner of the law of our fathers, being zealous for God as you all are this day. I persecuted this Way to the death, binding and delivering to prison both men and women, as the high priest and the whole council of elders bear me witness. From them I received letters to the brethren, and I journeyed to Damascus to take those also who were there and bring them in bonds to Jerusalem to be punished. As I made my journey and drew near to Damascus, about noon a great light from heaven suddenly shone about me. And I fell to the ground and heard a voice saying to me, 'Saul, Saul, why do you persecute me?' And I answered, 'Who are you, Lord?' And he said to me, 'I am

Jesus of Nazareth whom you are persecuting.' Now those who were with me saw the light but did not hear the voice of the one who was speaking to me. And I said, 'What shall I do, Lord?' And the Lord said to me, 'Rise, and go into Damascus, and there you will be told all that is appointed for you to do.' And when I could not see because of the brightness of that light, I was led by the hand by those who were with me, and came into Damascus. And one Anani'as, a devout man according to the law, well spoken of by all the Jews who lived there, came to me, and standing by me said to me, 'Brother Saul, receive your sight.' And in that very hour I received my sight and saw him. And he said, 'The God of our fathers appointed you to know his will, to see the Just One and to hear a voice from his mouth; for you will be a witness for him to all men of what you have seen and heard. And now why do you wait? Rise and be baptized, and wash away your sins, calling on his name.'"

A Reading (Lesson) from the Gospel according to Luke
[6:12-26]

In those days Jesus went out to the mountain to pray; and all night he continued in prayer to God. And when it was day, he called his disciples, and chose from them twelve, whom he named apostles; Simon, whom he named Peter, and Andrew his brother, and James and John, and Philip, and Bartholomew, and Matthew, and Thomas, and James the son of Alphaeus, and Simon who was called the Zealot, and Judas the son of James, and Judas Iscariot, who became a traitor. And he came down with them and stood on a level place, with a great crowd of his disciples and a great multitude of people from all Judea and Jerusalem and the seacoast of Tyre and Sidon, who came to hear him and to be healed of their diseases; and those who were troubled with unclean spirits were cured. And the crowd sought to touch him, for power came forth from him and healed them all. And he lifted up his eyes on his disciples, and said: "Blessed are you poor, for yours is the kingdom of God. Blessed are you that hunger now, for you shall be satisfied. Blessed are you that weep now, for you shall laugh. Blessed are you when men hate you, and when they exclude you and revile you, and cast out your name as evil, on account of the Son of man! Rejoice in that day, and leap for joy, for behold, your reward is great in heaven; for so their fathers did to the prophets. But woe to you that are rich, for you have received your consolation. Woe to you that are full now, for you shall hunger. Woe to you that laugh now, for you shall mourn and weep. Woe to you, when all men speak well of you, for so their fathers did to the false prophets."

Saturday

Psalm 107:33-43 [page 748],
Psalm 108:1-6(7-13) [page 749]   ❖   *Psalm 33* [page 626]

A Reading (Lesson) from the Book of Hosea [11:1-9]

When Israel was a child, I loved him, and out of Egypt I called my son. The more I called them, the more they went from me; and kept sacrificing to the Ba'als, and burning incense to idols. Yet it was I who taught E'phraim to walk, I took them up in my arms; but they did not know that I healed them. I led them with cords of compassion, with the bands of love, and I became to them as one who eases the yoke on their jaws, and I bent down to them and fed them. They shall return to the land of Egypt, and Assyria shall be their king, because they have refused to return to me. The sword shall rage against their cities, consume the bars of their gates, and devour them in their fortresses. My people are bent on turning away from me; so they are appointed to the yoke, and none shall remove it. How can I give you up, O E'phraim! How can I hand you over, O Israel! How can I make you like Admah! How can I treat you like Zeboi'im! My heart recoils within me, my compassion grows warm and tender. I will not execute my fierce anger,

I will not again destroy E'phraim; for I am God and not man, the Holy One in your midst, and I will not come to destroy.

A Reading (Lesson) from the Acts of the Apostles
[22:17-29]

Paul spoke to the people in the Hebrew language: "When I had returned to Jerusalem and was praying in the temple, I fell into a trance and saw him saying to me, 'Make haste and get quickly out of Jerusalem, because they will not accept your testimony about me.' And I said, 'Lord, they themselves know that in every synagogue I imprisoned and beat those who believed in thee. And when the blood of Stephen thy witness was shed, I also was standing by and approving, and keeping the garments of those who killed him.' And he said to me, 'Depart; for I will send you far away to the Gentiles.'" Up to this word they listened to him; then they lifted up their voices and said, "Away with such a fellow from the earth! For he ought not to live." And as they cried out and waved their garments and threw dust into the air, the tribune commanded him to be brought into the barracks, and ordered him to be examined by scourging, to find out why they shouted thus against him. But when they had tied him up with the thongs, Paul said to the centurion who was standing by, "Is it lawful for you to scourge a man who is a Roman citizen, and uncondemned?" When the centurion heard that, he went to the tribune and said to him, "What are you about to do? For this man is a Roman citizen." So the tribune came and said to him, "Tell me, are you a Roman citizen?" And he said, "Yes." The tribune answered, "I bought this citizenship for a large sum." Paul said, "But I was born a citizen." So those who were about to examine him withdrew from him instantly; and the tribune was also afraid, for he realized that Paul was a Roman citizen and that he had bound him.

A Reading (Lesson) from the Gospel according to Luke
[6:27-38]

Jesus lifted up his eyes on his disciples, and said: "I say to you that hear, Love your enemies, do good to those who hate you, bless those who curse you, pray for those who abuse you. To him who strikes you on the cheek, offer the other also; and from him who takes away your coat do not withhold even your shirt. Give to every one who begs from you; and of him who takes away your goods do not ask them again. And as you wish that men would do to you, do so to them. If you love those who love you, what credit is that to you? For even sinners love those who love them. And if you do good to those who do good to you, what credit is that to you? Even sinners do the same. And if you lend to those from whom you hope to receive, what credit is that to you? Even sinners lend to sinners, to receive as much again. But love your enemies, and do good, and lend, expecting nothing in return; and your reward will be great, and you will be sons of the Most High; for he is kind to the ungrateful and the selfish. Be merciful, even as your Father is merciful. Judge not, and you will not be judged; condemn not, and you will not be condemned; forgive, and you will be forgiven; give, and it will be given to you; good measure, pressed down, shaken together, running over, will be put into your lap. For the measure you give will be the measure you get back."

Proper 22   *Week of the Sunday closest to October 5*

Sunday

Psalm 118 [page 760]   ❖   *Psalm 145* [page 801]

A Reading (Lesson) from the Book of Hosea [13:4-14]

I am the Lord your God from the land of Egypt; you know no God but me, and besides me there is no savior. It was I who knew you in the wilderness, in the land of drought; but when they had fed to the full, they were filled, and their heart was lifted up; therefore they forgot me. So I will be to them like a lion, like a leopard I will lurk beside the way. I will fall upon them like a bear robbed of her cubs, I will tear open their breast, and there I will devour them like a lion, as a wild beast would rend them. I will destroy you, O Israel; who can help you? Where now is your king, to save you; where are all your princes, to defend you—those of whom you said, "Give me a king and princes"? I have given you kings in my anger, and I have taken them away in my wrath. The iniquity of E'phraim is bound up, his sin is kept in store. The pangs of childbirth come for him, but he is an unwise son; for now he does not present himself at the mouth of the womb. Shall I ransom them from the power of Sheol? Shall I redeem them from Death? O Death, where are your plagues? O Sheol, where is your destruction? Compassion is hid from my eyes.

A Reading (Lesson) from the First Letter of Paul to the Corinthians [2:6-16]

Among the mature we do impart wisdom, although it is not a wisdom of this age or of the rulers of this age, who are doomed to pass away. For we impart a secret and hidden wisdom of God, which God decreed before the ages for our glorification. None of the rulers of this age understood this; for if they had, they would not have crucified the Lord of glory. But, as it is written, "What no eye has seen, nor ear heard, nor the heart of man conceived, what God has prepared for those who love him," God has revealed to us through the Spirit. For the Spirit searches everything, even the depths of God. For what person knows a man's thoughts except the spirit of the man which is in him? So also no one comprehends the thoughts of God except the Spirit of God. Now we have received not the spirit of the world, but the Spirit which is from God, that we might understand the gifts bestowed on us by God. And we impart this in words not taught by human wisdom but taught by the Spirit, interpreting spiritual truths to those who possess the Spirit. The unspiritual man does not receive the gifts of the Spirit of God, for they are folly to him, and he is not able to understand them because they are spiritually discerned. The spiritual man judges all things, but is himself to be judged by no one. "For who has known the mind of the Lord so as to instruct him?" But we have the mind of Christ.

Matthew 14:1-12   [page 64 above]

Monday

Psalm 106:1-18 [page 741]   ❖   *Psalm 106:19-48* [page 743]

A Reading (Lesson) from the Book of Hosea [14:1-9]

Return, O Israel, to the Lord your God, for you have stumbled because of your iniquity. Take with you words and return to the Lord; say to him, "Take away all iniquity; accept that which is good and we will render the fruit of our lips. Assyria shall not save us, we will not ride upon horses; and we will say no more, 'Our God,' to the work of our hands. In thee the orphan finds mercy." I will heal their faithlessness; I will love them freely, for my anger has turned from them. I will be as the dew to Israel; he shall blossom as the lily, he shall strike root as the poplar; his shoots shall spread out; his beauty shall be like the olive, and his fragrance like Lebanon. They shall return and dwell beneath my shadow, they shall flourish as a garden; they shall blossom as the vine, their fragrance shall be like the wine of Lebanon. O E'phraim, what have I to do with idols? It is I who answer and look after you. I am like an evergreen cypress, from me comes your fruit. Whoever is wise, let him understand these things; whoever is discerning, let him know them; for the ways of the Lord are right, and the upright walk in them, but transgressors stumble in them.

Acts 22:30—23:11   [page 183 above]

A Reading (Lesson) from the Gospel according to Luke
[6:39-49]

Jesus also told his disciples a parable: "Can a blind man lead a blind man? Will they not both fall into a pit? A disciple is not above his teacher, but every one when he is fully taught will be like his teacher. Why do you see the speck that is in your brother's eye, but do not notice the log that is in your own eye? Or how can you say to your brother, 'Brother, let me take out the speck that is in your eye,' when you yourself do not see the log that is in your own eye? You hypocrite, first take the log out of your own eye, and then you will see clearly to take out the speck that is in your brother's eye. For no good tree bears bad fruit, nor again does a bad tree bear good fruit; for each tree is known by its own fruit. For figs are not gathered from thorns, nor are grapes picked from a bramble bush. The good man out of the good treasure of his heart produces good, and the evil man out of his evil treasure produces evil; for out of the abundance of the heart his mouth speaks. Why do you call me 'Lord, Lord,' and not do what I tell you? Every one who comes to me and hears my words and does them, I will show you what he is like: he is like a man building a house, who dug deep, and laid the foundation upon rock; and when a flood arose, the stream broke against that house, and could not shake it, because it had been well built. But he who hears and does not do them is like a man who built a house on the ground without a foundation; against which the stream broke, and immediately it fell, and the ruin of that house was great."

Tuesday

(Psalm 120 [page 778]), *Psalm 121* [page 779],
Psalm 122 [page 779], *Psalm 123* [page 780] ❖
Psalm 124 [page 781], *Psalm 125* [page 781],
Psalm 126 [page 782], *(Psalm 127* [page 782])

A Reading (Lesson) from the Book of Micah [1:1-9]

The word of the Lord that came to Micah of Mo'resheth in
the days of Jotham, Ahaz, and Hezeki'ah, kings of Judah,
which he saw concerning Samar'ia and Jerusalem. Hear,
you peoples, all of you; hearken, O earth, and all that is in
it; and let the Lord God be a witness against you, the Lord
from his holy temple. For behold, the Lord is coming forth
out of his place, and will come down and tread upon the
high places of the earth. And the mountains will melt
under him and the valleys will be cleft, like wax before the
fire, like waters poured down a steep place. All this is for
the transgression of Jacob and for the sins of the house of
Israel. What is the transgression of Jacob? Is it not
Samar'ia? And what is the sin of the house of Judah? Is it
not Jerusalem? Therefore I will make Samar'ia a heap in
the open country, a place for planting vineyards; and I will
pour down her stones into the valley, and uncover her
foundations. All her images shall be beaten to pieces, all
her hires shall be burned with fire, and all her idols I will
lay waste; for from the hire of a harlot she gathered them,
and to the hire of a harlot they shall return. For this I will
lament and wail; I will go stripped and naked: I will make
lamentation like the jackals, and mourning like the
ostriches. For her wound is incurable; and it has come to
Judah, it has reached to the gate of my people, to
Jerusalem.

A Reading (Lesson) from the Acts of the Apostles
[23:12-24]

When it was day, the Jews made a plot and bound
themselves by an oath neither to eat nor drink till they had
killed Paul. There were more than forty who made this
conspiracy. And they went to the chief priests and elders,
and said, "We have strictly bound ourselves by an oath to
taste no food till we have killed Paul. You therefore, along
with the council, give notice now to the tribune to bring
him down to you, as though you were going to determine
his case more exactly. And we are ready to kill him before
he comes near." Now the son of Paul's sister heard of their
ambush; so he went and entered the barracks and told
Paul. And Paul called one of the centurions and said, "Take
this young man to the tribune; for he has something to tell
him." So he took him and brought him to the tribune and
said, "Paul the prisoner called me and asked me to bring
this young man to you, as he has something to say to you."
The tribune took him by the hand, and going aside asked
him privately, "What is it that you have to tell me?" And
he said, "The Jews have agreed to ask you to bring Paul
down to the council tomorrow, as though they were going
to inquire somewhat more closely about him. But do not
yeild to them; for more than forty of their men lie in
ambush for him, having bound themselves by an oath
neither to eat nor drink till they have killed him; and now
they are ready, waiting for the promise from you." So the
tribune dismissed the young man, charging him, "Tell no
one that you have informed me of this." Then he called
two of the centurions and said, "At the third hour of the
night get ready two hundred soldiers with seventy
horsemen and two hundred spearmen to go as far as
Caesare'a. Also provide mounts for Paul to ride, and bring
him safely to Felix the governor."

A Reading (Lesson) from the Gospel according to Luke
[7:1-17]

After Jesus had ended all his sayings in the hearing of the people he entered Caper′na-um. Now a centurion had a slave who was dear to him, who was sick and at the point of death. When he heard of Jesus, he sent to him elders of the Jews, asking him to come and heal his slave. And when they came to Jesus, they besought him earnestly, saying, "He is worthy to have you do this for him, for he loves our nation, and he built us our synagogue." And Jesus went with them. When he was not far from the house, the centurion sent friends to him, saying to him, "Lord, do not trouble yourself, for I am not worthy to have you come under my roof; therefore I did not presume to come to you. But say the word, and let my servant be healed. For I am a man set under authority, with soldiers under me: and I say to one, 'Go,' and he goes; and to another, 'Come,' and he comes; and to my slave, 'Do this,' and he does it." When Jesus heard this he marveled at him, and turned and said to the multitude that followed him, "I tell you, not even in Israel have I found such faith." And when those who had been sent returned to the house, they found the slave well. Soon afterward he went to a city called Na′in, and his disciples and a great crowd went with him. As he drew near to the gate of the city, behold, a man who had died was being carried out, the only son of his mother, and she was a widow; and a large crowd from the city was with her. And when the Lord saw her, he had compassion on her and said to her, "Do not weep." And he came and touched the bier, and the bearers stood still. And he said, "Young man, I say to you, arise." And the dead man sat up, and began to speak. And he gave him to his mother. Fear seized them all; and they glorified God, saying, "A great prophet has arisen among us!" and "God has visited his people!" And this report concerning him spread through the whole of Judea and all the surrounding country.

Wednesday

Psalm 119:145-176 [page 775] ❖ *Psalm 128* [page 783],
Psalm 129 [page 784], *Psalm 130* [page 784]

A Reading (Lesson) from the Book of Micah [2:1-13]

The word of the Lord that came to Micah: Woe to those
who devise wickedness and work evil upon their beds!
When the morning dawns, they perform it, because it is in
the power of their hand. They covet fields, and seize them;
and houses, and take them away; they oppress a man and
his house, a man and his inheritance. Therefore thus says
the Lord: Behold, against this family I am devising evil,
from which you cannot remove your necks; and you shall
not walk haughtily, for it will be an evil time. In that day
they shall take up a taunt song against you, and wail with
bitter lamentation, and say, "We are utterly ruined; he
changes the portion of my people; how he removes it from
me! Among our captors he divides our fields." Therefore
you will have none to cast the line by lot in the assembly of
the Lord. "Do not preach"—thus they preach—"one
should not preach of such things; disgrace will not
overtake us." Should this be said, O house of Jacob? Is the
Spirit of the Lord impatient? Are these his doings? Do not
my words do good to him who walks uprightly? But you
rise against my people as an enemy; you strip the robe
from the peaceful, from those who pass by trustingly with
no thought of war. The women of my people you drive out
from their pleasant houses; from their young children you
take away my glory for ever. Arise and go, for this is no
place to rest; because of uncleanness that destroys with a
grievous destruction. If a man should go about and utter
wind and lies, saying, "I will preach to you of wine and
strong drink," he would be the preacher for this people! I
will surely gather all of you, O Jacob, I will gather the
remnant of Israel; I will set them together like sheep in a
fold, like a flock in its pasture, a noisy multitude of men.

He who opens the breach will go up before them; they will break through and pass the gate, going out by it. Their king will pass on before them, the Lord at their head.

A Reading (Lesson) from the Acts of the Apostles
[23:23-35]

The tribune called two of the centurions and said, "At the third hour of the night get ready two hundred soldiers with seventy horsemen and two hundred spearmen to go as far as Caesare'a. Also provide mounts for Paul to ride, and bring him safely to Felix the governor." And he wrote a letter to this effect: "Claudius Lys'ias to his Excellency the governor Felix, greeting. This man was seized by the Jews, and was about to be killed by them, when I came upon them with the soldiers and rescued him, having learned that he was a Roman citizen. And desiring to know the charge on which they accused him, I brought him down to their council. I have found that he was accused about questions of their law, but charged with nothing deserving death or imprisonment. And when it was disclosed to me that there would be a plot against the man, I sent him to you at once, ordering his accusers also to state before you what they have against him." So the soldiers, according to their instructions, took Paul and brought him by night to Antip'atris. And on the morrow they returned to the barracks, leaving the horsemen to go on with him. When they came to Caesare'a and delivered the letter to the governor, they presented Paul also before him. On reading the letter, he asked to what province he belonged. When he learned that he was from Cili'cia he said, "I will hear you when your accusers arrive." And he commanded him to be guarded in Herod's praetorium.

A Reading (Lesson) from the Gospel according to Luke
[7:18-35]

The disciples of John told him of all these things. And

John, calling to him two of his disciples, sent them to the Lord, saying, "Are you he who is to come, or shall we look for another?" And when the men had come to him, they said, "John the Baptist has sent us to you, saying, 'Are you he who is to come, or shall we look for another?'" In that hour he cured many of diseases and plagues and evil spirits, and on many that were blind he bestowed sight. And he answered them, "Go and tell John what you have seen and heard: the blind receive their sight, the lame walk, lepers are cleansed, and the deaf hear, the dead are raised up, the poor have good news preached to them. And blessed is he who takes no offense at me." When the messengers of John had gone, he began to speak to the crowds concerning John: "What did you go out into the wilderness to behold? A reed shaken by the wind? What then did you go out to see? A man clothed in soft clothing? Behold, those who are gorgeously appareled and live in luxury are in kings' courts. What then did you go out to see? A prophet? Yes, I tell you, and more than a prophet. This is he of whom it is written, 'Behold, I send my messenger before thy face, who shall prepare the way before thee.' I tell you, among those born of women none is greater than John; yet he who is least in the kingdom of God is greater than he." (When they heard this all the people and the tax collectors justified God, having been baptized with the baptism of John; but the Pharisees and the lawyers rejected the purpose of God for themselves, not having been baptized by him.) "To what then shall I compare the men of this generation, and what are they like? They are like children sitting in the market place and calling to one another, 'We piped to you, and you did not dance; we wailed, and you did not weep.' For John the Baptist has come eating no bread and drinking no wine; and you say, 'He has a demon.' The Son of man has come eating and drinking; and you say, 'Behold, a glutton and a drunkard, a friend of tax collectors and sinners!' Yet wisdom is justified by all her children."

Thursday

Psalm 131 [page 785], *Psalm 132* [page 785],
(Psalm 133 [page 787]) ❖ *Psalm 134* [page 787],
Psalm 135 [page 788]

A Reading (Lesson) from the Book of Micah [3:1-8]

I said: Hear, you heads of Jacob and rulers of the house of
Israel! Is it not for you to know justice?—you who hate the
good and love the evil, who tear the skin from off my
people, and their flesh from off their bones; who eat the
flesh of my people, and flay their skin from off them, and
break their bones in pieces, and chop them up like meat in
a kettle, like flesh in a caldron. Then they will cry to the
Lord, but he will not answer them; he will hide his face
from them at that time, because they have made their
deeds evil. Thus says the Lord concerning the prophets
who lead my people astray, who cry "Peace" when they
have something to eat, but declare war against him who
puts nothing into their mouths. Therefore it shall be night
to you, without vision, and darkness to you, without
divination. The sun shall go down upon the prophets, and
the day shall be black over them; the seers shall be
disgraced, and the diviners put to shame; they shall all
cover their lips, for there is no answer from God. But as for
me, I am filled with power, with the Spirit of the Lord, and
with justice and might, to declare to Jacob his
transgression and to Israel his sin.

A Reading (Lesson) from the Acts of the Apostles [24:1-23]

After five days the high priest Anani′as came down with
some elders and a spokesman, one Tertul′lus. They laid
before the governor their case against Paul; and when he
was called, Tertul′lus began to accuse him, saying: "Since
through you we enjoy much peace, and since by your
provision, most excellent Felix, reforms are introduced on
behalf of this nation, in every way and everywhere we

accept this with all gratitude. But, to detain you no further, I beg you in your kindness to hear us briefly. For we have found this man a pestilent fellow, an agitator among all the Jews throughout the world, and a ringleader of the sect of the Nazarenes. He even tried to profane the temple, but we seized him. By examining him yourself you will be able to learn from him about everything of which we accuse him." The Jews also joined in this charge, affirming that all this was so. And when the governor had motioned to him to speak, Paul replied: "Realizing that for many years you have been judge over this nation, I cheerfully make my defense. As you may ascertain, it is not more than twelve days since I went up to worship at Jerusalem; and they did not find me disputing with any one or stirring up a crowd, either in the temple or in the synagogues, or in the city. Neither can they prove to you what they now bring up against me. But this I admit to you, that according to the Way, which they call a sect, I worship the God of our fathers, believing everything laid down by the law or written in the prophets, having a hope in God which these themselves accept, that there will be a resurrection of both the just and the unjust. So I always take pains to have a clear conscience toward God and toward men. Now after some years I came to bring to my nation alms and offerings. As I was doing this, they found me purified in the temple, without any crowd or tumult. But some Jews from Asia—they ought to be here before you and to make an accusation, if they have anything against me. Or else let these men themselves say what wrongdoing they found when I stood before the council, except this one thing which I cried out while standing among them, 'With respect to the resurrection of the dead I am on trial before you this day.'" But Felix, having a rather accurate knowledge of the Way, put them off, saying, "When Lys'ias the tribune comes down, I will decide your case." Then he gave orders to the centurion that he should be kept in custody but should have some liberty, and that none of his friends should be prevented from attending to his needs.

A Reading (Lesson) from the Gospel according to Luke
[7:36-50]

One of the Pharisees asked Jesus to eat with him, and he
went into the Pharisee's house, and took his place at table.
And behold, a woman of the city, who was a sinner, when
she learned that he was at table in the Pharisee's house,
brought an alabaster flask of ointment, and standing
behind him at his feet, weeping, she began to wet his feet
with her tears, and wiped them with the hair of her head,
and kissed his feet, and anointed them with the ointment.
Now when the Pharisee who had invited him saw it, he
said to himself, "If this man were a prophet, he would have
known who and what sort of woman this is who is
touching him, for she is a sinner." And Jesus answering
said to him, "Simon, I have something to say to you." And
he answered, "What is it, Teacher?" "A certain creditor
had two debtors; one owed five hundred denarii, and the
other fifty. When they could not pay, he forgave them both.
Now which of them will love him more?" Simon
answered, "The one, I suppose, to whom he forgave
more." And he said to him, "You have judged rightly."
Then turning toward the woman he said to Simon, "Do
you see this woman? I entered your house, you gave me no
water for my feet, but she has wet my feet with her tears
and wiped them with her hair. You gave me no kiss, but
from the time I came in she has not ceased to kiss my feet.
You did not anoint my head with oil, but she has anointed
my feet with ointment. Therefore I tell you, her sins, which
are many, are forgiven, for she loved much; but he who is
forgiven little, loves little." And he said to her, "Your sins
are forgiven." Then those who were at table with him
began to say among themselves, "Who is this, who even
forgives sins?" And he said to the woman, "Your faith has
saved you; go in peace."

Friday

Psalm 140 [page 796], *Psalm 142* [page 798] ❖
Psalm 141 [page 797], *Psalm 143:1-11(12)* [page 798]

A Reading (Lesson) from the Book of Micah [3:9—4:5]

Hear this, you heads of the house of Jacob and rulers of the house of Israel, who abhor justice and pervert all equity, who build Zion with blood and Jerusalem with wrong. Its heads give judgment for a bribe, its priests teach for hire, its prophets divine for money; yet they lean upon the Lord and say, "Is not the Lord in the midst of us? No evil shall come upon us." Therefore because of you Zion shall be plowed as a field; Jerusalem shall become a heap of ruins, and the moutain of the house a wooded height. It shall come to pass in the latter days that the mountain of the house of the Lord shall be established as the highest of the mountains, and shall be raised up above the hills; and peoples shall flow to it, and many nations shall come, and say: "Come, let us go up to the mountain of the Lord, to the house of the God of Jacob; that he may teach us his ways and we may walk in his paths." For out of Zion shall go forth the law, and the word of the Lord from Jerusalem. He shall judge between many peoples, and shall decide for strong nations afar off; and they shall beat their swords into plowshares, and their spears into pruning hooks; nation shall not lift up sword against nation, neither shall they learn war any more; but they shall sit every man under his vine and under his fig tree, and none shall make them afraid; for the mouth of the Lord of hosts has spoken. For all the peoples walk each in the name of its god, but we will walk in the name of the Lord our God for ever and ever.

A Reading (Lesson) from the Acts of the Apostles
[24:24—25:12]

After some days Felix came with his wife Drusilla, who

was a Jewess; and he sent for Paul and heard him speak upon faith in Christ Jesus. And as he argued about justice and self-control and future judgment, Felix was alarmed and said, "Go away for the present; when I have an opportunity I will summon you." At the same time he hoped that money would be given him by Paul. So he sent for him often and conversed with him. But when two years had elapsed, Felix was succeeded by Porcius Festus; and desiring to do the Jews a favor, Felix left Paul in prison. Now when Festus had come into his province, after three days he went up to Jerusalem from Caesare'a. And the chief priests and the principal men of the Jews informed him against Paul; and they urged him, asking as a favor to have the man sent to Jerusalem, planning an ambush to kill him on the way. Festus replied that Paul was being kept at Caesare'a, and that he himself intended to go there shortly. "So," said he, "let the men of authority among you go down with me, and if there is anything wrong about the man, let them accuse him." When he had stayed among them not more than eight or ten days, he went down to Caesare'a; and the next day he took his seat on the tribunal and ordered Paul to be brought. And when he had come, the Jews who had gone down from Jerusalem stood about him, bringing against him many serious charges which they could not prove. Paul said in his defense, "Neither against the law of the Jews, nor against the temple, nor against Caesar have I offended at all." But Festus, wishing to do the Jews a favor, said to Paul, "Do you wish to go up to Jerusalem, and there be tried on these charges before me?" But Paul said, "I am standing before Caesar's tribunal, where I ought to be tried; to the Jews I have done no wrong, as you know very well. If then I am a wrongdoer, and have committed anything for which I deserve to die, I do not seek to escape death; but if there is nothing in their charges against me, no one can give me up to them. I appeal to Caesar." Then Festus, when he had conferred with his council, answered, "You have appealed to Caesar; to Caesar you shall go."

A Reading (Lesson) from the Gospel according to Luke
[8:1-15]

Soon after being anointed by the woman who was a sinner he went on through cities and villages, preaching and bringing the good news of the kingdom of God. And the twelve were with him, and also some women who had been healed of evil spirits and infirmities: Mary, called Mag'dalene, from whom seven demons had gone out, and Jo-an'na, the wife of Chu'za, Herod's steward, and Susanna, and many others, who provided for them out of their means. And when a great crowd came together and people from town after town came to him, he said in a parable: "A sower went out to sow his seed; and as he sowed, some fell along the path, and was trodden under foot, and the birds of the air devoured it. And some fell on the rock; and as it grew up, it withered away, because it had no moisture. And some fell among thorns; and the thorns grew with it and choked it. And some fell into good soil and grew, and yielded a hundredfold." As he said this, he called out, "He who has ears to hear, let him hear." And when his disciples asked him what this parable meant, he said, "To you it has been given to know the secrets of the kingdom of God; but for others they are in parables, so that seeing they may not see, and hearing they may not understand. Now the parable of the seed is this: The seed is the word of God. The ones along the path are those who have heard; then the devil comes and takes away the word from their hearts, that they may not believe and be saved. And the ones on the rock are those who, when they hear the word, receive it with joy; but these have no root, they believe for a while and in time of temptation fall away. And as for what fell among the thorns, they are those who hear, but as they go on their way they are choked by the cares and riches and pleasures of life, and their fruit does not mature. And as for that in the good soil, they are those who, hearing the word, hold it fast in an honest and good heart, and bring forth fruit with patience."

Saturday

Psalm 137:1-6(7-9) [page 792],   *Psalm 144* [page 801]
❖   *Psalm 104* [page 735]

A Reading (Lesson) from the Book of Micah [5:1-4,10-15]

Now you are walled about with a wall; siege is laid against us; with a rod they strike upon the cheek the ruler of Israel. But you, O Bethlehem Eph'rathah, who are little to be among the clans of Judah, from you shall come forth for me one who is to be ruler in Israel, whose origin is from of old, from ancient days. Therefore he shall give them up until the time when she who is in travail has brought forth; then the rest of his brethren shall return to the people of Israel. And he shall stand and feed his flock in the strength of the Lord, in the majesty of the name of the Lord his God. And they shall dwell secure, for now he shall be great to the ends of the earth. And in that day, says the Lord, I will cut off your horses from among you and will destroy your chariots; and I will cut off the cities of your land and throw down all your strongholds; and I will cut off sorceries from your hand, and you shall have no more soothsayers; and I will cut off your images and your pillars from among you, and you shall bow down no more to the work of your hands; and I will root out your Ashe'rim from among you and destroy your cities. And in anger and wrath I will execute vengance upon the nations that did not obey.

A Reading (Lesson) from the Acts of the Apostles
[25:13-27]

When some days had passed, Agrippa the king and Berni'ce arrived at Caesare'a to welcome Festus. And as they stayed there many days, Festus laid Paul's case before the king, saying, "There is a man left prisoner by Felix; and when I was at Jerusalem, the chief priests and the elders of the Jews gave information about him, asking for sentence against him. I answered them that it was not the custom of the Romans to give up any one before the accused met the accusers face to face, and had opportunity to make his defense concerning the charge laid against him. When therefore they came together here, I made no delay, but on the next day took my seat on the tribunal and ordered the man to be brought in. When the accusers stood up, they brought no charge in his case of such evils as I supposed; but they had certain points of dispute with him about their own superstition and about one Jesus, who was dead, but whom Paul asserted to be alive. Being at a loss how to investigate these questions, I asked whether he wished to go to Jerusalem and be tried there regarding them. But when Paul had appealed to be kept in custody for the decision of the emperor, I commanded him to be held until I could send him to Caesar." And Agrippa said to Festus, "I should like to hear the man myself." "Tomorrow," said he, "you shall hear him." So on the morrow Agrippa and Berni'ce came with great pomp, and they entered the audience hall with the military tribunes and the prominent men of the city. Then by command of Festus Paul was brought in. And Festus said, "King Agrippa and all who are present with us, you see this man about whom the whole Jewish people petitioned me, both at Jerusalem and here, shouting that he ought not to live any longer. But I found that he had done nothing deserving death; and as he himself appealed to the emperor. I decided to send him. But I have nothing definite to write to my lord about him. Therefore I have brought him before you, and, especially before you, King Agrippa, that, after we have examined him, I may have something to write. For it seems to me unreasonable, in sending a prisoner, not to indicate the charges against him."

A Reading (Lesson) from the Gospel according to Luke [8:16-25]

Jesus said to the disciples, "No one after lighting a lamp

covers it with a vessel, or puts it under a bed, but puts it on a stand, that those who enter may see the light. For nothing is hid that shall not be made manifest, nor anything secret that shall not be known and come to light. Take heed then how you hear; for to him who has will more be given, and from him who has not, even what he thinks that he has will be taken away." Then his mother and his brothers came to him, but they could not reach him for the crowd. And he was told, "Your mother and your brothers are standing outside, desiring to see you." But he said to them, "My mother and my brothers are those who hear the word of God and do it." One day he got into a boat with his disciples, and he said to them, "Let us go across to the other side of the lake." So they set out, and as they sailed he fell asleep. And a storm of wind came down on the lake, and they were filling with water, and were in danger. And they went and woke him, saying, "Master, Master, we are perishing!" And he awoke and rebuked the wind and the raging waves; and they ceased, and there was a calm. He said to them, "Where is your faith?" And they were afraid, and they marveled, saying to one another, "Who then is this, that he commands even wind and water, and they obey him?"

Proper 23 *Week of Sunday closest to October 12*

Sunday

Psalm 146 [page 803], *Psalm 147* [page 804] ❖
Psalm 111 [page 754], *Psalm 112* [page 755]
Psalm 113 [page 756]

A Reading (Lesson) from the Book of Micah [6:1-8]

Hear what the Lord says: Arise, plead your case before the mountains, and let the hills hear your voice. Hear, you mountains, the controversy of the Lord, and you enduring foundations of the earth; for the Lord has a controversy with his people, and he will contend with Israel. "O my people, what have I done to you? In what have I wearied you? Answer me! For I brought you up from the land of Egypt, and redeemed you from the house of bondage; and I sent before you Moses, Aaron, and Miriam. O my people, remember what Balak king of Moab devised, and what Balaam the son of Be'or answered him, and what happened from Shittim to Gilgal, that you may know the saving acts of the Lord." "With what shall I come before the Lord, and bow myself before God on high? Shall I come before him with burnt offerings, with calves a year old? Will the Lord be pleased with thousands of rams, with ten thousands of rivers of oil? Shall I give my first-born for my transgression, the fruit of my body for the sin of my soul?" He has showed you, O man, what is good; and what does the Lord require of you but to do justice, and to love kindness, and to walk humbly with your God?

A Reading (Lesson) from the First Letter of Paul to the Corinthians [4:9-16]

I think that God has exhibited us apostles as last of all, like men sentenced to death; because we have become a spectacle to the world, to angels and to men. We are fools for Christ's sake, but you are wise in Christ. We are weak, but you are strong. You are held in honor, but we in disrepute. To the present hour we hunger and thirst, we are ill-clad and buffeted and homeless, and we labor, working with our own hands. When reviled, we bless; when persecuted, we endure, when slandered, we try to conciliate; we have become, and are now, as the refuse of the world, the off-scouring of all things. I do not write this to make you ashamed, but to admonish you as my beloved children. For though you have countless guides in Christ, you do not have many fathers. For I became your father in Christ Jesus through the gospel. I urge you, then, be imitators of me.

Matthew 15:21-28   [page 75 above]

Monday

Psalm 1 [page 585],   *Psalm 2* [page 586],
Psalm 3 [page 587]   ❖   *Psalm 4* [page 587],
Psalm 7 [page 590]

A Reading (Lesson) from the Book of Micah [7:1-7]

Woe is me! For I have become as when the summer fruit
has been gathered, as when the vintage has been gleaned:
there is no cluster to eat, no first-ripe fig which my soul
desires. The godly man has perished from the earth, and
there is none upright among men; they all lie in wait for
blood, and each hunts his brother with a net. Their hands
are upon what is evil, to do it diligently; the prince and the
judge ask for a bride, and the great man utters the evil
desire of his soul; thus they weave it together. The best of
them is like a brier, the most upright of them a thorn
hedge. The day of their watchmen, of their punishment,
has come; now their confusion is at hand. Put no trust in a
neighbor, have no confidence in a friend; guard the doors
of your mouth from her who lies in your bosom; for the
son treats the father with contempt, the daughter rises up
against her mother, the daughter-in-law against her
mother-in-law; a man's enemies are the men of his own
house. But as for me, I will look to the Lord, I will wait for
the God of my salvation; my God will hear me.

A Reading (Lesson) from the Acts of the Apostles [26:1-23]

Agrippa said to Paul, "You have permission to speak for
yourself." Then Paul stretched out his hand and made his
defense: "I think myself fortunate that it is before you,
King Agrippa, I am to make my defense today against all
the accusations of the Jews, because you are especially
familiar with all customs and controversies of the Jews;

therefore I beg you to listen to me patiently. My manner of life from my youth, spent from the beginning among my own nation and at Jersualem, is know by all the Jews. They have known for a long time, if they are willing to testify, that according to the strictest party of our religion I have lived as a Pharisee. And now I stand here on trial for hope in the promise made by God to our fathers, to which our twelve tribes hope to attain, as they earnestly worship night and day. And for this hope I am accused by Jews, O king! Why is it thought incredible by any of you that God raises the dead? I myself was convinced that I ought to do many things in opposing the name of Jesus of Nazareth. And I did so in Jerusalem; I not only shut up many of the saints in prison, by authority from the chief priests, but when they were put to death I cast my vote against them. And I punished them often in all the synagogues and tried to make them blaspheme; and in raging fury against them, I persecuted them even to foreign cities. Thus I journeyed to Damascus with the authority and commission of the chief priests. At midday, O king, I saw on the way a light from heaven, brighter than the sun, shining round me and those who journeyed with me. And when we had all fallen to the ground, I heard a voice saying to me in the Hebrew language, 'Saul, Saul, why do you persecute me? It hurts you to kick against the goads.' And I said, 'Who are you, Lord?' And the Lord said, 'I am Jesus whom you are persecuting. But rise and stand upon your feet; for I have appeared to you for this purpose, to appoint you to serve and bear witness to the things in which you have seen me and to those in which I will appear to you, delivering you from the people and from the Gentiles—to whom I send you to open their eyes, that they may turn from darkness to light and from the power of Satan to God, that they may receive forgiveness of sins and a place among those who are sanctified by faith in me.' Wherefore, O King Agrippa, I was not disobedient to the heavenly vision, but declared first to those at Damascus, then at Jerusalem and throughout all the country of Judea, and also to the Gentiles, that they should repent and turn to God and perform deeds worthy of their repentance. For this reason the Jews seized me in the temple and tried to kill me. To this day I have had the help that comes from God, and so I stand here testifying both to small and great, saying nothing but what the prophets and Moses said would come to pass: that the Christ must suffer, and that, by being the first to rise from the dead, he would proclaim light both to the people and to the Gentiles."

A Reading (Lesson) from the Gospel according to Luke
[8:26-39]

Jesus and the disciples arrived at the country of the Ger'asenes, which is opposite Galilee. And as he stepped out on land, there met him a man from the city who had demons; for a long time he had worn no clothes, and he lived not in a house but among the tombs. When he saw Jesus, he cried out and fell down before him, and said with a loud voice, "What have you to do with me, Jesus, Son of the Most High God? I beseech you, do not torment me." For he had commanded the unclean spirit to come out of the man. (For many a time it had seized him; he was kept under guard, and bound with chains and fetters, but he broke the bonds and was driven by the demon into the desert.) Jesus then asked him, "What is your name?" And he said, "Legion"; for many demons had entered him. And they begged him not to command them to depart into the abyss. Now a large herd of swine was feeding there on the hillside; and they begged him to let them enter these. So he gave them leave. Then the demons came out of the man and entered the swine, and the herd rushed down the steep bank into the lake and were drowned. When the herdsmen saw what had happened, they fled, and told it in the city and in the country. Then people went out to see what had happened, and they came to Jesus, and found the man from whom the demons had gone, sitting at the feet of

Jesus, clothed and in his right mind; and they were afraid. And those who had seen it told them how he who had been possessed with demons was healed. Then all the people of the surrounding country of the Ger'asenes asked him to depart from them; for they were seized with great fear; so he got into the boat and returned. The man from whom the demons had gone begged that he might be with him; but he sent him away, saying, "Return to your home, and declare how much God has done for you." And he went away, proclaiming throughout the whole city how much Jesus had done for him.

Tuesday

Psalm 5 [page 588], *Psalm 6* [page 589] ❖
Psalm 10 [page 594], *Psalm 11* [page 596]

A Reading (Lesson) from the Book of Jonah [1:1-17a]

Now the word of the Lord came to Jonah the son of Amit'tai, saying, "Arise, go to Nin'eveh, that great city, and cry against it; for their wickedness has come up before me." But Jonah rose to flee to Tarshish from the presence of the Lord. He went down to Joppa and found a ship going to Tarshish; so he paid the fare, and went on board, to go with them to Tarshish, away from the presence of the Lord. But the Lord hurled a great wind upon the sea, and there was a mighty tempest on the sea, so that the ship threatened to break up. Then the mariners were afraid, and each cried to his god; and they threw the wares that were in the ship into the sea, to lighten it for them. But Jonah had gone down into the inner part of the ship and had lain down, and was fast asleep. So the captain came and said to him, "What do you mean, you sleeper? Arise, call upon your god! Perhaps the god will give a thought to us, that we do not perish." And they said to one another, "Come, let us cast lots, that we may know on whose account this evil has come upon us." So they cast lots, and the lot fell upon Jonah. Then they said to him, "Tell us, on whose account this evil has come upon us? What is your occupation? And whence do you come? What is your country? And of what people are you?" And he said to them, "I am a Hebrew; and I fear the Lord, the God of heaven, who made the sea and the dry land." Then the men were exceedingly afraid, and said to him, "What is this that you have done!" For the men knew that he was fleeing from the presence of the Lord, because he had told them. Then they said to him, "What shall we do to you, that the sea may quiet down for us?" For the sea grew more and more tempestuous. He said to them, "Take me up and throw me into the sea; then the sea will quiet down for you; for I know it is because of me that this great tempest has come upon you." Nevertheless the men rowed hard to bring the ship back to land, but they could not, for the sea grew more and more tempestuous against them. Therefore they cried to the Lord, "We beseech thee, O Lord, let us not perish for this man's life, and lay not on us innocent blood; for thou, O Lord, has done as it pleased thee." So they took up Jonah and threw him into the sea; and the sea ceased from its raging. Then the men feared the Lord exceedingly, and they offered a sacrifice to the Lord and made vows. And the Lord appointed a great fish to swallow up Jonah.

A Reading (Lesson) from the Acts of the Apostles
[26:24—27:8]

As Paul made his defense, Festus said with a loud voice, "Paul, you are mad; your great learning is turning you mad." But Paul said, "I am not mad, most excellent Festus, but I am speaking the sober truth. For the king knows about these things, and to him I speak freely, for I am persuaded that none of these things has escaped his notice, for this was not done in a corner. King Agrippa, do you believe the prophets? I know that you believe." And

Agrippa said to Paul, "In a short time you think to make me a Christian!" And Paul said, "Whether short or long, I would to God that not only you but also all who hear me this day might become such as I am—except for these chains." Then the king rose, and the governor and Berni'ce and those who were sitting with them; and when they had withdrawn, they said to one another, "This man is doing nothing to deserve death or imprisonment." And Agrippa said to Festus, "This man could have been set free if he had not appealed to Caesar." And when it was decided that we should sail for Italy, they delivered Paul and some other prisoners to a centurion of the Augustan Cohort, named Julius. And embarking in a ship of Adramyt'tium, which was about to sail to the ports along the coast of Asia, we put to sea, accompanied by Aristar'chus, a Macedo'nian from Thessaloni'ca. The next day we put in at Sidon; and Julius treated Paul kindly, and gave him leave to go to his friends and be cared for. And putting to sea from there we sailed under the lee of Cyprus, because the winds were against us. And when we had sailed across the sea which is off Cili'cia and Pamphyl'ia, we came to Myra in Ly'cia. There the centurion found a ship of Alexandria sailing for Italy, and put us on board. We sailed slowly for a number of days, and arrived with difficulty off Cni'dus, and as the wind did not allow us to go on, we sailed under the lee of Crete off Salmo'ne. Coasting along it with difficulty, we came to a place called Fair Havens, near which was the city of Lase'a.

A Reading (Lesson) from the Gospel according to Luke
[8:40-56]

When Jesus returned, the crowd welcomed him, for they were all waiting for him. And there came a man named Ja'irus, who was a ruler of the synagogue; and falling at Jesus' feet he besought him to come to his house, for he had an only daughter, about twelve years of age, and she was dying. As he went, the people pressed round him. And a woman who had had a flow of blood for twelve years and could not be healed by any one, came up behind him, and touched the fringe of his garment; and immediately her flow of blood ceased. And Jesus said, "Who was it that touched me?" When all denied it, Peter said, "Master, the multitudes surround you and press upon you!" But Jesus said, "Some one touched me; for I perceive that power has gone forth from me." And when the woman saw that she was not hidden, she came trembling, and falling down before him declared in the presence of all the people why she had touched him, and how she had been immediately healed. And he said to her, "Daughter, your faith has made you well; go in peace." While he was still speaking, a man from the ruler's house came and said, "Your daughter is dead; do not trouble the Teacher any more." But Jesus on hearing this answered him, "Do not fear; only believe, and she shall be well." And when he came to the house, he permitted no one to enter with him, except Peter and John and James, and the father and mother of the child. And all were weeping and bewailing her; but he said, "Do not weep; for she is not dead but sleeping." And they laughed at him, knowing that she was dead. But taking her by the hand he called, saying, "Child, arise." And her spirit returned, and she got up at once; and he directed that something should be given her to eat. And her parents were amazed; but he charged them to tell no one what had happened.

Wednesday

Psalm 119:1-24 [page 763]   ❖   *Psalm 12* [page 597],
Psalm 13 [page 597],   *Psalm 14* [page 598]

A Reading (Lesson) from the Book of Jonah [1:17—2:10]

The Lord appointed a great fish to swallow up Jonah; and Jonah was in the belly of the fish three days and three nights. Then Jonah prayed to the Lord his God from the belly of the fish, saying, "I called to the Lord, out of my distress, and he answered me; out of the belly of Sheol I cried, and thou didst hear my voice. For thou didst cast me into the deep, into the heart of the seas, and the flood was round about me; all thy waves and thy billows passed over me. Then I said, 'I am cast out from thy presence; how shall I again look upon thy holy temple?' The waters closed in over me, the deep was round about me; weeds were wrapped about my head at the roots of the mountains. I went down to the land whose bars closed upon me for ever; yet thou didst bring up my life from the Pit, O Lord my God. When my soul fainted within me, I remembered the Lord; and my prayer came to thee, into thy holy temple. Those who pay regard to vain idols forsake their true loyalty. But I with the voice of thanksgiving will sacrifice to thee; what I have vowed I will pay. Deliverance belongs to the Lord!" And the Lord spoke to the fish, and it vomited out Jonah upon the dry land.

A Reading (Lesson) from the Acts of the Apostles [27:9-26]

As much time had been lost, and the voyage was already dangerous because the fast had already gone by, Paul advised them, saying, "Sirs, I perceive that the voyage will be with injury and much loss, not only of the cargo and the ship, but also of our lives." But the centurion paid more attention to the captain and to the owner of the ship than to what Paul said. And because the harbor was not suitable to winter in, the majority advised to put to sea from there, on the chance that somehow they could reach Phoenix, a harbor of Crete, looking northeast and southeast, and winter there. And when the south wind blew gently, supposing that they had obtained their purpose, they weighed anchor and sailed along Crete, close inshore. But soon a tempestuous wind, called the northeaster, struck down from the land; and when the ship was caught and could not face the wind, we gave way to it and were driven. And running under the lee of a small island called Cauda, we managed with difficulty to secure the boat; after hoisting it up, they took measures to undergird the ship; then, fearing that they should run on the Syrtis, they lowered the gear, and so were driven. As we were violently storm-tossed, they began next day to throw the cargo overboard; and the third day they cast out with their own hands the tackle of the ship. And when neither sun nor stars appeared for many a day, and no small tempest lay on us, all hope of our being saved was at last abandoned. As they had been long without food, Paul then came forward among them and said, "Men, you should have listened to me, and should not have set sail from Crete and incurred this injury and loss. I now bid you take heart; for there will be no loss of life among you, but only of the ship. For this very night there stood by me an angel of the God to whom I belong and whom I worship, and he said, 'Do not be afraid, Paul; you must stand before Caesar; and lo, God has granted you all those who sail with you.' So take heart, men, for I have faith in God that it will be exactly as I have been told. But we shall have to run on some island."

A Reading (Lesson) from the Gospel according to Luke
[9:1-17]

Jesus called the twelve together and gave them power and authority over all demons and to cure diseases, and he sent them out to preach the kingdom of God and to heal. And he said to them, "Take nothing for your journey, no staff, nor bag, nor bread, nor money; and do not have two tunics. And whatever house you enter, stay there, and from there depart. And wherever they do not receive you, when you leave that town shake off the dust from your feet as a testimony against them." And they departed and went through the villages, preaching the gospel and healing everywhere. Now Herod the tetrarch heard of all that was done, and he was perplexed, because it was said by some that John had been raised from the dead, by some that

Eli'jah had appeared, and by others that one of the old prophets had risen. Herod said, "John I beheaded; but who is this about whom I hear such things?" And he sought to see him. On their return the apostles told him what they had done. And he took them and withdrew apart to a city called Beth-sa'ida. When the crowds learned it, they followed him; and he welcomed them and spoke to them of the kingdom of God, and cured those who had need of healing. Now the day began to wear away; and the twelve came and said to him, "Send the crowd away, to go into the villages and country round about, to lodge and get provisions; for we are here in a lonely place." But he said to them, "You give them something to eat." They said, "We have no more than five loaves and two fish—unless we are to go and buy food for all these people." For there were about five thousand men. And he said to his disciples, "Make them sit down in companies, about fifty each." And they did so, and made them all sit down. And taking the five loaves and the two fish he looked up to heaven, and blessed and broke them, and gave them to the disciples to set before the crowd. And all ate and were satisfied. And they took up what was left over, twelve baskets of broken pieces.

Thursday

Psalm 18:1-20 [page 602]   ❖   *Psalm 18:21-50* [page 604]

A Reading (Lesson) from the Book of Jonah [3:1—4:11]

The word of the Lord came to Jonah the second time, saying, "Arise, go to Nin'eveh, that great city, and proclaim to it the message that I tell you." So Jonah arose and went to Nin'eveh, according to the word of the Lord. Now Nin'eveh was an exceedingly great city, three days' journey in breadth. Jonah began to go into the city, going a day's journey. And he cried, "Yet forty days, and Nin'eveh shall be overthrown!" And the people of Nin'eveh believed God;

they proclaimed a fast, and put on sackcloth, from the greatest of them to the least of them. Then tidings reached the king of Nin'eveh, and he arose from his throne, removed his robe, and covered himself with sackcloth, and sat in ashes. And he made proclamation and published through Nin'eveh, "By the decree of the king and his nobles: Let neither man nor beast, herd nor flock, taste anything; let them not feed, or drink water, but let man and beast be covered with sackcloth, and let them cry mightily to God; yea, let every one turn from his evil way and from the violence which is in his hands. Who knows, God may yet repent and turn from his fierce anger, so that we perish not?" When God saw what they did, how they turned from their evil way, God repented of the evil which he had said he would do to them; and he did not do it. But it displeased Jonah exceedingly, and he was angry. And he prayed to the Lord and said, "I pray thee, Lord, is not this what I said when I was yet in my country? That is why I made haste to flee to Tarshish; for I knew that thou art a gracious God and merciful, slow to anger, and abounding in steadfast love, and repentest of evil. Therefore now, O Lord, take my life from me, I beseech thee, for it is better for me to die than to live." And the Lord said, "Do you do well to be angry?" Then Jonah went out of the city and sat to the east of the city, and made a booth for himself there. He sat under it in the shade, till he should see what would become of the city. And the Lord God appointed a plant, and made it come up over Jonah, that it might be a shade over his head, to save him from his discomfort. So Jonah was exceedingly glad because of the plant. But when dawn came up the next day, God appointed a worm which attacked the plant, so that it withered. When the sun rose, God appointed a sultry east wind, and the sun beat upon the head of Jonah so that he was faint; and he asked that he might die, and said, "It is better for me to die than to live." But God said to Jonah, "Do you do well to be angry for the plant?" And he said, "I do well to be angry, angry enough to die." And the Lord said, "You pity the plant, for which you did not labor, nor did you make it grow, which came into being in a night, and perished in a night. And should not I pity Nin'eveh, that great city, in which there are more than a hundred and twenty thousand persons who do not know their right hand from their left, and also much cattle?"

A Reading (Lesson) from the Acts of the Apostles
[27:27-44]

When the fourteenth night had come, as we were drifting across the sea of A'dria, about midnight the sailors suspected that they were nearing land. So they sounded and found twenty fathoms; a little farther on they sounded again and found fifteen fathoms. And fearing that we might run on the rocks, they let out four anchors from the stern, and prayed for day to come. And as the sailors were seeking to escape from the ship, and had lowered the boat into the sea, under pretense of laying out anchors from the bow, Paul said to the centurion and the soldiers, "Unless these men stay in the ship, you cannot be saved." Then the soldiers cut away the ropes of the boat, and let it go. As day was about to dawn, Paul urged them all to take some food, saying, "Today is the fourteenth day that you have continued in suspense and without food, having taken nothing. Therefore I urge you to take some food; it will give you strength, since not a hair is to perish from the head of any of you." And when he had said this, he took bread, and giving thanks to God in the presence of all he broke it and began to eat. Then they all were encouraged and ate some food themselves. (We were in all two hundred and seventy-six persons in the ship.) And when they had eaten enough, they lightened the ship, throwing out the wheat into the sea. Now when it was day, they did not recognize the land, but they noticed a bay with a beach, on which they planned if possible to bring the ship ashore. So they cast off the anchors and left them in the sea, at the same time loosening the ropes that tied the rudders; then hoisting the foresail to the wind, they made for the beach. But striking a shoal they ran the vessel aground; the bow stuck and remained immovable, and the stern was broken up by the surf. The soldiers' plan was to kill the prisoners, lest any should swim away and escape; but the centurion, wishing to save Paul, kept them from carrying out their purpose. He ordered those who could swim to throw themselves overboard first and make for the land, and the rest on planks or on pieces of the ship. And so it was that all escaped to land.

A Reading (Lesson) from the Gospel according to Luke
[9:18-27]

Now it happened that as Jesus was praying alone the disciples were with him; and he asked them, "Who do the people say that I am?" And they answered, "John the Baptist; but others say, Eli′jah; and others, that one of the old prophets has risen." And he said to them, "But who do you say that I am?" And Peter answered, "The Christ of God." But he charged and commanded them to tell this to no one, saying, "The Son of man must suffer many things, and be rejected by the elders and chief priests and scribes, and be killed, and on the third day be raised." And he said to all, "If any man would come after me, let him deny himself and take up his cross daily and follow me. For whoever would save his life will lose it; and whoever loses his life for my sake, he will save it. For what does it profit a man if he gains the whole world and loses or forfeits himself? For whoever is ashamed of me and of my words, of him will the Son of man be ashamed when he comes in his glory and the glory of the Father and of the holy angels. But I tell you truly, there are some standing here who will not taste death before they see the kingdom of God."

Friday

Psalm 16 [page 599],   *Psalm 17* [page 600]   ❖
Psalm 22 [page 610]

A Reading (Lesson) from the Book of Ecclesiasticus
[1:1-10,18-27]

All wisdom comes from the Lord and is with him for ever.
The sand of the sea, the drops of rain, and the days of
eternity—who can count them? The height of heaven, the
breadth of the earth, the abyss, and wisdom—who can
search them out? Wisdom was created before all things,
and prudent understanding from eternity. The root of
wisdom—to whom has it been revealed? Her clever
devices—who knows them? There is One who is wise,
greatly to be feared, sitting upon his throne. The Lord
himself created wisdom; he saw her and apportioned her,
he poured her out upon all his works. She dwells with all
flesh according to his gift, and he supplied her to those
who love him. The fear of the Lord is the crown of
wisdom, making peace and perfect health to flourish. He
saw her and apportioned her; he rained down knowledge
and discerning comprehension, and he exalted the glory of
those who held her fast. To fear the Lord is the root of
wisdom, and her branches are long life. Unrighteous anger
cannot be justified, for a man's anger tips the scale to his
ruin. A patient man will endure until the right moment,
and then joy will burst forth for him. He will hide his
words until the right moment, and the lips of many will tell
of his good sense. In the treasuries of wisdom are wise
sayings, but godliness is an abomination to a sinner. If you
desire wisdom, keep the commandments, and the Lord will
supply it for you. For the fear of the Lord is wisdom and
instruction, and he delights in fidelity and meekness.

A Reading (Lesson) from the Acts of the Apostles [28:1-16]

After we had escaped, we then learned that the island was called Malta. And the natives showed us unusual kindness, for they kindled a fire and welcomed us all, because it had begun to rain and was cold. Paul had gathered a bundle of sticks and put them on the fire, when a viper came out because of the heat and fastened on his hand. When the natives saw the creature hanging from his hand, they said to one another, "No doubt this man is a murderer. Though he has escaped from the sea, justice has not allowed him to live." He, however, shook off the creature into the fire and suffered no harm. They waited, expecting him to swell up or suddenly fall down dead; but when they had waited a long time and saw no misfortune come to him, they changed their minds and said that he was a god. Now in the neighborhood of that place were lands belonging to the chief man of the island, named Publius, who received us and entertained us hospitably for three days. It happened that the father of Publius lay sick with fever and dysentery; and Paul visited him and prayed, and putting his hands on him healed him. And when this had taken place, the rest of the people on the island who had diseases also came and were cured. They presented many gifts to us; and when we sailed, they put on board whatever we needed. After three months we set sail in a ship which had wintered in the island, a ship of Alexandria, with the Twin Brothers as figurehead. Putting in at Syracuse, we stayed there for three days. And from there we made a circuit and arrived at Rhe′gium; and after one day a south wind sprang up, and on the second day we came to Pute′oli. There we found brethren, and were invited to stay with them for seven days. And so we came to Rome. And the brethren there, when they heard of us, came as far as the Forum of Ap′pius and Three Taverns to meet us. On seeing them Paul thanked God and took courage. And when we came into Rome, Paul was allowed to stay by himself, with the soldier that guarded him.

A Reading (Lesson) from the Gospel according to Luke
[9:28-36]

Now about eight days after these sayings Jesus took with
him Peter and John and James, and went up the mountain
to pray. And as he was praying, the appearance of his
countenance was altered, and his raiment became dazzling
white. And behold, two men talked with him, Moses and
Eli'jah, who appeared in glory and spoke of his departure,
which he was to accomplish at Jerusalem. Now Peter and
those who were with him were heavy with sleep, and when
they wakened they saw his glory and the two men who
stood with him. And as the men were parting from him,
Peter said to Jesus, "Master, it is well that we are here; let
us make three booths, one for you and one for Moses and
one for Eli'jah"—not knowing what he said. As he said
this, a cloud came and overshadowed them; and they were
afraid as they entered the cloud. And a voice came out of
the cloud, saying, "This is my Son, my Chosen; listen to
him!" And when the voice had spoken, Jesus was found
alone. And they kept silence and told no one in those days
anything of what they had seen.

Saturday

Psalm 20 [page 608], *Psalm 21:1-7(8-14)* [page 608] ❖
Psalm 110:1-5(6-7) [page 753],
Psalm 116 [page 759], *Psalm 117* [page 760]

A Reading (Lesson) from the Book of Ecclesiasticus
[3:17-31]

My son, perform your tasks in meekness; then you will be
loved by those whom God accepts. The greater you are,
the more you must humble yourself; so you will find favor
in the sight of the Lord. For great is the might of the Lord;
he is glorified by the humble. Seek not what is too difficult
for you, nor investigate what is beyond your power.

Reflect upon what has been assigned to you, for you do not
need what is hidden. Do not meddle in what is beyond
your tasks, for matters too great for human understanding
have been shown you. For their hasty judgment has led
many astray, and wrong opinion has caused their thoughts
to slip. A stubborn mind will be afflicted at the end, and
whoever loves danger will perish by it. A stubborn mind
will be burdened by troubles, and the sinner will heap sin
upon sin. The affliction of the proud has no healing, for a
plant of wickedness has taken root in him. The mind of the
intelligent man will ponder a parable, and an attentive ear
is the wise man's desire. Water extinguishes a blazing fire:
so alms giving atones for sin. Whoever requites favors
gives thought to the future; at the moment of his falling he
will find support.

A Reading (Lesson) from the Acts of the Apostles
[28:17-31]

After three days in Rome Paul called together the local
leaders of the Jews; and when they had gathered, he said to
them, "Brethren, though I had done nothing against the
people or the customs of our fathers, yet I was delivered
prisoner from Jerusalem into the hands of the Romans.
When they had examined me, they wished to set me at
liberty, because there was no reason for the death penalty
in my case. But when the Jews objected, I was compelled to
appeal to Caesar—though I had no charge to bring against
my nation. For this reason therefore I have asked to see
you and speak with you, since it is because of the hope of
Israel that I am bound with this chain." And they said to
him, "We have received no letters from Judea about you,
and none of the brethren coming here has reported or
spoken any evil about you. But we desire to hear from you
what your views are; for with regard to this sect we know
that everywhere it is spoken against." When they had
appointed a day for him, they came to him at his lodging in

great numbers. And he expounded the matter to them from morning till evening, testifying to the kingdom of God and trying to convince them about Jesus both from the law of Moses and from the prophets. And some were convinced by what he said, while others disbelieved. So, as they disagreed among themselves, they departed, after Paul had made one statement: "The Holy Spirit was right in saying to your fathers through Isaiah the prophet: 'Go to this people, and say, You shall indeed hear but never understand, and you shall indeed see but never perceive. For this people's heart has grown dull, and their ears are heavy of hearing, and their eyes they have closed; lest they should perceive with their eyes, and hear with their ears, and understand with their heart, and turn for me to heal them.' Let it be known to you then that this salvation of God has been sent to the Gentiles; they will listen." And he lived there two whole years at his own expense, and welcomed all who came to him, preaching the kingdom of God and teaching about the Lord Jesus Christ quite openly and unhindered.

A Reading (Lesson) from the Gospel according to Luke [9:37-50]

On the next day, when Jesus and the disciples had come down from the mountain, a great crowd met him. And behold, a man from the crowd cried, "Teacher, I beg you to look upon my son, for he is my only child; and behold, a spirit seizes him, and he suddenly cries out; it convulses him till he foams, and shatters him, and will hardly leave him. And I begged your disciples to cast it out, but they could not." Jesus answered, "O faithless and perverse generation, how long am I to be with you and bear with you? Bring your son here." While he was coming, the demon tore him and convulsed him. But Jesus rebuked the unclean spirit, and healed the boy, and gave him back to his father. And all were astonished at the majesty of God.

But while they were all marveling at everything he did, he said to his disciples, "Let these words sink into your ears; for the Son of man is to be delivered into the hands of men." But they did not understand this saying, and it was concealed from them, that they should not perceive it; and they were afraid to ask him about this saying. And an argument arose among them as to which of them was the greatest. But when Jesus peceived the thought of their hearts, he took a child and put him by his side, and said to them, "Whoever receives this child in my name receives me, and whoever receives me receives him who sent me; for he who is least among you all is the one who is great." John answered, "Master, we saw a man casting out demons in your name, and we forbade him, because he does not follow with us." But Jesus said to him, "Do not forbid him; for he that is not against you is for you."

Proper 24   *Week of the Sunday closest to October 19*

Sunday

Psalm 148 [page 805],   *Psalm 149* [page 807],
Psalm 150 [page 807]   ❖   *Psalm 114* [page 756],
Psalm 115 [page 757]

A Reading (Lesson) from the Book of Ecclesiasticus [4:1-10]

My son, deprive not the poor of his living, and do not keep needy eyes waiting. Do not grieve the one who is hungry, nor anger a man in want. Do not add to the troubles of an angry mind, nor delay your gift to a beggar. Do not reject an afflicted suppliant, nor turn your face away from the poor. Do not avert your eye from the needy, nor give a man occasion to curse you; for if in bitterness of soul he calls down a curse upon you, his Creator will hear his prayer. Make yourself beloved in the congregation; bow your head low to a great man. Incline your ear to the poor, and

answer him peaceably and gently. Deliver him who is
wronged from the hand of the wrongdoer; and do not be
fainthearted in judging a case. Be like a father to orphans,
and instead of a husband to their mother; you will then be
like a son of the Most High, and he will love you more
than does your mother.

*A Reading (Lesson) from the First Letter of Paul
to the Corinthians* [10:1-13]

I want you to know, brethren, that our fathers were all
under the cloud, and all passed through the sea, and all
were baptized into Moses in the cloud and in the sea, and
all ate the same supernatural food and all drank the same
supernatural drink. For they drank from the supernatural
Rock which followed them, and the Rock was Christ.
Nevertheless with most of them God was not pleased; for
they were overthrown in the wilderness. Now these things
are warnings for us, not to desire evil as they did. Do not
be idolaters as some of them were; as it is written, "The
people sat down to eat and drink and rose up to dance."
We must not indulge in immorality as some of them did,
and twenty-three thousand fell in a single day. We must not
put the Lord to the test, as some of them did and were
destroyed by serpents; nor grumble, as some of them did
and were destroyed the Destroyer. Now these things
happened to them as a warning, but they were written
down for our instruction, upon whom the end of the ages
has come. Therefore let any one who thinks that he stands
take heed lest he fall. No temptation has overtaken you
that is not common to man. God is faithful, and he will not
let you be tempted beyond your strength, but with the
temptation will also provide the way of escape, that you
may be able to endure it.

Matthew 16:13-20 [page 82 above]

Monday

Psalm 25 [page 614] ❖ Psalm 9 [page 593],
Psalm 15 [page 599]

A Reading (Lesson) from the Book of Ecclesiasticus
[4:20—5:7]

Observe the right time, and beware of evil; and do not bring shame on yourself. For there is a shame which brings sin, and there is a shame which is glory and favor. Do not show partiality, to your own harm, or deference, to your downfall. Do not refrain from speaking at the crucial time, and do not hide your wisdom. For wisdom is known through speech, and education through the words of the tongue. Never speak against the truth, but be mindful of your ignorance. Do not be ashamed to confess your sins, and do not try to stop the current of a river. Do not subject yourself to a foolish fellow, nor show partiality to a ruler. Strive even to death for the truth and the Lord God will fight for you. Do not be reckless in your speech, or sluggish and remiss in your deeds. Do not be like a lion in your home, nor be a faultfinder with your servants. Let not your hand be extended to receive, but withdrawn when it is time to repay. Do not set your heart on your wealth, nor say, "I have enough." Do not follow your inclination and strength, walking according to the desires of your heart. Do not say, "Who will have power over me?" for the Lord will surely punish you. Do not say, "I sinned, and what happened to me?" for the Lord is slow to anger. Do not be so confident of atonement that you add sin to sin. Do not say, "His mercy is great, he will forgive the multitude of my sins," for both mercy and wrath are with him, and his anger rests on sinners. Do not delay to turn to the Lord, nor postpone it from day to day; for suddenly the wrath of the Lord will go forth, and at the time of punishment you will perish.

A Reading (Lesson) from the Revelation to John [7:1-8]

After the Lamb opened the sixth seal I saw four angels standing at the four corners of the earth, holding back the four winds of the earth, that no wind might blow on earth or sea or against any tree. Then I saw another angel ascend from the rising of the sun, with the seal of the living God, and he called with a loud voice to the four angels who had been given power to harm earth and sea, saying, "Do not harm the earth or the sea or the trees, till we have sealed the servants of our God upon their foreheads." And I heard the number of the sealed, a hundred and forty-four thousand sealed, out of every tribe of the sons of Israel, twelve thousand sealed out of the tribe of Judah, twelve thousand of the tribe of Reuben, twelve thousand of the tribe of Gad, twelve thousand of the tribe of Asher, twelve thousand of the tribe of Naph'tali, twelve thousand of the tribe of Manas'seh, twelve thousand of the tribe of Simeon, twelve thousand of the tribe of Levi, twelve thousand of the tribe of Is'sachar, twelve thousand of the tribe of Zeb'ulun, twelve thousand of the tribe of Joseph, twelve thousand sealed out of the tribe of Benjamin.

A Reading (Lesson) from the Gospel according to Luke [9:51-62]

When the days drew near for Jesus to be received up, he set his face to go to Jerusalem. And he sent messengers ahead of him, who went and entered a village of the Samaritans, to make ready for him; but the people would not receive him, because his face was set toward Jerusalem. And when his disciples James and John saw it, they said, "Lord, do you want us to bid fire come down from heaven and consume them?" But he turned and rebuked them. And they went on to another village. As they were going along the road, a man said to him, "I will follow you wherever you go." And Jesus said to him, "Foxes have holes, and birds of the air have nests; but the Son of man has nowhere to lay his head." To another he said, "Follow me." But he said, "Lord, let me first go and bury my father." But he said to him, "Leave the dead to bury their own dead; but as for you, go and proclaim the kingdom of God." Another said, "I will follow you, Lord; but let me first say farewell to those at my home." Jesus said to him, "No one who puts his hand to the plow and looks back is fit for the kingdom of God."

Tuesday

Psalm 26 [page 616], *Psalm 28* [page 619] ❖
Psalm 36 [page 632], *Psalm 39* [page 638]

A Reading (Lesson) from the Book of Ecclesiasticus
[6:5-17]

A pleasant voice multiplies friends, and a gracious tongue multiplies courtesies. Let those that are at peace with you be many, but let your advisers be one in a thousand. When you gain a friend, gain him through testing, and do not trust him hastily. For there is a friend who is such at his own convenience, but will not stand by you in your day of trouble. And there is a friend who changes into an enemy, and will disclose a quarrel to your disgrace. And there is a friend who is a table companion, but will not stand by you in your day of trouble. In your prosperity he will make himself your equal, and be bold with your servants; but if you are brought low he will turn against you, and will hide himself from your presence. Keep yourself far from your enemies, and be on guard toward your friends. A faithful friend is a sturdy shelter: he that has found one has found a treasure. There is nothing so precious as a faithful friend, and no scales can measure his excellence. A faithful friend is an elixir of life; and those who fear the Lord will find him. Whoever fears the Lord directs his friendship aright, for as he is, so is his neighbor also.

A Reading (Lesson) from the Revelation to John [7:9-17]

After the servants of God were sealed I looked, and
behold, a great multitude which no man could number,
from every nation, from all tribes and peoples and
tongues, standing before the Lamb, clothed in white robes,
with palm branches in their hands, and crying out with a
loud voice, "Salvation belongs to our God who sits upon
the throne, and to the Lamb!" And all the angels stood
round the throne and round the elders and the four living
creatures, and they fell on their faces before the throne and
worshiped God, saying, "Amen! Blessing and glory and
wisdom and thanksgiving and honor and power and might
be to our God for ever and ever! Amen." Then one of the
elders addressed me, saying, "Who are these, clothed in
white robes, and whence have they come?" I said to him,
"Sir, you know." And he said to me, "These are they who
have come out of the great tribulation; they have washed
their robes and made them white in the blood of the Lamb.
Therefore are they before the throne of God, and serve him
day and night within his temple; and he who sits upon the
throne will shelter them with his presence. They shall
hunger no more, neither thirst any more; the sun shall not
strike them, nor any scorching heat. For the Lamb in the
midst of the throne will be their shepherd, and he will
guide them to springs of living water; and God will wipe
away every tear from their eyes."

A Reading (Lesson) from the Gospel according to Luke
[10:1-16]

Jesus appointed seventy others, and sent them on ahead of
him, two by two, into every town and place where he
himself was about to come. And he said to them, "The
harvest is plentiful, but the laborers are few; pray therefore
the Lord of the harvest to send out laborers into his
harvest. Go your way; behold, I send you out as lambs in
the midst of wolves. Carry no purse, no bag, no sandals;

and salute no one on the road. Whatever house you enter, first say, 'Peace be to this house!' And if a son of peace is there, your peace shall rest upon him; but if not, it shall return to you. And remain in the same house, eating and drinking what they provide, for the laborer deserves his wages; do not go from house to house. Whenever you enter a town and they receive you, eat what is set before you; heal the sick in it and say to them, 'The kingdom of God has come near to you.' But whenever you enter a town and they do not receive you, go into its streets and say, 'Even the dust of your town that clings to our feet, we wipe off against you; nevertheless know this, that the kingdom of God has come near.' I tell you, it shall be more tolerable on that day for Sodom than for that town. Woe to you, Chora'zin! woe to you, Beth-sa'ida! for if the mighty works done in you had been done in Tyre and Sidon, they would have repented long ago, sitting in sackcloth and ashes. But it shall be more tolerable in the judgment for Tyre and Sidon than for you. And you, Caper'na-um, will you be exalted to heaven? You shall be brought down to Hades. He who hears you hears me, and he who rejects you rejects me, and he who rejects me rejects him who sent me."

Wednesday

Psalm 38 [page 636], ❖ *Psalm 119:25-48* [page 765]

A Reading (Lesson) from the Book of Ecclesiasticus
[7:4-14]

Do not seek from the Lord the highest office, nor the seat of honor from the king. Do not assert your righteousness before the Lord, nor display your wisdom before the king. Do not seek to become a judge, lest you be unable to remove iniquity, lest you be partial to a powerful man, and thus put a blot on your integrity. Do not offend against the public, and do not disgrace yourself among the people. Do not commit a sin twice; even for one you will not go unpunished. Do not say, "He will consider the multitude of my gifts, and when I make an offering to the Most High God he will accept it." Do not be fainthearted in your prayer, nor neglect to give alms. Do not ridicule a man who is bitter in soul, for there is One who abases and exalts. Do not devise a lie against your brother, nor do the like to a friend. Refuse to utter any lie, for the habit of lying serves no good. Do not prattle in the assembly of the elders, nor repeat yourself in your prayer.

A Reading (Lesson) from the Revelation to John [8:1-13]

When the Lamb opened the seventh seal, there was silence in heaven for about half an hour. Then I saw the seven angels who stand before God, and seven trumpets were given to them. And another angel came and stood at the altar with a golden censer; and he was given much incense to mingle with the prayers of all the saints upon the golden altar before the throne; and the smoke of the incense rose with the prayers of the saints from the hand of the angel before God. Then the angel took the censer and filled it with fire from the altar and threw it on the earth; and there were peals of thunder, voices, flashes of lightning, and an earthquake. Now the seven angels who had the seven trumpets made ready to blow them. The first angel blew his trumpet, and there followed hail and fire, mixed with blood, which fell on the earth; and a third of the earth was burnt up, and a third of the trees were burnt up, and all green grass was burnt up. The second angel blew his trumpet, and something like a great mountain, burning with fire, was thrown into the sea; and a third of the sea become blood, and a third of the living creatures in the sea died, and a third of the ships were destroyed. The third angel blew his trumpet, and a great star fell from heaven, blazing like a torch, and it fell on a third of the rivers and on the fountains of water. The name of the star is Wormwood. A third of the waters became wormwood, and many men died of the water, because is was made bitter. The fourth angel blew his trumpet, and a third of the sun was struck, and a third of the moon, and a third of the stars, so that a third of their light was darkened; a third of the day was kept from shining, and likewise a third of the night. Then I looked, and I heard an eagle crying with a loud voice, as it flew in midheaven, "Woe, woe, woe to those who dwell on the earth, at the blasts of the other trumpets which the three angels are about to blow!"

A Reading (Lesson) from the Gospel according to Luke
[10:17-24]

The seventy returned with joy, saying, "Lord, even the demons are subject to us in your name!" And he said to them, "I saw Satan fall like lightning from heaven. Behold, I have given you authority to tread upon serpents and scorpions, and over all the power of the enemy; and nothing shall hurt you. Nevertheless do not rejoice in this, that the spirits are subject to you; but rejoice that your names are written in heaven." In that same hour he rejoiced in the Holy Spirit and said, "I thank thee, Father, Lord of heaven and earth, that thou hast hidden these things from the wise and understanding and revealed them to babes; yea, Father, for such was thy gracious will. All things have been delivered to me by my Father; and no one knows who the Son is except the Father, or who the Father is except the Son and any one to whom the Son chooses to reveal him." Then turning to the disciples he said privately, "Blessed are the eyes which see what you see! For I tell you that many prophets and kings desired to see what you see, and did not see it, and to hear what you hear, and did not hear it."

Thursday

Psalm 37:1-18 [page 633] ❖ *Psalm 37:19-42* [page 634]

A Reading (Lesson) from the Book of Ecclesiasticus
[10:1-18]

A wise magistrate will educate his people, and the rule of an understanding man will be well ordered. Like the magistrate of the people, so are his officials; and like the ruler of the city, so are all its inhabitants. An undisciplined king will ruin his people, but a city will grow through the understanding of its rulers. The government of the earth is in the hands of the Lord, and over it he will raise up the right man for the time. The success of a man is in the hands of the Lord, and he confers his honor upon the person of the scribe. Do not be angry with your neighbor for any injury, and do not attempt anything by acts of insolence. Arrogance is hateful before the Lord and before men, and injustice is outrageous to both. Sovereignty passes from nation to nation on account of injustice and insolence and wealth. How can he who is dust and ashes be proud? for even in life his bowels decay. A long illness baffles the physician; the king of today will die tomorrow. For when a man is dead, he will inherit creeping things, and wild beasts, and worms. The beginning of man's pride is to depart from the Lord; his heart has forsaken his Maker. For the beginning of pride is sin, and the man who clings to it pours out abominations. Therefore the Lord brought upon them extraordinary afflictions, and destroyed them utterly. The Lord has cast down the thrones of rulers, and has seated the lowly in their place. The Lord has plucked up the roots of the nations, and has planted the humble in their place. The Lord has overthrown the lands of the nations, and has destroyed them to the foundations of the earth. He has removed some of them and destroyed them, and has extinguished the memory of them from the earth. Pride was not created for men, nor fierce anger for those born of women.

A Reading (Lesson) from the Revelation to John [9:1-12]

The fifth angel blew his trumpet, and I saw a star fallen from heaven to earth, and he was given the key of the shaft of the bottomless pit; he opened the shaft of the bottomless pit, and from the shaft rose smoke like the smoke of a great furnace, and the sun and the air were darkened with the smoke from the shaft. Then from the smoke came locusts on the earth, and they were given power like the power of scorpions of the earth; they were told not to harm the grass of the earth or any green growth or any tree, but only those of mankind who have not the seal of God upon their foreheads; they were allowed to torture them for five months, but not to kill them, and their torture was like the torture of a scorpion, when it stings a man. And in those days men will seek death and will not find it; they will long to die, and death will fly from them. In appearance the locusts were like horses arrayed for battle; on their heads were what looked like crowns of gold; their faces were like human faces, their hair like women's hair, and their teeth like lions' teeth; they had scales like iron breastplates, and the noise of their wings was like the noise of many chariots with horses rushing into battle. They have tails like scorpions, and stings, and their power of hurting men for five months lies in their tails. They have as king over them the angel of the bottomless pit; his name in Hebrew is Abaddon, and in Greek he is called Apol'lyon. The first woe has passed; behold, two woes are still to come.

A Reading (Lesson) from the Gospel according to Luke
[10:25-37]

And behold, a lawyer stood up to put Jesus to the test, saying, "Teacher, what shall I do to inherit eternal life?" He said to him, "What is written in the law? How do you read?" And he answered, "You shall love the Lord your God with all your heart, and with all your soul, and with all your strength, and with all your mind; and your neighbor as yourself." And he said to him, "You have answered right; do this, and you will live." But he, desiring to justify himself, said to Jesus, "And who is my neighbor?" Jesus replied, "A man was going down from Jerusalem to Jericho, and he fell among robbers, who stripped him and beat him, and departed, leaving him half dead. Now by chance a priest was going down that road; and when he saw him he passed by on the other side. So likewise a Levite, when he came to the place and saw him, passed by on the other side. But a Samaritan, as he journeyed, came to where he was; and when he saw him, he had compassion, and went to him and bound up his wounds, pouring on oil and wine; then he set him on his own beast and brought him to an inn, and took care of him. And the next day he took out two denarii and gave them to the innkeeper, saying, 'Take care of him; and whatever more you spend, I will repay you when I come back.' Which of these three, do you think, proved neighbor to the man who fell among the robbers?" He said, "The one who showed mercy on him." And Jesus said to him, "Go and do likewise."

Friday

Psalm 31 [page 622]   ❖   *Psalm 35* [page 629]

A Reading (Lesson) from the Book of Ecclesiasticus [11:2-20]

Do not praise a man for his good looks, nor loathe a man because of his appearance. The bee is small among flying creatures, but her product is the best of sweet things. Do not boast about wearing fine clothes, nor exalt yourself in the day that you are honored; for the works of the Lord are wonderful, and his works are concealed from men. Many kings have had to sit on the ground, but one who was never thought of has worn a crown. Many rulers have been greatly disgraced, and illustrious men have been handed over to others. Do not find fault before you investigate; first consider, and then reprove. Do not answer before you have heard, nor interrupt a speaker in the midst of his words. Do not argue about a matter which does not concern you, nor sit with sinners when they judge a case. My son, do not busy yourself with many matters; if you multiply activities you will not go unpunished, and if you pursue you will not overtake, and by fleeing you will not escape. There is a man who works, and toils, and presses on, but is so much the more in want. There is another who is slow and needs help, who lacks strength and abounds in poverty; but the eyes of the Lord look upon him for his good; he lifts him out of his low estate and raises up his head, so that many are amazed at him. Good things and bad, life and death, poverty and wealth, come from the Lord. The gift of the Lord endures for those who are godly, and what he approves will have lasting success. There is a man who is rich through his diligence and self-denial, and this is the reward allotted to him: when he says, "I have found rest, and now I shall enjoy my goods!" he does not know how much time will pass until he leaves them to others and dies. Stand by your covenant and attend to it, and grow old in your work.

A Reading (Lesson) from the Revelation to John [9:13-21]

The sixth angel blew his trumpet, and I heard a voice from the four horns of the golden altar before God, saying to the sixth angel who had the trumpet, "Release the four angels who are bound at the great river Eu-phra'tes." So the four angels were released, who had been held ready for the hour, the day, the month, and the year, to kill a third of mankind. The number of the troops of cavalry was twice ten thousand times ten thousand; I heard their number. And this was how I saw the horses in my vision: the riders wore breastplates the color of fire and of sapphire and of sulphur, and the heads of the horses were like lions' heads, and fire and smoke and sulphur issued from their mouths. By these three plagues a third of mankind was killed, by the fire and smoke and sulphur issuing from their mouths. For the power of the horses is in their mouths and in their tails; their tails are like serpents, with heads, and by means of them they wound. The rest of mankind, who were not killed by these plagues, did not repent of the works of their hands nor give up worshiping demons and idols of gold and silver and bronze and stone and wood, which cannot either see or hear or walk; nor did they repent of their murders or their sorceries or their immorality or their thefts.

A Reading (Lesson) from the Gospel according to Luke [10:38-42]

As Jesus and the disciples went on their way, he entered a village; and a woman named Martha received him into her house. And she had a sister called Mary, who sat at the Lord's feet and listened to his teaching. But Martha was distracted with much serving; and she went to him and said, "Lord, do you not care that my sister has left me to serve alone? Tell her then to help me." But the Lord answered her, "Martha, Martha, you are anxious and troubled about many things; one thing is needful. Mary has chosen the good portion, which shall not be taken away from her."

Saturday

Psalm 30 [page 621],   *Psalm 32* [page 624]   ❖
Psalm 42 [page 643],   *Psalm 43* [page 644]

A Reading (Lesson) from the Book of Ecclesiasticus [15:9-20]

A hymn of praise is not fitting on the lips of a sinner, for it has not been sent from the Lord. For a hymn of praise should be uttered in wisdom, and the Lord will prosper it. Do not say, "Because of the Lord I left the right way"; for he will not do what he hates. Do not say, "It was he who led me astray"; for he has no need of a sinful man. The Lord hates all abominations, and they are not loved by those who fear him. It was he who created man in the beginning, and left him in the power of his inclination. If you will, you can keep the commandments, and to act faithfully is a matter of your own choice. He has placed before you fire and water: stretch out your hand for whichever you wish. Before a man are life and death, and whichever he chooses will be given to him. For great is the wisdom of the Lord; he is mighty in power and sees everything; his eyes are on those who fear him, and he knows every deed of man. He has not commanded any one to be ungodly, and he has not given any one permission to sin.

A Reading (Lesson) from the Revelation to John [10:1-11]

I saw another mighty angel coming down from heaven, wrapped in a cloud, with a rainbow over his head, and his face was like the sun, and his legs like pillars of fire. He has a little scroll open in his hand. And he set his right foot on the sea, and his left foot on the land, and called out with a loud voice, like a lion roaring; when he called out, the seven thunders sounded. And when the seven thunders had sounded, I was about to write, but I heard a voice from heaven saying, "Seal up what the seven thunders have said, and do not write it down." And the angel whom I saw standing on the sea and land lifted up his right hand to heaven and swore by him who lives for ever and ever, who created heaven and what is in it, the earth and what is in it, and the sea and what is in it, that there would be no more delay, but that in the days of the trumpet call to be sounded by the seventh angel, the mystery of God, as he announced to his servants the prophets, should be fulfilled. Then the voice which I had heard from heaven spoke to me again, saying, "Go, take the scroll which is open in the hand of the angel who is standing on the sea and on the land." So I went to the angel and told him to give me the little scroll; and he said to me, "Take it and eat; it will be bitter to your stomach, but sweet as honey in your mouth." And I took the little scroll from the hand of the angel and ate it; it was sweet as honey in my mouth, but when I had eaten it my stomach was made bitter. And I was told, "You must again prophesy about many peoples and nations and tongues and kings."

Luke 11:1-13   [page 56 above]

Proper 25   *Week of the Sunday closest to October 26*

Sunday

Psalm 63:1-8(9-11) [page 670],
Psalm 98 [page 727]   ❖   *Psalm 103* [page 733]

A Reading (Lesson) from the Book of Ecclesiasticus
[18:19-33]

Before you speak, learn, and before you fall ill, take care of your health. Before judgment, examine yourself, and in the hour of visitation you will find forgiveness. Before falling ill, humble yourself, and when you are on the point of sinning, turn back. Let nothing hinder you from paying a vow promptly, and do not wait until death to be released from it. Before making a vow, prepare yourself; and do not be like a man who tempts the Lord. Think of his wrath on the day of death, and of the moment of vengeance when he turns away his face. In the time of plenty think of the time of hunger; in the days of wealth think of poverty and need. From morning to evening conditions change, and all things move swiftly before the Lord. A wise man is cautious in everything, and in days of sin he guards against wrongdoing. Every intelligent man knows wisdom, and he praises the one who finds her. Those who understand sayings become skilled themselves, and pour forth apt proverbs. Do not follow your base desires, but restrain your appetites. If you allow your soul to take pleasure in base desire, it will make you the laughingstock of your enemies. Do not revel in great luxury, lest you become impoverished by its expense. Do not become a beggar by feasting with borrowed money, when you have nothing in your purse.

A Reading (Lesson) from the First Letter of Paul to the Corinthians [10:15-24]

I speak as to sensible men; judge for yourselves what I say. The cup of blessing which we bless, is it not a participation in the blood of Christ? The bread which we break, is it not a participation in the body of Christ? Because there is one bread, we who are many are one body, for we all partake of the one bread. Consider the people of Israel; are not those who eat the sacrifices partners in the altar? What do I imply then? That food offered to idols is anything, or that an idol is anything? No, I imply that what pagans sacrifice they offer to demons and not to God. I do not want you to be partners with demons. You cannot drink the cup of the Lord and the cup of demons. You cannot partake of the table of the Lord and the table of demons. Shall we provoke the Lord to jealousy? Are we stronger than he? "All things are lawful," but not all things are helpful. "All things are lawful," but not all things build up. Let no one seek his own good, but the good of his neighbor.

A Reading (Lesson) from the Gospel according to Matthew [18:15-20]

Jesus said to the disciples, "If your brother sins against you, go and tell him his fault, between you and him alone. If he listens to you, you have gained your brother. But if he does not listen, take one or two others along with you, that every word may be confirmed by the evidence of two or three witnesses. If he refuses to listen to them, tell it to the church; and if he refuses to listen even to the church, let him be to you as a Gentile and a tax collector. Truly, I say to you, whatever you bind on earth shall be bound in heaven, and whatever you loose on earth shall be loosed in heaven. Again I say to you, if two of you agree on earth about anything they ask, it will be done for them by my Father in heaven. For where two or three are gathered in my name, there am I in the midst of them."

Monday

Psalm 41 [page 641], *Psalm 52* [page 657] ❖
Psalm 44 [page 645]

A Reading (Lesson) from the Book of Ecclesiasticus
[19:4-17]

One who trusts others too quickly is lightminded, and one who sins does wrong to himself. One who rejoices in wickedness will be condemned, and for one who hates gossip evil is lessened. Never repeat a conversation, and you will lose nothing at all. With friend or foe do not report it, and unless it would be a sin for you, do not disclose it; for some one has heard you and watched you, and when the time comes he will hate you. Have you heard a word? Let it die with you. Be brave! It will not make you burst! With such a word a fool will suffer pangs like a woman in labor with a child. Like an arrow stuck in the flesh of the thigh, so is a word inside a fool. Question a friend, perhaps he did not do it; but if he did anything, so that he may do it no more. Question a neighbor, perhaps he did not say it; but if he said it, so that he may not say it again. Question a friend, for often it is slander; so do not believe everything you hear. A person may make a slip without intending it. Who has never sinned with his tongue? Question your neighbor before you threaten him; and let the law of the Most High take its course.

A Reading (Lesson) from the Revelation to John [11:1-14]

Then I was given a measuring rod like a staff, and I was told: "Rise and measure the temple of God and the altar and those who worship there, but do not measure the court outside the temple; leave that out, for it is given over to the nations, and they will trample over the holy city for forty-two months. And I will grant my two witnesses power to prophesy for one thousand two hundred and sixty days, clothed in sackcloth." These are the two olive trees and the two lampstands which stand before the Lord of the earth. And if any one would harm them, fire pours from their mouth and consumes their foes; if any one would harm them, thus he is doomed to be killed. They have power to shut the sky, that no rain may fall during the days of their prophesying, and they have power over the waters to turn them into blood, and to smite the earth with every plague, as often as they desire. And when they have finished their testimony, the beast that ascends from the bottomless pit will make war upon them and conquer them and kill them, and their dead bodies will lie in the street of the great city which is allegorically called Sodom and Egypt, where their Lord was crucified. For three days and a half men from the peoples and tribes and tongues and nations gaze at their dead bodies and refuse to let them be placed in a tomb, and those who dwell on the earth will rejoice over them and make merry and exchange presents, because these two prophets had been a torment to those who dwell on the earth. But after three and a half days a breath of life from God entered them, and they stood up on their feet, and great fear fell on those who saw them. Then they heard a loud voice from heaven saying to them,

"Come up hither!" And in the sight of their foes they went up to heaven in a cloud. And at that hour there was a great earthquake, and a tenth of the city fell; seven thousand people were killed in the earthquake, and the rest were terrified and gave glory to the God of heaven. The second woe has passed; behold, the third woe is soon to come.

A Reading (Lesson) from the Gospel according to Luke [11:14-26]

Jesus was casting out a demon that was dumb; when the demon had gone out, the dumb man spoke, and the people marveled. But some of them said, "He casts out demons by Be-el'zebul, the prince of demons"; while others, to test him, sought from him a sign from heaven. But he, knowing their thoughts, said to them, "Every kingdom divided against itself is laid waste, and a divided household falls. And if Satan also is divided against himself, how will his kingdom stand? For you say that I cast out demons by Be-el'zebul. And if I cast out demons by Be-el'zebul, by whom do your sons cast them out? Therefore they shall be your judges. But if it is by the finger of God that I cast out demons, then the kingdom of God has come upon you. When a strong man, fully armed, guards his own palace, his goods are in peace; but when one stronger than he assails him and overcomes him, he takes away his armor in which he trusted, and divides his spoil. He who is not with me is against me, and he who does not gather with me scatters. When the unclean spirit has gone out of a man, he passes through waterless places seeking rest; and finding none he says, 'I will return to my house from which I came.' And when he comes he finds it swept and put in order. Then he goes and brings seven other spirits more evil than himself, and they enter and dwell there; and the last state of that man becomes worse than the first."

Tuesday

Psalm 45 [page 647] ❖ *Psalm 47* [page 650],
Psalm 48 [page 651]

A Reading (Lesson) from the Book of Ecclesiasticus
[24:1-12]

Wisdom will praise herself, and will glory in the midst of her people. In the assembly of the Most High she will open her mouth, and in the presence of his host she will glory: "I came forth from the mouth of the Most High, and covered the earth like a mist. I dwelt in high places, and my throne was in a pillar of cloud. Alone I have made the circuit of the vault of heaven and have walked in the depths of the abyss. In the waves of the sea, in the whole earth, and in every people and nation I have gotten a possession. Among all these I sought a resting place; I sought in whose territory I might lodge. Then the Creator of all things gave me a commandment, and the one who created me assigned a place for my tent. And he said, 'Make your dwelling in Jacob, and in Israel receive your inheritance.' From eternity, in the beginning, he created me, and for eternity I shall not cease to exist. In the holy tabernacle I ministered before him, and so I was established in Zion. In the beloved city likewise he gave me a resting place, and in Jerusalem was my dominion. So I took root in an honored people, in the portion of the Lord, who is their inheritance."

A Reading (Lesson) from the Revelation to John [11:14-19]

The second woe has passed; behold, the third woe is soon to come. Then the seventh angel blew his trumpet, and there were loud voices in heaven, saying, "The kingdom of the world has become the kingdom of our Lord and of his Christ, and he shall reign for ever and ever." And the twenty-four elders who sit on their thrones before God fell on their faces and worshiped God, saying, "We give thanks to thee, Lord God Almighty, who art and who wast, that thou hast taken thy great power and begun to reign. The nations raged, but thy wrath came, and the time for the dead to be judged, for rewarding thy servants, the prophets and saints, and those who fear thy name, both small and great, and for destroying the destroyers of the earth." Then God's temple in heaven was opened, and the ark of his covenant was seen within his temple; and there were flashes of lightning, voices, peals of thunder, an earthquake, and heavy hail.

A Reading (Lesson) from the Gospel according to Luke
[11:27-36]

As Jesus spoke, a woman in the crowd raised her voice and said to him, "Blessed is the womb that bore you, and the breasts that you sucked!" But he said, "Blessed rather are those who hear the word of God and keep it!" When the crowds were increasing, he began to say, "This generation is an evil generation; it seeks a sign, but no sign shall be given to it except the sign of Jonah. For as Jonah became a sign to the men of Nin'eveh, so will the Son of man be to this generation. The queen of the South will arise at the judgment with the men of this generation and condemn them; for she came from the ends of the earth to hear the wisdom of Solomon, and behold, something greater than Solomon is here. The men of Nin'eveh will arise at the judgment with this generation and condemn it; for they repented at the preaching of Jonah, and behold, something greater than Jonah is here. No one after lighting a lamp puts it in a cellar or under a bushel, but on a stand, that those who enter may see the light. Your eye is the lamp of your body; when your eye is sound, your whole body is full of light; but when it is not sound, your body is full of darkness. Therefore be careful lest the light in you be darkness. If then your whole body is full of light, having no part dark, it will be wholly bright, as when a lamp with its rays gives you light."

Wednesday

Psalm 119:49-72 [page 767] ❖ *Psalm 49* [page 652],
(Psalm 53 [page 658])

A Reading (Lesson) from the Book of Ecclesiasticus
[28:14-26]

Slander has shaken many, and scattered them from nation
to nation, and destroyed strong cities, and overturned the
houses of great men. Slander has driven away courageous
women, and deprived them of the fruit of their toil.
Whoever pays heed to slander will not find rest, nor will he
settle down in peace. The blow of a whip raises a welt, but
a blow of the tongue crushes the bones. Many have fallen
by the edge of the sword, but not so many as have fallen
because of the tongue. Happy is the man who is protected
from it, who has not been exposed to its anger, who has
not borne its yoke, and has not been bound with its fetters;
for its yoke is a yoke of iron, and its fetters are fetters of
bronze; its death is an evil death, and Hades is preferable
to it. It will not be master over the godly, and they will not
be burned in its flame. Those who forsake the Lord will fall
into its power; it will burn among them and will not be put
out. It will be sent out against them like a lion; like a
leopard it will mangle them. See that you fence in your
property with thorns, lock up your silver and gold, make
balances and scales for your words, and make a door and a
bolt for your mouth. Beware lest you err with your tongue,
lest you fall before him who lies in wait.

A Reading (Lesson) from the Revelation to John [12:1-6]

A great portent appeared in heaven, a woman clothed with
the sun, with the moon under her feet, and on her head a
crown of twelve stars; she was with child and she cried out
in her pangs of birth, in anguish for delivery. And another
portent appeared in heaven; behold, a great red dragon,
with seven heads and ten horns, and seven diadems upon

his heads. His tail swept down a third of the stars of heaven, and cast them to the earth. And the dragon stood before the woman who was about to bear a child, that he might devour her child when she brought it forth; she brought forth a male child, one who is to rule all the nations with a rod of iron, but her child was caught up to God and to his throne, and the woman fled into the wilderness, where she has a place prepared by God, in which to be nourished for one thousand two hundred and sixty days.

A Reading (Lesson) from the Gospel according to Luke [11:37-52]

While Jesus was speaking, a Pharisee asked him to dine with him; so he went in and sat at table. The Pharisee was astonished to see that he did not first wash before dinner. And the Lord said to him, "Now you Pharisees cleanse the outside of the cup and of the dish, but inside you are full of extortion and wickedness. You fools! Did not he who made the outside make the inside also? But give for alms those things which are within; and behold, everything is clean for you. But woe to you Pharisees! for you tithe mint and rue and every herb, and neglect justice and the love of God; these you ought to have done, without neglecting the others. Woe to you Pharisees! for you love the best seat in the synagogues and salutations in the market places. Woe to you! for you are like graves which are not seen, and men walk over them without knowing it." One of the lawyers answered him, "Teacher, in saying this you reproach us also." And he said, "Woe to you lawyers also! for you load men with burdens hard to bear, and you yourselves do not touch the burdens with one of your fingers. Woe to you! for you build the tombs of the prophets whom your fathers killed. So you are witnesses and consent to the deeds of your fathers; for they killed them, and you build their tombs. Therefore also the Wisdom of God said, 'I will send them prophets and apostles, some of whom they will kill and persecute,' that the blood of all the prophets, shed from the foundation of the world, may be required of this generation, from the blood of Abel to the blood of Zechari'ah, who perished between the altar and the sanctuary. Yes, I tell you, it shall be required of this generation. Woe to you lawyers! for you have taken away the key of knowledge; you did not enter yourselves and you hindered those who were entering."

Thursday

Psalm 50 [page 654]   ❖   *(Psalm 59* [page 665],
Psalm 60 [page 667])   *or*   *Psalm 103* [page 733]

A Reading (Lesson) from the Book of Ecclesiasticus
[31:12-18,25—32:2]

Are you seated at the table of a great man? Do not be greedy at it, and do not say, "There is certainly much upon it!" Remember that a greedy eye is a bad thing. What has been created more greedy than the eye? Therefore it sheds tears from every face. Do not reach out your hand for everything you see, and do not crowd your neighbor at the dish. Judge your neighbor's feelings by your own, and in every matter be thoughtful. Eat like a human being what is set before you, and do not chew greedily, lest you be hated. Be the first to stop eating, for the sake of good manners, and do not be insatiable, lest you give offense. If you are seated among many persons, do not reach out your hand before they do. Do not aim to be valiant over wine, for wine has destroyed many. Fire and water prove the temper of steel, so wine tests hearts in the strife of the proud. Wine is like life to men, if you drink it in moderation. What is life to a man who is without wine? It has been created to make men glad. Wine drunk in season and temperately is rejoicing of heart and gladness of soul. Wine drunk to excess is bitterness of soul, with provocation and stumbling. Drunkenness increases the anger of a fool to his injury, reducing his strength and adding wounds. Do not reprove your neighbor at a banquet of wine, and do not despise him in his merrymaking; speak no word of reproach to him, and do not afflict him by making demands of him. If they make you master of the feast, do not exalt yourself; be among them as one of them; take good care of them and then be seated; when you have fulfilled your duties, take your place, that you may be merry on their account and receive a wreath for your excellent leadership.

A Reading (Lesson) from the Revelation to John [12:7-17]

Now war arose in heaven, Michael and his angels fighting against the dragon; and the dragon and his angels fought, but they were defeated and there was no longer any place for them in heaven. And the great dragon was thrown down, that ancient serpent, who is called the Devil and Satan, the deceiver of the whole world—he was thrown down to the earth, and his angels were thrown down with him. And I heard a loud voice in heaven, saying, "Now the salvation and the power and the kingdom of our God and the authority of his Christ have come, for the accuser of our brethren has been thrown down, who accuses them day and night before our God. And they have conquered him by the blood of the Lamb and by the word of their testimony; for they loved not their lives even unto death. Rejoice then, O heaven and you that dwell therein! But woe to you, O earth and sea, for the devil has come down to you in great wrath, because he knows that his time is short!" And when the dragon saw that he had been thrown down to the earth, he pursued the woman who had borne the male child. But the woman was given the two wings of the great eagle that she might fly from the serpent into the wilderness, to the place where she is to be nourished for a time, and times, and half a time. The serpent poured water like a river out of his mouth after the woman, to sweep her away with the flood. But the earth came to the help of the woman, and the earth opened its mouth and swallowed the river which the dragon had poured from his mouth. Then the dragon was angry with the woman, and went off to make war on the rest of her offspring, on those who keep the commandments of God and bear testimony to Jesus. And he stood on the sand of the sea.

A Reading (Lesson) from the Gospel according to Luke
[11:53—12:12]

As Jesus went away from there, the scribes and the Pharisees began to press him hard, and to provoke him to speak of many things, lying in wait for him, to catch at something he might say. In the meantime, when so many thousands of the multitude had gathered together that they trod upon one another, he began to say to his disciples first, "Beware of the leaven of the Pharisees, which is hypocrisy. Nothing is covered up that will not be revealed, or hidden that will not be known. Therefore whatever you have said in the dark shall be heard in the light, and what you have whispered in private rooms shall be proclaimed upon the housetops. I tell you, my friends, do not fear those who kill the body, and after that have no more that they can do. But I will warn you whom to fear: fear him who, after he has killed, has power to cast into hell; yes, I tell you, fear him! Are not five sparrows sold for two pennies? And not one of them is forgotten before God. Why, even the hairs of your head are all numbered. Fear not; you are of more value than many sparrows. And I tell you, every one who acknowledges me before men, the Son of man also will acknowledge before the angels of God; but he who denies me before men will be denied before the angels of God. And every one who speaks a word against the Son of man will be forgiven; but he who blasphemes against the Holy Spirit will not be forgiven. And when they bring you before the synagogues and the rulers and the authorities, do not be anxious how or what you are to answer or what you are to say; for the Holy Spirit will teach you in that very hour what you ought to say."

Friday

Psalm 40 [page 640], *Psalm 54* [page 659]   ❖
Psalm 51 [page 656]

A Reading (Lesson) from the Book of Ecclesiasticus
[34:1-8,18-22]

A man of no understanding has vain and false hopes, and dreams give wings to fools. As one who catches at a shadow and pursues the wind, so is he who gives heed to dreams. The vision of dreams is this against that, the likeness of a face confronting a face. From an unclean thing what will be made clean? And from something false what will be true? Divinations and omens and dreams are folly, and like a woman in travail the mind has fancies. Unless they are sent from the Most High as a visitation, do not give your mind to them. For dreams have deceived many, and those who put their hope in them have failed. Without such deceptions the law will be fulfilled, and wisdom is made perfect in truthful lips. If one sacrifices from what has been wrongfully obtained, the offering is blemished; the gifts of the lawless are not acceptable. The Most High is not pleased with the offerings of the ungodly; and he is not propitiated for sins by a multitude of sacrifices. Like one who kills a son before his father's eyes is the man who offers a sacrifice from the property of the poor. The bread of the needy is the life of the poor; whoever deprives them of it is a man of blood. To take away a neighbor's living is to murder him; to deprive an employee of his wages is to shed blood.

A Reading (Lesson) from the Revelation to John [13:1-10]

I saw a beast rising out of the sea, with ten horns and seven heads, with ten diadems upon its horns and a blasphemous name upon its heads. And the beast that I saw was like a leopard, its feet were like a bear's, and its mouth was like a lion's mouth. And to it the dragon gave his power and his throne and great authority. One of its heads seemed to have a mortal wound, but its mortal wound was healed, and the whole earth followed the beast with wonder. Men worshiped the dragon, for he had given his authority to the beast, and they worshiped the beast, saying, "Who is like the beast, and who can fight against it?" And the beast was given a mouth uttering haughty and blasphemous words, and it was allowed to exercise authority for forty-two months; it opened its mouth to utter blasphemies against God, blaspheming his name and his dwelling, that is, those who dwell in heaven. Also it was allowed to make war on the saints and to conquer them. And authority was given it over every tribe and people and tongue and nation, and all who dwell on earth will worship it, every one whose name has not been written before the foundation of the world in the book of life of the Lamb that was slain. If any one has an ear, let him hear: If any one is to be taken captive, to captivity he goes; if any one slays with the sword, with the sword must he be slain. Here is a call for the endurance and faith of the saints.

A Reading (Lesson) from the Gospel according to Luke [12:13-31]

One of the multitudes said to Jesus, "Teacher, bid my brother to divide the inheritance with me." But he said to him, "Man, who made me a judge or divider over you?" And he said to them, "Take heed, and beware of all covetousness; for a man's life does not consist in the abundance of his possessions." And he told them a parable, saying, "The land of a rich man brought forth plentifully; and he thought to himself, 'What shall I do, for I have nowhere to store my crops?' And he said, 'I will do this: I will pull down my barns, and build larger ones; and there I will store all my grain and my goods. And I will say to my soul, Soul, you have ample goods laid up for many years; take your ease, eat, drink, be merry.' But God said to him, 'Fool! this night your soul is required of you; and the things you have prepared, whose will they be?' So is he who lays up treasure for himself, and is not rich toward God." And he said to his disciples, "Therefore I tell you, do not be anxious about your life, what you shall eat, nor about your body, what you shall put on. For life is more than food, and the body more than clothing. Consider the ravens: they neither sow nor reap, they have neither storehouse nor barn, and yet God feeds them. Of how much more value are you than the birds! And which of you by being anxious can add a cubit to his span of life? If then you are not able to do as small a thing as that, why are you anxious about the rest? Consider the lilies, how they grow; they neither toil nor spin; yet I tell you, even Solomon in all his glory was not arrayed like one of these. But if God so clothes the grass which is alive in the field today and tomorrow is thrown into the oven, how much more will he clothe you, O men of little faith! And do not seek what you are to eat and what you are to drink, nor be of anxious mind. For all the nations of the world seek these things; and your Father knows that you need them. Instead, seek his kingdom, and these things shall be yours as well."

Saturday

Psalm 55 [page 660]   ❖   *Psalm 138* [page 793],
Psalm 139:1-17(18-23) [page 794]

A Reading (Lesson) from the Book of Ecclesiasticus
[35:1-17]

He who keeps the law makes many offerings; he who

heeds the commandments sacrifices a peace offering. He who returns a kindness offers fine flour, and he who gives alms sacrifices a thank offering. To keep from wickedness is pleasing to the Lord, and to forsake unrighteousness is atonement. Do not appear before the Lord empty-handed, for all these things are to be done because of the commandment. The offering of a righteous man anoints the altar, and its pleasing odor rises before the Most High. The sacrifice of a righteous man is acceptable, and the memory of it will not be forgotten. Glorify the Lord generously, and do not stint the first fruits of your hands. With every gift show a cheerful face, and dedicate your tithe with gladness. Give to the Most High as he has given, and as generously as your hand has found. For the Lord is the one who repays, and he will repay you sevenfold. Do not offer him a bribe, for he will not accept it; and do not trust to an unrighteous sacrifice; for the Lord is the judge, and with him is no partiality. He will not show partiality in the case of a poor man; and he will listen to the prayer of one who is wronged. He will not ignore the supplication of the fatherless, nor the widow when she pours out her story. Do not the tears of the widow run down her cheek as she cries out against him who has caused them to fall? He whose service is pleasing to the Lord will be accepted, and his prayer will reach to the clouds. The prayer of the humble pierces the clouds, and he will not be consoled until it reaches the Lord; he will not desist until the Most High visits him, and does justice for the righteous, and executes judgment.

A Reading (Lesson) from the Revelation to John [13:11-18]

Then I saw another beast which rose out of the earth; it had two horns like a lamb and it spoke like a dragon. It exercises all the authority of the first beast in its presence, and makes the earth and its inhabitants worship the first beast, whose mortal wound was healed. It works great signs, even making fire come down from heaven to earth in the sight of men; and by the signs which it is allowed to work in the presence of the beast, it deceives those who dwell on earth, bidding them make an image for the beast which was wounded by the sword and yet lived; and it was allowed to give breath to the image of the beast so that the image of the beast should even speak, and to cause those who would not worship the image of the beast to be slain. Also it causes all, both small and great, both rich and poor, both free and slave, to be marked on the right hand or the forehead, so that no one can buy or sell unless he has the mark, that is, the name of the beast or the number of its name. This calls for wisdom: let him who has understanding reckon the number of the beast, for it is a human number, its number is six hundred and sixty-six.

A Reading (Lesson) from the Gospel according to Luke
[12:32-48]

Jesus said to the disciples, "Fear not, little flock, for it is your Father's good pleasure to give you the kingdom. Sell your possessions, and give alms; provide yourselves with purses that do not grow old, with a treasure in the heavens that does not fail, where no thief approaches and no moth destroys. For where your treasure is, there will your heart be also. Let your loins be girded and your lamps burning, and be like men who are waiting for their master to come home from the marriage feast, so that they may open to him at once when he comes and knocks. Blessed are those servants whom the master finds awake when he comes; truly, I say to you, he will gird himself and have them sit at table, and he will come and serve them. If he comes in the second watch, or in the third, and finds them so, blessed are those servants! But know this, that if the householder had known at what hour the thief was coming, he would not have left his house to be broken into. You also must be ready; for the Son of man is coming at an unexpected hour." Peter said, "Lord, are you telling this parable for us or for all?" And the Lord said, "Who then is the faithful and wise steward, whom his master will set over his household, to give them their portion of food at the proper time? Blessed is that servant whom his master when he comes will find so doing. Truly, I say to you, he will set him over all his possessions. But if that servant says to himself, 'My master is delayed in coming,' and begins to beat the menservants and the maidservants, and to eat and drink and get drunk, the master of that servant will come on a day when he does not expect him and at an hour he does not know, and will punish him, and put him with the unfaithful. And that servant who knew his master's will, but did not make ready or act according to his will, shall receive a severe beating. But he who did not know, and did what deserved a beating, shall receive a light beating. Every one to whom much is given, of him will much be required; and of him to whom men commit much they will demand the more."

Proper 26 *Week of the Sunday closest to November 2*

Sunday

Psalm 24 [page 613], *Psalm 29* [page 620] ❖
Psalm 8 [page 592], *Psalm 84* [page 707]

A Reading (Lesson) from the Book of Ecclesiasticus
[36:1-17]

Have mercy upon us, O Lord, the God of all, and look upon us, and cause the fear of thee to fall upon all the nations. Lift up thy hand against foreign nations and let them see thy might. As in us thou hast been sanctified before them, so in them be thou magnified before us; and let them know thee, as we have known that there is no God but thee, O Lord. Show signs anew, and work further wonders; make thy hand and thy right arm glorious.

Rouse thy anger and pour out thy wrath; destroy the adversary and wipe out the enemy. Hasten the day, and remember the appointed time, and let people recount thy might deeds. Let him who survives be consumed in the fiery wrath, and may those who harm thy people meet destruction. Crush the heads of the rulers of the enemy, who say, "There is no one but ourselves." Gather all the tribe of Jacob, and give them their inheritance, as at the beginning. Have mercy, O Lord, upon the people called by thy name, upon Israel, whom thou hast likened to a first-born son. Have pity on the city of thy sanctuary, Jerusalem, the place of thy rest. Fill Zion with the celebration of thy wondrous deeds, and thy temple with thy glory. Bear witness to those whom thou didst create in the beginning, and fulfil the prophecies spoken in thy name. Reward those who wait for thee, and let thy prophets be found trustworthy. Hearken, O Lord, to the prayer of thy servants, according to the blessing of Aaron for thy people, and all who are on the earth will know that thou art the Lord, the God of the ages.

A Reading (Lesson) from the First Letter of Paul to the Corinthians [12:27—13:13]

Now you are the body of Christ and individually members of it. And God has appointed in the church first apostles, second prophets, third teachers, then workers of miracles, then healers, helpers, administrators, speakers in various kinds of tongues. Are all apostles? Are all prophets? Are all teachers? Do all work miracles? Do all possess gifts of healing? Do all speak with tongues? Do all interpret? But earnestly desire the higher gifts. And I will show you a still more excellent way. If I speak in the tongues of men and of angels, but have not love, I am a noisy gong or a clanging cymbal. And if I have prophetic powers, and understand all mysteries and all knowledge, and if I have all faith, so as to remove mountains, but have not love, I am nothing. If I give away all I have, and if I deliver my body to be burned, but have not love, I gain nothing. Love is patient and kind; love is not jealous or boastful; it is not arrogant or rude. Love does not insist on its own way; it is not irritable or resentful; it does not rejoice at wrong, but rejoices in the right. Loves bears all things, believes all things, hopes all things, endures all things. Love never ends; as for prophecies, they will pass away; as for tongues, they will cease; as for knowledge, it will pass away. For our knowledge is imperfect and our prophecy is imperfect; but when the perfect comes, the imperfect will pass away. When I was a child, I spoke like a child, I thought like a child, I reasoned like a child; when I became a man, I gave up childish ways. For now we see in a mirror dimly, but then face to face. Now I know in part; then I shall understand fully, even as I have been fully understood. So faith, hope, love abide, these three; but the greatest of these is love.

Matthew 18:21-35   [page 102 above]

Monday

Psalm 56 [page 662],   *Psalm 57* [page 663],
(Psalm 58 [page 664])   ❖   *Psalm 64* [page 671],
Psalm 65 [page 672]

A Reading (Lesson) from the Book of Ecclesiasticus [38:24-34]

The wisdom of the scribe depends on the opportunity of leisure; and he who has little business may become wise. How can he become wise who handles the plow, and who glories in the shaft of a goad, who drives oxen and is occupied with their work, and whose talk is about bulls? He sets his heart on plowing furrows, and he is careful about fodder for the heifers. So too is every craftsman and master workman who labors by night as well as by day;

those who cut the signets of seals, each is diligent in making a great variety; he sets his heart on painting a lifelike image, and he is careful to finish his work. So too is the smith sitting by the anvil, intent upon his handiwork in iron; the breath of the fire melts his flesh, and he wastes away in the heat of the furnace; he inclines his ear to the sound of the hammer, and his eyes are on the pattern of the object. He sets his heart on finishing his handiwork, and he is careful to complete its decoration. So too is the potter sitting at his work and turning the wheel with his feet; he is always deeply concerned over his work, and all his output is by number. He molds the clay with his arm and makes it pliable with his feet; he sets his heart to finish the glazing, and he is careful to clean the furnace. All these rely upon their hands, and each is skilful in his own work. Without them a city cannot be established, and men can neither sojourn nor live there. Yet they are not sought out for the council of the people, nor do they attain eminence in the public assembly. They do not sit in the judge's seat, nor do they understand the sentence of judgment; they cannot expound discipline or judgment, and they are not found using proverbs. But they keep stable the fabric of the world, and their prayer is in the practice of their trade.

A Reading (Lesson) from the Revelation to John [14:1-13]

Then I looked, and lo, on Mount Zion stood the Lamb, and with him a hundred and forty-four thousand who had his name and his Father's name written on their foreheads. And I heard a voice from heaven like the sound of many waters and like the sound of loud thunder; the voice I heard was like the sound of harpers playing on their harps, and they sing a new song before the throne and before the four living creatures and before the elders. No one could learn that song except the hundred and forty-four thousand who had been redeemed from the earth. It is these who have not defiled themselves with women, for they are chaste; it is these who follow the Lamb wherever he goes; these have been redeemed from mankind as first fruits for God and the Lamb, and in their mouth no lie was found, for they are spotless. Then I saw another angel flying in midheaven, with an eternal gospel to proclaim to those who dwell on earth, to every nation and tribe and tongue and people; and he said with a loud voice, "Fear God and give him glory, for the hour of his judgment has come; and worship him who made heaven and earth, the sea and the fountains of water." Another angel, a second, followed, saying, "Fallen, fallen is Babylon the great, she who made all nations drink the wine of her impure passions." And another angel, a third, followed them, saying with a loud voice, "If any one worships the beast and its image, and receives a mark on his forehead or on his hand, he also shall drink the wine of God's wrath, poured unmixed into the cup of his anger, and he shall be tormented with fire and sulphur in the presence of the holy angels and in the presence of the Lamb. And the smoke of their torment goes up for ever and ever; and they have no rest, day or night, these worshipers of the beast and its image, and whoever receives the mark of its name." Here is a call for the endurance of the saints, those who keep the commandments of God and the faith of Jesus. And I heard a voice from heaven saying, "Write this: Blessed are the dead who die in the Lord henceforth." "Blessed indeed," says the Spirit, "that they may rest from their labors, for their deeds follow them!"

A Reading (Lesson) from the Gospel according to Luke
[12:49-59]

Jesus said to the disciples, "I came to cast fire upon the earth; and would that it were already kindled! I have a baptism to be baptized with; and how I am constrained until it is accomplished! Do you think that I have come to give peace on earth? No, I tell you, but rather division; for henceforth in one house there will be five divided, three against two and two against three; they will be divided, father against son and son against father, mother against daughter and daughter against her mother, mother-in-law against her daughter-in-law and daughter-in-law against her mother-in-law." He also said to the multitudes, "When you see a cloud rising in the west, you say at once, 'A shower is coming'; and so it happens. And when you see the south wind blowing, you say, 'There will be scorching heat'; and it happens. You hypocrites! You know how to interpret the appearance of earth and sky; but why do you not know how to interpret the present time? And why do you not judge for yourselves what is right? As you go with your accuser before the magistrate, make an effort to settle with him on the way, lest he drag you to the judge, and the judge hand you over to the officer, and the officer put you in prison. I tell you, you will never get out till you have paid the very last copper."

Tuesday

Psalm 61 [page 668],   *Psalm 62* [page 669]   ❖
Psalm 68:1-20(21-23)24-36 [page 676]

A Reading (Lesson) from the Book of Ecclesiasticus
[43:1-22]

The pride of the heavenly heights is the clear firmament, the appearance of heaven in a spectacle of glory. The sun, when it appears, making proclamation as it goes forth, is a marvelous instrument, the work of the Most High. At noon it parches the land; and who can withstand its burning heat? A man tending a furnace works in burning heat, but the sun burns the mountains three times as much; it breathes our fiery vapors, and with bright beams it blinds the eyes. Great is the Lord who made it; and at his command it hastens on its course. He made the moon also, to serve in its season to mark the times and to be an everlasting sign. From the moon comes the sign for feast

days, a light that wanes when it has reached the full. The
month is named for the moon, increasing marvelously in
its phases, an instrument of the hosts on high shining forth
in the firmament of heaven. The glory of the stars is the
beauty of heaven, a gleaming array in the heights of the
Lord. At the command of the Holy One they stand as
ordered, they never relax in their watches. Look upon the
rainbow, and praise him who made it, exceedingly
beautiful in its brightness. It encircles the heaven with its
glorious arc; the hands of the Most High have stretched it
out. By his command he sends the driving snow and speeds
the lightnings of his judgment. Therefore the storehouses
are opened, and the clouds fly forth like birds. In his
majesty he amasses the clouds, and the hailstones are
broken in pieces. At his appearing the mountains are
shaken; at his will the south wind blows. The voice of his
thunder rebukes the earth; so do the tempest from the
north and the whirlwind. He scatters the snow like birds
flying down, and its descent is like locusts alighting. The
eye marvels at the beauty of its whiteness, and the mind is
amazed at its falling. He pours the hoarfrost upon the
earth like salt, and when it freezes, it becomes pointed
thorns. The cold north wind blows, and ice freezes over the
water; it rests upon every pool of water, and the water puts
it on like a breastplate. He consumes the mountains and
burns up the wilderness, and withers the tender grass like
fire. A mist quickly heals all things; when the dew appears,
it refreshes from the heat.

A Reading (Lesson) from the Revelation to John
[14:14—15:8]

Then I looked, and lo, a white cloud, and seated on the
cloud one like a son of man, with a golden crown on his
head, and a sharp sickle in his hand. And another angel
came out of the temple, calling with a loud voice to him
who sat upon the cloud, "Put in your sickle, and reap, for

the hour to reap has come, for the harvest of the earth is fully ripe." So he who sat upon the cloud swung his sickle on the earth, and the earth was reaped. And another angel came out of the temple in heaven, and he too had a sharp sickle. Then another angel came out from the altar, the angel who has power over fire, and he called with a loud voice to him who had the sharp sickle, "Put in your sickle, and gather the clusters of the vine of the earth, for its grapes are ripe." So the angel swung his sickle on the earth and gathered the vintage of the earth, and threw it into the great wine press of the wrath of God; and the wine press was trodden outside the city, and blood flowed from the wine press, as high as a horse's bridle, for one thousand six hundred stadia. Then I saw another portent in heaven, great and wonderful, seven angels with seven plagues, which are the last, for with them the wrath of God is ended. And I saw what appeared to be a sea of glass mingled with fire, and those who had conquered the beast and its image and the number of its name, standing beside the sea of glass with harps of God in their hands. And they sing the song of Moses, the servant of God, and the song of the Lamb, saying, "Great and wonderful are thy deeds, O Lord God the Almighty! Just and true are thy ways, O Kings of the ages! Who shall not fear and glorify thy name, O Lord? For thou alone art holy. All nations shall come and worship thee, for thy judgments have been revealed." After this I looked, and the temple of the tent of witness in heaven was opened, and out of the temple came the seven angels with the seven plagues, robed in pure bright linen, and their breasts girded with golden girdles. And one of the four living creatures gave the seven angels seven golden bowls full of the wrath of God who lives for ever and ever; and the temple was filled with smoke from the glory of God and from his power, and no one could enter the temple until the seven plagues of the seven angels were ended.

A Reading (Lesson) from the Gospel according to Luke
[13:1-9]

There were some present at that very time who told Jesus of the Galileans whose blood Pilate had mingled with their sacrifices. And he answered them, "Do you think that these Galileans were worse sinners than all the other Galileans, because they suffered thus? I tell you, No; but unless you repent you will all likewise perish. Or those eighteen upon whom the tower in Silo'am fell and killed them, do you think that they were worse offenders than all the others who dwelt in Jerusalem? I tell you, No; but unless you repent you will all likewise perish." And he told this parable: "A man had a fig tree planted in his vineyard; and he came seeking fruit on it and found none. And he said to the vinedresser, 'Lo, these three years I have come seeking fruit on this fig tree, and I find none. Cut it down; why should it use up the ground?' And he answered him, 'Let it alone, sir, this year also, till I dig about it and put on manure. And if it bears fruit next year, well and good; but if not, you can cut it down.'"

Wednesday

Psalm 72 [page 685],   ❖   *Psalm 119:73-96* [page 769],

A Reading (Lesson) from the Book of Ecclesiasticus
[43:23-33]

By his counsel he stilled the great deep and planted islands in it. Those who sail the sea tell of its dangers, and we marvel at what we hear. For in it are strange and marvelous works, all kinds of living things, and huge creatures of the sea. Because of him his messenger finds the way, and by his word all things hold together. Though we speak much we cannot reach the end, and the sum of our words is: "He is the all." Where shall we find strength to praise him? For he is greater than all his works. Terrible is the Lord and very great, and marvelous is his power. When you praise the Lord, exalt him as much as you can; for he will surpass even that. When you exalt him, put forth all your strength, and do not grow weary, for you cannot praise him enough. Who has seen him and can describe him? Or who can extol him as he is? Many things greater than these lie hidden, for we have seen but few of his works. For the Lord has made all things, and to the godly he has granted wisdom.

A Reading (Lesson) from the Revelation to John [16:1-11]

Then I heard a loud voice from the temple telling the seven angels, "Go and pour out on the earth the seven bowls of the wrath of God." So the first angel went and poured his bowl on the earth, and foul and evil sores came upon the men who bore the mark of the beast and worshiped its image. The second angel poured his bowl into the sea, and it became like the blood of a dead man, and every living thing died that was in the sea. The third angel poured his bowl into the rivers and the fountains of water, and they became blood. And I heard the angel of water say, "Just art thou in these judgments, thou who art and wast, O Holy One. For men have shed the blood of saints and prophets, and thou hast given them blood to drink. It is their due!" And I heard the altar cry, "Yea, Lord God the Almighty, true and just are thy judgments!" The fourth angel poured his bowl on the sun, and it was allowed to scorch men with fire; men were scorched by the fierce heat, and they cursed the name of God who had power over these plagues, and they did not repent and give him glory. The fifth angel poured his bowl on the throne of the beast, and its kingdom was in darkness; men gnawed their tongues in anguish and cursed the God of heaven for their pain and sores, and did not repent of their deeds.

Luke 13:10-17 [page 128 above]

Thursday

(Psalm 70 [page 682]), *Psalm 71* [page 683] ❖
Psalm 74 [page 689]

A Reading (Lesson) from the Book of Ecclesiasticus
[44:1-15]

Let us now praise famous men, and our fathers in their
generations. The Lord apportioned to them great glory, his
majesty from the beginning. There were those who ruled in
their kingdoms, and were men renowned for their power,
giving counsel by their understanding, and proclaiming
prophecies; leaders of the people in their deliberations and
in understanding of learning for the people, wise in their
words of instruction; those who composed musical tunes,
and set forth verses in writing; rich men furnished with
resources, living peaceably in their habitations—all these
were honored in their generations, and were the glory of
their times. There are some of them who have left a name,
so that men declare their praise. And there are some who
have no memorial, who have perished as though they had
not lived; they have become as though they had not been
born, and so have their children after them. But these were
men of mercy, whose righteous deeds have not been
forgotten; their prosperity will remain with their
descendants, and their inheritance to their children's
children. Their descendants stand by the covenants; their
children also, for their sake. Their posterity will continue
for ever, and their glory will not be blotted out. Their
bodies were buried in peace, and their name lives to all
generations. Peoples will declare their wisdom, and the
congregation proclaims their praise.

A Reading (Lesson) from the Revelation to John [16:12-21]

The sixth angel poured his bowl on the great river
Eu-phra'tes, and its water was dried up, to prepare the way
for the kings from the east. And I saw, issuing from the

mouth of the dragon and from the mouth of the beast and from the mouth of the false prophet, three foul spirits like frogs; for they are demonic spirits, performing signs, who go abroad to the kings of the whole world, to assemble them for battle on the great day of God the Almighty. ("Lo, I am coming like a thief! Blessed is he who is awake, keeping his garments that he may not go naked and be seen exposed!") And they assembled them at the place which is called in Hebrew Armaged'don. The seventh angel poured his bowl into the air, and a loud voice came out of the temple, from the throne, saying, "It is done!" And there were flashes of lightning, voices, peals of thunder, and a great earthquake such as had never been since men were on the earth, so great was that earthquake. The great city was split into three parts, and the cities of the nations fell, and God remembered great Babylon, to make her drain the cup of the fury of his wrath. And every island fled away, and no mountains were to be found; and great hailstones, heavy as a hundredweight, dropped on men from heaven, till men cursed God for the plague of the hail, so fearful was that plague.

A Reading (Lesson) from the Gospel according to Luke
[13:18-30]

Jesus said to his adversaries, "What is the kindgom of God like? And to what shall I compare it? It is like a grain of mustard seed which a man took and sowed in his garden; and it grew and became a tree, and the birds of the air made nests in its branches." And he said again, "To what shall I compare the kingdom of God? It is like leaven which a woman took and hid in three measures of flour, till it was all leavened." He went on his way through towns and villages, teaching, and journeying toward Jerusalem. And some one said to him, "Lord, will those who are saved be few?" And he said to them, "Strive to enter by the narrow door; for many, I tell you, will seek to enter and will not be able. When once the householder has risen up and shut the door, you will begin to stand outside and to knock at the door, saying, 'Lord, open to us.' He will answer you, 'I do not know where you come from.' Then you will begin to say, 'We ate and drank in your presence, and you taught in our streets.' But he will say, 'I tell you, I do not know where you come from; depart from me, all you workers of iniquity!' There you will weep and gnash your teeth, when you see Abraham and Isaac and Jacob and all the prophets in the kingdom of God and you yourselves thrust out. And men will come from east and west, and from north and south, and sit at table in the kingdom of God. And behold, some are last who will be first, and some are first who will be last."

Friday

Psalm 69:1-23(24-30)31-38 [page 679] ❖
Psalm 73 [page 687]

A Reading (Lesson) from the Book of Ecclesiasticus
[50:1,11-24]

The leader of his brethren and the pride of his people was Simon the high priest, son of Oni'as, who in his life repaired the house, and in his time fortified the temple. When he put on his glorious robe and clothed himself with superb perfection and went up to the holy altar, he made the court of the sanctuary glorious. And when he received the portions from the hands of the priests, as he stood by the hearth of the altar with a garland of brethren around him, he was like a young cedar on Lebanon; and they surrounded him like the trunks of palm trees, all the sons of Aaron in their splendor with the Lord's offering in their hands, before the whole congregation of Israel. Finishing the service at the altars, and arranging the offering to the Most High, the Almighty, he reached out his hand to the cup and poured a libation of the blood of the grape; he poured it out at the foot of the altar, a pleasing odor to the Most High, the King of all. Then the sons of Aaron shouted, they sounded the trumpets of hammered work, they made a great noise to be heard for remembrance before the Most High. Then all the people together made haste and fell to the ground upon their faces to worship their Lord, the Almighty, God Most High. And the singers praised him with their voices in sweet and full-toned melody. And the people besought the Lord Most High in prayer before him who is merciful, till the order of worship of the Lord was ended; so they completed his service. Then Simon came down, and lifted up his hands over the whole congregation of the sons of Israel, to pronounce the blessing of the Lord with his lips, and to glory in his name; and they bowed down in worship a second time, to receive the blessing from the Most High. And now bless the God of all, who in every way does great things; who exalts our days from birth, and deals with us according to his mercy. May he give us gladness of heart, and grant that peace may be in our days in Israel, as in the days of old. May he entrust to us his mercy! And let him deliver us in our days!

A Reading (Lesson) from the Revelation to John [17:1-18]

Then one of the seven angels who had the seven bowls came and said to me, "Come, I will show you the judgment of the great harlot who is seated upon many waters, with whom the kings of the earth have committed fornication, and with the wine of whose fornication the dwellers on earth have become drunk." And he carried me away in the Spirit into a wilderness, and I saw a woman sitting on a scarlet beast which was full of blasphemous names, and it had seven heads and ten horns. The woman was arrayed in purple and scarlet, and bedecked with gold and jewels and pearls, holding in her hand a golden cup full of abominations and the impurities of her fornication; and on her forehead was written a name of mystery: "Babylon the great, mother of harlots and of earth's abominations." And I saw the woman, drunk with the blood of the saints and the blood of the martyrs of Jesus. When I saw her I marveled greatly. But the angel said to me, "Why marvel? I will tell you the mystery of the woman, and of the beast with seven heads and ten horns that carries her. The beast that you saw was, and is not, and is to ascend from the bottomless pit and go to perdition; and the dwellers on earth whose names have not been written in the book of life from the foundation of the world, will marvel to behold the beast, because it was and is not and is to come. This calls for a mind with wisdom: the seven heads are seven mountains on which the woman is seated; they are also seven kings, five of whom have fallen, one is, the other has not yet come, and when he comes he must remain only a little while. As for the beast that was and is not, it is an eighth but it belongs to the seven, and it goes to perdition. And the ten horns that you saw are ten kings who have not yet received royal power, but they are to receive authority as kings for one hour, together with the beast. These are of one mind and give over their power and authority to the beast; they will make war on the Lamb, and the Lamb will conquer them, for he is Lord of lords and King of kings, and those with him are called and chosen and faithful." And he said to me, "The waters that you saw, where the harlot is seated, are peoples and multitudes and nations and tongues. And the ten horns that you saw, they and the beast will hate the harlot; they will make her desolate and naked, and devour her flesh and burn her up with fire, for God has put into their hearts to carry out his purpose by being of one mind and giving over their royal power to the beast, until the words of God shall be fulfilled. And the woman that you saw is the great city which has dominion over the kings of the earth."

A Reading (Lesson) from the Gospel according to Luke
[13:31-35]

At that very hour some Pharisees came, and said to Jesus, "Get away from here, for Herod wants to kill you." And he said to them, "Go and tell that fox, 'Behold, I cast out demons and perform cures today and tomorrow, and the third day I finish my course. Nevertheless I must go on my way today and tomorrow and the day following; for it cannot be that a prophet should perish away from Jerusalem.' O Jerusalem, Jerusalem, killing the prophets and stoning those who are sent to you! How often would I have gathered your children together as a hen gathers her brood under her wings, and you would not! Behold, your house is forsaken. And I tell you, you will not see me until you say, 'Blessed is he who comes in the name of the Lord!'"

Saturday

Psalm 75 [page 691],   *Psalm 76* [page 692]   ❖
Psalm 23 [page 612],   *Psalm 27* [page 617]

A Reading (Lesson) from the Book of Ecclesiasticus
[51:1-12]

I will give thanks to thee, O Lord and King, and will praise thee as God my Savior. I give thanks to thy name, for thou hast been my protector and helper and hast delivered my body from destruction and from the snare of a slanderous tongue, from lips that utter lies. Before those who stood by thou wast my helper, and didst deliver me, in the greatness of thy mercy and of thy name, from the gnashings of teeth about to devour me, from the hand of those who sought my life, from the many afflictions that I endured, from choking fire on every side and from the midst of fire which I did not kindle, from the depths of the belly of Hades,

from an unclean tongue and lying words—the slander of
an unrighteous tongue to the king. My soul drew near to
death, and my life was very near to Hades beneath. They
surrounded me on every side, and there was no one to help
me; I looked for the assistance of men, and there was none.
Then I remembered thy mercy, O Lord, and thy work from
of old, that thou dost deliver those who wait for thee and
dost save them from the hand of their enemies. And I sent
up my supplication from the earth, and prayed for
deliverance from death. I appealed to the Lord, the Father
of my lord, not to forsake me in the days of affliction, at
the time when there is no help against the proud. I will
praise thy name continually, and will sing praise with
thanksgiving. My prayer was heard, for thou didst save me
from destruction and rescue me from an evil plight.
Therefore I will give thanks to thee and praise thee, and I
will bless the name of the Lord.

A Reading (Lesson) from the Revelation to John [18:1-14]

After this I saw another angel coming down from heaven,
having great authority; and the earth was made bright
with his splendor. And he called out with a mighty voice,
"Fallen, fallen is Babylon the great! It has become a
dwelling place of demons, a haunt of every foul spirit, a
haunt of every foul and hateful bird; for all nations have
drunk the wine of her impure passion, and the kings of the
earth have committed fornication with her, and the
merchants of the earth have grown rich with the wealth of
her wantonness." Then I heard another voice from heaven
saying, "Come out of her, my people, lest you take part in
her sins, lest you share in her plagues; for her sins are
heaped high as heaven, and God has remembered her
iniquities. Render to her as she herself has rendered, and
repay her double for her deeds; mix a double draught for
her in the cup she mixed. As she glorified herself and
played the wanton, so give her a like measure of torment

and mourning. Since in her heart she says, 'A queen I sit, I am no widow, mourning I shall never see,' so shall her plagues come in a single day, pestilence and mourning and famine, and she shall be burned with fire; for mighty is the Lord God who judges her." And the kings of the earth, who committed fornication and were wanton with her, will weep and wail over her when they see the smoke of her burning; they will stand far off, in fear of her torment, and say, "Alas! alas! thou great city, thou mighty city, Babylon! In one hour has thy judgment come." And the merchants of the earth weep and mourn for her, since no one buys their cargo any more, cargo of gold, silver, jewels and pearls, fine linen, purple, silk and scarlet, all kinds of scented wood, all articles of ivory; all articles of costly wood, bronze, iron and marble, cinnamon, spice, incense, myrrh, frankincense, wine, oil, fine flour and wheat, cattle and sheep, horses and chariots, and slaves, that is, human souls. "The fruit for which thy soul longed has gone from thee, and all thy dainties and thy splendor are lost to thee, never to be found again!"

A Reading (Lesson) from the Gospel according to Luke [14:1-11]

One sabbath when Jesus went to dine at the house of a ruler who belonged to the Pharisees, they were watching him. And behold, there was a man before him who had dropsy. And Jesus spoke to the lawyers and Pharisees, saying, "Is it lawful to heal on the sabbath, or not?" But they were silent. Then he took him and healed him, and let him go. And he said to them, "Which of you, having a son or an ox that has fallen into a well, will not immediately pull him out on a sabbath day?" And they could not reply to this. Now he told a parable to those who were invited, when he marked how they chose the places of honor, saying to them, "When you are invited by any one to a marriage feast, do not sit down in a place of honor, lest a more eminent man than you be invited by him; and he who invited you both will come and say to you, 'Give place to this man,' and then you will begin with shame to take the lowest place. But when you are invited, go and sit in the lowest place, so that when your host comes he may say to you, 'Friend, go up higher'; then you will be honored in the presence of all who sit at table with you. For every one who exalts himself will be humbled, and he who humbles himself will be exalted."

Proper 27   *Week of the Sunday closest to November 9*

Sunday

Psalm 93 [page 722],   *Psalm 96* [page 725]   ❖
Psalm 34 [page 627]

A Reading (Lesson) from the Book of Ecclesiasticus
[51:13-22]

While I was still young, before I went on my travels, I sought wisdom openly in my prayer. Before the temple I asked for her, and I will search for her to the last. From blossom to ripening grape my heart delighted in her; my foot entered upon the straight path; from my youth I followed her steps. I inclined my ear a little and received her, and I found for myself much instruction. I made progress therein; to him who gives me wisdom I will give glory. For I resolved to live according to wisdom, and I was zealous for the good; and I shall never be put to shame. My soul grappled with wisdom, and in my conduct I was strict; I spread out my hands to the heavens, and lamented my ignorance of her. I directed my soul to her, and through purification I found her. I gained understanding with her from the first, therefore I will not be forsaken. My heart was stirred to seek her, therefore I have gained a good possession. The Lord gave me a tongue as my reward, and I will praise him with it.

A Reading (Lesson) from the First Letter of Paul to the Corinthians [14:1-12]

Make love your aim, and earnestly desire the spiritual gifts, especially that you may prophesy. For one who speaks in a tongue speaks not to men but to God; for no one understands him, but he utters mysteries in the Spirit. On the other hand, he who prophesies speaks to men for their upbuilding and encouragement and consolation. He who speaks in a tongue edifies himself, but he who prophesies edifies the church. Now I want you all to speak in tongues, but even more to prophesy. He who prophesies is greater than he who speaks in tongues, unless some one interprets, so that the church may be edified. Now, brethren, if I come to you speaking in tongues, how shall I benefit you unless I bring you some revelation or knowledge or prophecy or teaching? If even lifeless instruments, such as the flute or the harp, do not give distinct notes, how will any one know what is played? And if the bugle gives an indistinct sound, who will get ready for battle? So with yourselves; if you in a tongue utter speech that is not intelligible, how will any one know what is said? For you will be speaking into the air. There are doubtless many different languages in the world, and none is without meaning; but if I do not know the meaning of the language, I shall be a foreigner to the speaker and the speaker a foreigner to me. So with yourselves; since you are eager for manifestations of the Spirit, strive to excel in building up the church.

Matthew 20:1-16 [page 117 above]

Monday

Psalm 80 [page 702] ❖ *Psalm 77* [page 693], *(Psalm 79* [page 701])

A Reading (Lesson) from the Book of Joel [1:1-13]

The word of the Lord that came to Jo'el, the son of
Pethu'el: Hear this, you aged men, give ear, all inhabitants
of the land! Has such a thing happened in your days, or in
the days of your fathers? Tell your children of it, and let
your children tell their children, and their children another
generation. What the cutting locust left, the swarming
locust has eaten. What the swarming locust left, the
hopping locust has eaten, and what the hopping locust left,
the destroying locust has eaten. Awake, you drunkards,
and weep; and wail, all you drinkers of wine, because of
the sweet wine, for it is cut off from your mouth. For a
nation has come up against my land, powerful and without
number; its teeth are lions' teeth, and it has the fangs of a
lioness. It has laid waste my vines, and splintered my fig
trees; it has stripped off their bark and thrown it down;
their branches are made white. Lament like a virgin girded
with sackcloth for the bridegroom of her youth. The cereal
offering and the drink offering are cut off from the house
of the Lord. The priests mourn, the ministers of the Lord.
The fields are laid waste, the ground mourns; because the
grain is destroyed, the wine fails, the oil languishes. Be
confounded, O tillers of the soil, wail, O vinedressers, for
the wheat and the barley; because the harvest of the field
has perished. The vine withers, the fig tree languishes.
Pomegranate, palm, and apple, all the trees of the field are
withered; and gladness fails from the souls of men. Gird on
sackcloth and lament, O priests, wail, O ministers of the
altar. Go in, pass the night in sackcloth, O ministers of my
God! Because cereal offering and drink offering are
withheld from the house of your God.

A Reading (Lesson) from the Revelation to John [18:15-24]

The merchants of these wares, who gained wealth from
her, will stand far off, in fear of her torment, weeping and
mourning aloud, "Alas, alas, for the great city that was

clothed in fine linen, in purple and scarlet, bedecked with gold, with jewels, and with pearls! In one hour all this wealth has been laid waste." And all shipmasters and seafaring men, sailors and all whose trade is on the sea, stood far off and cried out as they saw the smoke of her burning, "What city was like the great city?" And they threw dust on their heads, as they wept and mourned, crying out, "Alas, alas, for the great city where all who had ships at sea grew rich by her wealth! In one hour she has been laid waste. Rejoice over her, O heaven, O saints and apostles and prophets, for God has given judgment for you against her!" Then a mighty angel took up a stone like a great millstone and threw it into the sea, saying, "So shall Babylon the great city be thrown down with violence, and shall be found no more; and the sound of harpers and minstrels, of flute players and trumpeters, shall be heard in thee no more; and a craftsman of any craft shall be found in thee no more; and the light of a lamp shall shine in thee no more; and the voice of bridegroom and bride shall be heard in thee no more; for thy merchants were the great men of the earth, and all nations were deceived by thy sorcery. And in her was found the blood of prophets and of saints, and of all who have been slain on earth."

A Reading (Lesson) from the Gospel according to Luke
[14:12-24]

Jesus said to the Pharisee who had invited him, "When you give a dinner or a banquet, do not invite your friends or your brothers or your kinsmen or rich neighbors, lest they also invite you in return, and you be repaid. But when you give a feast, invite the poor, the maimed, the lame, the blind, and you will be blessed, because they cannot repay you. You will be repaid at the resurrection of the just." When one of those who sat at table with him heard this, he said to him, "Blessed is he who shall eat bread in the kingdom of God!" But he said to him, "A man once gave a great banquet, and invited many; and at the time for the banquet he sent his servant to say to those who had been invited, 'Come; for all is now ready.' But they all alike began to make excuses. The first said to him, 'I have bought a field, and I must go out and see it; I pray you, have me excused.' And another said, 'I have bought five yoke of oxen, and I go to examine them; I pray you, have me excused.' And another said, 'I have married a wife, and therefore I cannot come.' So the servant came and reported this to his master. Then the householder in anger said to his servant, 'Go out quickly to the streets and lanes of the city, and bring in the poor and maimed and blind and lame.' And the servant said, 'Sir, what you commanded has been done, and still there is room.' And the master said to the servant, 'Go out to the highways and hedges, and compel people to come in, that my house may be filled. For I tell you, none of those men who were invited shall taste my banquet.'"

Tuesday

Psalm 78:1-39 [page 694]   ❖   *Psalm 78:40-72* [page 698]

A Reading (Lesson) from the Book of Joel [1:15—2:2(3-11)]

Alas for the day! For the day of the Lord is near, and as destruction from the Almighty it comes. Is not the food cut off before our eyes, joy and gladness from the house of our God? The seed shrivels under the clods, the storehouses are desolate; the granaries are ruined because the grain has failed. How the beasts groan! The herds of cattle are perplexed because there is no pasture for them; even the flocks of sheep are dismayed. Unto thee, O Lord, I cry. For fire has devoured the pastures of the wilderness, and flame has burned all the trees of the field. Even the wild beasts cry to thee because the water brooks are dried up, and fire has devoured the pastures of the wilderness. Blow the trumpet in Zion; sound the alarm on my holy mountain!

Let all the inhabitants of the land tremble, for the day of the Lord is coming, it is near, a day of darkness and gloom, a day of clouds and thick darkness! Like blackness there is spread upon the mountains a great and powerful people; their like has never been from of old, nor will be again after them through the years of all generations.

Fire devours before them, and behind them a flame burns. The land is like the garden of Eden before them, but after them a desolate wilderness, and nothing escapes them. Their appearance is like the appearance of horses, and like war horses they run. As with the rumbling of chariots, they leap on the tops of the mountains, like the crackling of a flame of fire devouring the stubble, like a powerful army drawn up for battle. Before them peoples are in anguish, all faces grow pale. Like warriors they charge, like soldiers they scale the wall. They march each on his way, they do not swerve from their paths. They do not jostle one another, each marches in his path; they burst through the weapons and are not halted. They leap upon the city, they run upon the walls; they climb up into the houses, they enter through the windows like a thief. The earth quakes before them, the heavens tremble. The sun and the moon are darkened, and the stars withdraw their shining. The Lord utters his voice before his army, for his host is exceedingly great; he that executes his word is powerful. For the day of the Lord is great and very terrible; who can endure it?

A Reading (Lesson) from the Revelation to John [19:1-10]

After this I heard what seemed to be the loud voice of a great multitude in heaven, crying, "Hallelujah! Salvation and glory and power belong to our God, for his judgments are true and just; he has judged the great harlot who corrupted the earth with her fornication, and he has avenged on her the blood of his servants." Once more they cried, "Hallelujah! The smoke from her goes up for ever and ever." And the twenty-four elders and the four living creatures fell down and worshiped God who is seated on the throne, saying, "Amen. Hallelujah!" And from the throne came a voice crying, "Praise our God, all you his servants, you who fear him, small and great." Then I heard what seemed to be the voice of a great multitude, like the sound of many waters and like the sound of mighty thunderpeals, crying, "Hallelujah! For the Lord our God the Almighty reigns. Let us rejoice and exult and give him the glory, for the marriage of the Lamb has come, and his Bride has made herself ready; it was granted her to be clothed with fine linen, bright and pure"—for the fine linen is the righteous deeds of the saints. And the angel said to me, "Write this: Blessed are those who are invited to the marriage supper of the Lamb." And he said to me, "These are true words of God." Then I fell down at his feet to worship him, but he said to me, "You must not do that! I am a fellow servant with you and your brethren who hold the testimony of Jesus. Worship God." For the testimony of Jesus is the spirit of prophecy.

A Reading (Lesson) from the Gospel according to Luke
[14:25-35]

Great multitudes accompanied Jesus; and he turned and said to them, "If any one comes to me and does not hate his own father and mother and wife and children and brothers and sisters, yes, and even his own life, he cannot be my disciple. Whoever does not bear his own cross and come after me, cannot be my disciple. For which of you, desiring to build a tower, does not first sit down and count the cost, whether he has enough to complete it? Otherwise, when he has laid a foundation, and is not able to finish, all who see it begin to mock him, saying, 'This man began to build, and was not able to finish.' Or what king, going to encounter another king in war, will not sit down first and take counsel whether he is able with ten thousand to meet him who comes against him with twenty thousand? And if not, while the other is yet a great way off, he sends an embassy and asks terms of peace. So therefore, whoever of you does not renounce all that he has cannot be my disciple. Salt is good; but if salt has lost its taste, how shall its saltness be restored? It is fit neither for the land nor for the dunghill; men throw it away. He who has ears to hear, let him hear."

Wednesday

Psalm 119:97-120 [page 771] ❖ *Psalm 81* [page 704]
Psalm 82 [page 705]

A Reading (Lesson) from the Book of Joel [2:12-19]

"Yet even now," says the Lord, "return to me with all your heart, with fasting, with weeping, and with mourning; and rend your hearts and not your garments." Return to the Lord, your God, for he is gracious and merciful, slow to anger, and abounding in steadfast love, and repents of evil. Who knows whether he will not turn and repent, and leave a blessing behind him, a cereal offering and a drink offering for the Lord, your God? Blow the trumpet in Zion; sanctify a fast; call a solemn assembly; gather the people. Sanctify the congregation; assemble the elders; gather the children, even nursing infants. Let the bridegroom leave his room, and the bride her chamber. Between the vestibule and the altar let the priests, the ministers of the Lord, weep and say, "Spare thy people, O Lord, and make not thy heritage a reproach, a byword among the nations. Why should they say among the peoples, 'Where is their God?'" Then the Lord became jealous for his land, and had pity on his people. The Lord answered and said to his people, "Behold, I am sending to you grain, wine, and oil, and you will be satisfied; and I will no more make you a reproach among the nations."

A Reading (Lesson) from the Revelation to John [19:11-21]

Then I saw heaven opened, and behold, a white horse!
He who sat upon it is called Faithful and True, and in
righteousness he judges and makes war. His eyes are like a
flame of fire, and on his head are many diadems; and he
has a name inscribed which no one knows but himself. He
is clad in a robe dipped in blood, and the name by which
he is called is The Word of God. And the armies of heaven,
arrayed in fine linen, white and pure, followed him on
white horses. From his mouth issues a sharp sword with
which to smite the nations, and he will rule them with a
rod of iron; he will tread the wine press of the fury of the
wrath of God the Almighty. On his robe and on his thigh
he has a name inscribed, King of kings and Lord of lords.
Then I saw an angel standing in the sun, and with a loud
voice he called to all the birds that fly in midheaven,
"Come, gather for the great supper of God, to eat the flesh
of kings, the flesh of captains, the flesh of mighty men, the
flesh of horses and their riders, and the flesh of all men,
both free and slave, both small and great." And I saw the
beast and the kings of the earth with their armies gathered
to make war against him who sits upon the horse and
against his army. And the beast was captured, and with it
the false prophet who in its presence has worked the signs
by which he deceived those who had received the mark of
the beast and those who worshiped its image. These two
were thrown alive into the lake of fire that burns with
sulphur. And the rest were slain by the sword of him who
sits upon the horse, the sword that issues from his mouth;
and all the birds were gorged with their flesh.

A Reading (Lesson) from the Gospel according to Luke
[15:1-10]

The tax collectors and sinners were all drawing near to
hear Jesus. And the Pharisees and the scribes murmured,
saying, "This man receives sinners and eats with them."

So he told them this parable: "What man of you, having a hundred sheep, if he has lost one of them, does not leave the ninety-nine in the wilderness, and go after the one which is lost, until he finds it? And when he has found it, he lays it on his shoulders, rejoicing. And when he comes home, he calls together his friends and his neighbors, saying to them, 'Rejoice with me, for I have found my sheep which was lost.' Just so, I tell you, there will be more joy in heaven over one sinner who repents than over ninety-nine righteous persons who need no repentance. Or what woman, having ten silver coins, if she loses one coin, does not light a lamp and sweep the house and seek diligently until she finds it? And when she has found it, she calls together her friends and neighbors, saying, 'Rejoice with me, for I have found the coin which I had lost.' Just so, I tell you, there is joy before the angels of God over one sinner who repents."

Thursday

(Psalm 83 [page 706]) *or Psalm 23* [page 612],
Psalm 27 [page 617] ❖ *Psalm 85* [page 708],
Psalm 86 [page 709]

A Reading (Lesson) from the Book of Joel [2:21-27]

The Lord said to his people, "Fear not, O land; be glad and rejoice, for the Lord has done great things! Fear not, you beasts of the field, for the pastures of the wilderness are green; the tree bears its fruit, the fig tree and vine give their full yield. Be glad, O sons of Zion, and rejoice in the Lord, your God; for he has given the early rain for your vindication, he has poured down for you abundant rain, the early and the latter rain, as before. The threshing floors shall be full of grain, the vats shall overflow with wine and oil. I will restore to you the years which the swarming locust has eaten, the hopper, the destroyer, and the cutter, my great army, which I sent among you. You shall eat in plenty and be satisfied, and praise the name of the Lord your God, who has dealt wondrously with you. And my people shall never again be put to shame. You shall know that I am in the midst of Israel, and that I, the Lord, am your God and there is none else. And my people shall never again be put to shame."

A Reading (Lesson) from the Letter of James [1:1-15]

James, a servant of God and of the Lord Jesus Christ, To the twelve tribes in the Dispersion: Greeting. Count it all joy, my brethren, when you meet various trials, for you know that the testing of your faith produces steadfastness. And let steadfastness have its full effect, that you may be perfect and complete, lacking in nothing. If any of you lacks wisdom, let him ask God, who gives to all men generously and without reproaching, and it will be given him. But let him ask in faith, with no doubting, for he who doubts is like a wave of the sea that is driven and tossed by the wind. For that person must not suppose that a double-minded man, unstable in all his ways, will receive anything from the Lord. Let the lowly brother boast in his exaltation, and the rich in his humiliation, because like the flower of the grass he will pass away. For the sun rises with its scorching heat and withers the grass; its flower falls, and its beauty perishes. So will the rich man fade away in the midst of his pursuits. Blessed is the man who endures trial, for when he has stood the test he will receive the crown of life which God has promised to those who love him. Let no one say when he is tempted, "I am tempted by God"; for God cannot be tempted with evil and he himself tempts no one; but each person is tempted when he is lured and enticed by his own desire. Then desire when it has conceived gives birth to sin; and sin when it is full-grown brings forth death.

A Reading (Lesson) from the Gospel according to Luke
[15:1-2,11-32]

The tax collectors and sinners were all drawing near to
hear Jesus. And the Pharisees and the scribes murmured,
saying, "This man receives sinners and eats with them."
And he said, "There was a man who had two sons; and the
younger of them said to his father, 'Father, give me the
share of property that falls to me.' And he divided his
living between them. Not many days later, the younger son
gathered all he had and took his journey into a far country,
and there he squandered his property in loose living. And
when he had spent everything, a great famine arose in that
country, and he began to be in want. So he went and joined
himself to one of the citizens of that country, who sent him
into his fields to feed swine. And he would gladly have fed
on the pods that the swine ate; and no one gave him
anything. But when he came to himself he said, 'How
many of my father's hired servants have bread enough and
to spare, but I perish here with hunger! I will arise and go
to my father, and I will say to him, "Father, I have sinned
against heaven and before you; I am no longer worthy to
be called your son; treat me as one of your hired
servants." ' And he arose and came to his father. But while
he was yet at a distance, his father saw him and had
compassion, and ran and embraced him and kissed him.
And the son said to him, 'Father, I have sinned against
heaven and before you; I am no longer worthy to be called
your son.' But the father said to his servants, 'Bring quickly
the best robe, and put it on him; and put a ring on his
hand, and shoes on his feet; and bring the fatted calf and
kill it, and let us eat and make merry; for this my son was
dead, and is alive again; he was lost, and is found.' And
they began to make merry. Now his elder son was in the
field; and as he came and drew near to the house, he heard
music and dancing. And he called one of the servants and
asked what this meant. And he said to him, 'Your brother

has come, and your father has killed the fatted calf, because he has received him safe and sound.' But he was angry and refused to go in. His father came out and entreated him, but he answered his father, 'Lo, these many years I have served you, and I never disobeyed your command; yet you never gave me a kid, that I might make merry with my friends. But when this son of yours came, who has devoured your living with harlots, you killed for him the fatted calf!' And he said to him, 'Son, you are always with me, and all that is mine is yours. It was fitting to make merry and be glad, for this your brother was dead, and is alive; he was lost, and is found.'"

Friday

Psalm 88 [page 712]   ❖   *Psalm 91* [page 719],
Psalm 92 [page 720]

A Reading (Lesson) from the Book of Joel [2:28—3:8]

The Lord said to his people, "It shall come to pass afterward, that I will pour out my spirit on all flesh; your sons and your daughters shall prophesy, your old men shall dream dreams, and your young men shall see visions. Even upon the menservants and maidservants in those days, I will pour out my spirit. And I will give portents in the heavens and on the earth, blood and fire and columns of smoke. The sun shall be turned to darkness, and the moon to blood, before the great and terrible day of the Lord comes. And it shall come to pass that all who call upon the name of the Lord shall be delivered; for in Mount Zion and in Jerusalem there shall be those who escape, as the Lord has said, and among the survivors shall be those whom the Lord calls. For behold, in those days and at that time, when I restore the fortunes of Judah and Jerusalem, I will gather all the nations and bring them down to the valley of Jehosh'aphat, and I will enter into judgment with them there, on account of my people and my heritage Israel, because they have scattered them among the nations, and have divided up my land, and have cast lots for my people, and have given a boy for a harlot, and have sold a girl for wine, and have drunk it. What are you to me, O Tyre and Sidon, and all the regions of Philistia? Are you paying me back for something? If you are paying me back, I will requite your deed upon your own head swiftly and speedily. For you have taken my silver and my gold, and have carried my rich treasures into your temples. You have sold the people of Judah and Jerusalem to the Greeks, removing them far from their own border. But now I will stir them up from the place to which you have sold them, and I will requite your deed upon your own head. I will sell your sons and your daughters into the hand of the sons of Judah, and they will sell them to the Sabe'ans, to a nation far off; for the Lord has spoken."

A Reading (Lesson) from the Letter of James [1:16-27]

Do not be deceived, my beloved brethren. Every good endowment and every perfect gift is from above, coming down from the Father of lights with whom there is no variation or shadow due to change. Of his own will he brought us forth by word of truth that we should be a kind of first fruits of his creatures. Know this, my beloved brethren. Let every man be quick to hear, slow to speak, slow to anger, for the anger of man does not work the righteousness of God. Therefore put away all filthiness and rank growth of wickedness and receive with meekness the implanted word, which is able to save your souls. But be doers of the word, and not hearers only, deceiving yourselves. For if any one is a hearer of the word and not a doer, he is like a man who observes his natural face in a mirror; for he observes himself and goes away and at once forgets what he was like. But he who looks into the perfect law, the law of liberty, and perseveres, being no hearer that forgets but a doer that acts, he shall be blessed in his doing. If any one thinks he is religious, and does not bridle his tongue but deceives his heart, this man's religion is vain. Religion that is pure and undefiled before God and the Father is this: to visit orphans and widows in their affliction, and to keep oneself unstained from the world.

A Reading (Lesson) from the Gospel according to Luke [16:1-9]

Jesus said to the disciples, "There was a rich man who had a steward, and charges were brought to him that this man was wasting his goods. And he called him and said to him, 'What is this that I hear about you? Turn in the account of your stewardship, for you can no longer be steward.' And the steward said to himself, 'What shall I do, since my master is taking the stewardship away from me? I am not strong enough to dig, and I am ashamed to beg. I have decided what to do, so that people may receive me into their houses when I am put out of the stewardship.' So, summoning his master's debtors one by one, he said to the first, 'How much do you owe my master?' He said, 'A hundred measures of oil.' And he said of him, 'Take your bill, and sit down quickly and write fifty.' Then he said to another, 'And how much do you owe?' He said, 'A hundred measures of wheat.' He said to him, 'Take your bill, and write eighty.' The master commended the dishonest steward for his shrewdness; for the sons of this world are more shrewd in dealing with their own generation than the sons of light. And I tell you, make friends for yourselves by means of unrighteous mammon, so that when it fails they may recieve you into the eternal habitations."

Saturday

Psalm 87 [page 711], *Psalm 90* [page 717] ❖
Psalm 136 [page 789]

A Reading (Lesson) from the Book of Joel [3:9-17]

Proclaim this among the nations: Prepare war, stir up the mighty men. Let all the men of war draw near, let them come up. Beat your plowshares into swords, and your pruning hooks into spears; let the weak say, "I am a warrior." Hasten and come, all you nations round about, gather yourselves there. Bring down thy warriors, O Lord. Let the nations bestir themselves, and come up to the valley of Jehosh'aphat; for there I will sit to judge all the nations round about. Put in the sickle, for the harvest is ripe. Go in, tread, for the wine press is full. The vats overflow, for their wickedness is great. Multitudes, multitudes, in the valley of decision! For the day of the Lord is near in the valley of decision. The sun and the moon are darkened, and the stars withdraw their shining. And the Lord roars from Zion, and utters his voice from Jerusalem, and the heavens and the earth shake. But the Lord is a refuge to his people, a stronghold to the people of Israel. "So you shall know that I am the Lord your God, who dwell in Zion, my holy mountain. And Jerusalem shall be holy and strangers shall never again pass through it.

A Reading (Lesson) from the Letter of James [2:1-13]

My brethren, show no partiality as you hold the faith of our Lord Jesus Christ, the Lord of glory. For if a man with gold rings and in fine clothing comes into your assembly, and a poor man in shabby clothing also comes in, and you pay attention to the one who wears the fine clothing and say, "Have a seat here, please," while you say to the poor man, "Stand there," or "Sit at my feet," have you not made distinctions among yourselves, and become judges with evil thoughts? Listen, my beloved brethren. Has not God chosen those who are poor in the world to be rich in faith and heirs of the kingdom which he has promised to those who love him? But you have dishonored the poor man. Is it not the rich who oppress you, is it not they who drag you into court? Is it not they who blaspheme the honorable name which was invoked over you? If you really fulfil the royal law, according to scripture, "You shall love your neighbor as yourself," you do well. But if you show partiality, you commit sin, and are convicted by the law as transgressors. For whoever keeps the whole law but fails in one point has become guilty of all of it. For he who said, "Do not commit adultery," said also, "Do not kill." If you do not commit adultery but do kill, you have become a transgressor of the law. So speak and so act as those who are to be judged under the law of liberty. For judgment is without mercy to one who has shown no mercy; yet mercy triumphs over judgment.

A Reading (Lesson) from the Gospel according to Luke [16:10-17(18)]

Jesus said to the disciples, "He who is faithful in a very little is faithful also in much; and he who is dishonest in a very little is dishonest also in much. If then you have not been faithful in the unrighteous mammon, who will entrust to you the true riches? And if you have not been faithful in that which is another's, who will give you that which is your own? No servant can serve two masters; for either he will hate the one and love the other, or he will be devoted to the one and despise the other. You cannot serve God and mammon." The Pharisees, who were lovers of money, heard all this, and they scoffed at him. But he said to them, "You are those who justify yourselves before men, but God knows your hearts; for what is exalted among men is an abomination in the sight of God. The law and the prophets were until John; since then the good news of the kingdom of God is preached, and every one enters it violently. But it is easier for heaven and earth to pass way, than for one dot of the law to become void."

> "Every one who divorces his wife and marries another commits adultery, and he who marries a woman divorced from her husband commits adultery."

Proper 28 *Week of the Sunday closest to November 16*

Sunday

Psalm 66 [page 673], *Psalm 67* [page 675] ❖
Psalm 19 [page 606], *Psalm 46* [page 649]

A Reading (Lesson) from the Book of Habakkuk
[1:1-4(5-11)12—2:1]

The oracle of God which Habak'kuk the prophet saw. O
Lord, how long shall I cry for help, and thou wilt not hear?
Or cry to thee "Violence!" and thou wilt not save? Why
dost thou make me see wrongs and look upon trouble?
Destruction and violence are before me; strife and
contention arise. So the law is slacked and justice never
goes forth. For the wicked surround the righteous, so
justice goes forth perverted.

> Look among the nations, and see; wonder and be
> astounded. For I am doing a work in your days that you
> would not believe if told. For lo, I am rousing the
> Chalde'ans, that bitter and hasty nation, who march
> through the breadth of the earth, to seize habitations
> not their own. Dread and terrible are they; their justice
> and dignity proceed from themselves. Their horses are
> swifter than leopards, more fierce than the evening
> wolves; their horsemen press proudly on. Yea, their
> horsemen come from afar; they fly like an eagle swift to
> devour. They all come for violence; terror of them goes
> before them. They gather captives like sand. At kings
> they scoff, and of rulers they make sport. They laugh at
> every fortress, for they heap up earth and take it. Then
> they sweep by like the wind and go on, guilty men,
> whose own might is their god!

Art thou not from everlasting, O Lord my God, my Holy
One? We shall not die. O Lord, thou hast ordained them as
a judgment; and thou, O Rock, hast established them for

chastisement. Thou who art of purer eyes than to behold evil and canst not look on wrong, why dost thou look on faithless men, and art silent when the wicked swallows up the man more righteous than he? For thou makest men like the fish of the sea, like crawling things that have no ruler. He brings all of them up with a hook, he drags them out with his net, he gathers them in his seine; so he rejoices and exults. Therefore he sacrifices to his net and burns incense to his seine; for by them he lives in luxury, and his food is rich. Is he then to keep on emptying his net, and mercilessly slaying nations for ever? I will take my stand to watch, and station myself on the tower, and look forth to see what he will say to me, and what I will answer concerning my complaint.

A Reading (Lesson) from the Letter of Paul to the Philippians [3:13—4:1]

Brethren, I do not consider that I have made it my own; but one thing I do, forgetting what lies behind and straining forward to what lies ahead, I press on toward the goal for the prize of the upward call of God in Christ Jesus. Let those of us who are mature be thus minded; and if in anything you are otherwise minded, God will reveal that also to you. Only let us hold true to what we have attained. Brethren, join in imitating me, and mark those who so live as you have an example in us. For many, of whom I have often told you and now tell you even with tears, live as enemies of the cross of Christ. Their end is destruction, their god is the belly, and they glory in their shame, with minds set on earthly things. But our commonwealth is in heaven, and from it we await a Savior, the Lord Jesus Christ, who will change our lowly body to be like his glorious body, by the power which enables him even to subject all things to himself. Therefore, my brethren, whom I love and long for, my joy and crown, stand firm thus in the Lord, my beloved.

A Reading (Lesson) from the Gospel according to Matthew
[23:13-24]

Jesus said to the crowds and to his disciples, "But woe to you, scribes and Pharisees, hypocrites! because you shut the kingdom of heaven against men; for you neither enter yourselves, nor allow those who would enter to go in. Woe to you, scribes and Pharisees, hypocrites! for you traverse sea and land to make a single proselyte, and when he becomes a proselyte, you make him twice as much a child of hell as yourselves. Woe to you, blind guides, who say, 'If any one swears by the temple, it is nothing; but if any one swears by the gold of the temple, he is bound by his oath.' You blind fools! For which is greater, the gold or the temple that has made the gold sacred? And you say, 'If any one swears by the altar, it is nothing; but if any one swears by the gift that is on the altar, he is bound by his oath.' You blind men! For which is greater, the gift or the altar that makes the gift sacred? So he who swears by the altar, swears by it and by everything on it; and he who swears by the temple, swears by it and by him who dwells in it; and he who swears by heaven, swears by the throne of God and by him who sits upon it. Woe to you, scribes and Pharisees, hypocrites! for you tithe mint and dill and cummin, and have neglected the weightier matters of the law, justice and mercy and faith; these you ought to have done, without neglecting the others. You blind guides, straining out a gnat and swallowing a camel!"

Monday

Psalm 89:1-18 [page 713] ❖ *Psalm 89:19-52* [page 715]

A Reading (Lesson) from the Book of Habakkuk
[2:1-4,9-20]

I will take my stand to watch, and station myself on the tower, and look forth to see what he will say to me, and I

will answer concerning my complaint. And the Lord
answered me "Write the vision; make it plain upon tablets,
so he may run who reads it. For still the vision awaits its
time; it hastens to the end—it will not lie. If it seem slow,
wait for it; it will surely come, it will not delay. Behold, he
whose soul is not upright in him shall fail, but the
righteous shall live by his faith." Woe to him who gets evil
gain for his house, to set his nest on high, to be safe from
the reach of harm! You have devised shame to your house
by cutting off many peoples; you have forfeited your life.
For the stone will cry out from the wall, and the beam
from the woodwork respond. Woe to him who builds a
town with blood, and founds a city on iniquity! Behold, is
it not from the Lord of hosts that peoples labor only for
fire, and nations weary themselves for nought? For the
earth will be filled with the knowledge of the glory of the
Lord, as the waters cover the sea. Woe to him who makes
his neighbors drink of the cup of his wrath, and makes
them drunk, to gaze on their shame! You will be sated with
contempt instead of glory. Drink, yourself, and stagger!
The cup in the Lord's right hand will come around to you,
and shame will come upon your glory! The violence done
to Lebanon will overwhelm you; the destruction of the
beasts will terrify you, for the blood of men and violence to
the earth, to cities and all who dwell therein. What profit is
an idol when its maker has shaped it, a metal image, a
teacher of lies? For the workman trusts in his own creation
when he makes dumb idols! Woe to him who says to a
wooden thing, Awake; to a dumb stone, Arise! Can this
give revelation? Behold, it is overlaid with gold and silver,
and there is no breath at all in it. But the Lord is in his holy
temple; let all the earth keep silence before him.

A Reading (Lesson) from the Letter of James [2:14-26]

What does it profit, my brethren, if a man says he has faith
but has not works? Can his faith save him? If a brother or

sister is ill-clad and in lack of daily food, and one of you says to them, "Go in peace, be warmed and filled," without giving them the things needed for the body, what does it profit? So faith by itself, if it has no works, is dead. But some one will say, "You have faith and I have works." Show me your faith apart from your works, and I by my works will show you my faith. You believe that God is one; you do well. Even the demons believe—and shudder. Do you want to be shown, you shallow man, that faith apart from works is barren? Was not Abraham our father justified by works, when he offered his son Isaac upon the altar? You see that faith was active along with his works, and faith was completed by works, and the scripture was fulfilled which says, "Abraham believed God, and it was reckoned to him as righteousness"; and he was called the friend of God. You see that a man is justified by works and not by faith alone. And in the same way was not also Rahab the harlot justified by works when she received the messengers and sent them out another way? For as the body apart from the spirit is dead, so faith apart from works is dead.

A Reading (Lesson) from the Gospel according to Luke [16:19-31]

Jesus said to the Pharisees, "There was a rich man, who was clothed in purple and fine linen and who feasted sumptuously every day. And at his gate lay a poor man named Laz'arus, full of sores, who desired to be fed with what fell from the rich man's table; moreover the dogs came and licked his sores. The poor man died and was carried by the angels to Abraham's bosom. The rich man also died and was buried; and in Hades, being in torment, he lifted up his eyes, and saw Abraham far off and Laz'arus in his bosom. And he called out, 'Father Abraham, have mercy upon me, and send Laz'arus to dip the end of his finger in water and cool my tongue; for I am in anguish in this flame.' But Abraham said, 'Son, remember that you in your lifetime received your good things, and Laz'arus in like manner evil things; but now he is comforted here, and you are in anguish. And besides all this, between us and you a great chasm has been fixed, in order that those who would pass from here to you may not be able, and none may cross from there to us.' And he said, 'Then I beg you, father, to send him to my father's house, for I have five brothers, so that he may warn them, lest they also come into this place of torment.' But Abraham said, 'They have Moses and the prophets; let them hear them.' And he said, 'No, father Abraham; but if some one goes to them from the dead, they will repent.' He said to him, 'If they do not hear Moses and the prophets, neither will they be convinced if some one should rise from the dead.'"

Tuesday

Psalm 97 [page 726], *Psalm 99* [page 728], *(Psalm 100* [page 729]) ❖ *Psalm 94* [page 722], *(Psalm 95* [page 724])

A Reading (Lesson) from the Book of Habakkuk [3:1-10(11-15)16-18]

A prayer of Habak'kuk the prophet, according to Shigion'oth. O Lord, I have heard the report of thee, and thy work, O Lord, do I fear. In the midst of the years renew it; in the midst of the years make it known; in wrath remember mercy. God came from Teman, and the Holy One from Mount Paran. His glory covered the heaven, and the earth was full of his praise. *Selah*. His brightness was like the light, rays flashed from his hand; and there he veiled his power. Before him went pestilence, and plague followed close behind. He stood and measured the earth; he looked and shook the nations; then the eternal mountains were scattered, the everlasting hills sank low.

His ways were as of old. I saw the tents of Cushan in affliction; the curtains of the land of Mid'ian did tremble. Was thy wrath against the rivers, O Lord? Was thy anger against the rivers, or thy indignation against the sea, when thou didst ride upon thy horses, upon thy chariot of victory? Thou didst strip the sheath from thy bow, and put the arrows to the string. *Selah*. Thou didst cleave the earth with rivers. The mountains saw thee, and writhed; the raging waters swept on; the deep gave forth its voice, it lifted its hands on high.

> The sun and moon stood still in their habitation at the light of thine arrows as they sped, at the flash of thy glittering spear. Thou didst bestride the earth in fury, thou didst trample the nations in anger. Thou wentest forth for the salvation of thy people, for the salvation of thy anointed. Thou didst crush the head of the wicked, laying him bare from thigh to neck. *Selah*. Thou didst pierce with thy shafts the head of his warriors, who came like a whirlwind to scatter me, rejoicing as if to devour the poor in secret. Thou didst trample the sea with thy horses, the surging of mighty waters.

I hear, and my body trembles, my lips quiver at the sound; rottenness enters into my bones, my steps totter beneath me. I will quietly wait for the day of trouble to come upon people who invade us. Though the fig tree do not blossom, nor fruit be on the vines, the produce of the olive fail and the fields yield no food, the flock be cut off from the fold and there be no herd in the stalls, yet I will rejoice in the Lord, I will joy in the God of my salvation.

A Reading (Lesson) from the Letter of James [3:1-12]

Let not many of you become teachers, my brethren, for you know that we who teach shall be judged with greater strictness. For we all make many mistakes, and if any one makes no mistakes in what he says he is a perfect man, able to bridle the whole body also. If we put bits into the mouths of horses that they may obey us, we guide their whole bodies. Look at the ships also; though they are so great and are driven by strong winds, they are guided by a very small rudder wherever the will of the pilot directs. So the tongue is a little member and boasts of great things. How great a forest is set ablaze by a small fire! And the tongue is a fire. The tongue is an unrighteous world among our members, staining the whole body, setting on fire the cycle of natures, and set on fire by hell. For every kind of beast and bird, of reptile and sea creature, can be tamed and has been tamed by humankind, but no human being can tame the tongue—a restless evil, full of deadly poison. With it we bless the Lord and Father, and with it we curse men, who are made in the likeness of God. From the same mouth come blessing and cursing. My brethren, this ought not to be so. Does a spring pour forth from the same opening fresh water and brackish? Can a fig tree, my brethren, yield olives, or a grapevine figs? No more can salt water yield fresh.

A Reading (Lesson) from the Gospel according to Luke
[17:1-10]

Jesus said to his disciples, "Temptations to sin are sure to come; but woe to him by whom they come! It would be better for him if a millstone were hung round his neck and he were cast into the sea, than that he should cause one of these little ones to sin. Take heed to yourselves; if your brother sins, rebuke him, and if he repents, forgive him; and if he sins against you seven times in the day, and turns to you seven times, and says, 'I repent,' you must forgive him." The apostles said to the Lord, "Increase our faith!" And the Lord said, "If you had faith as a grain of mustard seed, you could say to this sycamine tree, 'Be rooted up, and be planted in the sea,' and it would obey you. Will any one of you, who has a servant plowing or keeping sheep, say to him when he has come in from the field, 'Come at once and sit down at table'? Will he not rather say to him,

'Prepare supper for me, and gird yourself and serve me, till I eat and drink; and afterward you shall eat and drink'? Does he thank the servant because he did what was commanded? So you also, when you have done all that is commanded you, say, 'We are unworthy servants; we have only done what was our duty.'"

Wednesday

Psalm 101 [page 730],
Psalm 109:1-4(5-19)20-30 [page 750] ❖
Psalm 119:121-144 [page 773]

A Reading (Lesson) from the Book of Malachi [1:1,6-14]

The oracle of the word of the Lord to Israel by Mal'achi. "A son honors his father, and a servant his master. If then I am a father, where is my honor? And if I am a master, where is my fear? says the Lord of hosts to you, O priests, who despise my name. You say, 'How have we despised thy name?' By offering polluted food upon my altar. And you say, 'How have we polluted it?' By thinking that the Lord's table may be despised. When you offer blind animals in sacrifice, is that no evil? And when you offer those that are lame or sick, is that no evil? Present that to your governor; will he be pleased with you or show you favor? says the Lord hosts. And now entreat the favor of God, that he may be gracious to us. With such a gift from your hand, will he show favor to any of you? says the Lord of hosts. Oh, that there were one among you who would shut the doors, that you might not kindle fire upon my altar in vain! I have no pleasure in you, says the Lord of hosts, and I will not accept an offering from your hand. For from the rising of the sun to its setting my name is great among the nations, and in every place incense is offered to my name, and a pure offering; for my name is great among the nations, says the Lord of hosts. But you profane it when you say that the Lord's table is polluted, and the food for it may be despised. 'What a weariness this is,' you say, and you sniff at me, says the Lord of hosts. You bring what has been taken by violence or is lame or sick, and this you bring as your offering! Shall I accept that from your hand? says the Lord. Cursed be the cheat who has a male in his flock, and vows it, and yet sacrifices to the Lord what is blemished; for I am a great King, says theLord of hosts, and my name is feared among the nations."

A Reading (Lesson) from the Letter of James
[3:13—4:12]

Who is wise and understanding among you? By his good life let him show his works in the meekness of wisdom. But if you have bitter jealousy and selfish ambition in your hearts,do not boast and be false to the truth. This wisdom is not such as comes down from above, but is earthly, unspiritual, devilish. For where jealousy and selfish ambition exist, there will be disorder and every vile practice. But the wisdom from above is first pure, then peaceable, gentle, open to reason, full of mercy and good fruits, without uncertainty or insincerity. And the harvest of righteousness is sown in peace by those who make peace. What causes wars, and what causes fightings among you? Is it not your passions that are at war in your members? You desire and do not have; so you kill. And you covet and cannot obtain; so you fight and wage war. You do not have, because you do not ask. You ask and do not receive, because you ask wrongly, to spend it on your passions. Unfaithful creatures! Do you not know that friendship with the world is enmity with God? Therefore whoever wishes to be a friend of the world makes himself an enemy of God. Or do you suppose it is in vain that the scripture says, "He yearns jealously over the spirit which he has made to dwell in us"? But he gives more grace; therefore it says, "God opposes the proud, but gives grace to the humble." Submit yourselves therefore to God. Resist the devil and he will flee from you. Draw near to God and he will draw near to you. Cleanse your hands, you sinners, and purify your hearts, you men of double mind. Be wretched and mourn and weep. Let your laughter be turned to mourning and your joy to dejection. Humble yourselves before the Lord and he will exalt you. Do not speak evil against one another, brethren. He that speaks evil against a brother or judges his brother, speaks evil against the law and judges the law. But if you judge the law, you are not a doer of the law but a judge. There is one lawgiver and judge, he who is able to save and to destroy. But who are you that you judge your neighbor?

A Reading (Lesson) from the Gospel according to Luke [17:11-19]

On the way to Jerusalem Jesus was passing along between Samaria and Galilee. And as he entered a village, he was met by ten lepers, who stood at a distance and lifted up their voices and said, "Jesus, Master, have mercy on us." When he saw them he said to them, "Go and show yourselves to the priests." And as they went they were cleansed. Then one of them, when he saw that he was healed, turned back, praising God with a loud voice; and he fell on his face at Jesus' feet, giving him thanks. Now he was a Samaritan. Then said Jesus, "Were not ten cleansed? Where are the nine? Was no one found to return and give praise to God except this foreigner?" And he said to him, "Rise and go your way; your faith has made you well."

Thursday

Psalm 105:1-22 [page 738]   ❖   *Psalm 105:23-45* [page 739]

A Reading (Lesson) from the Book of Malachi [2:1-16]

The oracle of the word of the Lord to Israel by Malachi.

"And now, O priests, this command is for you. If you will not listen, if you will not lay it to heart to give glory to my name, says the Lord of hosts, then I will send the curse upon you and I will curse your blessings; indeed I have already cursed them, because you do not lay it to heart. Behold, I will rebuke your offspring, and spread dung upon your faces, the dung of your offerings, and I will put you out of my presence. So shall you know that I have sent this command to you that my covenant with Levi may hold, says the Lord of hosts. My covenant with him was a covenant of life and peace, and I gave them to him, that he might fear; and he feared me, he stood in awe of my name. True instruction was in his mouth, and no wrong was found on his lips. He walked with me in peace and uprightness, and he turned many from iniquity. For the lips of a priest should guard knowledge, and men should seek instruction from his mouth, for he is the messenger of the Lord of hosts. But you have turned aside from the way; you have caused many to stumble by your instruction; you have corrupted the covenant of Levi, says the Lord of hosts, and so I make you despised and abased before all the people, inasmuch as you have not kept my ways but have shown partiality in your instruction." Have we not all one father? Has not one God created us? Why then are we faithless to one another, profaning the covenant of our fathers? Judah has been faithless, and abomination has been committed in Israel and in Jerusalem; for Judah has profaned the sanctuary of the Lord, which he loves, and has married the daughter of a foreign God. May the Lord cut off from the tents of Jacob, for the man who does this, any to witness or answer, or to bring an offering to the Lord of hosts! And this again you do. You cover the Lord's altar with tears, with weeping and groaning because he no longer regards the offering or accepts it with favor at your hand. You ask, "Why does he not?" Because the Lord was witness to the covenant between you and the wife of your youth, to whom you have been faithless, though she is

your companion and your wife by covenant. Has not the
one God made and sustained for us the spirit of life? And
what does he desire? Godly offspring. So take heed to
yourselves, and let none be faithless to the wife of his
youth. "For I hate divorce, says the Lord the God of Israel,
and covering one's garment with violence, says the Lord of
hosts. So take heed to yourselves and do not be faithless."

A Reading (Lesson) from the Letter of James [4:13—5:6]

Come now, you who say, "Today or tomorrow we will go
into such and such a town and spend a year there and trade
and get gain"; whereas you do not know about tomorrow.
What is your life? For you are a mist that appears for a
little time and then vanishes. Instead you ought to say, "If
the Lord wills, we shall live and we shall do this or that."
As it is, you boast in your arrogance. All such boasting is
evil. Whoever knows what is right to do and fails to do it,
for him it is sin. Come now, you rich, weep and howl for
the miseries that are coming upon you. Your riches have
rotted and your garments are moth-eaten. Your gold and
silver have rusted, and their rust will be evidence against
you and will eat your flesh like fire. You have laid up
treasure for the last days. Behold, the wages of the laborers
who mowed your fields, which you kept back by fraud, cry
out; and the cries of the harvesters have reached the ears of
the Lord of hosts. You have lived on the earth in luxury
and in pleasure; you have fattened your hearts in a day of
slaughter. You have condemned, you have killed the
righteous man; he does not resist you.

A Reading (Lesson) from the Gospel according to Luke
[17:20-37]

Being asked by the Pharisees when the kingdom of God
was coming, Jesus answered them, "The kingdom of God
is not coming with signs to be observed; nor will they say,
'Lo, here it is!' or 'There!' for behold, the kingdom of God

is in the midst of you." And he said to the disciples, "The days are coming when you will desire to see one of the days of the Son of man, and you will not see it. And they will say to you, 'Lo, there!' or 'Lo, here!' Do not go, do not follow them. For as the lightning flashes and lights up the sky from one side to the other, so will the Son of man be in his day. But first he must suffer many things and be rejected by this generation. As it was in the days of Noah, so will it be in the days of the Son of man. They ate, they drank, they married, they were given in marriage, until the day when Noah entered the ark, and the flood came and destroyed them all. Likewise, as it was in the days of Lot—they ate, they drank, they bought, they sold, they planted, they built, but on the day when Lot went out from Sodom fire and sulphur rained from heaven and destroyed them all—so will it be on the day when the Son of man is revealed. On that day, let him who is on the housetop, with his goods in the house, not come down to take them away; and likewise let him who is in the field not turn back. Remember Lot's wife. Whoever seeks to gain his life will lose it, but whoever loses his life will preserve it. I tell you, in that night there will be two in one bed; one will be taken and the other left. There will be two women grinding together; one will be taken and the other left." And they said to him, "Where, Lord?" He said to them, "Where the body is, there the eagles will be gathered together."

Friday

Psalm 102 [page 731] ❖ *Psalm 107:1-32* [page 746]

A Reading (Lesson) from the Book of Malachi [3:1-12]

"Behold, I send my messenger to prepare the way before me, and the Lord whom you seek will suddenly come to his temple; the messenger of the covenant in whom you delight, behold, he is coming, says the Lord of hosts. But who can endure the day of his coming, and who can stand when he appears? For his is like a refiner's fire and like fullers' soap; he will sit as a refiner and purifier of silver, and he will purify the sons of Levi and refine them like gold and silver, till they present right offerings to the Lord. Then the offering of Judah and Jerusalem will be pleasing to the Lord as in the days of old and as in former years. Then I will draw near to you for judgment; I will be a swift witness against the sorcerers, against the adulterers, against those who swear falsely, against those who oppress the hireling in his wages, the widow and the orphan, against those who thrust aside the sojourner, and do not fear me, says the Lord of hosts. For I the Lord do not change; therefore you, O sons of Jacob, are not consumed. From the days of your fathers you have turned aside from my statutes and have not kept them. Return to me, and I will return to you, says the Lord of hosts. But you say, 'How shall we return?' Will man rob God? Yet you are robbing me. But you say, 'How are we robbing thee?' In your tithes and offerings. You are cursed with a curse, for you are robbing me; the whole nation of you. Bring the full tithes into the storehouse, that there may be food in my house; and thereby put me to the test, says the Lord of hosts, if I will not open the windows of heaven for you and pour down for you an overflowing blessing. I will rebuke the devourer for you, so that it will not destroy the fruits of your soil; and your vine in the field shall not fail to bear, says the Lord of hosts. Then all nations will call you blessed, for you will be a land of delight, says the Lord of hosts."

A Reading (Lesson) from the Letter of James [5:7-12]

Be patient, therefore, brethren, until the coming of the Lord. Behold, the farmer waits for the precious fruit of the earth, being patient over it until it receives the early and the late rain. You also be patient. Establish your hearts, for the coming of the Lord is at hand. Do not grumble, brethren, against one another, that you may not be judged; behold, the Judge is standing at the doors. As an example of suffering and patience, brethren, take the prophets who spoke in the name of the Lord. Behold, we call those happy who were steadfast. You have heard of the steadfastness of Job, and you have seen the purpose of the Lord, how the Lord is compassionate and merciful. But above all, my brethren, do not swear, either by heaven or by earth or with any other oath, but let your yes be yes and your no be no, that you may not fall under condemnation.

A Reading (Lesson) from the Gospel according to Luke
[18:1-8]

Jesus told the disciples a parable, to the effect that they ought always to pray and not lose heart. He said, "In a certain city there was a judge who neither feared God nor regarded man; and there was a widow in that city who kept coming to him and saying, 'Vindicate me against my adversary.' For a while he refused; but afterward he said to himself, 'Though I neither fear God nor regard man, yet because this widow bothers me, I will vindicate her, or she will wear me out by her continual coming.'" And the Lord said, "Hear what the unrighteous judge says. And will not God vindicate his elect, who cry to him day and night? Will he delay long over them? I tell you, he will vindicate them speedily. Nevertheless, when the Son of man comes, will he find faith on earth?"

Saturday

Psalm 107:33-43 [page 748],
Psalm 108:1-6(7-13) [page 749] ❖
Psalm 33 [page 626]

A Reading (Lesson) from the Book of Malachi [3:13—4:6]

"Your words have been stout against me, says the Lord. Yet
you say, 'How have we spoken against thee?' You have
said, 'It is vain to serve God. What is the good of our
keeping his charge or of walking as in mourning before the
Lord of hosts? Henceforth we deem the arrogant blessed;
evildoers not only prosper but when they put God to the
test they escape.'" Then those who feared the Lord spoke
with one another; the Lord heeded and heard them, and a
book of remembrance was written before him of those
who feared the Lord and thought on his name. "They shall
be mine, says the Lord of hosts, my special possession on
the day when I act, and I will spare them as a man spares
his son who serves him. Then once more you shall
distinguish between the righteous and the wicked, between
one who serves God and one who does not serve him. For
behold, the day comes, burning like an oven, when all the
arrogant and all evildoers will be stubble; the day that
comes shall burn them up, says the Lord of hosts, so that it
will leave them neither root nor branch. But for you who
fear my name the sun of righteousness shall rise, with
healing in its wings. You shall go forth leaping like calves
from the stall. And you shall tread down the wicked, for
they will be ashes under the soles of your feet, on the day
when I act, says the Lord of hosts. Remember the law of
my servant Moses, the statutes and ordinances that I
commanded him at Horeb for all Israel. Behold, I will send
you Eli'jah the prophet before the great and terrible day of
the Lord comes. And he will turn the hearts of fathers to
their children and the hearts of children to their fathers,
lest I come and smite the land with a curse."

A Reading (Lesson) from the Letter of James [5:13-20]

Is any one among you suffering? Let him pray. Is any
cheerful? Let him sing praise. Is any among you sick? Let
him call for the elders of the church, and let them pray over

him, anointing him with oil in the name of the Lord; and the prayer of faith will save the sick man, and the Lord will raise him up; and if he has committed sins, he will be forgiven. Therefore confess your sins to one another, that you may be healed. The prayer of a righteous man has great power in its effects. Eli'jah was a man of like nature with ourselves and he prayed fervently that it might not rain, and for three years and six months it did not rain on the earth. Then he prayed again and the heaven gave rain, and the earth brought forth its fruit. My brethren, if any one among you wanders from the truth and some one brings him back, let him know that whoever brings back a sinner from the error of his way will save his soul from death and will cover a multitude of sins.

A Reading (Lesson) from the Gospel according to Luke
[18:9-14]

Jesus told this parable to those who trusted in themselves that they were righteous and despised others: "Two men went into the temple to pray, one a Pharisee and the other a tax collector. The Pharisee stood and prayed thus with himself, 'God, I thank thee that I am not like other men, extortioners, unjust, adulterers, or even like this tax collector. I fast twice a week, I give tithes of all that I get.' But the tax collector, standing far off, would not even lift up his eyes to heaven, but beat his breast, saying, 'God, be merciful to me a sinner!' I tell you, this man went down to his house justified rather than the other; for every one who exalts himself will be humbled, but he who humbles himself will be exalted."

Proper 29   *Week of the Sunday closest to November 23*

Sunday

Psalm 118 [page 760]   ❖   *Psalm 145* [page 801]

A Reading (Lesson) from the Book of Zechariah [9:9-16]

Rejoice greatly, O daughter of Zion! Shout aloud, O
daughter of Jerusalem! Lo, your king comes to you;
triumphant and victorious is he, humble and riding on an
ass, on a colt the foal of an ass. I will cut off the chariot
from E'phraim and the war horse from Jerusalem; and the
battle bow shall be cut off, and he shall command peace to
the nations; his dominion shall be from sea to sea, and
from the River to the ends of the earth. As for you also,
because of the blood of my covenant with you, I will set
your captives free from the waterless pit. Return to your
stronghold, O prisoners of hope; today I declare that I will
restore to you double. For I have bent Judah as my bow; I
have made E'phraim its arrow. I will brandish your sons O
Zion, over your sons, O Greece, and wield you like a
warrior's sword. Then the Lord will appear over them, and
his arrow go forth like lightning; the Lord God will sound
the trumpet, and march forth in the whirlwinds of the
south. The Lord of hosts will protect them, and they shall
devour and tread down the slingers; and they shall drink
their blood like wine, and be full like a bowl, drenched like
the corners of the altar. On that day the Lord their God
will save them for they are the flock of his people; for like
the jewels of a crown they shall shine on his land.

A Reading (Lesson) from the First Letter of Peter [3:13-22]

Now who is there to harm you if you are zealous for what
is right? But even if you do suffer for righteousness' sake,
you will be blessed. Have no fear of them, nor be troubled,
but in your hearts reverence Christ as Lord. Always be

prepared to make a defense to any one who calls you to account for the hope that is in you, yet do it with gentleness and reverence; and keep your conscience clear, so that, when you are abused, those who revile your good behavior in Christ may be put to shame. For it is better to suffer for doing right, if that should be God's will, than for doing wrong. For Christ also died for sins once for all, the righteous for the unrighteous, that he might bring us to God, being put to death in the flesh but made alive in the spirit; in which he went and preached to the spirits in prison, who formerly did not obey, when God's patience waited in the days of Noah, during the building of the ark, in which a few, that is, eight persons, were saved through water. Baptism, which corresponds to this, now saves you, not as a removal of dirt from the body but as an appeal to God for a clear conscience, through the resurrection of Jesus Christ, who has gone into heaven and is at the right hand of God, with angels, authorities, and powers subject to him.

A Reading (Lesson) from the Gospel according to Matthew [21:1-13]

When Jesus and the disciples drew near to Jerusalem and came to Beth'phage, to the Mount of Olives, then Jesus sent two disciples, saying to them, "Go into the village opposite you, and immediately you will find an ass tied, and a colt with her; untie them and bring them to me. If any one says anything to you, you shall say, 'The Lord has need of them,' and he will send them immediately." This took place to fulfil what was spoken by the prophet, saying, "Tell the daughter of Zion, Behold, your king is coming to you, humble, and mounted on an ass, and on a colt, the foal of an ass." The disciples went and did as Jesus had directed them; they brought the ass and the colt, and put their garments on them, and he sat thereon. Most of the crowd spread their garments on the road, and others cut branches from the trees and spread them on the road. And the crowds that went before him and that followed him shouted, "Hosanna to the Son of David! Blessed is he who comes in the name of the Lord! Hosanna in the highest!" And when he entered Jerusalem, all the city was stirred, saying, "Who is this?" And the crowds said, "This is the prophet Jesus from Nazareth of Galilee." And Jesus entered the temple of God and drove out all who sold and bought in the temple, and he overturned the tables of the moneychangers and the seats of those who sold pigeons. He said to them, "It is written, 'My house shall be called a house of prayer'; but you make it a den of robbers."

Monday

Psalm 106:1-18 [page 741]   ❖   *Psalm 106:19-48* [page 743]

A Reading (Lesson) from the Book of Zechariah [10:1-12]

Ask rain from the Lord in the season of the spring rain, from the Lord who makes the storm clouds, who gives men showers of rain, to every one the vegetation in the field. For the teraphim utter nonsense, and the diviners see lies; the dreamers tell false dreams, and give empty consolation. Therefore the people wander like sheep; they are afflicted for want of a shepherd. "My anger is hot against the shepherds, and I will punish the leaders; for the Lord of hosts cares for his flock, the house of Judah, and will make them like his proud steed in battle. Out of them shall come the cornerstone, out of them the tent peg, out of them the battle bow, out of them every ruler. Together they shall be like mighty men in battle, trampling the foe in the mud of the streets; they shall fight because the Lord is with them, and they shall confound the riders on horses. I will strengthen the house of Judah, and I will save the house of

Joseph. I will bring them back because I have compassion on them, and they shall be as though I had not rejected them; for I am the Lord their God and I will answer them. Then E'phraim shall become like a mighty warrior, and their hearts shall be glad as with wine. Their children shall see it and rejoice, their hearts shall exult in the Lord. I will signal for them and gather them in, for I have redeemed them, and they shall be as many as of old. Though I scattered them among the nations, yet in far countries they shall remember me, and with their children they shall live and return. I will bring them home from the land of Egypt, and gather them from Assyria; and I will bring them to the land of Gilead and to Lebanon, till there is no room for them. They shall pass through the sea of Egypt, and the waves of the sea shall be smitten, and all the depths of the Nile dried up. The pride of Assyria shall be laid low, and the scepter of Egypt shall depart. I will make them strong in the Lord and they shall glory in his name," says the Lord.

*A Reading (Lesson) from the Letter of Paul
to the Galatians* [6:1-10]

Brethren, if a man is overtaken in any trespass, you who are spiritual should restore him in a spirit of gentleness. Look to yourself, lest you too be tempted. Bear one another's burdens, and so fulfil the law of Christ. For if any one thinks he is something, when he is nothing, he deceives himself. But let each one test his own work, and then his reason to boast will be in himself alone and not in his neighbor. For each man will have to bear his own load. Let him who is taught the word share all good things with him who teaches. Do not be deceived; God is not mocked, for whatever a man sows, that he will also reap. For he who sows to his own flesh will from the flesh reap corruption; but he who sows to the Spirit will from the Spirit reap eternal life. And let us not grow weary in well-doing, for in due season we shall reap, if we do not lose heart. So then, as we have opportunity, let us do good to all men, and especially to those who are of the household of faith.

A Reading (Lesson) from the Gospel according to Luke [18:15-30]

Now they were bringing even infants to Jesus that he might touch them; and when the disciples saw it, they rebuked them. But Jesus called them to him, saying, "Let the children come to me, and do not hinder them; for to such belongs the kingdom of God. Truly, I say to you, whoever does not receive the kingdom of God like a child shall not enter it." And a ruler asked him, "Good Teacher, what shall I do to inherit eternal life?" And Jesus said to him, "Why do you call me good? No one is good but God alone. You know the commandments: 'Do not commit adultery, Do not kill, Do not steal, Do not bear false witness, Honor your father and mother.'" And he said, "All these I have observed from my youth." And when Jesus heard it, he said to him, "One thing you still lack. Sell all that you have and distribute to the poor, and you will have treasure in heaven; and come, follow me." But when he heard this he became sad, for he was very rich. Jesus looking at him, said, "How hard it is for those who have riches to enter the kingdom of God! For it is easier for a camel to go through the eye of a needle than for a rich man to enter the kingdom of God." Those who heard it said, "Then who can be saved?" But he said, "What is impossible with men is possible with God." And Peter said, "Lo, we have left our homes and followed you." And he said to them, "Truly, I say to you, there is no man who has left house or wife or brothers or parents or children, for the sake of the kingdom of God, who will not receive manifold more in this time, and in the age to come eternal life."

Tuesday

(Psalm 120 [page 778]),   *Psalm 121* [page 779],
Psalm 122 [page 779],   *Psalm 123* [page 780]   ❖
Psalm 124 [page 781],   *Psalm 125* [page 781],
Psalm 126 [page 782],   *(Psalm 127* [page 782])

A Reading (Lesson) from the Book of Zechariah [11:4-17]

Thus said the Lord my God: "Become shepherd of the flock doomed to slaughter. Those who buy them slay them and go unpunished; and those who sell them say, 'Blessed be the Lord, I have become rich'; and their own shepherds have no pity on them. For I will no longer have pity on the inhabitants of this land, says the Lord. Lo, I will cause men to fall each into the hand of his shepherd, and each into the hand of his king; and they shall crush the earth, and I will deliver none from their hand." So I became the shepherd of the flock doomed to be slain for those who trafficked in the sheep. And I took two staffs; one I named Grace, the other I named Union. And I tended the sheep. In one month I destroyed the three shepherds. But I became impatient with them, and they also detested me. So I said, "I will not be your shepherd. What is to die, let it die; what is to be destroyed, let it be destroyed; and let those that are left devour the flesh of one another." And I took my staff Grace, and I broke it, annulling the covenant which I had made with all the peoples. So it was annulled on that day, and the traffickers in the sheep, who were watching me, knew that it was the word of the Lord. Then I said to them, "If it seems right to you, give me my wages; but if not, keep them." And they weighed out as my wages thirty shekels of silver. Then the Lord said to me, "Cast it into the treasury'—the lordly price at which I was paid off by them. So I took the thirty shekels of silver and cast them into the treasury in the house of the Lord. Then I broke my second staff Union, annulling the brotherhood between Judah and Israel. Then the Lord said to me, "Take once more the implements of a worthless shepherd. For lo, I am raising up in the land a shepherd who does not care for the perishing, or seek the wandering, or heal the maimed, or nourish the sound, but devours the flesh of the fat ones, tearing off even their hoofs. Woe to my worthless shepherd, who deserts the flock! May the sword smite his arm and his right eye! Let his arm be wholly withered, his right eye utterly blinded!"

A Reading (Lesson) from the First Letter of Paul to the Corinthians [3:10-23]

According to the grace of God given to me, like a skilled master builder I laid a foundation, and another man is building upon it. Let each man take care how he builds upon it. For no other foundation can any one lay than that which is laid, which is Jesus Christ. Now if any one builds on the foundation with gold, silver, precious stones, wood, hay, straw—each man's work will become manifest; for the Day will disclose it, because it will be revealed with fire, and the fire will test what sort of work each one has done. If the work which any man has built on the foundation survives, he will receive a reward. If any man's work is burned up, he will suffer loss, though he himself will be saved, but only as through fire. Do you not know that you are God's temple and that God's Spirit dwells in you? If any one destroys God's temple, God will destroy him. For God's temple is holy, and that temple you are. Let no one deceive himself. If any one among you thinks that he is wise in this age, let him become a fool that he may become wise. For the wisdom of this world is folly with God. For it is written, "He catches the wise in their craftiness," and again, "The Lord knows that the thoughts of the wise are futile." So let no one boast of men. For all things are yours, whether Paul or Apol'los or Cephas or the world of life or death or the present or the future, all are yours; and you are Christ's; and Christ is God's.

A Reading (Lesson) from the Gospel according to Luke
[18:31-43]

Taking the twelve, Jesus said to them, "Behold, we are going up to Jerusalem, and everything that is written of the Son of man by the prophets will be accomplished. For he will be delivered to the Gentiles, and will be mocked and shamefully treated and spit upon; they will scourge him and kill him, and on the third day he will rise." But they understood none of these things; this saying was hid from them, and they did not grasp what was said. As he drew near to Jericho, a blind man was sitting by the roadside begging; and hearing a multitude going by, he inquired what this meant. They told him, "Jesus of Nazareth is passing by." And he cried, "Jesus, Son of David, have mercy on me!" And those who were in front rebuked him, telling him to be silent; but he cried out all the more, "Son of David, have mercy on me!" And Jesus stopped, and commanded him to be brought to him; and when he came near, he asked him, "What do you want me to do for you?" He said, "Lord, let me receive my sight." And Jesus said to him, "Receive your sight; your faith has made you well." And immediately he received his sight and followed him, glorifying God; and all the people, when they saw it, gave praise to God.

Wednesday

Psalm 119:145-176 [page 775] ❖ *Psalm 128* [page 783],
Psalm 129 [page 784],   *Psalm 130* [page 784]

A Reading (Lesson) from the Book of Zechariah [12:1-10]

The word of the Lord concerning Israel: Thus says the Lord, who stretched out the heavens and founded the earth and formed the spirit of man within him: "Lo, I am about to make Jerusalem a cup of reeling to all the peoples round about; it will be against Judah also in the siege against

Jerusalem. On that day I will make Jerusalem a heavy stone for all the peoples; all who lift it shall grievously hurt themselves. And all the nations of the earth will come together against it. On that day, says the Lord, I will strike every horse with panic, and its rider with madness. But upon the house of Judah I will open my eyes, when I strike every horse of the peoples with blindness. Then the clans of Judah shall say to themselves, 'The inhabitants of Jerusalem have strength through the Lord of hosts, their God.' On that day I will make the clans of Judah like a blazing pot in the midst of wood, like a flaming torch among sheaves; and they shall devour to the right and to the left all the peoples round about, while Jerusalem shall still be inhabited in its place, in Jerusalem. And the Lord will give victory to the tents of Judah first, that the glory of the house of David and the glory of the inhabitants of Jerusalem may not be exalted over that of Judah. On that day the Lord will put a shield about the inhabitants of Jerusalem so that the feeblest among them on that day shall be like David, and the house of David shall be like God, like the angel of the Lord, at their head. And on that day I will seek to destroy all the nations that come against Jerusalem. And I will pour out on the house of David and the inhabitants of Jerusalem a spirit of compassion and supplication, so that, when they look on him whom they have pierced, they shall mourn for him, as one mourns for an only child, and weep bitterly over him, as one weeps over a first-born."

A Reading (Lesson) from the Letter of Paul to the Ephesians [1:3-14]

Blessed be the God and Father of our Lord Jesus Christ, who has blessed us in Christ with every spiritual blessing in the heavenly places, even as he chose us in him before the foundation of the world, that we should be holy and blameless before him. He destined us in love to be his sons through Jesus Christ, according to the purpose of his will, to the praise of his glorious grace which he freely bestowed on us in the Beloved. In him we have redemption through his blood, the forgiveness of our trespasses, according to the riches of his grace which he lavished upon us. For he has made known to us in all wisdom and insight the mystery of his will, according to his purpose which he set forth in Christ as a plan for the fulness of time, to unite all things in him, things in heaven and things on earth. In him, according to the purpose of him who accomplishes all things according to the counsel of his will, we who first hoped in Christ have been destined and appointed to live for the praise of his glory. In him you also, who have heard the word of truth, the gospel of your salvation, and have believed in him, were sealed with the promised Holy Spirit, which is the guarantee of our inheritance until we acquire possession of it, to the praise of his glory.

A Reading (Lesson) from the Gospel according to Luke
[19:1-10]

Jesus entered Jericho and was passing through. And there was a man named Zacchae'us; he was a chief tax collector, and rich. And he sought to see who Jesus was, but could not, on account of the crowd, because he was small of stature. So he ran on ahead and climbed up into a sycamore tree to see him, for he was to pass that way. And when Jesus came to the place, he looked up and said to him, "Zacchae'us, make haste and come down; for I must stay at your house today." So he made haste and came down, and received him joyfully. And when they saw it they all murmured, "He has gone in to be the guest of a man who is a sinner." And Zacchae'us stood and said to the Lord, "Behold, Lord, the half of my goods I give to the poor; and if I have defrauded any one of anything, I restore it fourfold." And Jesus said to him, "Today salvation has come to this house, since he also is a son of Abraham. For the Son of man came to seek and to save the lost."

Thursday

Psalm 131 [page 785],   *Psalm 132* [page 785],
(Psalm 133 [page 787])   ❖   *Psalm 134* [page 787],
Psalm 135 [page 788]

A Reading (Lesson) from the Book of Zechariah [13:1-9]

Thus says the Lord: "On that day there shall be a fountain opened for the house of David and the inhabitants of Jerusalem to cleanse them from sin and uncleanness. And on that day, says the Lord of hosts, I will cut off the names of the idols from the land, so that they shall be remembered no more; and also I will remove from the land the prophets and the unclean spirit. And if any one again appears as a prophet, his father and mother who bore him will say to him, 'You shall not live, for you speak lies in the name of the Lord'; and his father and mother who bore him shall pierce him through when he prophesies. On that day every prophet will be ashamed of his vision when he prophesies; he will not put on a hairy mantle in order to deceive, but he will say, 'I am no prophet, I am a tiller of the soil; for the land has been my possession since my youth.' And if one asks him, 'What are these wounds on your back?' he will say, 'The wounds I received in the house of my friends.'" "Awake, O sword, against my shepherd, against the man who stands next to me," says the Lord of hosts. "Strike the shepherd, that the sheep may be scattered; I will turn my hand against the little ones. In the whole land, says the Lord, two thirds shall be cut off and perish, and one third shall be left alive. And I will put this third into the fire, and refine them as one refines silver, and test them as gold is tested. They will call on my name, and I will answer them. I will say, 'They are my people'; and they will say, 'The Lord is my God.'"

*A Reading (Lesson) from the Letter of Paul
to the Ephesians* [1:15-23]

For this reason, because I have heard of your faith in the
Lord Jesus and your love toward all the saints, I do not
cease to give thanks for you, remembering you in my
prayers, that the God of our Lord Jesus Christ, the Father
of glory, may give you a spirit of wisdom and of revelation
in the knowledge of him, having the eyes of your hearts
enlightened, that you may know what is the hope to which
he has called you, what are the riches of his glorious
inheritance in the saints, and what is the immeasurable
greatness of his power in us who believe, according to the
working of his great might which he accomplished in
Christ when he raised him from the dead and made him sit
at his right hand in the heavenly places, far above all rule
and authority and power and dominion, and above every
name that is named, not only in this age but also in that
which is to come; and he has put all things under his feet
and has made him the head over all things for the church,
which is his body, the fulness of him who fills all in all.

A Reading (Lesson) from the Gospel according to Luke
[19:11-27]

As they heard these things, Jesus proceeded to tell a
parable, because he was near to Jerusalem, and because
they supposed that the kingdom of God was to appear
immediately. He said therefore, "A nobleman went into a
far country to receive a kingdom and then return. Calling
ten of his servants, he gave them ten pounds, and said to
them, 'Trade with these till I come.' But his citizens hated
him and sent an embassy after him, saying, 'We do not
want this man to reign over us.' When he returned, having
received the kingdom, he commanded these servants, to
whom he had given the money, to be called to him, that he
might know what they had gained by trading. The first
came before him, saying, 'Lord, your pound has made ten

pounds more.' And he said to him, "Well done, good servant! Because you have been faithful in a very little, you shall have authority over ten cities.' And the second came, saying, 'Lord, your pound has made five pounds.' And he said to him, 'And you are to be over five cities.' Then another came, saying, 'Lord, here is your pound, which I kept laid away in a napkin; for I was afraid of you, because you are a severe man; you take up what you did not lay down, and reap what you did not sow.' He said to him, "I will condemn you out of your own mouth, you wicked servant! You knew that I was a severe man, taking up what I did not lay down and reaping what I did not sow? Why then did you not put my money into the bank, and at my coming I should have collected it with interest?' And he said to those who stood by, 'Take the pound from him, and give it to him who has the ten pounds.' (And they said to him, 'Lord he has ten pounds!') 'I tell you, that to every one who has will more be given; but from him who has not, even what he has will be taken away. But as for these enemies of mine, who did not want me to reign over them, bring them here and slay them before me.'"

Friday

Psalm 140 [page 796], *Psalm 142* [page 798] ❖
Psalm 141 [page 797], *Psalm 143:1-11(12)* [page 798]

A Reading (Lesson) from the Book of Zechariah [14:1-11]

Behold, a day of the Lord is coming, when the spoil taken from you will be divided in the midst of you. For I will gather all the nations against Jerusalem to battle, and the city shall be taken and the houses plundered and the women ravished; half of the city shall go into exile, but the rest of the people shall not be cut off from the city. Then the Lord will go forth and fight against those nations as when he fights on a day of battle. On that day his feet shall stand on the Mount of Olives which lies before Jerusalem on the east; and the Mount of Olives shall be split in two from east to west by a very wide valley; so that one half of the Mount shall withdraw northward, and the other half southward. And the valley of my mountains shall be stopped up, for the valley of the mountains shall touch the side of it; and you shall flee as you fled from the earthquake in the days of Uzzi'ah king of Judah. Then the Lord your God will come, and all the holy ones with him. On that day there shall be neither cold nor frost. And there shall be continuous day (it is known to the Lord), not day and not night, for at evening there shall be light. On that day living waters shall flow out from Jerusalem, half of them to the eastern sea and half of them to the western sea; it shall continue in summer as in winter. And the Lord will become king over all the earth; on that day the Lord will be one and his name one. The whole land shall be turned into a plain from Geba to Rimmon south of Jerusalem. But Jerusalem shall remain aloft upon its site from the Gate of Benjamin to the place of the former gate, to the Corner Gate, and from the Tower of Han'anel to the king's wine presses. And it shall be inhabited, for there shall be no more curse; Jerusalem shall dwell in security.

A Reading (Lesson) from the Letter of Paul to the Romans [15:7-13]

Welcome one another, therefore, as Christ has welcomed you, for the glory of God. For I tell you that Christ became a servant to the circumcised to show God's truthfulness, in order to confirm the promises given to the patriarchs, and in order that the Gentiles might glorify God for his mercy. As it is written, "Therefore I will praise thee among the Gentiles, and sing to thy name"; and again it is said, "Rejoice, O Gentiles, with his people"; and again, "Praise the Lord, all Gentiles, and let all the peoples praise him"; and further Isaiah says, "The root of Jesse shall come, he who rises to rule the Gentiles; in him shall the Gentiles hope." May the God of hope fill you with all joy and peace in believing, so that by the power of the Holy Spirit you may abound in hope.

A Reading (Lesson) from the Gospel according to Luke [19:28-40]

When Jesus had said this, he went on ahead, going up to Jerusalem. When he drew near to Beth'phage and Bethany, at the mount that is called Olivet, he sent two of the disciples, saying, "Go into the village opposite, where on entering you will find a colt tied, on which no one has ever yet sat; untie it and bring it here. If any one asks you, 'Why are you untying it?' you shall say this, 'The Lord has need of it.'" So those who were sent away and found it as he had told them. And as they were untying the colt, its owners said to them, "Why are you untying the colt?" And they said, "The Lord has need of it." And they brought it to Jesus, and throwing their garments on the colt they set Jesus upon it. And as he rode along, they spread their garments on the road. As he was now drawing near, at the descent of the Mount of Olives, the whole multitude of the disciples began to rejoice and praise God with a loud voice for all the mighty works that they had seen, saying, "Blessed is the King who comes in the name of the Lord! Peace in heaven and glory in the highest!" And some of the Pharisees in the multitude said to him, "Teacher, rebuke your disciples." He answered, "I tell you, if these were silent, the very stones would cry out."

Saturday

Psalm 137:1-6(7-9) [page 792], *Psalm 144* [page 801] ❖
Psalm 104 [page 735]

A Reading (Lesson) from the Book of Zechariah [14:12-21]
This shall be the plague with which the Lord will smite all

the peoples that wage war against Jerusalem: their flesh shall rot while they are still on their feet, their eyes shall rot in their sockets, and their tongues shall rot in their mouths. And on that day a great panic from the Lord shall fall on them, so that each will lay hold on the hand of his fellow, and the hand of the one will be raised against the hand of the other; even Judah will fight against Jerusalem. And the wealth of all the nations round about shall be collected, gold, silver, and garments in great abundance. And a plague like this plague shall fall on the horses, the mules, the camels, the asses, and whatever beasts may be in those camps. Then every one that survives of all the nations that have come against Jerusalem shall go up year after year to worship the King, the Lord of hosts, and to keep the feast of booths. And if any of the families of the earth do not go up to Jerusalem to worship the King, the Lord of hosts, there will be no rain upon them. And if the family of Egypt do not go up and present themselves, then upon them shall come the plague with which the Lord afflicts the nations that do not go up to keep the feast of booths. This shall be the punishment to Egypt and the punishment to all the nations that do not go up to keep the feast of booths. And on that day there shall be inscribed on the bells of the horses, "Holy to the Lord." And the pots in the house of the Lord shall be as the bowls before the altar; and every pot in Jerusalem and Judah shall be sacred to the Lord of hosts, so that all who sacrifice may come and take of them and boil the flesh of the sacrifice in them. And there shall no longer be a trader in the house of the Lord of hosts on that day.

A Reading (Lesson) from the Letter of Paul to the Philippians [2:1-11]

If there is any encouragement in Christ, any incentive of love, any participation in the Spirit, any affection and sympathy, complete my joy by being of the same mind, having the same love, being in full accord and of one mind. Do nothing from selfishness or conceit, but in humility count others better than yourselves. Let each of you look not only to his own interests, but also to the interests of others. Have this mind among yourselves, which is yours in Christ Jesus, who, though he was in the form of God, did not count equality with God a thing to be grasped, but emptied himself, taking the form of a servant, being born in the likeness of men. And being found in human form he humbled himself and became obedient unto death, even death on a cross. Therefore God has highly exalted him and bestowed on him the name which is above every name, that at the name of Jesus every knee should bow, in heaven and on earth and under the earth, and every tongue confess that Jesus Christ is Lord, to the glory of God the Father.

A Reading (Lesson) from the Gospel according to Luke [19:41-48]

When Jesus drew near and saw Jerusalem he wept over it, saying, "Would that even today you knew the things that make for peace! But now they are hid from your eyes. For the days shall come upon you, when your enemies will cast up a bank about you and surround you, and hem you in on every side, and dash you to the ground, you and your children within you, and they will not leave one stone upon another in you; because you did not know the time of your visitation." And he entered the temple and began to drive out those who sold, saying to them, "It is written, 'My house shall be a house of prayer'; but you have made it a den of robbers." And he was teaching daily in the temple. The chief priests and the scribes and the principal men of the people sought to destroy him; but they did not find anything they could do, for all the people hung upon his words.

Holy Days

Eve of the Visitation   *May 30*

(Evening Prayer)   *Psalm 132* [page 785]

A Reading (Lesson) from the Book of Isaiah [11:1-10]

There shall come forth a shoot from the stump of Jesse, and a branch shall grow out of his roots. And the Spirit of the Lord shall rest upon him, the spirit of wisdom and understanding, the spirit of counsel and might, the spirit of knowledge and the fear of the Lord. And his delight shall be in the fear of the Lord. He shall not judge by what his eyes see, or decide by what his ears hear; but with righteousness he shall judge the poor, and decide with equity for the meek of the earth; and he shall smite the earth with the rod of his mouth, and with the breath of his lips he shall slay the wicked. Righteousness shall be the girdle of his waist, and faithfulness the girdle of his loins. The wolf shall dwell with the lamb, and the leopard shall lie down with the kid, and the calf and the lion and the fatling together, and a little child shall lead them. The cow and the bear shall feed; their young shall lie down together; and the lion shall eat straw like the ox. The sucking child shall play over the hole of the asp, and the weaned child shall put his hand on the adder's den. They shall not hurt or destroy in all my holy mountain; for the earth shall be full of the knowledge of the Lord as the waters cover the sea. In that day the root of Jesse shall stand as an ensign to the peoples; him shall the nations seek, and his dwellings shall be glorious.

A Reading (Lesson) from the Letter to the Hebrews [2:11-18]

He who sanctifies and those who are sanctified have all

one origin. That is why he is not ashamed to call them brethren, saying, "I will proclaim thy name to my brethren, in the midst of the congregation I will praise thee." And again, "I will put my trust in him." And again, "Here am I, and the children God has given me." Since therefore the children share in flesh and blood, he himself likewise partook of the same nature, that through death he might destroy him who has the power of death, that is, the devil, and deliver all those who through fear of death were subject to lifelong bondage. For surely it is not with angels that he is concerned but with the descendants of Abraham. Therefore he had to be made like his brethren in every respect, so that he might become a merciful and faithful high priest in the service of God, to make expiation for the sins of the people. For because he himself has suffered and been tempted, he is able to help those who are tempted.

The Visitation   *May 31*

(Morning Prayer)   *Psalm 72* [page 685]

A Reading (Lesson) from the First Book of Samuel [1:1-20]

There was a certain man of Ramatha'im-zo'phim of the hill country of E'phraim, whose name was Elka'nah the son of Jero'ham, son of Eli'hu, son of Tohu, son of Zuph, an E'phraimite. He had two wives; the name of the one was Hannah, and the name of the other Penin'nah. And Penin'nah had children, but Hannah had no children. Now this man used to go up year by year from his city to worship and to sacrifice to the Lord of hosts at Shiloh, where the two sons of Eli, Hophni and Phin'ehas, were priests of the Lord. On the day when Elka'nah sacrificed, he would give portions to Penin'nah his wife and to all her sons and daughters; and, although he loved Hannah, he would give Hannah only one portion, because the Lord had closed her womb. And her rival used to provoke her sorely, to irritate her, because the Lord had closed her womb. So it went on year by year; as often as she went up to the house of the Lord, she used to provoke her. Therefore Hannah wept and would not eat. And Elka'nah, her husband said to her, "Hannah, why do you weep? And why do you not eat? And why is your heart sad? Am I not more to you than ten sons?" After they had eaten and drunk in Shiloh, Hannah rose. Now Eli the priest was sitting on a seat beside the doorpost of the temple of the Lord. She was deeply distressed and prayed to the Lord, and wept bitterly. And she vowed a vow and said, "O Lord of hosts, if thou wilt indeed look on the affliction of thy maidservant, and remember me, and not forget thy maidservant, but wilt give to thy maidservant a son, then I will give him to the Lord all the days of his life, and no razor shall touch his head." As she continued praying before the Lord, Eli observed her mouth. Hannah was speaking in her heart; only her lips moved, and her voice was not heard; therefore Eli took her to be a drunken woman. And Eli said to her, "How long will you be drunken? Put away your wine from you." But Hannah answered, "No, my lord, I am a woman sorely troubled; I have drunk neither wine nor strong drink, but I have been pouring out my soul before the Lord. Do not regard your maidservant as a base woman, for all along I have been speaking out of my great anxiety and vexation." Then Eli answered, "Go in peace, and the God of Israel grant your petition which you have made to him." And she said, "Let your maidservant find favor in your eyes." Then the woman went her way and ate, and her countenance was no longer sad. They rose early in the morning and worshiped before the Lord; then they went back to their house at Ramah. And Elka'nah knew Hannah his wife, and the Lord remembered her; and in due time Hannah conceived and bore a son, and she called his name Samuel, for she said, "I have asked him of the Lord."

A Reading (Lesson) from the Letter to the Hebrews
[3:1-6]

Therefore, holy brethren, who share in a heavenly call, consider Jesus, the apostle and high priest of our confession. He was faithful to him who appointed him, just as Moses also was faithful in God's house. Yet Jesus has been counted worthy of as much more glory than Moses as the builder of a house has more honor than the house. (For every house is built by some one, but the builder of all things is God.) Now Moses was faithful in all God's house as a servant, to testify to the things that were to be spoken later, but Christ was faithful over God's house as a son. And we are his house if we hold fast our confidence and pride in our hope.

(Evening Prayer) *Psalm 146* [page 803], *Psalm 147* [page 804]

A Reading (Lesson) from the Book of Zechariah [2:10-13]

Thus said the Lord of hosts: "Sing and rejoice, O daughter of Zion; for lo, I come and I will dwell in the midst of you, says the Lord. And many nations shall join themselves to the Lord in that day, and shall be my people; and I will dwell in the midst of you, and you shall know that the Lord of hosts has sent me to you. And the Lord will inherit Judah as his portion in the holy land, and will again choose Jerusalem." Be silent, all flesh, before the Lord; for he has roused himself from his holy dwelling.

A Reading (Lesson) from the Gospel according to John
[3:25-30]

A discussion arose between John's disciples and a Jew over purifying. And they came to John, and said to him, "Rabbi, he who was with you beyond the Jordan, to whom you bore witness, here he is, baptizing, and all are going to him." John answered, "No one can receive anything except what is given him from heaven. You yourselves bear me witness, that I said, I am not the Christ, but I have been sent before him. He who has the bride is the bridegroom; the friend of the bridegroom, who stands and hears him, rejoices greatly at the bridegroom's voice; therefore this joy of mine is now full. He must increase, but I must decrease."

St. Barnabas   *June 11*

(Morning Prayer)   *Psalm 15* [page 599],   *Psalm 67* [page 675]

A Reading (Lesson) from the Book of Ecclesiasticus
[31:3-11]

The rich man toils as his wealth accumulates, and when he rests he fills himself with his dainties. The poor man toils as his livelihood diminishes, and when he rests he becomes needy. He who loves gold will not be justified, and he who pursues money will be led astray by it. Many have come to ruin because of gold, and their destruction has met them face to face. It is a stumbling block to those who are devoted to it, and every fool will be taken captive by it. Blessed is the rich man who is found blameless, and who does not go after gold. Who is he? And we will call him blessed, for he has done wonderful things among his people. Who has been tested by it and been found perfect? Let it be for him a ground for boasting. Who has had the power to transgress and did not transgress, and to do evil and did not do it? His prosperity will be established, and the assembly will relate his acts of charity.

A Reading (Lesson) from the Acts of the Apostles [4:32-37]

The company of those who believed were of one heart and soul, and no one said that any of the things which he possessed was his own, but they had everything in common. And with great power the apostles gave their testimony to the resurrection of the Lord Jesus, and great grace was upon them all. There was not a needy person among them, for as many as were possessors of lands or houses sold them, and brought the proceeds of what was sold and laid it at the apostles' feet; and distribution was made to each as any had need. Thus Joseph who was surnamed by the apostles Barnabas (which means, Son of encouragement), a Levite, a native of Cyprus, sold a field which belonged to him, and brought the money and laid it at the apostles' feet.

(Evening Prayer)   *Psalm 19* [page 606],   *Psalm 146* [page 803]

A Reading (Lesson) from the Book of Job [29:1-16]

Job again took up his discourse, and said: "Oh, that I were as in the months of old, as in the days when God watched over me; when his lamp shone upon my head, and by his light I walked through the darkness; as I was in my autumn days, when the friendship of God was upon my tent; when the Almighty was yet with me, when my children were about me: when my steps were washed with milk, and the rock poured out for me streams of oil! When I went out to the gate of the city, when I prepared my seat in the square, the young men saw me and withdrew, and the aged rose and stood; the princes refrained from talking, and laid their hand on their mouth; the voice of the nobles were hushed, and their tongue cleaved to the roof of their mouth. When the ear heard, it called me blessed, and when the eye saw, it approved; because I delivered the poor who cried, and the fatherless who had none to help him. The blessing of him who was about to perish came upon me, and I caused the widow's heart to sing for joy. I put on righteousness, and it clothed me; my justice was like a robe and a turban. I was eyes to the blind, and feet to the lame. I was father to the poor, and I searched out the cause of him whom I did not know.

A Reading (Lesson) from the Acts of the Apostles [9:26-31]

When Paul had come to Jerusalem he attempted to join the disciples; and they were all afraid of him, for they did not believe that he was a disciple. But Barnabas took him, and brought him to the apostles, and declared to them how on the road he had seen the Lord, who spoke to him, and how at Damascus he had preached boldly in the name of Jesus. So he went in and out among them at Jerusalem, preached boldly in the name of the Lord. And he spoke and disputed against the Hellenists; but they were seeking to kill him. And when the brethren knew it, they brought him down to Caesare'a, and sent him off to Tarsus. So the church throughout all Judea and Galilee and Samar'ia had peace and was built up; and walking in the fear of the Lord and in the comfort of the Holy Spirit it was multiplied.

Eve of St. John the Baptist   *June 23*

(Evening Prayer)   *Psalm 103* [page 733]

A Reading (Lesson) from the Book of Ecclesiasticus
[48:1-11]

The prophet Eli'jah arose like a fire, and his word burned like a torch. He brought a famine upon them, and by his zeal he made them few in number. By the word of the Lord he shut up the heavens, and also three times brought down fire. How glorious you were, O Eli'jah, in your wondrous deeds! And who has the right to boast which you have? You have raised a corpse from death and from Hades, by the word of the Most High; who brought kings down to destruction, and famous men from their beds; who heard rebuke at Sinai and judgments of vengeance at Horeb; who anointed kings to inflict retribution, and prophets to succeed you. You who were taken up by a whirlwind of fire, in a chariot with horses of fire; you who are ready at the appointed time, it is written, to calm the wrath of God before it breaks out in fury, to turn the heart of the father to the son, and to restore the tribes of Jacob. Blessed are those who saw you, and those who have been adorned in love; for we also shall surely live.

A Reading (Lesson) from the Gospel according to Luke [1:5-23]

In the days of Herod, king of Judea, there was a priest named Zechari'ah, of the division of Abi'jah; and he had a wife of the daughters of Aaron, and her name was Elizabeth. And they were both righteous before God, walking in all the commandments and ordinances of the Lord blameless. But they had no child, because Elizabeth was barren, and both were advanced in years. Now while he was serving as priest before God when his division was on duty, according to the custom of the priesthood, it fell to him by lot to enter the temple of the Lord and burn incense. And the whole multitude of the people were praying outside at the hour of incense. And there appeared to him an angel of the Lord standing on the right side of the altar of incense. And Zechari'ah was troubled when he saw him, and fear fell upon him. But the angel said to him, "Do not be afraid, Zechari'ah, for your prayer is heard, and your wife Elizabeth will bear you a son, and you shall call his name John. And you will have joy and gladness, and many will rejoice at his birth; for he will be great before the Lord, and he shall drink no wine nor strong drink, and he will be filled with the Holy Spirit, even from his mother's womb. And he will turn many of the sons of Israel to the Lord their God, and he will go before him in the spirit and power of Eli'jah, to turn the hearts of the fathers to the children, and the disobedient to the wisdom of the just, to make ready for the Lord a people prepared." And Zechari'ah said to the angel, "How shall I know this? For I am an old man, and my wife is advanced in years."

And the angel answered him, "I am Gabriel, who stand in the presence of God; and I was sent to speak to you, and to bring you this good news. And behold, you will be silent and unable to speak until the day that these things come to pass, because you did not believe my words, which will be fulfilled in their time." And the people were waiting for Zechari'ah, and they wondered at his delay in the temple. And when he came out, he could not speak to them, and they perceived that he had seen a vision in the temple; and he made signs to them and remained dumb. And when his time of service was ended, he went to his home.

Nativity of St. John the Baptist   *June 24*

(Morning Prayer)   *Psalm 82* [page 705],   *Psalm 98* [page 727]

A Reading (Lesson) from the Book of Malachi [3:1-5]

"Behold, I send my messenger to prepare the way before me, and the Lord whom you seek will suddenly come to his temple; the messenger of the covenant in whom you delight, behold, he is coming, says the Lord of hosts. But who can endure the day of his coming, and who can stand when he appears? For he is like a refiner's fire and like fullers' soap; he will sit as a refiner and purifier of silver, and he will purify the sons of Levi and refine them like gold and silver, till they present right offerings to the Lord. Then the offering of Judah and Jerusalem will be pleasing to the Lord as in the days of old and in former years. Then I will draw near to you for judgment; I will be a swift witness against the sorcerers, against the adulterers, against those who swear falsely, against those who oppress the hireling in his wages, the widow and the orphan, against those who thrust aside the sojourner, and do not fear me, says the Lord of hosts."

A Reading (Lesson) from the Gospel according to John [3:22-30]

Jesus and his disciples went into the land of Judea; there he remained with them and baptized. John also was baptizing at Ae'non near Salim, because there was much water there; and people came and were baptized. For John had not yet been put in prison. Now a discussion arose between John's disciples and a Jew over purifying. And they came to John, and said to him, "Rabbi, he who was with you beyond the Jordan, to whom you bore witness, here he is, baptizing, and all are going to him." John answered, "No one can receive anything except what is given him from heaven. You yourselves bear me witness, that I said, I am not the Christ, but I have been sent before him. He who has the bride is the bridegroom; the friend of the bridegroom, who stands and hears him, rejoices greatly at the bridegroom's voice; therefore this joy of mine is now full. He must increase, but I must decrease."

(Evening Prayer)   *Psalm 80* [page 702]

A Reading (Lesson) from the Book of Malachi [4:1-6]

"For behold, the day comes, burning like an oven, when all the arrogant and all the evildoers will be stubble; the day that comes shall burn them up, says the Lord of hosts, so that it will leave them neither root nor branch. But for you who fear my name the sun of righteousness shall rise, with healing in its wings. You shall go forth leaping like calves from the stall. And you shall tread down the wicked, for they will be ashes under the soles of your feet, on the day when I act, says the Lord of hosts. Remember the law of my servant Moses, the statutes and ordinances that I commanded him at Horeb for all Israel. Behold, I will send you Eli'jah the prophet before the great and terrible day of the Lord comes. And he will turn the hearts of fathers to their children and the hearts of children to their fathers, lest I come and smite the land with a curse."

A Reading (Lesson) from the Gospel according to Matthew
[11:2-19]

When John heard in prison about the deeds of the Christ, he sent word by his disciples and said to him, "Are you he who is to come, or shall we look for another?" And Jesus answered them, "Go and tell John what you hear and see: the blind receive their sight and the lame walk, lepers are cleansed and the deaf hear, and the dead are raised up, and the poor have good news preached to them. And blessed is he who takes no offense at me." As they went away, Jesus began to speak to the crowds concerning John: "What did you go out into the wilderness to behold? A reed shaken by the wind? Why then did you go out? To see a man clothed in soft raiment? Behold, those who wear soft raiment are in kings' houses. Why then did you go out? To see a prophet? Yes, I tell you, and more than a prophet. This is he of whom it is written, 'Behold, I send my messenger before thy face, who shall prepare thy way before thee.' Truly, I say to you, among those born of woman there has risen no one greater than John the Baptist; yet he who is least in the kingdom of heaven is greater than he. From the days of John the Baptist until now the kingdom of heaven has suffered violence, and men of violence take it by force. For all the prophets and the law prophesied until John; and if you are willing to accept it, he is Eli'jah who is to come. He who has ears to hear, let him hear. But to what shall I compare this generation? It is like children sitting in the market places and calling to their playmates, 'We piped to you, and you did not dance; we wailed, and you did not mourn.' For John came neither eating nor drinking, and they say, 'He has a demon'; the Son of man came eating and drinking, and they say, 'Behold, a glutton and a drunkard, a friend of tax collectors and sinners!' Yet wisdom is justified by her deeds."

St. Peter and St. Paul *June 29*

(Morning Prayer) *Psalm 66* [page 673]

A Reading (Lesson) from the Book of Ezekiel [2:1-7]

And the Lord said to me, "Son of man, stand upon your feet, and I will speak with you." And when he spoke to me, the Spirit entered into me and set me upon my feet; and I heard him speaking to me. And he said to me, "Son of man, I send you to the people of Israel, to a nation of rebels, who have rebelled against me; they and their fathers have transgressed against me to this very day. The people also are impudent and stubborn: I send you to them; and you shall say to them, 'Thus says the Lord God.' And whether they hear or refuse to hear (for they are a rebellious house) they will know that there has been a prophet among them. And you, son of man, be not afraid of them, nor be afraid of their words, though briers and thorns are with you and you sit upon scorpions; be not afraid of their words, nor be dismayed at their looks, for they are a rebellious house. And you shall speak my words to them, whether they hear or refuse to hear; for they are a rebellious house."

Acts 11:1-18 [page 300 above]

(Evening Prayer) *Psalm 97* [page 726], *Psalm 138* [page 793]

A Reading (Lesson) from the Book of Isaiah [49:1-6]

Listen to me, O coastlands, and hearken, you peoples from afar. The Lord called me from the womb, from the body of my mother he named my name. He made my mouth like a sharp sword, in the shadow of his hand he hid me; he made me a polished arrow, in his quiver he hid me away. And he said to me, "You are my servant, Israel, in whom I will be glorified." But I said, "I have labored in vain, I have spent my strength for nothing and vanity; yet surely my right is with the Lord, and my recompense with my God." And now the Lord says, who formed me from the womb to be his servant, to bring Jacob back to him, and that Israel might be gathered to him, for I am honored in the eyes of the Lord, and my God has become my strength—he says: "It is too light a thing that you should be my servant to raise up the tribes of Jacob and to restore the preserved of Israel; I will give you as a light to the nations, that my salvation may reach to the end of the earth."

A Reading (Lesson) from the Letter of Paul to the Galatians [2:1-9]

After fourteen years I went up again to Jerusalem with Barnabas, taking Titus along with me. I went up by revelation; and I laid before them (but privately before those who were of repute) the gospel which I preach among the Gentiles, lest somehow I should be running or had run in vain. But even Titus, who was with me, was not compelled to be circumcised, though he was a Greek. But because of false brethren secretly brought in, who slipped in to spy out our freedom which we have in Christ Jesus, that they might bring us into bondage—to them we did not yield submission even for a moment, that the truth of the gospel might be preserved for you. And from those who were reputed to be something (what they were makes no difference to me; God shows no partiality)—those, I say, who were of repute added nothing to me; but on the contrary, when they saw that I had been entrusted with the gospel to the uncircumcised, just as Peter had been entrusted with the gospel to the circumcised (for he who worked through Peter for the mission to the circumcised worked through me also for the Gentiles), and when they perceived the grace that was given to me, James and Cephas and John, who were reputed to be pillars, gave to me and Barnabas the right hand of fellowship, that we should go to the Gentiles and they to the circumcised.

Independence Day *July 4*

(Morning Prayer)   *Psalm 33* [page 626]

A Reading (Lesson) from the Book of Ecclesiasticus
[10:1-8,12-18]

A wise magistrate will educate his people, and the rule of
an understanding man will be well ordered. Like the
magistrate of the people, so are his officials; and like the
ruler of the city, so are all its inhabitants. An undisciplined
king will ruin his people, but a city will grow through the
understanding of its rulers. The government of the earth is
in the hands of the Lord, and over it he will raise up the
right man for the time. The success of a man is in the hands
of the Lord, and he confers his honor upon the person of
the scribe. Do not be angry with your neighbor for any
injury, and do not attempt anything by acts of insolence.
Arrogance is hateful before the Lord and before men, and
injustice is outrageous to both. Sovereignty passes from
nation to nation on account of injustice and insolence and
wealth. The beginning of man's pride is to depart from the
Lord; his heart has forsaken his Maker. For the beginning
of pride is sin, and the man who clings to it pours out
abominations. Therefore the Lord brought upon them
extraordinary afflictions, and destroyed them utterly. The
Lord has cast down the thrones of rulers, and has seated
the lowly in their place. The Lord has plucked up the roots
of the nations, and has planted the humble in their place.
The Lord has overthrown the lands of the nations, and has
destroyed them to the foundations of the earth. He has
removed some of them and destroyed them, and has
extinguished the memory of them from the earth. Pride
was not created for men, nor fierce anger for those born of
women.

A Reading (Lesson) from the Letter of James [5:7-10]

Be patient, therefore, brethren, until the coming of the
Lord. Behold, the farmer waits for the precious fruit of the
earth, being patient over it until it receives the early and
the late rain. You also be patient. Establish your hearts, for
the coming of the Lord is at hand. Do not grumble,
brethren, against one another, that you may not be judged;
behold, the Judge is standing at the doors. As an example
of suffering and patience, brethren, take the prophets who
spoke in the name of the Lord.

(Evening Prayer)   *Psalm 107:1-32* [page 746]

A Reading (Lesson) from the Book of Micah [4:1-5]

It shall come to pass in the latter days that the mountain of
the house of the Lord shall be established as the highest of
the mountains, and shall be raised up above the hills; and
peoples shall flow to it, and many nations shall come, and
say: "Come, let us go up to the mountain of the Lord, to
the house of the God of Jacob; that he may teach us his
ways and we may walk in his paths." For out of Zion shall
go forth the law, and the word of the Lord from Jerusalem.
He shall judge between many peoples, and shall decide for
strong nations afar off; and they shall beat their swords
into plowshares, and their spears into pruning hooks;
nation shall not lift up sword against nation, neither shall
they learn war any more; but they shall sit every man
under his fig tree, and none shall make them afraid; for the
mouth of the Lord of hosts has spoken. For all the peoples
walk each in the name of its god, but we will walk in the
name of the Lord our God for ever and ever.

A Reading (Lesson) from the Revelation to John [21:1-7]

I saw a new heaven and a new earth; for the first heaven
and the first earth had passed away, and the sea was no
more. And I saw the holy city, new Jerusalem, coming

down out of heaven from God, prepared as a bride adorned for her husband; and I heard a loud voice from the throne saying, "Behold, the dwelling of God is with men. He will dwell with them, and they shall be his people, and God himself will be with them; he will wipe away every tear from their eyes, and death shall be no more, neither shall there be mourning nor crying nor pain any more, for the former things have passed away." And he who sat upon the throne said, "Behold, I make all things new." Also he said, "Write this, for these words are trustworthy and true." And he said to me, "It is done! I am the Alpha and the Omega, the beginning and the end. To the thirsty I will give from the fountain of the water of life without payment. He who conquers shall have this heritage, and I will be his God and he shall be my son."

St. Mary Magdalene   *July 22*

(Morning Prayer)   *Psalm 116* [page 759]

A Reading (Lesson) from the Book of Zephaniah [3:14-20]

Sing aloud, O daughter of Zion; shout, O Israel! Rejoice and exult with all your heart, O daughter of Jerusalem! The Lord has taken away the judgments against you, he has cast out your enemies. The King of Israel, the Lord, is in your midst; you shall fear evil no more. On that day it shall be said to Jerusalem: "Do not fear, O Zion; let not your hands grow weak. The Lord, your God, is in your midst, a warrior who gives victory; he will rejoice over you with gladness, he will renew you in his love; he will exult over you with loud singing as on a day of festival. "I will remove disaster from you, so that you will not bear reproach for it. Behold, at that time I will deal with all your oppressors. And I will save the lame and gather the outcast, and I will change their shame into praise and renown in all the earth. At that time I will bring you home, at the time when I gather you together; yea, I will make you renowned and praised among all the peoples of the earth, when I restore your fortunes before your eyes," says the Lord.

A Reading (Lesson) from the Gospel according to Mark [15:47—16:7]

Mary Mag'dalene and Mary the mother of Joses saw where Jesus was laid. And when the sabbath was past, Mary Mag'dalene, and Mary the mother of James, and Salo'me, bought spices, so that they might go and anoint him. And very early on the first day of the week they went to the tomb when the sun had risen. And they were saying to one another, "Who will roll away the stone for us from the door of the tomb?" And looking up, they saw that the stone was rolled back—it was very large. And entering the tomb, they saw a young man sitting on the right side, dressed in a white robe; and they were amazed. And he said to them, "Do not be amazed; you seek Jesus of Nazareth, who was crucified. He has risen, he is not here; see the place where they laid him. But go, tell his disciples and Peter that he is going before you to Galilee; there you will see him, as he told you."

(Evening Prayer)   *Psalm 30* [page 621],   *Psalm 149* [page 807]

A Reading (Lesson) from the Book of Exodus [15:19-21]

When the horses of Pharaoh with his chariots and his horsemen went into the sea, the Lord brought back the waters of the sea upon them; but the people of Israel walked on dry ground in the midst of the sea. Then Miriam, the prophetess, the sister of Aaron, took a timbrel in her hand; and all the women went out after her with timbrels and dancing. And Miriam sang to them: "Sing to the Lord, for he has triumphed gloriously; the horse and his rider he has thrown into the sea."

A Reading (Lesson) from the Second Letter of Paul to the Corinthians [1:3-7]

Blessed be the God and Father of our Lord Jesus Christ, the Father of mercies and God of all comfort, who comforts us in all our affliction, so that we may be able to comfort those who are in any affliction, with the comfort with which we ourselves are comforted by God. For as we share abundantly in Christ's sufferings, so through Christ we share abundantly in comfort too. If we are afflicted, it is for your comfort and salvation; and if we are comforted, it is for your comfort, which you experience when you patiently endure the same sufferings that we suffer. Our hope for you is unshaken; for we know that as you share in our sufferings, you will also share in our comfort.

St. James   *July 25*

(Morning Prayer)   *Psalm 34* [page 627]

A Reading (Lesson) from the Book of Jeremiah [16:14-21]

The word of the Lord came to me: "Therefore, behold, the days are coming, says the Lord, when it shall no longer be said, 'As the Lord lives who brought up the people of Israel out of the land of Egypt,' but 'As the Lord lives who brought up the people of Israel out of the north country and out of all the countries where he had driven them.' For I will bring them back to their own land which I gave to their fathers. Behold, I am sending for many fishers, says the Lord, and they shall catch them; and afterwards I will send for many hunters, and they shall hunt them from every mountain and every hill, and out of the clefts of the rocks. For my eyes are upon all their ways; they are not hid from me, nor is their iniquity concealed from my eyes. And I will doubly recompense their iniquity and their sin, because they have polluted my land with the carcasses of their detestable idols, and have filled my inheritance with their abominations." O Lord, my strength and my stronghold, my refuge in the day of trouble, to thee shall the nations come from the ends of the earth and say: "Our fathers have inherited nought but lies, worthless things in which there is no profit. Can man make for himself gods? Such are no gods!" "Therefore, behold, I will make them know, this once I will make them know my power and my might, and they shall know that my name is the Lord."

Mark 1:14-20   [page 146 above]

(Evening Prayer)   *Psalm 33* [page 626]

A Reading (Lesson) from the Book of Jeremiah   [26:1-15]

In the beginning of the reign of Jehoḯakim the son of Josḯah, king of Judah, this word came from the Lord, "Thus says the Lord: Stand in the court of the Lord's house, and speak to all the cities of Judah which come to worship in the house of the Lord all the words that I command you to speak to them; do not hold back a word. It may be they will listen, and every one turn from his evil way, that I may repent of the evil which I intend to do to them because of their evil doings. You shall say to them, 'Thus says the Lord: If you will not listen to me, to walk in my law which I have set before you, and to heed the words of my servants the prophets whom I send to you urgently, though you have not heeded, then I will make this house like Shiloh, and I will make this city a curse for all the nations of the earth.'" The priests and the prophets and all the people heard Jeremiah speaking these words in the house of the Lord. And when Jeremiah had finished speaking all that the Lord had commanded him to speak to all the people, then the priests and the prophets and all the people laid hold of him, saying, "You shall die! Why have you prophesied in the name of the Lord, saying, 'This house shall be like Shiloh, and this city shall be desolate, without inhabitant'?" And all the people gathered about Jeremiah in the house of the Lord. When the princes of Judah heard these things, they came up from the king's house to the house of the Lord and took their seat in the entry of the New Gate of the house of the Lord. Then the priests and the prophets said to the princes and to all the people, "This man deserves the sentence of death, because he has prophesied against this city, as you have heard with your own ears." Then Jeremiah spoke to all the princes and all the people, saying, "The Lord sent me to prophesy against this house and this city all the words you have heard. Now therefore amend your ways and your doings, and obey the voice of the Lord your God, and the Lord will repent of the evil which he has pronounced against you. But as for me, behold, I am in your hands. Do with me as seems good and right to you. Only know for certain that if you put me to death, you will bring innocent blood upon yourselves and upon this city and its inhabitants, for in truth the Lord sent me to you to speak all these words in your ears."

A Reading (Lesson) from the Gospel according to Matthew [10:16-32]

Jesus sent out the twelve, charging them, "Behold, I send you out as sheep in the midst of wolves; so be wise as serpents and innocent as doves. Beware of men; for they will deliver you up to councils, and flog you in their synagogues, and you will be dragged before governors and kings for my sake, to bear testimony before them and the Gentiles. When they deliver you up, do not be anxious how you are to speak or what you are to say; for what you are to say will be given to you in that hour; for it is not you who speak, but the Spirit of your Father speaking through you. Brother will deliver up brother to death, and the father his child, and children will rise against parents and have them put to death; and you will be hated by all for my name's sake. But he who endures to the end will be saved. When they persecute you in one town, flee to the next; for truly, I say to you, you will not have gone through all the towns of Israel, before the Son of man comes. A disciple is not above his teacher, nor a servant above his master; it is enough for the disciple to be like his teacher, and the servant like his master. If you have called the master of the house Be-el'zebul, how much more will they malign those of his household. So have no fear of them; for nothing is covered that will not be revealed, or hidden that will not be known. What I tell you in the dark, utter in the light; and what you hear whispered, proclaim upon the housetops. And do not fear those who kill the body but cannot kill the soul; rather fear him who can destroy both soul and body in hell. Are not two sparrows sold for a penny? And not one of them will fall to the ground without your Father's will. But even the hairs of your head are all numbered. Fear not, therefore; you are of more value than many sparrows. So every one who acknowledges me before men, I also will acknowledge before my Father who is in heaven."

Eve of the Transfiguration   *August 5*

(Evening Prayer)   *Psalm 84* [page 707]

A Reading (Lesson) from the First Book of the Kings
[19:1-12]

Ahab told Jez'ebel all that Eli'jah had done, and how he had slain all the prophets with the sword. Then Jez'ebel sent a messenger to Eli'jah, saying, "So may the gods do to me, and more also, if I do not make your life as the life of one of them by this time tomorrow." Then he was afraid, and he arose and went for his life, and came to Beer-sheba, which belongs to Judah, and left his servant there. But he himself went a day's journey into the wilderness, and came and sat down under a broom tree; and he asked that he might die, saying, "It is enough; now, O Lord, take away my life; for I am no better than my fathers." And he lay down and slept under a broom tree; and behold, an angel touched him, and said to him, "Arise and eat." And he looked, and behold, there was at his head a cake baked on hot stones and a jar of water. And he ate and drank, and lay down again. And the angel of the Lord came again a second time, and touched him, and said, "Arise and eat, else the journey will be too great for you." And he arose and ate and drank, and went in the strength of that food forty days and forty nights to Horeb the mount of God. And there he came to a cave, and lodged there; and behold, the word of the Lord came to him, and he said to him, "What are you doing here, Eli'jah?" He said, "I have been very jealous for the Lord, the God of hosts; for the people of Israel have forsaken thy covenant, thrown down thy altars, and slain thy prophets with the sword; and I, even I only, am left; and they seek my life, to take it away." And he said, "Go forth, and stand upon the mount before the Lord." And behold, the Lord passed by, and a great strong wind rent the mountains, and broke in pieces the rocks before the Lord, but the Lord was not in the wind; and after the wind an earthquake, but the Lord was not in the earthquake; and after the earthquake a fire, but the Lord was not in the fire; and after the fire a still small voice.

A Reading (Lesson) from the Second Letter of Paul to the Corinthians [3:1-9,18]

Are we beginning to commend ourselves again? Or do we need, as some do, letters of recommendation to you, or from you? You yourselves are our letter of recommendation, written on your hearts, to be known and read by all men; and you show that you are a letter from Christ delivered by us, written not with ink but with the Spirit of the living God, not on tablets of stone but on tablets of human hearts. Such is the confidence that we have through Christ toward God. Not that we are competent of ourselves to claim anything as coming from us; our competence is from God, who has made us competent to be ministers of a new covenant, not in a written code but in the Spirit; for the written code kills, but the Spirit gives life. Now if the dispensation of death, carved in letters on stone, came with such splendor that the Israelites could not look at Moses' face because of its brightness, fading as this was, will not the dispensation of the Spirit be attended with greater splendor? For if there was splendor in the dispensation of condemnation, the dispensation of righteousness must far exceed it in splendor. And we all, with unveiled face, beholding the glory of the Lord, are being changed into his likeness from one degree of glory to another; for this comes from the Lord who is the Spirit.

The Transfiguration   *August 6*

(Morning Prayer)   *Psalm 2* [page 586],   *Psalm 24* [page 613]

A Reading (Lesson) from the Book of Exodus [24:12-18]

The Lord said to Moses, "Come up to me on the mountain, and wait there; and I will give you the tables of stone, with the law and the commandment, which I have written for their instruction." So Moses rose with his servant Joshua, and Moses went up into the mountain of God. And he said to the elders, "Tarry here for us, until we come to you again; and, behold, Aaron and Hur are with you; whoever has a cause, let him go to them." Then Moses went up on the mountain, and the cloud covered the mountain. The glory of the Lord settled on Mount Sinai, and the cloud covered it six days; and on the seventh day he called to Moses out of the midst of the cloud. Now the appearance of the glory of the Lord was like a devouring fire on the top of the mountain in the sight of the people of Israel. And Moses entered the cloud, and went up on the mountain. And Moses was on the mountain forty days and forty nights.

*A Reading (Lesson) from the Second Letter of Paul
to the Corinthians* [4:1-6]

Therefore, having this ministry by the mercy of God, we
do not lose heart. We have renounced disgraceful,
underhanded ways; we refuse to practice cunning or to
tamper with God's word, but by the open statement of the
truth we would commend ourselves to every man's
conscience in the sight of God. And even if our gospel is
veiled, it is veiled only to those who are perishing. In their
case the god of this world has blinded the minds of the
unbelievers, to keep them from seeing the light of the
gospel of the glory of Christ, who is the likeness of God.
For what we preach is not ourselves, but Jesus Christ as
Lord, with ourselves as your servants for Jesus' sake. For it
is the God who said, "Let light shine out of darkness," who
has shone in our hearts to give the light of the knowledge
of the glory of God in the face of Christ.

(Evening Prayer)   *Psalm 72* [page 685]

A Reading (Lesson) from the Book of Daniel
[7:9-10,13-14]

As I looked, thrones were placed and one that was ancient
of days took his seat; his raiment was white as snow, and
the hair of his head like pure wool; his throne was fiery
flames, its wheels were burning fire. A stream of fire issued
and came forth from before him; a thousand thousands
served him, and ten thousand times ten thousand stood
before him; the court sat in judgment, and the books were
opened. I saw in the night visions, and behold, with the
clouds of heaven there came one like a son of man, and he
came to the Ancient of Days and was presented before
him. And to him was given dominion and glory and
kingdom, that all peoples, nations, and languages should
serve him; his dominion is an everlasting dominion which
shall not pass away, and his kingdom one that shall not be
destroyed.

John 12:27-36a   [page 349 above]

St. Mary the Virgin   *August 15*

(Morning Prayer)   *Psalm 113* [page 756],   *Psalm 115* [page 757]

A Reading (Lesson) from the First Book of Samuel   [2:1-10]

Hannah prayed and said, "My heart exults in the Lord; my strength is exalted in the Lord. My mouth derides my enemies, because I rejoice in thy salvation. There is none holy like the Lord, there is none besides thee; there is no rock like our God. Talk no more so very proudly, let not arrogance come from your mouth; for the Lord is a God of knowledge, and by him actions are weighed. The bows of the mighty are broken, but the feeble gird on strength. Those who were full have hired themselves out for bread, but those who were hungry have ceased to hunger. The barren has borne seven, but she who has many children is forlorn. The Lord kills and brings to life; he brings down to Sheol and raises up. The Lord makes poor and makes rich; he brings low, he also exalts. He raises up the poor from the dust; he lifts the needy from the ash heap, to make them sit with princes and inherit a seat of honor. For the pillars of the earth are the Lord's, and on them he has set the world. He will guard the feet of his faithful ones; but the wicked shall be cut off in darkness; for not by might shall a man prevail. The adversaries of the Lord shall be broken to pieces; against them he will thunder in heaven. The Lord will judge the ends of the earth; he will give strength to his king, and exalt the power of his anointed."

John 2:1-12   [page 239 above]

(Evening Prayer)   *Psalm 45* [page 647]   or
                   Psalm 138 [page 793],   *Psalm 149* [page 807]

A Reading (Lesson) from the Book of Jeremiah [31:1-14]

These are the words which the Lord spoke concerning Israel and Judah: "At that time, says the Lord, I will be the God of all the families of Israel, and they shall be my people." Thus says the Lord: "The people who survived the sword found grace in the wilderness; when Israel sought for rest, the Lord appeared to him from afar. I have loved you with an everlasting love; therefore I have continued my faithfulness to you. Again I will build you, and you shall be built, O virgin Israel! Again you shall adorn yourself with timbrels, and shall go forth in the dance of the merrymakers. Again you shall plant vineyards upon the mountains of Samar'ia; the planters shall plant, and shall enjoy the fruit. For there shall be a day when watchmen will call in the hill country of E'phraim: 'Arise, and let us go up to Zion, to the Lord our God.'" For thus says the Lord: "Sing aloud with gladness for Jacob, and raise shouts for the chief of the nations; proclaim, give praise, and say, 'The Lord has saved his people, the remnant of Israel.' Behold, I will bring them from the north country, and gather them from the farthest parts of the earth, among them the blind and the lame, the woman with child and her who is in travail, together; a great company, they shall return here. With weeping they shall come, and with consolations I will lead them back, I will make them walk by brooks of water, in a straight path in which they shall not stumble; for I am a father to Israel, and E'phraim is my first-born. Hear the word of the Lord, O nations, and declare it in the coastlands afar off; say, 'He who scattered Israel will gather him, and will keep him as a shepherd keeps his flock.' For the Lord has ransomed Jacob, and has redeemed him from hands too strong for him. They shall come and sing aloud on the height of Zion, and they shall be radiant over the goodness of the Lord, over the grain, the wine, and the oil, and over the young of the flock and the herd; their life shall be like a watered garden, and they shall languish no more. Then shall the maidens rejoice in the dance, and the young men and the old shall be merry. I will turn their mourning into joy, I will comfort them, and give them gladness for sorrow. I will feast the soul of the priests with abundance, and my people shall be satisfied with my goodness, says the Lord."

or this

Zechariah 2:10-13   [page 550 above]

A Reading (Lesson) from the the Gospel according to John [19:23-27]

When the soldiers had crucified Jesus they took his garments and made four parts, one for each soldier; also his tunic. But the tunic was without seam, woven from top to bottom; so they said to one another, "Let us not tear it, but cast lots for it to see whose it shall be." This was to fulfil the scripture, "They parted my garments among them, and for my clothing they cast lots." So the soldiers did this. But standing by the cross of Jesus were his mother, and his mother's sister, Mary the wife of Clopas, and Mary Mag'dalene. When Jesus saw his mother, and the disciple whom he loved standing near, he said to his mother, "Woman, behold your son!" Then he said to the disciple, "Behold, your mother!" And from that hour the disciple took her to his own home.

or this

A Reading (Lesson) from the Acts of the Apostles [1:6-14]

When the disciples had come together, they asked Jesus, "Lord, will you at this time restore the kingdom to Israel?" He said to them, "It is not for you to know times or seasons which the Father has fixed by his own authority. But you shall receive power when the Holy Spirit has come upon you; and you shall be my witnesses in Jerusalem and

in all Judea and Samar'ia and to the end of the earth." And
when he had said this, as they were looking on, he was
lifted up, and a cloud took him out of their sight. And
while they were gazing into heaven as he went, behold,
two men stood by them in white robes, and said, "Men of
Galilee, why do you stand looking into heaven? This Jesus,
who was taken up from you into heaven, will come in the
same way as you saw him go into heaven." Then they
returned to Jerusalem from the mount called Olivet, which
is near Jerusalem, a sabbath day's journey away; and when
they had entered, they went up to the upper room, where
they were staying, Peter and John and James and Andrew,
Philip and Thomas, Bartholomew and Matthew, James the
son of Alphaeus and Simon the Zealot and Judas the son of
James. All these with one accord devoted themselves to
prayer, together with the women and Mary the mother of
Jesus, and with his brothers.

St. Bartholomew *August 24*

(Morning Prayer) *Psalm 86* [page 709]

A Reading (Lesson) from the Book of Genesis [28:10-17]

Jacob left Beer-sheba, and went toward Haran. And he
came to a certain place, and stayed there that night,
because the sun had set. Taking one of the stones of the
place, he put it under his head and lay down in that place
to sleep. And he dreamed that there was a ladder set up on
the earth, and the top of it reached to heaven; and behold,
the angels of God were ascending and descending on it!
And behold, the Lord stood above it and said, "I am the
Lord, the God of Abraham your father and the God of
Isaac; the land on which you lie I will give to you and to
your descendants; and your descendants shall be like the
dust of the earth, and you shall spread abroad to the west
and to the east and to the north and to the south; and by

you and your descendants shall all the families of the earth bless themselves. Behold, I am with you and will keep you wherever you go, and will bring you back to this land; for I will not leave you until I have done that of which I have spoken to you." Then Jacob awoke from his sleep and said, "Surely the Lord is in this place; and I did not know it." And he was afraid, and said, "How awesome is this place! This is none other than the house of God, and this is the gate of heaven."

John 1:43-51   [page 236 above]

(Evening Prayer)   *Psalm 15* [page 599],   *Psalm 67* [page 675]

A Reading (Lesson) from the Book of Isaiah   [66:1-2,18-23]

Thus says the Lord: "Heaven is my throne and the earth is my footstool; what is the house which you would build for me, and what is the place of my rest? All these things my hand has made, and so all these things are mine, says the Lord. But this is the man to whom I will look, he that is humble and contrite in spirit, and trembles at my word. For I know their works and their thoughts, and I am coming to gather all nations and tongues; and they shall come and shall see my glory, and I will set a sign among them. And from them I will send survivors to the nations, to Tarshish, Put, and Lud, who draw the bow, to Tubal and Javan, to the coastlands afar off, that have not heard my fame or seen my glory; and they shall declare my glory among the nations. And they shall bring all your brethren from all the nations as an offering to the Lord, upon horses, and in chariots, and in litters, and upon mules, and upon dromedaries, to my holy mountain Jerusalem, says the Lord, just as the Israelites bring their cereal offering in a clean vessel to the house of the Lord. And some of them also I will take for priests and for Levites, says the Lord. For as the new heavens and the new earth which I will make shall remain before me, says the Lord; so shall your descendants and your name remain. From new moon to new moon, and from sabbath to sabbath, all flesh shall come to worship before me, says the Lord."

A Reading (Lesson) from the First Letter of Peter [5:1-11]

I exhort the elders among you, as a fellow elder and a witness of the sufferings of Christ as well as a partaker in the glory that is to be revealed. Tend the flock of God that is your charge, not by constraint but willingly, not for shameful gain but eagerly, not as domineering over those in your charge but being examples to the flock. And when the chief Shepherd is manifested you will obtain the unfading crown of glory. Likewise you that are younger be subject to the elders. Clothe yourselves, all of you, with humility toward one another, for "God opposes the proud, but gives grace to the humble." Humble yourselves therefore under the mighty hand of God, that in due time he may exalt you. Cast all your anxieties on him, for he cares about you. Be sober, be watchful. Your adversary the devil prowls around you like a roaring lion, seeking some one to devour. Resist him, firm in your faith, knowing that the same experience of suffering is required of your brotherhood throughout the world. And after you have suffered a little while, the God of all grace, who has called you to his eternal glory in Christ, will himself restore, establish, and strengthen you. To him be the dominion for ever and ever. Amen.

Eve of Holy Cross   *September 13*

(Evening Prayer)   *Psalm 46* [page 649],   *Psalm 87* [page 711]

A Reading (Lesson) from the First Book of the Kings [8:22-30]

Solomon stood before the altar of the Lord in the presence of all the assembly of Israel, and spread forth his hands toward heaven; and said, "O Lord, God of Israel, there is no God like thee, in heaven above or on earth beneath, keeping covenant and showing steadfast love to thy servants who walk before thee with all their heart; who hast kept with thy servant David my father what thou didst declare to him; yea, thou didst speak with thy mouth, and with thy hand hast fulfilled it this day. Now therefore, O Lord, God of Israel, keep with thy servant David my father what thou hast promised him, saying, 'There shall never fail you a man before me to sit upon the throne of Israel, if only your sons take heed to their way, to walk before me as you have walked before me.' Now therefore, O God of Israel, let thy word be confirmed, which thou hast spoken to thy servant David my father. But will God indeed dwell on the earth? Behold, heaven and the highest heaven cannot contain thee; how much less this house which I have built! Yet have regard to the prayer of thy servant and to his supplication, O Lord my God, hearkening to the cry and to the prayer which thy servant prays before thee this day; that thy eyes may be open night and day toward this house, the place of which thou hast said, 'My name shall be there,' that thou mayest hearken to the prayer which thy servant offers toward this place. And hearken thou to the supplication of thy servant and of thy people Israel, when they pray toward this place; yea, hear thou in heaven thy dwelling place; and when thou hearest, forgive."

A Reading (Lesson) from the Letter of Paul to the Ephesians [2:11-22]

Therefore remember that at one time you Gentiles in the flesh, called the uncircumcision by what is called the circumcision, which is made in the flesh by hands— remember that you were at that time separated from Christ, alienated from the commonwealth of Israel, and strangers to the covenants of promise, having no hope and without God in the world. But now in Christ Jesus you who once were far off have been brought near in the blood of Christ. For he is our peace, who has made us both one, and has broken down the dividing wall of hostility, by abolishing in his flesh the law of commandments and ordinances, that he might create in himself one new man in place of the two, so making peace, and might reconcile us both to God in one body through the cross, thereby bringing the hostility to an end. And he came and preached peace to you who were far off and peace to those who were near; for through him we both have access in one Spirit to the Father. So then you are no longer strangers and sojourners, but you are fellow citizens with the saints and members of the household of God, built upon the foundation of the apostles and prophets, Christ Jesus himself being the cornerstone, in whom the whole structure is joined together and grows into a holy temple in the Lord; in whom you also are built into it for a dwelling place of God in the Spirit.

Holy Cross Day *September 14*

(Morning Prayer) *Psalm 66* [page 673]

A Reading (Lesson) from the Book of Numbers [21:4-9]

From Mount Hor Israel set out by the way to the Red Sea, to go around the land of Edom; and the people became impatient on the way. And the people spoke against God and against Moses, "Why have you brought us up out of Egypt to die in the wilderness? For there is no food and no water, and we loathe this worthless food." Then the Lord sent fiery serpents among the people, and they bit the people, so that many people of Israel died. And the people came to Moses, and said, "We have sinned, for we have spoken against the Lord and against you; pray to the Lord that he take away the serpents from us." So Moses prayed for the people. And the Lord said to Moses, "Make a fiery serpent, and set it on a pole; and every one who is bitten, when he sees it, shall live." So Moses made a bronze serpent, and set it on a pole; and if a serpent bit any man, he would look at the bronze serpent and live.

A Reading (Lesson) from the Gospel according to John [3:11-17]

Jesus answered Nicode᷍mus, "Truly, truly, I say to you, we speak of what we know, and bear witness to what we have seen; but you do not receive our testimony. If I have told you earthly things and you do not believe, how can you believe if I tell you heavenly things? No one has ascended into heaven but he who descended from heaven, the Son of man. And as Moses lifted up the serpent in the wilderness, so must the Son of man be lifted up, that whoever believes in him may have eternal life." For God so loved the world that he gave his only Son, that whoever believes in him should not perish but have eternal life. For God sent the Son into the world, not to condemn the world, but that the world might be saved through him.

(Evening Prayer)   *Psalm 118* [page 760]

A Reading (Lesson) from the Book of Genesis [3:1-15]

Now the serpent was more subtle than any other wild creature that the Lord God had made. He said to the woman, "Did God say, 'You shall not eat of any tree of the garden'?" And the woman said to the serpent, "We may eat of the fruit of the trees of the garden; but God said, 'You shall not eat of the fruit of the tree which is in the midst of the garden, neither shall you touch it, lest you die.'" But the serpent said to the woman, "You will not die. For God knows that when you eat of it your eyes will be opened, and you will be like God, knowing good and evil." So when the woman saw that the tree was good for food, and that it was a delight to the eyes, and that the tree was to be desired to make one wise, she took of its fruit and ate; and she also gave some to her husband, and he ate. Then the eyes of both were opened, and they knew that they were naked; and they sewed fig leaves together and made themselves aprons. And they heard the sound of the Lord God walking in the garden in the cool of the day, and the man and his wife hid themselves from the presence of the Lord God among the trees of the garden. But the Lord God called to the man, and said to him, "Where are you?" And he said, "I heard the sound of thee in the garden, and I was afraid, because I was naked; and I hid myself." He said, "Who told you that you were naked? Have you eaten of the tree of which I commanded you not to eat?" The man said, "The woman whom thou gavest to be with me, she gave me fruit of the tree, and I ate." Then the Lord God said to the woman, "What is this that you have done?" The woman said, "The serpent beguiled me, and I ate." The Lord God said to the serpent, "Because you have done this, cursed are you above all cattle, and above all wild animals; upon your belly you shall go, and dust you shall eat all the days of your life. I will put enmity between you and the woman, and between your seed and her seed; he shall bruise your head, and you shall bruise his heel."

A Reading (Lesson) from the First Letter of Peter [3:17-22]

It is better to suffer for doing right, if that should be God's will, than for doing wrong. For Christ also died for sins once for all, the righteous for the unrighteous, that he might bring us to God, being put to death in the flesh but made alive in the spirit; in which he went and preached to the spirits in prison, who formerly did not obey, when God's patience waited in the days of Noah, during the building of the ark, in which a few, that is, eight persons, were saved through water. Baptism, which corresponds to this, now saves you, not as a removal of dirt from the body but as an appeal to God for a clear conscience, through the resurrection of Jesus Christ, who has gone into heaven and is at the right hand of God, with angels, authorities, and powers subject to him.

St. Matthew   *September 21*

(Morning Prayer)   *Psalm 119:41-64* [page 766]

A Reading (Lesson) from the Book of Isaiah [8:11-20]

For the Lord spoke thus to me with his strong hand upon me, and warned me not to walk in the way of this people, saying: "Do not call conspiracy all that this people call conspiracy, and do not fear what they fear, nor be in dread. But the Lord of hosts, him you shall regard as holy; let him be your fear, and let him be your dread. And he will become a sanctuary, and a stone of offense, and a rock of stumbling to both houses of Israel, a trap and a snare to the inhabitants of Jerusalem. And many shall stumble thereon; they shall fall and be broken; they shall be snared and taken." Bind up the testimony, seal the teaching among my disciples. I will wait for the Lord, who is hiding his face from the house of Jacob, and I will hope in him. Behold, I and the children whom the Lord has given me are signs and portents in Israel from the Lord of hosts, who dwells on Mount Zion. And when they say to you, "Consult the mediums and the wizards who chirp and mutter," should not a people consult their God? Should they consult the dead on behalf of the living? To the teaching and to the testimony! Surely for this word which they speak there is no dawn.

A Reading (Lesson) from the Letter of Paul to the Romans [10:1-15]

Brethren, my heart's desire and prayer to God for them is that they may be saved. I bear them witness that they have a zeal for God, but it is not enlightened. For, being ignorant of the righteousness that comes from God, and seeking to establish their own, they did not submit to God's righteousness. For Christ is the end of the law, that every one who has faith may be justified. Moses writes that the man who practices the righteousness which is based on the law shall live by it. But the righteousness based on faith says, Do not say in your heart, "Who will ascend into heaven?" (that is, to bring Christ down) or "Who will descend into the abyss?" (that is, to bring Christ up from the dead). But what does it say? The word is near you, on your lips and in your heart (that is, the word of faith which we preach); because, if you confess with your lips that Jesus is Lord and believe in your heart that God raised him from the dead, you will be saved. For man believes with his heart and so is justified, and he confesses with his lips and so is saved. The scripture says, "No one who believes in him will be put to shame." For there is no distinction between Jew and Greek; the same Lord is Lord of all and bestows his riches upon all who call upon him. For, "every one who calls upon the name of the Lord will be saved." But how are men to call upon him in whom they have not believed? And how are they to believe in him of whom they have never heard? And how are they to hear without a preacher? And how can men preach unless they are sent? As it is written, "How beautiful are the feet of those who preach good news!"

(Evening Prayer) *Psalm 19* [page 606], *Psalm 112* [page 755]

A Reading (Lesson) from the Book of Job [28:12-28]

Job took up his discourse, and said: "Where shall such wisdom be found? And where is the place of understanding? Man does not know the way to it, and it is not found in the land of the living. The deep says, 'It is not in me,' and the sea says, 'It is not with me.' It cannot be gotten for gold, and silver cannot be weighed as its price. It cannot be valued in the gold of Ophir, in precious onyx or sapphire. Gold and glass cannot equal it, nor can it be exchanged for jewels of fine gold. No mention shall be made of coral or of crystal; the price of wisdom is above pearls. The topaz of Ethiopia cannot compare with it, nor can it be valued in pure gold. Whence then comes wisdom? And where is the place of understanding? It is hid from the eyes of all living, and concealed from the birds of the air. Abaddon and Death say, 'We have heard a rumor of it with our ears.' God understands the way to it, and he knows its place. For he looks to the ends of the earth, and sees everything under the heavens. When he gave to the wind its weight, and meted out the waters by measure; when he made a decree for the rain, and a way for the lightning of the thunder; then he saw it and declared it; he established it, and searched it out. And he said to man, 'Behold, the fear of the Lord, that is wisdom; and to depart from evil is understanding.'"

Matthew 13:44-52   [page 59 above]

St. Michael & All Angels   *September 29*

(Morning Prayer)   *Psalm 8* [page 592],   *Psalm 148* [page 805]

A Reading (Lesson) from the Book of Job [38:1-7]

The Lord answered Job out of the whirlwind: "Who is this that darkens counsel by words without knowledge? Gird up your loins like a man, I will question you, and you shall declare to me. Where were you when I laid the foundation of the earth? Tell me, if you have understanding. Who determined its measurements—surely you know! Or who stretched the line upon it? On what were its bases sunk, or who laid its cornerstone, when the morning stars sang together, and all the sons of God shouted for joy?"

A Reading (Lesson) from the Letter to the Hebrews [1:1-14]

In many and various ways God spoke of old to our fathers
by the prophets; but in these last days he has spoken to us
by a Son, whom he appointed the heir of all things,
through whom also he created the world. He reflects the
glory of God and bears the very stamp of his nature,
upholding the universe by his word of power. When he
had made purification for sins, he sat down at the right
hand of the Majesty on high, having become as much
superior to angels as the name he has obtained is more
excellent than theirs. For to what angel did God ever say,
"Thou art my Son, today I have begotten thee"? Or again,
"I will be to him a father, and he shall be to me a son"? And
again, when he brings the first-born into the world, he
says, "Let all God's angels worship him." Of the angels he
says, "Who makes his angels winds, and his servants
flames of fire." But of the Son he says, "Thy throne, O
God, is for ever and ever, the righteous scepter is the
scepter of thy kingdom. Thou hast loved righteousness and
hated lawlessness; therefore God, thy God, has anointed
thee with the oil of gladness beyond thy comrades." And,
"Thou, Lord, didst found the earth in the beginning, and the
heavens are the work of thy hands; they will perish, but
thou remainest; they will all grow old like a garment, like a
mantel thou wilt roll them up, and they will be changed.
But thou art the same, and thy years will never end." But to
what angel has he ever said, "Sit at my right hand, till I
make thy enemies a stool for thy feet"? Are they not all
ministering spirits sent forth to serve, for the sake of those
who are to obtain salvation?

(Evening Prayer)   *Psalm 34* [page 626],   *Psalm 150* [page 807]
                     or   *Psalm 104* [page 735]

A Reading (Lesson) from the Book of Daniel [12:1-3]

One having the appearance of a man said to me, "At that

time shall arise Michael, the great prince who has charge of your people. And there shall be a time of trouble, such as never has been since there was a nation till that time; but at that time your people shall be delivered, every one whose name shall be found written in the book. And many of those who sleep in the dust of the earth shall awake, some to everlasting life, and some to shame and everlasting contempt. And those who are wise shall shine like the brightness of the firmament; and those who turn many to righteousness, like the stars for ever and ever."

or this

A Reading (Lesson) from the Second Book of the Kings
[6:8-17]

Once when the king of Syria was warring against Israel, he took counsel with his servants, saying, "At such and such a place shall be my camp." But the man of God sent word to the king of Israel, "Beware that you do not pass this place, for the Syrians are going down there." And the king of Israel sent to the place of which the man of God told him. Thus he used to warn him, so that he saved himself there more than once or twice. And the mind of the king of Syria was greatly troubled because of this thing; and he called his servants and said to them, "Will you not show me who of us is for the king of Israel?" And one of his servants said, "None, my lord, O king; but Eli'sha, the prophet who is in Israel, tells the king of Israel the words that you speak in your bedchamber." And he said, "Go and see where he is, that I may send and seize him." It was told him, "Behold, he is in Dothan." So he sent there horses and chariots and a great army; and they came by night, and surrounded the city. When the servant of the man of God rose early in the morning and went out, behold, an army with horses and chariots was round about the city. And the servant said, "Alas, my master! What shall we do? He said,

"Fear not, for those who are with us are more than those who are with them." Then Eli'sha prayed, and said, "O Lord, I pray thee, open his eyes that he may see." So the Lord opened the eyes of the young man, and he saw; and behold, the mountain was full of horses and chariots of fire around Eli'sha.

A Reading (Lesson) from the Gospel according to Mark
[13:21-27]

Jesus said to the disciples, "And then if any one says to you, 'Look, here is the Christ!' or 'Look, there he is!' do not believe it. False Christs and false prophets will arise and show signs and wonders, to lead astray, if possible, the elect. But take heed; I have told you all things beforehand. But in those days, after that tribulation, the sun will be darkened, and the moon will not give its light, and the stars will be falling from heaven, and the powers in the heavens will be shaken. And then they will see the Son of man coming in clouds with great power and glory. And then he will send out the angels, and gather his elect from the four winds, from the ends of the earth to the ends of heaven."

or this

Revelation 5:1-14   [page 303 above]

St. Luke   *October 18*

(Morning Prayer)   *Psalm 103* [page 733]

Ezekiel 47:1-12   [page 24 above]

A Reading (Lesson) from the Gospel according to Luke
[1:1-4]

Inasmuch as many have undertaken to compile a narrative

of the things which have been accomplished among us, just as they were delivered to us by those who from the beginning were eyewitnesses and ministers of the word, it seemed good to me also, having followed all things closely for some time past, to write an orderly account for you, most excellent The-oph′ilus, that you may know the truth concerning the things of which you have been informed.

(Evening Prayer) *Psalm 67* [page 675], *Psalm 96* [page 725]

A Reading (Lesson) from the Book of Isaiah [52:7-10]

How beautiful upon the mountains are the feet of him who brings good tidings, who publishes peace, who brings good tidings of good, who publishes salvation, who says to Zion, "Your God reigns." Hark, your watchmen lift up their voice, together they sing for joy; for eye to eye they see the return of the Lord to Zion. Break forth together into singing, you waste places of Jerusalem; for the Lord has comforted his people, he has redeemed Jerusalem. The Lord has bared his holy arm before the eyes of all the nations; and all the ends of the earth shall see the salvation of our God.

A Reading (Lesson) from the Acts of the Apostles [1:1-8]

In the first book, O The-oph′ilus, I have dealt with all that Jesus began to do and teach, until the day when he was taken up, after he had given commandment through the Holy Spirit to the apostles whom he had chosen. To them he presented himself alive after his passion by many proofs, appearing to them during forty days, and speaking of the kingdom of God. And while staying with them he charged them not to depart from Jerusalem, but to wait for the promise of the Father, which, he said, "you heard from me, for John baptized with water, but before many days you shall be baptized with the Holy Spirit." So when they had come together, they asked him, "Lord, will you at this time restore the kingdom to Israel?" He said to them, "It is not for you to know times or seasons which the Father has fixed by his own authority. But you shall receive power when the Holy Spirit has come upon you; and you shall be my witnesses in Jerusalem and in all Judea and Samar'ia and to the end of the earth."

St. James of Jerusalem   *October 23*

(Morning Prayer)   *Psalm 119:145-168* [page 775]

A Reading (Lesson) from the Book of Jeremiah [11:18-23]

The Lord made it known to me and I knew; then thou didst show me their evil deeds. But I was like a gentle lamb led to the slaughter. I did not know it was against me they devised schemes, saying, "Let us destroy the tree with its fruit, let us cut him off from the land of the living, that his name be remembered no more." But, O Lord of hosts, who judgest righteously, who triest the heart and the mind, let me see thy vengeance upon them, for to thee have I committed my cause. Therefore thus says the Lord concerning the men of An'athoth, who seek your life, and say, "Do not prophesy in the name of the Lord, or you will die by our hand"—therefore thus says the Lord of hosts: "Behold, I will punish them; the young men shall die by the sword; their sons and their daughters shall die by famine; and none of them shall be left. For I will bring evil upon the men of An'athoth, the year of their punishment."

A Reading (Lesson) from the Gospel according to Matthew [10:16-22]

Jesus sent out the twelve, charging them, "Behold, I send you out as sheep in the midst of wolves; so be wise as serpents and innocent as doves. Beware of men; for they will deliver you up to councils, and flog you in their synagogues, and you will be dragged before governors and kings for my sake, to bear testimony before them and the Gentiles. When they deliver you up, do not be anxious how you are to speak or what you are to say; for what you are to say will be given to you in that hour; for it is not you who speak, but the Spirit of your Father speaking through you. Brother will deliver up brother to death, and the father his child, and children will rise against parents and have them put to death; and you will be hated by all for my name's sake. But he who endures to the end will be saved."

(Evening Prayer)   *Psalm 122* [page 779],   *Psalm 125* [page 781]

A Reading (Lesson) from the Book of Isaiah [65:17-25]

Thus says the Lord God: "Behold, I create new heavens and a new earth; and the former things shall not be remembered or come to mind. But be glad and rejoice for ever in that which I create; for behold, I create Jerusalem a rejoicing, and her people a joy. I will rejoice in Jerusalem, and be glad in my people; no more shall be heard in it the sound of weeping and the cry of distress. No more shall there be in it an infant that lives but a few days, or an old man who does not fill out his days, for the child shall die a hundred years old, and the sinner a hundred years old shall be accursed. They shall build houses and inhabit them; they shall plant vineyards and eat their fruit. They shall not build and another inhabit; they shall not plant and another eat; for like the days of a tree shall the days of my people be, and my chosen shall long enjoy the work of their hands. They shall not labor in vain, or bear children for calamity; for they shall be the offspring of the blessed of the Lord, and their children with them. Before they call I will answer, while they are yet speaking I will hear. The wolf and the lamb shall feed together, the lion shall eat straw like the ox; and dust shall be the serpent's food. They shall not hurt or destroy in all my holy mountain, says the Lord."

A Reading (Lesson) from the Letter to the Hebrews
[12:12-24]

Lift your drooping hands and strengthen your weak knees, and make straight paths for your feet, so that what is lame may not be put out of joint but rather be healed. Strive for peace with all men, and for the holiness without which no one will see the Lord. See to it that no one fail to obtain the grace of God; that no "root of bitterness" spring up and cause trouble, and by it the many become defiled; that no one be immoral or irreligious like Esau, who sold his birthright for a single meal. For you know that afterward, when he desired to inherit the blessing, he was rejected, for he found no chance to repent, though he sought it with tears. But you have not come to what may be touched, a blazing fire, and darkness, and gloom, and a tempest, and the sound of a trumpet, and a voice whose words made the hearers entreat that no further messages be spoken to them. For they could not endure the order that was given, "If even a beast touches the mountain, it shall be stoned." Indeed, so terrifying was the sight that Moses said, "I tremble with fear." But you have come to Mount Zion and to the city of the living God, the heavenly Jerusalem, and to innumerable angels in festal gathering, and to the assembly of the first-born who are enrolled in heaven, and to a judge who is God of all, and to the spirits of just men made perfect, and to Jesus, the mediator of a new covenant, and to the sprinkled blood that speaks more graciously than the blood of Abel.

St. Simon and St. Jude   *October 28*

(Morning Prayer)   *Psalm 66* [page 673]

A Reading (Lesson) from the Book of Isaiah [28:9-16]

"Whom will he teach knowledge, and to whom will he explain the message? Those who are weaned from the milk, those taken from the breast? For it is precept upon precept, precept upon precept, line upon line, line upon line, here a little, there a little." Nay, but by men of strange lips and with an alien tongue the Lord will speak to this people, to whom he has said, "This is rest; give rest to the weary; and this is repose"; yet they would not hear. Therefore the word of the Lord will be to them precept upon precept, precept upon precept, line upon line, line upon line, here a little, there a little; that they may go, and fall backward, and be broken, and snared, and taken. Therefore hear the words of the Lord, you scoffers, who rule this people in Jerusalem! Because you have said, "We have made a covenant with death, and with Sheol we have an agreement; when the overwhelming scourge passes through it will not come to us; for we have made lies our refuge, and in falsehood we have taken shelter"; therefore thus says the Lord God, "Behold, I am laying in Zion for a foundation a stone, a tested stone, a precious cornerstone, of a sure foundation: 'He who believes will not be in haste.'"

A Reading (Lesson) from the Letter of Paul to the Ephesians [4:1-16]

I therefore, a prisoner for the Lord, beg you to lead a life worthy of the calling to which you have been called, with all lowliness and meekness, with patience, forbearing one another in love, eager to maintain the unity of the Spirit in the bond of peace. There is one body and one Spirit, just as you were called to the one hope that belongs to your call, one Lord, one faith, one baptism, one God and Father of us all, who is above all and through all and in all. But grace was given to each of us according to the measure of Christ's gift. Therefore it is said, "When he ascended on high he led a host of captives, and he gave gifts to men." (In saying, "He ascended," what does it mean but that he had also descended into the lower parts of the earth? He who descended is he who also ascended far above all the heavens, that he might fill all things.) And his gifts were that some should be apostles, some prophets, some evangelists, some pastors and teachers, to equip the saints for the work of ministry, for building up the body of Christ, until we all attain to the unity of the faith and of the knowledge of the Son of God, to mature manhood, to the measure of the stature of the fulness of Christ; so that we may no longer be children, tossed to and fro and carried about with every wind of doctrine, by the cunning of men, by their craftiness in deceitful wiles. Rather, speaking the truth in love, we are to grow up in every way into him who is the head, into Christ, from whom the whole body, joined and knit together by every joint with which it is supplied, when each part is working properly, makes bodily growth and upbuilds itself in love.

(Evening Prayer)   *Psalm 116* [page 759],   *Psalm 117* [page 760]

A Reading (Lesson) from the Book of Isaiah [4:2-6]

In that day the branch of the Lord shall be beautiful and glorious, and the fruit of the land shall be the pride and glory of the survivors of Israel. And he who is left in Zion and remains in Jerusalem will be called holy, every one who has been recorded for life in Jerusalem, when the Lord shall have washed away the filth of the daughters of Zion and cleansed the bloodstains of Jerusalem from its midst by a spirit of judgment and by a spirit of burning. Then the Lord will create over the whole site of Mount Zion and over her assemblies a cloud by day, and smoke and the shining of a flaming fire by night; for over all the glory there will be a canopy and a pavilion. It will be for a shade by day from the heat, and for a refuge and a shelter from the storm and rain.

A Reading (Lesson) from the Gospel according to John
[14:15-31]

Jesus said to the disciples, "If you love me, you will keep my commandments. And I will pray the Father, and he will give you another Counselor, to be with you for ever, even the Spirit of truth, whom the world cannot receive, because it neither sees him nor knows him; you know him, for he dwells with you, and will be in you. I will not leave you desolate; I will come to you. Yet a little while, and the world will see me no more, but you will see me; because I live, you will live also. In that day you will know that I am in my Father, and you in me, and I in you. He who has my commandments and keeps them, he it is who loves me; and he who loves me will be loved by my Father, and I will love him and manifest myself to him." Judas (not Iscariot) said to him, "Lord, how is it that you will manifest yourself to us, and not to the world?" Jesus answered him, "If a man loves me, he will keep my word, and my Father will love him, and we will come to him and make our home with him. He who does not love me does not keep my words; and the word which you hear is not mine but the Father's who sent me. These things I have spoken to you, while I am still with you. But the Counselor, the Holy Spirit, whom the Father will send in my name, he will teach you all things, and bring to your remembrance all that I have said to you. Peace I leave with you; my peace I give to you; not as the world gives do I give to you. Let not your hearts be troubled, neither let them be afraid. You heard me say to you, 'I go away, and I will come to you.' If you loved me, you would have rejoiced, because I go to the Father; for the Father is greater than I. And now I have told you before it takes place, so that when it does take place, you may believe. I will no longer talk much with you, for the ruler of this world is coming. He has no power over me; but I do as the Father has commanded me, so that the world may know that I love the Father. Rise, let us go hence."

Eve of All Saints   *October 31*

A Reading (Lesson) from the Book of Wisdom [3:1-9]

The souls of the righteous are in the hand of God, and no torment will ever touch them. In the eyes of the foolish they seemed to have died, and their departure was thought to be an affliction, and their going from us to be their destruction; but they are at peace. For though in the sight of men they were punished, their hope is full of immortality. Having been disciplined a little, they will receive great good, because God tested them and found them worthy of himself; like gold in the furnace he tried them, and like a sacrificial burnt offering he accepted them. In the time of their visitation they will shine forth, and will run like sparks through the stubble. They will govern nations and rule over peoples, and the Lord will reign over them for ever. Those who trust in him will understand truth, and the faithful will abide with him in love, because grace and mercy are upon his elect, and he watches over his holy ones.

A Reading (Lesson) from the Revelation to John [19:1,4-10]

I heard what seemed to be the loud voice of a great multitude in heaven, crying, "Hallelujah! Salvation and glory and power belong to our God." And the twenty-four elders and the four living creatures fell down and worshiped God who is seated on the throne, saying, "Amen. Hallelujah!" And from the throne came a voice crying, "Praise our God, all you his servants, you who fear him, small and great." Then I heard what seemed to be the voice of a great multitude, like the sound of many waters and like the sound of mighty thunderpeals, crying, "Hallelujah! For the Lord our God the Almighty reigns.

Let us rejoice and exult and give him the glory, for the marriage of the Lamb has come, and his Bride has made herself ready; it was granted her to be clothed with fine linen, bright and pure"—for the fine linen is the righteous deeds of the saints. And the angel said to me, "Write this: Blessed are those who are invited to the marriage supper of the Lamb." And he said to me, "These are true words of God." Then I fell down at his feet to worship him, but he said to me, "You must not do that! I am a fellow servant with you and your brethren who hold the testimony of Jesus. Worship God." For the testimony of Jesus is the spirit of prophecy.

All Saints' Day   *November 1*

(Morning Prayer)   *Psalm 111* [page 754],   *Psalm 112* [page 755]

A Reading (Lesson) from the Second Book of Esdras [2:42-47]

I, Ezra, saw on Mount Zion a great multitude, which I could not number, and they were all praising the Lord with songs. In their midst was a young man of great stature, taller than any of the others, and on the head of each of them he placed a crown, but he was more exalted than they. And I was held spellbound. Then I asked an angel, "Who are these, my lord?" He answered and said to me, "These are they who have put off mortal clothing and have put on the immortal, and they have confessed the name of God; now they are being crowned, and receive palms." Then I said to the angel, "Who is that young man who places crowns on them and puts palms in their hands?" He answered and said to me, "He is the Son of God, whom they confessed in the world." So I began to praise those who had stood valiantly for the name of the Lord.

A Reading (Lesson) from the Letter to the Hebrews
[11:32—12:2]

What more shall I say? For time would fail me to tell of
Gideon, Barak, Samson, Jephthah, of David and Samuel
and the prophets—who through faith conquered
kingdoms, enforced justice, received promises, stopped the
mouths of lions, quenched raging fire, escaped the edge of
the sword, won strength out of weakness, became mighty
in war, put foreign armies to flight. Women received their
dead by resurrection. Some were tortured, refusing to
accept release, that they might rise again to a better life.
Others suffered mocking and scourging, and even chains
and imprisonment. They were stoned, they were sawn in
two, they were killed with the sword; they went about in
skins of sheep and goats, destitute, afflicted, ill-treated—of
whom the world was not worthy—wandering over deserts
and mountains, and in dens and caves of the earth. And all
these, though well attested by their faith, did not receive
what was promised, since God had foreseen something
better for us, that apart from us they should not be made
perfect. Therefore, since we are surrounded by so great a
cloud of witnesses, let us also lay aside every weight,
and sin which clings so closely, and let us run with
perseverance the race that is set before us, looking to Jesus
the pioneer and perfecter of our faith, who for the joy that
was set before him endured the cross, despising the shame,
and is seated at the right hand of the throne of God.

(Evening Prayer)   *Psalm 148* [page 805],   *Psalm 150* [page 807]

A Reading (Lesson) from the Book of Wisdom [5:1-5,14-16]

Then the righteous man will stand with great confidence in
the presence of those who have afflicted him, and those
who make light of his labors. When they see him, they will
be shaken with dreadful fear, and they will be amazed at
his unexpected salvation. They will speak to one another

in repentance, and in anguish of spirit they will groan, and say, "This is the man whom we once held in derision and made a byword of reproach—we fools! We thought that his life was madness and that his end was without honor. Why has he been numbered among the sons of God? And why is his lot among the saints?" Because the hope of the ungodly man is like chaff carried by the wind, and like a light hoarfrost driven away by a storm; it is dispersed like smoke before the wind, and it passes like the remembrance of a guest who stays but a day. But the righteous live for ever, and their reward is with the Lord; the Most High takes care of them. Therefore they will receive a glorious crown and a beautiful diadem from the hand of the Lord, because with his right hand he will cover them, and with his arm he will shield them.

A Reading (Lesson) from the Revelation to John
[21:1-4,22—22:5]

I saw a new heaven and a new earth; for the first heaven and the first earth had passed away, and the sea was no more. And I saw the holy city, new Jerusalem, coming down out of heaven from God, prepared as a bride adorned for her husband; and I heard a loud voice from the throne saying, "Behold, the dwelling of God is with men. He will dwell with them, and they shall be his people, and God himself will be with them; he will wipe away every tear from their eyes, and death shall be no more, neither shall there be mourning nor crying nor pain any more, for the former things have passed away." And I saw no temple in the city, for its temple is the Lord God the Almighty and the Lamb. And the city has no need of sun or moon to shine upon it, for the glory of God is its light, and its lamp is the Lamb. By its light shall the nations walk; and the kings of the earth shall bring their glory into it, and its gates shall never be shut by day—and there shall be no night there; they shall bring into it the glory and the honor of the nations. But nothing unclean shall enter it, nor any one who practices abomination or falsehood, but only those who are written in the Lamb's book of life. Then he showed me the river of the water of life, bright as crystal, flowing from the throne of God and of the Lamb through the middle of the street of the city; also, on either side of the river, the tree of life with its twelve kinds of fruit, yielding its fruit each month; and the leaves of the tree were for the healing of the nations. There shall no more be anything accursed, but the throne of God and of the Lamb shall be in it, and his servants shall worship him; they shall see his face, and his name shall be on their foreheads. And night shall be no more; they need no light of lamp or sun, for the Lord God will be their light and they shall reign for ever and ever.

Thanksgiving Day

(Morning Prayer)   *Psalm 147* [page 804]

A Reading (Lesson) from the Book of Deuteronomy [26:1-11]

Moses summoned all Israel, and said to them, "When you come into the land which the Lord your God gives you for an inheritance, and have taken possession of it, and live in it, you shall take some of the first of all the fruit of the ground, which you harvest from your land that the Lord your God gives you, and you shall put it in a basket, and you shall go to the place which the Lord your God will choose, to make his name to dwell there. And you shall go to the priest who is in office at that time, and say to him, 'I declare this day to the Lord your God that I have come into the land which the Lord swore to our fathers to give us.' Then the priest shall take the basket from your hand, and set it down before the altar of the Lord your God. And you shall make response before the Lord your God, 'A wandering Aramean was my father; and he went down into Egypt and sojourned there, few in number; and there he became a nation, great, mighty, and populous. And the Egyptians treated us harshly, and afflicted us, and laid upon us hard bondage. Then we cried to the Lord the God of our fathers, and the Lord heard our voice, and saw our affliction, our toil, and our oppression; and the Lord brought us out of Egypt with a mighty hand and an outstretched arm, with great terror, with signs and wonders; and he brought us into this place and gave us this land, a land flowing with milk and honey. And behold, now I bring the first of the fruit of the ground, which thou, O Lord, has given me.' And you shall set it down before the Lord your God, and worship before the Lord your God; and you shall rejoice in all the good which the Lord your God has given to you and to your house, you, and the Levite, and the sojourner who is among you."

A Reading (Lesson) from the Gospel according to John
[6:26-35]

Jesus said to the people, "Truly, truly, I say to you, you seek me, not because you saw signs, but because you ate your fill of the loaves. Do not labor for the food which perishes, but for the food which endures to eternal life, which the Son of man will give to you; for on him has God the Father set his seal." Then they said to him, "What must we do, to be doing the works of God?" Jesus answered them, "This is the work of God, that you believe in him whom he has sent." So they said to him, "Then what sign do you do, that we may see, and believe in you? What work do you perform? Our fathers ate manna in the wilderness; as it is written, 'He gave them bread from heaven to eat.'" Jesus then said to them, "Truly, truly, I say to you, it was not Moses who gave you the bread from heaven; my Father gives you the true bread from heaven. For the bread of God is that which comes down from heaven, and gives life to the world." They said to him, "Lord, give us this bread always." Jesus said to them, "I am

the bread of life; he who comes to me shall not hunger, and
he who believes in me shall never thirst."

(Evening Prayer)   *Psalm 145* [page 801]

Joel 2:21-27   [page 504 above]

*A Reading (Lesson) from the First Letter of Paul
to the Thessalonians* [5:12-24]

We beseech you, brethren, to respect those who labor
among you and are over you in the Lord and admonish
you, and to esteem them very highly in love because of
their work. Be at peace among yourselves. And we exhort
you, brethren, admonish the idlers, encourage the
fainthearted, help the weak, be patient with them all. See
that none of you repays evil for evil, but always seek to do
good to one another and to all. Rejoice always, pray
constantly, give thanks in all circumstances; for this is the
will of God in Christ Jesus for you. Do not quench the
Spirit, do not despise prophesying, but test everything;
hold fast what is good, abstain from every form of evil.
May the God of peace himself sanctify you wholly; and
may your spirit and soul and body be kept sound and
blameless at the coming of our Lord Jesus Christ. He who
calls you is faithful, and he will do it.